Quran & History

Quran & History

by

Dr. Rafat Amari

A Religion Research Institute Publication

Printed in the United States of America.
First Edition, November 2018
Second Print, 2022

Index

Introduction

Investigating the history of how a religion arose is one of the most important tests in examining the credibility of its claims. Despite whatever claims and arguments, later proponents of the religion added to the founders' sayings to lend support to the founders' claims, the facts regarding the religion remain limited to the period in which the founder lived. Therefore, the most important guiding principles for examining his claims and evaluating his religion are these: Studying the life of the founder, analyzing the religious and social environment in which he lived, and investigating the sources upon which he depended in founding his religion.

It is easy today to trace the developmental stages of any religion in the world. Apart from the faith proclaimed in the Bible, all other religions appeared during a certain epoch of history and were influenced greatly by local factors related to where the founder lived. Thus, all such religions were considered as "local" religions, in spite of whatever bridges the founder built with other religions and the elements he adopted from other faiths and religions. The increase of historical knowledge and archaeology has facilitated the process of examining the developmental stages of a religion. To understand the developmental stages of the worship of "Allah" in Arabia, I refer the reader to my book The Star Akbar: The History of Allah in Arabia.

The faith declared in the Bible, however, was not a claim born in a generation of a claimant. Rather, it is God's revelation that He revealed in various epochs, confirming His revelation with miracles and prodigies, such as Moses' bringing the Israelites out of Egypt (the Exodus). God's revelation continued in other stages of history. He called prophets such as Elijah and Elisha through whom He performed great miracles. The most important and remarkable consideration of all is that those prophets who lived hundreds (and even well over a thousand) years apart - from the time of

Abraham to the time of John the Baptist – accurately prophesied about the incarnation of God in human form, His death as a man for humanity's redemption, and His resurrection. The prophets prophesied with accurate details about the second coming of Christ, with emphases on the political and moral signs that will precede His return.

Therefore, the revelation contained in the Bible is not the result of the claim of one man who lived at a certain time in a certain environment that influenced his doctrines. Nor is it the outgrowth of one individual who relied on other religious claims as was the case with Mohammed and Islam. Rather, it is God's revelation throughout all epochs; thus, its historical credibility is based on the fact that God, as its source and origin, exists in all epochs because He spoke in each epoch. His word revealed in all epochs has a purpose: It declares and reveals His identity and plans in history. No religion can boast such credibility.

When we study the books of the Old Testament, we find that they were written by individuals who lived in the time they wrote. Though some of them lived several centuries before the Christian era, their writings accurately reflect the social and political times in which they lived. Thus, we find Moses writing in the 15th century B.C. about the epoch in which the Patriarchs (Abraham, Isaac, and Jacob) lived, reflecting perfectly the characteristics of the epoch in which those Patriarchs lived (i.e., the beginning of the second millennium B.C.). This indicates that, in addition to being led by the Holy Spirit to write, Moses depended on records written by one of the Patriarchs, passed down to him through Joseph, who thanks to God's grace became a responsible man in Egypt. (To verify these facts, I refer the reader to the chapter in which I discuss Abraham in the Quran and the Bible.)

Furthermore, when we compare the Middle Eastern inscriptions, especially those of the Assyrians and the Chaldeans, with the historical chronology of the books of the Old Testament, which corresponds with it, we find that the narration of the Old Testament agrees with the historical facts. This confirms the fact that we are reading writings penned by the prophets themselves who lived during the epochs they described – not writings written much later and attributed to the prophets.

The prophecies made by the writers of the Old Testament Holy Scriptures were fulfilled in the New Testament. This reveals not only that they lived during the time they declared they lived in, but that God spoke through them to reveal His message whose main subject – the coming of God in the flesh as Christ, His death as a man for man's redemption, His resurrection from the dead, and His return to judge the living and dead – they all agreed on.

By contrast, when we analyze the Quran, we find it was written by one individual – Mohammed – who lived in the 7th century A.D. In the few instances in which he wrote about history, he depended on the notions of various ignorant groups of his time. In no case did he succeed in presenting accurate data, and in fact failed when it comes to historical credibility. Furthermore, he included in his Quran the names of various figures (such as Luqman) whom he mistakenly believed were prophets who lived in history. Yet, these figures were not historical characters at all, but rather imaginary and fictitious figures mentioned in mythological writings with dates well-known to us. Furthermore, Mohammed incorporated in his Quran famous classical myths. How then could we give any credibility to the claim that he wrote under God's direction, when we know for a fact that he lacks any historical credibility?! Many who lived in his time, such as the Byzantines among whom lived historians of high reputation for historical accuracy, were better aware than Mohammed regarding historical facts. Thus, they were better able than he to discern between the mythological and the true. Even the inhabitants of Mecca, who distinguished many of his myths as the "the myths of the ancients," were aware of how the myths Mohammed incorporated in his Quran had spread among the ignorant groups in their generation. They made light of the Surahs of the Quran that presented those myths as spiritual facts inspired by Allah.

I sought to examine each historical reference in the Quran, and thus refute the claims of the Quran based on the official history substantiated by historical documentation and various historical and archaeological records. In some cases, I exposed the sources upon which Mohammed depended in formulating his Quran and disclosed the societies, cultures, and religions prior to Mohammed that had adopted the myths he included in the Quran.

Can we know?

We live in an era in which we can distinguish the ancients' mistakes, based on the facts we have discovered since and know in our times. Many of the ancient methods of treating diseases are rejected by the physicians of our day based on their greatly enhanced knowledge of anatomy, pathology and microbiology. Over time the body of medical knowledge has grown so that they are aware of each organ's tissues, the kinds of cells they are formed of, and the nerves, veins, and arteries that comprise these organs. In most cases, our doctors know the factors that cause various diseases. They understand the way such diseases should be treated, whether through modern surgery or the use of medicines such as antibiotics and antivirals. No rational man today could claim that he does not know if our knowledge of medicine is more accurate and better than the knowledge of the people who lived during or prior to Mohammed's time.

The same principle is valid when we discuss our knowledge of history and archaeology. Our knowledge of various inscriptions, such as those found in Arabia, whether they be Thamudic, Lahyanic, Sabaean, or other, provides us with information and facts that far exceed what the contemporaries of Mohammed could perceive. Our knowledge about the Middle Eastern inscriptions in general, such as the ones in Mesopotamia, Egypt, Syria, and Israel, provides us with data about the various nations and tribes who lived there. Findings from archeological digs have provided us with new information about ancient history. There are also the historical books written by famous Greek and Roman historians and copies of various ancient books that have been translated and analyzed and greatly contributed to our knowledge. All these factors lend far greater credibility on historical matters to today's researchers than to the views of any group who lived in old times, especially those who lived in Arabia during the 7th century A.D. Those Arabians were disconnected from civilization as it flourished in the Byzantine Empire and in some European regions. Thus, no man today who possesses any level of wisdom could claim that the knowledge that the pre-Islamic Arabians in Mohammed's time had about the ancient history of the Middle East that preceded Mohammed by thousands of years, is more accurate than the schools of history taught in our contemporary universities.

Therefore, clear logic leads us to acknowledge that we can know and discern between the true and the mythological. The fact that the mythological is dressed in religious attire and claims to be of heavenly inspiration does not exempt it from being examined in light of official and documented history, to expose its true affiliations with the ignorant and with groups of limited knowledge at Mohammed's time. No one is excused when they insist upon holding to the Quran, which reflects the errant historical views of the Jahiliyyah peoples of Arabia. One can know and discern truth from falsehood when they compare the Quranic views regarding history with the historical facts of well-documented history.

Dressing up a false treasure with the veneer of a true treasure does not turn the false treasure into a true treasure. The reader is encouraged to put aside the writings of the Muslim writers, who during centuries that followed the 7th century A.D., created a new history that is distinct from the authentic history. They invented this new history without any prior documentation. They based it instead on information born in their own generation.

Studying without a heart open to God's will and readiness to do His will results in general information that quickly evaporates from the soul. It will be vaporized by narrow-mindedness of religious preconception, which will never admit the truth even when the truth is obvious.

Ad

The Tribe of Ad in Quran and in History

Confusion on the Timing of the Tribes of Ad and Thamud

The narration of the Quran is distinguished by the ignorance of its author in historical chronology, as documented through our knowledge of the history of the nations and the date in which those nations appeared in history. No author or historian in our generation would claim that the Romans appeared prior to Abraham's time, which was 2,000 years before Christ. If any Italian today were to claim that the Romans had a history that preceded the Sumerians, and that the Roman Empire known to us is only a "second Rome," which followed the first Rome by thousands of years, modern historians would consider them to be ignorant at best and irrationally delirious at worst. Yet, this is precisely what some Muslims resort to in order to gloss over the egregious errors in the Quran and its fallacious chronology. For example, when they find that the Quran claims that some tribes known to have appeared in a certain time actually appeared in remote epochs, such as in the time of Noah, they will attempt to resolve the dilemma by making the spurious claim that those tribes had a double appearance – one very remote and another in a more recent time that is substantiated by real history. The one adopting such an excuse is similar to the one who would claim that the Roman Empire arose thousands of years prior to the true historical date when it actually arose.

Here is an example of Mohammed's confusion regarding historical chronology and Muslims' attempts to resolve the dilemma. In the Quran Mohammed placed the tribe of Ad as the second generation after Noah. The historical fact is that Ad, if it even existed in history at all, might have appeared in the 2nd century A.D. Muslims, however, claimed that the

Quran intended the "first Ad," but made the claim without any documentation whatsoever.

Ad was a small Arabian tribe that might have lived in northern Arabia in the 2nd century A.D. Claudius Ptolemy of Alexandria, Egypt, who was born in the year 90 A.D. and died in 168 A.D., wrote his famous book of geography in the first part of the 2nd century A.D. Among the tribes he listed on one of his maps was Oaditae, which some identify as Ad. Many scholars, among them Forster, had identified the tribe of Oaditae with Ad and held that it was located in the northern part of Arabia.[1]

Scholars such as Wellhausen believe that Ad did not exist in history. He pointed out that "instead of the expression 'since the time of Ad' the expression min al-'ad also occurs"; therefore, he supposed that originally 'Ad was a common noun ("the ancient time"; adj. 'adi, "very ancient") and that the mythical nation arose from a misinterpretation of that expression."[2]

Ptolemy placed Oaditae in the area east of Gulf Aqaba. No other geographer had previously mentioned this tribe, although classical authors such as Pliny (who wrote around the years 69-70 A.D.) who mentioned all tribes in the region did not mention this tribe. Prior to him, Strabo wrote about the same region without mentioning this tribe. Other classical Greek authors, such as Agatharchides of Alexandria who wrote between 145-132 B.C., described the region but did not mention this tribe. All this shows that the tribe of Ad, if it existed in history, was a small tribe that appeared in the 2nd century A.D. It is not known how long it existed there, but most probably it was absorbed by greater tribes in the area, such as Thamud.

Although we have seen from the descriptions of the geographers that if Oaditae was Ad, it was a small tribe that occupied a limited area near the Aqaba Gulf. Mohammed claimed that members of this tribe inhabited the earth in the second generation after Noah. We read in Surah al-A'raf 7, 69:

> Call to your remembrance that he made you inheritors after the people of Noah, and gave you a stature tall among the nations.

And in Sura 23: 31 and 32:

> Then we raised another generation after them - by which he means after the people who died in the flood at the time of Noah - and we sent a messenger to them from among themselves saying, "Worship Allah.

According to the Quran, one century after Noah, a giant people called Ad inhabited several regions of the earth. The Quran calls these people Erm

"إِرَمَ ذَاتِ الْعِمَادِ", (Surah 89:7) which means in Arabic, "the Aram of Pillars," meaning that Ad built cities in Aram which had pillars or columns. Because of the pillars, many Muslims thought that Damascus was one of the cities of Ad.

We question how Noah and his family of only eight people, according to Genesis 7:6, 7, could became so numerous within a hundred years that they were able to build so many cities. We know that Noah was six hundred years old when the floodwaters came on the earth. Noah, his wife, his sons and their wives entered the ark to escape the waters of the flood. In Genesis 9:18, 19, we read, "The sons of Noah who came out of the ark were Shem, Ham and Japheth. Ham was the father of Canaan. These were the three sons of Noah, and from them came the people who were scattered over all the earth."

Genesis 10:1 reveals the sons of Noah had sons after the flood. In Genesis 10:21-31 Shem's children are mentioned:

> Sons were also born to Shem, whose older brother was Japheth; Shem was the ancestor of all the sons of Eber. The sons of Shem: Elam, Asshur, Arphaxad, Lud and Aram. The sons of Aram: Uz, Hul, Gether and Meshech. Arphaxad was the father of Shelah, and Shelah the father of Eber. Two sons were born to Eber: One was named Peleg because in his time the earth was divided; his brother was named Joktan. Joktan was the father of Almodad, Sheleph, Hazarmaveth, Jerah, Hadoram, Uzal, Diklah, Obal, Abimael, Sheba, Ophir, Havilah and Jobab. All these were sons of Joktan. The region where they lived stretched from Mesha toward Sephar, in the eastern hill country. These are the sons of Shem by their clans and languages, in their territories and nations.

Although the Bible mentioned the sons of Shem who became fathers of known nations in history, we do not see any mention of Ad or Thamud, as the Quran claims. Furthermore, history did not list Ad and Thamud with the ancient nations mentioned by the book of Genesis. On the contrary, Thamud appeared in the 8th century B.C, while Ad appeared in the 2nd century A.D., a clear refutation of the claim of the Quran that these Arabian tribes appeared in the 1st and 2nd centuries after Noah.

There is another thing to consider. When were the sons of Shem born? Genesis 11:10 says:

> This is the account of Shem. Two years after the flood, when Shem was 100 years old, he became the father of Arphaxad.

Between Arphaxad and Joktan, from whom came the tribes which inhabited eastern and southern Arabia, there were three generations. From Genesis 11:12, 14, 16, and 18 we learn the exact time Joktan was born:

> When Arphaxad had lived 35 years, he became the father of Shelah. When Shelah had lived 30 years, he became the father of Eber. When Eber had lived 34 years, he became the father of Peleg. When Peleg had lived 30 years, he became the father of Reu.

This is probably how the source on which Mohammed depended fell into this mistake: We assume that some groups of Jahiliyyah heard from the Jews that Joktan was the father of the tribes that lived in Arabia and that he was born a hundred years after the Flood. Thinking that Ad and Thamud were among the sons of Joktan, they stated that Ad existed one century after Noah.

However, one century after the Flood, the descendants of Shem could not have been more than 80 to 180 people. When we start from Joktan, his descendants could not have been born 100 years after the flood. Two centuries after the flood, no Arabian tribe yet existed. Only small families were born to Joktan. How could Mohammed insist Ad was a great tribe that filled the earth, within 100 years from the time of Noah?

If Mohammed were to make Ad and Thamud descendants of Aram, the fifth son of Shem, he would have faced the same problem. After two centuries, the sons of Aram, according to Genesis 10:23 were Uz, Hul, Gether and Meshech, from whom the Aramaic tribes descended. They were not yet tribes, but they were still small families.

We find the claim that Ad was the first nation after Noah in the poetry of some pre- Islamic Jahiliyyah poets such as Baathu Tay:

> The two mounts that we mounted and occupied, that was in remote times, after Noah and before Ad.[3]

Mohammed created a dilemma for Muslims by placing the Arabian tribes, Ad and Thamud, in a period connected with Noah that is prior to 6000 B.C., so they sought a remedy or a way out of this problem by fabricating "history." The first Muslim who proposed a remedy for this contradiction was Ibn Ishak, who died around 774 A.D. (152 years after Mohammed's emigration to Medina). Ibn Ishak changed the genealogies in Genesis to fit the Quran's historical mistakes. He added names to the genealogy of Shem, son of Noah; Arabic names of his generation style that were not known as style even in four or five centuries prior to his times. He inserted the name of Ad as son of Uz who is mentioned in Genesis 10:21-24. "as son of Aram, son of Shem, son of Noah." He then changed the genealogy of Noah, arabizing it.[4]

When ibn Ishak made Ad the son of Uz, he had no way of knowing that Uz, an Aramaic tribe at the time of Job, was still one tribe, not yet divided into tribes. How could he paste Ad to this tribe?

Job lived between the 6th and the 9th century B.C. Yet, ibn Ishak placed the tribe of Ad as the first tribe of Uz, in the second century after the Flood. He created his claim in order to substantiate the enormous mistake Mohammed wrote in the Quran. This certainly causes a great dilemma for Muslims who believe in such thing: history of the Aramaic peoples, including the Aramaic tribe of Uz, did not know a tribe descending from it under the name of Ad.

For the sake of argument, even if we would accept ibn Ishack's claim that Ad was the son of Uz, who was the son of Aram, and who was the son of Shem, this wouldn't resolve the problem or find a solution for the mistake the Quran had made. Aram, as the fifth son of Shem, could not have been born earlier than 40 or 50 years after the flood. Uz as the son of Aram cold not have been born earlier than 70 or 80 years after the Flood. Ad, if we want to admit to him being the son of Uz, either he would have to have been born within one century after the flood, or he would have been only a few years old. How then could he have children during the same century or even the century that came after that, and be the tribe that built cities with pillars? Any great tribe that inhabited large areas had it is own prophet–in this case Hudo–after the flood and have been famous and well-known among the nations as the Quran claimed.

Ibn Ishak was considered by the educated people of his time as one "who fabricates false genealogies" and as a "liar and deceiver."[5] Since no one before him or who wrote between the 7th-9th centuries A.D. had cited such modified genealogies, his educated Islamic contemporaries considered him to be a false historian. Yet, in the generations that followed, Ibn Ishak's writings - along with the writings of Wahab bin Munabeh, Ibn Abbass, Ibn al Kalbi, and Ubeid bin Sharayeh - became the foundation for a new "history" that backs the Quran. Based on the genealogy that Ibn Ishak invented, Ibn Khaldun (1332-1406 A.D.) claimed that Ad occupied the south of Arabia, part of western Africa, and Egypt, and built the city of Damascus.[6]

He invented this claim without any precedent from history to draw upon. We find no support for his historical fabrication in any archaeological find or writing. The Muslims found an old tomb in Hadramawt among the tombs of southern Arabia and attributed it to Hud as his tomb, without any evidence to support such a claim prior to the Islamic era.

Mohammed sources about Ad

The tribe of Ad, if it even existed in history at all, was an Arabian tribe that lived a Bedouin lifestyle, and knew nothing of civilization or architectural accomplishments which could have distinguished it from other nations and made it appear to be superior to all the other cities on earth, as the Quran claims. Yet myths were spread among superstitious people of Jahiliyyah who embraced them.

In fact, Myths about Ad appearing among ignorant groups during the time of Mohammed. Among the poets who spoke about Ad was Umayyah bin Abi al Salet,[7] the cousin of Mohammed on his mother side. He had an uncanny way of adopting myths and spreading them among superstitious people, who tended to believe the myths were true. We find myths about Ad in the poetry of Mutmem bin Nuwaireh متمم بن نُوَيْرَة, who lived until the rise of Islam. We cannot attribute the poetry of Mutmem or Umayyah to periods distant from Islam. It is easy to see that Mohammed took his ideas about Ad from Umayyah and he did not come up with anything new. He was misled by Umayyah.

The question is how did those poems, dated about the time of the rise of Islam, be trusted when they speak about the time of Noah, who lived thousands of years before? The oldest poems are, for the most part, only one century before Islam. Pre-Islamic poetry failed to record with any accuracy the things that happened only a century prior to Islam. Jawad Ali said:

> How can we trust the accuracy of those sayings which are attributed to distant times; long before Islam, when Islamic writers failed to give us a correct accounting of incidents that happened within the times before Islam and during the rise of Islam.[8]

Al Taberi says that people would tell Mohammed stories about Ad[9] confirming that the myths about Ad which Mohammed recited as Quranic verses, were spread among certain groups of the people of Jahiliyyah at the time of Mohammed.

The sources of the Quran's claim regarding the excessive tallness of the inhabitants of Ad. The Mandaean and Manichaean influence and the spread of the Manichaean myths in Mecca.

The phrase "stature tall among the nations" in Surah 7:69 indicates that Mohammed was influenced by Manichaean literature, which claimed that the people who lived on earth at the time of the flood were giants very tall in stature. Mani, the founder of Manichaeism, wrote a book entitled The Giants. We also find this idea in other Gnostic literature the Manichaeans embraced in the 4th century A.D. The roots of these myths are taken from the book of 1 Enoch, which dates to the 4th–3rd centuries B.C. In 1 Enoch we read that the angels married the human women "...and the women became pregnant and bore great giants, having heights of three thousand cubits (about 4,500 feet)."[10] We know that the Ethiopian church considered the book of Enoch to be a canonical book. The Ethiopians were great in number in Mecca at the time of Mohammed.

The Quran's claim that two angels, Harut and Marut, came down to Babel and taught magic to people is taken from different sources influenced by 1 Enoch. That an angel would come down and live among men is a familiar idea in the Mandaean literature. For example, the Mandaean book Haran Gawaita mentions that Ruha-Surbis, an angel of darkness, came down and lived amid the Mandaeans to deceive men. [11] This reminds us of the Quran's claim that Harut and Marut descended and lived in Babylon to teach magic and to separate husbands and wives. In the magical Mandaean books, there is something that accurately reflects the Quranic story regarding Harut and Marut. We read that the angels of the planets descended in the main cities of Mesopotamia (including Babylon) and said:

> In the name of the angels that separate and divide, let it be separations and divisions between men and their wives...[12]

This reflects the same Quranic idea. We know about the influence of the Mandaeans on Mohammed through the group Ahnaf. Zayd bin Amru bin Nufayl, the founder of Ahnaf, used to go to the area of Mosul in northern Iraq where groups of Mandaeans lived in order to inquire about religion.

Regarding those myths, the Manichaeans definitely influenced Mohammed since we find similar myths in the book Giant of Mani. [13]

The connection between Mohammed and the Manichaeans is affirmed by the fact that many people in the tribe of Quraysh, from which Mohammed came, embraced Manichaeism. The Manichaeans were called Zandik at Mecca.[14]

When the Arabs mentioned al Zanadikeh, they were referring to the followers of Mani, who believed in dualism –a good creator for the world of light and wicked creator for the world of darkness.

The fact that the term "Zanadikeh" referred to the Manichaeans is obvious from the writings of Arabic historians. For example, writing about villages in China and nearby regions, Yaqut al Hamawi stated that most of their inhabitants were Zanadikeh who followed the doctrine of Mani. He distinguished them from the Magus (the Persian Magi religion adherents). Yaqut wrote:

> **Most of the inhabitants are worshipers of fire on the doctrines of Magi, among them are the Zanadikeh who are on the doctrine of Mani.[15]**

This confirms that the title of Zanadikeh that was used by the Arabic narrators was intended to be the Manichaeans, the followers of Mani.

Al Abshihi الابشــيهي spoke about the religions which spread in some Arabian tribes:

> **Al Zandakeh was in Quraysh which they took from al Jazireh.[16]**

Al Jazireh a region in northeastern Syria, which bordered Asia Minor and Iraq. Manichaeism in Quraysh spread because of its trade with Iraq and Syria.

Among Arabian names, we find the name of Mani, the founder of Manichaeism. Al Hakem الحاكم in his book, Al Mustrak ala al Sahihein المســـتدرك على الصـــحيحين, says, "...We were told by Ali the son of Abdel Rahman, son of Mani."[17] Al Yaqubi اليعقوبي mentioned about the Arabians, "Some of them 'Tazandek' and believed in dualism."[18] Dualism is one of the principles of Persian Zoroastrianism, which Mani embraced and promoted.

Manichaeism has had a strong influence over north Arabia since early times. Amru, the governor of Arabic Hira lived between 270 and 300. He embraced Manichaeism, supported it and helped it spread into other Arabian regions.[19] The Arabic geographer, ibn Rasteh ابن رسته, confirmed that Manichaean missionaries reached Mecca from al Hirah. Furthermore,

Arabic historians, such as ibn Qutaibeh ابن قتيبة , mentioned that some people in the tribe of Quraysh brought Manichaeism to Mecca.[20] These historical facts demonstrate that Mecca and Quraysh were familiar with Manichaeism. Mohammed copied many Manichaean doctrines, especially regarding the concept of inspiration. Furthermore, when the Christians, such as Ephraim the Syriac, refuted Manichaeism, many Manichaeans left for north Arabia and Mecca. [21]

Other factors also come into play. The Persians made use of the Manichaeans against the Romans. This created grounds for the persecution of the Manichaeans in the Roman provinces. Something that induced the Manichaeans to look for regions such as Arabia, where the Romans has no authority. Asmussen wrote:

> The reign of Shapur's son Hormized I was too short (about one year) for Mani to find out exactly what the situation was, but in any case, the position of the new religion was tolerable. This religion, called "Righteousness" (e.g., the Coptic Homilies 67, 22, and the Parthian M 4575) was quickly introduced into the whole area of the eastern and central Mediterranean, into Syria, Palestine (e.g. the mission of the Manichaean Julia in Ghaza, described by Marcus Diaconus in his Life of Porphyrios), and into Northern Arabia.[22]

The issue of "the first Ad and the second Ad"

Some Muslims today look to Surah 53, verse 50, where it says, "he destroyed the ancient Ad," to claim that there were two Ads: the ancient one (which they placed in southern Arabia) and another Ad that appeared in the north in the area of the Gulf of Aqaba. But the Quran called Ad "ancient" because Mohammed placed it as second generation after Noah; he did not intend to distinguish it from another more recent Ad.

Some Muslims also look to Surah 46, verse 21, where it says, "mention the brother of Ad who warned his people about the winding sand-tracts." in Arabic the "winding sand tracts" is Ahqaf. They say the first Ad lived in Al-Ahqaf, which they considered as a place in southern Arabia in the desert of Rub al-Khali at the border of Hadramawt. I do not know how the Rub al-Khali, which is uninhabited and considered to be among the most scorched and arid deserts of the world, according to Muslims, could have been home to a powerful people who occupied all southern Arabia and western Africa, and, according to the Quran, had cities with pillars. But the Quran spoke about Hud as a prophet who, according to the Quran, was a prophet to Ad, and who warned Ad of a destruction which would come to Ad through winding sand–tracts. This is what the Quran intended by this verse. In verse 24, we find the Quran describing the coming of this wind over the tribe of Ad which, according to the Quran, destroyed everything.

Early Islamic writers such as al Aini spoke about "Ahqaf" as high wind-blown sand,[23] and Al Bakri al Andulsi understood the word "Ahqaf" not as a place but as wind-blown sand.[24]

The Quran intended in this ancient Ad a place in northern Arabia and not in the south. The Quran intended that this ancient Ad inhabit the same area that Thamud inhabited immediately after Ad's destruction through wind. The Quran specified the area where ancient Ad and Thamud lived by describing the area where houses are being hewed in the rock of the mountains, which we know existed only in a certain place in northern Arabia near the city of al Hijr. In reality, it was a Nabataean city where some Thamud lived in northwestern Arabia. In Surah 7, called al-A'raf, verse 69, we see that Mohammed spoke of Ad existing one generation after Noah, and he dealt with destroying them. Then, immediately in verses 73 and 74, he began speaking about the tribe of Thamud as coming a generation after Ad and inheriting their land:

> To the Thamud we sent Salih, one of their brothers... Remember how he made you inheritors after the Ad people and gave you habitation in the land; you build for yourselves palaces and castles in the plains and hew homes from the mountains.

It is clear that Mohammed placed this ancient Ad (which he placed after Noah) in the area where houses were hewed in the rocks which, in Surah al-Hijr 15:80-82, he specified that the area was the city Hegra (known also as Hijr):

> The inhabitants of Hijr have rejected the messengers. We sent them our signs, but they turned away from them. Out of mountains they hewed homes where they were safe. But the cry seized them one morning and gave them no avail.

We know that Hijr is in northwestern Arabia, and was built by the Nabataeans, who alone were known as people who hew their houses in rocks. So we see that Mohammed meant by the "ancient Ad" a tribe who lived before Thamud in the area of Hijr in north-western Arabia, and not a tribe who lived in southern Arabia. He placed such a tribe as second generation after Noah, though we know that Thamud appeared in the 8th century B.C. (as I will discuss later). Ad appeared in the same area of Thamud only in the 2nd century A.D.

Some Muslim writers claim that the "ancient Ad" lived in southern Arabia and disappeared two or three centuries before the Christian era. But there is no tribe or nation who lived in southern Arabia whose history lacks archaeological documentation. Not even one archaeological finding supports this Islamic position. No inscriptions in southern Arabia speak of Ad, though the southern Arabian Inscriptions are the richest in the whole world. Even the smallest nations are richly attested to with hundreds of inscriptions.

What is the origin of the myth of Hud, the prophet which the Quran assigned to the tribe of Ad

The Quran speaks of a prophet, named Hud, whom Allah sent to the tribe of Ad. Hud cannot be an Arabian name; No Arabian in history was ever named Hud. Hud is a Jewish name which we find in the Old Testament book of Judges. Hud was a judge in Israel during the time of the Judges. Probably this Hud was a Jewish man from the Jewish settlements of northern Arabia, where there were Jewish cities such as Kheiber.

Arabians at the time of Mohammed often referred to Jews by the name Hud. This is confirmed by the way the Quran used the word Hud referring to Jews in Surah 2, al-Baqarah, verses 111, 135 and 140.

Certain scholars connect the Hud of the Quran with a Jewish man named Hud, who had a son named Daniel. Hud was a Jewish preacher who called many Arabians to Judaism. Among those scholars were men like R.B. Sergeant,[25] W. L. Reed and F. V. Winnett. They were scholars who specialized in the history of Arabia. They maintain that Hud was a Jewish preacher who tried to proselyte Arabians to Judaism during the 6th century A.D.[26] Judaism spread in Arabia, especially in the south and in some cities to the north of Arabia as well.

Myths concerning Hud arose later, and these myths were attributed to the tribe of Ad. This corresponds with the Arabian custom in Mohammed's day of mythologizing names and places.

Without any documentation to support their claim, some Muslims identified a place in Hadhramaut in southern Arabia as the burial place of

Hud. Scholars who studied the place, such as Von Kremer[27] discovered, however, that this alleged burial site of Hud was the location of an old volcano that had once erupted and killed many people. Arabic writings state that this place once brought forth lava accompanied by loud thunderous noises, which confirms that it was in fact a volcano.

The Quran is full of unrealistic conceptions and contradictions when it comes to the way judgments against tribes and nations are executed.

Mohammed filled the Quran with contradictions in the same way he treated the extermination of the tribe of Ad. In Surah 23, Al Mu'minun, verse 41, he brought doom with a loud cry, "Then the cry overtook them with justice and we made them as rubbish or dead leaves." The expositors of the Quran, depending on other Islamic resources, attributed this cry to Gabriel.[28] The Mandaeans attributed a similar cry to Pthael, a personality of light, whom they called Gabriel. (I will discuss this in detail in the chapter on the sources of the cries in the Quran.)

But in Sura 46, Al Ahqaf, the judgment of Ad comes through a wind. Mohammed often contradicted himself in the Quran, probably because he repeated the same stories in the Quran many times, often forgetting the way he handled the events and judgments earlier. For example, he judged the tribe of Midian with a cry in one Surah, and with an earthquake in another Surah.

We read in Sura 46, Al Ahqaf, verses 24 and 25, about a wind destroying the tribe of Ad:

> When they saw a cloud coming to meet their valleys, they said 'this cloud will give us rain.' No, it is the calamity which you wanted to come over you—a wind that is a tormenting gloom. It will destroy everything by the command of its lord. Then, in the morning, nothing was seen except their ruins.

In other words, the Quran claims that they saw a cloud traversing the sky, coming to meet their valleys. They came to be under the cloud, and then a wind came and destroyed all of them including their houses.

In the Quran, Mohammed portrayed the tribe of Ad as a small group of people like a tiny village, so that they could be under one limited cloud, even though this description contradicts what he had previously mentioned in the Quran about the tribe – that it was the first nation on earth following the time of Noah and had great cities with pillars. No cloud could be so large as to bring them together to accommodate the claims of the Quran found here, which said that they were gathered before their prophet under a single cloud so that their prophet could address them and remind them of their penalty before they were destroyed. We see, then, that Mohammed treated this nation, which he claimed to be the first nation to spread on earth, as if they were a small neighborhood in an Arabian village. It is like a man addressing a group of small children to narrate a story about God's gathering all the Europeans under a cloud, admonishing them, and then destroying them. Mohammed was apparently unaware that he was establishing great dimensions in history for the nations he wanted to destroy. But when he wanted to destroy them, he treated them as the inhabitants of one village or one city — as he did with the Thamudic people, whom he imprisoned in the city of al Hijr and then removed them from history. He brought all this "great nation of Ad" under one cloud and then exterminated them all.

Mohammed was not aware of the contradictions he made. As we have seen, he previously mentioned in Surah 23, Al Mu'minun, verse 41, that he brought doom, destroying them with a loud cry, "Then the cry overtook them with justice and we made them as rubbish or dead leaves." This was Gabriel's cry. But he later made them appear to have been destroyed by the wind, after which he gathered them under a cloud. It seems that Mohammed either did not review the verses he had previously recited to avoid contradicting himself, or simply forgot these verses. Most probably, he believed that his listeners were not aware of the contradictions or, if they were, that they did not care to examine them because they so enjoyed the rhyming in these verses.

Not only were they supposed to be under one cloud, but the Quran says the judgment came to the tribe through a great wind. Judgment in the Quran always comes either through a wind or through a shout or cry from the mouth of the angel Gabriel.

Mohammed's Zoroastrian sources for the Judgment Through Wind in Zoroastrianism

The Quran makes the judgment to the tribe come through the wind. The judgment in the Quran is always either through the wind, or through a shout or blast from the mouth of the angel Gabriel.

Mohammed had a Persian counselor by the name of Salman Al- farisi. This man was a priest in Zoroastrianism before becoming Muslim. When he met Mohammed and became Muslim, Mohammed gave him a golden egg, which was considered a great fortune at that time. Evidently, Mohammed saw in Salman Al-Farsi a great resource which would give him access and knowledge to Zoroastrianism.

Although the Medinan verses of the Quran that were borrowed from Zoroastrianism relied in part on Salman the Persian, he was not Mohammed's only source on Zoroastrianism. Some Quranic Meccan verses preceded the time when Salman embraced Islam. The Persian religion was well known as one of the main religions in Arabia. Zoroastrianism spread in the tribe of Tamim, which was in intimate connection with Quraysh, the tribe of Mohammed. There are also indications that Zoroastrianism spread among the Quraysh itself. Arabic narrators said that "Zandakah" spread in Quraysh. Al Abshihi said this about the religions that penetrated into some Arabian tribes: "Zandakah was in Quraysh. They took it from al Jazirah."[29]

Though the word Zandakah came to represent Manichaeism, the original meaning referred to the Zoroastrian religion. This is for two reasons. First, the word Zend (Zand) or Zenda (Zanda) meant "interpretation"; it referred to the interpretation of the Zoroastrian books of Avesta. Thus, the term Zand-i-Avesta means the interpretation of Avesta. Later, some Persian Zoroastrian manuscripts were called Avesta-o-Zand (or Zand-i-Avesta) meaning the book of the Avesta with its interpretation. Thus, the word Zandiq was a title for one who believes in the books of Zenda Avesta.

The other reason is that the word Zandaqa was connected with dualism which was the most important Zoroastrian doctrine. Yaqubi wrote this about the Arabians, "some of them Tazandaka (became Zandiq) declaring dualism."[30]

Dualism was originally a Persian principle that was later adopted by Mani. It is safe to say that "Zandaqa" referred to those who embraced dualism, such as the Zoroastrians and the Manichaeans.

It is not strange that Zoroastrianism spread among the Quraysh because Quraysh was connected with the city of Hirah, the Arabic city in Iraq that was under the Persians. The Quraysh used to send their children to study the Persian culture and education. For example, al Nather bin Harith studied in Hirah and was schooled in Persian history and religion. It was natural that the Meccans learned about the Persian religion.

Zoroastrianism data was at the disposal of Mohammed at Mecca. This was before he came to meet Salman the Persian in Medina. It was at Mecca that the Meccans accused Mohammed's Quran of being in Ajami (Persian) tongue. This we see in the Meccan surah al Nahl 103 and verse 16:

> **We know indeed that they say, 'It is a man that teaches him.' The tongue of him they wickedly point to is notably Ajami (Persian), while this is Arabic, pure and clear.**

This verse states that Mohammed was taught by a Persian, revealing that Mohammed received information at Mecca from either a Persian or a person with Persian education.

This explains the great data of Zoroastrianism in the Quran. In fact, the Quran as Cosmology and Eschatology depends in the major part on Zoroastrianism.

The judgment through wind is the way to execute judgments on peoples like we encounter in Zoroastrianism. In Ram Yast I, (Ram Yast is part of the sacred Zoroastrian literature), Ahura Mazda, the god in Zoroastrianism, presents offerings to Vayu, the god of the air or wind, asking him to judge the creation of wickedness.[31] The god of air or wind has great potency, with the ability to evacuate the whole earth from its inhabitants. In Ram Yast, Azi Dahaka, a mythological potency as enemy of the Iranian nation, presented a request to the god of the air, Vayu, to evacuate the earth from its inhabitants, but Vayu refused to grant him this request.[32]

All judgments in Zoroastrianism are done by the god of air, or by a blast shouted by the god of the air as an angel. We find the Quran also giving the judgment to the wind or to Gabriel shouting a blast. Gabriel has replaced the angel of wind in Zoroastrianism in this role of judging through blast.

The Quran has copied the style of judgment from Zoroastrianism. There is a good wind which executes judgment toward the creation of Ahriman, the god of evil. In the other part, there is wind as a devil appertaining to Ahriman, who carries out works of destruction toward the good creation of Ahura Mazda, the god of goodness. Zoroastrianism is known for such dualism. The wind devil, or the storm devil, destroyed the city where Zoroaster was born. With just one blast, part of the city was elevated up to the sky, and then made to go upside down. (This we find, for example, in Dinkard, VII, chapter II).[33] The same concept is borrowed by the Quran, where Gabriel with his blast elevated the cities of Sodom and Gomorrah; then he turned them upside down.

The god of wind or air in Zoroastrianism is portrayed as a judge who executes judgments against persons or peoples who do not believe in Zoroaster's message. We find him carrying two kings who refuse to believe, carrying them too high and keeping them in that state as judgment.[34]

The same concept we encounter in the Quran as judgment toward the tribe of Ad who refused to believe in "Hud," created by Mohammed for the tribe as prophet. Ibn Abbas, the cousin of Mohammed and the narrator of his important Hadith, says that the wind which came to Ad used to carry the men and livestock and fly in them in the sky, then strike them against the earth. [35]

Early Islamic writers such as al Aini, spoke about "Ahqaf," as high wind-blown sand that has distortion.[36] and Al Bakri al Andulsi understood the word "Ahqaf," not as a place, but as wind-blown sand. [37]

The Quran is filled with such errors. For instance, the Quran places an Arabian tribe, Ad, in the second generation after Noah. If this tribe ever in fact existed in history, which is not an established historical fact, it lived during the 2nd century A.D.

The Quran claimed that the tribe of Ad filled the earth with cities with pillars; whereas, the tribe of questionable existence was known to have lived a Bedouin life style. The Quran adopted a well-known myth that claims that people after the flood were giants. Mohammed applied this myth to the members of this Arabian tribe that lived in North Arabia during the 2nd century A.D.

The Quran took a man with the Jewish name of Hud and made him an Arabian prophet for the tribe. Then it brought judgement in the Zoroastrian style in which the devil, or the god of the air, carried it out.

Based on the archeological progress in our day, we have come to know the story of the tribes of northern Arabia better than the superstitious people who lived at the time of Mohammed, and whose myths Mohammed recorded in his Quran. I believe, when we compare the true data of archeology and history, the myths of the groups with whom Mohammed had contact, and the Zoroastrian myths which influenced Arabia at the time of Mohammed, these would help evaluate the claims of Mohammed in light of documented history, and not attribute divine inspiration to them.

We simply cannot embrace the point of view of the pre-Islamic Jahiliyyah people regarding the antiquity of some tribes. The Jahiliyyah people considered tribes that were close to their time, such as Ad, as the most ancient. We now know the names of the tribes that descended from Shem as well their languages. Archaeological discoveries have proved that these tribes are identical to those described in the Old Testament book of Genesis. On the other hand, the Quran's narration reflects the unhistorical views of the pre-Islamic Jahiliyyah people. Thus, we cannot annul the discoveries of our scientific age regarding history and archaeology and embrace these Jahiliyyah views upon which the Quran was based.

Thamud

The Tribe of Thamud in History and in the Quran

We now come to the tribe of Thamud in the Quran. Mohammed claimed that the inhabitants of the city of Hijr were Thamudi. Hijr was a Lahynite site, occupied by the Nabataeans in the 1st century B.C. Their houses and sepulchers were hewn in the rocks by the Nabataeans in the 1st century A.D or the 1st century B.C. Mohammed placed Thamud in the 3rd generation after Noah, immediately after Ad whom he placed as the 2nd generation after Noah.

Mohammed claimed that the Thamudi were exterminated in the 3rd generation or century after Noah. Mohammed claimed that Ad came immediately after the generation of the people of Noah who perished through the Flood. We know this from Surah 23 Verse 31 (called Al-Mumenoon) which says this about Ad:

Then We raised after them another generation or century.

Thamud comes as the generation after Ad (Surah 7, called al-Araf, verses 73-74):

To the Thamud people (we sent) Saleh, one of their own brethren. He said, 'And remember how He made you inheritors after the 'Ad people and gave you habitations in the land: Ye build for yourselves palaces and castles in (open) plains, and carve out homes in the mountains; so bring to remembrance the benefits (ye have received) from Allah, and refrain from evil and mischief on the earth.'

The verse claims Thamud inherited the land after 'Ad was destroyed. Taberi, the most important expositor of the Quran, explained the verse in these words, "Remember O people the grace of Allah upon you. He made you to inherit Ad after they were perished."

Thus, since Ad was the second generation after the flood, Thamud was the third generation. The Quran uses the word Qarn قرن, which means century, in Surah 23:31 (called Al-Mumenoon). A "generation" in the Quran can be interpreted as a "century." The Quran intended to say that the Thamud were the 3rd generation or 3rd century after Noah.

The extermination of the people of Thamud, according to the Quran's claim, was caused by the same cry which resulted in the deaths of a great many people. As we see in Surah Hud 11:67,

> The cry overtook the wrongdoers and they lay dead, prostrate in their homes before morning.

We know historically that the claims of the Quran are incorrect. The people of Thamud were never exterminated. The tribe appeared in the 8th century B.C. at the time of King Sargon II, who defeated it when the tribe attacked his southwestern borders.[38] In fact, in 715 B.C. Sargon II, the King of Assyria, dealt with the Arabian tribes menacing the southern Assyrian borders. The tribes were Khaiapa, Thamud, Ibadidi, and Marsimani. [39] Thumad remained, as we will see later, an organized tribe until the fifth century A.D.

Before the 8th century B.C., the tribe was unknown, but Mohammed claimed that it was combined with another tribe named Ad, a prominent nation only one century after Noah. This claim places the two Arabian tribes as the main nations in history after Noah, and those tribes were judged through the cry of Gabriel which totally exterminated them.

When Mohammed passed by the ruins of Hijr, he reminded Muslims that all Thamud had been condemned and perished. Mohammed told his followers that these houses which were hewed in the rock were the houses of the Thamuds. In his campaign against Tabuk, Sahih al Bukhari and Sahih Muslim said:

> When the prophet of Allah passed by al Hijr he said, 'Do not enter the houses of those who committed injustice or tyranny, unless you are weeping, so their punishment will not happen to you.' Then while he was on his camel, he veiled his face using his robe.

Also, ibn Omar reported:

> When the apostle of Allah campaigned against Tabuk, he came to al Hijr. Then he ordered his followers not to drink from the well of the city, nor to give its water to their animals. They said to him, 'We already made our baking dough from the city and took water from it as well.' He ordered them to throw away the dough and the water.[40]

This explains how he described them in the Surah with these words, "out of mountains they did hew homes." Yet we know his unhistorical statement about the city of Hijr should have been attributed to the Nabataeans.

Contrary to the historical facts, Muslims throughout history have believed that Thamud disappeared from history in the 3rd century after Noah.

We see that through various epochs of their history, Muslims (such as al Hajjaj) have believed that Thamud disappeared completely in the 3rd century after Noah. Thaqif was the main tribe of the city of Taif. Some Arabian genealogists say that the tribe of Thaqif was descended from Thamud. But al Hajjaj, who was from the tribe of Thaqif and eventually became governor of Iraq, said that those who claim that the Thaqif are descendants from Thamud either lied or were deceived because Thamud perished just as the Quran said. [41] We see how the Quran convinced Muslims, even governors and rulers, that Thamud had perished.

Evidently, Mohammed was ignorant of the true history of Thamud, which appeared in the 8th century B.C., and continued as an organized tribe until the 5th century A.D. when they were mingled with other Arabian tribes in north Arabia. No judgment or extermination of the tribe was ever reported by historians.

It is easy to see that when Mohammed wanted to bring a nation into judgment, he invented a cry or wind to deliver magical judgments to nations even though their activities were known to historians; and civilized nations reported their wars, their kings and many of their commercial activities.

The nation of Thamud appeared in Assyrian and Chaldean inscriptions and chronicles, as well in the writings of most of the Greek and Roman historians who visited the area where the Thamuds lived.

Historians recorded events involving the tribe, starting from the 5th century B.C. through the 5th century A.D. near the time of Mohammed. However, no one ever mentioned that this large tribe had been condemned and exterminated.

Yet, in full view of historical accounts, the extermination of Thamud through the cry is found in the Quran, Surah Al Hijr 15:80- 84. The Quran claims the inhabitants of Hijr, a city of North Arabia, were condemned by a cry:

> The inhabitants of Hijr have rejected the messengers. We sent them our signs, but they turned away from them. Out of mountains they hewed homes. The cry seized them in the morning and of no avail to them was all that they gained.

Thus, contrary to historical facts, Muslims believed that the Thamudi ceased to exist during the 3rd century after Noah.

The true history of Hijr

Hijr is about 24 Kilometers from the old city of Dedan. Muslims gave the name Mada'in Salih to the city of Hijr. Mada'in Salih, more accurately means "the gardens of Salih." According to the Quran, Salih was the prophet that was sent to the people of Thamud.

The city historically was not an ancient one, as the Quran claims. Dedan which was built at an oasis, was the first city to appear in that region. Scholars think it was built in the 9th century B.C. by the tribe of Dedan that descended from Dedan, son of Jokshan, the second son whom Keturah begot to Abraham after Sarah died as we see in Genesis 25:1.

Hijr was a Nabataean city, since the first century B.C.[42] When the Romans invaded western Arabia around 23 B.C., Strabo mentioned the city of Hegra which was also called Egra. He mentioned that Aretas was a Nabataean governor for the city, describing him as the kinsman of Obodas, King of the Nabataeans.[43]

The Nabataeans were known as those who hewed their homes into the rocks. We do not find any people in Arabia who did this other than the Nabataeans. This completely disproves the Quranic claim that the Thamud tribe hewed their homes into the rocks. Thamuds were not known in any of the places they inhabited to have done this. This phenomenon was known in the middle East to be exclusively Nabataean. Mohammed thought these houses hewed into the rocks were built by the Thamuds.

The city of Hegra originally was a Lihyanite site. The presence of some Lihyanite graffiti confirmed that the city was a Lihyanite before the

Nabataeans occupied it and built their city which was hewn from the rocks.[44]

We know the occupation of Lihyanite by the city of Dedan took place during the Persian period in Mesopotamia and during the Hellenistic period.[45] Therefore, Hijr as a Lihyanite site must have existed sometime after the 4th century B.C. The founder of the Lihyanite kingdom reigned approximately from 330-320 B.C. Information concerning the kings who succeeded him is well-documented. King Shahru II reigned between 320-305 B.C. The line ended with the tenth king, Mas'udu, who reigned from 120-100 B.C.[46] After the reign of King Mas'udu, the Nabataeans took over.

The city of Hijr as a Nabataean city. The true date when some Thamudi came to live outside the city.

Mohammed thought the Thamuds were the inhabitants of the city claimed they hewed their houses from the rock. Evidently, he confused them with the Nabataeans who were indeed the inhabitants of Hijr and who hewed their houses from the rock. Hijr was a Lahyanite city that appeared after the fourth century B.C., and was occupied by the Nabataeans in the first century B.C.

The Thamuds who emigrated to Hijr after the second century A.D. were in the minority. But Mohammed claimed the city was totally Thamudic and that they were the third generation after Noah.

Mohammed also said they were totally exterminated with a loud cry. This is an enormous historical mistake. He assumed that all the Thamud people had lived in Hijr, but, the Thamuds were known to have spread throughout a vast area between the Red Sea and the Mesopotamia border. Archeologists have discovered many of their sites in various parts of North Arabia. History tells us that Thamud was a strong tribe with numerous people–enough to conduct an attack on the Assyrian empire.

Thamud inscriptions were found, not in Hijr, but in neighboring areas of the city. However, these inscriptions are quite few to consider the indigenous inhabitants of the city as Thamudic. Modern archaeologists such as Winnet and Reed, specialist in the archeology of North Arabia, say these kinds of inscriptions are bilingual, Nabataean and Thamudic, which come from 267 A.D. This shows us that some Thamuds did come to the Hijr area, but not before the second or even the third century A.D., a few centuries after the Nabataean occupation of the city. The Thamuds came to

Hijr searching for a living. This was after the route connecting Yemen with North Arabia adjacent to the Red Sea flourished, and we know this occurred in the second and third centuries A.D. The Thamud groups did not live in the city itself, but, as was their custom, they lived a Bedouin lifestyle camping around the city.

Hijr as a Nabataean city is second in importance to their capital city of Petra. Their hewed houses are seen with very rich inscriptions, which are still seen on buildings, tombs and monuments in the city.

The Saudi Archaeologists and Hijr

Muslim archaeologists admit that the Thamudi did not inhabit the city of Hijr. Halimeh Muthafer wrote in al Sharq al Awsat, an Arabic magazine, in article No. 10146, dated September 8, 2006. Muthafer quoted Arabic archaeologists who stated that several archaeologists confirmed to al Sharq al Awsat that, until now, their excavations had turned up no archaeological or scientific evidence to indicate that the Thamudi lived in the city called Madaen Saleh, which was the Islamic name for Hijr. The city of Madaen Saleh is about 22 Kilometers from al Ula, which is the Islamic name for the city of Dedan. About the ruins and rocks that are hewn as castles, in reality they were burial places for the Nabataeans. The tombs were cut from the rocks as far back as 2,100 years ago.

The archaeologist Farajallah Ahmed Yusef told al Sharq al Awsat magazine that all the rocks that were cut in the city of Hijr were Nabataean burial places. The most ancient of them dates back to 100 years B.C. Those burial places have nothing to do with Thamud. Farajallah added that Madain Saleh, the new name given to the city of Hijr, did not refer to the prophet Saleh but rather to a man named Saleh from the clan of Beni Abbass. The city was named after him in the 14th century A.D. The writings and research of Saudi archaeologist Abed al Rahman al Ansari also confirms Yusef's findings.

Farajallah continued, "While excavating the areas where people lived in the city of Hijr, we did not find any inscriptions – not even a single word that suggests the Thamudi lived in the area." Everything we found were either Lahyanite or Nabataean. However, we found one Thamudic word south of Tabuk but not in Ula [Dedan]. The Islamic religious authority in Saudi Arabia issued a verdict, prohibiting people from living in Madain

Saleh [Hijir], claiming that it was the place where the Thamudic people of "prophet Saleh" lived. Farajallah said that the religious authority had issued this verdict, that people were not to live there based on the interpretation of a Hadith, which showed that Mohammed passed quickly through the area, and told the people they were not to drink or eat there, because the Thamudi, who were considered the people of Saleh, were tormented there. The religious authority issued this verdict without consulting the archeologists or the archeological discoveries in the area."

Although the evidence these men uncovered and the reports they gave were impressive, they were further confirmed by Mutlaq Suleiman Mutlaq, the vice-director of archeological sites and Museums in the region of al Ula [Dedan]. He said 132 rocks hewed in and around al Hijir were all Nabataean burial places and the analysis of human bones found in the burial places date back to 100 B. C. when the Nabataean civilization began in that area. He also said it is not true that the rocks in which the cutting took place were never finished were Thamudic. This claim was refused because there was no scientific proof."

While accompanying the representatives of al Sharq al Awsat magazine in a tour of al Hijir and al Ula, Al Mutlaq told them that their argument about Hijir as the place of Thamud was only based on the Quran and Hadith, but this judgment is without any scientific or archeological evidence.

Dr. Khaled Ascobi, of the Archeology and Tourism Agency in Saudi Arabia, refuted the claim that there are some rocky hills in Madain Saleh, which is al Hijir, which were not hewed, so they were Thamudic. He said, "During my scientific research and study I never heard of such claim. This is not a scientific claim. Until now, three excavations have been accomplished in the area of al Hijir. We did not find any archeological proof that appertains to Thamud. All what we have found was surely Nabataean."

Representatives of al Sharq al Awsat magazine visited the area on May 14, 2006. Based on the opinions of western scientists and archaeologists who conducted surveys in the region, the representatives reported in detail about the ruins found in the area. Among those scientists was the British archaeologist John Hily from Manchester University. Through his research, which was published in Atlal, Saudi archeological literature, Hily confirmed that all the hewed rocks belonged to the Nabataeans. He excluded the

Muslim claim about al Hijir that it was the city where the Thamudi lived. He said the people of Thamud had nothing to do with the region."

So, we see that both western and Arabic archeologists confirmed that al Hijir was not the place where the Thamudi lived. Even though the Arabic archeologists, are Muslims, they could not agree with the claim of the Quran and with Mohammed. Their courage is something to admire.

An article written by Abed Aziz al Anzi عبد العزيز العنزي was published in many Saudi magazines, including Ukkath, which is a weekly Saudi magazine produced in Jeddah. In issue 2112 from March 30, 2007, he said, "Many people seem to think that Madain Saleh is named after the prophet Saleh. This is a mistake of which people must be made aware. People have been calling the city by this name since the 14th century. Ibn Nasser al Deen Mohammed Abdellah reported that Abi Mohammed al Qassem al- Barzali determined that Madain Saleh was named after Saleh, who was from the clan of Abbass, the son of Abdel Mutaleb. Before that, the city was known for its true name, al Hijir."

Muslims tried to connect the archeological findings to the story mentioned in the Quran about the camel of Saleh and Thamud. They tried to make the myth of the Quran look as though it was documented in archeology. Among the false documentation of the Quran lays a large stone cylinder, whose diameter is over 12 feet and it has a depth of seven feet. Many Muslims think that the stone cylinder was a pail used by Saleh to milk his camel. Archeologists, such as Jaussen and Savignac, found evidence that the stone cylinder was part of an ancient temple at Dedan "which stood in the center of an open court along two sides of which ran arcades containing statues set on pedestals bearing dedicatory inscriptions."[47]

The educated people of Saudi Arabia admit that the stone cylinder was part of a pagan temple, and has nothing to do with Saleh or his camel. For example, the daily Riad newspaper from Friday, November 15, 2002, issue 12565, ran an article written by Turki bin Ibrahim al Qahidan تركي بن ابراهيم القهيدان. Qahidan speaks about the stone, saying that its best-known as the vessel where the camel of Saleh put her milk, but it was part of an ancient temple, which comes from the third century B.C. Qahidan continues to say that scholars think the stone was in the middle of a temple dedicated to the gods of the Lahyanites. This idea is confirmed by the number of idols and statues which surrounded the stone. The stone was a rock and was hewed in this form to keep the water in the temple.

According to the Quran there was a complete extermination of the Thamudi in the third century after Noah.

Mohammed claimed that the Thamudi tribe was exterminated through a cry and ceased to exist. No trace of the tribe remained. We read in surah Hud 11:67-68:

> The cry overtook the wrongdoers, and they lay prostrate in their homes before the morning, as if they had never dwelt and flourished there. Ah! Behold! For the Thamud rejected their Lord! Ah! Behold! Removed (from sight) were the Thamud!

According to the Arabic language of the Quran the last verse means they were completely exterminated and existed no more. But we know that Thamud remained as an organized tribe in north Arabia until the 5th century A.D.

Some Muslims may contend that a few who believed and followed Saleh survived and multiplied to form the tribe once again. We answer by saying that, according to the Quran, all the Thamudi were in the city of Hijr and were thus all exterminated. Not one person remained from the tribe. In Surah Hud 11:67-68, Mohammed claimed that the tribe was condemned through a cry, and ceased to exist:

> And the cry overtook the wrong-doers, so they lay (dead), prostrate in their homes, as if they had never lived there. No doubt! Verily, Thamud disbelieved in their lord. So away with Thamud!

Expositors of the Quran, such as Taberi, quoting ibn Abbass, also said that the Thamudi were removed completely as if they never existed.[48]As a matter of fact, when the Quran used the term "away with" in the above verses against Thamud he meant that the nation would be completely destroyed – i.e., that all the Thamudi would die and be removed from history. In the same Surah of Hud, verse 44, the Quran used the same term "away with" in condemning the generation of Noah, saying that all inhabitants of the earth perished through the flood:

> Then the word went forth: 'O earth! swallow up thy water, and O sky! Withhold (thy rain)!' and the water abated, and the matter was ended. The Ark rested on Mount Judi, and the word went forth: 'Away with those who do wrong!'

A question may be asked of those who claim that a group of Thamudi, who followed Saleh, had escaped from this cry and that the descendants of this group were the Thamudi who later appeared: Why do we not see in the

Thamudic inscriptions any mention of Saleh, the she-camel, and the cry of Gabriel who destroyed their people? Why is there no monotheistic heritage of the progenies of those monotheistic groups who followed Saleh?

Saleh

The Quran claimed that Saleh, an Arabic name, was a prophet who lived in the 3rd generation after Noah

The Quran claims that Allah sent a prophet by the name of Saleh to the Arabian tribe of Thamud. The name Saleh in Arabic means "righteous" and belongs to a later generation. It cannot be associated with the time of Noah or the 3rd century after Noah.

The name Saleh does not belong to old Arabic. This name is not found in the Semitic languages, which were closer to the time of Noah than Arabic was

The Arabic language was not spoken before the 10th century B.C. The oldest Thamudic inscriptions were totally different from the Arabic language in which the name Saleh is found. Scholars and archaeologists could not even read old Thamudic inscriptions with accuracy because of the great variation in the Arabic. [49]

Compared to other Semitic languages, Arabic is more recent. Arabic was born from the North Arabian dialects. The language of Yemen is very different from the Arabic. The most ancient Arabian dialect of North Arabia is the Thamudic dialect; yet, it is very different from the Arabic of Quraysh, which is the language of the Quran, which became the language spoken in the Arab world. The Thamudic inscriptions, which go back to the 6th century B.C., are not understood by archaeologists.

The oldest inscription of the Arabic language, which archaeologists attest is close to the Arabic of the Quran, is the 'Ijel bin Haf'am عجل بن هفعم inscription. It dates to the 1st century B.C. and was written in the Musnad letters (handwriting) — the handwriting that the ancient Yemeni and Ethiopians used. This inscription was found in the village of al Faw in Saudi Arabia. Another inscription called Ain Abdat عين عبدات was written in Nabataean letters. This inscription was found in the desert of Najef and dates to the 2nd century A.D. There is also the inscription of al Namara

النمارة, which was found in the Syrian Desert and dates to the year 328 A.D. It was written in Nabataean letters similar to Arabic letters. This inscription describes Emri al Qais bin Amru, the king of Hira, as the King of the Arabs.

If the name Saleh were an ancient name used in an epoch close to the time of Noah, as the Quran state, this name would have also appeared in the Semitic languages (such as Akkadian, Aramaic, and Hebrew), which were closer than Arabic to the time of Noah. Yet, according to Semitic language experts, this name does not exist in those languages. Professor Richard Averbeck, an expert in Semitic languages and is considered an authority in those languages at American universities, made a search for this word Saleh in the Semitic languages. Averbeck concluded that this word did not exist in those languages, either as a name or as an adjective. Thus, we conclude that Saleh is a late Arabic name. This is important historical, linguistic, and archaeological evidence for excluding the claim of the existence of a prophet by the name of Saleh who lived in North Arabia.

Suppose someone claimed that a prophet lived in Italy 2,000 years ago. We would not look for this person's name in an Italian dictionary because Italian is a relatively recent language whose dialects stemmed from Latin during the 10th century A.D. Two thousand years ago Italians did not speak Italian, but Latin. Therefore, we would look for this name in Latin dictionaries – not in Italian ones. Thus, the inhabitants of North Arabia, as a Semitic population living close to the time of Noah, did not speak Arabic, a language that appeared in the 10th century B.C. Instead, they must have spoken an ancient Semitic language. We would look for the name of Saleh in the old Semitic languages, such as Akkadian, Aramaic, and Hebrew. Since Saleh did not exist in those languages, how then could this name be connected to a period close to the time of Noah or even to a time closer to us than that, such as the Akkadian era? The Akkadian era started around 2,500 B.C. and Akkadian was the dominant language in the region. It was followed by Aramaic, from which Hebrew and other Semitic languages were born. If Saleh did not exist in those languages, how then could we connect it to a period which preceded those languages?!

The name Saleh is an Arabic name that belongs to a more recent era. It has a specific meaning – "good or righteous" – and is derived from the word for goodness. It was found in the Safaitic inscriptions as one of the good names of the Safaitic gods, where the names of Rahm (meaning Rahim) and Rahmen (meaning al Rahman) were also found.[50] Safaitic inscriptions belonged to the tribes that emigrated from North Arabia to Jordan, Syria, and Israel, and they are dated between the 1st century B.C. and the 4th century A.D. They were called Safaitic because they were discovered for the first time in the area of Safa — the volcanic lands southwest of Damascus.

What is the true identity of Saleh?

The name Saleh can be found in later Arabic periods but not before the Christian era. F.V. Winnett and W.L. Reed, famous scholars of the history of North Arabia, believe that Saleh was a Christian who preached in North Arabia around al-Hijr after the collapse of the Nabataean domain. According to these scholars, the name Saleh is a substitute for this Christian's actual name.[51]

Christians sent missionaries to the northern part of Arabia. In fact, archaeologists found a Thamudic inscription dedicated to Jesus Christ with an accompanying sign of the cross. The inscription, known as inscription No. 476, dates back to the 3rd century A.D., reflecting the early spread of Christianity in North Arabia.[52]

The names that appeared after the Christian era were perceived by some pre-Islamic groups at the time of Mohammed as belonging to ancient epochs of history, before the history our present scientific age could attest to or know about, despite the progress of archaeology and the study of ancient historical writings. For example, the tribe of Ad (which as we have seen before appeared in the 2nd century A.D.) became for those Jahiliyyah groups, at the time of Mohammed, the most ancient nation that appeared on Earth after Noah's time. No wonder that the name of an evangelist who visited North Arabia at a time after the Christian era became for those Jahiliyyah groups a prophet who belonged to the 3rd century after Noah. These groups misunderstood because they lacked any historical chronology. When they heard names such as Ad, Thamud, and Saleh attributed to periods very close to the time of Noah, they were easily deceived. In his narration, Mohammed was a victim of this phenomenon of Jahiliyyah ignorance.

Mohammed introduced the pre-Islamic Jahiliyyah elements of chronology as part of his narration about Biblical names.

An obvious trend in the Quran is this: In his narration, Mohammed adopted the myths that some naïve groups believed about historical figures in his time, especially myths about names the Bible mentioned. Mohammed did this so that he would appear knowledgeable of Biblical stories. This is similar to someone who would dare to introduce the myths of the "Arabian One Thousand Nights" into Roman history as if they were historical facts that could complete the documented Roman history.

Mohammed placed the Thamud and Ad and their prophets on the tongue of Moses, as if they were known in Egyptian history or were as famous as Noah. On the contrary, Moses made no mention of them whatsoever. To give the reader an idea of this, I quote Surah 14, called Ibrahim:

> And Moses said: 'If ye show ingratitude, ye and all on earth together, yet is Allah free of all wants, worthy of all praise. Has not the story reached you, (O people!), of those who (went) before you? – of the people of Noah, and Ad, and Thamud? – And of those who (came) after them? None knows them but Allah. To them came apostles with Clear (Signs); but they put their hands up to their mouths, and said: 'We do deny (the mission) on which ye have been sent, and we are really in suspicious (disquieting) doubt as to that to which ye invite us.' (Surah 14:8-9)

There is also a Quranic narration about "a believer from the people of Pharaoh" who admonished Pharaoh and the Egyptians that they would suffer what the people of Ad and Thamud went through:

> And he who believed said: 'O my people! Verily, I fear for you a fate like that day (of disaster) of the Confederates (of old)! Like the fate of the people of Nuh (Noah), and Ad, and Thamud and those who came after them. And Allah wills no injustice for (his) slaves.' (Surah Ghafer 40:30-31)

This is stated as if Thamud and Ad were famous tribes the Egyptians and Moses knew about in the 15th century B.C. and that existing famous judgments in world history happened to those two Arabian tribes to the extent that a "believer of the clan of Pharaoh" admonished the Egyptians that they would suffer the same fate! How could Moses admonish the Egyptian people of the fate of those Arabian tribes when he neither mentioned them within the genealogies of the tribes of Earth nor listed them in the book of Genesis. Nor did he mention the myths attributed to them by the Quran, such as the she-camel of Saleh, though he wrote five books?! They were not mentioned by any of the prophets of the Old Testament or any writers of the New Testament.

The Myth of Saleh's She-Camel

The story of the Thamud and Saleh is narrated in the Quran in summary form. We know few of the details from the Quran. We get the details from the expositors of the Quran and from the poetry of Umayyah bin abi al Salt. For example, the Quran did not mention how the she-camel came, but we know from outside sources that it came out from a rock.[53]

The expositors of the Quran explained that the rock went into travail and gave birth to a she-camel. The she-camel came out of the rock pregnant and gave birth to its child.[54]The expositors claimed that the rock's name was Katibah. The people of Saleh asked Saleh to bring a she-camel out of the rock; he brought out a camel who was pregnant and in a state of travail.[55]

There is a Hadith in al Taberi attributed to Mohammed in which he gave details about how the she-camel was killed and how its son escaped to a mountain. Allah made the mountain rise until it reached a height that the birds could not reach.[56] Mohammed thus depended upon a myth already existing in his generation that he summarized in his Quran in a few sentences. These sentences are not understood without the details found outside the Quranic text.

The original detail of the she-camel myth is found in the poetry of Umayyah bin abi al Salt.

There is poetry of Umayyah, in which he speaks about the she-camel and how it was killed.[57] This suggests that he was an important source of the Quranic myth. In some stanzas Umayyah spoke about the Thamud and how it abandoned religion. In other stanzas he mentioned the son of the she-camel and its return to enter the rock whence his mother had come out and how it cried in a loud voice — in addition to other details of the myth.[58] Thus, Umayyah gave many more details of the myth than the Quran. The story of the she-camel in the Quranic narration, and how it was a direct inspiration from Allah to Mohammed, cannot be spoken of. Since Muslims do not believe that Umayyah was a prophet, the Quranic narration is therefore not an inspiration of Allah to Umayyah. It is a myth propagated at the time of Umayyah.

The style of the she-camel myth agrees with the style of the ancient pagan myths, especially those that were widespread in Arabia.

This mythological style, which often brought gods or deified animals out of rocks, was not strange in pagan literature. In the Roman tradition, Mithra came from a rock; therefore, the rock became his mother, who was called Genetrix. [59]

The mythical style also agrees with Arabian mythology. For example, the people of Thaqif believed that Ellat was a man from the tribe of Thaqif who entered the rock and was worshiped. There is a famous phrase attributed to Amru bin Lahi addressing the people of Thaqif: "...your lord was Ellat; he entered inside the rock."[60]

We see here that the pre-Islamic people of Jahiliyyah believed that beings could enter into and come out of a rock. Animal or human gods, who were worshiped in the Jahiliyyah period, could enter into rocks and come out of them. This explains the Quranic myth of the she-camel of Saleh, which is in accordance with Arabian Jahiliyyah myths. Its existence, as we will later see, is of Persian Zoroastrian origin.

We notice that the son of the she-camel had entered into the rock after its mother was killed. This confirms that the she-camel story agrees with the nature of the Jahiliyyah myths. Therefore, we understand how big rocks in Arabia gave the impression to the Arabians that they were gods, or that gods came out of them, or entered into them. An example is the Mount of al Howarah: it is a smooth rocky mountain from which most Muslims believe the she-camel came out, and to which its son, called Howar حوار, returned.

She-camels had special importance to some Arabian tribes. Some tribes, such as Iyad, even believed that they were blessed by the she-camels[61] in the same way that the Hindus believe they are blessed by the cows. This makes us assume that the she-camel of Saleh was a camel some Arabian tribes worshiped in the time of Mohammed or in a previous generation. The idea that the she-camel came out of a certain rock in the area of Hijr suggests that the inhabitants of that region worshiped that rock. Also, the idea that the she-camel drank all the water appointed for the people reflects the notion that she came was deified by the superstitious people of Jahiliyyah.

The pre-Islamic people of Jahiliyyah looked to some she-camels as good or righteous beings. That is why they bound a she-camel near the tombs of their fathers — so that when their fathers are led to the Seat of Judgment, they can mount these camels. We see an example in the poem of Juraibah bin Ashim, stirring his son to select for him a righteous and good she-camel that he can mount in the Day of Judgment. [62]

The Zoroastrian origin of the myth of the deified camel

When the Quran comments on the Thamud, on Saleh, and on the she-camel, it adopts information from a Zoroastrian myth. It is easy to verify the origin of the Quran's myth when you compare the Zoroastrian version with the Quran's version.

Zoroastrian literature speaks about a mythological bull that is presented in their sacred literature as having great roles. We see this in Zad-Sparam, which is part of the Pahlavi Texts.[63] The story here is about a bull, but the Arabians adopted this myth as the She-camel of Thamud and used a she-camel instead of a bull because the camel is the main domestic animal of the Arabians.

The Zoroastrian myth can be simplified as following:

The Persians were in continuous war with the people of Turan who often attacked Persian borders. Because the Turanians continuously violated their borders, the priest made glowing supplications to Ahura Mazda, the main deity of the Zoroastrians. Ahura Mazda answered their prayers by miraculously bringing forth a bull. The Zoroastrian texts did not specify how their god brought forth the bull. It could have come from a rock or a plant or in some other way, but certainly it was in a magical way. [64]

This bull presented a challenge to all the people of Turan. Its assignment was to watch the borders, hoofing and pawing its feet, threatening everyone who wanted to cross the border to attack the Persians. When the bull informed the Persians that the Turanians violated their borders, the bull was used to punish the big nation. The book of Dincard describes the bull's role and how he carried it out. [65]

The Turrians conspired against the bull, they sent a man to injure the bull, which then led to its death. [66]

As a result, Ahura Mazda became angry at the people of Turan, and retaliated by condemning them to violent deaths. (see the story in Selection of Zad -Sparam XII: 7 –21)

The Arabians before the time of Mohammed copied the myth in an Arabian form. Then the Quran incorporated the Zoroastrian myth, reflecting similar wording and content but taking in consideration the culture of Arabia. The Quran repeats the myth of the bull but calls it a she-camel. After continuous contention between Saleh, the prophet of Allah according to the Quran, and the people of Thamud, Allah brought forth the she-camel from a rock. It was an instant miracle. The camel was created instantly as Ahura Mazda instantly created the bull.

Allah brought forth the camel to punish the people of Thamud, because they violated his orders. Therefore, the she-camel became a continuous threat to the people of Thamud, in the same way the bull became a continuous threat to the people of Turan. Saleh chose a regulation to enable the she-camel to control the people of Thamud, in such a way that the people of Thamud became under the mercy of the she-camel. This regulation consisted in controlling the spring of water from which the people of Thamud drank water, by alternating access to the spring: On one day all the people of Thamud could drink from the spring of water, but the following day only the she-camel could drink. As a result, the people of Thamud were distressed by this special she-camel, because when it became the camel's turn, she drank all the water forcing the people of Thamud to obey the tough regulations of Allah and his servant, Saleh. It is exactly the same way the people of Turan were distressed by the bull, which made them submit to the regulation of Ahura Mazda in observing the borders with the Persians.

The Persian myth was clothed in Arabian attire in the Quran. But its elements are clear in both narrations. In reality, this Persian myth took on an Arabian nature considering the water was the important border in Arabia. There were no contentions over borders between the Arabian tribes. Instead, due to the rarity of water springs in Arabia, they now fought over the water itself. With this in mind, we understand how the borders between Turan and the Persians were placed in the Arabian form and the Quran as a myth about the water and the she-camel was in a position to compel the people of Thamud to observe the law imposed by Saleh and Allah, in the same way the bull put the Turanians under obligation to respect the borders defined by Ahura Mazda.

The myths converge again. The Quran claims the people of Thamud conspired against the she-camel, because she opposed their plot to violate the rules imposed upon them by Allah and Saleh. In the same way, the people of Turan conspired against the bull which compelled them to respect the borders imposed by Ahura Mazda. As the bull was injured by a Turanian after a plot was prepared by the people, so the she-camel was injured by a Thamudian after a plot was prepared by the people. Likewise, as Ahura Mazda retaliated against the people of Turan, so Allah retaliated against the people of Thamud exterminating them with a loud cry.

Usually myths are not restricted by borders. Although they vary by degree, they readily cross from one nation into another. The Zoroastrian myth of the bull crossed into Arabia with limited variations making it easily recognizable. As the hunter recognizes the gazelle that crosses the border of one nation into another nation, even though the deer suffer from the drought and aridity of the deserted land of the country where it enters, the bull's myth crossed into Arabia, even though it added Arabian character and proprieties.

The Thamudi lived outside of the Nabataean city

Mohammed claimed that all the Thamudi tribe lived in the city of al Hijr. The fact was, however, that Thamud was a great tribe, one of the largest tribes of northern Arabia, whose extensive territory included a large portion of the region. Mohammed saw the buildings excavated in the rocks in the area of al Hijr and attributed these houses to the Thamudi. It is known, however, that these structures were not houses but mostly tombs, which were excavated by the Nabataeans who built the city after they occupied it from the Lahyanites. The place dates to the 4th century B.C. As we mentioned before, after the 2nd century A.D. some Thamudi had erected their tents in the area of Hijr. They were not the main inhabitants of the city; the Nabataeans were the main inhabitants. Mohammed, however, considered them to have been the inhabitants of the city since the time of Noah – in spite of the fact that the Thamudi did not appear before the 8th century B.C. Not one of them had inhibited the city of Hijr before the Nabataeans built the city during the 1st century B.C. or A.D.

Furthermore, Mohammed claimed that the Thamudi were exterminated through a cry, as if all the people of Thamud lived in the city of Hijr and their extermination occurred in ancient times, that is, in the third generation after Noah. Those are serious historical and geographical mistakes, which were accepted by some ignorant groups of Jahiliyyah.

The Thamudi had never been part of the Hijr population, they never hewed their houses in the rock, as the Quran claims. The Nabataeans were those who hewed those houses, for this kind of architecture was known to be theirs. The houses and tombs that were hewn in the rocks in the city of Hijr where documented historically to have been built by the Nabataeans, through the numerous Nabataean inscriptions, which still exist on the houses, tombs, and buildings. As a whole, they are considered second in importance after those found in their capital city Petra.

In reality, the Thamudi inscriptions on stones were not found in the city of Hijr but in the surroundings. Very few consider the original inhabitants of the city to be Thamudi. To verify these facts, we refer the reader to the research of archaeologists such as Winnet and Reed, who are specialists in the archaeology of Northern Arabia.

We learn another thing from those scholars: Those inscriptions that are attributed to the Thamud were written in both Nabataean and Thamudi languages. They go back to a late date, beginning in the year 267 A.D.[67]

This indicates that the coming of the Thamudi to that region did not occur before the 2nd or 3rd century, that is some centuries after the Nabataeans occupied the city. The Thamudi came to the suburbs of the city in search of a place to live. This was after the land route adjacent to the Red Sea had flourished. This route connected Yemen with northern Arabia. We know that during the beginning of the second or third century A. D. those groups of Thamudi did not live in the city but lived rather in tents around the city because the Thamudi were known to have lived a semi-nomadic or bedouin lifestyle.

The Thamudi existence was attested in the Roman army during the 4th century A.D.

The Greek and Roman geographers and historians mentioned the tribe of Thamud before and after the beginning of the Christian era. The Thamudi were part of the Roman army during the 4th century A.D., as we see in the famous Roman document Notitia Dignitatum.[68] The same document speaks about two Thamudi military units that were part of the Byzantine army: one in Israel and the other in Egypt.[69] The Thamudi cavalry unit was in Veteranorum Scenae, a Roman territory in Egypt.[70] Mohammed, however, claimed that the Thamudi were removed from history during the 3rd generation after Noah as we have seen in Surah Hud, verses 67 and 68.

Summary of the historical mistakes of the Quran regarding Thamud

First, according to the Quran, Thamud appeared in the 3rd century after Noah; the fact is that the Thamud appeared at the beginning of the 8th century B.C.

Second, the Quran claims that the Thamudi built the city of Hijr and that hewed their houses in the rocks; the fact is that the Thamudi neither built the city of Hijr nor hewed houses in the rocks. The Nabataeans built the city of Hijr; they were the only nation known in the Middle East to hew their houses in the rocks.

Third, the Quran states that the entire tribe of Thamud lived in the Nabataean city of Hijr. In reality, Thamud was a great tribe that extended into most of the region north of Arabia, as well as into the desert regions between Arabia and Mesopotamia.

Fourth, the Quran claims that Thamud had a prophet by the name of Saleh during the 3rd century after Noah. We have seen that this name does not match the ancient Semitic names.

Fifth, the Quran claims that the Thamudi perished and were exterminated completely through a cry in the 3rd century after the Noahic flood. In fact, they continued as an organized tribe until the 5th century A.D., that is until a period close to the rise of Islam.

Objections to the she-camel myth

At the end of this study, I present the following objections to the she-camel of Saleh:

First, the story is formed in an unhistorical frame that contradicts both archaeology and history – a fact that Arabic archaeologists have admitted.

Second, when the story claimed to bring forth living beings from a stone or rock, it contradicts divine principles. God will not create another Adam from the dust because God established a principle that the entire human race should be born naturally from Adam. This kind of Arabian myth is similar to the Arabian myths of al Maskh, which features the phenomenon of beings changing into stones. Also, it is similar to the entrance of gods into rocks, as we have seen that Ellat entered a rock.

Third, God never created an animal such as a cow or she-camel in a unique way or separately to be a subject of special creation. God made Adam important when He created him from dust and then breathed the breath of life into him. Then He created Eve from one of Adam's ribs to show the importance of the oneness of the family formed from one man and one woman. But God never created a special animal in order to make its creation a prodigy or a significant sign. Why? Because man is the crown of creation created in the very image of God, and for whom all creation was made. The animals were not the subject and aim of creation. All the animals were created one time, without any focus on a special animal, as if they had special importance to compete with man's position in the sight of God. We see in this Quranic myth, however, an elevation of the she-camel, as if it became the crown of creation. In effect, as a prodigy that God created the she-camel became more important than man. The she-camel was given privileges over all the inhabitants of Thamud: On one day it alone drinks the water; on the next day, all the people drink.

Fourth, the she-camel is portrayed as the most important creature over all humans in history. God never condemned a nation because of the death of one man. The people of Israel often killed their prophets, but God did not retaliate by exterminating the Israelites and destroying their cities. In our day, we see thousands of devout Christian believers killed by hostile governments and populations, and yet God does not retaliate by destroying their cities or exterminating their populations. According to this myth, however, Allah condemned all the Thamudi, exterminating them for the sake of this she-camel. This act makes this deified she-camel as a goddess of great value more important than the human race. The god of the Quran has more concern and feelings for the she-camel than for the members of the tribe — as if they were insects that could readily be exterminated for killing one camel.

We notice that in the Quran all judgments executed against nations were without justification, such as in this case of the she-camel, or when the Quran claimed that the city of Antioch was destroyed because some people there did not receive the "two missionaries" sent to it. Or, when the Quran claimed that the Midianites were exterminated because they did not give just measures and weights in their commerce. God never exterminated a whole population or nation because they did not receive the message of a prophet. God never executed judgments of extermination against nations because they were pagans.

Fifth, the mythological nature of the story of the she-camel and Saleh is very clear. It is also obvious that those who embraced the myth were ignorant, especially when we consider the great size of the tribe of Thamud and its expansion, as we see in the history of Arabia. It is absurd this notion that on one day the she-camel drank alone and on the second day all the tribes people drank and that the people of this massive tribe complained because the she-camel drank their water. Furthermore, the claim that the large tribe milked the she-camel and fed on its milk is ludicrous.

All these things prove that Mohammed ignored the size of the tribe of Thamud, which inhabited a large region of North Arabia, and was the most powerful of North Arabian tribes. In fact, the Thamudi led a war against the Assyrian kingdom, the greatest kingdom in the world during the 8th century B.C.

The expansion of the Thamud tribe in North Arabia is attested by the richness of their inscriptions in many regions. The Thamudic inscriptions are classified in three categories: the Najd, the Hejaz, and the Tabuk inscriptions. This reflects the spread of the Thamudi population in these regions.[71] The Thamud tribe also had villages in the deserts. In fact, Thamudic inscriptions were found in distant places far from Arabia, such as on the furthest border of Jordan with Iraq. All these historical facts show how great the tribe was in size and in expansion.

The Quranic notions about the struggle of the Thamudi against a she-camel, and the judgment of the tribe and their extermination in the way the Quran describes it, makes any student of history chuckle. The Quran stated that the extermination of the whole tribe occurred in the city of Hijr, which was not a Thamudic city at all. This Quranic narration is contradictory to the expansion of the Thamud tribe into most of North Arabia, part of the southern Jordan desert, and into Iraqi deserts.[72]

Saying that a she-camel drinks in one day from a well of water, and on the second day all the Thamud tribe drinks, assumes that well was the size of a large lake. This, however, does not agree with the geography of Arabia, which does not have lakes. Furthermore, there is no lake in the city of Hijr that would justify the Quranic narration. The story also contradicts logic: it is like saying that a cow drinks the waters of a country like Jordan or Syria, and then the second day all the inhabitants of Jordan or Syria drink. Or, in one day they all drink the milk of the cow and are fed on its milk.

Furthermore, it is not feasible that the whole Thamud tribe would be imprisoned in a city where they never lived (the city of Hijr) and then summarily exterminated with a cry. That would be like claiming that all the inhabitants of Jordan and Syria lived in the Jordanian city of Irbid and all perished through a cry. Thus, the she-camel story is a primitive and naïve myth that reflects Mohammed's lack of understanding of its mythological nature and the naïveté and ignorance of the group who accepted it in his generation.

Sixth, neither the she-camel myth nor the name of Saleh exists in the Thamudic inscriptions. If the Thamudi who had lived throughout history were descendants of Saleh and his friends who had not perished by the cry, they would have been believers in God. The name and memory of their ancestor Saleh would have remained in their culture. They would certainly have mentioned something about the story and about Saleh.

The Quran made Saleh a great Arabian prophet in history, just as Moses was for the Israelites. Had a prophet by the name of Saleh existed, God would not have allowed the Thamudi to forget the name of their prophet. God would not have allowed all the prophets of the Bible to miss Saleh's name and the story of his people. God ensured that the story of Job was mentioned in both the Old and New Testaments, although he was not a Hebrew prophet.

It is impossible for someone to succeed in inserting new revelations or information to what God had already inspired through history. This is one of many aspects that distinguishes the Biblical truth from the Quranic claims: The Quran added names of prophets, such as Saleh, Hud, and Shaib, to tribes and nations without there being any documentation or attestation of those names in the records of these tribes and nations.

The Midianites
The Case of the Midianites in the Quran and History

The Thamuds were not the only people for whom Mohammed claimed extinction. Mohammed placed the Midianites close to the time of Sodom and Gomorra and eventually removed them completely from history. In Surah Hud 11, verse 89, Mohammed claimed that they had a prophet, called Shuyeb. Shuyeb addresses his people:

> Oh my people. Let not my dissent with you cause you to suffer a fate similar to what occurred to the people of Noah or of Hud or of Salih nor are the people of Lut far off from you.

It is interesting to note that Mohammed treated both Saleh and Hud as if they were famous prophets like Noah, prominent in the worship of God throughout history. Mohammed assumed those two names were familiar to the people of Midian. We know that the Midianites lived in the Sinai region in their early history; thus, Mohammed claimed that the Midianites knew as much about Saleh and Hud as they knew about various important figures in their history. In Surah 14, called Ibrahim, verse 9, Mohammed assumed that Thamud and Ad, and the prophets he created for them, were names known to the Egyptians and their Pharaoh at the time of Moses in the 15th century B.C. The Quran claims that Moses warned Pharaoh that what happened to the people of Noah, Thamud, and Ad, would happen also to him.

Such unhistorical assertions are ludicrous because (as we have previously seen) there is no historical record of the tribe of Thamud before the 8th century B.C. As for Ad, if it existed in history, it was a small tribe that no one outside of Arabia had ever heard of. It appeared in the 2nd century A.D. and was absorbed by other North Arabian tribes. If Saleh and Hud had existed and performed the miracles attributed to them, God could not possibly have disregarded them and neglected to reveal in the Holy Bible their astonishing acts – such as Saleh bringing forth a she-camel from a rock and prophesying the coming of judgment to their people through a strong wind or an ear-splitting cry. We must also ask why God, in the Old and New Testaments, did not warn other peoples, such as the people of Israel, of judgment through wind and cries? We find no reference to either Thamud or Ad in either the Old Testament nor the New Testament.

The Bible describes judgments against many people who lived great distances from Thamud and Ad. However, the judgments which the Quran says took place between Noah's flood and the judgment of Sodom and Gomorrah, were the judgments of Ad and Thamud. How could God forget to mention this to any of His prophets? The Bible tells us about judgments against hundreds of peoples, many of whom were farther more remote than where Thamud and Ad. In reality, the Quran inserted Arabian myths, which spread during Mohammed's time to a few Arabian tribes around Mecca and Medina, as if they were great historical facts. Mythological figures were treated as great historical figures, greater than Noah. Even Pharaoh and the Egyptians were familiar with those judgments and the mythological figures which Mohammed described in the Quran.

The Quran added a new judgment against Midian, placing it in a very remote and distant time

Hud and Saleh were the names of the prophets that Mohammed assigned to the tribes of Ad and Thamud. He dated Midian very close to God's judgment of Lot, only one or two generations removed from the destruction of Sodom and Gomorrah, which occurred in the beginning of the 2nd millennium B.C. According to Mohammed's chronology, the Midianites would have lived in the 20th or 19th century B.C.

The Bible tells a different story. The Midianites came from Keturah, whom Abraham married after Sarah died, as reported in Genesis 25:1-4:

> Abraham again took a wife, and her name was Keturah. And she bore him Zimran, Jokshan, Medan, Midian, Ishbak and Shuah. Jokshan begot Sheba and Dedan. The sons of Dedan were Ashurim, Letushim and Leummim, and the sons of Midian were Ephah, Epher, Hanoch, Abidah and Eldaah. All these were the children of Keturah.

It was not until the 17th century B.C. that the descendants of Midian became a nation.

The following is Mohammed's account of the cry that removed the Midianites from history (Surah Hud 11:94-95):

The Cry seized the wrongdoers and they lay prostrate in their houses
in the morning, as if they had never dwelt and flourished there. So away
with Midian, as away with Thamud!

Expositors of the Quran agree that these verses imply that Midian no
longer existed. We have already seen that the term "away with" in the Quran
(as it is used in the above verses against Midian as well as in the case of the
extermination of Thamud) means a complete destruction of the nation in
which all would be dead and removed from history. In the same Surah of
Hud, verse 44, the Quran again uses the term "away with" in condemning
the generation of Noah to indicate that all inhabitants of the earth perished
through the flood:

Then the word went forth: "O earth! swallow up thy water, and O sky!
Withhold (thy rain)!" and the water abated, and the matter was ended.
The Ark rested on Mount Judi, and the word went forth: "Away with
those who do wrong!"

Removing the Midianites from history at a time close to when Lot lived
shows how Mohammed simply dealt promptly and quickly with the people
of the world by using magical cries. He was completely ignorant of their
history. Not only did he display total ignorance about the chronology of the
people as to when they appeared in history, but he also completely removed
nations from history who lived close to his time. He claimed that they had
been exterminated in ancient times.

The Midianites in the Bible

The Midianites are mentioned 39 times in the Bible, beginning in the
time of Joseph and subsequently in various epochs of Biblical history. They
first lived in southern Sinai and then expanded toward the regions around
the Gulf of Aqaba and southern Moab. The Midianites were known for
their trade with neighboring nations, especially Egypt and Israel. The Bible
speaks about them from their first stages of growth as a tribe. We read in
Genesis 37:28:

So when the Midianite merchants came by, his brothers pulled Joseph
up out of the cistern and sold him for twenty shekels[a] of silver.

At the time of Joseph, the Midianites were not yet a nation but rather
groups of merchants who traded between Gilead and Egypt.

In the book of Exodus, we read that after Moses fled from Egypt he went to live with the Midianites. This indicates that, as of around 1525 B.C., southern Sinai was part of Midian territory. In fact, Moses lived among them for 40 years when he was in southern Sinai. He married a Midianite woman. Though Moses' own father-in-law, Jethro, was a priest of the Midianites, Moses never reported what the Quran alleges to be the extermination of the tribe of Midian. In the book of Genesis, Moses gave details about various tribes and nations that were very distant from where the Midianites lived. Without doubt, Moses' knowledge of the Midianites surpassed even our knowledge about them. Furthermore, Moses mentioned men of God who were not Israelites; yet, he never mentioned that there existed a prophet by the name of Shu'aib. Moses had intimate knowledge of the Midianites, whereas the pre-Islamic people of Jahiliyyah were ignorant of accurate Midianite history. The people of Jahiliyyah had no knowledge of archeology or references about the Midianites. In Genesis 25:4, Moses mentioned the five sons from whom descended the five Midianite tribes.

Had this "cry" occurred, Moses would certainly have mentioned it! In fact, it would have been the main subject in telling about the Midianites. Moses mentioned Melchizedek, Anoth, and Enoch. If indeed there had been a prophet by the name of Shu'aib, he would have been closer to Moses, in time and location, than the other men and tribes Moses mentioned.

Moses defeated the Midianites in the Sinai desert.

The book of Judges records that, in the time of Gideon, there was an alliance between the Midianites and the Ishmaelites. They lived together when they fought against Gideon during the 12th century B.C. In 1 Chronicles 1:46, the Bible mentions the name of an Edomite king named Hadad, son of Bedad, who defeated Midian in the land of Moab. This suggests that Midian expanded its domain into some of the Moabite regions.

The prophets of the Old Testament mentioned that the Midianites traded with Israel and Saba-Yemen. The book of Isaiah mentions Midian and Ephah, and their trade in gold and incense. Habakkuk, who wrote around 619 B.C., mentioned the tents of Midian in Habakkuk 3:7.

The Midianites in Official History

The Quran, as we have seen, claims that a cry destroyed (did "away with") the Midianites such that it was as if they had never existed. The cry removed them, just as it removed the Thamudi. The plain fact is that only a person who has never studied history could believe such sayings. What if somebody claimed that all the Assyrians had perished in a remote period of history? Historians and scholars would recognize the assertion at once as absurd, for we know that Assyrian descendants have continued to exist throughout history until this day. The Quranic claim about the Midianites is no less absurd.

The Midianites, especially the tribe of Ephah, that descended from the first-born of Midian, were mentioned several times in the Assyrian inscriptions. For example, an inscription of Sargon II, dating to the year 715 or 716, mentions Ephah. Ephah and the rest of the Midianite tribes who traded on the spice route that ran from India and passed through Yemeni coasts were directed to the Fertile Crescent. Ephah also formed alliances with other tribes against the Assyrians and the Chaldeans.

The book of Judith, an apocryphal book that dates to the 4th century B.C., mentioned the campaign of Nebuchadnezzar in North Arabia and Midian. In Judith 2:26 we read:

> He surrounded all the Midianites, and burned their tents and plundered their sheepfolds.

The classical Greek geographers who lived prior to Christ mentioned the Midianites many times. Ptolemy, a Greek geographer of the 2nd century A.D., mentioned the city of Modiama, [73] which Musil identified as Midian.[74] Josephus Flavius (37-101 A.D.) mentioned the city of Madiané. Eusebius, who lived between 260-339 A.D., says that Madiam is named after one of the sons of Abraham and Keturah. In other words, he intended Midian, one of the sons of Qatturah. Eusebius specified the location of the city, He said it was toward the desert of the Saracens,[75] southeast of Aqaba. All these historical facts indicate that the Midianites lived many centuries after the advent of Christianity.

The Midianites were mentioned under the name of Maddeni by the Procopius of Caesarea, the Byzantine historian, who was born at the end of the fifth century A.D. He wrote near the beginning of the sixth century A.D. He said that the Midianites lived during his time in Gulf of Aqaba.[76] It gives us further historical evidence that the Midianites were a nation through the fifth and sixth centuries A.D. The city was attested by archaeologists and was identified as the city of the Midianites. One of these archaeologists was

Sir R. Burton. In chapter 12 of his book The Gold Mines of Midian, he presents detailed research about the capital of the Midianites.[77]

The Midianites Remained in Existence Until After the Rise of Islam

Confirming that the Midianites remained after the rise of Islam, Jawad Ali mentioned Midian, as a nation. They were active in the Islamic era during the incursion led by Zayd bin Harithah against Jutham جـذام in Hasmaحسـمى.[78] Islamic writers mention that Midian existed in the land of Jutham during Islamic times. Yaqut al Hamawi wrote about Midian or Median:

> Maden is situated on the sea of Qalsem القلزم –another name for the Red Sea–about six Marahel from Tabuk. A Marahalah is the distance a man could walk in one day, and Marahalah the singular form of Marahel. Tabuk lies between the mount of Hasma and Mount Sharuriشـرورى. Hasma is west of Median and Sharuri is east.

Reporting data from his contemporaries, Yaqut also mentioned that Maden was both a city and a tribe. He reported that Abu Zayd said:

> Median, although larger than Tabuk, is on the Red Sea, a 6-day walk from Tabuk. Median has the well from which Moses drank. I saw it was well concealed, and a house was built over the well. The inhabitant of the city took their water from a flowing spring. Median is the name of a tribe as well as a city.

He mentioned that monks were found in Median, [79] which demonstrates the spread of Christianity in the tribe.

We understand from the aforementioned quotations that the tribe of Midian existed in the Islamic era. Its capital, Maden, was a big city, larger than Tabuk. It remained around the Aqaba Gulf, in the same area throughout its history.

Ibn Manthur mentioned abu al Hamisaابو الهميسـع, a poet of Midian. Ibn Manthur wrote, "Abu al Hamisa was from a Bedouin tribe of Midian. We hardly understood him when he talked."[80]

From this we learned there were Bedouins in Midian, whose language– even at the time of ibn Manthur–differed from Arabic, to the extent it was difficult for ibn Manthur to comprehend the words of one of their poets.

The ignorance of Mohammed's companions regarding basic historical facts. The Quran's unreliability because of its inaccurate and immature narration of history.

The Quran's claim in Surah 11:94-95 about the Midianites' removal from history at a time close to Lot is an enormous historical mistake! It is clear that the companions of Mohammed lacked even a very basic knowledge of history. They ignored the tribes who lived not very far from them, such as the Midianites who lived in the far end of North Arabia.

Unfortunately, however, many fail to acknowledge that Mohammed's claim that the Midianites were from earth at a time close to Lot despite the clear historical fact that the Midianites continued to exist for centuries after the rise of Islam completely annuls the credibility both of Mohammed as a true prophet and of the Quran itself. Many of the Quran's expositors, such as Qurtubi, supported the claim that the Midianites were condemned and removed from history through Gabriel's Cry.[81] There was no willingness to compare the claims of the Quran with the historical facts.

Reasons that Mohammed Narrated these Judgments and Stories

Mohammed readily presented examples of judgments on nations that were known to have existed to some of his listeners. He ignored the history of these nations. Mohammed's purpose was to make a good impression on his listeners by claiming that he received revelation from Allah about these nations and populations, and that through the inspiration he knew everything about any nation that the Arabians knew existed. Often in the Quran, Mohammed attributed to Allah that he is al 'Aleem العليم (meaning he knows everything). Thus, because Allah is omniscient, Mohammed is omniscient, all-knowing. Mohammed usually asked his followers if they knew about elements of cosmos or any other subject. They answered him, "Allah and his apostle know better."

Mohammed never objected to this answer, nor did he rebuke them by telling them that only God knows what they asked. He always enjoyed have his followers consider him as a prophet who, like Allah, knows everything. Mohammed wanted to appear as if he were God: knowing everything because Allah immediately provided him with all knowledge about everything. Therefore, Mohammed could not remain silent on any subject, including the history of all nations. Thus, he was ready to present any narration, such as his narration about Dhu al Qarnayn (the one with two horns), using the myths spread in his time about Alexander the Great that were taken from the book of Pseudo-Callisthenes, as we will see when discussing this subject. Mohammed cast Alexander as a Muslim who made Jihad to spread Islam, and who imprisoned Gog and Magog behind a dam between two mountains until the last day of history.

As Mohammed claimed to know all things about all tribes, he could not be silent about the subject of the Midianites. He had to define them, a part of history, through his Quranic revelation. Thus, he placed them as a nation at the time of Lot and removed them through the cry of the archangel Gabriel.

In reality, Mohammed and his companions were ignorant about the Midianites, and unaware that various Byzantine scholars and historians wrote about them, and that there was much documented knowledge about them. They even ignored the fact that the Midianites' main city existed in their own day. Mohammed and his followers ignored the accuracy of the Bible about the Midianites. Thus, instead of taking care that his sayings would one day be examined by historical critics, Mohammed chose instead to impress his listeners about "his knowledge which Allah gave him."

Another reason why Mohammed created stories and judgments was in response to criticism by the inhabitants of Mecca, who used to say that he merely was a man like just them and possessed no spiritual superiority. They did not see in him a life of holiness and piety. Instead, they noticed how he lusted after women. They also accused him of being a Kahen (a priest of the Jinn devils) and a magician. Debates and disputes arose between Mohammed and the Meccans. Mohammed claimed that the same disputes, discussions, and confrontations occurred between the prophets of the Old Testament (or the prophets created by some Jahiliyyah groups) and the ancestors of people of Mecca. Thus, he wanted to annul the accusations of the Meccans against him by claiming that the prophets throughout history were charged with the same accusations that the Meccans leveled against him.

Analyzing Mohammed's Claim about Shu'aib.

The Midianites never claimed a monotheistic faith. Whenever a prophet appeared in a nation, that nation would never forget about its prophet. Even if he had been rejected in his own generation, God would have revived his message in subsequent generations. This we know through what occurred to the prophets of the Old Testament. For example, the kings and people of Israel rejected Jeremiah. His message, however, lived on in Israel, and he was later revered as one of their greatest prophets. The same can be said about Micah and others. Elijah was persecuted by King Ahab and his wife Jezebel and his son. Later generations considered Elijah to be one of the Israelites' major prophets. When we examine Mohammed's claim regarding Shu'aib, however, we find no mention of him in history. In fact, no historical documents in Arabia mention that Shu'aib was a prophet in Midian. This leads us to assume that Shu'aib was a fictional (rather than a historical) character created in Mohammed's time or close to his time. Some Jahiliyyah groups or Arabian tribes who embraced Judaism used the name Shu'aib to refer to Isaiah.

Reason to Assume that Shu'aib was the Prophet Isaiah for Some Jahiliyyah Groups.

Mohammed mentioned Shu'aib شعيب in one of his Hadiths. He said that Shu'aib was the "orator of the prophets,"[82] making him the most important prophet in history.

This is something strange, because God did not forget any prophet. He even mentioned Job, who lived in the land of Uz on the western border of Babel. Job was not even an Israelite. Uz was a greater distance from Israel than Israel was to the Sinai, the homeland of the Midianites. None of the prophets of Israel ever mentioned Shuayb's name.

Although they had close contact with Moses, the Midianites never mentioned that they had a prophet named Shuayb. We know that Moses lived among the Midianites for 40 years before leading Israel out of Egypt.

When we examine the Islamic tradition concerning Shuyeb, we find Islamic writers, such as al Masudi, place Shuayb at the time of the kings of Judah. [83]

The most important prophet in Israel was Isaiah. He prophesied during the reign of four kings who ruled Judah. Mohammed said Shuayb was the orator of the prophets, a term that could be applied to Isaiah, whose prophecies had a distinguished poetical style. We assume Mohammed heard the Jews in Arabia repeating the prophecies and the words of Isaiah. who spoke about Midian and their caravans. Therefore, Mohammed could have thought Isaiah was a prophet to Midian. This opinion is strengthened by the similarities in Arabic between Isaiah, called in Arabic Ashiya, and Shu'aib. We assume that Shu'aib was the Arabic name which some Arabian Judaic tribes adopted for Isaiah. However, Mohammed failed to record that Isaiah lived in the 8th century B.C., not in the 19th or 18th century B.C. Mohammed placed Shu'aib, the prophet to Midian, close to the time of Sodom and Gomorrah. In addition, Isaiah was not a prophet to Midian, but he lived all his life in the city of Jerusalem as a prophet to the kingdom of Judah.

Some Islamic writers want to identify Shu'aib with Yathron or Jethro, the father in law of Moses. But there are no similarities between the two names, and Jethro was never called Shu'aib.

A Call to Re-evaluate the Quran's Claims

The Quran has serious historical mistakes such as the one discussed above. The members of Aws and Khazraj, the two tribes of Medina, and the Muslims of Mecca who followed Mohammed, were quite ignorant and naive in matters of history, and thus failed to notice the unhistorical sayings of Mohammed.

Antioch

The Quran's claim that a magical cry destroyed the city of Antioch in the 1st century A.D.

In the Quran. the use of a cry to destroy people and to remove them from history was used by Mohammed to exterminate the people of Antioch in the 1st century A.D. We read the text of the Quran in Surah Ya Sin, Surah 36, starting from verse 13:

By way of a parable, I set forth the story of the inhabitants of the city. Then the messengers came to it. We sent to them two messengers whom they rejected, but we strengthened those two with a third. They said to the inhabitants, "We have been sent on a mission to you." The people replied, "You are only men like ourselves, and the Rahman sent no sort of revelation. You do nothing but lie." They replied, "Our lord does know that we have been sent on a mission to you, and our duty is only to proclaim the clear message." The people replied, "for us, we conjured an evil omen from you. If you desist not, we will certainly stone you and we will inflict a grievous punishment on you."

The Quran claims in verse 36:29:

It was no more than a single mighty Blast, and behold! they were (like ashes) quenched and silent.

Antioch was the city intended by Mohammed, when he claimed it was destroyed by a cry

The reporters of the Hadith of Mohammed and his biographers confirmed that the city intended by the Quran is Antioch in Asia Minor. Ibn Ishak agreed with Wahab ben Munabbeh and ibn Abbass that the city was Antioch.[84] Al Allusi said:

The city, as told by ibn Abbass, Barideh بريدة, and Akraham عكرمة, was Antioch.[85]

Al Qurtubi reported that al Mauridi الماوردي said, "According to all expositors of the Quran the city was Antioch."[86]

Among the expositors of the Quran who identified Antioch as the city were al Qurtubi,[87] abu Hayyan,[88] and ibn al Kathir.[89] Among the Islamic historians was al Masudi.[90]

Many Islamic authors wrote books that state the missionaries sent to the city of Antioch were apostles of Christ. These are main Islamic writings, considered significant in defining the circumstances and the purpose for which each verse of the Quran was written. They all confirm that Antioch was the city intended by the Quran. Among those books are Al Tashil fi al-'Ulum al-Tansil.[91]

The Quran text surely demonstrates that Mohammed had in mind Barnabas and Paul, the two apostles who preached and taught in Antioch. Then their testimony in the city was strengthened by the arrival of Silas, which the Quranic text expresses clearly by the words "we strengthened them with a third."

The threat of stoning the apostles did not occur in Antioch as the Quran portrays, but in another Antioch, the Antioch in Pisidia. Evidently Mohammed failed to accurately remember the early mission to Antioch, and the rest of the missionary trips, as reported in the book of Acts. We read in the book of Acts that the Holy Spirit sent Paul and Barnabas on a mission trip where they were joined by Mark. In Antioch of Pisidia, the people wanted to stone them. Evidently Mohammed, thinking that Antioch of Pisidia was the main city Antioch, combined the events of the mission to Antioch with the events of Antioch of Pisidia to form one event which he expressed in one paragraph. He had a habit of reporting great chapters of the Bible in small confused sentences and paragraphs.

Expositors of the Quran, such as ibn Kathir, quote other writers who mentioned Mark, whom they called John. You may remember that the name of the New Testament writer of the Gospel of Mark was actually John Mark. This was not unusual. Paul was called Paulis.[92] Al Masudi mentioned Paul as one whom the Quran intended in its narration.[93] Confirming that Islamic expositors verified what Mohammed intended in the Quran about the trips Paul made to Antioch, accompanied by his companions, such as John Mark.

Then we read in the same Surah 36, verse 29, that the magic cry which judged and destroyed the inhabitants of Antioch, "Was just one cry, and behold they were quenched like ashes."

The main reporters of the Hadith of Mohammed confirm that the city of Antioch was destroyed with its king and inhabitants because of this cry. One of the reporters was Khutadeh, a main reference in interpreting the Hadith of Mohammed. Another was Abdullah Ibn Abbas,[94] the cousin of Mohammed:

> Gabriel cried a Cry, and all the infidels who remained in the city died.[95]

We encounter judgment through magical cries in the literature of many Middle Eastern religions, such as the sacred books of the Sabian Mandaeans. The Mandaeans attributed cries to their gods which were similar to those reported by Mohammed. Civilized people at the time of Mohammed abstained from repeating what Mohammed said about the cries.

The Islamic Writers Explained the Story of the Quran

In spite of these facts, the fathers of Islamic tradition, such as Ibn Ishak, depended on Wahab Ben Munabbeh who embraced the irrational claims of Mohammed without question and made a frail attempt to conform them to something that resembled historical fact. While Mohammed inserted these myths into the Quran in a context that totally disregarded history, the fathers of Islamic tradition created their own history to substantiate the myths of Mohammed. They wanted the Quran to appear to be a credible document in the eyes of people who were naive because they had not been taught the elements of history. As one might expect, the people became eager to defend the claims of Mohammed, even though they would be required to exchange recognized history for a new history rewritten by the fathers of Islamic tradition.

Ibn Ishak, depending on Wahab Ben Munabbah and Kaab al Ahbar, says that in Antioch there was a pharaoh whose name was Antikos, son of Antikos and grandson of Antikos. He worshiped idols, so Allah sent three missionaries to him whose names were S'adik and S'aduk and Shalum. Pharaoh refused to believe the first two missionaries, so Allah strengthened the testimony by sending the third missionary. All three were considered disciples sent from Christ. When Pharaoh insisted his people kill the disciples, Allah exterminated Pharaoh and all the inhabitant of Antioch. They all disappeared from the face of the earth. No one remained.[96]

What the fathers of Islamic tradition said was endorsed by the testimonies of others, such as Khutadeh قتادة, one of the main reporters of the Hadith of Mohammed, and by Abdullah ibn Abbass,[97] a cousin of Mohammed and another main reporter of Mohammed's Hadiths. The Hadiths were considered by Muslims as part of their canonical creed, and second only to the Quran in importance.

The stories they told to justify Mohammed's myths, demonstrate the irrational and incoherent arguments the fathers of Islamic tradition used to get around true documented history. It also shows how incredibly naive the people were who listened to their claims and believed the history they invented.

Pharaohs disappeared many centuries before the time of Christ. The city of Antioch was built by Selecus Nicator, one of the four leaders who succeeded Alexander the Great. Selecus built Antioch around the year 300 BC. in memory of Antiochus, a member of his family. In addition to the fact that the pharaohs had died long before the city of Antioch was founded, the pharaohs lived in Egypt, not on the border between North Syria and Asia Minor.

The name assigned by the Islamic fathers to the pharaoh who allegedly ruled Antioch was Antikos, son of Antikos, and grandson of Antikos. This series of titles was used for the dynasty of the Greek kings of the royal family of Selecus who controlled Syria after Alexander the Great died. They no longer reigned after the Romans came to power and during the Christian era.

This shows how little the Islamic fathers knew when they rewrote history to support the myths of the Quran. They mixed ancient times with more recent times, and they placed important historical figures, like pharaohs, in other countries and in cities which were unknown at the time of the pharaohs.

Mohammed's Christian Sources Enabled Him to Mention Something about the Mission of Paul and Barnabas in Antioch.

How could Mohammed have been so confused? Where did he learn about the mission in Antioch as reported in the Book of Acts? When we study the life of Mohammed, we know he was taught by many individuals who were in some way related to the Christian faith, or were part of the Christian heretics at Mecca. One of them was Waraqa Ben Nofel.

Khadijah sought Warqa's help in order to transform Mohammed's negative experiences into prophecy

Waraqa Ben Nofel was the cousin of Mohammed's first wife, Khadijah. Mohammed was sent by Khadijah to Waraqa, in order to convert the negative experiences of Mohammed into a prophetic call. This was after Mohammed returned to his wife, Khadijah, from his cave in Harra' near Mecca, where he used to spend long periods of time. When Mohammed returned to her. He reported that a spirit who claimed to be Gabriel, ordered him to read a book. He choked Mohammed three times. Mohammed returned very frightened and depressed. He accused the devil of giving him negative experiences.

Sahih al Bukhari states:

> The angel came to him while he was in the cave of Hira' and said to him: 'Read.' He answered: 'I am not a reader.' Mohammed continued: 'Then he took me and (Ghatani) (choked me) until I could not breathe, then he released me and said: 'Read.' I said: 'I am not a reader.' He took me and choked me the second time until I could not breathe, then released me and said: 'Read.' I answered: 'I am not a reader.' He took me and choked me for the third time, then released me and said: 'Read in the name of your lord who created man from a clot. Read and your lord is the most honorable.' The apostle of Allah returned with his heart shaking. He entered to Khadijah bin Khuwailed and said: 'Fold me in garments.' They wrapped him in garments until his fear had subsided. He told Khadijah about it and said: 'I am scared on my soul.'[98]

Al-Aini commented on the "Ghatani," saying that it is choking.[99] This confirms that Mohammed claimed that "Gabriel" had choked him. The narrators have used another verb, which confirms the choking. Ibn Manthur wrote:

> He saaba means choked him until he killed him. In the story when Mohammed was called we read: 'Gabriel took my throat and Saabani until I wept heavily, and he wanted to choke me.' It is said Saabtahu if I

choke him. ibn Al- Athir said: 'al Saab is squeezing the throat as choking.'[100]

Ibn al Athir wrote:

Saaba: in the Hadith of Mohammed's call 'Gabriel hold my throat and Saabani until I wept heavily,' Saab means squeezing the throat as in choking.'[101]

Al Suheili wrote:

He said in the Hadith Ghatani "saabani and Saatani. Also, Thaatani. All these have one meaning, which is choking.[102]

Ibn Hisham used another verb that is Ghatani "he choked me."[103] This word Gattahu (he choked him), which is used by Mohammed's biographers, is defined in the Munjed, the famous Arabic dictionary, as "choked him." [104]

Analysis of how this spirit treated Mohammed makes it clear that it was more than one incident but rather a series of such chokings administered with the intent of inducing Mohammed to finally yield to him and would remain terrorized that he would never dare to disobey him. When we analyze the first episode in which Gabriel attempted to chock Mohammed, we notice that Mohammed did not read what "Gabriel" ordered him to read. The fact that it was a series of episodes is clear from al Halabieh:

It is not hidden that he (Gabriel) came to him the night of Saturday and the night of Sunday. Then appeared to him the day of Monday.[105]

It is clear that "Gabriel" visited Mohammed many times and choked him. During the first visit Mohammed refused to read. Although the narrators, including ibn Athir, report that the spirit choked Mohammed by holding, squeezing, and compressing his throat but did not accomplish his goal because Mohammed did not read. Mohammed attempted to withdraw from dealing with a dreadful spirit who humiliated and choked him. Mohammed's excuse was that he did not read. The narrators' reports here concerning the first visit of this spirit who impersonated the angel Gabriel. At this point Mohammed had not yet been disciplined by this spirit and attempted to avoid him. He did, however, found it difficult to breathe.

That those who are subject to demonic discipline designed to get them to submit to the devil's will often resist, as Mohammed did, is well known in anthropology.

In order for Mohammed to get rid of the spirit posing Gabriel, he attempted to throw himself from a mountain:

> Then I crawled with my face shaking and entered to Khadijah and said: 'Wrap me with garments until the terror leaves me." Then he came to me and said: 'O Mohammed, you are the apostle of Allah.' I began to throw myself from a high place on a mountain. When I started to do so, he appeared to me and said: 'O Mohammed, I am Gabriel, and you are the apostle of Allah.' Then he said: 'Read.' I said: 'I do not read.' He took me and choked me three times until I became unable to breathe.[106]

We know from anthropology that when those whom the devil seeks to recruit as mediums fail to get rid of the devil, they often attempt to commit suicide. "Gabriel" continued to go after Mohammed. But later, after this spirit choked him in a more aggressive manner by putting a Namat on Mohammed's mouth and nose, Mohammed felt as though he was facing death. Mohammed yielded so as to prevent the spirit from returning for another attempt and replaying the awful experience. A Namat is a wool fabric formed of many layers that the Arabians used to put on camels. We notice that when "Gabriel" choked Mohammed with the Namat, Mohammed yielded for the first time, saying: "What shall I read?" Here are the words of Mohammed:

> He came to me in a Namat while sleeping. The Namat contained a writing. And he said to me: 'Read.' I said 'I do not read.' He choked me through that Namat, putting it on my mouth and nose until I saw death, then he released me and said: 'Read.' I said: 'What shall I read?' I said so in order to get rid of him so that he would not return to do again what he had done. I asked what to read and did not deny lest he repeat the same experience. I read, then he left me.'[107]

Thus, Mohammed yielded after the spirit choked him by a putting Namat over his mouth and nose, which made Mohammed feel that he was at the point of death. Only then did he finally submit to the spirit and begin reading. This yielding was borne of despair, where the soul did not find any way to get rid of the power of the devil who disciplined it as victim. This phenomenon is well-known phenomenon in anthropology: The devil's persists in disciplining (via choking) those he has chosen for a role of oracle and mediumship until the victim yields.

Mohammed's wife used Waraqa to convince Mohammed that he had a prophetical call.

Then Waraqa became a source to guide Mohammed, especially in the heretical doctrines of the Ebionite sect which Waraqa had joined after he embraced Judaism. The doctrines concerning Jesus as a prophet, and the claim that Jesus was not crucified, but someone resembling Jesus was crucified instead, were among the heretical doctrines that Waraqa taught to Mohammed. We know the later idea was first claimed by Simon, the magician of Samaria, who was rebuked by Peter. Later, Simon, the magician, claimed to be the Messiah, and taught that Jesus was never crucified. It only appeared to the Jews that he was crucified.[108] Simon the Magician founded a heresy which was known as Simonianism. His ideas were later embraced by many of the Gnostics and other heretics. Some of these sects operated in Mecca at the time of Mohammed. Some Gnostics later adopted Simon's claims. For instance, Basilides claimed that Simon the Cyrenian, whom the Romans compelled to bear Jesus' cross, had acquired the identity of Jesus. Thus, the Jews crucified Simon thinking that he was Jesus.[109] This notion was adopted into the Quran by Waraqa bin Nofel.

After Waraqa died, Mohammed searched for new sources

After Waraqa died, Mohammed's biographers and the authors such as Bukhari who kept his Hadith reported that "the inspiration cooled down."[110] This led Mohammed to look to other sources who could teach him the Bible, other Christian doctrines, the Byzantine myths, as well as other myths and legislations of other groups and sects such as the Zoroastrians and Sabians.

We read in Ibn Hisham, the biographer of Mohammed:

> The prophet of Allah very often used to set with a Christian man named Jaber, who was a slave to the children of Al Khathrami. The people of Mecca used to say: "Many things Mohammed teaches, were taught to him by Jaber, the Christian, the slave of the children of Al Khathrami."[111]

Here is a Christian slave who never became a Muslim, yet Mohammed took time every day to go to him. The fact that Mohammed came to Jaber rather than Jaber coming to Mohammed, reveals the importance of Jaber as a source for understanding the Bible and Christian doctrine. Arabic sources tell us Jaber was a "Roman," the term used in Arabia for a citizen of the Byzantine empire. They say also that he gathered many books.

Mohammed had a working relationship with other Christians as well as with Jaber. The same old narrators mentioned that the family of Al Khathrami had two slaves, Jaber and Yasar. They used to read the Bible to Mohammed who would visit them and listen to their readings. Mohammed's Christian sources were not reliable sources of accurate information, which is quite obvious in the myth of the sleeping of Ephesus.

Another Byzantine Christian whom Mohammed often contacted was Balaam, or Yaish. He was a slave to Beni al Hathrami. The people of Mecca often saw Mohammed when he met with Balaam and they said Balaam used to teach Mohammed.[112]

Mohammed was in contact with certain Christians, especially monks, who promoted various other heresies. Among them was the monk Buhaireh who lived on the caravan route to Mecca. As a youth, Mohammed would go with his uncle, Abu Taleb, to trade in Syria, and they would stop in the city of Busrah al Sham where Buhaireh lived,[113] in the region known as Horan.[114] The books that narrated the life of Mohammed admit that "Mohammed and his uncle often stopped by to visit Buhaireh."[115]

I mentioned these facts to demonstrate that Mohammed was not deprived of Biblical resources which provided background for many of the Biblical events and verses he inserted in the Quran. The story of the missionary trip of Barnabas, Paul and Silas is one of these. However, when Mohammed was finished, he left behind only mythological narrations.

Mohammed possessed Syriac books and ordered Zayd bin Thabet to learn the Syriac language in order to translate them to him. I will discuss this fact later.

Verifying the falsity of a myth is easy.

Mohammed said the cry occurred in the first century. He also said it happened, not in a distant African country where it would have been difficult for researchers to examine it and refute it, but Mohammed said it occurred in Antioch, a significantly important city known by everyone in the Roman empire because Antioch had a strategic location between Syria and Asia Minor in the heart of the Greek and Roman civilizations. Events which occurred in Antioch were known by everyone in that generation, and Antioch's history was studied by many people in the following centuries.

It is impossible to add a story, such as this one, to the book of the Acts of the Apostles.

There is something else worth mentioning. How could the apostles of Christ have failed to record a significant event such as this that occurred in front of three important people: Paul, Barnabas, and Silas?

Such a miraculous event, if it really had taken place, would have deserved more attention than many of the other incidents that took place in Antioch and in other cities of Palestine, Syria and Asia Minor. For example, the book of Acts mentions the judgment of a sorcerer named Elymas. He was struck with blindness because he resisted the Gospel proclaimed by Paul and Barnabas to the Roman proconsul in a city in Cyprus. The account is found in Acts 13: 6-12. How much more important the judgment of Antioch would have been, especially if it came through the cry of an angel. It would have been a central and major incident in the book of Acts.

This story could not be missed by the Fathers of the Church.

How could the many fathers of the church in Antioch and other surrounding cities, have failed to mention the cry in their writings? Many details were written by the fathers of the church who lived in Antioch and surrounding cities where the apostles and early Christian missionaries went. The fathers of the church did not miss refuting things of secondary importance, such as mythological stories that never happen. How could all those fathers miss anything which, according to the Quran, is a catastrophic tragic calamity, never attributed to a city before?

This story could not be missed by The Greek and Roman Historians

There is no mention in the Roman records of this event occurring in Antioch, which means that it is not history, but rather a Quranic myth.

It is claimed that the judgment expressed in the "cry" destroyed the inhabitants of Antioch, a large city at the time Christianity was growing popular. Numerous Greek and Roman historians did not fail to mention insignificant incidents that happened in their times, in places distant from their cities. In fact they even mentioned the tiny villages in Arabia since the fifth century B.C. They described the myths the people of far Asia embraced, the customs of tribes in eastern Africa, and many of the myths and events common to the local populations. They reported nearly everything that had occurred in their midst. How, then, could they fail to mention Gabriel's great "cry" that, according to the claims of Mohammed in the Quran, had destroyed the inhabitants of Antioch in just one instant?

Those who still believe the Quran was an inspired book that came down from heaven to Mohammed by the angel Gabriel, want us to believe that the imaginary "cry" would have been missed by tens of Roman and Greek historians who lived at the same time the Quran claimed the incident occurred even though events in the city of Rome, Athens and Antioch were recoded with accurate precision.

The city of Antioch in the Christian era was full of Greek philosophers and geographers. We have much literature coming from Antioch which relates even secondary things that happened in the city. We have Roman historians who precisely recorded the deeds done in each city in the empire. Although Antioch was the third most important city in the empire after Rome and Alexandria, no one mentioned a magical cry which destroyed the inhabitants, or even part of them. Mohammed, when he applied his habitual cry to destroy and remove nations in ancient times, was unaware that Antioch in Asia Minor was ineligible to receive his claims. This reveals the ignorance of Mohammed's companions who accepted his claims. They were ignorant of the civilized world which was in existence in their time.

The Roman Historians' Accuracy in Reporting the News and Historical Facts

If the great catastrophe claimed by Mohammed had happened, it would have shaken the whole Roman Empire. Indeed, it would have become the main news, in all Roman literature of the first century and centuries that followed.

This event would have become more important than the Vesuvius volcano that erupted around the year 79 A.D. and struck the city of Pompeii, near the Italian city of Naples which was close in time to the ministries of Paul and Barnabas in the city of Antioch. We find Roman historians mentioning detailed description of what happened each day because of the volcano. They described it as accurately as modern reporters would describe the eruptions today.

Pliny the Younger, the famous Roman historian, was an eyewitness of the volcano and wrote about it. The small earthquakes that preceded the eruption of the volcano were accurately recorded. One of the earthquakes that occurred in the vicinity of the volcano occurred in the year 64 A.D. Suetonius mentioned this in his book about the life of the emperor Nero, De Vita Caesarum.[116] Tacitus also mentioned it in the 15th book of Annales, "An earthquake demolished a large part of Pompeii, a populous town in Campania."[117]

This small earthquake occurred only a few years after the time during which Paul and Barnabas ministered in Antioch.

Surely the destruction of Antioch would have merited significant attention from the Roman and Greek historians. A small earthquake would of course receive less attention than a calamity of the proportions claimed by the Quran.

The absurdity of Mohammed's Claim about the Destruction of Antioch in the 1st Christian Century

If one claimed that a terrible catastrophe befell the inhabitants of a large modern city such as Geneva, Switzerland. And if he said a loud cry suddenly killed all or part of the people, but he did not have support for his claim from the city itself or from the surrounding cities, whether Swiss or some other European city, he would be looked on as a person who talks incoherently and irrationally. He would also have to assume that no one possessed enough knowledge to expose his plan, disagree or contradict him.

The Quran displays an inadequate knowledge of historical chronology when it presents unsubstantiated statements, confuses the personalities of the Bible, and adulterates history. Mohammed took advantage of his local environment at Medina where the people were generally deficient in the knowledge of history. Mohammed was able to use the ignorance of his companions who were unable to compare his narrations with the true facts of history. Can the Quran be defended today in our generation when the knowledge of documented history reveals the obvious mistakes it makes?

The Cries

The mythological roots of the cry talked about in the Quran

What were Mohammed's sources for those magical judgments that he used in the Quran to destroy tribes, nations, and cities? We must ask ourselves, where Mohammed got this kind of magical judgment which he used to destroy kingdoms, tribes and cities so many times in the Quran?

We do not see this method of judgment in the Bible. God never brought judgment against a city or a tribe through a cry. God used many different ways to perform His judgments. At times He used a strong nation to defeat a kingdom that opposed his moral principles. At times God used other methods as He did in His judgments against Pharaoh in Egypt. Sodom and Gomorrah were completely morally corrupt. God used a fire from heaven to destroy them. But never we find God using a cry like the mythological cries used in the Quran.

The Cry in the Persian Zoroastrianism

The cry of destruction is nothing new or limited to Mohammed. It is the means through which many ancient sects and religions handled the idea of judgment. For example, Zoroastrianism of Persia used this kind of cry in much of its literature. In the book of Bundahis it speaks about a deified donkey which had three legs, and stood in the midst of a celestial ocean which the Zoroastrians placed between earth and the "ceiling of the sky." The donkey had six eyes, nine mouths, two ears and one horn. The donkey was considered a righteous being; his body was white, and his food was spiritual.[118]

Many scholars believe that the donkey myth had its roots in meteorology, which is the study of weather. Among those scholars is professor Darmesteter who wrote the book, "Ormazd et Ahriman."[119] The donkey mentioned in Zoroastrian literature was the incarnation of clouds,

---

hurricanes and windstorms which enabled him to bring extensive judgment through his cry. The power of his cry is seen by the nine mouths, each mouth is big as a house. The size of the donkey, according to Bundahis, was as big as the mountains of the Himalayas.[120]

The donkey's golden horn had the power to eliminate all the wickedness created by wicked creatures.[121] The cry of the donkey coming through the horn, causes the wicked creation to lie prostrate on earth, without life. Furthermore, when this animal raises his neck in the ocean and moves his ears, the ocean shakes and the mountains quake. When the donkey cries all the wicked creatures abort their children.[122]

Both Zoroastrianism and the Quran claim that the world will be destroyed through a cry and that humanity will be brought again to life through a cry.

Eschatology deals with the events of the last days or how the world will end. The picture of judgement found in the Quran is attributed to an angel named Israfil. It is similar to what the Zoroastrians said about their deified donkey. It is said that one cry from Israfil brings death to every creature and makes the entire earth shake and quake causing the end of the world. The eschatological idea called Rajifah means "quaking and shaking." According to the Quran, Surah al-Naziat 79, verses 6 and 7, the cry is attributed to Israfil, and will befall all humans in the last day.

Destruction by a cry is also a common theme in Persian mythology. Here, the end of the world comes by the angel-storm. The world, according to Zoroastrians, is formed over 12 thousand years, but it ends with the cry of a storm.[123]

Here's how the Quran reports the end of the world with a cry from Israfil. The text is written for us in Surah Ya sin, Surah 36, and verse 49:

> They will not hear but a single cry. It will seize them while they are yet disputing among themselves.

In Surah Sad 38:15 Mohammed threatened the inhabitants of Mecca saying they would be destroyed during his lifetime by a similar cry,

> These people today wait for only one cry which will come without warning.

Evidently Mohammed believed the end of the world was imminent in his time, so he threatened the people of Mecca telling them that very soon they would be destroyed by the cry.

The Persians not only have a cry to end the world, but they have another cry through which humans return to earth alive. The angel Neryosang, in the end time, cries one last cry through which he awakens the hero, Keresasp, who has been sleeping for centuries.[124]

The same concept of the return to life in the Quran is attributed to Israfil. He first makes a cry through which he kills all the humans on earth. Then he makes second cry through which he brings to life all who were killed by his first cry. We read in Surah, Ya sin 36:53:

> It will be no more than one cry, then all of them will be brought before us.

The cry in Persian mythology was often a way to liberate one from opposing powers. Because devils oppose the falling of the rain, there are always struggles when rain is about to come. These struggles continue until the god of fire, who is also the god of thunder, comes and makes a big cry, then the rain comes down. It lasts for another ten days.[125]

The Cry in Manichaeism

The Cry in Zoroastrianism had left its imprint on the religions that were born in the regions dominated by the Persians, such as Mesopotamia. They adopted the principles that the Persians attributed to their gods regarding how to operate and how to accomplish their works. Manichaeism, the religion founded by Mani in Mesopotamia during the 3rd century A.D., borrowed many concepts from Zoroastrianism, including the idea of the "Cry." In Manichaeism the Cry was considered as a divine dimension or as a god. We see this in the Manichaean psalms.[126]

Manichaeans attributed a creative role to this Cry. This is seen in Paraphrase of Shem, one of the books found in the Gnostic library in Naji Hamadi-Egypt that belonged to a Manichaean Gnostic sect.[127]

The Cry became the routine means of justifying the happening of everything and why it was a possibility for anything to occur, however great it may be. The Cry also exempted the founders of these religions, or authors of their sacred books, from giving an account of what they created in their myths or doctrines – whether mythological judgments or irrational thoughts, such as the Manichaean claim that "the Cry transformed the primordial man into a god."[128]

In the Quran Mohammed adopted this practice of using the mythological Cry to explain the occurrence of anything. The Cry is used to explain how the world will end, how the inhabitants of the earth will come back to life in order to be judged, how to destroy nations and tribes in an instant, and so on. This indicates that the idea of the Cry, that some pagan religions of the Middle East adopted, was known to some groups in Arabia, such as the Ahnaf, in Mohammed's day. The Ahnaf had relations with some religious sects, such as the Mandaeans, for whom the Cry was the primary means by which their gods worked and accomplished things.

Manichaeans spread amongst the Quraysh, the tribe of Mohammed at Mecca, and were called Zanadikeh. This made their doctrines and myths accessible for Mohammed to learn and adopt.

The Cry in Mandaeanism

The cry is not limited to Persian and Manichaean mythology. If we study Sabian-Mandaean literature, we find that a cry, or shout, is the way Mandaeans handled the judgments of their deities. They lacked a knowledge about God, His attributes, and how His divine judgments were carried out against nations in ancient history. The problem was a common one. Many sects in the Middle East gave their gods a "cry" through which they created, judged and performed miraculous and supernatural things. The Mandaeans were very well-known and specialized in adopting these Cries.

In the sacred Mandaean book, "The Thousand and Twelve Questions," we find that a "cry" explains everything that exists and everything that happens.[129] The fifth book of "Ginza Rba," the main sacred book of the Mandaeans, mentions that Ur, the prince of darkness in Mandaeanism, came out of the turbulent waters which, according to their mythology, exists in the underground world. When Ur cried, he brought the water from the underground world, and the walls of the worlds shook to the point where everything was in danger of collapse.[130]

To the Mandaeans, a cry is a powerful method of judgment. Through a great shout, they confront the powers of devils, and their deities display authority in opposing the foes of their religion. Mandaeans, like

Zoroastrians, consider some animals, particularly reptiles, as wicked incarnations of devils. [131] This concept influenced Mohammed who condemned reptiles. The book, Thousand and Twelve Questions, tells us that a cry came from the world of light creating ten creatures to fight these diabolic reptiles and animals.[132]

So, we see that these ancient people thought that a cry was the way to deal with demons. The Mandaean sacred literature, Alma Risaia RBA: The Great First World, describes it this way:

> A swift messenger travels every place, uttering a cry which makes hell-beasts and purgatory demons betake themselves to the depths of the earth.[133]

In this way the Mandaeans had invented a way for their deities to deal with opposing forces. The cry in their sacred literature, does great things including the shaking of the earth and the mountains. One of their gods and messengers of light was Mara- d- Rabutha, who cried and the mountains began to quake.[134] In the Scroll of Exalted Kingship, Diwan Malkuta Laita, another sacred Mandaean book, a Mandaean god cries aloud, shaking the worlds and ages.[135]

We see how the Mandaeans shook nations, earths and cities and destroyed them through a cry. The cry, however, was to be uttered by a god or a messenger of light who was an angel. The Mandaeans do not have any other way for their gods to execute judgment. The size of the nation or the dimensions of the judgement is always through the same cry. This explains how most of the judgments in the Quran, were carried out through a similar cry. Though most judgments in the Quran are carried out through a cry, some judgements are accomplished by the wind. Judgment through wind comes from Zoroastrianism which depict the wind as a god responsible to judge cities and nations.

In the Mandaean sacred scriptures Pthael-Gabrael was the one who executed these Cries. In the Quran, Gabriel was the one who executed the Cries.

It is interesting to note that in Mandaean literature the cries are attributed particularly to Pthael, who was also known as Gabriel. We read in Ginza Rba 15 that Pthael spoke about his cries saying:

> Through my fifth cry all the wicked reptiles were formed. Through my sixth cry all the elements of the darkness were formed. Through my

seventh cry, Ruha, a god of darkness, appeared before me with her seven sons.

The same text mentions four Cries of Pthael:

Through my first Cry I condensed the earth from water, and it became solid, and I upholstered the sky. Through my second Cry I made the rivers and streams. Through my third Cry I created the fish in the seas and the birds in the sky. Through my fourth Cry I formed all the plants and their seeds.[136]

In the Quran, most of the cries that judged the nations, tribes and cities are attributed to Gabriel, a further proof that Mohammed depended on the Sabian Mandaeans for a way to explain how judgments came in history.

In Mandaean literature, magical cries are seen as the way through which their gods accomplish great things because the Mandaeans, as well as some adherents of other religions in the Middle East like the Manichaeans, imagined that great occurrences in creation, are caused by phenomenal magical things such as the cries. In Mandaean literature the word "Khritha" قريثا, translated as "cry", expresses or explains the accomplishments of their god.

In Both the Old Testament and the New Testament, God Accomplished great works Without a Cry.

This teaching is contrary to Biblical concepts concerning the accomplishments of the Triune God. In the Bible, we see that the Godhead's accomplishments are attributed to His everlasting Wisdom who is Christ. In the New Testament, Christ is clearly seen accomplishing great creative works like when He multiplied the five loaves and two fish which He used to feed thousands of people in the desert. Christ calmed the violent wind and raging sea instantly. He did all this without invoking power outside Himself. He depended on His own potency, eternal authority and wisdom through which He created the universe out of nothing. What He accomplished in the New Testament, He did without resorting to a magical cry or anything else to justify the great dimensions of what He was doing.

The Mandaeans' claim that the judgement cries came from Pthael, or Gabriel, is derived from primitive Mesopotamian mythology, in which gods are portrayed as giants able to make great noises. People who try to explain the greatness of creation to a giant who cries ignore the true God, and the absolute power which the Bible attributes to Him. He simply divided the Red Sea, not through a cry designed to impress the two million Israelites who were present, but without any effort from a giant body with a huge shout. Men can never explain how God accomplish His great works except by an expression of His infinite omnipotence and wisdom.

The Sabian Mandaean Cry was transferred into use by Mohammed.

In the Quran, the cry of the Mandaean gods, especially Pthael who was later called Gabriel, were transplanted into the service of Mohammed. It is common knowledge that Mohammed was discipled to accept Mandaean thoughts primarily because of his contacts with the Sabians in Arabia. In the Quran, Mohammed called the Sabians "people of the book," or people who had received a book from heaven as the Jews and Christians did. Some scholars identify those Sabians as the Mandaeans and the Harranians. Other scholars see the Manichaeans as part of the Sabians in Arabia.

Another factor that contributed to Mohammed's involvement with Mandaean thought came through Ahnaf, a group he joined in his youth. Ahnaf was a conglomeration of some heretical Christians, Gnostic heretics and Sabians, with some occult followers of the Kuhhan who practiced the Jinn religion of Arabia. The founders of the Ahnaf, such as Zayd bin Amru bin Nufayl, accompanied by Waraqa bin Nofel (the cousin of Khadijah, the first wife of Mohammed), often visited northern Iraq, specifically the region around the city of Mosul where there were concentrations of Mandaeans.

They also traveled to Jazireh, in northeastern Syria and northwestern Iraq where Harran is located. Harran was known as the center of the Harranian Sabians. We are told that those founders went to these cities in their search for religious knowledge.

Is there documentation of the relation of Zayd bin Amru bin Nufayl and Waraqa bin Nofel with the Mandaeans and Harranians?

Ibn Hisham said this about Zayd:

He went inquiring about the religion of Abraham, asking the monks and rabbis, until he reached Musil and al Jazirah. Then he wandered in all the regions of Sham.[137]

Ibn Kathir reported that Zayd went with Waraqa to Mosul in order to inquire about the religion.[138] Further, he mentioned that Zayd went to al Jazirah for the same purpose.[139] In an encounter between Zayd and Mohammed, Zayd told Mohammed about his travels to al Jazirah to search and how an old man there told him about the religion of Allah and the angels:

> I came out until I came to the rabbis of Ila (on the Gulf of Aqaba) whom I found worshipping Allah, but they ascribed to him partners. I told them: 'This is not the religion which I desire.' One of the rabbis of Damascus told me: 'You ask about a religion. No one worships Allah except a sheik (or old man) in Jazirah.' I went to Jazireh and came to visit this man, and I told him the purpose for which I had come. He said: 'All what you have seen is deceit. You ask about a religion that is the religion of Allah and the angels.[140]

We notice that it was not a monk or a rabbi that shared those claims with him, but rather a sheik. This points to the connections of Zayd with the Sabians. "The religion of Allah and the angels" is a Sabian term, whether for the Mandaeans or the Harranians, since both worshiped the angels.

According to the Arabic historians, Mosul was the center of the Sabian Mandaeans. In the book of Umdit al Qari of al 'Aini we read:

> Ibn Zayd said that the Sabians are people of a religion in Jazirah of Musil. They say: "There is no god except Allah." ... reported by al Hassan that Ziad said that the Sabians pray according to the Qublah (they direct themselves toward Mecca when they pray) and they pray five times daily. He said that he wanted to impose on them the Jeziah (the Islamic tribute), but he was told that they worship the angels. Qatadah and al Razi reported that the Sabians were a people who worship the angels, pray the Qublah, and read the psalms.[141]

We notice in the above quotation that the Sabians were in Jazirah of Mosul, which explains why Zayd Bin Amru bin Nufayl went to Mosul – to meet with the Mandaean Sabians. If his intent was to contact monks, he would not have needed to travel so far in those days to reach Mosul. Monks were close to him in Trans Jordan.

Some Sabian rituals and slogans were incorporated into Islam, such as "there is no god except Allah," their respect for the Qublah of Mecca in their prayers, and their practice of praying five times daily. It is also clear that these Sabians were Mandaeans because they worshiped angels.

The Origin of the Word "Hanif" and its Roots Prior to Islam

The designation "Hanif" was used to designate the Harranian worshipers of planets who were later called in Islam "Sabians." We understand from Thabet bin Qurrah, a Harranian scholar born in 836 A.D., that the Sabian Harranian was called Hanpi or Hanifi.[142] According to many scholars, the word Hanif was derived from the Syriac word "hanpo" or "hanpi," which means "pagan." Sometimes, however, the word meant a man with Hellenistic culture. [143] From famous scholars such as Noldeke we understand that prior to Islam the word hanif meant "pagan."[144]

It seems the Syriacs called the Harranians hanif or hanpi because they were worshipers of the planets and the moon. This title or designation spread to the extent that Zayd bin Amru bin Nufayl, who used to visit the region of al Jazirah where many Harranians resided, thought the title hanif was a positive one. Thus, he adopted it without being aware of its negative meaning. After he returned from visiting the places where the Sabians resided, he became known as Hanif because he began spreading the religion of the Sabians who were known by the Syriacs by their negative title "hanif." This explains the presence of many Sabian doctrines in the Quran since the Ahnaf were the bridge of contact between Mohammed and the Sabians doctrines.

This explains how many of Mohammed rituals and thoughts came from the Sabians whether they were originally Mandaeans or Harranians. The connection was so strong that when Mohammed built his religion and established its rituals, the people of Mecca thought he was a Sabian. Muslims also were considered to be Sabians because their rituals and slogans were identified with what the Sabians displayed in Mecca before the rise of Islam.

It is easy for us to see that Islam was not created in a vacuum, but relied heavily on what many of the Sabians and other Middle Eastern sects attributed to their gods. Mohammed in the Quran simply repeated these teachings to his people who were easily impressed by the primitive religious concepts of their time, including the cry. One reason Mohammed found acceptance for these teachings was that his followers were without a strong Biblical education concerning the one true God. Had they possessed that knowledge, they would have recognized how God accomplished his great works without any magical cries or irrational means used in Persian mythology, such as claiming a nation was judged by a wind as recorded in the Quran.

The cry or loud shout Mohammed adopted from the Mandaeans was cited many times in the Quran as the main means through which the power of Allah is displayed. The Sabians and other Mesopotamian sects used these events when they wanted to display the power of an idol or a god or wished to justify the alleged domain and works of their false deities. Thus, we see that Gabriel's Cry brought about the extermination of the peoples of Ad, Thamud, and Midian, as well as the city of Antioch. The Cry made the inhabitants fall prostrate and dead.

Quran's Eschatology
Eschatology in Zoroastrianism and the Quran

Do we wonder that the Quran presents the Zoroastrian eschatology? The great similarities between the eschatology of the Quran and that of the Zoroastrian literature proves that the Persian myths had spread widely in Arabia. This was due in part to the Persian domain in eastern Arabia and later in Yemen. This was also due to the fact that some Arabian tribes embraced the Persian religion. As the Jewish myths spread in Arabia due to some Arabian tribes that embraced Judaism, and the Christian heretical myths spread with the increase of Christian heretics, especially north of Arabia, likewise the Zoroastrian myths spread for the same reasons. Zoroastrian myths were more widespread because Persians had stronger influence over Arabia than the Christian kingdoms such as the Byzantine Empire.

Add to this another factor: Salman the Persian, who previously embraced Islam, was a priest of fire in Zoroastrianism. Thus, he was very learned and diligent in Zoroastrianism.

Salman al Farisi confessed that he was very diligent in Majusieh—the Maghi religion—a term referring to Zoroastrianism in Arabia. He said:

> I was very diligent in Zoroastrianism as a servant of fire who used to light it up.[145]

Fire was one of the worshiped deities in Zoroastrianism. Certain priests were consecrated to the rituals of fire worship. Salman al Farisi was a Zoroastrian priest to whom Mohammed gave an amount of gold the size of an egg.[146] Mohammed attracted Salman with money, and Salman embraced Islam. Mohammed saw in Salman an important source for Zoroastrianism and used him in formulating many doctrines of Zoroastrian origin. The priest of fire had significant importance in the Zoroastrian rituals.[147] From this we understand the importance of Salman al Farisi in the Persian religion. In the Zoroastrian book called Sad Dar, we find the implication that every priest must know the Avesta.[148]

This is behind the knowledge of Salman of the doctrines and myths in the Zoroastrian books. For example, we find in the book of Dinkard, the 7th book, a Persian legislation regarding the digging of trenches and canals.[149] This enabled Salman to advise Mohammed to dig a trench around the city when the tribe of Quraysh planned to attack Medina. The military plans were in the Zoroastrian books as part of legislation. Therefore, Salman studied those books and was knowledgeable in them. Salman became an important source for the Quran and Hadiths of Mohammed.

The fact that Mohammed took Salman's advice and completed a strange project – that is, digging a trench around the city of Medina, something the Arabians had never done before –proves that Mohammed viewed Salman's recommendations as words of "inspiration or revelation." How, then, could one conclude that Salman was not one of Mohammed's guides to the Zoroastrian doctrines, considering that Mohammed was eager to be seen through these doctrines as a distinguished, knowledgeable prophet who knew about many things, such as the cosmos, the journey of the soul after death, and eschatology? Mohammed adopted all of these notions from Zoroastrianism.

Mohammed's use of the Persian doctrines was not limited to the contribution of Salman al Farisi. Before Salman came to Medina and embraced Islam, Mohammed had connections in Mecca with persons who were competent in the Persian religion. This fact was not something concealed from the Meccans.

Many of the Quranic myths are of Persian origin, and the many of Mohammed's contemporaries were well aware of this fact. They described Mohammed's Quran as influenced by a man described as 'Ajami, a word that means "Persian." In fact, the people of Iraq used to call the Persians 'Ajam. The accusation that Mohammed was influenced by an 'Ajam man is expressed in Surah An-Nahl:

> And indeed we know that they say: 'It is only a human being who teaches him (Mohammed).' The tongue of the man they refer to is 'Ajami, while this (the Quran) is a clear Arabic tongue. (Surah 16, called An-Nahl, verse 103).

The above verse is the reaction of Mohammed to the people of Mecca who recognized that there were in the Quran many myths of Persian origin

— more than the myths and stories of other sources and religions — that were spread in their time. This reveals Mohammed's connections with people who had religious Persian education. This was possible because of the relationship of the tribe of Quraysh with the city of Hira, an Arabic city in Iraq under the Persians, where the Meccans used to send their sons to study and receive a Persian education.

A reminder of the Cry of Israfil and its Zoroastrian Root

In examining the roots of the "Cries," we saw that the Cry of "Israfil" in the Quran (79:6-7) shakes everything and will cause the destruction of the world. We have seen in Surah Ya Sin, verse 49, that life on earth will be removed through a Cry of Israfil. We mentioned that such an idea is derived from Zoroastrianism that claims that mankind on earth will be removed through a Cry of a storm.[150]

We have also seen how Israfil will utter two Cries: The first Cry will make all humans on earth die. The second Cry (as we see in Surah Ya Sin, verse 53) will revive all so that they can come before the Judgment Seat. We have seen that this Cry was derived from Zoroastrianism.

The Dam of Gog and Magog and its Zoroastrian Root

In addition to the two cries attributed to Israfil, Mohammed borrowed other elements of Zoroastrian eschatology. One of these elements concerns Gog and Magog. Mohammed in the Quran says Alexander the Great imprisoned Gog and Magog between two mountains in a dam of iron and brass. This dam, according to the Quran, will be destroyed at the last day so that Gog and Magog can attack the world.

In this volume, I dedicated an entire chapter writing about Dhu al Qarnayn in the Quran –his journey to the ends of the earth and his building of a mythological dam. These myths are derived from the book of Pseudo-Callisthenes, whose author mentioned an imprisonment of savage people behind a dam. The author relied on a Persian Zoroastrian myth about Anzi Dahak who, according to Zoroastrians, was a descendant of devils. According to Zoroastrian mythology, Dahak is fettered to a mountain in the East. Later, Dahak was followed by diabolical people who became fettered with him on the same mountain. They will be released in the final days of history in order to attack the whole world. Dahak and his people were fettered by Fredun, another Persian mythological figure, who sleeps for thousands of years on the same mountain.

The Zoroastrians believe that throughout history Dahak and his diabolical people are bound continuously on a mountain in the East. This is the root of Pseudo-Callisthenes when he claimed that Alexander the Great imprisoned a savage people on the ends of the earth until the final days of history. A Syriac writing attributed to Jacob Sarugh stated that the savage people imprisoned by Alexander were Gog and Magog. The Syriac author also wrote that the destruction of the dam, and the release of Gog and Magog, will be a sign of the last days. This was adopted in the Quran. (For details of this myth and its correspondence with the Quranic myth, consult the chapter "Dhu al Qarnayn" in this volume.)

The Influence of the "Liberators" Awaited by the Zoroastrians on Mohammed and the Quran

Zoroastrians believed that a series of saviors or liberators would appear throughout history:

1 Hushedar was expected to appear in the year 341 A.D. Zoroastrians believed that when Hushedar appeared that the sun would stop for a period of 10 days. The Bahman Yast, part of the Pahlavi Texts, says that Hushedar will come to a conference with Ahura Mazda and receive the religion. When he comes away from the conference he cries to the sun: "stand still." The sun will stand still 10 days. And when this happens all the people of the world will "abide by the good religion of the Mazda." Then Mitro will order Hushedar to cry to the sun to move on. Hushedar will cry to the sun, and the sun will move on and all mankind will fully believe in the Zoroastrian religion.[151] Mohammed adopted a similar concept when he claimed that in the last days there will be a great sign: the sun will rise from the west and set in the east, as we read his Hadith in Sahih al Bukhari :

> Reported by Abi Hurrerah: The apostle of Allah said: The last day of history will not come before the sun rises from the west. When it rises from the west all inhabitants of the earth will believe.[152]

The year 341 A.D. passed without the world's seeing the sun rising from the West and setting in the East, yet Muslims still hold onto this myth as an important sign of the last days.

This Zoroastrian concept must have been in the mind of Mohammed when he recited Surah 2, al Baqarah, in which verse 258 claims that Abraham challenged Nimrod to cause the sun to rise in the west. Mohammed believed Allah would cause the sun to rise in the west in the last day. It would be seen by all the inhabitants of the earth as sign for them causing all of them to believe.

The Hindus believed that the sun has two faces, one dark and the other radiant. Through the night, they believe the sun returns from the west with its dark face toward the earth, and therefore we do not see it.[153] This Hindu myth influenced the Persians who believed that Mithra, a symbol of the sunshine, followed the sun in its course from east to west during the day, changing its direction to return from the west at night.[154]

This mythology strongly influenced Mohammed. In more than one Hadith, Mohammed explains how the sun goes to worship Allah before his throne in heaven. When the sun is dismissed, it returns to rise from the west.[155] We read in another Hadith of Mohammed:

> Reported by Abu Ther, who said: 'I entered the mosque where the prophet of Allah sat.' When the sunset came, Mohammed said: 'O Abu Ther, do you know where the sun goes?' I said: 'Allah and his prophet better know.' He said: 'It goes asking permission to worship. It is given permission to worship. Then it is ordered: Return back from where you came. So it rises from the west.'[156]

Evidently Mohammed had in mind the same idea the Persians had that the dark face of the sun enables it to return during the night from the west without being seen. But in the last day all the inhabitants of the earth will see the bright face of the sun rising in the west.

Aushedar-Mah: The Zoroastrians expected Aushedar-Mah to come in the year 1341 A.D. and restore the glory of Zoroastrianism to Iran. He was to spread justice and peace among humanity. The Mahdi, whose appearance the Muslims await, is derived from the second part of the name of this liberator — i.e., Mah. The Zoroastrians prophesied that the sun would stop for 20 days when this liberator appeared.[157]

Muslims claim that the last hour will not come before an imam called al Mahdi, from the progeny of Mohammed, will appear. He will spread peace and justice among humanity and support the message of Mohammed. Some Muslims claim that al Mahdi will be a descendant of al Hasan, son of Ali bin Abu Taleb, Mohammed's son-in-law. Others think he will be a descendant of Hussein, the brother of Hasan. He will appear first at Mecca, where the people of Mecca will swear allegiance to him. Then the inhabitants of Medina will swear allegiance to him; gradually, all the inhabitants of the earth will swear allegiance to him.

This Mahdi, as stated above, is a reflection of Aushedar-Mah, awaited by the Zoroastrians, who will be from the progeny of Zoroaster. Likewise, we see that al Mahdi will be from the progeny of Mohammed.

Aushedar-Mah will restore the glory of Zoroastrianism to Iran and spread justice and peace in the world. We notice that Aushedar-Mah will perform some duties, which the Muslims later attributed to al Mahdi — that is, restoring the glory of Islam and spreading peace and justice in the world. The year 1341 A.D. passed and the Mahdi did not show up. Yet, Muslims are still awaiting the coming of this Mah or Mahdi. They made his appearance an important sign of the last days.

Soshans: Soshans was expected to appear in the year 2341 A.D. The Zoroastrians claimed Soshans would appear after the appearance of Azi Dahak, the mythological figure mentioned above. The Zoroastrians claimed Azi Dahak was fettered on a mountain in the East. This Azi Dahak would be unfettered in the last days of history in order to attack the world. Azi Dahak would be followed by his people (the devil's progeny). (Pseudo-Callisthenes and the Syriac authors based their account of Gog and Magog upon this myth, which was later incorporated into the Quran.) After this attack, Soshans will appear and remove wickedness from the earth. He will destroy the idols the nations worship, thus allowing Zoroastrianism to dominate the whole earth.[158] Without doubt, this is the origin of the Islamic myth about the return of Jesus to destroy the idols, break the Cross, and kill the people who believe in the Cross. Also, the return of Jesus would kill the pig and the people who have pigs and make Islam dominate the whole world.

The Sun and Moon in Zoroastrianism and the Quran in the Last Days

We find in the Quran myths of Zoroastrian origin regarding the sun in the last days - myths we do not encounter in any other religion prior to Zoroastrianism. These myths influenced the Quranic eschatology about the last days.

Contrary to the Bible, the pagan religions of the Middle East attribute special importance to the sun and the moon as spiritual beings.

The sun and moon in the Bible are created as sources of light and not as personalities or beings. As such, they do not have any spiritual responsibilities or liabilities. Contrary to the Biblical view, the pagan religions of the Middle East had bestowed importance on the moon and the sun as beings. In some religions, they are good beings; in others, they are wicked. After the star Athtar (a title of Venus in ancient Arabia) snatched the title of Allah from the moon, the sun and the moon became two slaves subjected to Allah, the Star Akbar. We see this principle clearly in Surah al Ankabut, chapter 29, verse 61:

He subjected the sun and the moon in order to say 'O Allah.'

That is, they acknowledged the authority of Allah, the Star Akbar, over them and were compelled to cooperate with Allah. (For more on this subject, see my book The Star Akbar.)

The Zoroastrian Doctrine of the Incarnation of the Sun and the Moon in the Last Days and its Reflection on Mohammed

Another element of Persian eschatology found in the Quran concerns the sun. According to Zoroastrian eschatology, the sun will stop rising and setting for a period of time and will meet with certain personalities of the restoration. The Zoroastrians believe that after the resurrection heavenly stars and planets such as the sun and the moon will be dressed in different bodies so that they appear as human beings and angels and will walk among people and meet with them in the time of the restoration.[159]

The Zoroastrians embodied and personified the elements they worshiped, especially the stellar (astral) ones. They connected them as beings with their prophecies of the last days. The Zoroastrians created prophecies concerning the last days in which they gave their gods various roles to play.

Mohammed adopted this Zoroastrian practice. In the authoritative book that contains the Hadiths of Mohammed, Sahih a Bukhari, there is a Hadith in which Mohammed explains how the sun will be gathered with different beings in the Day of Judgment. [160]

Thus, as it is in the Zoroastrian prophecies, the sun will come close to humans in the Day of Judgment and will come in contact with people. Mohammed adopted this prophecy from Zoroastrianism.

The Spiritual Role the Zoroastrians Attributed to the Sun in the Last Days

Zoroastrians in their sacred literature, such as in Farvardin Yast, claim that in the past the sun and the moon gathered together in a specific place and they stopped their movements in order to oppose the devils. Once this was accomplished, they began to move again.[161] Zoroastrian mythology views the sun and the moon as personalities who stop their movements for spiritual reasons, either to meet to plan how to oppose devils, or to wait for decisions from superior gods to be taken for humanity. Zoroastrians assume the sun and the moon will gather in the last days and stop their movements until they are ordered by a liberator to resume them. As I mentioned previously, according to the Zoroastrian prophecies, the sun will stop moving for 30 days and nights at which point a liberator named Soshance will appear.[162]

Zoroastrian teaching that the sun and the moon will cease their movements in the last day until they are ordered to move again, influenced many sects in the Middle East before Islam. The Zoroastrians envisioned the sun and the moon as righteous deities who stop to converse with other personalities and plan to fight devils. The sun, along with other personalities, will be a witness in the last day, when Soshans judges the wicked creation. This certainly influenced the Hadith of Mohammed when he said the sun would appear with other personalities in the day of judgment, and it influenced the Quran when it talked about gathering the sun and the moon in the day of judgment.

The contradictory pagan Middle Eastern ideas about the gathering of the sun and the moon in the Day of Judgment. The Quran adopts the Zoroastrian notion.

The pagans of the Middle East who did not worship the sun and moon as their principle gods viewed them as rivals to their main gods. Some religions, such as Zoroastrianism and the Quran, considered them two good beings who were submitted to their gods. The sun and moon were often considered to be liable because people worshiped them and thus, they would be brought before the Judgment Seat to give account for this worship. We find this notion in the Quran.

But other sects looked to the sun and the moon as wicked creatures who will be gathered in the final day to be judged because many people have worshiped them. The Zoroastrian book, Sikand-Gumanik Vigar, mentions certain groups who believed that the sun and the moon will, in the day of judgment, be condemned as wicked creatures and will be sent to hell because people had worshiped them.[163] The Zoroastrian book tried to refute such an idea because their eschatology teaches the gathering of the sun and the moon in the last day is not because they are wicked, but because they are deities that have spiritual duties in the struggle against devils.

However, the two thoughts have influenced the Quran. We find in Surah 75, verse 9, called al Qiyamah or the resurrection, that the sun will be gathered with the moon at the day of judgment. Surah 25, called al-Furqan, in verse 17 speaks of Allah gathering everything that was worshiped by men including the men themselves in the day of judgment. This verse says, "In the day he gathers them and everything they worshiped besides Allah, he will say to them, 'it is you who led my servants astray or they did astray from the path.'" It is clear that everything that was worshiped will be gathered together in the day of judgment, and they will be judged. This explains the Quran's claim that the sun and the moon would be gathered in the day of judgment, an idea that was commonly embraced by many groups at the time of Mohammed. The Quran agrees with the Zoroastrian idea that the sun and the moon are righteous beings, and therefore in the judgment they will appear innocent from the guilt of those who worshiped them.

In Mohammed's time, the Quranic monotheism was an elevation of one worshiped god over the other local gods, which Mohammed continued to see as beings competing with Allah, the Star Akbar.

Mohammed's monotheism can be summed up as follows: He elevated one element – the Star Akbar – that was worshiped in his day over all the other elements of nature and stars that were worshiped and considered beings. Thus, Mohammed shared with the followers of many pagan Middle Eastern sects the religious struggle against the rest of the worshiped elements of nature, which he considered as beings who were rivals to Allah, the Star Akbar. In particular, Mohammed adopted the Zoroastrian doctrines that held the sun and moon to be less important beings than Allah, the Star Akbar. He minimized the role of the sun and moon in the last days by making them appear before the Judgment Seat. He cast them along with the rest of the worshiped elements that would be brought before the throne of Allah to give account of why men worshipped them.

Therefore, we see that the monotheism Mohammed promoted is a pagan monotheism founded on the elevation of one of the Arabian gods worshiped in his time over the rest of the gods. In fact, this was a well-known phenomenon in the Middle East from ancient times. For example, the Babylonian god Marduch became the main god who presided over the other Mesopotamian gods and thus diminished their power and roles. Ahura Mazda, the main Zoroastrian god, made the rest of the Ayres gods less important by making them his assistants, or spiritual beings like the sun and moon, charged with the task of resisting the devils. Likewise, Allah, the Star Akbar, who presided over the Arabian Star Family, became Allah Akbar-the-great, transforming the rest of the members of the Arabian Star Family — that is, Allat (the sun), Manat, and Uzza — into servants.

The claims of Mohammed regarding monotheism reflect the old claims of the Athtar star worship. That is, the head of the Star Family should have preeminence over the worship of the rest of the Star Family. Thus, Mohammed's contention with his tribe is the old Arabian claim that the Allah star should be more revered than his wife, Allat, representing the sun, or his daughters, al-'Uzza and Manat, representing two planets. The worship of the Star Akbar (Athtar-Venus) reached the point of reckoning the rest of the members of the Arabian Star Family as intercessors to Allah, the biggest star, and not as daughters. Moreover, the fanatical worshipers of the star monotheism centered on Athtar fought the rest of the worship in Arabia. A Yemeni inscription mentions "Abed Athtar (servant of Athtar) bin Moqas," who was a chief of the tribe of Khulan, a famous Yemeni tribe that was most probably a branch of the Himyarite tribe of Quthaa. Abed Athtar destroyed a temple of the worship of al Muqh (the Yemeni god of the moon) in a place called Olan. He was attacked and defeated by the armies of King Shaaram Autar. The author of the inscription considered this defeat as Abed Athtar's punishment for destroying the temple of the god al Muqh.[164]

Thus, we see that Abed Athtar was a leader sided with Athtar who considered the worship of any god other than Athtar to be illegal. He was so zealous that he was ready to destroy the temple of al Muqh, who was seen as the moon god and head of the Star Family in Yemen. Abed Athtar bin Moqas engaged in holy war because he reckoned the worship of al Muqh along with other gods as idol worship and set about to destroy their temples. This monotheistic campaign was counter to the history of worship in Yemen, which was based on tolerant reverence for all Star Family members with al Muqh as the head and the sun as his wife and Athtar his son. This change signaled the rise of monotheism based on Athtar, and its effects on the North of Arabia became obvious as Radhu or Radha (Venus) became known as Allah. This Arabian monotheism rejected the notion of the Star Family that held that Allah had a wife and daughters.

We find that Mohammed shared this concern. In fact, he wrote a verse of the Quran in the chapter known as Najm, that is, the star chapter, in which he discussed the roles of al-'Uzza and Manat and Allat, who are the daughters and wife of Allah according to the tribe of Mohammed. He recognized them as angels who can intercede as "al Gharaniq al Ula," important birds of the high, and that their intercessory role with Allah was important and should be respected.[165] But they were not daughters of Allah, the greatest star. Gharaniq, the plural of Gharnuq, is used for "a bird with a tall neck, known in the Middle East as al Kurki, which also flies on high."[166]

As a result, the pagan Arabians of Mecca worshipped together with him, because he recognized their deities and their deities' role as intercessors with Allah.[167]

This shows us that Mohammed was spreading the star monotheism doctrine of old Arabia which claimed the preeminence of the worship of the Allah star over the worship given to his wife and daughters.

I find it interesting to realize that all the companions of Mohammed bowed down and worshiped with Mohammed and with the pagans who respected the pagan words of the Quran which Mohammed uttered. He recognized the intercessory role of the gods of Quraysh. This indicates it was not the idea of monotheism which led the first Muslims to follow Mohammed. They followed him for other more selfish reasons, such as sex privileges and looting the caravans.

According to Islamic tradition, after the Jews criticized him, Mohammed omitted this verse from his Quran, claiming that the Devil had put them in his mouth.

In their struggle with other religions, the religions founded on pagan monotheism — that is, elevating a local god over the rest of the gods — cast the rest of the worshiped elements either as weak beings compared to their gods or as limited beings that could only intercede. In Zoroastrianism, these worshiped elements were viewed as beings under submission of the main Zoroastrian god. Mohammed adopted from Zoroastrian mythology this practice of minimizing the other worshiped gods who were contenders to Allah, the Star Akbar.

The rain and the resurrection of dead bodies in Zoroastrianism and in Mohammed's eschatology.

Both the Old and New Testaments spoke about the resurrection of bodies when Christ returns. Resurrection of bodies is a divine work that depends on the power of God as Creator to bring His creation back to life. Zoroastrians, however, have their own gods, such as the earth and water, to which they attributed the power of resurrecting bodies in the Last Day.

Zoroastrians taught that rain on the bones of the dead would cause bodies to be resurrected in the last day. We see this in the book of Bundahis, which says:

> One will demand bones from the spirit of the earth, blood from the water, and hair from the plants.[168]

The earth was a spirit, a holy deity in Zoroastrianism. The earth will present the bones of the dead to the rain which is a superior deity over the earth. The water will give blood to the bones and form a living body. They arrive at this thinking because the first man and woman, called Masye and Masyaoi by Zoroastrians, grew as plants from the earth, fertilized by Gayomard, a prototype of the human race.[169]

The water is a potent deity in Zoroastrianism and can create a human body. In Dinkard, book VII, the creation of Zoroaster's body is attributed to the water.[170] In the Zoroastrian book, Farvardin Yast I, the water creates the bones.[171] Therefore, the Zoroastrians believed the resurrection would occur when the water rains on the bones of the dead. Mohammed copied this eschatological Zoroastrian element. We read in al-Bukhari, a Hadith of

Mohammed, "Allah will rain water from heaven on the bones of the dead and they will grow like plants."[172]

Mohammed's choice of rain water as the power that will raise bodies in the Last Day reveals how greatly his doctrines were influenced by Salman al Farisi, his counselor in Zoroastrianism. Mohammed's adoption of this Zoroastrian doctrine reveals his lack of knowledge of the Biblical teaching about the resurrection. Instead, he leaned toward the Persian eschatology that honors the water and attributed to it the function of resurrecting bodies in the Last Day. In Zoroastrianism water is an important goddess by the name of Ardvi Sura whom the Zoroastrians worshiped.[173] The Zoroastrians had to honor water in the Last Day by attributing to it the power to resurrect bodies. Mohammed did not care that his adoption of Zoroastrian concepts would coronate the Zoroastrian gods and paganism in Islam.

Zoroastrianism and Mohammed on the Subject of Fire that will Compel Men to Move Toward the Judgment Seat

Testing human beings by making them walk over molten metal.

The Zoroastrians are distinguished in creating unique eschatology, one that no other religion shares with them. Since their sacred books were written prior to the rise of Islam and the correspondence between Mohammed's eschatology and the Zoroastrians' is something that cannot be denied, we cannot attribute the Islamic eschatology to anything other than Mohammed's Persian sources. We have seen that the Persian priest of fire, Salman, was the most prominent source available to Mohammed.

There were of course other Persian sources that were at Mohammed's disposal at Mecca. We know that the Meccans realized (and even accused Mohammed) that the Quran came with an Ajami (Persian) tongue as we have seen in surah al Nahl 103:16, which was a Meccan Surah (Mohammed recited when he was still in Mecca before emigrating to Medina).

The failure of Muslims today to study the Zoroastrian doctrines and compare them with Islam is why they insist that these doctrines were given to Mohammed through heavenly revelation.

Mohammed's adoption of Zoroastrian eschatology was not limited to a single point only, so that we could consider this phenomenon to be an accident. Rather, the more we examine both Persian eschatology and that of Mohammed the more we become aware of the fact that Mohammed adopted the full Zoroastrian eschatology.

Another element of eschatology that we find in Zoroastrianism is the molten metal that will test human beings. According to Zoroastrian eschatology, in the Last Day men and women will be compelled to walk on molten metal. The righteous will not suffer because of the fire, but sinners will suffer greatly.[174] The molten metal tests humanity as an ordeal for the wicked.[175]

This walking on fire was also applied to people who, according to Zoroastrianism, will be brought forth from hell. They will be purified through the molten metal in one final ordeal. The metal in the mountains will melt and flow like rivers. The righteous will also be brought from paradise to walk on the molten metal. To the righteous it will feel like walking through warm milk, but sinners will suffer greatly. Through this purgatorial act sin will be wiped out and sinners will be saved. [176]

Mohammed adopted these Zoroastrian ideas about fire-walking. We read the saying of Mohammed in Sahih al Bukhari, the book that is considered by Muslims to contain the confirmed Hadiths of Mohammed:

The fire will be from the east to the west of the earth, and it will compel the human beings to go toward the Judgment Seat.[177]

In another Hadith found in Sahih al Bukhari, Mohammed spoke of pouring molten lead in the ears of sinners when they were gathered for judgment.[178] He adopted this notion from the Zoroastrian myth concerning molten metal in the final judgment.

Finally, Mohammed speaks of forcing those released from hell to walk in the fire in order to purify them. Water of life will be poured on them and thus they will grow because of it as the seed grows when watered.[179] Also, "the straight path will be erected over Hell, and I will be the first among the apostles to lead his nation... They will come out of fire, the water of life will be poured on them, then they will grow under this water as the seed grows under the normal water."[180] This is the same Zoroastrian myth that holds that the souls from hell are saved by exposing them to the fire of molten metal.

It is the same Zoroastrian myth that the souls from hell are saved by exposing them to the fire of molten metal.

All these facts reveal just how greatly Mohammed depended on Persian eschatology when he wrote his eschatology for Muslims. The perfect similarity between Mohammedan and Zoroastrian eschatology could not have existed without a knowledgeable Zoroastrian informant, such as Salman al Farsi or a Meccan person who studied Zoroastrianism in the city of Hira or through a person who embraced Zoroastrianism.

When we examine the background of Islam and the problems that appear in the Quran we can come to only one conclusion: The Quran's main doctrines are based on the notions and myths of the pagan religions that were widespread in Mohammed's time: The Quranic eschatology is a faithful summary of the Zoroastrian eschatology.

Haman and the Tower

The Quran Placed Haman and the Tower of Mesopotamia in Egypt during Moses' time

We have to ask about Haman in the Quran and the Bible: Can the false imitator replace the authentic original? Mohammed's style in writing the Quran was to insert Biblical events into different periods of time and to place them in different countries and couch them in different circumstances. On the other hand, the Bible which is well documented and is older than any other book the Hebrews wrote, holds its integrity by being true to the events as they happened. No story mentioned in the Bible is more accurate in any other religious source, no matter how old that source is.

The Bible has more documentation showing its incorruptibility more than any other book in history. There are many ancient translations of the Bible, one of which is the Greek translation of the Hebrew Old Testament, called the Septuagint. It dates back to the 3rd century B.C. Scrolls uncovered in caves of Qumran date back to the 2nd century B.C. There are many other examples which show that the Bible has more manuscripts than any other book which has appeared in History. They all establish its authenticity.

Since this is the case, which religious book can question the correctness of the Biblical text? Which book written during these early years, can offer a more accurate historical text? The Hebrew tradition always respected the Bible as the unchangeable Word of God, whose books were inspired by the prophets and preserved through the following generations.

How can we give weight to what Mohammed recited in the beginning of the seventh century A.D. in the Quran? What caused him to take stories from the Bible and place them in other circumstances and other time periods? How can information, existing many centuries before Christ, and known as the only source for a specific incident, be doubted or disbelieved by some other religious text which appeared later in the 7th century A.D., when we know the author tried to copy the original source and make his own changes?

We examined how Mohammed often changed Biblical stories to suit his own purposes. He would often ignore the Biblical text (the primary source itself) about a Biblical name or character and rely instead on mythological texts that used the Biblical name or character as a main element in their myths.

For example, Mohammed tells the story of Gog and Magog, of whom the prophet Ezekiel also wrote about. But Mohammed ignored what Ezekiel wrote and instead adopted a story regarding a savage people narrated in the mythological book Pseudo Callisthenes. Other Syriac writings referred to this savage people as Gog and Magog but they, too, were based on the Pseudo Callisthenes. This mythological literature claimed that Alexander the Great had imprisoned Gog and Magog behind gates of iron and brass between two mountains until the final day when they were to be freed to attack the world. Mohammed adopted this myth and claimed it was inspired by Allah (later, I will discuss the myth of Dhu al Qarnayn, and Gog and Magog, in a separate chapter).

This is not the only passage in the Quran which Mohammed took from the Bible. All of them express his intention to change the Bible, and elevate himself so he appears to be directly inspired by Allah.

Mohammed was inept at being an imitator. He fabricated his tales with no regard for history or culture.

If Mohammed had been more skilled when he copied the stories of other nations, he would have been more circumspect. He would have presented a correct historical and cultural framework for his plagiarism. A simple imitator can be easily caught if his information shows huge inconsistencies, unhistorical and anti-cultural frame.

For example, suppose we find a paper written by a person who lived many centuries after Dante, the famous Italian author. Suppose that the paper reports about another Italian who is a friend of Dante, named Abdel Rahman. The paper asserts that Dante's friend had met Julius Caesar, the Roman Emperor. Because these two men were not living at the same time, the story is inconsistent with history and the culture of the times. The author of the paper would be considered as a primitive inventor of tales, even though he may have quoted some sentences that Dante did write.

Applying this reasoning to Mohammed, because he copied incidents from the Bible, and placed them in other time periods than those contained in the original text, he lacks credibility. The situation gets worse, when he changes names and habits to those which did not exist at the time the original text was written.

When Mohammed took information concerning the Mesopotamian tower of Babel mentioned in the Bible, he violated basic historical facts.

Mohammed copied the text in Genesis 11:1-4 concerning the descendants of Noah, who only few generations after the flood, wanted to make a tower of baked bricks to reach the sky. The Bible says:

> Now the whole world had one language and a common speech. As men moved eastward, they found a plane in Shinar and settled there. They said to each other, 'Come, let us make bricks and bake them thoroughly.' They used brick instead of stone, and they used tar for mortar. Then they said, "Come, let us build ourselves a city, with a tower that reaches to the heavens, so that we may make a name for ourselves and not be scattered over the face of the whole earth.

In Mohammed's version the event happened in Egypt at the time of Moses and the people constructed the tower of brick instead of stone and used tar instead of mortar.

If the flood during the time of Noah happened before 6,500 B.C., as many scholars think, then this incident reported in Genesis occurred around the 6th millennia B.C. This was the period that signaled the first Mesopotamian civilization, before the Sumerians appeared.

Mohammed copied the same text with some variations, and applied it to the time of Moses. The Quran says in Surah 28: 38, Al Qasas:

> Pharaoh said 'Oh people, no god do I know for except me.' Therefore, Oh Haman, light me a kiln to bake bricks out of clay and build me a lofty tower, that I may mount up to the god of Moses. I think he [meaning Moses] is a liar.

What Mohammed copied from Genesis 11 is very clear. but he inserted the Tower of Babel event into the time of Moses. But Moses was not born until about 1525 B.C. There is about 4000 years between the two Biblical events.

Not only was the timing wrong, but the construction was wrong. The type of towers used by the Mesopotamians were unknown in Egypt.

The Egyptians were unaware of the high towers which the Mesopotamians built to communicate with their gods. This kind of tower was characteristic of the Mesopotamian people. The Babylonians were experts at building high towers, which some scholars think they learned from the Sumerians. This kind of Mesopotamian building became known in Babylonian times as Ziggurat. The original name is Ziqquratu, which means "peak." About 26 Ziggurat towers were left by the Mesopotamians and remain today.

A Ziggurat was formed of stepped stages; at the top was the temple where the priest went to communicate with the gods. The stages were made from baked bricks made from mud. The Ziggurats were also used to watch the stars. The Egyptians had no knowledge of this kind of building.

The Egyptians did not use baked bricks in their buildings until the Roman occupation of Egypt.

Egyptians made their temples and pyramids from large stones that were especially cut and brought to Egypt from distant places. There are no ruined temples in Egypt made by baked bricks, so they cannot prove they used baked bricks for important and lofty buildings like temples. Normal construction used in buildings and houses were made of clay bricks, dried by the sun. In Egypt there was no need for baking the clay, because rain was very rare and the bricks lasted a long time. Many old Egyptian bricks which were dried in the sun, still conserve their form to this day demonstrating that baking the bricks was an unnecessary process for the Egyptians. Baking bricks was not only unnecessary, but it was expensive, because it required much fuel.

By the way, the ancient Egyptian word for brick was "debet," a word that has come into our modern vocabulary through the Spanish as "adobe," meaning sun-dried brick.[181]

However, some baked bricks have been discovered in limited quantities in a tomb at Nebesheh and in a few other places. Scholars believe that these few burned bricks were the results of accidental fires. Burned bricks in Egypt were introduced during the Roman occupation of the country.

It is clear that while some buildings in Egypt were built with brick dried by the sun, temples, pyramids and other monuments relied on hewn stones because large buildings required solid foundations. Why then, would Pharaoh use the weaker baked brick construction when he wanted to build a lofty tower which had to be stronger than the pyramids which his ancestors built? I suppose, for the pyramids, which were not particularly high, the big cut stones were fine, but, for a lofty tower, perhaps seven times higher than the pyramids, they would not have the necessary strength. In the Egyptian mentality, architecture relied on big stones, the true foundations for strong buildings.

No tower ruins exist in Egypt that could substantiate the Quran's claim concerning the construction of a Ziggurat tower by Pharaoh.

If the baked bricks were in use in Egypt at or before the time of Moses, why we do not see a single pyramid or temple built from baked bricks today? If Pharaoh had built a tower of baked brick, it would have been the only tower of its kind which the Egyptians built in their entire history. Certainly, it would have been an architectural accomplishment to compete with the tower of Babel, which reached the height of 300 feet.

A tower like this would have remained in Egypt, in whole or in part, as the tower of Babel is today, a most important artifact of the Babylonian civilization. Today 26 towers remain in Mesopotamia and Iran, yet there is no trace of a lofty baked brick tower in Egypt. There are, however, the ruins of many less significant buildings in addition to the pyramids that remain intact today – all of which were made of hewn stone not baked brick. The alleged lofty brick tower would have been more important than the pyramids. Furthermore, there are no traces in Egypt of any tower of this kind.

No historian, or Hebrew writer, including Moses, ever mentioned the construction of a Ziggurat tower in Egypt

A 300-foot tower would have been a great architectural accomplishment if it indeed existed. It would have been one of the significant wonders of the ancient world. It would have been mentioned by various historians, and listed in Egyptian literature as one of their main monuments and a reason to brag about.

The tower of Babel was described by historians like Herodotus who lived in the fifth century B.C. Herodotus visited Egypt in addition to the many other Greek historians who lived in Alexandria, Egypt, yet, none of them mentioned this tower or any other tower like the Ziggurat of Mesopotamia.

Moses was a contemporary of the Pharaoh who had constructed many of these structures, but he never mentioned that such a tower ever existed. And even though Moses described in detail the Pharaoh's reaction to God's order to let the Hebrews leave Egypt, he never mentions that Haman was the prime minister of Pharaoh, as Mohammed claims in the Quran, or that Qaroon (Qurah) had opposed him while Moses was still in Egypt.

Some have tried to defend this historical mistake in the Quran in Internet conversations or through articles. They often make a big deal of the few baked bricks, which were found in Egypt, as if they prove that Pharaoh, at the time of Moses, had built a lofty tower which reached the clouds.

Yet, none of these people have discussed another issue which is more important-whether the lofty towers which the Mesopotamians built to speak with their gods ever existed in Egypt. Let me illustrate the implications of the tower's location. If somebody dares to tell you there was a great crystal palace erected on the moon 3500 years ago because scientists discovered the presence of crystal material on the surface of the moon, you would say, "that cannot be possible."

Why would the presence of a crystal deposited on the moon prove that a mythological palace was erected on the moon 3500 years ago.? The same argument is made by those who held to the weak argument that the presence of few baked bricks found in Egypt defended the argument that the Egyptians built Ziggurat towers in Egypt.

Mohammed made another historical mistake, this time, involving Haman who appears in the book of Esther.

Mohammed took the name of Haman from the Bible, and built another myth around him. You may remember from the Bible that Haman was the counselor or prime minister to the Persian king, Ahasuerus. Ahasuerus is identified in the Greek language as Xerxes who lived between 485 and 465 B.C. Mohammed said Haman was the prime minister to Pharaoh at the time of Moses, who led the Israelites out of Egypt around 1445 B.C. Simple calculation will tell you there are nearly 1,000 years between Moses and Haman.

In an attempt to rectify the Quran's erroneous references to the book of Esther, some Muslims try to undermine the book of Esther and the Biblical narration concerning Haman and the plot against the Jews. This, however, did not annul the fact that Haman appeared for the first time in the book of Esther and that Mohammed used the name Haman out of context and place in history.

Mohammed wrongfully copied from the Bible

Problems arose in the mistakes Mohammed made when he copied Haman's name.

Haman never appeared in history before the Book of Esther where he is found as the prime minister, "second in authority to the king and his first counselor."

Mohammed's error was not only in his failure to copy the exact name, but also in stating the role which Haman had to the Persian king. Mohammed claimed Haman was "Prime Minster and first counselor to Pharaoh," showing us that Mohammed wanted to use Biblical figures, to impress his listeners. Mohammed created new events in an effort to compete with the Bible, without giving consideration to the historical frame in which those figures lived.

Changing Biblical stories was common for Mohammed. We saw that he borrowed from the book of Genesis concerning the lofty tower people built after the Flood to reach into heaven. Mohammed took the same idea, and nearly the same words, claiming that the event happened in Egypt at the time of Moses. which confirms that he depended on the Biblical narration to make his claims. Mohammed's use of the Bible is undisputable.

Today we have questioned the claims of the Quran concerning the historical accuracy of many things, including the lofty tower. We looked at how Moses in the Bible mentioned Pharaoh in detail, but never mentioned the "lofty tower." Nor it is mentioned in any source before the Quran.

The name Haman is not found in any of the Egyptian documents. It was a common practice for the Egyptian pharaohs to give a foreigner in their service an Egyptian name. For example, Joseph was given the name Zaphenath-Paneah by Pharaoh as recorded in Genesis 41:45. It remains a mystery, however, how the Persian name Haman, which belongs to the beginning of the 5th century B.C., could have been used in the time of a Pharaoh in the 15thth century B.C. This is evidence of Mohammed's practice of taking Biblical events and changing them to suit his objective of lending authority to the Quran.

At the end of our examination of this subject, we noted the desperate measures some Muslims have resorted to in their attempt to find a way out of this dilemma, which was created by Mohammed's egregious error regarding Haman. They searched the Egyptian writings recorded in the modern texts for a name similar to Haman. The fact, of course, is that in the writings of any civilization such as the Egyptian civilization with its rich body of inscriptions and writings, it is easy to find a name that contains some letters in common with the name you are looking for. Despite this, no credible name was found matching the Quranic criteria.

The book of Esther
Historical and Theological comments on the book of Esther

Let us consider the historical foundation of the Biblical narration about Haman. The Old Testament book of Esther mentioned that the Persian king Ahasuerus had chosen Esther, a Jewish girl, as his queen instead of the current queen, Vashti. Mordecai, the uncle of Esther, who also adopted her as his daughter, served at the king's gate. He discovered a plot against the king by two eunuchs who were the king's doorkeepers. Mordecai informed Esther, who in return informed the king. After investigation, the Eunuchs were put to death. The incident was then written into the kingdom's chronicles in the presence of the King.

Esther 3:1 also mentions how the king promoted Haman and gave him a position over all his assistants. The book describes Haman as "Son of Hammedatha, the Agagite." (Esther 3:1) Agag was a title used by the kings of Amalek, a strong tribe of Edomites who were the descendants of Esau, the rival brother of Jacob, the father of the Israelites.

One of these kings, Agag, is mentioned by Moses in Numbers 24:7. Another Agag, who was king of the Amalekites, was defeated by King Saul, the first king of Israel. The account of this battle is recorded in I Samuel, chapters 14 and 15.

Because Haman was an Agagite and a descendent of the Amalekite royal family, he viewed the Israelites, as people who were privileged to worship God and, who were appointed space in the land with a law and prophets. The Amalekites opposed the Israelites in the wilderness of Sinai, and fought against them, trying to prevent them from reaching the promised land. Moses defeated the Amalekites in the wilderness of Rephidim.

We see that the animosity between the Amalekites and the Israelites has historical foundations, it is not just something that the book of Esther invented. In fact, when Haman, the Agagite, noticed that Mordecai did not bow to him, he was furious, and wanted to use his position as prime minister, to exterminate the Jews in all the provinces which were part of the Persian kingdom which extended, at times from India to Ethiopia.

But, in Esther 3:8, Haman plans a scheme to destroy the Jews. He told the king:

> There is a certain people scattered and dispersed among the people in all the provinces of your kingdom, their laws are different from the laws of all the other people, and they do not keep the king's laws. Therefore, it is not fitting for the king to let them remain.

This conspiracy of Haman against the Jewish people is not something unrealistic, but historical. A similar discriminative conspiracy to exterminate the Jews took place in the past century at the hand of Hitler's Nazism, with the holocaust of 6 million Jews. It is understandable then, that a conspiracy could have occurred, led by an Agagite, the descendent of the royal family of the Amalekites, who were known to be traditional enemies of Israel.

Great spiritual facts and lessons are found in the book of Esther.

Great spiritual lessons are taught in the book of Esther which is unique among the books of the Bible. Its central message describes a spiritual warfare against the forces of evil. Esther represents the praying church that faces persecution planned by the devil, who is symbolized by Haman. The devil always schemes to destroy the church, as he makes false accusations against the believers who loves the Lord.

The book of Ester also has a great spiritual lesson about the importance of fasting when fighting the devil. During persecution, people humiliate themselves before God, moving the arm of God to act. We read in the fourth chapter of Esther:

> And in every province whithersoever the king's commandment and his decree came, there was great mourning among the Jews, and fasting and weeping and wailing; and many lay in sackcloth and ashes.

The book shows that Haman's conspiracy was met with fasting, not only by Esther, but by all the people. They completely fasted for three days.

The book of Esther is of great encouragement for faithful Christians who face oppression and tyranny, and who suffer unjust and unfair treatment at the hand of the people who have domain and political authority over them. Esther shows us that a person who is in close relationship with God-much like Esther was in close relationship with the king-can be given authority by God to pray and to intercede for the fate of others and their salvation. Often in the Bible, kings on earth are symbols of the real King of the Universe, who is the Lord.

Also, Christ is clearly symbolized in the book of Esther as the Savior and representative of the human race. He is the One who regained the fellowship of God for humanity.

The Book of Esther also has a prophetic meaning concerning Christ's role in saving humanity from perishing. The human race lost it is fellowship with God because all have sinned. In the Bible, the devil is called "the accuser" because he mentions our sins before God. Because God eternally condemned the devil for his rebellious sin, the devil insists that God cannot accept us because of our sins.

The devil sees us as people who have to perish, in the same way that Haman saw the Israelites as people to be destroyed.

In the book of Esther, fellowship with God is symbolized by the golden scepter. No matter what the reason, people standing in the court of the King of Persia could be immediately killed, unless the king held his golden scepter out to them, as a sign that they found favor with the king. Then, they were free to touch his golden scepter.

Rarely, only when they have a cause that involves the lives of their beloved ones, do servants in the kingdom venture to stand in the inner court of the king, hoping the king will extend the golden scepter to them, allowing them to present their cause. Despite being the king's wife, Esther acted as a servant in a very dangerous place. She could only hope that the king would hold out the golden scepter to her and permit her to express her concern about the Jews whom Haman intended to exterminate.

In this incident Esther was a symbol of Christ who, being in eternal unity with the Father, came to earth and sought fellowship with God the Father not as the Son of God (as He eternally is) but as a human servant. He waited for the Father to hold out the golden scepter to Him. Christ was seeking the fellowship with God that we all have lost, as all of us have sinned and are thus deprived of spiritual fellowship with God. We all came under the verdict of death. The devil pointed the finger at us, claiming that we cannot be a people of God but should instead all perish in Hell.

Jesus as our representative before a holy God, regained the spiritual fellowship with God for us through His perfect life. He lived in contrast to us who live on earth, who all are born in sin and live as sinners. Therefore, as Esther gained fellowship with the king, by standing in the place where servants stand, Jesus gained fellowship with God for us by standing as a servant. He became the representative of humanity, so he could regain fellowship with God for all who believe in Him.

Finally, Esther stood in danger of death. Although she was the queen and did not need to go through such risk, she stood there as a servant because she had a cause to present to the king. She had to annul Haman's decree to exterminate her people. Christ — although He was the essence of God and enjoyed the same glory as the Father and was worshiped by the angels in heaven — put His glory aside and accepted the assignment to be incarnated as a human being and to stand before God as a servant who carried our cause and interceded for us who were condemned to eternal death.

The devil, who is the enemy of our souls, accuses us before God, saying God cannot accept us, because God is holy and we are transgressors. Yet, Jesus stood as a perfect man and servant, asking God the Father to remove the condemnation from His people with whom Jesus shared their human nature. Jesus has the right to remove the curse and its condemnation from His people. He died on the cross paying for our transgressions.

Therefore, as Esther gained favor, and the king held out the golden scepter, he sat and listened to her as a representative of her people. Her pleading caused the king to remove the decree of death imposed by Haman. In the same way, Jesus was elevated in His humanity to the throne of God, where He represents humanity and is the mediator and intercessor for us, He removed the verdict of spiritual death from each person who believes in Him.

Unfounded claims against the book of Esther.

Some want to annul the enormous historical mistake regarding Haman which is recorded in the Quran. They want to attack the historical facts found in the book of Esther and nullify its authority. They have developed an elaborate scheme claiming that Esther is Ishtar, the goddess which was also called Venus. They also claim that Mordecai was Morduch, a significant Babylonian god and Haman was Hammun, an Elamite god. They claim that Purim, the festival which the Jews practiced in memory of their rescue from Haman's extermination scheme, was actually a long practiced Persian festival.

These claims also rely on unfounded ideas about king Ahasuerus, whom some identify as Xerxes I. They endeavor to discredit the book of Esther when it says Ahasuerus had 127 provinces and a wife named Vashti.

Later, I will respond to those critics in detail. Nevertheless, attacking the book of Esther does not change the fact that Mohammed copied Haman's name from the book of Esther, but he placed him in Egypt. These critics cannot hide the enormous mistake Mohammed made.

The book of Esther has always been regarded by the church as an important treasure in the canon, or selected books, of the Bible. The writer of Esther demonstrated that he was acquainted with many of the Persian customs at that time. He also was familiar with the laws of the king, and he gave many details.

Therefore, many believe the author must have lived in the same period about which he wrote. Josephus, 1st century A.D. Jewish Historian, and Clement of Alexandria, a church father CA200 A.D., suggested that Mordecai himself was the author of the book.

Who was Ahasuerus of the book of Esther?

There is some question however about who Ahasuerus was in the book of Esther.

Although modern Bible scholars disagree on who Ahasuerus was, most of them believe he was Xerxes, but others believe that Ahasuerus might have been an appellative title like the generic term Pharaoh. Richard Fix in an article supporting this view, quotes Sir Henry Rawlinson, Professor Sayce, The Encyclopedia Britannica, and The Century Encyclopedia of Names, all of which support the idea that Ahasuerus was a general name and not a proper name.[182]

Some scholars assert that the name Ahasuerus, which means "the mighty," is a title of more than one a Median and Persian king.[183] However, most Bible scholars agree with those who say that Ahasuerus is derived from the Persian "khshayarsha." In the papyri, "Elephantine Aramaic," the king appears under the name of "kys'rs". This is close to the Greek name Xerxes.

We read in the International Standard Bible Encyclopedia:

> There is absolute certainty that the Persian Khshayarsha, the Hebrew Achashverosh, the Greek Assoueros or Xerxes, and the Latin Ahasuerus, are the exact equivalents of one another.[184]

Mordecai's service to the Kings

Esther 2:5, 6, tells us about Mordecai:

> In the citadel, Shushan, there was a certain Jew whose name was Mordecai, the son of Jair, the son of Shimei, the son of Kish, a Benjamite. Kish had been carried away from Jerusalem with the captives who had been captured with Jeconiah king of Judah, whom Nebuchadnezzar the king of Babylon had carried away.

When Nebuchadnezzar carried the nobles of the land to Babel, Mordecai's grandfather was carried away from Jerusalem with Jeconiah and the other captives as we are told in 2 Kings 24. This occurred in 597 B.C. We know that Daniel was carried away previously with other captives around 605 B.C.

Daniel 1:1-6 shows how Nebuchadnezzar, trained and employed the sons of the Jewish nobles in his service in the palace. Daniel, with some of the Jews who served in the Chaldean kingdom, continued to serve in the subsequent Persian Kingdom. This explains why Mordecai was in the palace at the time of Ahasuerus, the king of Persia. Since Kish, the grandfather of Mordecai, was among the nobles whom Nebuchadnezzar carried away, it is likely that Kish, like Daniel, was among the young sons of the nobles who were trained in the palace and remained in service to monarchs who later occupied Mesopotamia.

We are told that Mordecai, had free access to different parts of the palace, because every day he watched the entrance to the court of the women's quarters in order to look for his adopted daughter, Esther, "And every day Mordecai paced in front of the court of the women's quarters, to learn of Esther's welfare and what was happening to her." (Esther 2: 11)

Often, we see him sitting at the king's gate. This shows that Mordecai was an important officer appointed by the king to watch the movements of the palace, and to insure the safety of the king. He was not just a simple guard, because normal palace guards were not free to enter all the areas of the palace. Mordecai proved he had authority. As Esther 2:21-23 tells us:

> While Mordecai watched all the other guards and workers in the palace he discovered a plot against the king which was schemed by two individuals who were guards of the king.

This suggests that Mordecai may have been a key intelligence officer appointed by the king for things like this. Ancient kings of the Middle East often trusted loyal people (such as Joseph) from among the minorities who lived in their country rather than relying totally on agents of their own nationality.

Mordecai served the Persian kings at the time of Cyrus II, called Cyrus the Great, who was the founder of the Achaemenian Empire.

In his writings the author of the book of Esther reflects the historical characteristics of the Achaemenian Empire at that time.

After Cyrus II defeated Astages, the Median King, in the battle of Pasargadae, around the year 550 A.D., he united the Medians and Persians to form the Achaemenian Empire. Historically, he was known for his wisdom in building his kingdom, recognizing the authority of the Median princes, and making them feel that they were represented in the affairs of the empire as much as the Persians themselves. When he united the two main Iranian tribes to form his empire, he incorporated the nobles of Media and Persia in his system of government.

The book of Esther confirms this historical decision. In Esther 1:13 and 14, we read:

> Then the king said to the wise men who understood the times for this was the king's manner toward all who knew law and justice, those closest to him being Carshena, Shethar, Admatha, Tarshish, Meres, Marsena, and Memucan, the seven princes of Persia and Media, who

had access to the king's presence, and who ranked highest in the kingdom.

Esther 1: 2, 3 says:

In those days when King Ahasuerus sat on the throne of his kingdom, which was in Shushan, the citadel, that in the third year of his reign he made a feast for all his officials and servants–the powers of Persia and Media, the nobles, and the princes of the provinces being before him.

This is characteristic of how Cyrus caused the Achaemenian Empire to represent the Meads and Persians in his reign and the reigns of successive kings. This is one of many proofs which confirm that the author of the book of Esther lived during this period, which began with Cyrus II and continued for some generations.

We can identify Mordecai as the one of the exiles who returned from the Persian palace to rebuild Jerusalem.

In the year 539 B.C. Cyrus entered the city of Babel and was welcomed as a liberator. He was welcomed by the Jewish population, which was in exile there, as well by the Babylonians. The Babylonians were not satisfied with King Nabonidus, who was from the city of Harran and worshiped the moon god, Sin, and was indifferent to the Babylonian worship of Morduch.

In 538 B.C., Cyrus issued a decree allowing the Jews to return to Jerusalem to build the Temple. There have been many returns since then to Jerusalem. One was under Zerubbabel, who was of the royal family of Judah, and was one of the Messianic ancestors in the genealogy leading to the birth of Jesus.

Zerubbabel was appointed by the Persians to govern Judah. Ezra 2:2 mentions Mordecai among the leaders who returned with Zerubbabel.

In addition to Zerubbabel himself, the leaders who returned with him were also mentioned by name, such as Joshua, the high priest, but they failed to mention their fathers' names. Because Mordecai is mentioned by name without mentioning his father, and because Ezra does not give details about him as he did with the others whom he listed, shows that Mordecai was already well known to his contemporaries, such as Zerubbabel and the high priest, Joshua.

It seems that Zerubbabel was close to the palace of the Persian kings, so that he was commissioned to lead a group of thousands to Jerusalem.

Then he was appointed to be the governor of Judah. The leaders who returned with him, were close to the Persian palace as well, confirming that Mordecai, who returned as a leader with Zerubbabel, was also close to the palace.

All this points to the fact that this Mordecai is the same Mordecai found in the book of Esther, and who lived in the palace, an idea also supported by rabbinic tradition.

For Mordecai the Jew was next unto king Ahasuerus, and great among the Jews and accepted of the majority of his brethren. Of the majority of his brethren but not of all his brethren; this informs us that some members of the Sanhedrin separated from him.

R. Joseph said:

> The study of the Torah is superior to the saving of life. For at first Mordecai was reckoned next after four, but afterwards next after five. At first it is written, who came with Zerubbabel, [namely] Joshua, Nehemiah, Serayah, Reelaiah, Mordecai, Bilshan, and subsequently it is written, who came with Zerubbabel, Joshua, Nehemiah, Azariah, Ramaiah, Nahamani, Mordecai, Bilshan.[185]

There was a tradition that Mordecai once went with a deputation to the king of Persia to ask permission for the Jews to rebuild the Temple.[186] People who were selected for leadership to accompany groups of Jews on their return to Palestine were always favored by the kings of Persia. Some of them were chosen to return so they might lead the people in building the city of Jerusalem. There was one condition, however. After their mission was accomplished, they were to return to the palace to serve the Persian king once more.

Nehemiah is an example of this. He was allowed to go to Jerusalem after he set a time when he would return to serve the king of Persia. This may also have been the case for Mordecai. He was allowed to lead the return with Zerubbabel and Joshua, the high priest, with the condition that he return to his service to the king. It seems that Mordecai, like Daniel, served during the reigns of many kings.

The return of Zerubbabel occurred during the reign of King Darius in the year 520 B.C. Mordecai must have been young at the time, perhaps 25–30 years of age. He must have already been in the palace at the Persian city of Susa. Cambyses, the son of Cyrus II, became king after the death of his father, and he moved the capital from Pasargadae to Susa.

In the year 521 B.C., Darius I became the king of Persia, and confirmed his capital at Susa, which is Shushan in Hebrew, and mentioned also in the book of Esther.

These facts agree with what is told in the book of Esther. Mordecai, it seems, lived in Susa during the time of Darius, and he accompanied Zerubbabel in his return to Jerusalem, as we find in Nehemiah 7:7.

The return of Mordecai must have taken only a short time, because neither Ezra nor Nehemiah gave many details about Mordecai. He probably did not stay long in the promised land, but returned to Susa to again take up his service to king Darius. It seems his delicate service as a guard officer, watching the other workers of the palace, did not allow him to leave his office for a long time.

Thus, we find Mordecai at the palace of Susa during the reign of Darius' son, Xerxes, who began his reign in the year 486 B.C. Thirty-four years elapsed since he visited Jerusalem under the reign of Darius. That would make him around the age of 60-64. I think that is why he is portrayed in the book of Esther as sitting in the gate of the palace, where business is conducted. Instead of standing with guards due to his relatively old age.

The historical facts about Xerxes match what is recorded in the book of Esther.

Many other historical traits point to Xerxes as described in the book of Esther. For example, Xerxes was known historically for easily changing his wives. We do not know just how many wives he had, but it seems that Vashti was the last wife he took before marrying Esther. The fact that he divorced her because she refused to let her beauty be seen by his guests, is indicative of his pride and strange character as described by the Greek historian, Herodotus.

The references in the book of Esther stating that there were 127 provinces in the empire agree with the historical facts. In fact, Darius was known in history to have divided the large empire into many small provinces. He was a great organizer. He subdued rebellions in many parts of his empire and extended his territory in Asia, especially in India. He occupied Thracia (southeastern Bulgaria), and added many cities — especially Ionian-Greek cities — to increase the provinces in his empire.

His son, Xerxes, found the empire already well-organized when he came to power. The increase in the number of provinces is understandable because he occupied so many cities in his military campaigns. That's how he extended his Empire. The book of Esther says:

> This is what happened during the time of Ahasuerus, who ruled over 127 provinces stretching from India to Cush.

The book of Esther is considered to be historically accurate.

Most of the life of Xerxes is obscure at best. Many documents have been found in Mesopotamia documenting Darius's reign, but there is little about Xerxes.

The main source is Herodotus. However, Herodotus focused mainly on Xerxes's military conflict with the Greeks during the year 480 B.C. Those conflicts culminated in the Battle of Salamis, September 28 of the same year, 480 B.C. The Persians lost the war.

Little is mentioned about Xerxes's family life, especially after he returned from this war. History reports he maintained a harem, but no one knows exactly how many wives were involved. Therefore, if Vashti is not mentioned in the limited sources we have about his life, that does not mean he did not have Vashti as his queen before he married Esther.

Regarding the historicity of the book of Esther

Many scholars, noting the writer's familiarity with Persian customs and institutions and with the character of King Ahasuerus, hold that the author of the book of Esther was a contemporary of Mordecai, whose historical records he used.

Biblical scholars consider the book of Esther to be an accurate historical account for many other reasons. In this regard, I would like to quote the detailed and historically rich work of A. L. McMaho:

> Biblical scholars base their conclusions especially on the following: the vivacity and simplicity of the narrative; the precise and circumstantial details, as, particularly, the naming of unimportant personages, the noting of dates and events; the references to the annals of the Persians; the absence of anachronisms; the agreement of proper names with the time in which the story is placed; the confirmation of details by history

and archeology; the celebration of the feast of Purim in commemoration of the deliverance of the Jews by Esther and Mardochai at the time of the Machabees (II Mach., xv, 37), at the time of <u>Josephus</u> (Antiq of the Jews, XI, vi, 13), and since.. Nor has any one else succeeded better in offering an explanation of the feast than that it had its origin as stated in the Book of Esther.[187]

The work of Herodotus (especially book 7, verses 8, 24, 35, and 37-39, and book 9, verse 108) confirms the fact that the book of Esther is historically accurate. For example, in the seventh book of Herodotus, verse 8, we see King Xerxes' policy of organizing his kingdom and respecting the two tribes of Iran: the Medes and the Persians. When we analyze the rest of the writings of Herodotus about Xerxes, we are even more convinced that the book of Esther agrees with history.

Dating the book of Esther

What about the book of Esther itself? Esther is part of the Septuagint, the Greek translation of the Old Testament. The Septuagint was translated by Ptolemy II Philadelphus, who reigned as the king of Egypt in 287 B.C. Ptolemy II established a library in Alexandria and wanted to enrich it by adding the Bible to it. The work was completed by the 2nd century B.C.. This, among other evidence such as from Ben Sira, Qumran, and others, suggests the book of Esther was considered as part of the Old Testament canon as early as the beginning of the third century B.C.

This also means that the Book of Esther was spread throughout the Jewish communities earlier than the 4th century B.C. This is significant because it proves that the author of Esther lived close to, or at the time of King Assuerus, who has been identified as Xerxes, and who reigned from 485-465 B.

Purim as a Jewish festival

To celebrate the decision to spare the Jews, the festival of Purim was established demonstrating to us that the festival of Purim was an old Hebrew celebration.

Purim never appeared before the time of Esther, and was not known to be a Persian or Babylonian festival, since no Persian or Babylonian script, chronicle or anal mentioned this festival. When we study the Persian sacred books such as the Zenda Avesta or the Pahlavi texts, which were the traditional interpretation of the original Avesta, all the religious festivals of the Persians are listed, yet, nowhere do we find the Festival of Purim. All these facts prove that Purim is purely and strictly a Jewish festival, which came as a result of Queen Esther.

Jews have celebrated this festival since the time of Esther, and we know that, historically, Jewish people never added festivals to those ordered by God. This connects Purim with that great event, giving us confidence that it really happened, and that the festival was ordered as stated in the book which was inspired by God.

In the apocryphal book, II Maccabees, 15:13, the writer stress the importance of celebrating Purim as it was celebrated since the time of Mordecai. Jews were to celebrate it in the 13th day of Adar, which is the mouth of March. The book of Maccabees dates from between 135 and 125 B.C.

The names found in the book of Esther supports the authenticity of the book.

As if these records are not enough to establish the credibility of Esther, names which appear in the Book of Esther support its authenticity. Some of these names are derived from pagan names, but rather than undermine the historical nature of the book, they actually lend support to its historical accuracy.

Esther's name was not her original Hebrew name. In Esther, chapter 2, her name first appears, "And he [Mordecai] brought up Hadassah, that is, Esther, his uncle's daughter, for she had neither father nor mother." So, we see the true name of Esther was Hadassah. Probably she was given the name of Esther by the authorities of the palace. Often Babylonian and Persian palace chiefs changed foreign names of people they wanted to employ in the palace, giving them Babylonian or Persian names.

No wonder they often chose pagan names. We have an example in Daniel and his friends who were trained to provide services for King Nebuchadnezzar. We read in Daniel 1:7:

> The chief eunuch gave them other names, calling Daniel Belteshazzar; Hananiah, Shadrach; Mishael, Meshach; and Azariah, Abed-Nego.

In Daniel 4:8 we know that Belteshazzar, the name which was given to Daniel, is a pagan name. Daniel was named to reflect a local pagan god that Nebuchadnezzar revered personally. Nebuchadnezzar himself said:

> But finally Daniel came in before me, whose name is Belteshazzar,
> according to the name of my god.

Similarly, there is a small probability that Mordecai's name was a Babylonian name. In this case, it must have been a Babylonian name given to Mordecai by the authorities of the palace, since his father had served in the palace as well. Although scholars have different opinions about his name, some scholars think it is related somehow to Morduch. Rabbinic tradition explains the name "Mordecai" (מרדכי) as a compound of מירא דכיא, the Aramaic form of מר דרור, which means "pure myrrh."[188]

As in two passages–Ezra 2: 2 and Neh. 7: 7– Mordecai is followed by the name Bilshan. Hebrew tradition considers that Mordecai and Bilshan were the names of one man,[189] which may suggest that Bilshan is the original Hebrew name of Mordecai.

Haman, who drafted the decree to have the Jews killed, is not the name of the Elamite god, Hammun, although it sounds similar. Haman is of Amalekite origin, but his name is Persian, Hamayun, meaning "magnificent.[190] It seems his family lived in Persia for many generations before the occurrence of the events reported in the Book of Esther.

Another possibility is that Haman was named by the King of Persia himself. Oriental kings often trusted foreigners rather than nationals for close service in their palaces.

At the end of this research on the book of Esther, we conclude that the book to be historically accurate. In history, the name of Haman was known because of the book of Esther. The Islamic attack on the book of Esther will not help to annul Mohammed's error in transferring the name of the Persian King Ahasuerus' counselor to a counselor to Pharaoh who lived nearly 1,000 years before the events recorded in the historically accurate book of Esther.

Simon

The Samaritan magician of the book of Acts transported to the time of Moses

Simon, the Samaritan magician who appears in the book of Acts, became part of the Quran when Mohammed inserted him in its pages. The problem is that he claims Simon lived at the time of Moses, not at the time of the New Testament. Mohammed made the character Simon, the Samaritan magician who lived in the 1st century A.D. as presented in the book of Acts of the Apostles and the apocryphal books of the early Church, live in Moses' time during the 15th century B.C.

In writing the Quran, Mohammed also copied a famous incident from the book of Exodus. It was the story of the golden calf which Aaron, under pressure from the Israelites, made in the wilderness, but the Quran attributed the calf to someone he called "the Samaritan."

The Quran quotes Allah in Surah Ta Ha 20: 85-97:

We have seduced your people in your absence. The Samaritan has led them astray." Moses returned to his people in a state of anger and sorrow. He said to them, 'Oh people, did not your lord make a good promise to you? Did waiting for the promise seem too long to you? Or perhaps you wanted wrath to come down on you from your lord, and so you broke your promise to me?'

They replied, 'As much as it was in our power, we did not break our promise to you, but we were forced to carry the heavy ornaments of the people, and we threw them into the fire, and that what the Samaritan threw'. Then the Samaritan brought forth the body of a calf before their eyes. It was lowing or mooing, and they said, 'This is your god, and the god of Moses...'

Then Moses said, 'What is the matter with you, Samaritan?' He replied, ' I saw what they did not see, so I took a handful of dust from the footprint of the apostle, and threw it into the calf...'.'Go,' Moses said to him, 'For your punishment in life, you will tell everyone, "touch me not," and you will have a day of punishment which will not fail, so look to your God from whom you have gone astray.'

As we see from these verses, the Quran claimed the person who made the golden calf was the Samaritan and not Aaron. Did you notice that Mohammed did not say "a Samaritan," but he said, "the Samaritan?" This indicates that he was speaking about a known Samaritan whose name was familiar to his listeners.

There is little doubt that this Samaritan was Simon, the Samaritan magician, who appears in the book of the Acts of the Apostles. Simon the magician, or sorcerer, seduced the Samaritans with his magic. We read about this in Acts 8: 9-24:

> But there was a certain man called Simon, who previously practiced sorcery in the city and astonished the people of Samaria, claiming that he was someone great, to whom they all gave heed, from the least to the greatest, saying, 'This man is the great power of God.' And they heeded him because he had astonished them with his sorceries for a long time. But when they believed Philip as he preached the things concerning the kingdom of God and the name of Jesus Christ, both men and women were baptized. Then Simon himself also believed; and when he was baptized, he continued with Philip, and was amazed, seeing the miracles and signs which were done.

The magician of Samaria and his mythological figure, the root of the Quranic claim that "the Samaritan" created a living calf in the desert.

Simon became famous in the centuries after Christ. He established a cult, called Simonianism, he claimed to be God, and he claimed to create life. He showed interest in Christianity when he saw the evangelist Philip doing great miracles in the name of Jesus. His interest, however, proved to be an admiration of the miracles that were performed in the city of Samaria rather than a real love for the truth. Evidently, he thought he could imitate the miracles and imagined he could learn the secret of how they were done.

When the apostles learned that many in the city of Samaria demonstrated faith in Jesus, they sent two apostles, Peter and John, to strengthen the new believers. Acts 8: 14-17:

> Now when the apostles who were at Jerusalem heard that Samaria had received the word of God, they sent Peter and John to them, who, when they had come down, prayed for them that they might receive the Holy Spirit. For as yet He had fallen upon none of them. They had only been baptized in the name of the Lord Jesus. Then they laid hands on them, and they received the Holy Spirit.

Simon the Samaritan thought that he could buy this gift with his money, proving that he was still thinking as magician and not as a real Christian. The account in Acts continues with verses 18-23:

> And when Simon saw that through the laying on of the apostles' hands the Holy Spirit was given, he offered them money, saying, 'Give me this power also, that anyone on whom I lay hands may receive the Holy Spirit.' But Peter said to him, "Your money perish with you, because you thought that the gift of God could be purchased with money! You have neither part nor portion in this matter, for your heart is not right in the sight of God. Repent, therefore, of this your wickedness, and pray [to] God if perhaps the thought of your heart may be forgiven you. For I see that you are poisoned by bitterness and bound by iniquity'.

The influence of this account on the Quran, is evident. The Quran refers to "the Samaritan" as a person capable of doing great signs, including creating the golden calf whose mooing meant it was alive. In the early centuries that followed, the ability to create was attributed to Simon by his followers. This sect continued for many centuries after Christ. From the writings of the early church fathers, we know that Simon, the magician, claimed to be God potentially existing in everyone.[191] as the infinite power.[192] Hippolytus, a father of the church in the end of second and the beginning of the third centuries A.D. said, "Now Simon affirms that he himself is He who stood in the past, stands now, and will stand in the future. He is a power that is above all things."[193]

Simon, the Samaritan magician, was given great prominence in Simonianism. The cult that he founded, made Simon appear as a force competing with God, creating bodies as God created bodies. His reputation grew as his followers claimed he could compete with the miracles only God can do. The Samaritan soon became a name which many believed became the negative competitor with God, capable of creating and imitating God. From this we see how the idea of creating, as described in the Quran by creating the body of a calf, complete with mooing, is attributed to "the Samaritan."

The image of Simon, the Samaritan magician, in the apocryphal books is the root of the Quranic myth about the Samaritan.

The portrait of the Samaritan who, according to the Quran, changed the golden calf into a lowing, living calf is derived from the image of Simon, the Samaritan magician, whom we encounter in several apocryphal books of the early church. For example, we read about Simon the magician in

Chapter 31 of Acts of Peter, an apocryphal book dating to the middle of the 2nd century A.D.:

> Though he had oft-times been convicted of sorcery, he made lame men seem whole for a little space, and blind likewise, and once he appeared to make many dead to live and move, as he did with Nicostratus.

This verse implies that Simon used magic to make dead men appear to be alive without actually raising them from the dead.

Simon the Samaritan magician was one who used magic to give life to lifeless bodies, such as stones, as we see in the Pseudo-Clementine writings. These writings are divided into two categories: The Clementine Homilies, which are formed of 20 books written originally in Greek, and the Clementine Recognitions. They were translated from Greek by Rufinus, the historian and theologian who died in the year 410 A.D. Some of Rufinus' translations of some Pseudo-Clementine writings were later translated into Arabic and Syriac.

The Clementine Recognitions

The second book of the Clementine Recognitions claims that Clementine, who later became a bishop of Rome, was a disciple of Simon the magician. He then became a Christian through the preaching of Zacchaeus, and followed the Apostle Peter.[194]

The second book of the Clementine Homilies reports that Aquila was Simon's disciple and then became a Christian. Aquila spoke to Peter about Simon the magician (Homily 2, chapter XXII):

> First Aquila began to speak in this wise: 'Listen, O dearest brother, that you may know accurately everything about this man, whose he is, and what, and whence; and what the things are which he does, and how and why he does them. This Simon is the son of Antonius and Rachel, a Samaritan by race, of the village of Gitthae, which is six schoeni distant from the city. He having disciplined himself greatly in Alexandria, and being very powerful in magic, and being ambitious, wishes to be accounted a certain supreme power, greater even than the God who created the world. 'And sometimes intimating that he is Christ, he styles himself the Standing One. And this epithet he employs, as intimating that he shall always stand, and as not having any cause of corruption so that his body should fall. And he neither says that the God who created the world is the Supreme, nor does he believe that the dead will be raised'[195]

These writings thus bestowed to the Samaritan magician the ability to give life to the statues. According to the second book of the Clementine Recognitions, Aquila spoke to Peter before a debate that was to take place between Peter and Simon and emphasized the danger of Simon's magic. Aquila recalled how Simon said to him and to others who, before turning to Christianity, were Simon's disciples:

> I can make the barriers open of their own accord; I can render statues animated, so that those who see suppose that they are men. I can make new trees suddenly spring up, and produce sprouts at once... I can change my countenance, so that I cannot be recognized...Whatever I wish, that I shall be able to do. For already I have achieved many things by way of experiment.[196]

Thus, according to these writings, Simon the Samaritan magician claimed that he was able to create life in the statues and thus change them into real men. This is actually the same type of work the Quran attributed to the "the Samaritan": that is, transforming the golden calf into a lowing, living calf.

These apocryphal writings established a mythological reputation for Simon the Samaritan magician that spread through several centuries after the period after Christ: that Simon had the capability of transforming lifeless materials into living creatures. For example, in the second book of the Pseudo-Clementine Homilies Clement said that he was informed about Simon the magician making the statues walk:

> And they told me that he makes statues walk, and that he rolls himself on the fire, and is not burnt; and sometimes he flies; and he makes loaves of stones; he becomes a serpent; he transforms himself into a goat; he becomes two-faced... he melts iron.... I wondered when I heard them speak thus; but many bore witness that they had been present, and had seen such things.[197]

Powers attributed to Simon in those writings include the ability to animate and make alive inanimate objects. Bernice, who according to these writings was previously Simon's disciple, speaks in the fourth book of these Homilies that when Simon walked, the statues moved and the shadows went before him:

> These things are indeed as you have heard; and I will tell you other things respecting this same Simon, which perhaps you do not know. For he astonishes the whole city every day, by making specters and ghosts appear in the midst of the market-place; and when he walks abroad, statues move, and many shadows go before him, which, he says, are souls of the dead.[198]

According to these Pseudo-Clementine writings, Simon claimed to have created a boy by giving life to a picture of a boy that he had drawn. According to this claim, this was a practical expression of his ability to give life to inanimate objects, such as a picture, a statue, or a metallic animal. This is similar to the Quranic story that the Samaritan gave life to the golden calf. According to the second book of the Clementine Homilies, the disciples of Simon who became Christians, however, interpret this claim as follows:

> For he even began to commit murder as he himself disclosed to us, as a friend to friends, that, having separated the soul of a child from its own body by horrid incantations, as his assistant for the exhibition of anything that he pleased, and having drawn the likeness of the boy, he has it set up in the inner room where he sleeps, saying that he once formed the boy of air, by divine arts, and having painted his likeness, he gave him back again to the air.

> And he explains that he did the deed thus. He says that the first soul of man, being turned into the nature of heat, drew to itself, and sucked in the surrounding air, after the fashion of a gourd; and then that he changed it into water, when it was within the form of the spirit; and he said that he changed into the nature of blood the air that was in it, which could not be poured out on account of the consistency of the spirit, and that he made the blood solidified into flesh; then, the flesh being thus consolidated, that he exhibited a man not made from earth, but from air.

> And thus, having persuaded himself that he was able to make a new sort of man, he said that he reversed the changes, and again restored him to the air. And when he told this to others, he was believed; but by us who were present at his ceremonies he was religiously disbelieved. Wherefore we denounced his impieties, and withdrew from him.[199]

According to the second book of the Clementine Recognitions, Simon claimed that he created a boy of air. He claimed that his work was superior to God the Creator's work in which God had created man from the dust of the earth. The disciples who withdrew from him and became Christians said that Simon spoke about the boy and said that after he killed him, separating his soul from his body, he used the boy's soul in the act he performed by inserting the boy's soul in the boy's picture, thus giving him life in the air.[200]

These writings attribute to Simon the ability to create new life by placing a soul into an insensible form. This is actually the foundation of the Quranic myth — that the Samaritan magician had inserted life into the golden calf.

As we have seen, however, even though Simon claimed to have created a boy of air, his disciples left him. They discovered the tricks by which he appeared to insert created lives into insensible lifeless elements. They discovered that he did not create life but rather borrowed life and, through magic, inserted this life into insensible lifeless things, making them live.

The Quranic verse says that the Samaritan took dust from under the horse of Gabriel, which means he borrowed life from Gabriel, and then poured it on the golden calf, and it became a lowing, living calf. This is actually the same ability attributed to Simon the Samaritan magician in these Pseudo-Clementine writings. This suggests that the myth current in Mohammed's time had borrowed a famous portrait about Simon the Samaritan magician and applied it to the story mentioned in the Bible about Aaron, who formed a golden calf in the wilderness. The Quranic verse is attributed to the "Samaritan magician" and presents the same characteristics of Simon that were presented in these Pseudo-Clementine writings. It is clear that Mohammed, who made Haman, the vizier of King Ahasuerus of Persia, to be a vizier of Pharaoh at the time of Moses, was capable of borrowings and mixing as it suited his own purposes without regard to historical accuracy. Here Mohammed borrowed a mythological claim attributed to Simon the Samaritan magician and inserted into the Quran a myth. He retained the name "the Samaritan" and the Samaritan magician's characteristic in animating the insensible elements and made him bestow life to the golden calf at the time of Moses.

How did the myths of the Pseudo-Clementine writings spread to Mecca?

Epiphanius of Salamis-Cyprus, who died in the year 403 A.D., wrote that the Ebionites used those Pseudo-Clementine writings, [201] because they opposed the Apostle Paul whom the Ebionites also opposed. For example, they used the name Simon as a nickname for Paul. Furthermore, these writings lent great importance to Moses and the Mosaic law and portrayed the Apostle Peter as zealous about the law. Those notions agree with the Ebionites' heretical doctrines. The Church Fathers reported that the Ebionites believed that Paul was a backslider from the doctrine and who taught against the Law.[202]

The spread of the Ebionites in North Arabia is confirmed. Epiphanius reported that some Christian heresies, such as the Alcasaite and Ebionite heresies, spread in the areas of Trans-Jordan and Nabataea and extended into North Arabia. In the 1st century B.C., when the Nabataeans occupied northwestern Arabia after defeating the Lahyanites, Hijr, a Lahyanite site in North Arabia, became a Nabataean city.

Epiphanius reported that Ebionism spread in his own time (during the 4th century A.D.) in the regions of Nabataea and Moab.[203] Epiphanius reports that the Ebionites began their activity in Trans-Jordan. He cited Arabia as one of the places where they were active.[204] This explains how the Ebionites were present in the region of Mecca at Mohammed's time.

The spread of the Ebionites at Mecca is a well-known fact. Waraqa bin Nofel, a cousin of Khadijah (Mohammed's first wife), and the second man, after Zayd bin Amru bin Nufayl, of the group of Ahnaf, was an Ebionite. This was proven by the fact that Waraqa translated the gospel according to Hebrews into Arabic. We read about Waraqa:

> He wrote the Hebrew Book. He wrote from Gospel in Hebrew what he desired to write.[205]

Furthermore, Waraqa influenced the Quran with many Ebionite doctrines. Waraqa was the first source of the Quranic verses – to the extent that, as we have previously mentioned, after he died it was said that "the inspiration cooled down." Mohammed found himself in crisis until he found other sources for his Quran.

The Ebionites influenced the Quran and Islam regarding alms. The issue of alms was a main pillar of Ebionite religion.[206] Alms became a main pillar in Islam, as well. As we understand from the writings of the Church Fathers, the Ebionites were a Jewish Christian cult that lived a life of asceticism and were fanatics for the Mosaic law. They venerated the city of Jerusalem in a particular manner.[207] This may explain the habit or practice of Waraqa bin Nofel and Khadijah in doing asceticism in the cave of Hirra' near Mecca. Later, Mohammed adopted the same ascetic practice. This also explains the existence of many Judaic laws and rituals in Islam and why Mohammed, when praying, used to direct his face toward Jerusalem. After he emigrated to Medina, he changed the direction of his prayer toward Mecca, so as to agree with the chiefs of the Aws and Khazraj tribes who prayed as pagans toward Mecca.

Through studying Panarion, Epiphanius' book refuting the heresies, we can see the Ebionites' influence on Islam. In addition to the fact the

Ebionites did not recognize the deity of Christ and instead considered Him to be just a man, various other Ebionite rituals and doctrines influenced Islam, such as:

> Ebion – the founder of Ebionism – added the rules about taking care not to touch a Gentile and how after a man has been with a woman and left her he must immerse himself in water – any water he can find, sea water or any other. Moreover, if he should meet anyone while returning from his bath in the water, he must run back again for another immersion, often even with his clothes on![208]

Here is the principle of defilement through touching the infidels, which was adopted in Islam. Also, the legislation in Islam of washing after intercourse with women – and purification through many washings and ablutions.

Their faith only in the gospel according to Mathew, calling it the gospel according to the Hebrews or the Hebrew Gospel. Epiphanius wrote:

> They too accept the Gospel according to Matthew. Like the Cerinthians and Merinthians, they too use it alone. They call it 'According to the Hebrews.[209]

He added:

> Though it is not the entire Gospel but is corrupt and mutilated — and they call this thing 'Hebrew.[210]

We recall that Waraqa bin Nofel used to translate the Hebrew Gospel, showing the relationship of Waraqa with the Ebionites.

They had a system of daily ablutions. They claimed that Peter used to make daily baptisms for purification as they did.[211] This gave rise to the idea of ablutions. But as Epiphanius reveals, the ablutions were because of their excessive sexual involvements. They took of the water to reassure themselves that they were purified by means of the ablutions.[212]

We see here a similarity with Islam, not only regarding ablutions, which is in Islam considered a means of purification, but also regarding indulgence in sex, as Mohammed, during the military campaigns, used to allow his companions to enjoy sex with conquered females. He permitted them to have sex with any female they captured.

Their boast in the circumcision[213] was also adopted in Islam.

They considered Aaron as great a prophet as Abraham and Moses.[214] Here we see a clear impact on Islam, in which Aaron is an important prophet, though according to the scriptures he did not obtain the role of prophecy.

They did not have commitment to the family values that the New Testament promoted. Their sexual indulgence made them not interested in the family and in building families on permanent bases according to the word of God. They gave their children for marriage when they were very young with the approval of their teachers.[215] Fulfilling their fleshly desires had priority over any consideration. This we see in Islam, for Mohammed married Aisha when she was 6 years old. Also, there is no commitment to the marriage. Epiphanius wrote about them in this regard:

> And they do not allow people to contract only one marriage; even if someone should want to be released from his first marriage and contract another, they permit it—they allow everything without hesitation—down to a second, and a third, and a seventh marriage.[216]

Thus, the influence of this Ebionite heresy upon Islam is clear. A Muslim can divorce by saying to his wife "you are divorced by the three." This is based on the Ebionites' principle of indulgence and fulfilling their lusts at the expense of marriage.

The Ebionites denied the deity of Christ and considered Jesus to be merely a prophet like Moses. They denied the redemption of Christ and His resurrection. Some of them denied the virgin birth of Jesus. The Ebionites' influence on the Islamic doctrines, especially regarding Jesus, is a fact that many scholars admit.[217]

The Ebionites' adoption of the Pseudo-Clementine writings made Simon the Samaritan magician (of whom these writings spoke in detail) an important figure who imitated God in creation. This helped the false notion that inanimate objects, such as metals or stones, can through magic be made alive spread in Arabia. These writings made the Samaritan magician a mythological figure known to Waraqa, the Ebionite, and to Mohammed, his disciple. So, when Mohammed wanted to resolve the dilemma of how the golden calf became a lowing, living body, he did not find anyone more suitable to the task of performing such magical and creative work than Simon the Samaritan magician.

On the one hand, there is a striking similarity between Peter's rebuke of Simon in the book of Acts and his punishment as it portrayed in the apocryphal writings, and, on the other hand, Moses' rebuke of the Samaritan in the Quran.

The Quran reveals Mohammed's dependence on some corrupted narration of the Biblical book of the Acts of the Apostles. According to the Quran, Moses revealed the Samaritan's present unhappy state, his future, and his punishment. He was asked to look to God in repentance. The Quran says, "Your punishment in this life will be that you will say, "Touch me not," meaning that no one should commune with him or touch him. Taberi, in explaining this verse, wrote:

> It was mentioned that Moses ordered the Israelites not to eat with him or commune with him. That is why he said to him, 'Your punishment in this life will be that you will say, 'Touch me not'[218]

Al Qurtubi wrote:

> Al Hasan said, 'Allah made the punishment of the Samaritan to be that he will neither touch people nor any one touches him or any of his followers until the day of judgment. As if Allah strengthened his affliction by making him not touch anyone or have anyone touch him. He made this as his punishment in life.'

Can you see how this was also taken from the book of Acts? Peter said to the Samaritan magician, "For I see that you are poisoned by bitterness and bound by iniquity" (Acts 8:23). This means a bitterness caused by punishment that will affect his soul, the bitterness of isolation from people.

The Quranic idea of the isolation of the Samaritan, who was not to be touched by anyone, is seen in the apocryphal writings. In the 14th book of the Acts of Peter, Simon is treated with harshness: All would beat him and avoid him so as not to be defiled by his infidelity, which he brought upon them before the arrival of Peter to Rome. In the 19th chapter, we see that Marcellus, in whose house Simon stayed, said to Peter:

> I cleansed mine whole house from the footsteps (traces) of Simon, and have wholly done away with even his wicked dust.

In the apocryphal letter called The Epistula Apostolorum (Letter of the Apostles), which the Ethiopian church adheres to, the letter dates back to the 2nd century A.D. where we find a warning not to come close to Simon the magician or to Cerinthus (another heretic):

> Cerinthos and Simon came... in the world. But these are enemies of Our Lord Jesus Christ, for they turn aside the words and the thing, that is Jesus Christ. So remove yourselves from them, for death is in them and a great destructive defilament.[219]

The Ethiopians were represented in great numbers in Mecca. Thus, the spread of stories in Mecca about Simon the Samaritan magician was not a strange thing.

We also find in the Quran that Moses showed the future state of the Samaritan: He is perished in eternity, and the day of punishment will not fail. Peter announced to the Samaritan magician that he is a doomed person, when he said, "Your money perishes with you."

All these passages show that Mohammed obviously had inaccurate translations of the book of Acts and that he had received from his Christian sources an inaccurate narration about the Samaritan mentioned in the book of Acts. Mohammed was also under the influence of the myths of the apocryphal writings, which the Ebionites ascribed to and spread in Arabia, in addition to the apocryphal books that the Ethiopians revered.

Mohammed and his sources understood that the golden calf was transformed into a real living calf.

In addition to Surah Ta Ha 20, the Quran says the calf lowed or mooed. Surah Al-A'raf 7:148 says, "In his absence, the people of Moses made the body of a lowing calf from their jewelry."

From the Hadiths of Mohammed, we see that, when he used the expression "an animal that has a lowing or a growl," he indicated it was a living animal. For example, in one Hadith as reported in al Bukhari, Mohammed used the terms "a camel that growls" and "a cow that lows" to mean a true, living camel and a true, living cow.[220] This shows that when he said "a body of a calf that has lowing" in the Quran Mohammed meant a true, living calf.

The companions of Mohammed also confirmed that the Quran intended a living calf. For example, Ibn Abbas, the cousin of Mohammed, and one of the main reporters of his Hadith, confirmed this.[221] And the most significant expositors of the Quran, such as Al Razi, spoke of a real living calf that came as the result of a miracle performed by the Samaritan.[222]

Al Qurtubi said that those golden ornaments were transformed into a true lowing, living calf:

> It was said that Allah changed it into flesh and blood. It was said when (the Samaritan) threw the dust into the fire the ornaments became a calf with lowing.[223]

Al Taberi quotes al Suddi, who said about the calf:

It became lowing and walking.[224]

The Quranic myth is formed of more than one component. One was a Jewish myth that holds that the golden calf that Aaron formed in the desert, in the absence of Moses, had lowing.

How the Quranic myth was developed in Mohammed's generation.

It seems the Jewish myths in Arabia made the golden calf be transformed into a lowing, living calf. But who would be able to change inanimate objects, such as a golden calf or the statues, into living bodies? According to mythology, the only figure who was a competitor and emulator of God, able to borrow life and insert it into lifeless things and thus transform them into living entities or creatures was Simon the Samaritan magician. At the time of Mohammed, we can assume that some groups (excluding Aaron, who according to mythology was also able to transform a golden calf into a living one) recalled the figure of Simon as the only emulator of God in these things. Thus, this magic procedure was attributed to Simon.

Another element that contributed to making these groups look to Simon the Samaritan magician as the hero of such an operation was the fact that the city of Samaria worshiped a metallic calf as god. (Hosea 8:6) This led them to think that the golden calf in the desert at the time of Moses belonged to the Samaritans, and that the Samaritan magician was the one who had transformed it into a living one.

It is clear that these groups ignored historical chronology. Simon the magician lived in the 1st century A.D., whereas Moses lived in the 15th century B.C. Mohammed, also ignorant of the historical chronology, was deceived by this myth. There is also the ignorance of both Mohammed and these groups that the term "Samaritans" did not exist before the 6th century B.C. and that Moses lived in the 15th century B.C.

The claim of creating a cow through magic and sorcery was also part of the Zoroastrian literature.

As we saw, the Quran claimed that a magician called "the Samaritan," created a cow, but that was not new to ancient literature. The concept that animals could be created through sorcery is found in Zoroastrian texts. We read in the book of Bundahis, from the Pahlavi Texts, that "Noktarga, through sorcery, formed a cow for tillage and begot children there."[225]

The idea, as it is found in the Quran, that a magician can create a living calf is without doubt the influence of Zoroastrian mythology as contrasted to the Bible, which says that only God can create. Neither spirit nor magician can imitate God in this unique function.

The mythology of Simon the magician's heresy, as well as that of Pthahil-Gabriel as a creator and apostle in Mandaeanism, left their fingerprints on the Quranic myth about the calf.

The text of the Quran is a mixture of various narrations, taken from here and there, and mingled with abbreviations of myths from various sources. The text of Surah 20:95-96 is a typical example of this mixture, or mishmash. Some Gnostic sects held that the one who created the world was not God but an angel. According to the 18th book of The Pseudo-Clementine Homilies, Simon said that the "dominant power" had sent two angels – the first angel to create the world and the second one to give the Law. [226] Here we see the idea of an angel as a creator sent by a superior power. This corresponds to the Quranic myth that the life that was given to the calf came from Gabriel, who was creative and known as "the apostle."

It is interesting to see that one component of this mixture is of Mandaean origin. We read in the Quran:

> Then Moses said : 'What is the matter with you O Samaritan?' who replied, ' I saw what they did not see, so that I took a handful of dust from the footprint of the messenger, and threw it into the calf. My soul suggested to me to do so,'

Who is this messenger mentioned in these verses? The term used is "Rasul," which means "apostle" or "messenger." This title is given specifically to the angel Gabriel in the Quran, as we see in Surah 17: 95 where the angel is called "Rasul," that is an apostle.

Al Sabuni, a famous expositor of the Quran, depending on previous expositions and Hadiths, gives the following interpretation of that text:

> I saw what they did not see; that Gabriel is coming to you mounted on the horse of life. My soul suggested to me to take a handful of dust from the footprint of his horse. Life would come to anything on which I threw

it. Thus, I took some dust from the footprint of the horse of Gabriel and I threw it onto the calf, and it began lowing [meaning it became alive].[227]

The term "apostle" when used as a title for the angel Gabriel is not found in the Bible. It is found only in Sabian Mandaean literature attributed to Pthael and Hibil Ziwa, two personalities of light who are type and prototype in the Mandaean mythology. Both Pthael and Hibil Ziwa are identified as the angel Gabriel. For example, we find the term "apostle" attributed to Hibil Ziwa in Ginza Rba, their main sacred book which dates back to the third century A.D., It says:

> Under your command every thing was created. Oh creator of Hibil Ziwa, who is Gabriel, the apostle, the one you have sent to the world of darkness.[228]

> Hibil Ziwa, as Gabriel, the apostle, is sent as a messenger to the seven heavens and seven earths, of which our earth is the superior. Hibil Ziwa came down to the seven earths, and organized "uthras," or angels, for each of the worlds and for each of the seven heavens. He set up rivers, and brought messages to these worlds.[229]

We find a detail about the visit of Hibil Ziwa to the seven earths mentioned in the Ginza Rba.[230] Distances are also given between one earth and another. Something that Mohammed imitated when he made our earth one of "seven earths." In his Hadiths he assigned distances between one earth and another:

> He said: Do you know what exists beneath you?' We answered: 'Allah and his prophet better know.' He said: 'Earth. Do you know what is beneath it?' We answered: 'Allah and his prophet better know.' He said: 'Another earth. Do you know the distance between the two earths?' We answered: 'Allah and his prophet better know.' He said seven hundred years of walk, then he counted seven earths. Then he said: In the name of Allah if you dangle one of you to the inferior earth, he would be landed there.[231]

The Quran repeated the Mandaean idea of seven heavens and seven earths, where inspired words carried by Gabriel to each world. In Surah 65, called Al Talaq, verse 12:

> Allah is the one who created seven heavens and a similar number of earths, the command of Allah comes down through the midst of them all.

This concept is not new to the Quran which borrowed it from the Mandaeans who claim the seven heavens and seven earths were created by

Pthael, called Gabriel. The command of the "king of lights," the main deity of the Mandaeans, comes to each of the heavens and earths.

The idea of the "inspiration for each heaven," which we saw in Mandaean literature, is also found in the Quran in Surah 41, called Faslit, and verse 12, which says, "he inspired to each heaven its duty and command." Which means in each heaven a chief for the inhabitants was selected in addition to angels and rivers etc. It is the same thing we encountered in Mandaean literature.

Pthael in Mandaean sacred literature is the creator of the seven heavens and the earth. He is also called "Gabriel" and "apostle." In Ginza Rba, Pthael is called "the glorified Gabriel, the apostle."[232]

Pthael, or Gabriel, the apostle, is portrayed as the creator who threw a spirit of life from his spirit into Adam, so that Adam could become alive.[233]

This Mandaean idea is used in the Quran, which claims that Gabriel breathed his spirit into the body of Mary for the creation of the body of Jesus. (Surah 21: 91 and 66:12)

Gabriel in the Quran is called "the Holy Spirit," a term derived from Mandaean and Gnostic literature. The title "Holy Spirit" is given in Manichaean and in some Gnostic literature to an angel. This we see in the Gnostic book "The Apocryphon of John,"[234] which was adopted by the Manichaeans, as found in Egypt in the famous Manichaean library called Nag Hammadi, which dates back to the 4th century A.D. The living spirit as an angel is the Creator described in the Manichaean sacred book, "The Kephalaia Of the Teacher." He is said to have created "ten heavens and eights earths."[235]

Pthael, or Gabriel, is a great creator in Mandaean literature. By magical movements he changed things into animated beings. He touched the black water condensing it to form the earth, as we see in Ginza Rba.[236]

With his touch he gave the sun and the moon their shine. As I previously mentioned, their sacred books call him the apostle. No wonder, dust of the footprint of his horse brought forth a living calf, {{as we saw in the Quranic verse,}} "I saw what they saw not, so that I took a handful of dust from the footprint of the apostle, and threw it into the calf." The Quran claims the Samaritan had seen what the Mandaeans called Pthael, Gabriel, the apostle, the magical creator. Gabriel is also in the Quran called "the apostle and the Holy Spirit." Many Gnostics said the angel Gabriel was the great angel, attributing the ability to create to him.

The Holy Spirit is the third person in the Triune God. He is not an angel, and he is not on the same level as the angels. In the Bible, the angel Gabriel is never given the ability to create life. The Holy Spirit appeared to Zacharias to proclaim the birth of John the Baptist, who came to prepare the way before Jesus. Then, Gabriel appeared a second time to Mary to announce the news of the virgin birth. Gabriel never performed a miracle or any creative role in the coming of Christ in a human body. All the divine functions attributed to Gabriel in the Quran came from Mandaeanism and Gnosticism.

Who are the Samaritans?

The city of Samaria was built by Umri, King of Israel, around the year 880 B.C. Umri named the city that he built after the owner of the hill upon which he built the city. We read in 1 Kings 16:24:

> And he bought the hill Samaria of Shemer for two talents of silver, and built on the hill, and called the name of the city which he built, after the name of Shemer, owner of the hill, Samaria.

It is clear that before the city of Samaria was built it was not possible to have the name of either "Samarians" or "Samaritans."

Shalmaneser V, King of Assyria, who reigned between 726 – 722 B.C. besieged the city of Samaria for three years. We read this in II Kings 17:3-6. Shalmaneser died during this siege, and Sargon II concluded the siege. We read in verse 6:

> In the ninth year of Hoshea, King of Israel, the King of Assyria took Samaria and carried Israel away to Assyria, and placed them in Halah and by the Harbor, the River of Gozan, and in the cities of the Medes.

The Israelites were replaced by other people as we read in II Kings 17:24:

> Then the king of Assyria brought people from Babylon, Cuthah, Ava, Hamath, and from Sepharvaim, and placed them in the cities of Samaria instead of the children of Israel; and they took possession of Samaria and dwelt in its cities.

Clearly the text shows these people took possession of Samaria.

The fact that Sargon II occupied Samaria, carried away its inhabitants and replaced them with other peoples, is confirmed from Sargon's inscriptions, which were discovered on a wall in his capital called Dur-Sharrukîn (now Khorsabad). These inscriptions, which were discovered in 1842 by the French archaeologist Paul Emil Botta, say:

> In my first year I captured Samaria. I took captive 27,290 people. People of other lands who never paid tribute, I settled in Samaria.

The religion of those whom the Assyrians brought to live in the city of Samaria

What kind of people moved into Samaria? We are told in II Kings 17:28-41 that at first, they did not fear the Lord. As a result, many of them were killed by the Lions. Then they asked the King of Assyria to send them a Hebrew priest to instruct them in God's law, so they would not be killed by the beasts of the land. The King of Assyria sent them one priest. This account says:

> Then one of the priests whom they had carried away from Samaria came and dwelt in Bethel, and taught them how they should fear the Lord. However every nation continued to make gods of its own, and put them in the shrines on the high places which the Samaritans had made, every nation in the cities where they dwelt.

> The men of Babylon made Succoth Benoth, the men of Cuth made Nergal, the men of Hamath made Ashima, and the Avites made Nibhaz and Tartak; and the Sepharvites burned their children in the fire to Adrammelech and Anammelech, the gods of Sepharvaim. So they feared the Lord, and from every class they appointed for themselves priests of the high places, who sacrificed for them in the shrines of the high places. They feared the Lord, yet served their own gods—according to the rituals of the nations from among whom they were carried away.

> To this day they continue practicing the former rituals; they do not fear the Lord, nor do they follow their statutes or their ordinances, or the law and commandment which the Lord had commanded the children of Jacob, whom He named Israel...However they did not obey, but they followed their former rituals. So these nations feared the Lord, yet served their carved images; also their children and their children's children have continued doing as their fathers did, even to this day.

This text shows us that the people whom the Assyrians brought to live in the northern part of Israel, where Samaria was its capitol, adopted a form of religion that recognized the name of the Lord, yet substantially continued their former pagan rituals and worshiped their own gods. They did this from the time they entered the land, soon after Samaria fell to the Assyrians. They continued this form of paganism during the time the book of II Kings was written, as seen in verse 41, "also their children and their children's children have continued doing as their fathers did, even to this day." These words were written by Ezra around 445 -440 B.C.

Later, Sargon II defeated the Arabian tribes of Thamud, Marsimani, Sheba and Ibadidi, along with some Ishmaelite tribes named Adbeel, Massa and Tema. Around the year 716 B.C., Sargon deported some of them to Samaria, as shown in his inscriptions.[237]

Esarhaddon, who reigned from 680- 669, brought other colonists to live in Samaria as we see in Ezra 4:2. Therefore, we see that each tribe whom Assyrian brought to live in Samaria over the years until the time of Ezra and Nehemiah, continued to have its own god, as we saw from II Kings 17.

The Samaritans opposed the Jews and imitated Jewish worship after the exile.

The Jews returned from the Babylonian exile which occurred in 586 B.C. They returned to Jerusalem and started rebuilding the temple and the walls of the city. They were opposed by three groups, as we see from Nehemiah 2:19-20. The first group was composed of people whom the Assyrians relocated in Samaria. From the Biblical text we see their opposition led by Sanballat during the time of Nehemiah. "But when Sanballat the Horonite, [who was the leader of the Samaritans], Tobiah the Ammonite official, and Geshem the Arab heard of it, they laughed at us and despised us, and said, "What is this thing that you are doing? Will you rebel against the king?" So I answered them, and said to them, 'The God of heaven Himself will prosper us. Therefore we, His servants, will arise and build, but you have no heritage or right or memorial in Jerusalem.'"

Sanballat is the leader of the Samaritans. "Samaritan" is the title with which those pagan peoples were called whom the Assyrian's brought.

When Sanballat failed to stop the Jews from building the walls of the city, and found the Temple of Jerusalem was rebuilt, he wanted to establish a competing form of worship, to the one God who had ordered the Jews to reestablish at Jerusalem. So, around the year 407 B.C., Sanballat built a Samaritan temple on Mount Gerizim.[238]

After the Samaritans built their temple, they claimed they were descended from the tribe of Manasseh, even though it is historically known they were not Israelites, and their ancestors were brought to Samaria by the Assyrians from many different lands, such as Babylon, Cuthah, Ava, Hamath, and Sepharvaim. Sargon II also brought other tribes to Samaria such as Thamud, Marsimani and Ibadidi. The Jews never considered these tribes as Jews, but they used to call them Kutim; because the largest part of these peoples came from the land of Cuthah.

In the 11th book of Antiquities, chapter 8, Josephus Flavius, the Jewish Roman Historian of the 1st century A.D., wrote about the Samaritans at the time that Alexander the Great conquered Jerusalem.

> The Samaritans, seeing that Alexander had so greatly honored the Jews, determined to profess themselves Jews; for such is the disposition of the Samaritans, as we have already elsewhere declared, that when the Jews are in adversity, they deny that they are of kin to them, and then they confess the truth; but when they perceive that some good fortune hath befallen them, they immediately pretend to have communion with them, saying that they belong to them, and derive their genealogy from the posterity of Joseph, Ephraim, and Manasseh.[239]

Historically, the Israelites never denied any true Israelite affiliation to their nation, yet, through their history they separated themselves from the Samaritans because the Samaritans were not Israelites.

The Samaritans change the Pentateuch.

The Samaritans built their temple at mount Gerizim. They retained the Old Testament books which Moses wrote called the Pentateuch, but they modified many of the verses in an attempt to make their worship appear legitimate. One of their changes is found in Deuteronomy 27:4, where it is written that the Lord ordered the Israelites to write down the Law given to Moses on stones, and set up those stones on Mount Ebal. In order to legitimatize. the temple they built, the Samaritans simply changed the words "Mount Ebal" to Mount Gerizim.

They made other changes in Exodus 20:1-17 and Deuteronomy 5: 6-21, Both these passages mention the Ten Commandments. The Samaritans added a new commandment claiming God ordered them to build an altar on Mount Gerizim and offer sacrifices on it. But we know that never in the history of the Israelites did anyone consider building a temple and an altar on Mount Gerizim.

In the Bible there is prophetical significance to the place where God ordered the Temple to be built. The Samaritans imitated the temple of Jerusalem when they built their temple

In the 10 century B.C., God ordered King Solomon to build the temple at Jerusalem. The exact location was chosen because it is on Mount Moriah where God ordered Abraham to sacrifice his son, Isaac.[240]

The Jewish virtual library published an article about Mount Moriah from the Hebrew University of Jerusalem which said:

> Mount Moriah is the name of the elongated north-south stretch of land lying between Kidron Valley and Hagai Valley, between Mount Zion to the west and the Mount of Olives to the east.The Jebusite "Zion" was situated on the southern slope of Mount Moriah, above the Gihon Spring. After King David captured the city, he made it his capital and named it for himself by calling it the "City of David." The northern area of the mountain's summit lay desolate long after Zion's capture by David. It was, in fact, still the private property of Araunah, the city's former Jebusite king. For various reasons David did not confiscate the site because he preferred to buy it from Araunah for its full value, "So David paid Ornan [Araunah] for the site 600 shekels' worth of gold. And David built there an altar to the Lord and sacrificed burnt offerings and offerings of well-being.[241]

The Old Testament indicates that Mount Moriah is important. This is reported in at least in two incidents in the Old Testament. One was a plague which came to the nation of Israel due to the sinful attitude of David when he counted the number of Israelites who were capable to go to war, instead of relying on the Lord. We read in 1 Chronicles 21:16 – 29:

> Then David lifted up his eyes and saw the angel of the Lord standing between earth and heaven, having in his hand a drawn sword stretched out over Jerusalem. So, David and the elders, clothed in sackcloth, fell on their faces. And David said to God, 'Was it not I who commanded the people to be numbered? I am the one who has sinned and done evil indeed; but these sheep, what have they done? Let Your hand, I pray, O Lord my God, be against me and my father's house, but not against Your people that they should be plagued.' Therefore, the angel of the Lord commanded Gad to say to David that David should go and erect an altar to the Lord on the threshing floor of Ornan the Jebusite. So, David went up at the word of Gad, which he had spoken in the name of the Lord... So, David gave Ornan six hundred shekels of gold by weight for the place. And David built there an altar to the Lord, and offered burnt offerings and peace offerings, and called on the Lord; and He answered him from heaven by fire on the altar of burnt offering. So the

> Lord commanded the angel, and he returned his sword to its sheath. At that time, when David saw that the Lord had answered him on the threshing floor of Ornan the Jebusite, he sacrificed there. For the tabernacle of the Lord and the altar of the burnt offering, which Moses had made in the wilderness, were at that time at the high place in Gibeon.

So we see that God instructed the Israelites to build the altar for the propitiation of sin on the hills of Mount Moriah at Jerusalem. Mount Moriah is same location where Abraham was ordered to sacrifice his son Isaac on the mountain of Moriah. Isaac was a symbol of Christ who was sacrificed on Mount Moriah two thousand years later.

When Abraham received the order to sacrifice his son he was living in the city of Beersheba, south of the land of Canaan. He traveled three days in order to reach this location. Although Isaac was placed on an altar on that mountain, God did not allow Abraham to sacrifice his son. Instead, God showed him a ram caught in a thicket on the mountain. Genesis 22:13 says, "Then Abraham lifted his eyes and looked, and there behind him was a ram caught in a thicket by its horns. So Abraham went and took the ram, and offered it up for a burnt offering instead of his son." This ram symbolized Christ who allowed himself to be bound in human flesh and brought to the same mountain range after 2,000 years, in order to be presented as a sin offering for mankind.

For this reason, in the Old Testament the Lord commanded the temple for the animal sacrifices would be built on Mount Moriah, around Jerusalem. The building of the Temple at Jerusalem was in accordance with the prophetical design which God announced in the book of Genesis. The great redemptive sacrifice of Christ was to be accomplished on a mountain range around Jerusalem.

The prophet Isaiah prophesied in chapter 25, verses 6-9, about the great redemption on the mountain of Moriah, (see also the chapter about Abraham at the end of this book) saying:

> And in this mountain shall the Lord of hosts make unto all people a feast of fat things, a feast of wines on the lees, of fat things full of marrow, of wines on the lees well refined. And he will destroy in this mountain the face of the covering cast over all people, and the vail that is spread over all nations. He will swallow up death in victory; and the Lord God will wipe away tears from off all faces; and the rebuke of his people shall he take away from off all the earth: for the Lord hath spoken it. And it shall

be said in that day, Lo, this is our God; we have waited for him, and he
will save us: this is the Lord; we have waited for him, we will be glad
and rejoice in his salvation.

In spite of the clarity of these prophecies about the redemption that
Christ performed, and the specific place where this redemption had to
happen, Sanballat, the Horonite, built the temple of the Samaritans on
Mount Gerizim in 407 B.C. in order to imitate the legitimate, scriptural
worship which God had established in the Old Testament to symbolize His
great design of redemption.

Although the Samaritans built their temple in 407 B.C. to imitate the
true worship which God ordered the Israelites to perform in the temple at
Jerusalem, they did not adhere to monotheism. In the year 165 B.C., there
was a great struggle between the Jewish Maccabees and Antiochus
Epiphanes, the Greek King of Syria. Antiochus wanted to suppress the
worship of God at Jerusalem, so the Samaritans cooperated with him by
dedicating their temple to the Greek god Zeus, expressing their original
paganism.

The Samaritan's claim that they were descendants of Ephraim and
Manasseh was outside the historical record

The Samaritan's claim that they were descended from the tribes of
Ephraim and Manasseh, also runs contrary to history. The Samaritans were
descendants from the people the Assyrians brought to live in Samaria,
instead of the Israelites, who were moved to other territories which were
under Assyrian control.

After they built their sanctuary on Mount Gerizim around the year 407
B.C., the Samaritans began to rewrite their history, they claimed a schism
occurred between them and the rest of the Israelites when Eli was the priest
in the 11th century B.C. In reality, no Biblical or historical book about
Israel ever mentioned a schism between them. If this split had occurred as
the Samaritans claimed, it would have been reported in the various books
of the Old Testament. Furthermore, no one mentioned people called
Samaritans before the time of Eli until the Assyrians transported people to
Samaria around the year 721 B.C. These people were not called Samaritans
until after the 6th century B.C.

We also notice that the Samaritans did not have prophets of their own,
once again proving they were not Israelites, and were not descendants of

either Manasseh nor Ephraim. After the time of Eli, many of the prophets of the Old Testament came from these two tribes.

Books written by the Samaritans, did not appear before the 3rd century B.C. Their two main books were Memar Markah, which means The Teaching of Markah, and Defter which was a prayer book. The Samaritans did not assign inspiration to these books. But the fact these Samaritan books were written at such a late date invalidates their claim that they descended from the Israelite tribes of Manasseh and Ephraim. This could not have happened before the time of Sanballat. On the other hand, we find the Israelites had books written by prophets since the time of Joshua, the person who succeeded Moses. These writings continued through the time of Samuel when Eli lived, and in almost every century after that.

The teachings of the Samaritans do not agree with the Old Testament. For example, their eschatology, or doctrines on the events of the last time, is derived from Zoroastrianism which waits for the coming of a savior whom they call Taheb. According to them, Taheb will initiate a period of peace when they will dominate the world in what they call "second kingdom."

Ideas like this were derived from Zoroastrianism which waited for three liberators. These liberators impose a kingdom of peace during which the Zoroastrians dominate the earth. Two of these liberators come from the descendants of Zoroaster.

I already discussed those liberators in the chapter on Eschatology. I mentioned that the first one they called Hushedar, who would have had to appear in the year 341 A.D., but that year passed without this "liberator" showing up. The second liberator they called Aushedar-Mah, who would have had to arrive at the beginning of the 10th millennium according to the Zoroastrian calendar, corresponding to the year 1341 A.D.

This second kingdom for the Zoroastrians is striking similar to the second kingdom for which the Samaritans are waiting. The year 1341 A.D. came and went, yet this liberator never appeared. Today, the Zoroastrians number only 200,000 people, most of them now live in Bombay, India, the remnants of those who fled from Persia after the Muslims occupied the country. The Mahdi, whom Muslims wait for, is derived from Aushedar-Mah, whom the Zoroastrians awaited. Most probably the Persians in Arabia called Aushedar-Mah by the abbreviation Mah. The Arabians then changed it to Mahdi to express the Arabic meaning "the one who brings guidance."

An important historical fact which excludes the Samaritans from being Israelites is that they never spoke the Hebrew language. Their fathers, who were relocated to Samaria from many different lands by the Assyrians, never learned to speak Hebrew. Their language was always a dialect of Aramaic. Only in the middle of the seventh century A.D., when the Muslims occupied Palestine, did the Samaritans abandon their own language, and began speaking Arabic. The Samaritans avoided speaking Hebrew, even when the Israelites returned to Palestine after the Babylon exile in the 6th century B.C. But Israel retuned to speaking Hebrew, the dominant language spoken by all the Israelites who lived in Palestine.

These facts clearly indicate the Samaritans did not want to identify themselves with the Israelites. They were attached to their various ancestral nationalities which the Assyrians brought to Samaria. One of the ways they did this was to keep their own original language.

There is no way of saving Mohammed's face from his enormous historical mistake regarding the Samaritans.

The Quran, in Surah Ta Ha, 20: 85-97 claims Moses in the desert addressed a man, who transformed the golden calf into a living calf which made a mooing or lowing sound. The Quran records, "Then Moses said, 'What is the matter with you Oh Samaritan?'"

According to the Quran, the Samaritans existed in the 15 century B.C. during the time Moses led Israel in the desert of Sinai. Yet, the name "Samaritans" was not used before the 6th century B.C. The city of Samaria, as we have seen previously, was built around the year 900 B.C. by Omri, the king of Israel. The term "Samarians", not "Samaritans" with a "t", was used once in II Kings 17:29 to designate the inhabitants of Samaria after the city was built. However, this term was not used before the city was built about 900 BC.

The Arabic word used in Surah, Ta Ha 20: 85-97, is "al-Samiri السـامري", which means "the Samaritan." The Samaritan were well known in Mohammed's generation especially due to the New Testament which referred to them on several occasions. Furthermore, Simon, the Samaritan from the city of Samaria, was well known. He is mentioned in the Acts of the Apostles as the one who deceived the people of Samaria with his magic. He also was a well-known figure during Mohammed's time as the one who founded a heresy which became known as "Simonism." Mohammed intimated that Simon was this "Samaritan man." This argument is ludicrous when we realize that 1,550 years lapsed between Moses and the Samaritan in the book of Acts, and 1000 years lapsed between the first time the Samaritans appeared and Moses.

Some Muslims, embarrassed by this enormous mistake, endeavored to save face for Mohammed by agreeing with the Samaritans, saying the Samaritans were the descendants of Manasseh and Ephraim. But the Samaritans' claim is not historical because it was made after they built their temple on Mount Gerizim in 407 B.C. We know the Samaritans were given this name after the 6th century B.C.

Nowhere do we find the tribes of Manasseh and Ephraim left the rest of the Israelites. Neither do we find any place they were called "Samaritans." Just for the sake of the argument, if we suppose the Samaritans had their beginning at the time of Eli as they claim, this does not give the Muslims an escape from the enormous historical mistake in the Quran. The Samaritans themselves hate the term "Samaritans." They confess the Israelites called them by this name after the 6th century B.C.

When we put the following facts together, we see just how ridiculous their arguments are. The Quran did not use the term "Samaritan" in the 11th century B.C. The Samaritans claimed a schism occurred in Israel at the time of Eli, during which they founded an independent nation We know their claim is false, because they were the descendants of the people whom the Assyrians relocated after the fall of Samaria in 721 B.C. Suppose, for the sake of argument, we would go with the Samaritan claim, this would not resolve the problem because the Quran used the term "Samaritan" four centuries before Eli was born. The Quran claims Moses addressed a man with a separate nationality calling him "the Samaritan". This happened in the desert when the Israelites were called Israelites, the tribe of Manasseh was called Manasseh, and the people of the tribe of Ephraim were called Ephramites.

The Samaritans readily admit the Israelites called them "Samaritans," after the sixth century B.C. They prefer to call themselves "Shamerim," which means the defenders of faith. They adopted this name after the fourth century B.C. to compete with the Israelites, but this doesn't help the Islamic case to erase the mistake of Mohammed. The Quran does not use the term "Shamerim," but it uses the term "Samaritan." Nowhere in the history of Israel before Eli or after him was there a nation called

"Shamerim." The Samaritans claim they began to be called Shamerims at the time of Eli in the 11century B.C. and not at the time of Moses. We know this claim is false, but, if for the sake of argument, if we would accept the claim, this would not help the Islamic case, since the Quran claims Moses addressed a man by the term "Samaritan" in the 15 century B.C. The tenacity of some Muslims not concede and admit the enormous mistake of the Quran, is hopeless.

Some Muslims even go further by claiming the "Samaritans" existed many centuries prior to the time the Samaritans themselves claimed to have existed. They created a special group claiming they existed as defenders of faith at the time of Moses when Moses himself was a defender of the faith which God has entrusted him to declare and communicate to the other Israelites. But these people claim there were others who were "defenders of faith" in addition to Moses. This becomes absurd when we realize even the Samaritans never dared to claim they lived at the time of Moses.

How did the expositors of the Quran regard the identity of the "Samaritan," and what was the effect of this on Muslims today?

Ibn Abbass, the cousin of Mohammed and a main authoritative reporter of Mohammed's Hadiths, reported that the Samaritan mentioned in the Quran came from the land of Bajerma باجرما,[242] the ancient name of the region of Karkuk in northern Iraq.[243]

The Hadith of ibn Abbass shows that Arabians at the time of Mohammed had certain knowledge about the origin of the Samaritans. I believe this knowledge came through the Jews around Medina where Mohammed emigrated. Many of the people whom the Assyrians relocated in Samaria came from Mesopotamia, which is today's Iraq. The land of Cuthah was a province in Assyria, and Sepharvaim was east of the Euphrates river in Mesopotamia. A good portion of those which the Assyrians brought to Samaria came from these two places, which were in northern Mesopotamia. It is logical to assume that the Jews also considered the Samaritans to have come mostly from Northern Mesopotamia. Evidently, Ibn Abbass, and those who lived in Arabia with him, heard the Assyrians brought those people from Assyrian provinces, and knew that the capital of Assyria was Nineveh. Then they placed the original location of the Samaritans to the area of Karkuk, which is near the old capital of the Assyrians in northern Mesopotamia.

What Ibn Abbass understood by the use of Quran's term "the Samaritan", is that he was not an Israelite, but one of the people whom the Assyrians brought from Assyrian provinces to live in Palestine. But neither Ibn Abbass nor Mohammed, knew the exact date on which this occurred. Evidently, they thought this was before the time of Moses.

Al- Allusi, in his famous expository book on the Quran called "Rooh al-Maani," locates Bejrema near Mosul, in northern Iraq. But he also presents the idea promoted by other Muslims who say the Samaritans were an Israelite tribe called "Samaria."[244]

They failed to recognize that Samaria was the name of the city which was built by Omri in the ninth century B.C., and there is no Israelite tribe called Samaria.

Al-Razi, another famous expositor of the Quran, reports an idea of the majority of Muslims of his generation that the Samaritan, was from the tribe of Samaria[245] Khutada, claim that the Samaritan was a great leader from an Israelite tribe called Samaria.[246]

Ibn al-Juzi, in his expository book about the Quran, called Zad al-Masir Fi Ilim al Tafsir, reports the various Muslim points of view concerning the Identity of the Samaritan. He explains the idea of Wahab bin Munabbeh that the Samaritan was a cousin of Moses. He also shares the idea of Musa bin Imran that the Samaritan was Micah, the prophet. He comments on the idea of Ibn Abbass that the Samaritan was not an Israelite. He also reports the idea of Said bin Jubier that the Samaritan was from Karman which is probably in northern Iraq. And he reports another idea coming from Wahab that the Samaritan was from Bajerma.[247]

We can only conclude that early Muslims knew the origin of the Samaritans took place mainly in northern Iraq, knowledge that came to them from the Jews of Arabia. But centuries later, expositors of the Quran became aware of Mohammed's historical mistake regarding the Samaritan as contemporary to Moses. Therefore, they tried to oppose the well-known fact that the Samaritans came from different areas mainly north of Iraq, and they were brought to Samaria in the year 720 B.C. So, they wanted to make the Samaritans one tribe of the 12 Israelite tribes, so they could place them in the time of Moses. They named this tribe after of the city of Samaria, which Omri built in the ninth century B.C.

Mohammed wanted to insert a historical figure into his version of the Biblical account, but he overlooked the historical frame surrounding these events. He was completely ignorant of the chronology of Biblical events, so he composed his own version, mixing different Biblical figures although they lived at various times distant from each other such as the case of Moses and the Samaritan of the Book of Acts.

Mohammed narrated his stories to a group of naive people, mainly composed of the members of Aws and Khazraj, the two savage tribes of Medina. Mohammed figured those around him would not question his words or compare the Quran with the documents of history and the Biblical text.

Mary

Mohammed in the Quran Confused Mary, the Mother of Jesus, with Mary, the Sister of Aaron and Moses.

One of the examples of historical and chronological confusion in the Quran concerns the dating of the life of Mary, the mother of Jesus. The Quran claims Mary, the mother of Jesus, was the sister of Aaron. You may remember that Aaron was the brother of Moses. In the Quran, Surah 19, verse 28, called the Surah of Maryam or Mary, she is addressed as sister of Aaron. The text says, "O sister of Aaron, your father was not a man of evil, nor your mother a woman who was unchaste."

The Quran confirms its historical mistake, when it talks about Amram, the father of Moses and Aaron. The Quran claims the wife of Amram, who was called Imran in the Quran, dedicated Mary, the mother of Jesus while she was pregnant with Jesus. In verses 35 and 36 of Surah 3 called, Al-'Imran, we read:

> Behold the woman of Imran said, 'O my Lord, I do dedicate unto thee what is in my womb for Thy special service. So accept this from me for You are the one who hears and knows.' When she delivered, she said, 'O my lord, I have delivered a female child. And Allah knew best what she brought forth. And in no wise is the male like the female. I have named her Mary.'

This shows that Mohammed was under a serious equivocation and was very confused, thinking that Mary, the mother of Jesus, was Mary, the sister of Aaron and Moses and the daughter of Amram and his wife, Jochebed, who are mentioned in the book of Exodus. To them were born Aaron, Moses and their sister, Miriam.

Is there additional evidence that the Quran identifies the family of Imran as the family of Moses and Aaron?

It is clear from Surah 3:33-34, called Imran, that the Quran uses the term "al Imran" to refer to the family of Moses and Aaron. The Quran says:

> Allah did choose Adam and Noah, the family of Abraham, and the family of Imran above all people and they were descendants of one another: And Allah heareth and knoweth all things.

In the above verse, the Quran cites the main Biblical figures and families from which the principal figures of the Old Testament descended. These include:

Adam, whom the Quran reveres as both the head of all humanity and as a great prophet.

Noah, who was the head of humanity after the flood.

The family of Abraham, which includes Isaac, Jacob, and Joseph (Jacob's son).

The family of Imran, which refers to Moses (the prophet of the law and Judaism, according to the Quran), Aaron, and Miriam (sister of Moses and Aaron).

No mention is made here of Jesus, but the Quran considers Him the prophet of Christianity.

Surah 3 continues in verse 35:

> The wife of Imran said: 'O my lord! I do dedicate unto you what is in my womb for your special service: So accept this of me: For you hear and know all things.'

This refers to the family of Imran mentioned in verse 34, which was the family of Moses and Aaron's father, whose mother was the wife of Imran. Mohammed made a serious historical mistake, however, when in the Quran he identifies the wife of Imram as the mother of Mary the mother of Jesus (likely because Moses and Aaron had a sister named Miriam, or Mary). Thus, in verse 35, the wife of Imran speaks about dedicating Mary, the mother of Jesus, in her womb to Allah.

The sequence of the three verses above reveals Mohammed's obvious confusion. Mohammed believed that Moses and Aaron's grandmother was the one who was pregnant with Mary, the mother of Jesus – this despite the fact that Moses died some 1,400 years before Jesus was born. In an attempt to resolve this dilemma, some Muslims claim that the Imran family was not Moses' family but another family who lived in the Virgin Mary's time. They deny that Mohammed's reference was to the family of Imran, the father of Moses and Aaron. The sequence of verses 33-35, however, makes it clear that this reference to the "family of Imran" was to the family of Moses and Aaron during the historical time period in which Moses and Aaron lived.

Mohammed's sources for verses 35-37 regarding Mary's mother dedicating Mary in the Temple of Jerusalem

Surah 3:37 says:

> So her Lord accepted her fully and protected her growing up, and gave her into the charge of Zachariah. Whenever Zachariah entered the Mihrab 'the holy of holiness in the sanctuary' to (see) her, he found her with food. He said: 'O Mary! Whence comes this to you?' She said: 'It is from Allah. Surely Allah gives to whom He pleases without measure.'

Verses 35-37 of Surah Imran are taken from The Proto-evangelion of James the Lesser, which dates to the 2nd century A.D. In chapters 7 and 11 we read these words:

> And Anna (wife of Joachim) answered, 'As the Lord my God liveth, whatever I bring forth, whether it be male or female, I will devote it to the Lord my God, and it shall minister to him in holy things, during its whole life'...and called her name Mary.... And the high-priest received her; and blessed her, and said, 'Mary, the Lord God hath magnified thy name to all generations'.... Mary was fed by angels in the Temple. When she was 12 years old the priests discussed what to do with her. The angel of the Lord warned Zachariah to call together all the widowers and have each bring a rod. The people met at the sound of a trumpet. Joseph threw down his hatchet and went to the meeting. A dove came forth from his rod and lighted on his head. He was chosen to betroth the Virgin and he took her home.

The similarities between the Quran's account of Imran's wife dedicating Mary and The Proto-Evangelion of James the Lesser's narration about Anna dedicating Mary are clear. In both instances we read that Mary was raised up in the Temple, that food was supernaturally provided for her, and that Zachariah took care of her.

The myth regarding the rod or the pen mentioned in The Proto-Evangelion's James the Lesser appears in a deviant form in the Quran where it is attributed to the one who was in charge of Mary. Verse 44 of Surah Imran says:

> This concerns the announcements relating to the unseen things that we reveal to you. You were not with them when they cast their pens (to decide) which of them should have Miriam in his charge, and you were not with them when they contended one with another.

We find another similarity in The Proto-Evangelion of James the Lesser11:8-13:

> We reveal this to you. You were not with them when they cast their pens (to decide) which of them should have Miriam in his charge, and you were not with them when they contended one with another and when with a flood of tears she answered, 'As the Lord my God lives, I am innocent in His sight, seeing I know no man.'

We notice that, according to The Proto-Evangelion of James the Lesser, Mary was brought up in the Holy of Holies, which the Quran calls Mihrab. In reality, Zachariah never entered the Holy of Holies. The chief priest was the only one to enter there once a year: In the day of great atonement, the chief priest entered with a ram, which he sacrificed to atone for the sins of the people. Furthermore, Mary was brought up in Nazareth and not in Jerusalem. Zachariah was the father of John the Baptist and used to come to the Temple 15 days each year to serve in the priestly division of Abijah.

Surah 19 called Miriam, verses 24 and 25 says:

> Then a voice {the babe 'Isa (Jesus)} cried unto her from below her, saying: 'Grieve not: your Lord has provided a water stream under you. And shake the trunk of the palm tree towards thyself: It will let fall fresh ripe dates upon thee.

This is taken from the book the birth of Mary and the childhood of the savior", we read in chapter 20:

> And it came to pass on the third day of their journey, while they were walking, that the blessed Mary was fatigued by the excessive heat of the sun in the desert; and seeing a palm tree, she said to Joseph: Let me rest a little under the shade of this tree. Joseph therefore made haste, and led her to the palm, and made her come down from her beast. And as the blessed Mary was sitting there, she looked up to the foliage of the palm, and saw it full of fruit, and said to Joseph: I wish it were possible to get some of the fruit of this palm. And Joseph said to her: I wonder that thou sayest this, when thou seest how high the palm tree is; and that thou thinkest of eating of its fruit. I am thinking more of the want of water, because the skins are now empty, and we have none wherewith to refresh ourselves and our cattle. Then the child Jesus, with a joyful countenance, reposing in the bosom of His mother, said to the palm:

> O tree, bend thy branches, and refresh my mother with thy fruit. And immediately at these words the palm bent its top down to the very feet of the blessed Mary; and they gathered from it fruit, with which they were all refreshed. And after they had gathered all its fruit, it remained bent down, waiting the order to rise from Him who bad commanded it to stoop.

Then Jesus said to it: Raise thyself, O palm tree, and be strong, and be the companion of my trees, which are in the paradise of my Father; and open from thy roots a vein of water which has been hid in the earth, and let the waters flow, so that we may be satisfied from thee. And it rose up immediately, and at its root there began to come forth a spring of water exceedingly clear and cool and sparkling. And when they saw the spring of water, they rejoiced with great joy, and were satisfied, themselves and all their cattle and their beasts. Wherefore they gave thanks to God.

This myth – "the birth of Mary and the childhood of the Savior" – that the tree bent toward Mary is taken from Buddhist myths. Thus, in the first chapter of Buddha Carita about Buddha's mother, who after giving birth to the infant Buddha sat under a tree and the branch of the tree bent toward her.

Could it be that the Quran intend that Mary, the mother of Jesus, was daughter of Aaron just like Jesus was called the son of David, in the New Testament?

Today some Muslims, aware of this serious historical mistake, endeavor to justify it by stating the Quran meant that referring to Mary, the mother of Jesus, as the sister of Aaron is metaphorically speaking, comparable to the Gospels when they call Jesus the Son of David. It simply emphasizes His descendancy from David.

But this comparison cannot be validated. When the New Testament refers to Jesus by the epithet "Son of David," it is a reference to the Old Testament which prophesied that the coming Messiah would be the Son of David according to the flesh. Or simply that He would be a descendent of David. But Mary, Jesus' mother, was not from the line of Aaron.

The Bible never used this kind of epithet for a person who was not an important forefather of the person in question. The Bible calls Joseph, the husband of Mary, "the son of David" because he was the last person in the Messianic genealogy from which the Messiah was to be born. The Bible never addresses prophets or other important persons in this way. For instance, it doesn't refer to a king from the tribe of Ephraim as "the son of Ephraim," the father of the tribe from whom descended the kings of Israel after the 10 tribes were separated from the tribe of Judah and Benjamin. Nor does it address him as "the son of Moses" or "the son of Aaron."

When it comes to Aaron, he was not an important figure among the men of the Old Testament. There is nothing about him that would make others claim his name. He was not a prophet like Moses or Abraham. Conversely, his name was connected with a great sin. He made the golden calf in the desert when Moses was on the mountain receiving the Ten Commandments. He convinced all the Israelites to worship such abomination which provoked the anger of the Lord.

That is why Aaron is never mentioned in the Bible as a hero of faith or as an example for others to follow. He is not mentioned among the Old Testament heroes of faith in Hebrews chapter 11. To be called a father of the faith was only given by the Scripture to men like Abraham who were important figures in the Old Testament. There is nothing about Aaron that would make anyone want to claim his name. How, then, would God call people by that name thousands of years later?

Aaron belonged to the tribe of Levi like his brother Moses. Mary was not from the tribe of Levi. If the Quran wanted to imitate the Messianic Genealogy of the Bible, it should have called Mary after David or at least by the name of a lesser person of the tribe of Judah because Mary belonged to Judah, not to the tribe of Levi, as did Aaron.

An indisputable confirmation of the confusion of Mohammed is demonstrated when the Quran claims the father of Aaron was the father of Mary who was the mother of Jesus, and the mother of Aaron dedicates Mary, the mother of Jesus, while she is pregnant in her.

Evidently, Mohammed thought that Mary the mother of Jesus was not only from the house of Aaron, but was a sister to Aaron and Moses and the daughter of Amram. This makes the argument of the Quran ridiculous when it says the wife of Amram dedicated Mary, the mother of Jesus, while she was pregnant as we saw in Surah 3, Al-Imran, verses 35 and 36. The Quran specifies that the wife of Amram, father of Moses and Aaron, was pregnant with Mary, the mother of Jesus.

It is clear from the Quran that the wife of Imram, the father of Aaron, is the one who was pregnant with Mary the mother of Jesus, and that his wife named her Mary. There is no ambiguity here. When the Quran said Mary was the mother of Jesus and the daughter of Aaron in Surah 19, he meant she was actually the sister of Aaron, and it was not a figurative or symbolic title for Mary. In fact, the Quran confirmed this by specifying the name of her father, Amram, the father of Aaron and Moses. The Quran also specified that the mother of Mary was the wife of Amram.

As if this were not enough, in Surah 66, Al Tahrim, verse 12, the Quran identifies the name of the father of Mary, the mother of Jesus, as Amram, the father of Aaron and Moses. "And Mary was the daughter of Imran, who guarded her chastity," it says.

Mohammed in his Hadith called Moses the "son of Amram," or Imran. For example, in his alleged ascension to heaven, Mohammed claimed to have seen Moses and asked Gabriel: "Who is this?" Gabriel answered: "This is Moses, son of Imran."[248]

The dilemma for those who want to save Mohammed from this enormous historical mistake is more than justifying the Quran when it mentions that Mary, the mother of Jesus, is the sister of Aaron. It is more than explaining how she is called the daughter of Amram who the father of Moses and Aaron was. The Quran claims the wife of Amram herself was pregnant with Mary, the mother of Jesus. Therefore, beyond any shadow of doubt, Mohammed's belief, which he recited into the Quran was that Mary, the mother of Jesus, was the true sister of Aaron and Moses and the daughter of Amram.

Mohammed never called anyone the son of Amram except Moses, Aaron and Mary the mother of Jesus. This demonstrates clearly that he thought Mary, the mother of Jesus, was daughter of Amram as Moses and Aaron were. Furthermore, he did not limit his definition to Mary as daughter of Imarm, but also, he calls her sister of Aaron. This confirmed his mistake showing that he thought Mary as was living at the time of Aaron and Moses.

The Mandaeans also share the blame for the Quran's mistake regarding Mary.

It is obvious that Mohammed was depending upon the writings of others who were also ignorant of the identities of the Biblical figures and their historical chronology. This egregious historical error (confusion of Mary the mother of Jesus with Mary, or Miriam, the sister of Moses and Aaron, the daughter of Imram) arose because Mohammed relied on unreliable sources of history. They contributed to this and other historical mistakes in the Quran.

Although about 1500 years passed between the Mary in the story of Amram and the Mary in the account of Jesus, there were some groups who thought Mary, the mother of Jesus, was member of the Aaron and Moses family. We find this mistake recorded in the Mandaean literature. The Mandaeans, who were called "Sabians" at the time of Mohammed, were also the sources for many mythological and historically inaccurate narrations in the Quran. The bridge between Mohammed and the Mandaeans was the Ahnaf group, whose founder, Zayd bin Amru bin Nufayl, used to go to Mosul (northern Iraq) to inquire about religion. Often Zayd was accompanied by Waraqa bin Nofel, the cousin of Khadijah, Mohammed's first wife. Waraqa played an important part in shaping the first Surahs of Mohammed's Quran. Waraqa was Mohammed's source for many Mandaean notions.

The Sabians Mandaeans too, thought that Mary, the mother of Jesus, lived at the time of Moses and Aaron, as the daughter of Moses and the brother of Aaron.

One of the Mandaean sacred books, Haran Gawaita, dates back to the third century after Christ. It claims Jesus was placed in "the womb of Mary, a daughter of Moses, where it was hidden in her womb for nine months. When the nine months were fulfilled and she was in labor, she brought forth the Messiah."[249]

This mistake could have occurred because the Mandaean's formed a religion that opposed the Bible. They created their own stories using Biblical figures placed in strange narrations filled with deception and without any knowledge of Biblical historical chronology. The Mandaean ignorance of history caused much confusion in the Quran, since Mohammed followed the Mandaean view on historical events. One of their confused teachings was that Moses and Aaron were contemporaries to John the Baptist and Jesus. We read about this serious historical mistake also in Haran-Gawaita. They said Moses built the temple of Jerusalem and he was a contemporary to John the Baptist, who was born few months before Jesus was born.[250]

With all these mistakes, it is easy to see why they claimed Mary the mother of Jesus lived at the time of Moses, as his daughter and was part of Moses and Aaron's family. Evidently, reading in the Old Testament about a woman named Mary who was the sister of Aaron and Moses, caused them to think that she was the Mary who was the mother of Jesus. Consequently, they thought that Moses and Aaron must have lived when John the Baptist and Jesus lived.

The Mandaeans were influenced by some naive Persian groups regarding the time in which Mary lived.

The Mandaeans were influenced by the Persians in many aspects of their religion, due to the fact they lived in northern and southern Mesopotamia when the Persians controlled the country. Al Taberi reports that, according to ancient Persian chronologists, Mary, the mother of Jesus, was born 65 years after Alexander the Great occupied Babel.[251] another historical mistake that contributed to the Mandaean's confusion about the true times in which Mary lived. In turn, they also confused Mohammed and caused him to fall in the same problem.

Mohammed accepted the Mandaeans and their doctrines and rites.

The Sabian Mandaeans were considered by Mohammed as "people of the book." In the Quran, Surah 2, Al Baqarah, verse 62, we read, "Those who believe in the Quran, and those who follow the Jewish Scriptures, and the Christians and the Sabians who believe in Allah and the last day, and who work for righteousness, shall have their reward with their lord. On them shall be no fear, nor shall they grieve." Mohammed made the Sabians equal to the Jews and Christians as people of the "inspired book." In Surah 5 of the Quran, Mohammed put the Sabians before the Christians as the people Allah had spoken to and they do not have to worry for their eternal security. We read, "Those who believe in the Quran, those who became Jewish, and the Sabians and Christians... on them shall be no fear, nor shall they grieve" Surah 5, al- Maidah, verse 69.

Therefore, we see the Sabians, whom Muslim historians identified as the Mandaean Sabians, were accepted by Mohammed, and consequently their books were accepted and respected like the Bible. They were placed at the same level as the Jews preceding the Christians. When he first claimed to be a prophet, his own citizens called him and his followers Sabians, because they were seen observing Sabian rituals, such as the five-day prayers, their movements of prayer like standing and bowing, and the ritual washing their hands, feet, and face before every prayer, which also the Sabian

Mandaeans do. And there were other rituals that characterized this religious sect.

The Meccans called Mohammed "Sabian." For example, while returning from one of his military campaigns Mohammed became thirsty. Two of his companions asked a woman who carried a skin of water to go and give Mohammed water. We present the text as it occurs in Sahih al Bukhari and other Islamic literature:

> They said to her: 'Go then.' She said: 'To where?' They said 'to the apostle of Allah.' She asked 'To the one who is called Sabian?' They answered, 'Yes, to the one you call by this name.' The woman returned to the city and said, 'I met two men, who brought me to the one called the Sabian.'[252]

From this we know that the inhabitants of Mecca called Mohammed "Sabian," which is a title for members of the Sabian sect. The Islamic narrators' books tell us that the tribe of Quraysh used to call Mohammed a Sabian.

Other tribes in north Arabia made the same judgment. When the tribe of Beni Amer بني عـامر sent Lubeid, in order to interview Mohammed, Lubeid met with Mohammed and he embraced Islam.

Lubeid returned to his tribe he made ablutions as the Sabian had done, bowing as the Sabians, and praying like them in the Fatihah rituals. The Arabians were familiar with those Sabian rituals. Their poet, Suraqa 'Auf bin al Ahwas سـراقة بن عوف بن الاحوص, recited a poem about Lubeid, describing him as the one who came to them with the religion of the Sabians.[253]

Among the things Mohammed copied from the Mandaeans was the name Muslim. We know the Sabian Mandaeans worshiped a variety of gods coming from Mesopotamian and Persian origins. They were among those who called themselves Shalmani, evidently a title known in Arabia as Muslim.

In their main book, Ginza Raba, the Sabian Mandaeans are called "the perfect." Kurt Adolph, an expert on the Mandaean religion, says that the term "perfect" in the Mandaean language is "Shalmani."[254]

The word "Shalmani" became "Shalma," which means to become Muslim or to be saved. It is part of their main doctrine that says, "everyone who is baptized is saved." This baptism refers to the kind of ablution they performed; it is derived from the Aramaic.[255] They recited this same sentence during Athan.[256]

The community of the Sabians used to call itself shalmania,[257] that is, Muslim, from where Mohammed took the name of Muslim. In fact, till today the Mandaeans recite in their prayers "O Muslims, do not go away from your covenant in which you pledged to God."[258]

Another historical confusion was evident at the time of Mohammed. It concerned the destruction of Jerusalem under Nebuchadnezzar and a later destruction under Titus.

Mohammed's confusion in historical events which came from primitive resources in his time is seen in the narrations of his companions

Al Taberi reports a Hadith from the companions of Mohammed who expressed thoughts held by Mohammed since he was their main source of knowledge. In their writings we see confusion between the destruction of Jerusalem by Nebuchadnezzar, which we know occurred in the year 586 B.C., and the destruction of Jerusalem, which occurred around 70 A.D. by Titus, the Roman leader.

His colleagues claimed that the destruction of Jerusalem came about because Herod killed John the Baptist. When this happened, the blood of John began to boil, so Nebuchadnezzar destroyed the city and took the captive Jews to Babylonia. Among those whom he deported was the prophet Daniel. This incident is reported by many authoritative companions and reporters of the Hadith of Mohammed such as his cousin Ibn Abbass.[259]

This shows the confusion Mohammed's companions had between the two destructions of Jerusalem, thinking that the second one which occurred in 70 A.D. was accomplished by Nebuchadnezzar who lived in the 6th century BC.

The confusion of Mohammed and his close companions is due partially to many uneducated Persian groups at the time of Mohammed who determined to rewrite history without any knowledge of the chronology of the main historical events. They determined the time between Nebuchadnezzar and John the Baptist was 51 years.[260]

This determination contributed to Mohammed's confusion as we can see from his Hadiths and the Quran. Mohammed depended on Suleiman

Al Farsi as the main source for Persian mythology and historical chronology. Suleiman was a priest of fire in Zoroastrianism before embracing Islam.

Unfortunately, the fathers of Islamic tradition, were so influenced by the confused statements of Mohammed concerning the chronology of historical events, that they criticized the Christians because they maintained that Nebuchadnezzar's campaign against Jerusalem was during the lifetime of the prophet Jeremiah, and the Christians said the time between Nebuchadnezzar and Christ was many hundreds of years.[261] We know today that what those early Christians said was true. Nebuchadnezzar's campaign against Jerusalem was at the time of Jeremiah, and the time between Nebuchadnezzar and the birth of Jesus was 586 years.

Aishah strongly defended the Quran's claim that the Mary, the mother of Jesus, was the sister of Aaron

Mohammed's companions, defending the claims of the Quran concerning Mary, all believed that she was the mother of Jesus as well as the sister of Aaron and Moses. One of those who held this belief was Aishah, the beloved wife of Mohammed, and the one who recorded many of his main authoritative Hadiths. Aishah is the best official source for what Mohammed intended in the Quran. Muslims count on her to confirm Mohammed's purpose and to interpret what he intended by many of his critical Hadiths or verses in the Quran.

A man called Kaab once said, "When the Quran said 'Mary, the sister of Aaron,' this is not Aaron, the brother of Moses." Evidently, Kaab tried to save face for Mohammed by keeping him from an enormous mistake. But Kaab neglected the other verses of the Quran which specify that Mary, the mother of Jesus, was the "daughter of Imram," and we know that Imram, according to the Hadiths of Mohammed, was the father of Aaron and Moses. Kaab also neglected the verse which states, "the wife of Imram dedicated Mary. When she was still in her bosom, she dedicated her to "Allah."

Thus, we find Aishah promptly opposing Kaab and rebuking him with harsh words, telling him, "You have lied."[262] It is a phrase that Aishah and other pillars of the Islamic faith used to accuse those who doubted the primary teachings of Islam or the statements Mohammed made in the Quran.

This reveals that Mohammed's closed-minded companions regarded the Quran's statement that Mary, the mother of Jesus, was the sister of Aaron, as an indisputable fact. However, after Mohammed died, Muslims came in contact with more knowledgeable Christian sources. Many Muslims who embraced this enormous historical mistake tried to find a remedy. Yet, the many teachings of the Quran on this issue made a remedy impossible. They could only admit how far Mohammed was from the knowledge of the historical chronology of the events recorded in the Bible and in documented history.

Solomon
The myths in the Quran about Solomon

There arose among the Jews and Gnostics a strain of literature that cast Solomon as a mythological figure who commanded armies of devils, Jinn, animals, and birds that fought on his behalf and subdued to him the kingdoms of the earth. The Jinn and the devils were subject to Solomon's service, and the wind was to carry him wherever he desired. He understood the languages of birds, animals, and ants. We find in the Old Testament books written by Solomon under the inspiration of the Holy Spirit no such tales as we find in these and other myths about Solomon. Solomon wrote some psalms and a good portion of the proverbs found in the book of Proverbs. He also wrote the books of Ecclesiastes and Song of Songs. None of these books mention any of the myths that were later attributed to him. Moreover, no mention of these myths occurs in any of the Old or New Testament books, despite the fact that these books were written much earlier than the books that contain the myths. These myths are in later literature that found special acceptance among the Arabian tribes that embraced Judaism.

The Quran, which reflected the myths common in Arabia in Mohammed's day, adopted these myths in its Surahs. This was in part because Mohammed was not familiar with the canonical books of the Old Testament and thus assumed that those myths were authentic.

These myths regarding Solomon were influenced not only by the Arabian mythology but by Persian, Mandaean, and various Gnostic sects as well. Some myths were born from a mixing of these mythologies with various Jewish myths. Since the myths attributed to Solomon are numerous, I included a summary of them in this volume.

Devils and Jinn as Subjected to Solomon

The Quran portrayed a close relationship between Solomon and the devils. It also made the devils active agents and servants in the service of Solomon, as found in Surah 21, called Al Anbiya', verse 82: "...of the devils were some who dived for him (Solomon) and performed other work, and we protected them." Al Sabuni, a modern expositor of the Quran from Saudi Arabia, commenting on this verse, said, "The devils dived for Solomon in the depths of the sea to bring out treasures and pearls. They constructed for him great works, such as palaces."[263]

The reason that devils enjoyed such a high position in the Quran is that the Jinn religion of Arabia replaced angels with devils and cast devils rather than angels as good servants of the prophets and of men. For example, one of the poets who had relationships with the Jinn devils was al 'Asha الأعشى who was known to have a devil who inspired him to recite poetry, including a poem that claimed that the Jinn devils were servants of Solomon. He called his devil "Mashal."[264]

Surah 38, called Sad, verses 36-39 also holds that the devils worked for Solomon:

> Then we subjected the wind to his power, to flow gently to his order, whithersoever he willed, and also the devils who were every kind of builder and diver. Such are our bounties whether you will them on others or withhold them, no account will be asked.

Other verses in the Quran portray the Jinn as great artists whom God employed in Solomon's service to build the Temple and make its sacred vessels. We read in Surah 34, called Saba', verses 12-13:

> And to Solomon the wind is obedient; its early morning journey was a month's journey, and its evening stride was a month's journey, and we made a spring of molten brass to flow for him, and there were Jinn that worked in front of him by the leave of his lord.... They worked for him as he desired, making sanctuaries, niches, images (statues), basins as large as reservoirs, and cauldrons fixed in their places. 'Work you, sons of David, with thanks.'

Further, we find in the Quran claims about the extra power of the devils and how Solomon used them in his service. The Quran contains a story about the Queen of Saba whose country, according to the Quran, was discovered by the hoopoe bird who told Solomon about the queen and her country. (This myth was sourced from the book of The Second Targum of Esther.) Surah 27, called An-Naml, verses 38-39 reports that after Solomon sent a message threatening her, he asked:

> 'O chiefs! Which of you can bring to me her throne before they come to me in submission?' One audacious among the Jinn said: 'I will bring it to you before you rise up from your place; and most surely I am strong (and) trusty for it.'

This strong Jinn was working for Solomon and was ready to bring the throne of Saba to Jerusalem in an instant. Here we find the claim that giant devils could be used to do the impossible, such as transporting objects in one second. This is actually the same language used in the occult sects, whose founders were involved in relationships with the devils.

Ancient roots of the myth that Solomon subjected the devils and Jinn

The devils in Mesopotamian mythology served as assistants to the gods in their works.

The myth in the Quran about the devils and Jinn being subject to Solomon has ancient roots in the Mesopotamian religions. Devils were believed to assist the gods – and especially Nergal – in their work. The myth holds that a group of seven devils from the offspring of An, the Sky god, and Ki, the goddess of the earth, worked for the god Nergal. [265] This mythology left its influence on the Persians who occupied Mesopotamia from the Persian Achmenid period in the 6th century B.C. The Persians lost Mesopotamia when Alexander the Great conquered them. They reoccupied it, however, in the Parthian era, and then again in the Sassanid period, which extended from the 3rd century A.D. till the Islamic conquest of Persia.

Persian roots of subjecting the devils and Jinn

The idea of subjecting devils to leaders and prophets was originally a pagan belief found in Zoroastrianism, which was influenced by the Mesopotamian mythology. In Zoroastrianism, however, the devils were no longer held to be subject to gods but rather to prophets and mythological kings.

Clemens Alexandrinus, a Greek theologian of about the 2nd century A.D., wrote that the Magi (a term that designates a religious Persian caste) boasted of subjecting the devils to their authority. Minucius Felix, a Christian apologist of the 2nd or 3rd century A.D., wrote the same thing.[266]

In Persian mythology the devils produced important and great artistic works for the kings. They built castles and bathrooms for King Jamshid.[267] They also built a great city for King Kaiquis.[268]

This Persian mythology influenced the religions and inhabitants of all the regions that the Persians touched or dominated as evidenced by that fact all these religions adopted the myth that the devils were subject to kings and prophets. Mythological characteristics were attributed to King Solomon in many Middle Eastern religions (including Judaism, the Gnostic sects, Mandaeanism, and the Arabian Jinn religion and its poets). Thus, Solomon was held to be the king who most subjected the devils.

The Jewish sources for the myth that the devils were subject to Solomon

From ancient times, the Persians influenced the Jews. This was after the Persian occupation of Mesopotamia under Cyrus in the 6th century B.C. and continued during the Jews' exile from Mesopotamia that brought them into contact with the Persians. Thus, later there appeared Judaic books (outside the Biblical canon of the Old Testament) filled with myths about Solomon, including the myth that he subjected the devils and Jinn. In these myths, the devils were servants of Solomon rather than of the Persian kings and built cities and artistic works in Solomon's service.

In some Jewish myths we even find the idea expressed in the Quran (in Surah Saba, verses 12 and 13) that Solomon subjected the devils in building the Temple. Thus, in the Talmud, Solomon employed the service of the devil Asmodai in building the Temple. Asmodai was considered a chief of devils[269] whose name was derived from aēšma-daēva, the Zoroastrian devil of anger. Other devils were made to work in constructing the Temple of Jerusalem. One such devil was Ornia who, according to the Gnostic book *The Testament of Solomon*, Solomon made to hew stones in the Jerusalem Temple.

The Second Targum of Esther dates back to the 4th century A.D. and was spread among the Arabians who embraced Judaism. This book was the source of the Quran myth about the visit of the Queen of Sheba with all of its mythical elements, such as the hoopoe bird revealing the existence of the Sheba kingdom to Solomon. (This myth will be discussed in detail later in this volume.) The Targum has this to say about Solomon's subjecting the devils:

> Devils, demons, and ferocious beasts, evil spirits and accidents, were delivered into his hands" [second chapter of the Targum]. "He commanded the wild beasts, the birds, the reptiles, the devils, demons, and spirits to be brought, that they should dance before him" [fourth chapter of the Targum]. "David was succeeded by his son Solomon whom the Holy One, blessed be He!, made to rule over all the beasts of the field, and over the fowls of the air, and over the creeping things of the earth, and over devils, demons, and spirits, whose language he understood as they also understood his" [fourth chapter of the Targum].

We find an echo of such myths in the Quran. In addition to the verses that claim that the devils and Jinn were subject to Solomon, we find references also to the notion that the birds were subject to him, such as the following verses:

> And We made Sulaiman (Solomon) to understand (the case); and to each of them We gave Hukm (right judgment of the affairs and Prophethood) and knowledge. And We subjected the mountains and the birds to glorify our Praises along with Dawud (David). And it was We who were the doer (of all these things) (Surah 21:79).

> The birds were likewise subjected to David:

> We subdued the hills to sing hymns of praise (to their Lord) with him at nightfall and sunrise. And the birds assembled; all were turning unto him (Surah Sad 38:19-20).

> Even the strange mythological animals were subjected to him, as we see in the following verse of Surah Sad, verse 31:

> There were displayed before him, in the afternoon, well-trained horses of the highest breed. (According to Taberi, saying number 22951, they were 20 winged horses.)

Gnostic Sources

It is well-known that the Gnostic sects were influenced by the Persian religion. So it is not surprising that we find this myth about demons being subject to Solomon in the Gnostic sources. Among the Gnostic books that mentioned the subject are Apocalypse of Adam, which dates from the 1st–2nd centuries A.D. In this book we read that Solomon sent an army of devils to search for a virgin who had fled from him. We also find a passage in The Second Targum of Esther that states that Solomon had an army of devils.

Likewise, The Testament of Solomon, a Gnostic book that dates from between the 1st and 5th centuries A.D., states that Solomon subjected the devils. A myth in this book mentions a devil by the name of Ornias who used to disturb a servant whom Solomon loved. Solomon prayed and in response the archangel Michael came and presented him with a ring bearing a seal that authorized him to subdue the devils. This ring became known in mythology as the Seal of Solomon. Solomon gave the ring to his servant who threw it on the chest of the devil Ornias and thus sealed and subjected him. Ornias was made to hew stones in the Temple.[270] This myth regarding Solomon subjecting the devils to build the Temple was one of the sources for the Quranic narrations in Surah Saba. When Solomon realized the ring's effectiveness, he ordered Ornias to go to Beelzebub, the chief of the devils, in order to seal him. When Beelzebub was sealed, all the devils came under the authority of Solomon.[271]

The devils dive for Solomon in the Gnostic literature and the Quran

Again let us review the Quranic verses that mention that the devils served as divers for Solomon. The first is verse 82 of Surah al Anbiya:

Of the devils were some who dived for him [i.e., Solomon] and performed other work, and we protected them.

The second in Surah Sad 38:36-39:

Then we subjected the wind to his power, to flow gently to his order, whithersoever he willed, and also the devils who are every kind of builders and divers.... Such are our bounties whether you will them on others or withhold them, no account will be asked.

This myth of the devils as divers for Solomon who brought him treasures from the deep was not something introduced in the Quran. It is among the myths that we find in mythological books such as the Testament of Solomon.

In the book Testament of Solomon we read that Ephippas, the wind devil, cooperated with Abezithibod, the Red Sea devil, in bringing a purple pillar from the Red Sea to Solomon.[272]

The Jinn subjected to Solomon in Mandaeanism

The Mandaeans were part of the Elcasaites (a Christian-Jewish cult that was born in Trans-Jordan). The Mandaeans separated from the Elcasaites and immigrated to the city of Harran, and ancient city in Mesopotamia, which is in the southeastern part of modern Turkey. Then they immigrated to North Iraq from which they spread to southern Iraq.

In addition to some Jewish myths, the Persian religion had a great influence on the Mandaean scriptures. In Ginza Rba, the main Mandaean sacred book, we find the notion that the Jinn were subjected and obedient to Solomon. The left Ginza Rbadates from the 3rd century A.D., whereas the Right Ginza Rba dates from between the 3rd and 6th centuries A.D. In the first hymn of the second book of Ginza Rbawe read the following:

> King Solomon, son of David, was born. He became the great king of Judah and the ruler of Jerusalem. The Jinn were obedient to him, revering his will, until he became a tyrant and misfortune came upon him.[273]

The Ahnaf, the group that Mohammed joined in his youth, were the bridge between Mohammed and the Sabian Mandaeans. Zayd bin Amru bin Nufayl, the founder of Ahnaf, used to go to Mosul, where groups of Mandaeans lived, to inquire about religion. Zayd was accompanied by Waraqa bin Nofel, the cousin of Khadijah, the first wife of Mohammed.

The Jinn are subjected to Solomon in the pre-Islamic Jahiliyyah poetry

The Quran was not the only Arabian source that claimed that Solomon subjected the Jinn. Certain Arabian poets preceded Mohammed in this claim, confirming that Jewish and Christian myths spread in Arabia before Mohammed's time. Among those poets was al Aasha who wrote the following in one of his poems:

> If any human were eternal, Solomon would have been the one. My God has seen him and chosen him. He gave him domain over the region between Pleiades and Egypt. He subjected to him nine Jinn angels. They worked before him without wages.[274]

Zubeidi quotes the same last stanza. But he mentions the word Mahareb (altars):

> He subjected to him nine Jinn angels. They worked before him to construct altars.[275]

We find in the Quran this same claim — that the Jinn devils constructed altars for Solomon. This indicates that the notion that Jinn devils worked in the Temple of Jerusalem was a mythological claim that preceded Mohammed's time.

There were pre-Islamic Jahiliyyah myths about Solomon, such as the myth that the Jinn built the city of Tadmur in the Syrian Desert for Solomon. In one of Nabighah's poems we read:

> I (Allah) allowed the Jinn to build the city of Tadmur with iron and pillars.
> 276

Mohammed perpetuated these myths of the pre-Islamic poets that claimed that Solomon that subjected the Jinn to himself. Mohammed transformed them into rhymed verses in the Quran.

Ahnaf and the claim that the Jinn were subject to Solomon

The group of Ahnaf, to which Mohammed had belonged since his youth, was in contact with many groups. In addition to the Mandaeans of Mosul, the Ahnaf also had contact with the Christian heretics and Gnostics. Waraqa bin Nofel, the cousin of Khadijah, Mohammed's first wife, embraced Ebionism, a Christian Gnostic heresy. These sects influenced the Ahnaf group, and especially Waraqa, who claimed that the Jinn worked for Solomon.[277] Khadijah used Waraqa to convince Mohammed that he was receiving inspiration from Allah at a time when Mohammed suspected that he had a devil inside and was possessed by a spirit of Kahana (priesthood of the Jinn devils). Mohammed reached this conclusion after the spirit who assumed the identity of the archangel Gabriel had threatened him and choked him three times to subdue him so that he would spread the "inspiration."

Waraqa played a major role in authoring the first Surahs of the Quran. Waraqa's influence on Mohammed was so great that after Waraqa died "the inspiration cooled down" because Mohammed found himself unable to come up with more Quranic verses until he came in contact with new sources.

The Jinn and the death of Solomon

Surah Saba mentioned that after Solomon died, his body continued to be supported by his staff as the Jinn continued to watch him, ignoring that he had died. The subjection of the Jinn to Solomon continued – and they carried on with their heavy labor for Solomon – until an earthworm ate up Solomon's staff and they discovered that he was dead. Here are the words of the Quranic verse:

> Then, when we decreed (Solomon's) death, nothing showed them his death except a little worm of the earth, which kept (slowly) gnawing away at his staff: so when he fell down, the Jinn realized that if they had known the unseen, they would not have tarried in the humiliating penalty (of their task). (Surah Saba, verse 14)

We read the words of Thaalabi:

> After his death, they (the Jinn) continued to work for him for one year. After that period, people realized that the Jinn had been deceiving them about their ability to know the unseen. For had they known the unseen, they would have known that Solomon had died and would not have remained suffering in their work for him for one year.[278]

Taberi mentioned a Hadith of Mohammed:

> Reported by ibn Abbass: The prophet said, 'Solomon was a prophet who, every time he prayed, he saw a tree on the palms of his hands.' He then would ask the tree: 'What is your name?' The tree answered: 'So and so.' Then he would ask it: 'For what benefit are you?' If it was to be planted, then he ordered to be planted. If it was for medicine, then it was prescribed as medicine. One day when he was praying he saw a tree on his hands. He asked it: 'What is your name?' It answered: 'Carob.' He asked: 'For what use are you?' It answered: 'For the destruction of this Temple.' Then Solomon prayed: 'O my God, make the Jinn to become ignorant about my death, so that the humans will know that the Jinn do not know the unseen.' Then Solomon hewed the tree into a staff and leaned against it as dead for one year, while the Jinn continued to work. When a worm had eaten up the staff, Solomon fell down. Through this, the humans knew that if the Jinn did in fact know the unseen, they would not have remained for one year performing the humiliating work in service to Solomon. Ibn Abbass used to write like this. The Jinn then thanked the worm and kept bringing water to it.[279]

The most accepted interpretation of the story of Solomon's death and the Jinn, as we see in expository books on the Quran, is that when Solomon was dying, he told his family not to tell the Jinn of his death until they finished the construction of the Temple, which required one year of work.

Thus, Solomon died one year before the work was completed, and the devils continued to work without knowing about his death. Al Nuiry put it in these words:

> While Solomon was in his altar, leaning against his staff, reading the Psalms and the Torah, the angel of death came to him. He gave him something to smell that made him die. Solomon remained standing without falling or moving. The Jinn feared him, not daring to come close to him, not know that he had died. The humans, Jinn, devils, fierce animals, and birds continued in obedience at work until one year elapsed. The worm came to eat the staff. This is what Allah said (in the Quran): {Then, when we decreed (Solomon's) death, nothing showed them his death except a little worm of the earth, which kept (slowly) gnawing away at his staff.} They continued in their work for that year, transporting the rocks and doing construction.[280]

In analyzing this Quranic story we conclude that it reveals Mohammed's ignorance not only of basic medical principles but of common human experience as well. A deceased body cannot possibly remain upright by leaning against a staff. According to the Quranic verse, the corpse of Solomon remained leaning against the staff in the presence of the Jinn, who thought he was alive. For one year his corpse remained standing before them, as if he continued to supervise them until they completed the construction of the Temple. He remained in this state until the worm ate up the staff. It took the worm a long time— at least months — to consume the staff, and only then did the corpse of Solomon fall down revealing to the Jinn that Solomon was dead.

Just hours after death bacteria and fungi operate on a body to begin the process of putrefaction and decomposition. How, then, could Solomon's corpse remain propped up against a staff for an entire year?!

But there is more to ponder: Solomon had many wives (hundreds, in fact) as well as sons and servants. How could they all be around and yet remain ignorant of Solomon's death for a year? Are we to believe that Solomon remained there against the staff for one year without any one seeing him or bringing him food? How could the kingdom remain intact without an heir or king for one year? Were the Jinn devils bereft of any intelligence – these who are reputed to be the slyest of all creatures – and so dense as to not notice that Solomon was without food or natural bodily functions for one whole year?! If someone of his household had known of Solomon's death, would the devil not have known men's thoughts, and immediately discovered that Solomon had died?!

The Quranic story stands in contradiction with history: Solomon began building the Temple immediately after he became king. It took him five years to build it. Then in 13 years he built his palace. People who were ignorant of the Bible and its accurate chronology were fooled by this myth, which is also irrational.

Some elements in Jewish mythology may point to the sources of this myth. We have already mentioned the myth about Solomon subjecting the devils to work in the construction of the Temple. There was also a worm by the name of Shamir, which hewed stones in the Temple. Upon touching the rocks, this worm cleaved and hewed them. According to Midrash Tehillim, an eagle brought this worm from paradise.[281]

We assume that the Quranic story about a worm hewing the staff in the Temple may indicate that the original Arabian myth from which Mohammed drew his story contained the presence of this Shamir worm among the devil-workers in the Temple. The Arabians apparently could not recall the worm's name as it was recorded in the Jewish mythology. The Quranic story was most likely a form of the myth spread among the Arabians who embraced Judaism at the time of Mohammed.

The Winged Horses and Solomon

Surah Sad 38:30-33 says:

And we gave to David Solomon, most excellent the servant! Surely he was frequent in returning (to Allah). When the Safinat horses were brought to him in the evening, he said: 'Surely I preferred the good things to the remembrance of my Lord' — until the sun set and time for Asr prayer was over. Then he said: 'Bring them back to me;' so he began to slash (their) legs and necks.

According to the narrators' sayings reported by Taberi, these horses were winged horses:

Ibn Zayd said, 'The safinat were horses with wings.'

Reported by Ibrahim al Taimi: 'The Quran saying: "When there were brought to him in the evening the Safinat horses," they were 20 winged horses.'[282]

Al Qurtubi quotes other narrators, including Ali bin Abi Taleb, the son-in-law of Mohammed:

Al-Hasan said: 'I was told that they were horses coming out from the sea bearing wings.' Al Dhahhak said that they were horses brought from the sea to Solomon and had wings. Ibn Zayd said: 'The devil brought the horses from the sea, from the herbs of the sea, and they were winged horses.' The same thing Ali, Allah blessing upon him, had said. Ali added that they were 20 horses with wings.[283]

Without doubt, Ali's interpretation expresses the true meaning of the above verses. Since he was the closest to Mohammed, he knew what Mohammed meant by obscure verses such as these.

The myth of the winged horses coming out of the sea is related to an Ethiopian myth. Pliny the Elder mentioned an Ethiopian myth about winged horses, called Pegasi, which had a unicorn and were native to an island in the Red Sea opposite Ethiopia.[284] The name Pegasi is derived from Pegasus, the famous winged horse in Greek mythology. Ancient Greeks had always longed for Pegasus to appear to them so that they could mount it and travel to distant places. Pegasus was the son of Poseidon, the god of the sea, and was sometimes called "The Thundering Horse of Jove." The Greeks believed that Pegasus carried Zeus' thunderbolts through the sky.

Given the large population of Ethiopians in Mecca at the time of Mohammed, we assume that the myths regarding these Pegasi — the winged horses of Ethiopian mythology — were the sources for the Quranic myth. The Pegasi (like the servant devils) were added to the mythological privileges of Solomon who, in Ethiopian mythology, enjoyed superstitious privileges similar to those that the Jewish myths bestowed upon him.

The notion that Solomon possessed winged camels is something that Aisha, the youngest wife of Mohammed, believed. Thus in the books narrating the life of Mohammed we read:

Aisha said that the apostle of Allah returned from Tabuk or the Hanin campaign. In her room was a barrier of clothing. The wind blew and revealed the various toys Aisha had stashed behind the clothes. Mohammed asked her: 'O Aisha, what are these?' She said: 'These are my daughters (toys).' Mohammed saw among them a horse with two wings. He said to her: 'What is this that I see in their midst?' She answered: 'A horse.' He said: 'What is the thing placed on it?' She said: 'Two wings.' He said: 'A horse with two wings!?' She answered: 'Did you not hear that Solomon had horses with wings?' Mohammed then smiled.[285]

Mohammed married Aisha when she was six years old, which is why she kept children's toys to play with, which she referred to as "my daughters." Her belief about Solomon's winged horses came from a myth common among many groups at Mecca, including Mohammed's group, for he added this myth to his Quran.

The Myth of a Devil Replacing Solomon on the Throne

In Surah 38, called Sad, verses 34-35, we read:

And indeed, we did try Sulaiman (Solomon) and we placed on his throne Jasad (a devil, so he lost his kingdom for a while) and he did return (to Allah with obedience and in repentance, and to his throne and kingdom by the Grace of Allah).He said: 'My Lord! Forgive me, and bestow upon me a kingdom such as shall not belong to any other after me. Verily, You are the Bestower.' (Translation from Arabic by Mohsin Khan.)

Al Taberi provides Mohammed's cousin Ibn Abbass' interpretation of the passage above:

Ibn Abbass, in explaining the verse which said 'And indeed, we did try Solomon and we placed on his throne Jasad and he did return,' he said: 'The Jasad was the devil to whom Solomon gave his ring. The devil threw the ring into the sea. The reign of Solomon was through his ring. The name of this Jinn devil was Sakher صخر.'[286]

Mujahed gave more details about the story, but he called the devil "Asef آصف."

According to Mujahed, the Quranic words 'on his throne Jasad' was a devil by the name of Asef. Solomon asked him: 'How do you deceive people?' The devil said: 'If you show me your ring, I will tell you.' When Solomon gave him the ring, the devil threw it into the sea. Solomon went astray and lost his reign. Asef sat on his throne. Allah prohibited Asef from cavorting with the women so he did not touch them. Solomon went around asking for food saying, 'Do not you know me? I am Solomon.' But people disbelieved him until one day a woman gave him a fish, and he found his ring inside the belly of the fish. Then he returned to the throne and resumed his reign. Asef fled off into the sea.[287]

The "Jasad" who sat on Solomon's throne is derived from a Jewish myth. The myth says that a devil named Ashmedai (in other writings the devil is called Asmodai)[1] was subjected by Solomon through his ring. One day Solomon asked him about the formula by which devils exercised power over man. In order to show Solomon in a practical way, the devil asked him for his ring. The devil then threw the ring into the sea, removing Solomon from his reign; and the devil sat on Solomon's throne. Solomon went away, wandering as a private person, until his reign was returned to him.

In some versions, the myth says that, during his wandering about as a private person, Solomon married a girl and went to fish. He captured a fish and found his ring in its belly. He then returned and subdued the devil through his ring. We see this myth repeated in the sayings of the expositors of the Quran (as we already have seen).

In reality, in the Jewish myths Solomon was a king who became a private citizen and then resumed his reign.[288] In some myths he lost his reign because an angel assumed his likeness and cast him away. Solomon thereafter went begging, decrying the fact that he had lost his throne. One day a woman put a plate of beans before him and stroked his head with a stick, telling him: "Solomon sits on his throne and you claim to be a king."[289]

In some Jewish myths, the story is connected with the devil Ashmedai, who brought the worm, Shamir, to Solomon – this same Shamir that hewed stones in the Temple. When Solomon said that he did not understand the devil's power, Ashmedai answered that he would reveal this to him if he would untie him and lend him the magical ring. When Solomon did so, the devil stood in front of him with one wing touching the sky and the other touching the earth. He pushed Solomon 400 parasangs away from Jerusalem and installed himself as king. (A parasang was a historical Iranian unit of itinerant distance.)

---

[1] The names of the devils Ashmedai and Asmodai are derived from the Zoroastrian writings attributed to a devil named Æshma. Darmesteter, an expert in Zoroastrianism, wrote:

"Originally a mere epithet of the storm fiend, Æshma was afterward converted into an abstraction, the demon of rage and anger, and became an expression for all wickedness, a mere name of Ahriman" ["Introduction to Vendidad," iv 22].

Solomon returned to claim his throne. At the beginning he was considered a mad person. Then the people began watching Ashmedai. They noticed that even Benaiah, who was the first to serve Solomon, was not summoned for a long time. Furthermore, Ashmedai did not observe the Jewish customs regarding marriage. Thus, they came to believe Solomon and gave him a magical ring, through which he once again fettered Ashmedai.[290]

The old version of the myth dates to the 2nd century A.D. Ashmedai was presented as a false Solomon in the Jewish writing the Babylonian Haggadah from Palestine. As punishment for Solomon's sins, an angel took his throne leaving Solomon to wander about living as a mendicant (beggar).[291]

In a similar story, Asmodeus, instead of Ashmedai, stole the throne from Solomon. Asmodeus first appeared in the book of Tobit as a wicked spirit and king of the devils.[292] Asmodeus also appeared in the book Testament of Solomon as a devil whom Solomon subjected to help construct the Temple. Asmodeus confessed to deceiving, intervening in marriages, and causing adultery.

The myth says that after Asmodeus separated Solomon from the throne by throwing him 400 miles away from Jerusalem, he threw the magic ring into the sea. Solomon spent three years away from his reign. That was his punishment for transgress of some of the commandments. He wandered daily until he became a cook for the king of Ammun. Naamah, the king's daughter, fell in love with Solomon, which displeased the king who was tried to persuade her to decline. But she insisted on her decision. The king decided to kill her along with Solomon. Both were taken to a desert so that they would die of hunger and thirst. But they escaped from the desert and reached a coastal city where they bought a fish. Upon opening the belly of the fish, Solomon found a ring with the Holy Name engraved on it. Solomon recognized it as his ring, and used it to drive out the devil Asmodeus and regain his throne.[293]

We encounter none of these myths in the books of the Bible that talk about Solomon. These myths were accepted by the Arabians who embraced a form of Judaism. Mohammed adopted these myths, mistakenly assuming that they were historically accurate accounts of Solomon's life.

The Reflection of this Mythology (of subjecting devils to Solomon) upon some Religious Sects

The devils and Jinn were subjected not only to Solomon but to the leaders of many religious sects, including the Gnostics, who also claimed to subject the devils and Jinn. In reality, these groups took advantage of the myth that Solomon had devils in his service as an excuse to justify their involvement in relationships with devils.

Among those to be mentioned are the followers of Carpocrates, a Gnostic heretic at the beginning of the 2nd century A.D. His followers practiced spells and incantations, and had relationships with devils. They claimed to control and rule over devils who served them.[294] We find this claim also in the Ahnaf group, and then again in the claims of Mohammed.

Some Gnostic sects promoted the idea that the devils were useful, and encouraged people to pray to them for intervention in their lives and so they could benefit from their service. The church fathers fought against these dangerous occultic ideas and practices. We find in the writings of Origen (beginning in the 3rd century A.D.) a refutation against the claims of Celsus and Ophiani, who claimed that the devils were useful and that prayer should be offered to them.[295]

I mentioned Waraqa bin Nofel previously and discussed his role in authoring the first Surahs of the Quran. Waraqa was a Christian heretical priest who belonged to a Gnostic sect called Ebionism. The idea of the relationship with the devils, and the service of the devils to such groups, became acceptable for those who were around Waraqa. Waraqa's family was known for its affiliation with the Jinn religion of Arabia; his sister Ruqieh was a Kahinah — that is, a priestess of the Jinn.[296]

Those Gnostic heretics admitted that each one had a devil as a spouse. Mohammed also had a devil as spouse. I quote a Hadith of Mohammed in which he admitted that he had a devil as qareen قرين ; qareen in Arabic means spouse:

> The apostle of Allah said: 'To every one of you was entrusted a qareen of Jinn.' They said to him: 'To you also O apostle of Allah?' He said: 'To me also. But Allah helped me that this Jinn became Muslim. He orders me only in good things.'[297]

In another Hadith of Mohammed reported by al Tabresi he admitted that he was ordained as a careen by a Jinn. This Hadith is a confirmed Hadith. The Islamic scholars consider it to be genuine.[298]

In anthropology, the idea of a qareen denotes a special relationship between a possessed man and his devil. The devil usually chooses among the possessed men some to be spouses for him; among those are the dangerous magicians, or mediums, chosen by the devil for special tasks. The devil ordered Mohammed, even after Mohammed claimed to be a prophet:

> Reported by Jaber bin Abed who said: 'While I was walking with the apostle of Allah, a serpent came and stood beside him, and it brought her mouth close to the ear of the apostle of Allah and began talking to him.' Then the apostle of Allah said to the serpent: 'Yes.' Then it left him. I asked Mohammed about this serpent. He said that it was a man of Jinn, and that he said to him to order his nation not to clean themselves with the dung and bones, because Allah made dung and bones food for the Jinn.[299]

We notice that Mohammed responded with the word "Yes" to the Jinn who appeared to him in the form of a serpent. This is an answer of obedience. We do not know what the devil had ordered him. But we call your attention to the words of Mohammed that he had a devil as spouse and that this devil became Muslim – and thus that the devil did not order him except with good things. We do not, however, believe that the devil orders good things even if he claims (or feigns or pretends) that he has become religious. It is not plausible to believe that the subject or the dialog that took place between Mohammed and the devil who appeared to him in the form of a serpent was about the dung and the bones of the desert. Furthermore, it is impossible to believe that the dung and bones of the desert are food for the devils. Devils do not have physical bodies that require nourishment. Had they materialistic bodies, they would not accept the idea of feeding on dung and the bones of dogs and cats, which were strewn across the wildernesses of Arabia. Without doubt, this incident, like many others, manifests the role Mohammed played in front of naive followers, revealing himself to be a follower and vassal of a Jinn devil. It is known that the serpent was a symbol of the devil, and that the devil took the form of a serpent in order to deceive Adam and Eve.

We find the devil, who is connected with Mohammed as a spouse, appearing to him in the form of a serpent in order to direct his wars and piracies. This is seen clearly in the following incident that occurred during Mohammed's campaign to Tabuk-North Arabia:

"During the Tabuk campaign, a giant serpent came across the road. People went aside because of fear. The serpent came to the apostle of Allah and stood speaking to him for a long period of time, while he was sitting on his camel. People were looking at the serpent. Then it went away. The prophet of Allah said: 'Do you know who this is ?' They said, 'Allah and his apostle better know.' He said, 'This is one of the eight Jinn who came to me to listen to the Quran.'"[300]

We see here that in his wars against the Arabian tribes, through which he exterminated many, Mohammed was directed by the Jinn devils. The books that narrated the life of Mohammed revealed that "Gabriel" was connected with Mohammed before Mohammed's began claiming his role as prophet.[301]

But we ask: How is it that the angel Gabriel was connected as a spouse to a man who had a devil as a spouse? Furthermore, angels never relate to humans in the form of a spouse. There is no example in the Bible of an angel connecting himself to a prophet. Angels used to appear for a few seconds or minutes to declare a message from God and then they would disappear. The idea of connecting as a spouse with a spirit is known in the world of magic – that is, the devil would take a medium as a spouse. Therefore, the one who was given the title of "Gabriel" and was connected with Mohammed was certainly his spouse: the devil himself.

The Bible is against any relationship with wicked spirits.

It is easy for a man who is without a divine guide to be deceived by these occultic and Gnostic excuses that justify their involvement in occults and relationships with devils. The Bible, being the true word of God, exposes these dangerous relationships and prohibits them absolutely. We read in the book of Leviticus:

'Give no regard to mediums and familiar spirits [the Jinn as spouses to the mediums]; do not seek after them, to be defiled by them: I am the LORD your God.' (Leviticus 19:31)

'And the person who turns to mediums and familiar spirits [Jinn] to prostitute himself with them, I will set My face against that person and cut him off from his people.' (Leviticus 20:6)

'A man or a woman who is a medium, or who has familiar spirits (Jinn), shall surely be put to death; they shall stone them with stones. Their blood shall be upon them.' (Leviticus 20:27)

Thus, the relationship with the devils, which were also the Jinn, was the most dangerous abomination to which man was liable; punishment for this occultic practice was stoning.

The Transfer of
the throne of the Queen of Sheba

The Quran claims that the 'Ifrits of the Jinn were ready to bring the throne of the Queen of Sheba to Solomon in Jerusalem in a mere second. Here is the verse:

An 'Ifrit (strong one) from the Jinn said: 'I will bring it to you before you rise from your place (council). And verily, I am indeed strong, and trustworthy for such work.' Surah Al Naml 27:39

We find this story about transferring the throne of the Queen of Saba (Sheba) to the Jinn in the Quran's narration about the Queen of Sheba's visit. It is taken from the apocryphal (non-canonical) book Second Targum of Esther. Also, according to the Quran, after the queen was ready to come to Jerusalem after Solomon threatened her, Solomon asked his counselors who would bring her throne to him immediately (i.e., before the queen arrived.) One 'Ifrit of Jinn guaranteed he could do it.

The roots of this myth are found in the same Targum. In the third chapter of the Targum we read that the eagles moved the throne of Solomon. In the second chapter we find the 'Ifrits of Jinn transporting the fish from the sea to Solomon:

He was called Yaka (commander of obediencze) because he was lord and ruler over all the kings of the earth, east and west.... All the kingdoms feared him, nations and languages were obedient to him; devils, demons, and ferocious beasts, evil spirits and accidents, were delivered into his hands. Imps brought him all kinds of fish from the sea, and the fowls of heaven, together with the cattle and wild animals, came of their own accord to his slaughter-house to be slaughtered for his banquet...and all the kings obeyed him.

Mythological roots of transporting the Queen of Sheba's throne by 'Ifrit Jinn or devil.

There are Middle Eastern roots of this myth that the 'Ifrit of Jinn transported the throne of the Queen of Sheba to Jerusalem in one second. In mythology, the most difficult tasks and impossible enterprises were attributed to the giant devils or Jinn. In the Manichaean writings we find that the giant devils were utilized in the creation and in moving the inferior heaven under the supervision of two angels. [302] The Gnostic book Testament of Solomon, mentioned above, tells how Ephibas, the devil of the air, moved the mountains and turned thrones upside down.[303]

The pre-Islamic Jahiliyyah people classified the Jinn devils as the following:

> If a spirit became malignant, then he is a devil. If he is more than that, then he is Mared (a giant devil). If he is more in power, then he is 'Ifrit.[304]

The 'Ifrits were the most powerful of the devils who were able to do impossible things. This reflects the influence of the Gnostic and Jewish myths upon the Jahiliyyah people. It is no wonder then that we find such myths incorporated into the Quran.

Solomon and the Ant

A particular Jewish myth holds that Solomon and his army of devils, humans, animals, and birds, flew by means of a large flying carpet. According to the myth, on one occasion Solomon was flying on the carpet in the company of the leaders of his four mythological troops when they reached the valley of ants. Solomon heard the voice of an ant advising her colleagues to enter because of Solomon's army.

The Quran presented this myth – and all other myths and stories it included – in a brief summary of rhymed verses. The Quran's version of the story is incomplete and devoid of any value because it lacks the true essence of the myth that we find in its original sources. Mohammed recalled something of the myth as he had heard it from Arabians who embraced Judaism. But he did not comprehend the deeper meaning the myth was created to convey. Readers will discover this fact when they study the original Jewish myth and compare it to the Quranic narration as related in Surah al Naml:

The Quran	Jewish Sources
And before Solomon were marshaled his hosts of Jinn, and men and birds, and they were all kept in order and ranks. (Surah 27, called al Naml, verse 17)	"When God appointed Solomon king over every created thing, He gave him a large carpet sixty miles long and sixty miles wide, made of green silk interwoven with pure gold, and ornamented with figured decorations. He was surrounded by his four princes, Asaph b. Berechiah, prince of men; Ramirat, prince of the demons; a lion, prince of beasts; and an eagle, prince of birds."
At length, when they came to a (lowly) valley of ants, one of the ants said: "O ye ants, get into your habitations, lest Solomon and his hosts crush you (underfoot) without knowing it." (Surah 27, called al Naml, verse 18)	"On another day, while sailing over a valley where there were many swarms of ants, Solomon heard one ant say to the others, 'Enter your houses; otherwise Solomon's legions will destroy you.'"
We see the ants as a nation that glorified Allah in the Hadith of Mohammed: "...reported by AbiHurrerah: 'I heard the apostle of Allah saying that an ant bit one of the prophets. The prophet ordered the village of the ants to be burnt. Allah then inspired him to say: "Because you have been bitten by an ant, you want to destroy one of the nations that praises Allah?"'" (Bukhari 4:22)	"The king asked why she spoke thus, and she answered that she was afraid that if the ants looked at Solomon's legions they might be turned from their duty of praising God, which would be disastrous to them.
The expository books of the Quran say that Solomon heard the ant speak from a great distance.	Another form of the Jewish myth: "Solomon had a magic carpet that only he could command. One day he was flying high above the earth, and he was very pleased with himself. He said, 'I am the greatest of all. I fly above the world. I understand all the languages of all creatures. I can even hear them speak from this great height.' "At that moment he heard a creature say, 'King Solomon is not so great.' Solomon looked down and saw that the words had been spoken by an ant. He commanded the carpet to stop and to descend to the earth. Solomon found the tiny ant. He bent down and picked it up so he could look at it eye to eye. He said to it, 'You little creature of the dust, I heard you say

The Quran	Jewish Sources
	that I am not so great. Tell me, who is greater than I am?' "The ant replied, 'I am greater than you.' "'How can you say that?' asked Solomon. "The ant answered, 'I am greater than you.' "'What!' said Solomon. 'How?' "The ant replied, 'I am greater than you because the greatest king in the world stopped when he heard me speak, he lowered himself to the earth, and he bent down in front of me. He raised me up so we were the same height, and he asked me a question that I could answer and he could not.'
So he smiled, amused at her speech; and he said: "O my Lord! So order me that I may be grateful for Thy favors, which Thou hast bestowed on me and on my parents, and that I may work the righteousness that will please Thee. And admit me, by Thy Grace, to the ranks of Thy righteous Servants." (Surah al Naml, verse 19) We notice that Solomon smiled in both narrations, humbling himself, and asked God that he might be grateful for His favors, which Hehad bestowed on him.	"Solomon smiled. He said, 'I am the king who stopped when you spoke and lowered himself, and bent down, raised you up, and asked you a question that he could not answer.' "'You are,' said the ant. 'And I am the creature who told you something you did not know.' "King Solomon gently lowered the ant back to the earth. 'O wise and mighty Ant, you are greater than I thought you were, and I am not as great as I thought I was. I still have much to learn from my fellow creatures.'"
	The Jewish sources of the myth: Bet Hamidrash, ed. Jellenek — Collection of Smaller Midrashim] V, 22-26; Louis Ginzberg, The Legends of the Jews, volume IV, chapter 5, Solomon; In his book Solomon and the Ant, Sheldon Oberman said that versions of the full story are found in Ma'asseh ha-Namalah, Ma'assehNissim; with versions in Moses Gaster's The Exempla of the Rabbis and Haim Schwarzhaum's Studies in Jewish and World Folklore. The story "The Ant and the Impenetrable Palace" can be found in Micha Joseph Bin Gorion's MimekorYisrael. "Story of the Ant" can be found in Nathan Ausubel's A Treasury of Jewish Folklore [305]

The Quranic story could not be the original. Without referring to the Jewish myth, the Quran is incomplete and void of its original intent and meaning. Mohammed wanted to impress his listeners by narrating mythological elements (such as Solomon's army formed of Jinn, humans, and birds) and relating that Solomon understood the languages of the ants. He did not pay attention, however, to the dialogue which, according to the Jewish myth, occurred between Solomon and the ant, through which the Jewish author wanted to convey the deeper meaning of how God taught Solomon humility through the least of His creatures, the ant.

Scientific questions regarding the ant and Solomon

We draw the attention of our Muslim friends, who consider the Quran to be a celestial book that contains historical stories, to the following facts: If the Jewish author of the myth had intended to say that the story actually happened, he would have important arguments against him, such as his ignorance of the scientific facts about ants. Most ants in fact do not see, and ants of the few species of African and American ants that do see are able to see only for a very short distance.[306] How could the ant have recognized the identity of Solomon and his army?!

Furthermore, ants are deaf to the acoustic waves or vibrations carried by air and thus do not hear the human voice. Ants are sensitive, however, to vibrations on the ground beneath them for a distance of a few centimeters.[307] How then could an ant distinguish the voice of Solomon, who was carried high up in the air, since the ant was unable to hear his voice or his army's noise?!

The claim that ants have languages

Some Muslims attribute scientific elements to the story of Solomon and the ant and contend that ants speak and have languages. They claim that the Quran preceded discoveries that prove it. This raises the question: Do ants speak and have distinguishing languages and words they use in communication within themselves?

Scientific research has proved that ants do not have languages or words that justify what the Quran attributed to them – that is, that they speak to one another. Furthermore, the idea that Solomon carried on a conversation with an ant in which both parties understood each other arises from Jewish myths that attributed to Solomon's knowledge of the languages of animals, birds, and insects. Furthermore, the noises such animals make are not languages. The Quran claims that Solomon understood the languages of animals and birds, including the hoopoe, which was his counselor, according to Surah al Naml:

> And he took a muster of the birds and said: 'Why is it I see not the Hoopoe? Or is he among the absentees? I will certainly punish him with a severe penalty, or execute him, unless he brings me a clear reason (for absence).' But the Hoopoe tarried not far; he (came up and) said: 'I have compassed (territory) which thou hast not compassed, and I have come to thee from Saba with tidings true. I found (there) a woman ruling over them and provided with every requisite; and she has a magnificent throne. 'I found her and her people worshiping the sun besides Allah. Satan has made their deeds seem pleasing in their eyes and has kept them away from the Path so they receive no guidance (Surah 27 called al Naml, verses 20-24).

In the same Surah al Naml, the Quran attributes a statement to Solomon in which he declared that he had been taught the birds' speech — that is, the language of the birds —and that he knows everything:

> And Solomon was David's heir. He said: 'O ye people! We have been taught the speech of birds, and on us has been bestowed knowledge of all things: this is indeed grace manifest (from Allah)' (27:16).

The Quranic story about the dialogue between Solomon and the ant is a part of the Jewish superstitious mythology, which attributed to Solomon knowledge of the languages of birds, animals, and insects. In the second Targum of Estherwe we read:

> He understood the languages of birds and of animals, steer and rams ran at his command, lions and tigers seized weapons before him. He understood languages better than all nations (Targum chapter 2).

We also read in the fourth chapter of the Targum the following:

> David was succeeded by his son Solomon, whom the Holy One, blessed be He!, made to rule over all the beasts of the field, and over the fowls of the air, and over the creeping things of the earth, and over devils, demons, and spirits, whose languages he understood as they also understood his.

We know that the myths of the second Targum of Esther spread among the Arabian tribes who embraced Judaism — especially that of the Quranic story of the hoopoe, Solomon and Queen of Saba — accurately reported the myth from this Targum.

Birds, animals, and insects do not have languages to communicate within their species. They emit noises not formal languages. Mohammed adopted these myths because he believed the noises of the animals and birds were true languages and that they had speech like humans and the capacity for logic that they expressed in languages.

The communication among the ants

Scientific research on ants enabled scientists to discover the ants' means of communication. Most of the communication among ants is chemical — the rest is by touch.[308]

Edward O. Wilson and Bert Hölldobler, two scientists who specialized in ants, describe the communication among ants as a chemical secretion by the insects to stimulate others of the same species to assume a behavior or to be alarmed.[309]

Ants also communicate via the sense of smell. The Jews apparently knew this because the Talmud mentions that when a grain of wheat fell from an ant all the ants came to smell the grain, without taking it, until the owner came and took it.[310]

There is a certain kind of noise that various insects produce. The noise comes either by rapping (drumming) or stridulation.

As for the drumming noise made by rapping, an organ works as a hammer that drums against another organ so as to produce this noise. This is the least primitive noise that man distinguishes. As Edward O. Wilson and Bert Hölldobler writes:

> The ants do not modify the drumming to identify the category of danger to the nest.[311]

Thus, such drumming noises are simple signals that many kinds of insects make. They are not languages or communicating words. They are similar to the wind, the noise of which does not carry special meaning or languages.

There are a few kinds of ants that produce noise through stridulation, "...it is generally as the rubbing of specialized body parts together to produce a 'chirp.' "This is the chirp that a number of species of insects emit. It is a unitary monotone signal and not words or language. Bert Hölldobler and Edward O. Wilson write:

No evidence exists to rank the chirps of stridulation as anything more than simple unitary signals. In other words, ants do not 'talk' by modulating sound through time.[312]

Just as we do not consider the buzz of bees as language, so we do not consider the chirp of ants as language or a formal means of communication. Thus, attributing to the Quran a scientific miracle — such as the tale of the ants and Solomon — is a false claim that contradicts science.

Man and other earthly creatures according to the Bible and to the Quran

At the end of our research about the myth of the ant and Solomon, which the Quran adopted from the Jewish myth, we say that this myth stands in contradiction with the word of God and His plan for His creation. Man is the only created being able to speak in languages. This is because man has a spirit that needs to communicate and fellowship with God — and to search for God and study His word. Man, being morally responsible before God, needs to communicate with his human colleagues and live according to the moral laws God has given him.

The rest of the creatures are not spiritual creatures; they are without eternal souls. Thus, they do not need a language but merely simple and limited signals for each species.

The Quranic notion, by contrast, is that all insects, animals, and birds are nations that have languages and are liable morally; thus, they are brought to judgment. This we see in Surah al Anaam:

There is not an animal in the earth, nor a flying creature flying on two wings, but they are nations like unto you. We have neglected nothing in the Book (of our decrees). Then unto their Lord they will be gathered (for Judgment) (Surah 6, called al Anaam, verse 38).

Those are notions adopted from Zoroastrianism. Zoroastrians categorized all animals, birds, reptiles, and insects as either good creatures who were followers of Ahura Mazda, or wicked creatures of the devil who were followers of Ahriman, the god of wickedness. These Zoroastrian thoughts influenced certain groups in the regions where the Persians dominated. They are doctrines that contradict science, the Bible, and reality.

Solomon and the Wind

The Quran claims that Allah made the wind subject to Solomon, to transport him to any place he desired. Of the Quranic verses concerning this topic, we mention:

> And to Sulaiman the wind blowing violent, pursuing its course by his command to the land which we had blessed, and we are knower of all things. (Surah 21:81).

> There is also the following verse from Surah Saba':

> And the wind to Sulaiman, which made a month's journey in the morning and a month's journey in the evening.

There is no mention in the Bible, which is the primary source of the life of Solomon, of Solomon riding the wind. This myth has deep pagan roots in mythologies that were present in many different regions of the Middle East at the time of Mohammed. Here are some of them:

The roots of subduing the wind in Persian Zoroastrianism

Like all other elements of nature, the wind was part of Zoroastrian dualism. In other words, some of the elements of nature were of a good nature and others were evil fighters of Ahura Mazda's world. Thus, we find the good wind as a servant for Ahura Mazda and the evil wind as a servant to Ahrimam, the god of wickedness. The wind as a devil in Zoroastrian literature is mentioned in multiple locations, such as in the book of Vendidad. [313] Zoroastrians made the wind an angel, and when the wind is a storm it is usually a devil.[314] There is the idea that the storm is a devil.[315] The wind is a dangerous character capable of overthrowing everything. Some imaginary personalities, however, such as Keresaspa, placed their feet on the wind and subdued it.[316]

The saying of the Quran in the Surah of the Prophets: "And to Sulaiman the wind blowing violent, pursuing its course by his command to the land which we had blessed" is in complete accordance with the Zoroastrian mythology. In fact, the wind in Zoroastrianism is an important vehicle for transportation, used by gods and prophets. That is why the wind is called "the horse of Ahura Mazda" in some Zoroastrian texts.[317]

The devils made a wheel from glass for Jamshid, a mythological Persian king, and the devils placed some shells on it. Jamshid drove it in the air from his home country when he was traveling to Babylon in one day— this day became a holy day for the Persians.[318]

The notion that Zoroastrian mythical characters subdued the wind and used it for transportation is clear in their texts. The book of Dinkard, a part of the Pahlavi texts, speaks of Kai-Khursoia, a mythical character and a prophet in Zoroastrianism. Kai-Khursoi transformed Vae, the god of the air, into a winged camel and rode it to visit those who "obtained eternity" in distant and heavenly places.[319]

These Persian myths had a profound effect on many groups in the Middle East, as I will discuss in the following sections.

Gnostic roots of Solomon and the Wind myth

In the book Testament of Solomon, we find the roots of the myth that Solomon subdued the wind to himself. In this Gnostic book we read that Solomon sent his boy with his ring to seal the wind devil who disturbed Arabia. (Many ignorant groups embraced the idea that Solomon dominated the whole world, including Arabia.) The plan was that the boy would carry an empty vessel and place the ring inside. Then he would open the vessel opposite the wind until the vessel was full of the wind and then close the vessel. The boy succeeded in his task. The wind devil's name was Ephippas. Solomon began using the wind in building the Temple. For example, when a cornerstone was difficult to carry, it was carried by this wind devil.[320]

Without doubt, the author of Testament of Solomon was influenced by Zoroastrianism, as we have seen from his adoption of the notion that Solomon subjected the wind borrowed from that religion.

We find in Islamic writings the idea of custody or imprisonment of the wind. For example, we read in al Masud's Muruj al Dhahab that Solomon imprisoned the wind in a place.[321] It is interesting to see the transfer of Jewish myths into Arabia, such as the wind as a servant or slave to Solomon, which he could humiliate, mount, or imprison in a place — all in accordance with the myth mentioned in the Testament of Solomon.

The idea that prophets travel as they are carried along by the wind is found in many Gnostic books. The angels in the Apocalypse of Enoch placed Enoch on a cart of wind and brought him to the furthest heavens.[322] Mohammed claimed to mount the Buraq, a winged animal, at night in the company of Gabriel in order to travel to the Temple of Jerusalem, which did not exist in his time. This idea of Buraq had roots in Zoroastrianism. We have already seen that Kai-Khursoi, one of their prophets, transformed the god of the air into a winged camel and traveled to distant and heavenly places. Some Gnostic writings reflected these myths. For instance, in The Paraphrase of Shem we read about a wind that is similar to the Buraq, a winged animal with one horn.[323]

Roots for Solomon and the wind in Mandaeanism

Mandaeanism has myths that reflect the Quranic myth about Solomon and the wind. In Mandaeanism, wind is a personality upon which kings sat in order to hold council.[324] On the wind sat royal personalities.[325] The notion of a prophet mounting a wind is found in the example of Shetel— that is, Seth, the third son of Adam. He became a great prophet in Mandaeanism. According to Ginza Rba, their main sacred book, Seth mounted the wind to travel.[326]

Manichaean roots for the wind and Solomon

The idea of the wind as a vehicle is found in Manichaeism, the religion established by Mani in Mesopotamia in the 3rd century A.D. According to The Kephalaia of the Teacher, a book attributed Mani's authorship, we find Jesus touring the cosmos through many vehicles, including the wind.[327] In other Manichaean literature, the cart of wind carried Adam to heaven.[328]

The myth of Solomon and wind in Judaism

In the Jewish mythological writings called Kabbalah, Solomon travels through a wind upon an eagle, sitting on a throne of light. He reached the doors of heaven. Solomon also reached beyond the "black mountains," where the two fallen angels, Uzza and Azael, were fettered. Solomon used his magical ring to force the two angels to reveal every secret that he wanted to know.[329] According to Jewish myths, Solomon traveled on a great eagle to go to Tadmur, a city in the Syrian desert.[330] These myths were spread in Arabia. We find similar myths of Arabian poets who had relationships with the Jinn, as in a poem of al Nabighah, in which he claimed that the Jinn worked for Solomon to build the city of Tadmur.[331]

The idea that Solomon sat on a carpet carried by the wind is actually a famous Jewish myth. Such a myth was highly regarded by the Jahiliyyah Arabians, who ignored the canonical books of the Old Testament, and the true life of Solomon in these books. They welcomed these myths as if they were true. Mohammed was one of those who believed these myths. The following is one of the Jewish myths about the wind carrying Solomon:

> When God appointed Solomon king over every created thing, He gave him a large carpet sixty miles long and sixty miles wide, made of green silk interwoven with pure gold, and ornamented with figured decorations. Surrounded by his four princes, Asaph b. Berechiah, prince of men; Ramirat, prince of the demons; a lion, prince of beasts; and an eagle, prince of birds; when Solomon sat upon the carpet he was caught up by the wind, and sailed through the air so quickly that he breakfasted at Damascus and supped in Media. One day Solomon was filled with pride at his own greatness and wisdom; and as a punishment, therefore, the wind shook the carpet, throwing down 40,000 men. Solomon chided the wind for the mischief it had done; but the latter rejoined that the king would do well to turn toward God and cease to be proud; whereupon Solomon felt greatly ashamed. [332]

When we compare the above Jewish myth with the expository interpretation of verse 12 of Surah Saba, we see that the Quran was influenced directly by the Jewish myth regarding the carpet that was carried by the wind and took Solomon to have his breakfast in Damascus. In explaining this Quranic verse, I quote the words of ibn Kathir:

> The carpet carried him to the land of Damascus. It was a carpet of wood, upon which were placed all that he needed of the affairs of the kingdoms, including horses, camels, tents, and soldiers. Then he ordered the wind to carry all...there were placed for Solomon 600 thousand seats: in the front seats sat the human believers, then the Jinn believers. Solomon then ordered the birds to make shadow over them. Then he ordered the wind to carry them all. [333]

According to Jahiliyyah mythology the wind carries Solomon

The spread of Jewish and Gnostic myths in Arabia is obvious through the pre-Islamic Arabian poetry. For example, we read in the poetry of al Ashaa:

> That was Solomon to whom the wind was subjected, in addition to the humans and Jinn. [334]

We find the myth about Solomon carried by the wind in the sayings of Waraqa bin Nofel. [335] Waraqa was known to inspire the content of the first Surahs that Mohammed recited in Mecca. All these citations prove that Mohammed had many sources for inserting this myth into the Quran. These kinds of myths were spread in his time among his relatives and the relatives of his first wife (knowing that Waraqa was Khadijah's cousin, Mohammed's first wife).

The effect of the myths attributed to Solomon on those who claimed to be prophets in Arabia, including Mohammed

Many claimed to be prophets at the time of Mohammed. They all were distinguished in imitating and claiming for themselves the mythological privileges attributed to Solomon. Given the nature of the myths attributed to Solomon, he became the most attractive of all the prophets of the Old Testament in the eyes of the Arabians who embraced Judaism, as well as in the eyes of many pre-Islamic Jahiliyyah people. The Arabian "prophets" wanted to imitate these superstitious elements attributed to Solomon, making out of them proofs for their prophetic role. Listeners to those false prophets of Arabia were deceived by their claims and mistook the myths attributed to Solomon for signs of prophecy. Among these "signs" I mention the following:

They claimed to understand the languages of birds and animals and made it a sign of their role as prophet

The "prophets" in Arabia were not the only ones who claimed to understand the languages of birds and animals. There were some among the Persians who claimed the same. Many Persians claimed to understand the language of birds. Ibn Khaldun reports the following:

> When in their return from hunting, al-Mubathan accompanied Bahram, the Persian king. They heard two owls talking. Bahram said: 'Has anyone understood the languages of the birds?' al-Mubathan answered: 'Yes, I know what they said, O king. They discussed a contract of marriage. The female required that the owl male dedicate to her 20 desolate villages. The male owl accepted this condition and said to her "As long as Bahram lives, I will give you one thousand instead of 20.'[336]

Those who claimed to be prophets in Arabia attributed spiritual features to the animals and birds, such as prayer and fasting, as if they were spiritual creatures. At the time of Mohammed there were "prophets," such as Taliha طليحة, who spread the idea that "al Surad," an Arabian bird, fasts. Taliha recited in one of his poems:

> I swear in the doves, pigeons, and the fasting al Surad.[337]

Mohammed supported this Arabian myth, as we see from the following:

> Reported by one of Mohammed's companions: 'The prophet of Allah saw me while I held al surad bird in my hand. And he said: "This is the first bird which fasted the fast of Ashura."'[338] (a fasting ritual which some Arabians, influenced by a Jewish ritual, fasted at the time of Mohammed.)

Museilimeh bin Habib was among those who claimed to be a prophet and preceded Mohammed in this claim. He claimed in the city of Yamameh to be the prophet to al Rahman. Museilimeh claimed to understand the languages of animals and said that animals came to him in order to tell him their problems and to serve him. He also claimed that a she deer used to come down from a mountain in order that he milk it.[339]

Umayyah bin Abi al Salt, a cousin of Mohammed from his mother's side, claimed to be a prophet and said that he understood the languages of animals and birds.[340] He had relationship with the Jinn: a Sheik of Jinn have taught him the term "Bismiki Allahhumma."[341]

Thus, when an animal passed near Umayyah, he stared at it and understood what the animal said. Then he explained the voice of the animal in words. Mohammed adopted the exact same behavior.

Mohammed had to homogenize, or harmonize, with what the Arabians of Jahiliyyah considered as the standard criterion for identifying a true prophet. Thus, he claimed to understand the languages of birds and animals. We read in Sahih al Bukhari that the livestock passed under his hands.[342] He claimed that some animals mentioned in the Quran will be in Paradise, such as the dog of the sleepers, the donkey of Aziz, and the she-camel of Thamud.[343] On many occasions he claimed to speak with cows, donkeys, and camels and resolved their problems. He also used to narrate stories in which animals speak. When people wondered at his stories, he affirmed that he believed that the animals do in fact speak. We present here a story mentioned in Bukhari:

> Reported by abi Hurrerah who said: 'The apostle of Allah prayed the morning prayer. Then he approached the people and said: "A man mounted on a cow and stroked it. She said to him: 'We are not created

for this task, but for ploughing and tilling.' The people said: 'Does a cow speak?' Mohammed answered: 'I believe so; Abu Baker and Omar believe, as well.' Then Mohammed told them: 'While a man was among his sheep, a wolf came and took one sheep. The man traced the wolf until he rescued the sheep. The wolf told him: "You have taken it from me. But when a strong animal will attack the sheep, where there it has no shepherd, she will have no shepherd except me." The People said: "Can a wolf speak?" Mohammed answered: "I believe so; Abu Baker and Omar believe, as well."'[344]

There are cases in which Mohammed claimed to understand the languages of birds, as in the following:

Reported by Anas bin Malek who said: 'I went with the prophet of Allah on a walk. We saw a blind bird hitting his beak against a tree. The apostle of Allah said: "Do you know what it says?" I said: "Allah and his prophet know better." He said: "It said: 'My God, you're the justice and you denied me vision, yet I am hungry.'"'[345]

While Mohammed traveled with his companions, one of them entered under the trees and then returned, having captured with his hand two baby larks cheeping in a low voice. It is well-known that if someone takes a bird's chicks the mother will follow its young, cheeping in a loud voice. The mother came out and began to fly over Mohammed and his companions. Mohammed looked to his companions and said: "Who made this lark to lose its baby birds?" Then Mohammed claimed that the lark complained to him about losing its small birds and asked that they be returned to it. Mohammed claimed that he understood the language of this lark.

Their subjection and utilization of the birds, animals, and reptiles

As according to mythology Solomon had authority over the animals, birds, and reptiles, so those who claimed to be prophets in Arabia also alleged to have this same kind of authority.

Aswad al Ansi, another Arabian who claimed to be a prophet in Mohammed's time, claimed to communicate with animals. Al Zebeidi wrote:

Aswad al Ansi claimed to be a prophet in Yemen. He had a black donkey that he used to order to worship. Then the donkey worshiped.[346]

Mohammed had a special donkey named Ya'for to which he used to speak. There are different opinions on how Mohammed got Ya'for. Ibn

Saad said that Ya'for was given to Mohammed along with Mary "the Coptic from al Muqauqas, the ruler of Alexandria":

> The prophet of Allah was given a gift: Mary the Coptic, her sister Nisreen, his donkey Ya'for, and his she mule Dalal.[347]

The Islamic sources tell us that the donkey Ya'for told Mohammed that he was a descendent of the donkeys that the prophets mounted. Mohammed asked him if he had lust for women. Ya'for answered no. As a result, Mohammed trusted Ya'for and used to send him to peoples' homes. Ya'for used to come and knock on the door with his head. When the owner of the house came out, Ya'for made a gesture that he should come to meet Mohammed.[348]

Talking and fellowshipping with the Jinn became signs of the role of prophet

Those who claimed to be prophets at the time of Mohammed were in relationships with devils. For example, Aswad al Anzi, the one who claimed to be a prophet in Yemen, had relationships with devils. Ibn Taimieh said:

> Aswad al Anzi, who claimed to be a prophet, had devils who informed him of secret things. When Muslims fought against him they feared that the devils would tell him about what they spoke about him.[349]

Yet, Aswad al Anzi considered his relationship with the devils as a sign of his role as a prophet.

Umayyah boasted of his relationships with the Jinn.[350] Mohammed used to meet with the Jinn. In his book Dalael al Nubwah, which means proofs of the prophecy, al Bahiqicited Mohammed's occult encounters with the Jinn as confirmation, or signs, that Mohammed was a prophet. Mohammed accompanied some of his companions to his occultic séances, which are known in our day among the practices of the priests of devils. Yet, such dangerous occultic acts became for Muslims "proofs of Mohammed's prophecy role."[351]

We see, then, that those who claimed to be prophets in Mohammed's day had used the myths attributed to Solomon of subjecting the demons in order to justify their encounters with the devils. They wanted to hide the fact that they were mediums and servants of the wicked spirits. Therefore, every time they met in their séances with the devils, they wanted to appear as if they had a message to the devils and authority over them. This is how they were seen by their naïve followers. Mohammed was not excluded from this phenomenon. He used to have his own seclusion in a cemetery near Mecca called al Hujun.

The life of Mohammed mentions his appointments with devils. Mohammed's appointments with the spirit who pretended to be Gabriel were occult experiences such as Mohammed had in al Hujuneحجون.

Hajun was a mountain near Mecca, as we understand from al Azruqi, where there was an old cemetery.[352] From the book of al Bukhari, we understand that Mohammed often stayed in al Hujune.[353] Mohammed used to accompany his assistants to al Hujune and participate inséances to encounter thousands of Jinn. In one of these encounters, he accompanied Ibn Masud.[354]

Ibn Masud is one of the four people Mohammed suggested read the Quran aloud. Mohammed returned often to al Hujune and spent nights there. The séance to which he brought Ibn Masud is one example of many that Mohammed conducted.[355] He used to spend the nights there, as we understand from Sahih Bukhari.[356]

The devils claimed that their heads were struck by stars when spying on the "ceiling of heaven" while the Quran was inspired to Mohammed. They were struck so that they would not hear the Quran. Then the devils searched for Mohammed and found him sitting under a tree on his return trip from Taif, where he was rejected by the tribe of Thaqif.

The devils who came "to listen to the Quran" under the tree where Mohammed sat claimed they came from Nasibin نصـيبين (a city south of Asia Minor). They came and entered into the tree where Mohammed sat and started talking to Mohammed. The books that narrate the life of Mohammed report that those devils returned and told the rest of the devils about the Quran and Islam. Thus, the delegations of the devils started visiting Mohammed in order to listen to the Quran and become Muslims. About this we read:

"When the seven Jinn of Nasibin left the tree they came to their people as monitors and admonishers. They returned as a delegation with others from their people to Mohammed while he was at Mecca. Their number was 300. They went to al Hujune. One of them came to the apostle of Allah and said to him, 'Our people came to al Hujune in order to meet with you.' The apostle of Allah gave him an appointment to meet with them in al Hujune during an hour of the night."[357]

Ibn Kathir reported that the Jinn became Muslims at al Hujune. They started calling others to Islam.[358]

How did these 300 Jinn devils come to know about al Hujune and propose to meet Mohammed there? Why exactly was the appointed meeting place in al Hujune, the cemetery where Mohammed used to have his occultic séances? This demonstrates that these devils had some familiarity with the daily routine of Mohammed and were familiar with the place where he had his occultic séances. It seems likely that they were the same devils of his old and continuing occultic séances in the same cemetery, al Hujune!

At the end our research on Solomon's myths, we conclude that these myths were not mentioned by the first source that mentioned Solomon – the Bible. Rather, they spread among groups, such as the Jahiliyyah people, who were inclined to believe theses myths. Although these type of myths – such as the wind carrying the prophets, or subjugating the devils and using them in great enterprises and for military service, and speaking with animals and bird – were of the primitive style and form of some ancient stories, those who claimed to be prophets in Arabia used them in their poems and claims. Mohammed, too, used them and incorporated them in his Quran. Thus, Mohammed belonged to a group of men who arose in his day claiming to be prophets.

The Queen of Saba
The Hoopoe, Solomon, and the Queen of Saba

We will contrast the Biblical narration of the visit of the Queen of Saba to Solomon with the narration of the Quran.

First of all, I'd like to turn your attention to the trading relationship between Saba, called Sheba, in Yemen and the Mediterranean countries such as Israel.

God gave Solomon a great gift of wisdom. So much so, that other rulers heard about his wisdom and came to him bearing gifts. The Queen of Sheba was among them. In I Kings, chapter 10, we read about the visit of the Queen of Sheba to King Solomon. The Bible says:

> Now when the Queen of Sheba heard of the fame of Solomon concerning the name of the Lord, she came to test him with hard questions. She came to Jerusalem with a very great retinue, with camels that bore spices, very much gold, and precious stones, and when she came to Solomon, she spoke with him about all that was in her heart. So Solomon answered all her questions; there was nothing so difficult for the king that he could not explain it to her. Then she gave the king one hundred and twenty talents of gold, spices in great quantity, and precious stones. There never again came such abundance of spices as the Queen of Sheba gave to King Solomon.

When did the Queen of Sheba visit Solomon?

The book of I Kings specifies that King Solomon had completed most of his important accomplishments before the visit of the Queen of Sheba. Among the things he did was the construction of the Temple at Jerusalem, the construction of his palace, and the building of his marine fleet with the help of Hiram, King of the Phoenician city of Tyre. (Solomon later married Hiram's daughter.) Solomon ascended to the throne in the year 971 B.C.

Five years later, he began building the Temple, which he finished in seven years. That takes us to around 959 B.C. Then he started building his palace. According to I Kings 7:1, "Solomon took thirteen years to build his own house." The completion of his palace brings us to about 945 B.C. Then he wanted to trade gold with Ophir on the Persian Gulf, so he built a fleet of ships in Ezion Geber near Elath on the Red Sea. We read about this in I Kings 9: 26-28, which says:

> King Solomon also built a fleet of ships at Ezion Geber, which is near Elath on the shore of the Red Sea, in the land of Edom. Then Hiram sent his servants with the fleet, seamen who knew the sea, to work with the servants of Solomon. And they went to Ophir and acquired four hundred and twenty talents of gold from there.

According to the Bible, all these accomplishments were made before the Queen of Sheba visited Jerusalem. When we add all the numbers, we conclude that the visit of the Queen of Sheba was between 940 and 935 B.C.

How the Queen of Sheba knew of the wisdom of Solomon

We could ask ourselves how the Queen of Sheba heard of the wisdom of Solomon. Perhaps Sabaean merchants were already traveling the land route through northern Arabia by the 10th century B.C. If so, the cities on the oases of northern Arabia, such as Teima, Dedan and Qedar, may have been only small villages, which facilitated trade along the land route from Yemen to Israel. This is probably the reason the Queen was convinced to travel by land to Jerusalem rather than by sea. In the previous century, it was impossible to make the trip by land.

I believe that Solomon's name was famous in Saba many years before the visit of the Queen of Sheba because of his ships, built many years before her visit. The fleet traveled across the Red Sea to Ophir on the Persian Gulf and made many stops along the way, many of which were to Sabaean ports, the most important ports on the Red Sea. The Sabaean ports were places where ships traded merchandise and re-supplied themselves with water and food. This made the King of Israel well-known among sailors for his wisdom and the beauty and greatness of his Temple which, along with the Great Wall of China and the pyramids, was already considered one of the greatest marvels of the ancient world. What else, other than the wisdom of Solomon, which impressed Israel and other kings of the earth, would have been the reason for the servants of Solomon, who served in the ships, to speak to the Sabaeans about him?

Many years before Solomon's fleet was constructed, King Hiram, the Phoenician king of Tyre, began sailing his fleet on the Red Sea to the Persian Gulf. Hiram traveled to Ophir, passing through the Sabaean ports. As we saw previously, Hiram traded in the Mediterranean and even provided Solomon, his son-in-law, with gold, special wood and precious stones. Mediterranean nations were connected to the Gulf region, where there were important kingdoms, such as Dilmun (which is present Bahrain) and Magan (which is present Oman). There were also rich ports, such as Jerra, which traded with India and made far-away Asian products available to the Phoenicians. So the main news of kings, like the wise and famous Solomon, was spread to many kingdoms through this international marine trade. This allowed other rulers to learn about the wisdom of Solomon and, consequently, prompted them to try to create friendships with him. We see this in the Biblical narrative of I Kings 4: 31, 34, where it is written:

> For he was wiser than any other man...Men of all nations came to listen to Solomon's wisdom, sent by all the kings of the world who had heard of his wisdom.

All the marine traffic from India to the Persian Gulf passed through the ports of Saba, carrying with it all the news of the Mediterranean, especially news of the famous King Solomon who was given special wisdom from God. He became known in the ports of Saba. So how would the Queen of Saba (Sheba) be the only woman in Saba to not hear about the wise king of Jerusalem? How would she be the only monarch of the earth who did not hear about him? The marine connection between Solomon and Ophir on the Gulf region through Saba leads us to believe that the Queen of Saba was the first monarch of the earth to hear about Solomon's kingdom. Also, this leads us to believe that the kingdom which Solomon was most acquainted with was the kingdom of Saba and her Queen.

The mythological Quranic narration regarding the visit of the Queen of Sheba to Solomon, copied from the II Targum of Esther.

You will find this difficult to believe, but the Quran claims that King Solomon never heard of the Kingdom of Saba or its famous Queen until a bird, a hoopoe, told him about her. The Quran in Surah 27, called al-Naml, or the chapter of ants, gives us a mythological narration of the visit of the Queen of Saba to Solomon. Solomon gathers his army composed of Jinn (meaning devils), men, and birds. Afterward Solomon missed the hoopoe and threatened to execute him. The hoopoe returned to announce the discovery of the Kingdom of Saba and its Queen. Then Solomon sent a message with the hoopoe threatening to wage war if the Queen did not submit to him. The Queen submitted but before she arrived, the Jinn, under the order of Solomon, brought her throne to Jerusalem in only one second.

This Quranic myth is copied with little variation from the mythological Jewish book called the Second Targum of Esther. The bird in the Targum is a wild rooster, while in the Quran it is the hoopoe. The wild rooster is another name for the hoopoe. The Targum uses eagles as carriers of great things to Solomon, whereas, the Quran uses the Jinn. Other than this, the Quranic narration is identical to the Targum.

The date of writing of The Second Targum of Esther

Scholars, such as S. Gelbhaus, date the writing of The Second Targum of Esther to the 4th century A.D.[359] Grossfeld, a professor of Hebrew and Aramaic languages at the University of Wisconsin, and a founding member of the Association for Targumic Studies, also maintains the 4th century A.D. as being the date for the writing. After mentioning the various scholars' ideas about the date of the Targum, he added:

> Perhaps even the 4th century C.E. The internal evidence for the earlier date is of a historical nature and concerns, as P. Churgin already pointed out, the derisive attitude towards Jewish laws and customs (3:8) ...An even more telling clue is contained in Ms P on 1:1 where the eighth of the ten kingdoms that ruled or were destined to rule, is described as that of wicked Rome, whom the God of Israel may speedily eradicate, and may the kingdom be taken away from them and given to the Messiah, son of David, who will be the ninth king. Such a period, describing an extreme state of persecution under the Roman yoke which could only be relieved by Messianic redemption, could very well fit the early 4th century C.E., as the time of composition of Targum Sheni.[360]

In analyzing The Second Targum of Esther, we are able to identify passages in the book that helps us easily assign a date during the Roman reign over Palestine. The book expresses the Jews' conditions during that period. In the version P and 1:1, which Grossfeld has quoted, the Roman

Empire is mentioned as reigning at the time of the author. Expressing the severe persecutions that the Jews were enduing at the hands of the Roman Empire, he described it as "the wicked Rome," hoping that God would remove it quickly, and remove the reign from the Romans and be given to the Messiah son of David. The description in this passage matches events occurring at the beginning of the fourth century A.D., as being the date of the Targum. In the fifth chapter of the second Targum of Esther we find the following sentence: "the guilty city Rome, may it be rooted from the world."[361] This is a further proof that the author was still under the authority of the Romans when he wrote his book. By analyzing the first chapter of the Targum, we notice further confirmation that the author lived under the reign of the Roman Empire: while he mentioned the kingdoms then reigning as being great empires, he did not mention the Byzantine Empire, but he did refer to Rome. He writes in the first chapter:

> And it came to pass in the days of Ahasuerus, one of the ten kings who once ruled and are to rule the world in the future. And these are the ten kings. The first kingdom is that of the King of kings, the Lord of hosts, — may it be speedily magnified upon us. The second is that of Nimrod; the third of Pharaoh, king of Egypt; the fourth of Israel; the fifth of Nebuchadnezzar, king of Babylon; the sixth of Ahasuerus; the seventh of Greece; the eighth of Rome; the ninth of the King Messiah, the son of David; the tenth (again) of the King of kings, the Lord of hosts — may it be speedily revealed to us, and to all the inhabitants of the earth.[362]

The author of the book mentioned the great kingdoms that reigned in the world, placing Nimrod's kingdom in Mesopotamia first, then the Pharaohs' kingdom, followed by the kingdom of Israel (he considered that Solomon reigned over all the earth). Then Nebuchadnezzar's kingdom, which was supplanted by the Persian kingdom, then the Greeks (he intended Alexander the Macedonian), and finally Rome. Then he spoke about the kingdoms which would come after: which would be the Kingdom of the Messiah, then the "the King of kings, the Lord of hosts." Thus, he lived when Rome still reigned.

Various opinions about the date of the book have resulted due to the wrong idea by some that the late editing of a book is an indication of its date of composition. But there are many books where we know the dates of their ancient composition, and yet they were later subjected to further editing by the copyists.

Mohammed's acquaintance with the myths of the Targum

Mohammed's acquaintance with the Targum is confirmed, not only through the myth of the hoopoe and the queen of Saba; but also through other information the Quran and Mohammed had mentioned in his Hadith, whose source is known to be the second Targum of Esther. As an example, in one of his Hadiths that I will discuss, in the chapter about Nimrod, Mohammed claimed Nimrod reigned on the whole earth. He claimed Solomon and Nebuchadnezzar reigned over the earth as well. He claimed that two of these kings were believers: Solomon and Alexander the Macedonian, while the other two, Nimrod and Nebuchadnezzar, were infidels.[363]

This Hadith of Mohammed is identical to what the second Targum of Esther stated. This mythological chronology belongs to the Targum.

The similarities of the Islamic expositions of the Quran and the Targum, such as the mention of the hair that was seen on the Queen of Saba's leg when she raised her clothes, is a clear demonstration that the Targum was spread throughout Arabia. The expositors of the Quran referred to the Targum myths in order to interpret the verse of Quran that says when the Queen entered where Solomon sat and thought it was water, she raised her clothes above her leg. It is known that the Islamic writers retuned to the sources of the Quran in order to interpret it. For example, Wahab bin Munabbeh spoke about the land of darkness, which Du Al Qarnayn entered in his search for immortality and the spring of life. Wahab also spoke about the fish which was revived in the spring of life. These myths are originally found in the book of Pseudo Callisthenes. Wahab was born in 36 H.

The Targum was spread in Arabia many centuries before Mohammed

The Second Targum of Esther was widely spread among Arabian tribes who embraced a form of Judaism. We find this myth in Arabian poems written before Mohammed's time, and in the poems of people claiming to be prophets in Arabia before Mohammed's time. One of these was Umayyah bin abi al-Salt, a cousin to Mohammed on his mother's side of the family.[364] Prior to Umayyah, Tubb'a, the Yemeni leader who occupied Mecca around the year 425 A.D., spoke about the hoopoe, as well as Solomon and the Queen of Saba.[365] This is because Tubb'a, when he occupied Yathrib (Medina), took two rabbis from the Jewish communities there and brought them to Yemen. Al Taberi mentioned the names of the two rabbis: Kaab and Asad.[366] كعبا وأسد

The rabbis instructed Tubb'a by teaching him many Judaic myths, which he then incorporated into his poems.[367] Many scholars, who specialize in the pre-Islamic history of Arabia, such as De Lacy O'Leary, maintain that some of the Jewish tribes in Arabia, such as Beni al Natheer and Beni Qarithah, the two tribes in Medina, were Arabian tribes who embraced Judaism. Others believe that most of the North Arabian Jews were Edomites.[368] The names of many Arabian Jewish tribes were actually Arabic tribes, such as Beni al Natheer and Beni Qarithah. Even their poetry had an Arabic style. In addition to this, other factors also point to an Arabic origin, causing us to believe they embraced Judaism. Some Jewish historians maintain that the Jews of Arabia were separated from the rest of the Jews because Arabian Jews did not observe the Mosaic Law and did not submit to the Talmud traditions. True Jews did not accept them as Jews because they did not share the same doctrines.[369]

However, Jewish mythology, such as the II Targum of Esther, found acceptance by the Arabian tribes who embraced Judaism. Those books were considered as legal canonical writings, equal to the books of Moses and the other prophets of the Old Testament. The superstitious nature of the Arabians caused them to believe in these and other mythological writings. This may explain why Jewish myths so easily spread through the Arabian Jewish tribes to people like Tubb'a ', who was discipled by the two rabbis of the tribe of Beni Qaritha. It also explains the presence of these myths in the poetry of Umayyah bin al Salt. Among such myths was the myth of the hoopoe which discovered the kingdom of Saba and announced such discovery to Solomon. This proves that the book of II Targum of Esther at the time of Tubb'a (in the first part of the 5th century A.D.) was spread among the Jewish communities of Arabia.

The accuracy of the Quranic borrowing from the Targum

This Quranic myth is copied from the II Targum of Esther, with little variation. As I mentioned above, most of the details are identical; for example:

And when the heart of King Solomon was once merry with wine, he sent to invite all the kings of the East and of the West who were near the land of Israel, and he lodged them in the royal palace. And when again merry with wine, he ordered that the violins, cymbals, tambourines, and harps upon which his father played should be brought to him. And, further merry with wine, he commanded the wild beasts, the birds, the reptiles, the devils, demons, and spirits to be brought, that they should dance before him, to show his greatness to the kings who were staying with him. The royal scribes called them all by their names, and they came together without being bound or ibrced, and without even a man leading them.

At that time, the cock of the wood was missed among the fowls, and was not found. Then the king commanded in anger that he should appear before him, or else he would destroy him. Then the cock of the wood answered and said to King Solomon : " lord of the earth, incline thine ears and hear my words. Are there not tln-ee months since thou hast put counsel in my heart and words of truth upon my tongue ? Since then I have not eaten any food, nor drank any water, and have flown all over the world and made an inspection. I thought, Is there a country or a kingdom which is not subject to my lord the king ? Then I saw a certain country, the name of whose fortified town is Kitor, whose dust is more precious than gold, and where silver lies about like dung in the streets. Trees also are there standing from primeval times, and are watered from the garden of Eden.

Great crowds of people are there from the garden of Eden, having crowns upon their heads, who know nothing of warfare, nor can they draw the bow. For, indeed, I have seen one woman who rules over them all, and her name is Queen of Saba. Now, if it please my lord the king, I shall gird my loins like a mighty man, and shall arise and go to the city of Kitor, in the land of Saba, and shall bind its kings and governor in chains of iron, and shall bring them to my lord the king.[370]

Here the verses of Surah An-Naml, which corresponds to the paragraphs of the Tagrum:

He inspected the birds; and he said: "Why is it I see not the Hoopoe? Or is he among the absentees? "I will certainly punish him with a severe penalty, or execute him, unless he bring me a clear reason (for absence)." But the Hoopoe tarried not far: he (came up and) said: "I have compassed (territory) which thou hast not compassed, and I have come to thee from Saba with tidings true. "I found (there) a woman ruling over them and provided with every requisite; and she has a magnificent throne. "I found her and her people worshipping the sun besides Allah. Satan has made their deeds seem pleasing in their eyes, and has kept them away from the path, so they receive no guidance. (Surah An-Naml 27:20-24

Let us compare between the narration of the Targum and the Quran. We notice that in both narrations:

1- Solomon in the Quran inspected the birds, whereas in the Targum he inspected the wild beasts, the birds, the reptiles, the devils, demons, and spirits. The Quran wanted to say that when Solomon reached the inspection of the birds, he noticed that the hoopoe was absent.

2- in both narrations we notice that cock of the wood(in the Targum) called the hoopoe (in the Quran) was absent. The cock of the wood is a title of the hoopoe.

3- in both narrations, Solomon threatened the cock of the wood-hoopoe if he does not appear before him.

4- in both narrations the cock of the wood-hoopoe declared his discovery of the kingdom of Saba, and that a woman reigns over them, and about the richness of the Queen and her kingdom.

The Targum continues its narration:

This speech pleased the king, and royal scribes were called, a letter was written and tied to the wings of the cock of the wood, who lifted up his wings and soared up in the air, and compelled other birds to fly with it. Then they came to the city of Kitor, in the land of Saba. Toward morning the queen went out to worship the sea, when the birds obscured the sunlight, so that the queen out of astonishment took hold of her clothes and tore them in pieces. The cock of the wood now came down, and she observed that a letter was tied to its wings, which she at once opened and read what was written therein, as follows : "From me. King Solomon, peace to thee and to thy princes. Thou must certainly know that the Holy One, blessed be He ! made me to rule over the wild beasts, over the fowls of the air, over devils, demons, and spirits, and that all the kings of the East and of the West, of the South and of the North, come to salute me. If thou wilt come and salute me, I shall show thee greater dignity than I shall show to all the kings that are sojourning with me ; but if thou wilt not come to salute me, I shall send kings, legions, and riders against thee. But if thou wilt ask. What sort of kings, legions, and riders has King Solomon ? So know, that the wild beasts are the kings and the legions, and the riders are the birds in the air. My army consists of devils, demons, and spirits, who will strangle you in your beds, the wild beasts will kill you in your houses, and the fowls of the air will devour your flesh in the field.[371]

We return to verses 28-31 to see points of similarities between both narrations:

Go you with this letter of mine, and deliver it to them, then draw back from them, and see what (answer) they return." She said: "O chiefs! Verily! Here is delivered to me a noble letter, "Verily it is from Sulaiman (Solomon), and verily, it (reads): In the Name of Allah, the Most Gracious, the Most Merciful: "Be you not exalted against me, but come to me as Muslims."(Surah An-Naml 27:28-31)

We notice that in both narrations, Solomon sent a letter to the Queen of Saba through the cock of the wood-hoopoe. The Targum uses a Hebrew greeting, whereas the Quran uses an Islamic greeting (In the Name of Allah, the Most Gracious, the Most Merciful). In both narrations, Solomon required from the queen and her army submission. We notice that the army of Solomon is formed of devils, Jinn, beasts and birds. We find in the same Surah An-Naml and verse 17 the following words:

And there were gathered before Solomon his hosts of jinn and men, and birds, and they all were set in battle order

The Targum narration continues:

When the queen heard the words of the letter she again rent her clothes. Then she sent for the elders and prominent men, and said to them, " Do you know what King Solomon has sent to me ? " They answered, " We do not know Solomon, nor do we esteem his kingdom." But she did not trust them, nor listen to their words, but caused all the ships to be collected and loaded with presents of pearls and of precious stones. And she also sent him six thousand boys and girls who were born in the same year, month, day, and hour, and who were of the same stature and of the same proportion; and they were all dressed in purple.[372]

Let us see the verses of the Quran that correspond to the So when (the messengers with the present) came to Sulaiman (Solomon), he said: "Will you help me in wealth? What Allah has given me is better than that which He has given you! Nay, you rejoice in your gift!" words of the Targum:

She said: "O chiefs! Advise me in (this) case of mine. I decide no case till you are present with me (and give me your opinions)." They said: "We have great strength, and great ability for war, but it is for you to command: so think over what you will command." She said: "Verily kings, when they enter a town (country), they defile it and make the most honourable amongst its people the lowest. And thus they do. But verily! I am going to send him a present, and see with what (answer) the messengers return." So when (the messengers with the present) came to Solomon, he said: "Will you help me in wealth? What Allah has given me is better than that which He has given you! Nay, you rejoice in your gift! Return unto them. We verily shall come unto them with hosts that they cannot resist, and we shall drive them out from thence with shame, and they will be abased. (Surah An-Naml 27:32-37)

We notice in both narrations the queen gathered her elders and chiefs of her kingdom, and from them an advice. In both narrations we find the chiefs refusing the idea of submitting to Solomon; they showed that they considered them strong and careless of the power of Solomon and his threat. In both narrations the queen did not listen to their advice, but she sent precious gifts to Solomon.

The Targum mentioned that when the Queen of Saba entered the palace of Solomon, she thought the king is setting in the water, so she lifted her clothes from her legs. The Quran copied this text from the Targum. I mention first the words of the Targum:

> Then Benayahu conducted her to the king, who, when he heard that she was coming, went and sat down in an apartment of glass. When the queen saw the king sitting there, she thought in her heart, and in fact dress to cross the water, when the king noticed that her foot was full of hair. He said to her, "Thy beauty is the beauty of women, and thy hair is the hair of men ; hair is becoming to a man, but to a woman it is a shame.[373]

We encounter the same idea in the Quran. We read in verse 44 of the same Surah An Naml:

> It was said unto her: Enter the hall. And when she saw it she deemed it a pool and bared her legs. (Solomon) said: Lo! it is a hall, made smooth, of glass. She said: My Lord! Lo! I have wronged myself, and I surrender with Solomon unto Allah, the Lord of the Worlds.

What is narrated in the Quran is a faithful abbreviation of the narration found in The Targum. The result of the acceptance of Jewish myths and the myths of other peoples, were incorporated into the Quran in an abbreviated form in its poetry and rhyming style. So those myths were translated into the Arabic stylings of those who claimed to be prophets, such as Umayyah ibn al Salt. However, this did not change the fact that they are still myths, and not inspired.

Nimrod

Nimrod in the Quran

According to Genesis 10:8-11, Nimrod was the first builder of the old cities in Mesopotamia. He was the son of Cush, the son of Ham, the son of Noah. Among the cities Nimrod built was Erech, identified by scholars as Uruk. It lies about 35 miles from the city of Ur and about 30 miles east of the Arabic city of Samawah in southern Iraq. Erech was found in the city's archeological findings that date back to the fourth millennium B.C. Archeologists today maintain that Uruk existed before 5000 B.C. in what is known as the Eridu period. Thus, it is highly probable that Nimrod built the city at the end of the 6th millennium B.C. Today, Uruk is considered the most ancient city in the world. Thus, the Bible mention of it as being one of the first cities built in the world is a proof of the truthiness of God's inspiration to Moses, who wrote the book of Genesis led by the Spirit of God. Uruk later lost its importance. In Moses' time, that is the 15th century B.C., Uruk was without importance and was not a candidate to be selected by any writer for the title of most ancient city in the world.

Islamic genealogies correctly state that Nimrod was the son of Cush. Sometimes they made him as son of Canaan, the father of Cush, but incorrectly state that he lived around the time of Abraham.[374]

This false claim about Nimrod was made to conform to a mistake in the Quran, which we understand from the expositors of the Quran, who claimed that the monarch with whom Abraham dealt with was Nimrod,[375] assuming Nimrod reigned at the time of Abraham, who lived in the 20 century B. C. The Quran says that the king, who is identified by Mohammed's companions and the expositors of the Quran as Nimrod, persecuted Abraham and cast him into a fire that did not harm him. We read this in Surah al-Anbiya' 21:51-70 and Surah al-Safat 37:95.

Midrash Rabbah, a mythological Jewish book, is the source of the Quranic narration about Nimrod and Abraham.

Many Jewish books were widely spread among Arabian tribes who embraced Judaism. At the time of Mohammed, the myth of the Quran regarding Abraham and Nimrod was taken from a Jewish book called Midrash Rabbah. The narration of the Quran corresponds perfectly to this Jewish book. A Jewish writer found in the Bible that Nimrod built the oldest Mesopotamian cities, but the writer incorrectly applied a story from the book of Daniel to Abraham. The book of Daniel told of the three Jewish young men who refused to worship a statue of Nebuchadnezzar, King of Babylon, and were cast into a fire that did not harm them. However, the writer of Midrash Rabbah ignored the fact that more than 3,000 years separated Abraham from Nimrod.

The confusion of Mohammed regarding the history of Alexander, Nimrod and Solomon.

In his Hadith, Mohammed claims that Nimrod reigned over the entire earth and that Solomon, Nebuchadnezzar and Dhu al-Qarnayn ruled over the entire earth, as well. Dhu al-Qarnayn means the "one with two horns," a title for Alexander the Great, as shown by the book of Pseudo Callisthenes and Syriac writings, that depended on this book.

Mohammed stated that two were believers: Solomon and Alexander the Great; and that two were infidels: Nimrod and Nebuchadnezzar.[376] This Hadith of Mohammed caused Islamic writers and the more prominent expositors of the Quran, such as Mujahed, al Qurtubi, ibn Kathir and ibn Hayyan, to embrace Mohammed's claim.[377]

This assertion is clearly incorrect because not one of these men ruled the whole earth. Alexander the Great did occupy a small part of Europe, in addition to his conquests in the Middle East and parts of Asia. Solomon extended his domain from Israel into parts of Syria and Trans Jordan. Nebuchadnezzar occupied the Fertile Crescent and Egypt. Nimrod's reign was limited to Mesopotamia. So none of them ruled the entire earth.

Mohammed's Hadith is also clearly incorrect regarding its claims about who believers were and who were infidels. Alexander the Great was known to be a pagan king with a passion for the idols of his conquered cities. In spite of this, Mohammed claimed that Alexander was a Muslim leader who made a holy war, or Jihad, to spread Islam throughout the world. Such myths of the Quran about Nimrod, Nebuchadnezzar, Alexander the Great and Solomon are derived from Jewish myths that were widespread in the area of Medina. They have as a source The Second Targum of Esther, the mythological book which I previously mentioned when discussing the Quranic myth about Solomon and the hoopoe. By analyzing the first chapter of The Targum, we notice that the author lived during the time of the Roman Empire. I quote the verses from the first chapter of this book, which I previously quoted:

> And it came to pass in the days of Ahasuerus, one of the ten kings who once ruled and are to rule the world in the future. And these are the ten kings. The first kingdom is that of the King of kings, the Lord of hosts, — may it be speedily magnified upon us. The second is that of Nimrod; the third of Pharaoh, king of Egypt; the fourth of Israel; the fifth of Nebuchadnezzar, king of Babylon; the sixth of Ahasuerus; the seventh of Greece; the eighth of Rome; the ninth of the King Messiah, the son of David; the tenth (again) of the King of kings, the Lord of hosts — may it be speedily revealed to us, and to all the inhabitants of the earth. [378]

The Hadith of Mohammed corresponds to what the author of the Targum claimed. We saw that the author listed among those who reigned the whole earth: Nimrod, Nebuchadnezzar, Alexander, Pharaoh, and the king of Israel (he intended Solomon. The idea of Mohammed that those who reigned in the whole earth were four, the ones mentioned above, proves the influence of the Targum on the Arabian Jews and Mohammed.

In the same first chapter of the Targum, the author mentioned five wicked people among them Nimrod.[379] We also read in the Targum:

> There were four men who ruled from one end of the world to the other. Two of them belonged to the nations of the world, and two to Israel. Solomon and Ahab were of Israel…The universal kings from the nations are Nebuchadnezzar and Achashverosh.[380]

We notice the similarity with Mohammed's idea. However, Mohammed depended on the beginning of the first chapter of The Targum, which mentioned Nimrod, Pharaoh, Nebuchadnezzar, Solomon, and the "Greece" (meaning Alexander the Great). Thus, he placed Ahab with Alexander, and Ahasuerus with Nebuchadnezzar. We also notice the influence of the Arabian Jews who depended on mythological Jewish literature, such as Midrash Rabbah and The Second Targum of Esther, in shaping Mohammed's language on history and the unhistorical chronology which he adopted.

Alexander

The Quranic myths about Alexander the great

Alexander the Great was known to be a zealot pagan and polytheistic worshiper of idols. But Mohammed claimed that Alexander was a servant of Allah, who made Jihads, or holy wars, to spread Islam throughout the ancient world.

Like the prophets of the Arabian Jinn religion, Mohammed wrote important historical figures into the religion of Islam. Mohammed also imitated Mani, the founder of Manichaeism, in making historical figures a part of his religion in order to make it appear as if the religions of Mani and Mohammed were known many centuries before they had lived!

For example, Mohammed claimed Alexander the Great was a Muslim leader who made Jihads to spread the religion of Allah throughout the world. At the time of Mohammed the Quran called him "Dhu al- Qarnayn," which means "the one with two horns." This term is also used in Pseudo-Callisthenes, a book written by an unknown man who lived in Alexandrian-Egypt around the year 200 A.D. The author attributed the book to Callisthenes, a companion of Alexander the Great. This book was second only to the Bible as the most distributed book in the Pre-Islamic centuries, and it was translated into many languages. Many versions of the book exist today. I'll discuss this in detail when we study the Pseudo-Callisthenes' book and the Syriac writings based on it. Old versions of The Romance of Alexander were found which carry the title of "Dhu al-Qarnayn."

Alexander the Great was portrayed on the coins of the kingdom with two horns to symbolize his conquests of the West and the East. Later we will see that the title "the one with two horns," was assigned to Alexander, and known in Arabia before Islam.

Alexander was known to be the most polytheistic pagan worshipper in history. He consulted the priests of the Greek gods before any military campaign, and worshipped the idols of each city he conquered. He claimed that he was a god, the son of the Greek god, Zeus. When Alexander heard that Philotas, the commander of the Companion Cavalry, had mocked his claim to be son of Zeus Ammon, Alexander was so angry that he arrested Philotas, put him on trial and condemned him to death. Alexander's claim to be deity was something mentioned by all the classical writers. The historian Agatharchides said:

> Alexander, who was invincible on the battlefield, was completely helpless in his personal relationships. For he was ensnared by praise, and when he called himself the son of Zeus he did not think he was being mocked, but thought he was being honored for his passion for the impossible and his forgetfulness of nature.[381]

Aristobulus, an eyewitness working as an engineer for Alexander, gives us the reason why Alexander was planning to conquer Arabia. Aristobulus says:

> When Alexander knew the Arabians worshipped two main deities, he took it for granted that they would worship him as a third deity if he conquered them and allowed them to keep their ancestral independence.[382]

Yet, Mohammed still claimed that Alexander was a Muslim devoted to Allah. Mohammed said Alexander's campaigns were Jihads for Allah in order to justify Mohammed's own campaigns against innocent Arabian and Jewish tribes.

Dhu al-Qarnayn's journey to the uttermost parts of the earth

Mohammed imprisoned his Quran in a myth that was widespread in his time regarding Alexander the Great's journey as described in the book Pseudo-Callisthenes, and the Syriac writings that were based on this book. A man from the city of Alexandria wrote a mythological book, which he falsely attributed to Callisthenes, a companion of Alexander. His book became known as Pseudo-Callisthenes, and spread throughout the ancient world, becoming second only to the Bible. The book dates to around 200 A.D. and Syriac writings dating back to the 5th and 6th centuries A.D. were built on this book.

The purpose of Alexander's journey, according to this mythological book, was to search for immortality, and subdue the nations to the gods.

There are similarities between Alexander's journey in Pseudo-Callisthenes, and Gilgamesh's journey in his search for immortality. (see Dr. Amari's upcoming book Eschatology in the Bible and the Quran.)

According to Pseudo-Callisthenes and the Syriac writings, there are three main destinations in Alexander's journey which are virtually identical to destinations mentioned in the Quran in abbreviated form, as in the following:

Alexander traveled to the western edge of the earth, where he found the sun setting near a fetid sea (in the Quran, the sun sets in a fetid spring).

The second destination is toward the eastern edge of the earth, where Alexander found the inhabitants living without protection from the blaze of the sun — since the sun melts even the rocks, no houses could be built there.

In the third destination Alexander reached two mountains that surrounded the whole earth; which had an aperture between their two edges. Behind those mountains lived a savage people who represented a danger for the rest of the inhabitants of the earth. The people there complained to Alexander about this savage people; resulting in Alexander building gates to close the aperture between the edges of the two mountains. By doing so, he imprisoned the savage people behind the gates until the last day of history. In one of the Syriac letters, this savage people became Gog and Magog. In the Quran, the gates became a big dam. Under the influence of the Syriac writing, the Quran also adopted the names of Gog and Magog for this savage people.

Mohammed's dependence upon the myths of Pseudo-Callisthenes and the Syriac writings, which depended upon the book, is confirmed from other excerpts of literature encountered in the Quran and the Hadiths.

In fact, in the Quran, an important part of the story of al Khader depended upon Pseudo-Callisthenes. In this book, Alexander was told that the spring of life is found in the land of darkness, where there are many springs. Alexander is advised to have his cook carry a dead salted fish, and expose it to the water of each spring he finds. The spring where the fish would be revived would be the spring of life. The cook washed the fish in a certain spring, and the fish returned to life and flew into the waters of the spring. The cook was afraid the king would ask him to bring the fish which returned to life, so he threw himself in the water to look for it, but failed to find the fish. He returned, telling the king that he had found the spring of life.[383]

A similar story is told in a Greek version of Pseudo-Callisthenes where Alexander passed by a spring in the region of darkness, and it gave new life to the dead salted fish.[384] This Greek version is known as β, to distinguish it from the Greek versions of Alpha and Gamma. The β version goes back to the third century - till before the year 550 A.D.[385]

The reality is that the author wanted to imitate the Epic of Gilgamesh, where we find Gilgamesh traveling in search of immortality. Then he reached Ut-napisti, the Sumerian hero of the flood, who advised him that, in order to become immortal, he should eat from the "plant of life." Gilgamesh failed, however, to eat from the plant, even after he found it, because it was stolen by a serpent. Pseudo-Callisthenes replaced the plant of life with the spring of life. Just as Gilgamesh failed to eat from the plant of immortality, likewise God hid the spring of life from the eyes of Alexander, even after he found it.

We find something similar in the Quran regarding the salt fish and the spring of life. Allah gave Moses an order to carry a whale in a vessel — which was, to the expositors of the Quran, interpreted as a big salted fish. Moses was told where the fish would be lost; where it would live and enter into the water, where there would be an immortal man called al Khader, who lived near the spring of life which gave him his immortality.

Joshua bin Nun, the servant of Moses, became worried because the fish came to life and flew in the water. But Moses, upon hearing this news, was pleased, saying that this is exactly the thing which he wanted to happen, because then he will meet al Khader near where the fish came to life.

In some versions of the book of Pseudo-Callisthenes, the cook immersed his body in the spring where the fish revived and obtained immortality. In other versions, we read that instead of the cook, a leader in the army of Alexander who was ordered by Alexander to enter the land of darkness in search of the spring of life, carrying a salted fish. After the fish was revived and he was immersed in the waters of the spring, he obtained immortality and obtained a special knowledge, which nobody else had.[386]

These cases formed the foundation for stories in the Quran of the immortal and wise al Khader and the dead whale which was suddenly revived.

There are many of Mohammed's Hadiths that indicate Mohammed's acquaintance of the myths of Pseudo-Callisthenes and the Syriac writings. (I refer the reader to my book Eschatology in the Bible and the Quran.) In this section I will focus on the three destinations of Dhu al Qarnayn's journey in the Quran, and the same destinations attributed to Alexander the Great in Pseudo-Callisthenes and the two main Syriac writings.

Dhu al Qarnayn's journey according to the Quran.

We find Dhu al Qarnayn's journey narrated in Surah al Kahf and the following verses:

> They ask thee concerning Zul-qarnain. Say, "I will rehearse to you something of his story." Verily We established his power on earth, and We gave him the ways and the means to all ends. One (such) way he followed, Until, when he reached the setting of the sun, he found it set in a fetid spring: Near it he found People: We said: "O Zul-qarnain! (thou hast authority,) either to punish them, or to treat them with kindness." He said: "Whoever doth wrong, him shall we punish; then shall he be sent back to his Lord; and He will punish him with a punishment unheard-of (before). But whoever believes, and works righteousness,- he shall have a goodly reward, and easy will be his task as We order it by our Command." Then followed he (another) way, (until) when he came to the rising of the sun, he found it rising on a people for whom we had provided no covering protection against the sun. (He left them) as they were: We completely understood what was before him. Then followed he (another) way, (till) when he came between the two mountains, he found upon their hither side a folk that scarce could understand a saying. They said: O Dhu'l-Qarneyn! Lo! Gog and Magog are spoiling the land. So may we pay thee tribute on condition that thou set a barrier between us and them? He said: "(The power) in which my Lord has established me is better (than tribute): Help me therefore with strength (and labour): I will erect a strong barrier between you and them: Give me pieces of iron - till, when he had leveled up (the gap) between the cliffs, he said: Blow! - till, when he had made it a fire, he said: Bring me molten copper to pour thereon. And (Gog and Magog) were not able to surmount, nor could they pierce (it). He said: This is a mercy from my Lord; but when the promise of my Lord cometh to pass, He will lay it low, for the promise of my Lord is true. And on that day we shall let some of them surge against others, and the Trumpet will be blown. Then we shall gather them together in one gathering. On that day we shall present hell to the disbelievers, plain to view.

From the above verses, we see that Sura al Kahf summarizes the three journey destinations of Dhu Al Qarnayn: in verse 86, he reaches the sunset where he found the sun setting in a fetid spring of water. In verse 90, his travel to the sunrise, where he found the inhabitants there without protection against the sun blaze. We will see later, through studying the Hadiths and the Syriac letter, that because the sun burns and melts everything — even the rocks — there were no buildings or houses there. In verse 93, and in the following verses, Dhu Al Qarnayn reaches the region of "Al Saddein," described by Mohammed as two smooth mountains — so smooth that everything slips down from them.[387] They reach the clouds of the sky. The people there complained against the wickedness of Gog and Magog. This induced Alexander to build a dam and close the aperture between the edges of the two mountains, through which he imprisoned Gog and Magog until "the promise of the Lord" would come to pass which, in the Quran, means the Last Day of history.

The Quran intended that the dam will remain until the last days

In the last days, the dam will be demolished allowing Gog and Magog to attack the world as we see in Surah 21 called al Anbiya', and verse 96, 97, "Until Gog and Magog's barrier is demolished, they will swiftly swarm from every hill. Then will the true promise become clear."

In Surah 18, Dhu al Qarnayn talks about the dam,

> He said "this is a mercy from my lord. When the promise of my lord, which is the last day, will come to pass, he will make it into dust. And the last day is true.

Demolishing the dam in the Quran is a major element in its eschatology. When he uses the phrase "by the promise of my lord" he is referring to the last day, and it coincides with the demolishing of the dam, which imprisoned a savage people according to Pseudo-Callisthenes. This people became Gog and Magog in the Syriac writings and the Quran.

The Quran uses the term "promise," or "promise of Allah," or "my lord," to express the last days or to obtain the promise to enter paradise. Nowhere do we have a better example than in Sura 4, called al Nisa', and verse 122, "Those who believed and performed deeds of righteousness, shall be admitted to gardens, with rivers flowing beneath them. They have become immortal forever. Allah's promise is truthful." In Surah al Isra', 17 and verse 7, he recalls the promise "the promise of the coming life."

We notice that the same "promise" is mentioned in Surah 21:96, 97 and it is fulfilled with the destruction of the dam and the freeing of Gog and Magog to destroy the world. Therefore, the "promise" is the Day of Judgment in which Allah uses Gog and Magog to destroy the infidels of the earth. And that is the main theme of some versions of Pseudo-Callisthenes's book and, the Syriac writings which depend on it.

The confirmation that the Quran intended for the dam to keep Gog and Magog imprisoned until the Judgment Day, are verses 99 and 100, which explained that day:

> And on that day we shall let some of them surge against others, and the Trumpet will be blown. Then we shall gather them together in one gathering. On that day we shall present hell to the disbelievers, plain to view.

The trumpet will be blown in the Day of Judgment when all inhabitants of the earth will be gathered. Hell will be presented to the disbelievers. Surah al Anbya, in verses 96 and 97, also mention the release of Gog and Magog from the dam to attack the world — that is, in the same "promise day," the Last Day of history:

> Until, when Gog and Magog are let loose, and they hasten out of every mound, And the True Promise draweth nigh; then behold them, staring wide (in terror), the eyes of those who disbelieve! (They say): 'Alas for us! We (lived) in forgetfulness of this. Ah, but we were wrong-doers!'

Clearly, the Quran meant the Day of Judgment when saying "in that day." Thus, according to the Quran, Gog and Magog are still there behind this dam of iron and molten brass — built, according to the Quran, by Dhul-Qarnain, a title of Alexander the Great. This is noteworthy when one considers that airplanes and satellites have flown over the area and have never revealed such a huge dam, and history has never showed in any of its stages the presence of a savage people imprisoned behind a metallic dam. This myth imprisoned the author of the Quran, as well as his Quran, into a trap from which it is impossible to be released, unless the Quran is rejected and considered merely a book that presents the myths of Mohammed's time.

Alexander's Journey according to Pseudo-Callisthenes and the Syriac writings

The three destinations which we already have seen in the Quran regarding Dhu al Qarnayn's journey are the same ones we encounter in Pseudo-Callisthenes and the Syriac writings upon which they were built. There are two main Syriac letters: the first is "A Christian Legend Concerning Alexander," dating back to the 5th century A.D. The second is Metrical Discourse of Jacob Serugh, going back to the 6th century A.D.

In the Quran, the fetid sea became a fetid spring

When the author of Pseudo-Callisthenes mentioned a sea that is difficult to cross, he was influenced by the Epic of Gilgamesh. In this Epic there was a difficult sea, and waters of death that nobody could cross except the sun. This sea, or waters of death, is adopted in Pseudo-Callisthenes as being a sea that nobody could cross and surrounded the whole earth.

Let us look first to the tablets where the Epic of Gilgamesh was recorded:

In the tenth tablet, Gilgamesh reaches to the fortress of goddess Siduri, who warns him of a devastating and troublesome sea before him. She tells him,

> "Of the ones who reached here since ancient times tried to cross this sea. Only the hero Shamsh, the sun, actually did cross this sea. Who else succeeded?"

We then conclude, that the Sumerian idea included a troublesome sea situated in the extremity of the earth, and only the sun when it was setting crossed this sea.

> Then goddess Siduri said to Gilgamesh,

> The place and the passage are difficult, and the waters of death are deep which flow between. Gilgamesh, how will you cross the Ocean? When you come to the waters of death what will you do?

This difficult sea and the waters of death described in the Epic of Gilgamesh, has its counterpart in Pseudo-Callisthenes. Here it is a sea or ocean that surrounds the earth which no one can cross. The story goes that some of Alexander's soldiers attempted to swim in the sea, but beast-like humans came out of the water and devoured them.[388] This sea is described in many versions of Pseudo-Callisthenes' book as a fetid sea full of pus making its crossing impossible.[389] According to "A Christian Legend concerning Alexander" near this fetid sea that the sun sets and enters into heaven through a gate placed there.[390]

It is clear that those ideas about the troublesome sea, which the sun crosses in the Sumerian mythology, is the foundation on which the fetid sea in the pseudo-Callisthenes' book is built. The sun passes over the fetid sea to set in a gate through which it enters heaven.

The fetid sea idea is used in the Quran where it is called "the Spring of Hammaah." In the Quran, Dhu al Qarnayn finds the setting sun.

Hammaah is an Arabic word which means fetid or fetid mud. Mohammed used Tubb'a a's idea regarding the sunset. Tubb'a was a Yemeni military leader who reigned in Yemen between 410-435 A.D., and occupied the cities of Medina and Mecca. Tubb'a a, influenced by a version of Pseudo-Callisthenes' book, described in a poem how Dhu al Qarnayn found the sun setting in a spring of fetid muddy water.

Due to a Hadith which says that the sun sets in a hot spring water, and other Hadiths which say that it sets in a fetid spring, there were two contradictory readings in the Quran regarding the nature of the spring. Muslims disagreed about which reading was more correct. For example, Muawiya bin Abi Sufyan, the first Umayyad Caliph, adopted the notion that the sun sets in a hot spring water. Whereas ibn Abbass, Mohammed's cousin, said it sets in a fetid spring. They agreed to make the poem of Tubb'a the rule in the matter. Tubb'a recited verses saying that Dhu al Qarnayn was a Muslim (Muslim was a term used in Arabia, as well as among the Mandaeans in Iraq, for their followers) who reached the sunset and sunrise, and found the sun setting in a fetid muddy spring.

قد كان ذو القرنين قبلي مسلما ملكا تدين له الملوك وتسجد

بلغ المغارب والمشارق يبتغي أسباب أمر من حكيم مرشد

فرأى مغيب الشمس عند غروبها في عين ذي خلب وثأط حرمد

الخلب: الطين؛ والثأط: الحمئة، والحرمد : الأسود391

Here we see that Tubb'a's poem was known prior to Islam and viewed as a trusted source without error. The idea of the sun setting in a fetid spring became an accepted notion in the area of Mecca, to the extent — in choosing the Quranic reading where the sun sets — they ruled according to Tubb'a's poem. This indicates that the myths of Pseudo-Callisthenes and the Syriac writings were widespread in Arabia since early times.

The fetid sea in "A Christian Legend Concerning Alexander"

The story, "A Christian Legend Concerning Alexander," tells how Alexander gathered the nobles, the wise men and the leaders of his army to ask them:

What is the extent of the earth," he asked. "How high are the heavens, and how many countries belong to my fellow kings? What are the heavens fixed upon? Do thick clouds and winds support them? Do pillars of fire rise up from the interior of the earth to support the heavens so that nothing can ever move them? Or do they depend on a silent call from God beckoning to them so they will not fall? Now this I desire to go and see, upon what the heavens rest, and what surrounds all creation."

The nobles answered him,

"The terrible seas which surround the world will not give you passage because there are eleven bright seas, on which the ships of men sail. Beyond these lies about ten miles of dry land, then in ten more miles lies the evil smelling fetid sea, called Okeyanos, or the ocean. This ocean surrounds all creation. Men are not able to come near the fetid sea, neither can ships sail thereon. No bird is able to fly over it, for if a bird should attempt to fly over it, it falls into the sea and suffocates therein. Its waters are like poison, and if men swim therein, they die at once. The leaves of the trees which are by its side are shriveled up by the smell of these waters as though fire had licked them.[392]

Then the king decided to travel to see the fetid sea, and subject in the way all the kingdoms. He prayed to God, asking for His help, and that if the Messiah will not come in his time, he (Alexander) will transfer his throne to Jerusalem in order that the Messiah sets on it.[393]

Here we see that the Syriac author of "A Christian Legend Concerning Alexander," planned to make use of Pseudo-Callisthenes. The Syriac author made Alexander the Great as a pious man who made war only to bring every kingdom into subjection to God. Alexander wanted to be the leader who prepared the world for the coming of Christ. This thought was also copied in the Quran in which Dhu al Qarnayn is portrayed as a pious man who made holy war to subject all the nations to Allah.

The author wrote that Alexander said in his prayer, that God placed two horns on his head. According to Pseudo-Callisthenes, Amon, the god of Libya, had two horns, so Alexander, as his son, also had two horns.

Then Alexander the Great asked the king of Egypt to send him seven thousand metalsmiths, who worked in iron and brass. The king of Egypt responded by fulfilling his request.[394]

As in Zoroastrian mythology, the fetid evil smelling sea was changed to a fetid spring in the Quran

The Syriac narration continues, as Alexander crossed the 11th sea(the bright sea,) and entered the arid land beyond the bright sea where he reached to the fetid sea. Alexander sent criminals who live in those regions, because he wanted to see if they would die when they came near the fetid sea. When they reached the shore of the fetid sea, they all died. So,

Alexander himself was afraid and he avoided the fetid sea. The author goes on to say:

> So the whole camp mounted their horses, and Alexander and his troops went up between the fetid sea and the bright sea to the place where the sun enters the window of heaven.[395]

It is obvious to the readers of "A Christian Legend Concerning Alexander," that these words form the foundation of the Quran's myth in Surah 18, al Kahf, where the Quran says that Dhu al Qarnayn reached the extremity of the West where he found the sun setting in a fetid muddy spring. This fetid muddy spring also reflects the concept of the fetid sea. When the Quran called it a "spring" instead of "sea," it was consistent with Zoroastrian-Persian mythology which believed the sun rose and set each day from a different spring situated on a mount Alburz, which they placed in a celestial sea between earth and heaven.

I assume that the lost Pahlavi version of Pseudo-Callisthenes, dated in the fourth or fifth century A.D., and was spread in the Sassanic-Persian period which continued until Islam, made the fetid sea, near where the sun sets, into fetid spring, paralleling the Zoroastrian concept which says the sun sets in a spring, and not in a sea or near a sea.

We see clearly that when the Quran spoke about Dhu al Qarnayn's visit to where the sun sets and rises, it depended on the Pahlavi version of Pseudo-Callisthenes as it is primary source, which certainly at the time of Mohammed was widespread in Arabia among the Persians. We know that many Persians accepted Islam, such as Salman al Farsi, called Solomon the Persian, who was the Zoroastrian priest who became Mohammed's counselor, accepted Islam and was close to Mohammed. As we have previously proved, however, Mohammed had connections in Mecca with individuals who enjoyed a Persian education, as the Meccans accused the Quran of being written in an Ajami (Persian) tongue.

Alexander's trip to the fetid-smelly sea according to the Syriac metrical discourse of Jacob Serugh

Jacob Serugh's metrical discourse mentioned about the fetid sea. Alexander's assistants speak to him about a great ocean, a fetid-evil smelling sea, which surrounds all the earth. Anyone who touches it will die. Despite this danger, Alexander decides to go to the extremities of the earth to see this fetid sea and examine for himself the extraordinary geography of the extremity of the earth.

Then Alexander asked the king of Egypt to provide him with:

> All the tradesmen who were workers in brass and iron, men full of skill, for the Lord had beckoned to Alexander to make a gate to contain Magog. Sorik, the king of Egypt, sent twelve thousand cunning workmen to Alexander, the son of Philip. Alexander provided iron and brass in great quantity, and in wisdom, he filled the ships therewith.[396]

After a long and arduous journey, Alexander reached to the fetid sea. The army fled from the bad smell of the fetid sea driving Alexander to the lofty mountain of Masis.

There are many similarities between the Syriac account and Epic of Gilgamesh. Gilgamesh who is in search for immortality, reached Mount Mashu, as Alexander had done. Mount Mashu is where the Sumerians believed the sun rose and set. In some versions of Pseudo-Callisthenes' book, Alexander also reached the mountain of Mashu but it was called Mount Maashi.[397] In the metrical homily written by Jacob Serugh, he also mentions mount Masis.

Analyzing Pseudo-Callisthenes and the two Syriac writings upon which they were based, we see that the authors believed in the existence of a fetid sea, near which the sun sets. Originally, this myth was derived from Epic of Gilgamesh, which mentions difficult waters nobody could cross except the sun, which stayed there.

The Quran made Dhu al Qarnayn reach the sunset, and discover that the sun sets in a fetid spring. Muslims argue about this, claiming that Dhu al Qarnayn thought the sun sets in a fetid spring. The Quran, however, does not say that Dhu al Qarnayn thought, but that he found the sun setting in a fetid spring. The Quran also says that "... he found near it (the sun) a people." Thus, the Quran recorded that Dhu al Qarnayn reached the place where the sun sets in a specific spot on earth.

A question to be asked is why would Tubb'a the Yemenite make the main subject of his poem the fact that Dhu al Qarnayn found the sun setting in a fetid spring, if the matter was just something he imagined to be so!? Everyone who looks to the sea during sunset will see that the sun sets in the sea. Actually, Tubb'a wanted to confirm a widespread myth in his time, which was based on the ancients' imagination regarding the geography of the earth, based on the views of Epic of Gilgamesh, and Pseudo-Callisthenes and the Syriac writings which were based on it.

Dhu- al Qarnayn-Alexander's journey to the place where the sun sets

The ancient Middle Easterners viewed the sunrise as occurring in a very distant spot on earth. They thought the diameter of the earth was as huge as the distance between the "ceiling of heaven" and earth. Thus, many believed that what Pseudo-Callisthenes described as the extremities of the earth was the true geography men would find if they could live so long and travel so far. Arabs thought that the diameter of the earth would require 500 years to walk across if a person was walking by foot. We see the same thought in the writings of al Masudi,[398] and in the writings of Yaqut al Hamawi.[399] Mohammed believed that if you could be carried by an angel or winged camel to explore the extremities of the earth, you would find the truth of Pseudo-Callisthenes — just as Mohammed claimed to find it when the angel Gabriel carried him on a winged camel to the temple of Jerusalem, then to the extremities of the earth, where he confirmed the discoveries of Dhu al Qarnayn as they were described in both the Quran and in Pseudo-Callisthenes.

According to Arabian mythology, Dhu al Qarnayn reached the most distant place in earth, near the place where the sun rises, according to Middle Eastern mythology. He could do so because he lived for two thousand years. Qais bin Saideh was an Arabian orator that Mohammed used to listen to before claiming to be a prophet. In one of his speeches, Qais mentioned that Dhu al Qarnayn lived for two thousand years. [400]

The rise of the sun from a distant place on earth was an ancient Sumerian notion, which we encounter in the Epic of Gilgamesh. We already saw that this Epic left its imprint on Pseudo-Callisthenes. Gilgamesh's journey to the east where the sun rises is found in the ninth tablet, where it is written that Gilgamesh decided to visit Uta-Napishtim, the one who obtained immortality and was deified. Gilgamesh wanted to consult Uta-Napishtim on how to obtain immortality for himself. Gilgamesh goes to the East where he is attacked by animals and humans with strange, anomalous or abnormal shapes, but he overcomes them. Then he reaches Mount Mashu, where it was believed the sun rose and rested.

The same thing happened to Alexander. He encountered humans with anomalous forms and mythological animals on his journey. Alexander also reached the Mount Mashu, called Mount Maashi. [401] Gilgamesh encountered the Scorpion-man, who warns him not to continue his travels because no one before him successfully crossed the land of darkness. Gilgamesh succeeds in crossing it. Similarly, Alexander the Great was advised not to attempt to cross the land of darkness, since all who tried to traverse it perished, and no one had ever crossed it.[402] However, Alexander succeeded in crossing the land of darkness.

In the Gilgamesh epic, we also notice that Mount Mashu is guarded by Scorpion men which are similar to the creatures and animals that Alexander encountered–half humans and half animals. Yet, there are still more striking similarities. Gilgamesh enters a garden full of fruitful trees, where he sees the "the tree of the gods." The sun speaks directly to him, telling him his request is useless. In like manner, Alexander goes to a garden in the extremity of the earth where he enters the temple of the sun, and sees that the garden is full of fruitful trees. There he sees two giant trees whose tops reach heaven–one is male and the other is female. The male is the sun, the female is the moon. The name of the tree-sun is Mitora, the tree-moon is Mayosa. These were Persian names: Mitora is derived from Mitra, which the Persian mythology symbolizes as the sun or the rays of the sun. Mayosa, on the other hand, is derived from the first man and woman in Persian mythology who grew like two plants from the seed of the primordial man called Gayomard. In Dinkard, book VIII, these two plants are called Masya and Mashyoi.[403] The presence of such Zoroastrian names in the Syriac version of Pseudo-Callisthenes confirms that it was built on the Pahlavi version of Pseudo-Callisthenes, which scholars think was lost. It returns to the fourth or fifth century A.D. In the garden, the sun speaks to Alexander telling him he will die in Babel, and discouraging him in his search for immortality.[404]

We see that, according to ancient mythology, the sun is seen or personally encountered in a spot located on the uttermost edge of the earth, where it rises. This mythology influenced the author of Pseudo-Callisthenes; and the Syriac writers, in describing the sunrise, had influenced the concept of sunrise in the Quran, also.

The facts confirm that the author of the Quran copied Alexander's journey, as it was portrayed in Pseudo-Callisthenes' book and in the Syriac writings that followed. Both of these sources tell us that, after conquering the Indians, Alexander went to the eastern extremity of the earth, to the place where the sun rises. There he found naked people living without shelter and they pastor in the fields like sheep.[405]

The Syriac writing called "A Christian Legend about Alexander" says:

He rises over the sea, and the people who dwell there flee away and hide themselves in the sea to avoid being burned by his rays as he passes through the midst of the heavens to where he enters the window of heaven. Wherever he passes, there are terrible mountains, and those who dwell there live in caves hollowed out from the rock. As soon as they see the sun passing over them, men and birds flee away from before him. They hide in the caves because the rocks are split in two by the blazing heat. Whether men or beasts, as the stones touch them they are consumed. When the sun enters the window of heaven, it immediately bows down to make obeisance before God it is creator. It descends through the heavens the whole night, until at length it finds itself where the sun rises.[406]

The author of "A Christian Legend Concerning Alexander" claims there is no covering to protect the people who live where the sun rises in the extremity of the East. There are no buildings to protect them because the blazing heat of the sun causes the rocks to split and the buildings to fall. Therefore, when the sun rises the inhabitants go to the water until the sun sets again.

The Quran expresses the same thought in Surah 18: 89 and 90:

Then he took another route until he reached the place where the sun rises. He found it (the sun) rising over a people to whom, because of the sun, we did not provide with covering protection.

Mohammed in his Hadith explained what he meant when he said, "We did not provide them with coverings to protect themselves." Sumra bin al Jundub سُمرَة بن جندب comments on the Hadith:

When the prophet of Allah explained this verse, he meant no building was ever built there. When the sun rises the people enter Asrab or the water courses. Another of Mohammed's Hadiths says. "Their land does not support any building to be built upon. Therefore, when the sun rises, they go into the water until the sun sets. Like the animals, they come out from the water seeking pasture.[407]

This Hadith of Mohammed was also affirmed by Taberi.[408] The notions that they go to water until the sun is lifted up and that their land does not support any building because of the heat of the sun are found also in the sayings of al Hassan, Qutadah, and ibn Jarih.[409]

Because Surah18:89 and 90 of the Quran perfectly match Mohammed's Hadith and the Syriac writing, these verses demonstrate Mohammed's rich knowledge of Alexander's mythological trip to the extremities of the earth. according to pseudo-Callisthenes' and the Syriac writings which were built on that book. But more importantly, Mohammed intended to prove, like the writings he depended on, that the sun really rises from a spot on earth. Dhu al Qarnayn reached the place where the sun rises directly over people, who hide themselves in water all day because of the sun.

The influence of the Quranic concept (regarding the sunrise) on the Islamic historians and scholars throughout history.

Before the advance in the science of geography of the earth, Muslim historians, writers and scholars believed that the sun rose from a spot in the eastern extremity of the earth. Throughout history, Muslims had a primitive geography based on the verse of the Quran which says that the sunrise occurs over people without protection; this was Mohammed's interpretation of the verse as well, as reported in his Hadith. Muslims imagined that the sun rose each day from a different spring existing in the extremity of the earth. This is because Mohammed claimed that he mounted the Buraq (winged animal) and saw the sun rising from those springs. He heard the noise of the sun when it rose from the springs.[410]

Muslims thought Alexander the Great crossed China and beyond, only to find the sun rising from the water over people with nothing to protect them against the blazing heat of the sun.

Even important Muslim historians revealed their belief in the sun rising from a spot on the earth. Ibn al Nadim tells of a mountain east of China behind which the sun rose.[411] Al Taberi has a definite place where the sun rises, and Dhu al Qarnany reached beyond the place where the sun rises.[412]

Yaqut al Hamawi, a famous Islamic geographer, said there was a dam that Dhu al Qarnany built. According to the Quran, he placed the dam beyond the spot where the sun rises.[413] Both ibn Hisham and al Thaalabi embrace this same thought. They claimed that Alexander had built the dam in an area beyond where the sunrises.[414]

The expositors of the Quran interpreted the Quranic verse about the sunrise ¯ that Dhu al Qarnayn reached the place where the sun rises from a spot on the earth. In fact, the Quran uses the words "Matlaa al Shams مطلع الشمس," which means in Arabic "the place where the sun rises." Ibn al Juzi, says:

> Al Hassan, Mujahid, Abu Majles, Abu Rajaa and Abu Mihisen all read it as 'Matlaa al Shams,' with accent on the Arabic letter, Lam." Al Anbari said, "There is controversy among the people of Arabia regarding the meaning of 'Matlaa,' weather it was with the accent on the Lam or not. Both ways, it means 'the place from where the sun rises.'

Ibn al Juzi explains the meaning of "Matlaa" in Arabic by giving an example:

> The Arabic word "Madkhal", means "the place through which a person enters," He said the same meaning is applied to "Matlaaمطلع", the place from which the sun comes out or rises.[415]

Al Qurtubi quotes al Jawhari confirming the same thing. Matlaa, with accent over the letter Lam or beneath it, has the same meaning–the place from where the sun rises.[416] All this tells us that experts in the Arabic language, confirm that the Quran intended for the sun to rise from a definite place in the extremity of the earth.

Taberi, Qurtubi, and ibn Kathir, all claim that an army went to the place where the sun rises. But the inhabitants warned them to not remain there till sunrise. The army saw a multitude of bones. When they asked about the bones, the inhabitants said they were the bones of an army which came to occupy their region, but when the sun rose upon them, they were immediately burned up. When the army heard the story they fled.[417] Muslims, inspired by the Quran and Mohammed's Hadith, endeavored to confirm that his claims were true.

The myth about Alexander building a barrier of gates, imprisoning a savage people until the last day of history

The Persian roots of Pseudo-Callisthenes and the Quranic myth about the imprisonment of wicked people until the Last Day of history

The ancient Middle Easterners imagined the existence of anti-human beings of devils' progenies, bound in the extremity of the East. Those enemies would be released in the Last Day of history to attack the world.

This is originally a Persian Zoroastrian myth. In reference to the Zoroastrian mythology found in their sacred books which claims the existence of a diabolic personality under the name of Azi Dahak. He is said to have descended from the devil, Ahriman, bound or fettered to a mountain in the extremity of the East.

Dahak was fettered by Fredun, a mythological Persian hero who had been sleeping for thousands of years on the mountain. Dahak is a devil in the form of a serpent, or a dragon, who had three heads with three mouths, six eyes and a thousand senses.[418] Later he became responsible for a diabolical people who were also bound with him in the same area.

According to Zoroastrians, Keresaspa was another hero who slept beside Dahak on the mountain. In the last days, Dahak will be untied from his fetters and will attack the whole world. Keresaspa will be awakened by two angels, and he will confront Dahak and kill him.

Zoroastrians throughout their history believed that Dahak is continually chained with his people to a mountain in the east. Pseudo-Callisthenes copied the Zoroastrian myth concerning the chaining of Dahak and his people, but he applied it to the savage people whom he claimed Alexander imprisoned behind gates. Those then became the Huns in "A Christian legend concerning Alexander," and became Gog and Magog according to The metrical homily on Alexander, which is attributed to Jacob Serugh. These resources took away the names of Dahak and his people, and replaced them with the names Gog and Magog which they borrowed from the book of Ezekiel. Ezekiel did not mention Gog and Magog as being people imprisoned in his time behind gates or a dam, but rather as a people who will appear in the last days. For details about this argument, I refer the leader to my book about Eschatology in the Quran and the Bible.

Regarding the Zoroastrian myth: the devils which are bound in the East are called Mazendarian Demons in the book of Dinkard, and portrayed as very dangerous.[419]

The people of the land Khvaniras complained against the Mazendarian Demons to Fredun, a mythological Persian hero, telling him they were dangerous.[420] It is the same complaint stated in the Quran. Referred to there as "The people who did not understand a saying," they complained about Gog and Magog to Alexander the Great. Fredun, gesturing with his nostril, separated these diabolic inhabitants until the end of days when they will be released. He separated them in an upland, which he created from his right nostril, where ice and cold winter persist. From his left nostril he created rocks. Fredun killed two thirds of these demonic inhabitants, and he imprisoned the rest.[421]

Certainly, the Zoroastrian myths are at the root of Pseudo-Callisthenes' myth about Alexander imprisoning dangerous savage people until the end times. Those people became Gog and Magog in the Syriac writings which followed Pseudo-Callisthenes' book.

With this mythological foundation, we understand Mohammed's words when he says, "The sun rises between the two horns of a devil."[422] Mohammed's myth is consistent with Persian mythology about Dahak and his progenies, the devils, who are bound in the extremity of the East. This is also consistent with the Syriac writing "A Christian Legend Concerning Alexander": "Devils live with Gog and Magog near where the sun rises." The Syriac author says:

> And by the side of every hundred men there seem to stand one hundred thousand bands of demons, for their sorceries are greater than those of all the other kingdoms.[423]

In like manner, this is based on Zoroastrian mythology, which portrays the imprisonment of diabolic inhabitants in the extremity of the East.

Later, in Dinkard, book nine, the diabolic inhabitants were imprisoned in a metallic settlement by a mythological king named Kai-Us. The text of the Dinkard say that Kai-Us erected these imprisoning places in the midst of a mountain range south of the Caspian Sea-. One prison was of gold, two were of silver, two were of steel, and two were of crystal. He used them to restrain the Mazonik demons who would ruin of the world, and he confined them to their own duty."[424]

The myth as it is portrayed in Pseudo-Callisthenes, and the Syriac letters that were based on Pseudo-Callisthenes.

We have seen that the final destination of Alexander's journey was the two "Saddin," which are two high mountains. A people there complained to Dhu al Qarnayn about Gog and Magog and how they did great mischief on the earth. They asked that he build a dam so that he could imprison them. Dhu al Qarnayn built a dam of iron through which he closed the aperture between the edges of the two mountains, imprisoning Gog and Magog until the Last Day of history — when this dam will be destroyed, and Gog and Magog will come out to fight the populations of the world.

This story we find in Pseudo-Callisthenes (though without mentioning Gog and Magog, but savage people) and the two Syriac writings which were built on this book. Reading from a Greek version of Pseudo-Callisthenes, we discover something interesting about the gates that were erected by Alexander. My information came from Carl Muller's edition of Pseudo-Callisthenes, in Cod. B (III, chap. 29 ed. Didot, p. 112 seq.). Code B was printed by Muller who edited it from one manuscript archived in the Bibliothèque Nationale of Paris –France; code B has number 1685.[425]

Alexander, according to the book, writes a letter to his mother. He says:

> I found there many people who ate the flesh of human beings and drank their blood like water. They did not bury their dead, but they ate them. And seeing people so wicked, and fearing that by this manner of eating, they would pollute the earth with their vile depravity, I petitioned the exalted Deity to proceed forcibly against them. I put the majority of them to the sword, and brought their land under subjection. From all sides arose their loud complaints, from the highest to the lowest. Hearing that Alexander, the King of the Macedonians, had come thither, they said, 'He will kill all, lay waste to our towns and overwhelm us.' So taking flight they followed one another, one people pressing upon another and all driving one another into a frenzy.

> "Of these there were twenty-two kings, and I pursued them with my troops until they entrenched themselves in the two great mountains which are called "The Breasts of the North," There is no other outlet or inlet in these great mountains since they reach in height above the clouds of the heavens, and the mountains stretch so far that they are as two walls right and left toward the north to the Great Sea, which is

the land of darkness. And I thought of every means of depriving them of the outlet through the great mountains into which they had been driven. Now the inlet between the great mountains was 46 Royal ells. Again, with all my heart I petitioned the exalted Deity, and he heard my prayer, and the exalted Deity commanded the two mountains and they moved and approached each other to a distance of twelve ells, and there I made copper gates, 12 ells broad, and 60 ells high. I smeared them over within and without so that neither fire nor iron, nor any other means should be able to loosen the copper since the fire was put out and the iron was shattered. Within these gates, I made another construction of stones, each of which was 11 ells broad, 20 ells high, and 60 ells thick. And having done this, I finished the construction by putting mixed tin and lead over the stones, and smearing the whole, so that no one might be able to do anything against the gates. I called them the Caspian Gates. Twenty and Two Kings did I shut up therein.[426]

When we compare this portion of Pseudo-Callisthenes with the Quran and Hadiths of Mohammed, we notice several items

The imagination of the author of the book is large indeed. He claimed there was a natural barrier formed between two mountains, which are so high that it reached above the clouds of heaven. They are so long that they are capable of imprisoning people from all over the rest of the world. We saw this in the letter Alexander wrote to his mother. We also discover that his idea is taken directly from the book of Pseudo-Callisthenes, which says:

I pursued them with my troops until they entrenched themselves in the two great mountains which are called 'The Breasts of the North. There is no other outlet or inlet to these great mountains. since they reach high above the clouds of the heavens, and they stretch so far that they are as two walls right and left towards the north to the Great Sea, which is.... and the land of darkness.[427]

The geography of the extremities of the earth as well the details about "the two mountains," mentioned in the Book of Pseudo-Callisthenes, are identical to what we read in the Quran. We notice that Pseudo-Callisthenes called the two mountains "barrier." The Quran called the two mountains barrier as well. Furthermore, according to the Quran, the depression between the two mountains is identical to the depression between the two Mountains where Dhu al Qarnayn erected the dam.

In Pseudo-Callisthenes we read:

Now the inlet between the great mountains was 46 Royal ells. Again, with all my heart I petitioned the exalted Deity, and he heard my prayer. The exalted Deity commanded the two mountains and they moved and approached each other to a width of twelve ells.

In Surah 18:96 we read this phrase:

He filled the space between the al-sadafein edges of the two mountains.

Al-Qurtubi says the edges of two mountains when they approach each other is called "al-sadafein."[428] The same meaning is rendered by al Razi.[429]

We see that it is the same description we find in Pseudo-Callisthenes except that Alexander prayed the two edges of the great mountains would approach each other. Mohammed said they were placed together without specifying how this came about.

Similarities in the descriptions of the savage people imprisoned both in Pseudo-Callisthenes and Hadiths of Mohammed

In Alexander's description, the savage people ate human flesh, and failed to bury their dead. preferring to eat them instead. Pseudo-Callisthenes says:

I found there many people who ate the flesh of human beings and drank their blood like water; since they did not bury their dead.

We find the same description about these savage people in the Hadiths of Mohammed. Both Al Qurtubi and al Thaalabi reported one Hadith describing Gog and Magog:

They once said to Mohammed,' O prophet of Allah, describe them for us.' Mohammed said: There are three kinds; one is like the trees of cedar in Syria. a tree of as much as 120 arms lengths, the other has equal length and width about one and half arms lengths. They never pass by an elephant or beast or pig without eating it. They eat their dead, and they drink the waters of the east.[430]

Ibn Al Juzi mentions another one of Mohammed's Hadiths as reported by Hadhifah, a companion of Mohammed and one of his known reporters. Hadhifah confirmed Mohammed's words about Gog and Magog who eat their dead.[431] In the writings of Ibn al Juzi and al Bukhari, Mohammed says Gog and Magog encompassed a large number of people, which matches the narration of Pseudo-Callisthenes. Mohammed said that in the last days:

The number of people who are Muslims compared to the number of people who follow Gog and Magog will be like one to 999.[432]

In other words, Gog and Magog followers will be one thousand times greater than the total number of Muslims. Islamic writers say Gog and Magog were composed of 21 tribes, in addition to the Turkish tribe which remained outside the dam.[433] The 22 tribes are the same as the number of kings who lead 22 tribes, whom pseudo-Callisthenes mentioned when he described the savage people Alexander wrote about to his mother.

The Quranic narration about the dam is consistent with the Syriac writings and the original Greek version of Pseudo-Callisthenes.

Alexander erected a gate between two mountains to imprison the Huns, as described in "A Christian Legend Concerning Alexander." The Huns came from Asia and settled in Hungary, before occupying regions of the eastern and western Roman Empire, making raids against the cities, and plundering the inhabitants. According to the Syriac writers, the Huns were the savage people who threatened the Roman Empire. The Syriacs formed a part of the nucleus of the Byzantine Empire in Asia Minor, which today is known as Turkey. The Syriac author wanted to imprison the Huns until the Last Day of history, using the myth of Pseudo-Callisthenes, in which Alexander imprisoned a savage people in the extremity of the earth.

We read in "A Christian Legend Concerning Alexander":

The king said, "Let us make a gate of brass and close up this breach." His troops said, 'As thy majesty commands we will do.' And Alexander commanded and fetched three thousand smiths, workers in iron, and three thousand men, workers in brass. And they put down brass and iron, and kneaded it as a man kneads when he works clay. Then they brought it and made a gate, the length of which was twelve cubits and its breadth eight cubits. And he made a lower threshold from mountain to mountain, the length of which was twelve cubits; and he hammered it into the rocks of the mountains, and it was fixed with brass and iron. The height of the lower threshold was three cubits. And he made an upper threshold from mountain to mountain, twelve cubits in length; and he hammered it into the rocks of the mountain, and fixed in it two bolts of each bolt being twelve cubits [long]; and the bolts went into the rock two cubits; and he made two bolts of iron from rock to rock behind the gate, and fixed the heads of the bolts into the rocks. He fixed the gate and the bolts, and he placed nails of iron and beat them down one by the other, so that if the Huns came and dug out the rock which was under the threshold of iron, even if footmen were able to pass through, horse with its rider would be unable to pass, so long as the gate that was hammered down with bolts stood. And he brought and hammered down a lower threshold and hinge for the gate, and he cast therein bolts of iron, and made it swing round on one side like the gates of Shushan the fortress. And the men brought and kneaded iron and brass and covered herewith the gate and its posts one by one, like a man when he moulds clay. And he made a bolt of iron in the rocks, and hammered out an iron key twelve cubits long, and made locks of brass turn therewith. And behold the gate was hung and stood.[434]

Muslims claim that the building of the dam is a miraculous narration of the Quran. But I consider the detailed Syriac narration about the dam as worthy of consideration; the Syriac author's imagination and description provide more than the brief sentences of the Quran.

The myth of erecting the gate in this Syriac writing is based on chapter 29 of the book of Pseudo-Callisthenes, according to Müller's Greek MS. C.[435] The Quran summarized the myth in few short sentences which is a characteristic of Mohammed. Here is verse 96 of Surah 18:

Bring me the blocks of iron. When he had filled up the space between the edges of the two mountains, he said 'blow on it.' When it became fire, he said 'bring me Qiter- which is molten brass-, that I may pour over it.'

The Quran tells us how Dhu al Qarnayn filled the space between two mountains with iron. When it was heated Dhu al Qarbayn poured the brass liquid on it. This summary is identical to the original Greek; with the exception that the original shows how the gate was erected and overlaid with iron and brass. Instead, the Quran made Alexander fill up the space between the two mountains with iron, forming a dam which he overlaid with "liquid brass."

To help the reader compare the accounts, we must look at the words of Pseudo-Callisthenes, according to Carl Müller's edition in Code B (III, cap. 29 ed. Didot, p. 112 seq.). Code B was printed by Müller, who edited it from a manuscript housed in the Bibliothèque Nationale of Paris, France — (Code B is number 1685).[436] I already mentioned part of the text regarding the imprisonment of savage people by Alexander, according to the Code B manuscript. I again quote the text to help the reader see the similarities with the Quranic narration:

"And the exalted Deity commanded the two mountains and they approached each other at a distance of twelve ells, and there I made.... copper gates 12 ells broad, and 60 ells high, and smeared them over within and without... so that neither fire nor iron, nor any other means should be able to loosen the copper; since it went through the fire. Even iron was shattered by it. Within these gates, I made another stone construction, each of which was eleven ells broad, 20 ells high, and 60 ells thick. And having done this I finished the construction by putting mixed tin and lead over the stones, and smearing the whole thing, so that no one was able to do anything against the gates. I called them the Caspian Gates. Twenty and Two Kings did I shut up therein.'"[437]

After overlaying the gates, no one could dig through them or scale them. This idea is also expressed in the Quran in verse 97:

Then they could not scale it nor to dig through it.

According to the Syriac writer, the Huns will come out of their imprisonment to attack the world.

According to the Syriac author of A Christian Legend Concerning Alexander, Alexander inscribed a prophecy on the gate in which he mentioned that wickedness will increase in the world in the last days to the extent that God will destroy the gate and release the imprisoned Huns who will devastate the world. According to the Syriac author, Alexander confirmed that the Lord will destroy the gate to condemn the nations of the world.[438]

The Quran repeated the same idea in verse 98:

He said 'this is a mercy from my lord. When the promise of my lord will come to pass, he will make it into dust. And the last day is true.

Mohammed claimed many times that the dam which Dhu al Qarnayn had built, is opened about the size of a small circle, which Mohammed showed with a gesture of his fingers.[439]

Zenab bint Jahsh, a wife of Mohammed who was previously married to Zayd, Mohammed's adopted son, said:

The prophet of Allah awoke one day with his checks very red. He said 'Woe to the Arabs because of the evil which is drawing near. Today the dam of Gog and Magog has been opened. There is a small opening this size,' and he made a gesture with his fingers to show the size of the opening, I said to him, 'O prophet of Allah, will we perish knowing that among us there are yet some righteous people?' He said, 'Yes, if the maliciousness continues to increase.'[440]

Mohammed's account of how the dam will be opened when the maliciousness increases in the world is identical to the Syriac myth.

Abi Hirrerah, a significant reporter and companion of Mohammed, reported on a similar Hadith of Mohammed.[441] Muslims believed, based on the words of Mohammed, that the dam in his generation had a small opening, but the aperture is increasing with the increase in wickedness in the world.[442]

There are similarities between the savage people whom, according to the Syriac author, Alexander imprisoned; and the description given by Mohammed regarding Gog and Magog.

The Syriac author of "A Christian Legend Concerning Alexander", described the savage people whom the legend claimed Alexander had imprisoned. The writer says about the speed of the savage people:

They are swifter than the blowing winds.[443]

The speed of Gog and Magog is expressed in the Quran in Surah 21 called al Anbiya' and verse 97:

Until the people of Gog and Magog are released from their barrier, they swiftly swarm from every hill.

Ibn al Juzi, commenting on the word, "Yansallun" used in this verse as "swiftly" he likened it to the wolf run.[444]

Other point is that they are swifter than the blowing wind. The noise of their outcry is more terrible than the voice of a lion.[445] This description is copied by Mohammed. In one Hadith, he mentioned the voices of the people of Gog and Magog and the people living adjacent to them where the sun rises from a spring of water. Mohammed said:

If it were not for the great number of people and the great noise they made, people everywhere in the world would have heard the noise of the sun when it rises.[446]

We see another important description of these savage people in the Syriac writing:

They are swifter than the wind that blows. For they are sorcerers, and they run between heaven and earth, and their chariots and swords and spears flash like fearful lightnings.[447]

This description shows how through sorcery, they became great fighters. Their magical spears reached heaven to harm the inhabitants of heaven. (According to Middle Eastern mythology, heaven was formed with seven layers; the first of them was close to the earth, and inhabited by men). This mythology about the seven layers of heaven is also encountered in Mohammed's alleged ascension to heaven.

The myth concerning savage people, is also expressed in the sayings of Mohammed. He says that when Gog and Magog will come out of the dam the population of the world will flee because of them. Then they point their spears and throw them toward heaven and when the spears return from heaven covered with blood. So, they will say, "We conquered the inhabitants of the earth, and prevailed against those who live in heaven."[448]

This Hadith of Mohammed is inspired by "A Christian Legend Concerning Alexander," in which the savage people are portrayed as powerful fighters between earth and heaven. Their spears flash like fearful lightnings capable of reaching the farthest place like heaven.

The Syriac author described how tall they were:

Each one of them stands six or seven cubits high.[449]

Describing them as tall giants is derived from a description, found in Zoroastrian sacred literature about the diabolic people who live in the land of the Mazandaran imprisoned until the end times by Fredun, the mythological hero. Their height, according to the book of Dinkard, is legendary.[450]

Mohammed's Hadiths confirm the legendary height of Gog and Magog, when he says that Gog and Magog differ in how tall they were. There were three categories. The first is like the cedar tree; 120 cubic tall.[451] The Syriac author says these savage people they drink the blood of men and of animals.[452] Concerning their atrocities, the author writes:

When they go forth to war, they fetch a pregnant woman, and pile up a fire, and bind her in front of the fire, and cook her child within her, and her belly bursts open and the child comes forth roasted.

We have seen that Mohammed gave a similar description of Gog and Magog, saying they eat human flesh, to the extent that they do not bury their dead but rather, they eat them.[453]

All these facts confirm that the Syriac myths about Gog and Magog were widespread in Arabia, and that Mohammed was very much acquainted with them.

The location of Paradise, beyond Gog and Magog, the Dog-men, and the nation of Menine: Mohammed knew this mythological geography.

Mohammed embraced the same mythological geography which was spread during his generation to other nations in the Middle East. We can see how Mohammed adopted the geography we encounter in Pseudo-Callisthenes and in the Syriac writings. According to the Syriac author of "A Christian Legend Concerning Alexander," Alexander asked the people at the extremity of the earth:

> Who are the nations that live beyond these? The old men replied, Those of Beth-Amardath, and the Dog-men. Beyond the Dog-men is the nation of the Menine. Beyond the nation of the Menine, there are no human beings, only terrible mountains, hills and valleys and plains and horrible caves, in which are serpents, adders and vipers. Men cannot go there without being immediately devoured by the serpents. The lands are waste, and there is nothing there except desolation. Living in all these mountains, the Paradise of God appears afar off.[454]

The Syriac notions were under the influence of Zoroastrian mythology. According to Dinkard, book nine, the mythological Persian figure called Kai-Us, built a metallic barrier and imprisoned the "Mazonik-demons," because they were dangerous to the world.[455] I think "Menine" is a misspelling of the Syriac writer for the "Mazonik" diabolic people, described in the Zoroastrian literature.

The dog men living in the extremity of the earth is derived from the book of Pseudo-Callisthenes, who was, in turn, influenced by the Epic of Gilgamesh. The Epic of Gilgamesh tells about men with the heads of animals who live in the extremity of the earth. Mohammed in his Hadiths placed the dog-men in the same area as did the author of "A Christian Legend Concerning Alexander." They both were beyond the people of Gog and Magog.[456]

Mohammed's dependence on the Syriac myths which were spread in his time is a fact that cannot be refuted, especially when we know the influence of the Syriacs on Arabia due to their missionary work there. Also, the fact that Mohammed possessed Syriac books and asked Zayd bin Thabet to study the Syriac language, in order to translate the books to him, I will discuss later.

The Metrical Homily on Alexander, attributed to Jacob Serugh

Previously mentioned was the influence on Mohammed and his Quran regarding Dhu al Qarnayn's journey by the myths of Pseudo-Callisthenes, which spread in Arabia through the lost Pahlavi version, and through the

Syriac version and other later versions based on them. There is evidence of a lost Arabic version which scholars believe was already spread in Arabia in the 4th or 5th century AD. One factor that points to the existence of this lost Arabic version from the end of the 4th, or the beginning of the 5th century AD is the poem of Tubb'a, the Himyarite king of Yemen, who reigned between 410-435 AD. He said in a poem, which is attributed to him when he occupied Mecca, that Dhu al Qarnayn saw the sun setting in a fetid muddy spring. It is known that the title of Dhu al Qarnayn was also known in Pseudo-Callisthenes, where we also find written that the sun sets near where Alexander reached a fetid sea. All these indicate that the lost Arabic version existed in this early period.

The Syriac writings, concerning Alexander's journey contain other important factors in the spread of the myths in Arabia. We already mentioned some influences on Mohammed by the Syriac writing, "A Christian Legend About Alexander." However, Syriac myths had a greater influence on Mohammed.

There were many Nestorian and Jacobite churches in Mesopotamia who had strong missionary work in many of the Arabian regions. The libraries of these churches include various books, many of which contained mythological characters, such as the metrical homilies of Jacob Serugh. He wrote at least two items which affected the Quran. The first is one which he translated from Greek is about the seven sleepers of Ephesus. The second is "The metrical homily on Alexander." These two writings of Jacob Serugh became part of Surah al-Kahf regarding the people who slept for hundreds of years in a cave, and the journey of Dhu al Qarnayn to the extremities of the earth. Jacob Serugh was known to the Arabians as Yaakub al Seruji. He wrote a letter to the church of Nijran, which is about 650 kilometers south of Mecca.[457]

This Syriac writing of "A Christian legend concerning Alexander," as well the one attributed to Jacob of Serugh, is based on Pseudo-Callisthenes according to Müller's Greek MS. C., chapters 37-39. The gate which Alexander built to imprison Gog and Magog is based on chapter 29 of the third book of Pseudo-Callisthenes, according to Müller's Greek MS. C.[458]

Jacob Serugh was born in 451 A.D. in Kurtam, a village on the Euphrates. He studied in the school of Raha, in the city of Edessa, located in northern Mesopotamia. Later, he became the bishop of Batnan, the main city of the province of Serugh in Asia Minor. He died in 521 A.D.

The transfer of the myths written or translated into Arabic by Jacob of Serugh came about because of his relationship with the churches in Arabia, especially the church of Nijran, about 200 miles south of Mecca. In fact, Jacob of Serugh wrote a letter to the church of Nijran.

The churches in Arabia were planted by the Jacobite and Nestorian Syriac churches. From this we see the influence of the Syriac church on the churches of western Arabia — not only regarding the Syriac doctrines, especially the Last Day, and other doctrines we encounter in the Quran, but also regarding the myths and the mythological books the Syriacs included along with their religious literature.

This explains the spread of these myths during Mohammed's time, such as the ones regarding Alexander and the myth about the Sleepers of Ephesus. Both myths are attributed to Jacob Serugh, and were adopted by Mohammed into Surah al Kahf.

Are there factors that favor Jacob of Serugh as the author of The Metrical Homily, and help determine the period and circumstances during which The Metrical Homily was written?

There are many factors that suggest Jacob of Serugh is the author of The Metrical Homily. One important factor is the bitterness which the author had against the Persians. This helps us frame the date of The Metrical Homily in the period during which the Persians committed atrocities, in the same region where Jacob Serugh lived and ministered.

When we study of the metrical homily on Alexander, we discover this bitterness the author had against the Persians. He says that the Gog and Magog "will come to Persia to strip it and destroy it."[459] The bitterness of Jacob of Serugh against the Persians was due to the violence and the atrocities the Persians committed when they occupied some regions of the Roman Empire. For example, in 503 A.D. after a siege lasting three months, the Persians occupied the city of Amid. They killed most the inhabitants with the sword, and made captives of the rest. The Christians living, in the adjacent regions, fled to the western regions of the Euphrates. Jacob of Serugh wrote to them encouraging them to stand firm. Thus, we see that Jacob of Serugh resented the Persians for their violence against the Christians, especially in the region of Serugh.

Jacob failed to mention the Huns, who were the main danger in the letter which we previously discussed, "A Christian legend concerning

Alexander." Toward the end of the 5th century, when Jacob composed this homily, the Huns did not exist and, therefore, posed no threat to the Eastern Roman Empire, but the Persians. When the Persians invaded of the city of Amid in 503 A.D., they killed most of the inhabitants with the sword, clearly demonstrating the cruelty of the Persian occupation replaced the Huns as their violent enemies and major threat. This made a great impact on the author of this metrical Homily. These factors make us strongly assume that the author was Jacob of Serugh, and that the homily dates back to the beginning of the 6th century A.D..

The similarity between the two Syriac writings, "A Christian Legend Concerning Alexander" and "The Metrical Homily on Alexander" by Jacob of Serugh, suggests that Jacob used a well-known Syriac text based on the book of Pseudo-Callisthenes.

This conclusion is supported by the fact that both Syriac writings were based on chapters 37-39 of the second book of Pseudo-Callisthenes, according to Müller's Greek MS. C. according to Müller's Greek MS. C. The gate, built by Alexander and referred to in both writings, came from chapter 29 of the third book of Pseudo-Callisthenes according to Müller's Greek MS. C. It is obvious that Jacob of Serugh had edited the existing Syriac text and added what encouraged his contemporary readers, reminding them of the violent crimes of the Persians and their final judgment. Thus, he replaced the Huns with the Persians.

The subject of imprisoning Gog and Magog in The Metrical Homily on Alexander and in the Quran

There are a lot of similarities between The Metrical Homily on Alexander and Dhu al Qarnayn in the Quran. Thus, analyzing The Metrical Homily is a determinant factor in tracing the sources of Islam regarding the dam built by Dhu al Qarnayn, given the place this dam has in the Quranic eschatology.

Like all tales about the savage peoples living on the extremity of the earth, the people living there complained to Alexander about them because they were corrupt and dangerous. Thus, Alexander decided to imprison them. Alexander asked if there were a mountain that would separate Gog and Magog. They answered him by saying there were lofty mountains which God placed between them:

> Then an old man said, "Look, my lord, the king, and see a wonder. God has set this mountain as a great boundary." King Alexander, the son of Philip then asked, "How far does this mountain extend?" and the man replied, "Beyond India it extends in its appearance." To which the King asked, "How far does this side come?" and the old man replied, "unto the ends of the earth." The king was seized with wonder at the counsel of the old man. The great king began to ask more questions because he wanted to learn more about everything.
>
> The king asked: "Who are these kings and the terrible people who are beyond this mountain?" to which the old man replied, Listen, O Master, and King, and we will tell thee. Behold, the families of Gog and the families of Magog are beyond us, terrible of aspect and hateful of form, and they are tall. The stature of each one is between six and seven cubits...
>
> The old man also said Gog and Magog, "bathe in blood, and in blood they wash their heads. They drink blood and they eat the flesh of men...They are more ferocious and have more wars than all the other nations... and they overturn the lands, and uproot mountains, and devour men."[460]

This reminds us of Mohammed's Hadith and his companions (including Ali bin Abi Taleb) sayings about the excessive stature of Gog and Magog.[461] Mohammed's cousin and son-in-law, Ali bin Abi Taleb was acquainted with Mohammed's myths. The description of Gog and Magog by the Syriac writings are also consistent with Mohammed's sayings about them: Their stature was like the cedar tree, and they do not bury the dead, but eat their flesh and drink their blood.

The metrical homily on Alexander says that after Alexander heard about the atrocities committed by Gog and Magog, he put in his heart to erect a gate in order to imprison them. Alexander looked to the mountain which God had set to be boundary, and asked:

> Where have the hosts come forth to plunder the land and all the world from of old?" They showed Alexander a place in the middle of the mountains—a narrow pass constructed by God. The king looked upon the pass with wonderment, and he saw that the mountain was excessively large and was terribly strong on all sides. Above it he saw a river of blood flowing down, against the people like a torrent of water. He examined the river and concluded that he would build a great and wonderful door for all the world to see. The Spirit of the Lord stirred the king, the son of Philip, to restrain wickedness from the land.[462]

There is Mohammed's Hadith about this mountain which separated Gog and Magog from the rest of the world. Mohammed called it "the barrier: two mountains are so smooth that everything slips down from them."[463]

While Alexander was considering erecting the gate, he fought the king of the Persians who had 62 other kings with him. God stood with Alexander in the camp so that he prevailed,[464] punished and severely destroyed them. This is one of the passages which the Quran copied when he said Alexander was given authority from Allah to punish the nations who are not submitted to Allah, as is portrayed in al Kahf, Surah 18, verses 86 and 87.

Filling the narrow pass with iron and brass as reported in the Syriac Homily and in the Quran

Later, Alexander erected the gate to imprison the people of Magog until the last day. He bought a great quantity of iron and brass, and ordered 12 thousand skilled workmen whom the king of Egypt sent to begin construction:

> He, the wise man, called the workmen and taught them how they should make the length and breadth of it, with great strength. He measured the ground of the narrow pass between the mountains, that he might shut in the peoples of the house of Magog until the end. The king in his wisdom measured from mountain to mountain, twelve cubits in the strength of his power. The king said "make you a threshold for the whole pass, and let it be sunk in the mountain on this side and on that."" Then he filled this distance between the two mountains with iron and brass, and fixed the edges of the gate with huge bolts through cunning work.[465]

Preparing the pass between the two mountains and filling it with iron and brass is summarized in the Quran, Surah 18: 96:

> Bring me the blocks of iron," he said. When he had filled up the space between the edges of the two mountains, he said. "blow on it, and it became fire. He said "bring me Qiter, (which is molten brass,) so I pour on it.

The Syriac author continues:

> They came over the peoples of the house of Magog who had not perceived the building.[466]

It means they failed to find an escape from the complicated and strong building, and they soon learned they could not dig it through it. This idea was also copied in the Quran and expressed in verse 97, where we read:

Then they could not scale it nor dig through it.

The most important accomplishment Alexander

Both Jacob Serugh's homily and the Quran said that erecting a gate or a dam in which to imprison Gog and Magog was the most important accomplishment Alexander ever had. However, no historian outside these sources ever mentioned such a feat.

Serugh's metrical homily on Alexander claims that ambassadors from all the nations of the earth came and saw the gate and told about this great work accomplished by Alexander. He claims that since this legendary gate was the most important accomplishment in the life of Alexander, everyone on earth knew about the gate and they were happy that it was erected. Without a doubt, Serugh's account was behind the narration of the Quran when it said a dam was the principal accomplishment of Dhu al Qarnayn through which he imprisoned Gog and Magog until the last day.

Although many of historical books, chronicled the life of Alexander and gave details of all his accomplishments, the dam was never mentioned. Many of these books were written by the companions of Alexander who were themselves witnesses to what he had done and what he had accomplished during his campaigns, but none of them ever mentioned the dam. The origin of the legendary work about the gate comes from pseudo-Callisthenes' book, and Syrian writings.

In both Jacob Serugh's homily and the Quran the opening of the gate in the last day is the central eschatological point.

The Syrian author claims that God spoke to Alexander through an angel saying in the final days, wickedness will increase. The angel told Alexander the gate will remain closed until the last days, then it will be opened and the world will come to an end.

Jacob Serugh mentions some of the signs of the last days and the opening of the gate. He says:

> And when these things have come to an end and passed away before the end. The earth shall quake and this door which you has made be opened. At the end of times creatures and men shall come evil to increase. And wickedness shall wax strong in all quarters of the earth … and the nation that is within this gate shall be roused up, and also the hosts of Agog and the peoples of Magog shall be gathered together. Those peoples, the fiercest of all creatures, of the mighty house of

Japheth of whom the Lord spake saying ' they shall go forth on the earth and cover all creation like a locust' the king marveled at these things which he had heard from the angel whom the Lord had sent to him a vision to teach him these things.[467]

The watcher said:

When all the things that written have been completed, the Lord will command, and by his beck will be opened this door. When the anger of the Lord waxes hot to slay men, in His ill will He will rouse up the people of the house of Magog against the lands. In the seven thousandth year, in which the heavens and the earth shall be dissolved, the hosts and troops shall go forth from their lands. The thousands and the ranks and the assemblies without number shall come. And shall stand behind this door ... and the voice of the Lord shall overthrow the height of this door. Over the threshold which carries this strong door, the hosts of horses and men shall tread and go forth. Another host which shall go forth after the hosts. The door and the bolts shall the Lord destroy and carry away."[468]

The pictures we see here are from Jacob Serugh's metrical homily on Alexander, but they are summarized in the Quran's story in Surah18, al Kahf, verse 98:

When the promise of my lord – the last day- comes to pass, he will make it into dust. And the promise of my lord about the last day is true.

But it doesn't stop here. Jacob Serugh describes in detail how the hosts of Gog and Magog swarm to destroy the world:

The hosts which shall go forth from thence shall cover the earth. In anger shall the hosts and the assemblies and the thousands go forth. With drawn swords and bent bows and sharp arrows, with wrath and murder and eager horses and pointed spears... they will fly and settle down upon the quarters of the whole world. And kings and hosts shall flee away before them... the whole creation shall totter and fall under the ruin... they shall rise up and go forth and fill the earth with their assemblies ...when the anger of the Lord waxes hot against the wicked, He will send over the earth the people of Agog and the people of Magog. Before the end of the world they shall go forth to destroy.[469]

This description about Gog and Magog, in the last days filling the earth with their hosts is expressed in al Anbiya', Surah 21: 96, 97:

Until the barrier is demolished, Gog and Magog they will swiftly swarm from every hill. Then the true promise (which is the end of the world,) will come near.

Mohammed's Hadith shows his dependence on the Syriac eschatology

In addition to what Mohammed adopted in his Quran about the imprisonment of Gog and Magog behind a dam — claiming that, as an eschatological sign, the dam will be demolished only on the Last Day of history — he also adopted other eschatological elements from the Syriacs.

In Mohammed's alleged ascension to heaven, he claimed to have met Abraham, Moses and Jesus. He discussed the signs of the end of the world. Abraham and Moses ignored the events of the end times, but Jesus said that "al Dajjal, the false prophet, will come first, and he will perish when he sees Jesus coming again. Then Gog and Magog will come out to the world, swarming from every hill. They will eat everything they encounter and drink all the waters of all the rivers. When people return to me and complain against them, I will call upon God, and He will kill them."[470]

In Mohammed's other Hadiths he repeats the same thing, adding that the earth will cry to God because of the bad smell of Gog and Magog and God will send rain that will carry their bodies to the sea.[471]

This indicates Mohammed was acquainted with some Syriac thoughts about the coming of Christ. A wicked personality will appear who will dominate the whole world. This personality is called the Anti-Christ. We read in 2 Thessalonians 2:7-8:

> However, the one who holds him back will do so until he is taken out of the way, and then the lawless one will be revealed, whom the Lord will destroy by the breath of his mouth and wipe out by the manifestation of his arrival.

Mohammed's Hadith connects Al Dajjal with the second coming of Christ, reflecting a Syriac teaching based on the New Testament. However, the Syriacs were not careful with the text of Ezekiel regarding an attack by a northern country against Israel at the end of the days. The northern country, called Gog and Magog, will lead an alliance of many nations against Israel. For despite the Bible does not mention a connection, the Syriacs linked this attack with the return of Christ.

The Syriacs adopted the myths of Pseudo-Callisthenes' book about Alexander which means that Gog and Magog were present throughout history, and have been imprisoned in that mythological dam. This shaped Mohammed's eschatology and he followed their path and their myths. In the Bible, Ezekiel in chapters 38 and 39 speaks about Gog and Magog, but he does not indicate they lived in his lifetime, nor does he believe they were imprisoned behind a gate or a dam.

It is abundantly clear that the teaching that the end of the world comes by opening a gate allowing the armies of Gog and Magog to cover the whole earth and destroy it is the same in Jacob Serugh's metrical homily, in the Quran and in "A Christian Legend Concerning Alexander." Both are based on the second book of pseudo-Callisthenes, according to Müller's Greek Manuscript C.

Many Syriac changes were introduced into the book between the 4th and 6th centuries A.D. The two Syriac writings which we have studied are two of these changes or edits.

The myths of The Metrical Homily spread to Nijran and to other northern regions of Arabia, including Mecca and Medina.

One may ask how the Syriac writings reached Mohammed? Without a doubt, the concepts contained in the Syriac writings concerning the Last Day were adopted by some Syriac groups.

The same myth was also adopted by other churches, which depended on the Syriac churches for their doctrines. They were mostly churches which existed in Mesopotamia and Arabia during the 6th century and at the beginning of the 7th century A.D. before the rise of Islam. These Syriac churches were known for their missionary activity in Arabia, especially in areas like Nijran, not far from Mecca. Many leaders in the Syriac churches, such as Jacob Serugh, were allied with the church of Nijran and with other churches in Yemen.

The Quran did not depend totally on ideas embraced by the Syriac churches. The Quran did not limit itself to Gog and Magog and the mythological journey of Alexander. In the Quran, Mohammed copied several doctrines which the Syriacs wrote such as The Legend of the Seven Sleepers of Ephesus which was reported in the Surah al Kahlf, chapter 18. The influence of the middle Eastern mythology carried by the Syriacs to many groups in Arabia at the time of Mohammed is easily seen. No wonder Mohammed could adapt the Syriac eschatology and include it in his Quran.

The Syriac myths and doctrines were well-known to Mohammed. He owned Syriac books, but was circumspect that no body of his companions could know about them, in order to prevent them from discovering his Syriac sources. As an example, we read in the book of Tabaqat al Kubra of ibn Saad and in the book of Kinz al Aamal by al Hindi:

> Zayd bin Thabet said: 'the apostle of Allah said to me: "some people gave books, but I do not like anybody to read them. Are you ready to learn the Syriac language?" I said: 'yes.' Then I learned it in 17 nights.'[472]

Answering Muslims who attempt to help the Quran save face for adopting the myths of Pseudo-Callisthenes and the Syriac writings

Today the science of comparative religions often depends on ancient literature, archeology and the writings of those religions. This study sheds light on the sources of the words that appear in the Quran. Recent discoveries have disturbed those who want to defend the Quran and attribute it to Allah.

The study of Dhu al Qarnayn in Surah al Kahf, the sources of the Surah from the book of Pseudo-Callisthenes, and the Syriac writings which were all based on Pseudo Callisthenes, is a fact which has come to light in the scholarly field. The relationship between the trip of Alexander the Great to the extremities of the earth as portrayed in the book of Pseudo-Callisthenes, and the trip of Dhu al Qarnayn in the Quran is a well-known fact.

The attempts by some Muslims to deal with the dilemma of the Quran's adopting the myths of Pseudo-Callisthenes and the Syriac writings have caused them to adopt two approaches. They wanted, in any case, to enable the Quran to save face because, in the eyes of the educated people of the world, it has become entangled and implicated in adopting well- known myths, based on a primitive mythological geography of the earth.

The first Islamic approach consists of creating doubt that Dhu al Qarnayn is actually Alexander the Great. They tend to make him an unknown personality in history. However, since claiming that Dhu al Qarnayn is an unknown personality in our history has become unrealistic and impractical, the ones who tried to ignore his being Alexander have become aware of the futility of persisting in this claim. In fact, the Jews of Mecca and al Nather bin Hareth, the educated man from Mecca who studied at Hira-Iraq, examined Mohammed regarding the personality of

Dhu al Qarnayn. He was well-known to them; otherwise, they would not have chosen his identity as a test for Mohammed. Thus, how could the Jews of Mecca and al Nather bin Hareth in Mohammed's generation have known about this important historical personality, though limited in knowledge when compared to the knowledge of our day? Whereas, we who possess immense historical knowledge due to the study of ancient manuscripts, in addition to archeological discoveries, are still unable to identify this personality.

Therefore, the personality of Dhu al Qarnayn at the time of Mohammed was famous, to the extent that the Jews in the area of Mecca, and others of Mecca such as al Nather, possessed enough knowledge to identify him.

Accordingly, some Muslims understood that insisting that the personality of Dhu al Qarnayn was unknown, and that it was before history, was no longer a useful approach in defending the Quran. Thus, they proposed persons such as Cyrus and others like Dhu al Qarnayn.

The second approach is adopted by some Muslims who, viewing the perfect correspondence between Dhu al Qarnayn's journey in the Quran and Alexander's journey in Pseudo-Callisthenes and the Syriac writings, became convinced that there is no way to escape this dilemma except by claiming that Pseudo-Callisthenes and the Syriac authors copied from the Quran. In the upcoming pages, I will refute both of these Islamic approaches.

Is Dhu al Qarnayn of the Quran also Alexander the Great?

Some Muslims tried to ignore the fact that Mohammed in the Quran referred to Dhu al Qarnayn when he intended Alexander. However, the correspondence between the trip of Alexander as we see it in the book of Pseudo-Callisthenes and the Syriac writings and the trip of Dhu al Qarnayn in Surah al Kahf, is sufficient in itself to prove that Mohammed had copied the myths which were spread in his time from those sources. When he wrote about Dhu al Qarnayn he meant none other than Alexander the Great.

Islamic attempts to avoid mixing Dhu al Qarnayn with Alexander appeared only recently when Muslims discovered that the source of Dhu al Qarnayn originated in the book of Pseudo-Callisthenes. Islamic attempts seem to contradict the Hadiths of Mohammed in which he clarifies that

Dhu al Qarnayn was indeed Alexander. To correct the problem they also would have to contradict all the famous expositors of the Quran, who all agreed that Dhu al Qarnayn was Alexander. They would also have to contradict the official history which states that the title "of two horns" which is the translation of Dhu al Qarnayn, is exclusive to Alexander.

Regarding Mohammed's Hadith about Dhu al Qarnayn being Alexander, we find that in various expository books on the Quran, such as al Taberi, al Qurtubi, ibn Kathir, and ibn Hajar. They all hold that view. Mohammad said that Dhu al Qarnayn built the city of Alexandria in Egypt. This confirms that Mohammed intended Alexander when he used the name Dhu al Qarnayn. Mohammed mentioned that an angel carried Dhu al Qarnayn high into the sky until the cities seemed very small. This actually is part of the myths of Pseudo-Callisthenes' book. Some versions of the book say that an eagle took flight carrying Alexander. Other versions say that an angel carried Alexander.

Mohammed mentioned other details which are characteristic of Pseudo-Callisthenes' book. He has the angel taking Alexander to the al Sad which was the barrier. Mohammed said the Sad was two very smooth mountains from which everything slips down from them. He said the angel carried Dhu al Qarnayn until they passed Gog and Magog. The angel accompanied him to another nation where the people have dogs' faces. This corresponds to the trip Alexander made in Pseudo-Callisthenes' book. According to the Syriac version, and the Syriac writings which depended upon this book, we find the Dog-men are located beyond the region where the savage people live, and became as Gog and Magog in the Metrical Syriac writings of Jacob Sarugh. Then Mohammed mentioned another nation after the Dog-men nation — something corresponding to what we see in the Syriac writings where, after the Dog-men, there is mentioned a nation before reaching the "Paradise of God."

Without a doubt, Mohammed's narration astonishingly agrees with the Pseudo-Callisthenes' book and the Syriac writings, which were based on this book, proving that Mohammed was acquainted with the myths of the book which were spread in his time.

Moreover, Mohammed's Hadith confirms the views of the scholars that an Arabic version of Pseudo-Callisthenes' book existed before the time of Mohammed. This version was based on the lost Pahlavi version. Scholars maintain that the Arabic version is closer to the existing Ethiopian version, which also was based on the lost Pahlavi version.

Here is Mohammed's Hadith. Mohammed said to a group of Christians who came to visit him:

> You came to ask me about Dhu al Qarnayn and what you find in your book. He was a young Rumi man [the word Rumi was used at the time of Mohammed for both the Greek and the Romans.] He came and built the city of Alexandria in Egypt. When he finished building the city, an angel came to him and flew away with him up to the sky. Then he asked him. What do you see ?' He answered, 'I see my city and other cities.' Then he went higher and he asked him, 'What do you see ?' He answered, 'I see my city.' Then he flew higher with him and asked again. 'What do you see?' He answered, 'I see the earth.' The angel said, 'This sea surrounds the world. Allah sent me to you in order that you could teach the ignorant and confirm the sapient.' Then he brought him to the Sad, which were the two very smooth mountains where everything slips down from the top. Then he accompanied him until they passed Gog and Magog. Then he brought him to the other nations composed of humans with the faces of dogs. They were fighting Gog and Magog. Then the angel accompanied him across other nations, who fought the dog faced people. Then he accompanied him until he crossed another nation.[473]

A study of Mohammed's Hadith fits perfectly with the myths of Pseudo-Callisthenes about the trips of Alexander on the extremities of the earth. The well-known expositors of the Quran, all confirm that Dhu al Qarnayn was Alexander. Ibn Hayyan says, "It was mentioned in the Hadith, 'Four men governed the earth. Two of them are believers: Solomon son of David and Dhu al Qarnayn.' Throughout history Dhu al Qarnayn, has had great fame and could be none other than Alexander. So it is necessary to ascertain with certainty the identity that Dhu al Qarnayn is Alexander, the son of Philipus the Greek."[474]

Al Razi said that Dhu al Qarnayn was Alexander because he reached the extremities of the West and East.[475] The same idea is confirmed by al Qurtubi who said: "Dhu al Qarnayn is Alexander, the Greek Macedonian king."[476] Al Allusi said the same thing.[477] Among the early famous writers who said that Dhu al Qarnayn was Alexander was Wahab bin Munabbeh.[478]

Dhu al Qarnayn was known by the pre-Islamic Jahiliyyah to be Alexander the Macedonian. For example, al A'sha الأعشى , a pre-Islamic poet, mentioned the death of Dhu al Qarnayn in Iraq. He meant Alexander who died in Babel, Iraq:

والصعب ذو القرنين أصبح بالحنو في جدث أميم مقيم ثاويا

وقوله بالحنو يريد حنو قراقر الذي مات فيه ذو القرنين بالعراق [479]

The same poem was reported also by al Zubeidi:

والصعب ذو القرنين أصبح ثاويا بالحنو في جدث، أميم، مقيم [480]

It is clear from all these incidents that Mohammed equated Alexander with Dhu al Qarnayn. However, today, when the accounts of Alexander's trip are known to many, and it corresponded to what the Quran said about the trip of Dhu al Qarnayn, Muslims are avoiding any verification that Dhu al Qarnayn is Alexander. In an attempt to avoid any verification, some Muslims have adopted the idea of the existence of two Dhu al Qarneins, one who lived at the time of Abraham [some say at the time of Moses.], and the second was Alexander the Macedonian. Yet, no leader existed in history who occupied the West and the East at the time of Abraham or Moses, so this cannot provide Muslims with an excuse. In fact, a leader like this did not appear before the Persian Achaemenian period, which began in the 6th century B.C. Before the Achaemenian Empire appeared, there was no empire which occupied both the West and East. Kingdoms in those periods did not stretch their domain outside their region. As an example, the most powerful of the ancient kingdoms was Egypt. During some periods of its history it expanded into the land of Canaan and part of Syria. The same thing is true for the kingdoms inside Mesopotamia. Only the kingdom of Ur spread in North Syria, and fell in the end around 2004 B.C. Later, strong kingdoms rose up in Mesopotamia, such as the Assyrian and Babylonian kingdoms which occupied the Fertile Crescent and, in certain periods, Egypt and part of Asia Minor, but they never occupied the West or the East.

The same is true for the kingdoms which were in Iranian territories. They were very limited until the Achaemenian period, which began in the 6th century B.C. Therefore, we cannot find Dhu al Qarnayn in ancient times.

Some Muslims claim that Dhu al Qarnayn was Fradun.[481] Those who attempted to identified Dhu al Qarnayn with Fradun, who according to the Persian mythology had fought Asi Dahak, ignored the idea that Fradun was an imaginary mythological figure who never lived at all. Asi Dahak is also a mythological figure, portrayed in Persian mythology as coming from the devil. On his head, were many serpents and he had three eyes and three mouths.

Still others tried to differentiate between Alexander the Greek and "the Alexander the Roman."[482] History showed us that Alexander did not reach the West beyond minor Greek regions. Some Muslims claim that Dhu al Qarnayn was a Roman Alexander and not a Greek one. However, he did not exist within the Romans emperors named Alexander who occupied the East and the West.

Still other Muslims tried to find Alexander among the Himyarite kings of Yemen to escape the fact that Dhu al Qarnayn was Alexander. These Muslims quote the poem of Tubb'a ', the Himyarite, in which he says, "Dhu al Qarnayn was a Muslim before me, a king to whom kings were subjected."[483] However, none of the kings of Yemen occupied the West and East. Furthermore, the kingdom of Himyar appeared as a tribe dominating only a small part of Yemen beginning in the year 115 B.C.[484] In the year 275 A.D. the Himyarites occupied Saba.)[485] However, they never expanded outside the Arabian peninsula. They never occupied Eastern Arabia, except for north and central Arabia. The history of the Himyarites is well known because of the writings and visits done by classical historians and geographers and through the rich Himyarite inscriptions. Nowhere do we read that they occupied parts of Asia or Europe, or reached outside Arabia.

Through his poetry, Tubb'a wanted to say that Dhu al Qarnayn lived in an earlier time. Tubb'a recited a poem when he occupied Mecca during the first part of the 5th century AD, mentioning that Dhu al Qarnayn found the sun setting in a fetid muddy spring. We now know that Tubb'a's ideas were derived from the writings of Pseudo-Callisthenes, and the Syriac writings, in which it is stated that the sun set near the fetid sea and entered a gate that led to heaven.

Can Dhu al Qarnayn be identified as Cyrus

To get rid of the dilemma of associating Dhu al Qarnayn with Alexander, many Muslims embraced the idea that Cyrus the Great was Dhu al Qarnayn.

Those who make this claim use the following verse in the book of Daniel:

I raised my eyes and saw, and behold, a ram standing on the bank of the canal. It had two horns, and both horns were high, but one was higher than the other, and the higher one came up last. (Daniel 8:3).

They say that the ram was Cyrus. Whereas, the ram here represented the Media-Persian kingdom, the higher horn represented the Medians, which were stronger than the Persians. But eventually the Persian element increased and dominated the kingdom. The book itself explains that the ram was the kingdom of Media and Persia with all its kings. This explanation came to Daniel through an angel:

> As for the ram that you saw with the two horns, these are the kings of Media and Persia. (Daniel 8:20)

In fact, in the same chapter, the goat that hit the ram was the Greek kingdom. When the Bible says the goat hit the ram, it referred to the Greek victory over the Persian Kingdom ruled by Darius III. Alexander the Great did not hit Cyrus, so it cannot be said that the ram was Cyrus.

Muslims also cite the following verse from Isaiah:

> Thus says the LORD to his anointed, to Cyrus, whose right hand I have grasped, to subdue nations before him and to loose the belts of kings, to open doors before him that gates may not be closed. (Isaiah 45:1)

The use of the phrase "anointed of the Lord" in the Old Testament does not necessarily mean that a person is righteous. We have people who had this title, yet were in a state of rebellion against God, such as King Saul. The term reflected God's choice for a person to fulfill a special task. The verse in Isaiah is a prophecy about God choosing Cyrus to judge Babylonia, and for the return of the Jews from their exile, and the rebuilding of the Temple in Jerusalem. Cyrus is not the only pagan leader in the Bible who was given a good title by God. Even though Nebuchadnezzar was a pagan king, God called him "my servant," as we see in Jeremiah 25:9:

> Behold, I will send for all the tribes of the north, declares the LORD, and for Nebuchadnezzar the king of Babylon, my servant, and I will bring them against this land and its inhabitants, and against all these surrounding nations. I will devote them to destruction, and make them a horror, a hissing, and an everlasting desolation.

The reason he is called God's servant is because God chose him to judge Judah and the surrounding kingdoms.

There is a good test. What did the Quran say about Dhu al Qarnayn, that does not match Cyrus?

Cyrus only reached as far west as Asia Minor, or modern-day Turkey. He did not reach the extremities of the West which the Quran described Dhu al Qarnayn as reaching. Furthermore, although historians such as

Herodotus wrote about Cyrus and his wars, and in addition to the many inscriptions we have about Cyrus, we never see any mention of the dam of Iron and brass that would have imprisoned a savage people throughout history.

Also, the Quran depicted Dhu al Qarnayn as being an invincible person that Allah says about him:

> Verily We established his power on earth, and We gave him the ways and the means to all ends.

This picture cannot apply to Cyrus who, as we understand through Herodotus, was killed during his war with the tribe of Massagetae, who inhabited the deserts of Khwarizmi, in the regions today known as Kazakhstan and Uzbekistan.

When we search Cyrus' religion and attitude toward the other religions, we see the picture of him is far removed from what the Quran narrated about Dhu al Qarnayn, who would have been a monotheistic leader fighting all other religions to subdue them to Allah. This picture matches in all its details what the pseudo-Callisthenes book and Syriac writings wrote about Alexander.

Mary Boyce, a scholar who is specialized in Zoroastrianism, proved that Cyrus the Great, was a Zoroastrian. Cyrus followed his ancestors in observing Zoroastrian rituals. In his palace he had Zoroastrian practices and rituals. Boyce quoted many Greek texts which confirm that Zoroastrian priests enjoyed a special authority in his palace and within his retinue.[486]

Cyrus was known for his tolerance and his respect for all the religions of his time. After Cyrus occupied Babel, he was coronated at Babel, On the first day of spring, he went to the temple of Marduch, the main god of the Babylonians. He announced new legislation which became an ancient form of human rights. He entered the temple of Marduch to honor the deity of the great Babylonian empire. Gezenfone, a Greek military officer and historian, recorded the celebration which took place at the coronation of Cyrus as the ruler of Babel.

Archaeologists found an important epigraph in the city of Ur. Here are some statements of this important epigraph which is now in the British National Library:

> Now by the grace of Mazda, I am crowned as the king of Iran, Babylonia and the four cardinal countries, I declare that: As long as I am alive and

favoured by Mazda, to lead the kingdom of Iran, Babylonia and the four cardinal countries, I will undertake to honor the religion and customs of all nations under my kingdom. Thus, no governor or other subordinates under my realm shall be allowed to humiliate or insult the religion or custom of the nations under my kingdom or of other nations. From now, that I am crowned, until I am alive and blessed by Mazda for this kingdom, I shall never impose my kingdom on any nation. The people are free to wage war or not to wage war.

As long as I am the king of Iran, Babylonia and the four cardinal countries, I shall not allow one person to oppress another. So, if anyone's right is injured, I shall punish the oppressor and and give what was taken from the oppressed. As long as I live, I shall not allow anyone to take some others' property by force, or take it without due consideration or satisfaction for the owner. As long as I live, I shall not allow anyone to use forced or unpaid labor.

Today I announce that everybody is free to choose any religion he believes in, and live any where he desires, provided he does not arrogate others' rights, and take any occupation he likes, and spend his property in any way he decides, providing he does not harm others' rights. I declare that every person is responsible for himself, and that no one shall be punished for actions committed by his relatives. Thus, punishment of a criminal's brother is forbidden. If a member of a family or tribe has committed a crime, he should by the person who is punished. Only the criminal and no one else.

So long as, with the grace of Mazda, I rule as the king, I shall not allow any man or woman to be sold as a slave. In this regard, my governors and other subordinates shall be responsible, within the sphere of their influence, to prevent the trade of slavery. This custom should be totally abolished throughout the world. And, I beg Mazda to succeed me in performing the obligations I have taken towards the nations of Iran, Babylonia and the four cardinal countries.

Cyrus

The Bible tells us that God appoints the kings and the rules of the earth, even though they were not believers, but they practiced pagan worship. In several verses, the Bible commends Cyrus. I believe it does so, because Cyrus respected the faith of the Israelites which was in God. Cyrus granted permission to the Jews to perform their religious rituals and their desire to return to Jerusalem to rebuild the Temple. What Cyrus did for Israel, he did for other nations. He addressed each nation using their own religious language and the name of their deities.

The Cyrus Cylinder discovered in 1879 confirms Cyrus' actions. This important Cylinder was found under the foundation of the temple of Marduch, the Babylonian god. It was discovered by Hormuzd Rassam, the famous British archeologist who discovered many important archeological items, including the tables of Gilgamesh. The Cyrus Cylinder, also known as Cyrus's inscription cylinder, was inscribed in Akkadian cuneiform on a clay barrel which now rests in the British Museum.

On this cylinder, Cyrus tells us about the mistake Nabonidus, the Babylon king whom Cyrus defeated, against the gods of Mesopotamia including Marduch, whom Cyrus calls "The king of the gods." Marduch looks for a new leader to replace Nabonidus and Marduch then announces that Cyrus had been chosen as the new leader over Babel. So Marduch gave Cyrus victory over Babel. Then Cyrus wrote on the cylinder how he returned the people to their own cities. These were the people whom the Babylonian kings had exiled to Babel. Cyrus also told how he rebuilt temples for the gods. Here is some of the text that appeared on the cylinder:

> As far as Ashur and Susa, Agade, Eshnunna, the towns of Zamban, Me-Turnu, Der as well as the region of the Gutians, I returned to (these) sacred cities on the other side of the Tigris, the sanctuaries of which have been ruins for a long time, the images which (used) to live therein and established for them permanent sanctuaries. I (also) gathered all their former inhabitants and returned (to them) their habitations. Furthermore, I resettled upon the command of Marduk, the great lord, all the gods of Sumer and Akkad whom Nabonidus has brought into Babylon to the anger of the lord of the gods, unharmed, in their (former) chapels, the places which made them happy.

> May all the gods whom I have resettled in their sacred cities ask Bel and Nebo for a long life for me and may they recommend me (to him); to Marduk, my lord, they may say this: "Cyrus, the king who worships you, and Cambyses , his son, ... all of them I settled in a peaceful place ... ducks and doves, ... I endeavored to fortify/repair their dwelling places.

You may study this important inscription by re-reading the text books of archeologists, like as James Bennett Pritchard. [487]

We notice that Cyrus addressed the Babylonians in their own religious language, claiming that Murdock gave him authority over the nations. We also see that Cyrus honored the religions of each group which means he rebuilt the temples of worship for their gods. He returned the people to their land which the Babylonians took. He also returned their gods to the people. Everyone was sent back to his holy city, and Cyrus rebuilt the temples where these gods were worshiped.

Thus, we understand why Cyrus said that God gave him all the nations, and commanded him to rebuild the temple in Jerusalem. That is why Cyrus addressed each group of people in the language of their religion. He did so, in order that he might be accepted by the people of each country he occupied.

To prove that Cyrus was Dhu al Qarnayn, some Muslims claim that Ahura Mazda was God, that Zoroastrianism was a monotheistic religion, and that Zoroaster was a prophet to the true God. This claim is made despite Zoroaster making Mithra an important deity along with Ahura Mazda, compromising with the Aryan religion that preceded him. He also accepted many pagan deities which were worshiped in his time: adopting fire, earth and water as gods. Also he made Tistrya, the star Sirius, as the lord of stars worthy of worship as Ahura Mazda.

The bottom line is that Cyrus the Great, was a Zoroastrian who respected and honored the religions of the people whom he subdued. But this picture doesn't match the picture which the Quran draws of Dhu al Qarnayn. the Quran portrays Dhu al Qarnayn as a Muslim leader, who made Jihad to impose Islam on the nations of the world, punishing each nation that refused Islam, and imposing Jezieh, the dreaded tribute.

By the same token, Cyrus never was called Dhu al Qarnayn. The picture which we find in the Quran of Dhu al Qarnayn fits perfectly with what we find in the book of Pseudo-Callisthenes about Alexander with two horns. All the details in Pseudo-Callisthenes are consistent with his trip in Surah al Kahf. It is so similar that it must be the one described for Alexander in Pseudo-Callisthenes.

Although Mohammed never mentioned the name Cyrus, he mentioned the name of Alexander as Dhu al Qarnayn. With that in mind, where do we get the idea that Cyrus was Dhu al Qarnayn, an idea which has only appeared in modern days? We get this idea because Muslims knew that Alexander was a pagan leader, and that the myths which the Quran tells concerning him first appeared in Pseudo-Callisthenes, and in the Syriac writings which were built on this book. Muslims also know that the myths of Pseudo-Callisthenes contradict the official history about Alexander, as seen in Greek historical books. Because of this, they desired to remove attention from the fact that Mohammed copied the myths of Pseudo-Callisthenes.

Alexander the Great claimed to be the "son of god named Amon." Usually shown with two horns. Thus, Alexander was honored by the Greeks who put his image on their coins. depicting him with the horns of Amon on his head. The title by which Alexander was known, "with two horns," translated into Arabic as Dhu al Qarnayn, was commonly spread in the ancient world long before Islam. When Mohammed used this title, it was understood by the average person that it referred to Alexander.

After Alexander occupied Egypt, he went to the temple of the god Amon in Libya, where he was coronated by Amon's priests as a son of Amon, who had the two horns of a ram, which symbolized fertility (others say it symbolized the western and eastern extremities of the earth). After this incident, Alexander began claiming that he was the son of Amon, who was portrayed with two horns. This explains the issuance of coins honoring Alexander with two horns on his head. Lysimachus, who was close to Alexander's time, became king over Macedonia and Asia Minor, issued the coins in 306 B.C.

Coins depicting Alexander with two horns were also issued in Arabia. The most ancient of these coins were issued in the city Gerra on the Persian Gulf. They go back to the third and second centuries B.C. Today these coins are in the British Museum.

This shows that the title of Alexander "with two horns," is a famous and ancient fact in Arabia as well as throughout the whole Middle East.

It seems the title of Dhu al Qarnayn (with two horns) is derived from the Aramaic: Alexander was known in Aramaic by the title "Tre-Qarnayia," which means "two horns."[488]

In many mythological writings that spread throughout the Middle East, especially in the Syriac, we find the title of Dhu al quarnein being attributed to Alexander the Great. As an example, we read in the Syriac writing attributed to Jacob Sarugh, which goes back to the sixth century A.D., and was based on the book of Pseudo-Callisthenes, the following:

O God... I know in my mind that thou hast exalted me above all kings, and thou hast made me horns upon my head, wherewith I might thrust down the kingdoms of the world.[489]

Thus, the title of Alexander being depicted with two horns is a well-known historical fact. It was spread in the Middle East before the rise of

Islam, so when Mohammed used this title "Dhu al Qarnayn," it was understood by the average person living in his time that he intended it to refer to Alexander the Macedonian.

The Islamic claim that Pseudo-Callisthenes and the Syriac authors copied from the Quran.

Many Muslims became aware of the striking similarities between Dhu al Qarnayn's journey in Surah al Kahf and Alexander's journey in Pseudo-Callisthenes, and the Syriac writings based on the book. They felt that if they wanted to defend the Quran from this accurate adoption, they had to claim that Pseudo-Callisthenes and the Syriac authors copied their material from the Quran, and that the Quran preceded those writings.

First of all, it is not an honor for the Quran to be the original source for those myths, such as: the sun setting in a fetid spring, and its rise from a spot on earth on a people without protection, and without buildings because the sun burns even the rocks, as Mohammed himself interpreted the Quranic verse regarding the sunrise. Also, the idea of imprisoning Gog and Magog by Alexander until the Last Day of history, and that the dam is still in existence in a distant place of the earth. Holding fast to the Quran, despite its presenting such myths is patently absurd. Nobody would hold fast to a book that narrates such myths, unless he ignores his mind, and refuses to distinguish between the truth and the lies, and not be willing to search for the true God.

Thus, trying to make the Quran the source of these myths does not alleviate the dilemma of the Quran, or make it less problematic than acknowledging that Mohammed adopted the myths of Pseudo-Callisthenes and the Syriac writings. However, the spread of Pseudo-Callisthenes is something well-known prior to Islam. There are also enough proofs that one of the two Syriac writings was written in the 5th century A.D., and the other in the 6th century A.D. I will discuss in the coming pages the dates of some versions of Pseudo-Callisthenes, in addition to the dates of the two Syriac writings.

It is impossible for the Pseudo-Callisthenes myths to have been copied from the Quran.

The idea that Pseudo-Callisthenes copied from the Quran is impossible, since it is well-established that Pseudo-Callisthenes was translated into many languages prior to Islam. Its myths were embedded into many writings long before the rise of Islam. Indeed, it was known as the most widespread book in the world, second only to the Bible.[490]

Muslims cannot save face for the Quran because its common knowledge the Pseudo-Callisthenes' book existed in a Greek text since the third century A.D., and eventually spread to many of the countries in the ancient world.

The noted historian, Colonel Yale, places the Greek text of the book as far back as 200 A.D.[491] Scholars established that the book was written in the Ptolemies' era. The Ptolemies reigned in Egypt after the death of Alexander the Great beginning as early as the fourth century B.C. Therefore, the myths which the book contains date hundreds of years before the third century A.D.[492]

Some scholars think myths about Alexander were spread among the Jews because it was suggested in the book of Maccabees[493] and in the writings of the Jewish Roman historian Josephus Flavius (in the 11th book of Antiquities, chapter 8) in which he narrates a myth about a dream Alexander had while in Macedonia wherein God granted him domain over Asia.[494] This, despite the fact that Alexander was one of the most pagan figures in all history. In fact, he claimed to be divine and promoted pagan worship in every city he conquered, presenting sacrifices to the deities of such cities. In reality, there was a trend for many groups to see that the victories of Alexander as signs of divine intervention, thus attributing those victories to God.

First Maccabees 1:2-3 report that Alexander "slew the kings of the earth, and went through to the ends of the earth." [495] This despite the fact that Alexander never reached as far west as Italy and reached only as far east as the river Indus in Pakistan. But we see that even in the 2nd century B.C. many outside Greek-educated circles, especially in the Middle East, began attributing to Alexander trips to the extremities of the earth. They ascribed to a mythological geography of the earth. They also ignored the secret behind the victories of Alexander, which was not divine intervention but his military tactics.

Here are some dates, and other information, regarding the versions of Pseudo-Callisthenes:

The Greek version of the book of Pseudo-Callisthenes

The Greek version which we have of the book of Pseudo-Callisthenes was dated in the third century A.D. Today, there are 20 manuscripts of the Greek version.[496] The most important manuscripts, A, B and C, are in the Bibliothèque Nationale at Paris. Those manuscripts represent the original Greek text of Pseudo Callisthenes.[497] The Greek text of these manuscripts can be found in a book written by Müller titled simply Pseudo-Callisthenes.[498] I quoted from the Greek manuscript B when we discussed the gates which Pseudo-Callisthenes claims were erected between two mountains, to imprison savage peoples until the final days. A copy of manuscript B is also in Leyden. β Versions goes back to the third century–550 A.D.[499] We find in these manuscripts the sources for some of the myths of Surah al Kahf in the Quran, such as the salted fish that was revived in the spring of life. It is the source of the myth we find in the story of Khather in the Quran.

In a study on the most ancient text of the book of Pseudo-Callisthenes, W. Kroll depended on a manuscript from the alpha series dated to the third century A.D.[500]

Regarding the antiquity of the book of Pseudo- Callisthenes: there are writings which borrowed from it, such as the Life of Apollonius of Tyana, which goes back to the third century A.D. Among the similar elements:

> Including a visit to the Brahmans, a visit to Meroe, and a visit to the Great King's palace. It is a secular or pagan analogue to the Christian Gospels. It belongs to the literary life of the imperial court circles of the early third century AD, when considerable interest was being shown in oriental religions.[501]

The Latin version

The Latin version was translated from the Greek text into Latin by Julius Valerius Alexander Polemius in the beginning of the fourth century A.D. Through the Latin version, the people of western and northwestern Europe came to know the mythological story of Alexander.[502] Since the fourth century, excerpts of Pseudo-Callisthenes were found in much of the European literature.

The manuscript extant today in Latin is kept in Turin, Italy, in the Royal Library of Turin, and dates back to the seventh century A.D.[503] This does not mean the book was translated into Latin in the seventh century.

Time often separates the date of the composing of a book from the date of the manuscripts themselves. Usually there are centuries between them.

A Latin manuscript from the seventh century, confirms that the reputation book of Pseudo-Callisthenes spread in the last half of the fifth century and into the sixth century A.D. This is additional confirmation as to the antiquity of this version. Historically, Pseudo-Callisthenes was translated by Julius Valerius at the beginning of the fourth century.

Other historical evidence points to the antiquity of the Latin version of Pseudo-Callisthenes. The Latin version was the main source for the book Itinerarium Alexandri, which dates back to 340-345 A.D. The author is unknown.

The Armenian version

The Armenian version of Pseudo-Callisthenes was translated in the fifth century by Moses of Khoren, the famous Armenian historian and scholar, also called Movses Xorenaci. His translation was based on an older Greek text.

Scholars noticed elements which confirm that the translator is actually Moses of Khoren. Among those are rich quotations in the book History of Movses Xorenaci from the Pseudo-Callisthenes according to the Armenian version. The book of Moses of Khoren is also known as History of Movses Xorenaci. It dates to the 5th century.

Wolohojian, mentions important scholars in Armenian literature such as Frederick C. Conybeare and S. Malxasian, who confirm, that the rich citations in the writings of Moses of Khoren from the Armenian version of pseudo-Callisthenes, indicate that the translation was made in the 5th century by Moses of Khoren.[504]

Dashian quotes significant textual places where Moses of Khoren borrowed from the Armenian version of Pseudo-Callisthenes, some portions are similar, others are verbatim.[505]

Scholars, such as Dashian, have concluded the latest date for the Armenian translation was the year 486.[506] One reason for this is that Lazar P'arpeci, an Armenian writer, quoted significantly from Pseudo-Callisthenes in his book, Towkt, which he wrote in 485 A.D.[507] This establishes the date of the translation of Pseudo-Callisthenes to be prior to 483 A.D.

The Syriac version

The Syriac version of Pseudo-Callisthenes ranks among the important works. Scholars, such as Zacher, suggest the Syriac version was written in the fifth century A.D.[508]

Scholars such as Nöldeke[509] and Dr. Ausfeld[510] say the Syriac version is based on a previous Pahlavi version. The Pahlavi version was written in the 5th century.[511] Pahlavi, a language of the Persian Sassanid period, was in use until the establishment of Islam.

The Quran replaced the fetid sea with the muddy or fetid spring. I attribute this to the Pahlavi version, since the Persians believed the sun sets and rises every day from a different spring of water situated on Mount Alburz, which they placed in a celestial sea.

The Syriac version, based on the Pahlavi's version, shows how extensively the Pahlavi version had spread, especially in countries Persia dominated, such as Mesopotamia, parts of eastern and south Arabia and parts of Asia Minor.

The lost Arabic version of the Book of Pseudo-Callisthenes

Scholars confirm that there was an Arabic version of Pseudo-Callisthenes, which has been lost. They draw this conclusion from Arabian quotations prior to Mohammed from the myths of Pseudo-Callisthenes. One example is that Tubb'a, the Yemen leader from the first part of the 5th century, speaks about Dhu'l-Qarneyn, which in Arabic means the one of two horns. This is also a title for Alexander in the Pseudo-Callisthenes. Tubb'a said that Dhu'l-Qarneyn went to the extremity of the earth and found the sun setting in a spring of fetid muddy water. This was later incorporated into the Quran.

There are also rich quotations by Arabian writers from the time of Mohammed from the Book of Pseudo-Callisthenes, as we have previously mentioned, such as the entrance of Dhu'l-Qarneyn into the land of darkness and the entrance of a leader of the army of Dhu'l-Qarneyn to the land of darkness, carrying a salted fish, which he washed in the spring of life. The fish was revived and the leader also became immortal.

Pseudo-Callisthenes mentions the "land of darkness." We also find this term in Arabic writings, in the writings of al Khurtubi, [512] Allusi, [513] and Wahab bin Munabeh, the Yemenite. [514] Those quotations indicate the Arabs were acquainted with the Book of Pseudo-Callisthenes.

Those who were contemporaries of Mohammed, as Mohammed himself, described the people of Gog according to Pseudo- Callisthenes. For example, Ali bin Abi Taleb, the son-in-law of Mohammed, described precisely the huge length of Gog, reflecting the idea of Pseudo-Callisthenes.

In addition to the precise description of Mohammed's Hadiths about the trip of Alexander, Mohammed mentioned the people living beyond Gog and Magog. You remember that they have faces like dogs, something we see in the Pseudo-Callisthenes. Mohammed described the people of Gog and Magog which were imprisoned behind the dam, which correspond perfectly to Pseudo-Callisthenes and the Syriac writings, which were based on this book.

Scholars maintain that both the lost Arabic and the Ethiopian versions depended on the lost Pahlavi version, which dates back to the fifth century A.D. When we compare the Ethiopic version and what's in Mohammed's Hadiths and the work done by Arabian writers, we note their similarities. Both versions depend on a previous version, which was the Pahlavi. They are similar in that Alexander was carried by an eagle or by an angel until he saw the earth very small. He described the geography of the earth as Pseudo-Callisthenes saw it. Also the name of the leader in Alexander's army who carried the salt fish was Al Khader, and that when he washed the fish in a spring of water the fish was revived and jumped in the water. When he entered the water in search of the fish, his face became green and he became wise and immortal.

We also encounter these particularities in the writings of Arabian such as Wahab bin Munabbeh who lived close to the time of Mohammed. Without doubt, they came from the lost Arabic version of Pseudo-Callisthenes, which was based on the Pahlavi text version. This helps to understand the sources of the Quran regarding the trip of Dhu'l-Qarneyn and the personality of al Khader who is also mentioned in Surah al Kahf.

Proofs that the two Syriac writings date prior to Islam

"A Christian Legend Around Alexander"

There are proofs that the author of "A Christian Legend Around Alexander" lived during the 5th century A.D.

There is little doubt the author had the horrible devastations caused by Attila, the king of the Huns, in mind when he wrote "A Christian Legend Concerning Alexander." Attila reigned from 434-453 A.D. in what is now Hungry, before he occupied many regions in Europe, He devastated the cities in a barbaric way.

Following the death of Attila, his kingdom was divided between his sons who warred with each other, which led the peoples and tribes subjected to them to rebel against them, and thus, regain control over their lands. The Huns were no longer a threat to the Roman Empire. Shortly the Huns lost their importance and their kingdom disappeared. The author of "A Christian Legend Concerning Alexander," lived when the Roman Empire was suffering from the campaigns of the Huns. The Syriacs inhabited the southern and the western parts of Asia Minor, which was the heart of the Eastern Roman Empire. Attila's campaigns against the Western and Eastern Roman Empire kept inhabitants in continual terror because of his violence and barbaric treatment of the cities. He burned and destroyed them.

Therefore, the Syriac author of "A Christian Legend Concerning Alexander," changed the people described by Pseudo-Callisthenes as "eaters the flesh of humans and drinkers their blood" into "Huns." He imprisoned them through the gates between two mountains because the Huns were seen by the author as a dangerous terror.

Had the author lived in the 6th century A.D., he wouldn't have changed these people into Huns. In the period in which the author lived, the Huns and their barbarous and atrocious attacks were the subject pressing on the minds of peoples dominating their lives. Certainly, they were not the Persians who threatened the Eastern Roman Empire in the six century nor were they Muslim Arabs who threatened the Empire in the seventh century. These factors cause us to place the date of the writing of "A Christian Legend Concerning Alexander," toward the end of the fifth century A.D.

There is no mention of Islam in the Syriac text. In the middle of the seventh century, Muslims occupied important parts of the Roman Byzantine Empire, such as Syria, Trans-Jordan, Palestine and Egypt. Had the author lived after Islam appeared, Muslims would have become enemies of the Empire. Surely, they would have occupied the place given in the Syriac writing to the Huns. All these considerations render it impossible for the author to have lived in the Islamic era.

There is another important factor which make us exclude that the author lived in the Islamic era. He claimed Alexander wrote an interesting prophecy on the gates with which he imprisoned the Huns. The prophecy contained a statement saying the Huns will occupy the empires of the Romans and the Persians after the gate is opened.[515] This statement shows us the Romans and the Persians were the two great powers in the world at that time. This statement fails to fit in the Islamic era, because the Persian Empire had ceased to exist by this time. The Muslims had defeated the Persians and annulled their kingdom, conquering all their regions as early as 651 A.D.

The author mentioned peoples and tribes several times, yet he mentioned the Arabs only once. He mentioned them when he spoke about the Persians, mentioning the Arabs in relation to the Persians, and placing them after the Persians.[516] Without a doubt, he meant the Lackamid Arabs who, since the third century A.D., were vassals of the Persians. the Lackamid Arabs, who lived in the south-western part of Mesopotamia, threatened the Syrians who were part of the Eastern Roman Empire. Having been the vassals of the Persians, explains why the author once placed them behind the Persians when he mentioned them in his writings.

More internal evidence supports a date as early as the fifth century for the Syriac writing.

There is more internal proof which confirms the author lived before the beginning of the sixth century A.D. He wrote that Alexander carved an inscription on the gate through which he imprisoned the Huns. He wrote that at the end of 826 years, the Huns will come out of the gate and occupy all the nations of the earth.[517] According to this prophecy, the 826 years must have begun around the year 330 B.C., in the middle of the campaigns of Alexander. Therefore, the author assigned the date around 496 A.D. This is definite confirmation that the author lived, not in the sixth century, but before the end of the fifth century A.D.

The author also had Alexander prophesied that the end of the world will happen after 940 years from the time Alexander wrote this prophecy on the gate. This would have occurred in the year 620 A.D.[518] Here we see that the author represented a fanatic group of Christian Syriacs, who saw the end of the world not far from the time in which they lived. The New Testament warns us against assigning dates for the end of the world, but the author violated this advice by fixing the date for the end of the world within a century or a century and half from their own time. These considerations mean the author lived at the end of the fifth century A.D.

The Metrical Homily of Sarugh was written in the 6th century A.D., prior to the rise of Islam in the 7th century A.D.

Serugh vicariously suffered from the pain and tribulation endured by his dear fellow Christians at the hands of the atrocities inflected by the Persian occupation in regions which were dear to his heart. He created Gog and Magog as the scourge of God against the Persian Empire in the last days. He claims Gog and Magog will destroy Persia,[519] and strip them of their dignity. It is clear from these statements that Serugh lived when the kingdom of Persia was still an important Empire.

No kingdom could accomplish such destruction which Serugh dearly hoped would fall on Persia, not even the Roman Empire itself. If Serugh had lived in Islamic times during which the Persian kingdom was conquered and forced out of existence, he would not have mentioned that Gog and Magog will destroy Persia and strip them of their dignity. The end of the world for Jacob Serugh is when the dominating kingdoms like the Persians and the Eastern Romans are destroyed.

Further evidence indicates the author did not live during Islamic times because he prophesied the fall of all the important countries known to him, yet, he did not mention the Arabs or the Muslims. Had he lived in the Islamic period, at least he would have mentioned the Arabic kingdom which was the main kingdom to fall, but he fails to even touch upon the matter. He fails to give even a hint indicating clearly that he lived in a period where there was no Arabic-Islamic kingdom, and the Arabs were tribes not worthy of the author's attention because they did not present a threat to the Eastern Roman Empire.

Additional internal evidence also points to the conclusion that the author lived before Islam appeared. He asserts that Gog and Magog will not enter the city of Jerusalem, "because the sign of the cross of the Lord shall drive them away from it, and they shall not enter it."[520] This certainly sounds like the conviction of a Christian who lived during the Byzantine Empire, when the city of Jerusalem was regarded as invincible and unconquerable. The common creed of that period, shared by his contemporaries, claims that Jerusalem was invincibility because it contained the Cross on which Jesus was crucified. Therefore, the author expressed a creed which had disappeared when Muslims conquered the city. Without doubt, this is a convincing indication that the author lived in a historical period before Muslims came to power in the Middle East, and occupied the city of Jerusalem.

The author of the Syriac metrical letter said that Gog and Magog will not enter Jerusalem, because the Cross of Jesus is there. There is a historical incident that reveals the author lived prior to the year 614 A.D. In this year, Khosrau II, the Sassanid Persian king, occupied the city of Jerusalem, and removed the remaining portion of the Cross. In the year 628 A.D, Heraclius, the Byzantine Emperor, won a battle against the Persians regaining their part of the cross, and brought it to Constantinople. Later, in the year 630 A.D, he placed it in Jerusalem once more. Thus, the fall of Jerusalem under the Persians and the removal of the Cross during these years, indicate that the author of this Syriac metrical letter had lived before the year 614 A.D, the date the cross was removed from the city.

The claims of Pseudo-Callisthenes, and the corresponding Quranic claims in light of official history.

At the end of this discussion about Dhu al Qarnayn's journey, we say this: the details of Dhu al Qarnayn's journey in the Quran, and Alexander's journey in Pseudo-Callisthenes, require us to judge both narrations according to official history in order to examine their credibility. It is known that Pseudo-Callisthenes does not match the official history which was recorded concerning Alexander, or even any leader who lived before or after Alexander. Pseudo-Callisthenes finished creating mythological stories regarding Alexander's journeys because of his ignorance of the Greek official history. He wanted to imitate Gilgamesh's journey in his search for immortality. Pseudo-Callisthenes made Alexander travel to the extremities of the earth in search of immortality. Thus, he had to describe imaginary things in agreement with his mythological purpose. At that time, the Greek historians recorded the official history about Alexander, and did not leave gaps to be filled later by Pseudo-Callisthenes.

The real Callisthenes, who accompanied Alexander in his campaigns, wrote about Alexander and his works. Other eyewitnesses wrote about Alexander, such as Onesicritus, his chief helmsman, who was another historian who followed him. So did Nearchus, Alexander's naval commander.

Chares, Alexander's chamberlain, was another person who recorded what he had seen as an eyewitness after the death of Alexander. Likewise, Ptolemy, one of Alexander's four main commanders who later founded the Ptolemy dynasty in Egypt, wrote about the expeditions of Alexander and his deeds.

Aristobulus, who worked as engineer for Alexander the Great, was also another eyewitness who wrote about Alexander's life, military expeditions and his deeds. Had Alexander built a dam between two mountains, Aristobulus certainly would have boasted in his writings of such great accomplishment. Yet, though he wrote about the works of Alexander and his campaigns, he did not mention that Alexander had built a dam of iron and brass through which he had imprisoned Gog and Magog.

We have fragments of the writings of the early eyewitnesses. Their writings were totally incorporated into the writings of many Greek historians' and classical writers who came one to three centuries later. The books of these early writers were still intact when Greek classical authors depended on them to describe the life and expeditions of Alexander.

A large list of classical authors wrote about life of Alexander the Great such as:

Diodorus Siculus, a Greek historian from the 1st century B.C.; in the 7-17th books of his work, called Bibliotheca Historica, writes details about Alexander.

Justin was a Roman historian of the third century A.D. who wrote about Alexander.

Curtius Rufus who a Roman historian wrote between 41-54 A.D. Curtius focused primarily upon the character and attributions of Alexander. Pompeius Trogus was a Roman historian from the first century B.C. His main work, The Historiae Philippicae, consists of 44 books. First, he focuses on the reign of Philip, the father of Alexander. Then he looks at the history of Alexander himself and those who reigned after his death.

Plutarch lived between 46-120 A.D. He wrote a book about the life of Alexander the Great, presenting unique information about him, mentioning everything that happened to him, even the rare and minuscule things which no other writer addressed.

Arrian, (86 to 146 A.D.) was a Greek historian Arrian wrote his famous work called Anabasis Alexandri, which means "The Expedition of Alexander." This is one of the oldest sources that is still intact. He used the writings of Callisthenes, the companion of Alexander, who was a nephew of Aristotle. Arrian also used the writings of the other people who were Alexander's companions. He used biographies written by Ptolemy.

Strabo (64 B.C. to 23 A.D.) was a famous Greek historian and geographer. His book, "Memoirs," was an expanded work about Alexander the Great. Although this work was lost, it was a major resource for many historians who wrote about Alexander. Among was Plutarch.

The life of Alexander and his deeds is one of the most covered of the ancient subjects. Yet none of them ever suggested Alexander erected a gigantic dam. Authors who accompanied Alexander on his campaigns wrote about minuscule things that happened but they never mentioned the dam. How could they ignore what would have been his greatest project? Nobody ever mentioned anything about Gog and Magog or a savage people living on the extremity of the earth; No one had complained to Alexander regarding this savage people who were supposedly dangerous to the entire world and that such a people should be imprisoned behind two mountains.

If this legendary metallic dam had really been built, not only the writers who accompanied Alexander would have made it a significant achievement in their histories, but the hundreds of Greek geographers who visited India and the Asia in consequent generations would have described the places Alexander built in great detail. Somewhere they would have mentioned the metallic dam as the most important construction feat the world had ever seen. But, none of them mentioned anything.

And there were Roman geographers who visited Asia following the routes that Alexander took during his campaigns. They certainly would have mentioned it .

Invitation to reflection

We see then, that the Quran contradicts the official history. It belongs to the myths of the times of Mohammed, which were held fast by the ignorant who did not study history, and believed in the primitive geography of the earth, which Pseudo-Callisthenes propagated. Those myths were believed by some Syriac groups. How, then, could we propose that the Quran is a divine book coming from heaven?!

Had the Arab Muslims considered Mohammed as being one who contributed in spreading Pseudo-Callisthenes in Arabia, no objections would have been raised. But honoring Mohammed to the level of a prophet because he transferred these myths of Pseudo-Callisthenes into a rhymed Arabic is something the Romans abstained from doing when Julius Valerius translated Pseudo-Callisthenes into a high linguistic level of their language — that is, Latin. The Armenians also did not fall into this mistake when Moses of Khoren translated it into their language. This is even though Khoren's version is considered by Armenian scholars to be a great piece of Armenian literature. However, the Armenians never considered Khoren as deserving the title of prophet just because he translated Pseudo-Callisthenes into a high Armenian language.

My prayer is that Muslims would go by the same rule as the Armenians did. They did not allow the rhyme and superiority of language to be the authority in determining the nature of the mythological substance which was translated into their languages. They were not driven to exalting the authors or translators to the role of prophet, making them spiritual guides for their lives, and making them control their eternal destinies.

The Seven Sleepers

The legend of the seven sleepers of Ephesus

Mohammed incorporated the Syriac legend of the "Seven Sleepers of Ephesus" into the Quran. The legend is about seven Christians who slept in a cave for 150-200 years. This was in the year 250 A.D., at the time of Decius, the Roman emperor who persecuted Christians. Decius, according to the legend, came to Ephesus to persecute Christians. He met with seven young, noble Christians and tried them in court. He then gave them time to consider the gravity of the situation and renounce their faith, but they decided to give what they owned to the poor, except for a few coins which they took with them. They did not deny their faith. They went to a cave in Mount Anchilos to prepare themselves for death. When Decius returned to Ephesus, he inquired about them, and his soldiers found them sleeping in the cave. Decius ordered his soldiers to seal the cave with big stones burying them alive.

At the time of the Christian emperor – either Theodosius the Great who lived between 379-395 A.D., or Theodosius the Younger, who lived between 408-450 A.D. – there was a controversy about the resurrection which many heretics denied. When a landowner opened the cave to use it as cattle stall, the sleepers awakened from their sleep and thought they had slept only one night. So the seven sent one of their number to buy food. The one sent by them went with the coins of Decius which they had kept when imprisoned in the cave. He was amazed to see the Cross over the churches and the name of Christ openly on the lips of everyone. The people were astonished to see the young man with the coins of Decius. They assumed he had found a treasure in the cave. The man then revealed the story of their sleep. Emperor Theodosius went to the cave to see the seven men, and used this miracle to confirm that bodies indeed can be resurrected. When the seven men eventually died, the king wanted to make tombs of gold for them, but the men appeared to the king in a dream asking him to bury them in a normal cave.

Many Muslims throughout history attempted to find the place where the sleepers slept for three centuries. Hundreds of caves were claimed as being the place where the sleepers slept.

Refutation of the claim that Amman would be the place where the sleepers slept

Some Muslims, conscious of the origin of the myth, and its place in Ephesian history, claim that the sleepers escaped from Ephesus and fled to the city of Amman in Trans-Jordan.

This myth was used by the church of Ephesus: they built a church over some tombs, claiming that the sleepers had slept there. If we admit, for the sake of argument, that the myth was a historical fact, would the sleepers, out of fear of the Romans flee thousands of miles towards Amman to seek refuge in a Roman city, as Amman was under the name of Philadelphia? Would it not have been easier, instead, to flee only a few hundred miles eastward where they would find themselves in regions dominated by the Persians?!

Furthermore, a professor of archeology in an American university, who is a friend of mine, visited the place in Amman. He examined it and stated that it was a Byzantine graveyard. If this were the place attributed to the myth of the sleepers, the church would have made a sanctuary out of it, where people would go to do a saint's pilgrimage throughout the many centuries before Islam, as the church of Ephesus did. But there are no traces or archeological findings pointing to such an event occurring. In reality, it was a Byzantine custom to bury the members of a family in one cave. Under the Persian influence, dogs became important, and were buried along with members of the family. That is why, in the Byzantine cave of Amman, a dog's bones were found alongside of the bones of family members.

The sources of the myth and how it spread

The Greek philosopher, Aristotle, tells a similar story about sleepers Sardinia.[521] Since Aristotle was born in 384 B.C. and died in 322 B.C., the Syriac version depended mainly on the old pagan version but replaced Ephesus with Sardinia. Koch, a scholar, demonstrated that there were other old pagan versions of the legend including Indian, Jewish and Chinese versions.[522] Today, the tale is considered a classical myth of wide-spread pagan origin, known in many parts of the world before Christianity.

The legend was Christianized by the Syriacs, probably translated by the Syriacs from the pagan Greeks because the Syriacs were known to have translated the works of Greek philosophers, such as Aristotle. The tale was known among Syriac resources before it was translated into other languages, proving that they had translated it from pagan Greek resources. The tale also appeared in the Homily of Jacob of Saruq, or Sarugh. He was a Monophyte priest, Syrian poet and writer who lived in the city of Edessa, a Syriac city in North Iraq. He studied in the Syriac school Raha. In the year 519 A.D., he became bishop of Batnan and died in 521 A.D The story was published in the Acta Sanctorum. Another 6th century version is available in a Syrian manuscript in the British Museum (Cat. Syr. Mss, p. 1090), and tells about eight sleepers.

Known to the Arabs as Yakub al- Saruji, Jacob of Sarugh had connections with Najran, a city between Yemen and Mecca. From the 3rd century A.D. until the time of Mohammed, Najran was home to many Christians. At one point, Jacob of Sarugh wrote a letter to the Christians at Najran.[523] We can only conclude that the spread of the legends to Najran, and then later to Mecca, was probably through Syriac sources connected to Jacob of Sarugh and his version of the Seven Sleepers of Ephesus.

The legend grows

The story remained within a limited circle of oriental Syriacs until it was translated into Latin in the late 6th century A.D. by Gregory of Tours (538-594 A.D.) and it gained legendary status. The legend is found in the 95th chapter of his book, De Gloria Martyrum, which means "the Glory of the Martyrs." Gregory says that he heard the legend from "a certain Syrian or Syriac." Gregory recorded the story as legend. The story is a legend because it originated in pagan circles before the Christian era. It was translated from the Greek pagan literature into Syriac, and spread among limited number of Syriacs in north Iraq.

Contrary to the Gospel that narrated Jesus' life, the myth lacks a historical foundation

Before Gregory translated it into Latin and popularized it, the legend was never mentioned in Ephesian literature, even though Ephesus was the city where the Syriacs say the story happened. This is an important criterion in refuting its history. Only after the legend was popularized by Gregory, a church was built over the tombs in the city of Ephesus, claiming they were the tombs of the Seven Sleepers of Ephesus. There is not one historical account in all of Ephesian literature to substantiate this legend. On the other hand, if we had such scant evidence on the life of Christ from Palestine, the land where Jesus lived, then we would have reason to doubt the existence of Jesus. But most of the authors of the New Testament were disciples of Jesus, men who accompanied him and observed His works and teachings. Moreover, we have evidence of the miracles and the death of Jesus from Josephus Flavius, the Hebrew writer who lived in Jerusalem. We also have historical confirmation about Christ and his crucifixion from other historians, such as Cornelius Tacitus,[524] who lived between 55-120 A.D., Lucian of Samosata,[525] who lived from 120-180 A.D., Pliny the Younger, from the beginning of the 2nd century A.D. There are two Roman historians, Thallus, who wrote in 52 A.D. and Phlegon who wrote at beginning of the second century A.D both mentioned the darkness, which covered the earth during the crucifixion as historical fact. However, they attributed the darkness to an eclipse of the sun. Julius Africanus, quoting these two historians, said the phenomenon could not be an eclipse, because at the time Christ died, the moon was full.[526]

Mara Bar-Serapion, the Syriac philosopher, also wrote about Christ around 70 A.D. Besides these writers, we also get information from the Talmud. The Babylonian Talmud tells us Jesus was crucified on the eve of Passover,[527] exactly as the Gospels narrated.

But when it comes to the legend of Ephesus, though the city was full of philosophers and historians during the 4th and the 5th centuries A.D., no one ever mentioned such an event. Neither the Roman records of Theodosius the Great, nor of Theodosius the Younger, say anything about the legend of the Seven Sleepers of Ephesus, which says that Theodosius met them personally and constructed a tomb for their burial.

Among the historians who lived at the time as Theodosius the Great and Theodosius the Younger, was Eunapius (349-414 A.D.). Of the

Byzantine historians who lived in the 6th century, we mention Jordanes, who wrote in the city of Constantinople around the year 551 or 552 A.D. In his book Romana, he wrote about the history of the world from the Roman point of view. There are other famous historians who lived in the 6th century, such as Procopius.

Choosing Theodosius the Great as the Emperor in whose time the sleepers awoke was because he made Christianity the official religion of the Roman Empire. He united the Eastern part of the Empire with its Western part. It came to be divided again, however, after he died. Others claimed the sleepers were awakened during the time of Theodosius II, who became emperor of the Eastern Roman Empire from 408-450 A.D.

Additional refutation of the claims regarding the historicity of the story

The myth appeared in Christendom first among the Syriacs, who translated it from Greek paganism. It also appeared in the writings of Jacob Sarugh, who died in the year 521 A.D. We draw the reader's attention to the fact that the Syriacs were not the inhabitants of Ephesus, where they claim the story took place, but the inhabitants were Greek. If the story really happened, would it not have been logical that the Christian Greeks would have been the first ones to carry this story to the world, rather than its being heard for the first time from the Syriacs.

Furthermore, scores of church fathers lived before Jacob Sarugh; with many of them living in Asia Minor, especially in the Greek regions, such as Constantinople, Ephesus and Sardis. Why had not one of them mentioned this story, if it truly happened?

Moreover, the story is dramatic and spectacular in a way that, if it had happened, would have been the greatest miracle to have occurred since the resurrection of Christ. Why did Gregory of Tour, as he himself admitted, have to hear the story from a Syriac speaking man? If it had happened, it would have been very well-known in the Christian world from the time of Theodosius the Great. The church would have been built from Theodosius' times, and would have been the most important church in the world, after the Church of the Resurrection in Jerusalem. We find, however, that the story was known among limited groups of Syriacs, before it became known by the inhabitants of Ephesus themselves. Therefore, the attempts to make the church in Ephesus as being built since the 5th or 6th century cannot be true. The church must have been built after Gregory of Tour died — that is, in the year 594 A.D. The writings, found in the church, must have been dated later, even though the one who wrote them wanted them to appear to have an older date, even to the point of recording wrong dates to deceive the worshipers.

Nather, a Relative of Mohammed, examines Mohammed on where he got his Legends

Mohammed copied the legend of the Seven Sleepers of Ephesus, as though it were historical fact. Mohammed included the legend in Surah 18, called al-Kahf, or "the chapter of the cave." Some leaders of Quraysh, the tribe from which Mohammed came, got together. Among them was Nather Bin al-Hareth. As a result of suggestions from some of the Jews, Nather Bin al-Hareth sought to expose the ignorance of Mohammed concerning history. They were concerned about his trend to incorporate all the myths he heard into Suras in his Quran. This incident was reported by Mohammed's biographers such as Ibn Hisham and ibn Kathir, in addition to important expositors of the Quran such as al Qurtubi.[528]

Nather Bin Hareth was known for exposing the origin of Mohammed's Persian myths. Every time Mohammed recited verses from the Quran which were of Persian origin, Nather would stand and recite the same Zoroastrian myths with more accuracy. We read about this in the book of Ibn Hisham. He writes:

Al Nather bin al Hareth went to Hira, where he learned about the kings of Persia and the news of Rustum and Isfendyar. When Mohammed used to warn his people about the judgments other nations would face, al Nather reprehended him saying, "I have, O Quraysh, better information than Mohammed. Listen to me; what I tell you is better than what Mohammed tells you."[529]

When Mohammed would sit and recite the Quran to the tribe of Quraysh, Al-Nather would speak when Mohammed was finished. He would recite the stories and myths of Rustam, Isfendyar and the Persian kings. Then, al-Nather would say, "Mohammed's narration is not better than mine. His narration is just ancient myths. He wrote them as I wrote them."[530]

We notice that al Nather bin al Hareth, who was a relative of Mohammed, said that Mohammed wrote the Persian myths. This is one proof that Mohammed was educated, and not illiterate as Islam claims. Al Nather would never dare to attribute to Mohammed the ability to write if it were not true because Quraysh was well aware of Mohammed's talents.

Nather was able to say this because he studied Persian history and mythology in Hira, a city governed by the Lakhmids, an Arabian tribe who were vassals to the Persians.[531]

Included in the questions Nather asked Mohammed was a question about the legend of Ephesus. The Jews and those who were well educated in Mecca knew the story was a myth popularized by Gregory. Thus, expecting that Mohammed would incorporate it as genuine history in the Quran, they would use this to prove to others the habit of Mohammed to include myths in the Quran and falsely claim them as historical fact. Nather and his companions also posed other questions of basic history to Mohammed. One of the questions concerned Alexander the Great, called Dhu al-Qarnayn, which means "the one with two horns." It was a topic which the average person at the time of Mohammed knew well. Greek Byzantine education was prevalent in the Middle East, especially at Mecca, where the inhabitants were rich traders in continuous contact with the Byzantine Empire in Syria and Palestine. Many of the inhabitants of Mecca were rich and had Byzantine slaves, such as Jaber, who was a servant to the Al Khadrami family. Mohammed was known to visit Jaber and listen to him while he read to him from his books, and learned the Byzantine myths from him. I previously mentioned Jaber and others whom Mohammed consulted when I discussed Mohammed's Christian sources. (see the myth of the destruction of Antioch in the first century A.D.)

Selecting Alexander, the most well-known figure in their history, became a test to Mohammed's integrity. It was not a random choice. The name, Dhu al Qarnayn, "the one with two horns," was a well-known title for Alexander the Great in the mythological book, Pseudo-Callisthenes. It is there that the author claims that Alexander reached the place where the sun rises and sets. Al Nather, his friends, and the Jews who followed behind, hoped that Mohammed would inquire about the myth, and then claim it to be a historical fact. Then he could connect it to his new religion, Islam. When we ponder the form of the question, which the Jews suggested al Nather ask Mohammed regarding Alexander the Great, we comprehend that they had in mind the myth of "Dhu al Qarnayn," which was spread in their time — that is, the mythological arrival of Alexander to the place where the sun sets and rises. They said:

> Ask him about a man who traveled until he reached where the sun sets and rises. What was your teaching about him?[532]

They knew the myth of "Dhu al Qarnayn," and could easily compare it to the story of Alexander:

At the time of Mohammed, the Persians believed that the sun rose each day from a different spring of the 180 springs, and set each day in a different spring. By this, they explained the difference in time between one day and another.[2] Mohammed embraced the same concept, as we see in his Hadith reported by al Taberi.[533]

Furthermore, the title of Alexander as Dhu al Qarnayn and His Trip to Where the Sun Sets and Rises, was well-known at the time of Mohammed, and even prior to him, as coming from the mythological book, Pseudo-Callisthenes, and the Syriac writings which depended on this book. Educated people in those times knew the myths because of the spread of this book. We assume these myths were popular at Mecca, and the educated

---

[2] The Persians believed about the movement of the sun, moon, and some stars through heights situated on Mount Alburz, which they imagined existing in the "Celestial Sea" from where the waters descend on earth. They believed about a rotation of the sun, moon and stars from these heights where there are springs waters, or apertures. They believed the sun, moon and stars passed through these springs, or apertures, from where they imagined the rains, coming from the stars, descended. According to the book of Vendidad, the sun passes or rises through this watery way which was opened by the gods. (Vendidad, Fargard XXI, IIIa, 5)

From here the Persians explained the difference between the length of the days; that is, in relation to the sunrise each day from a different spring or water aperture situated on these heights. Those springs, or apertures, are 180 in the East and 180 in the West. The total is 360 springs. Every day the sun rises from a spring, then returns from another spring. (Bundahis, Chapter V:5)

By this Persian mythology, we can understand Mohammed's Hadith in explaining the shortness or the length of the day: he attributed this to the rise of the sun each day from a different spring in the extremity of the East. He also made the total of the springs to be 360. Without a doubt, he was under the influence of the Persian mythology.

Jews along with the educated people of the tribe of Quraysh knew that such stories were merely myths.

Otherwise they would not have chosen its myths to test Mohammed, nor would they question another myth, the myth of the seven sleepers of Ephesus, a tale which was also known to the educated people as a myth.

Therefore, al Nather and his companions plotted a trap which they expected Mohammed to fall into, knowing his tendency to copy almost every myth spread in his generation. Mohammed should have known a majority of the people, especially those who were educated, were aware that it was a myth. Educated people in Quraysh and the educated Jews wanted to show how Mohammed dealt with important figures of history. Either he condemned them through a magical cry, or he made them Muslims. When Mohammed delayed two weeks before answering questions regarding the myths, everyone knew that Mohammed had consulted people who were the sources for many of the verses of the Quran.

When asked questions concerning Dhu al Qarnayn, Mohammed answered them as they were stated in the book of Pseudo Callisthenes. What Mohammed wrote is an Arabic summary of the trip Alexander took as it was written in the mythological book of Pseud Callisthenes. Even the Arabic poetry of Pre-Islamic times confirms the content of the book and how the story of Dhu al Qarnayn spread among the Arabians. The story of Dhu al Qarnayn was recited in poetical form by Tubb'a, the Himyarite king of Yemen who reigned between 410-435 A.D., and occupied Mecca, as well as by people who claimed to be prophets, such as Umayyah ibn al Salt, as well.

Others who traveled to Mecca and its surrounding villages, such as Qeis bin Saedeh, taught about Dhu al Qarnayn and the myths surrounding his trips

By copying the myths which were spread in his own generation, Mohammed confirmed what the educated men of his city said about him, that he came with the myths of the ancients.

Nather wanted to challenge Mohammed's ignorance concerning basic elements of history. He wanted to confirm the way in which Mohammed dealt with elements of history. Either Mohammed condemned ancient historical figures through magical ways such as a cry, or he made them devoted Muslims who embraced his myths. He did so after he consulted the primitive resources which provided him with the mythological narrations. We have seen, in part, how Mohammed answered the question about Alexander the Great. It only confirmed the idea which the Jews and the educated citizens of Mecca had about him and his claims.

The test put to Mohammed by Nather and his companions revealed Mohammed to be one who accumulated myths from primitive sources to appear as though he had all knowledge because, according to his claim, he was sent by Allah. The Quran lacks spiritual understanding. When he failed the test, Mohammed proved that he was unable to respond to the simplest spiritual questions.

The third question posed to Mohammed was, "What is the spirit?" This is a simple question every Jewish or Christian man should answer immediately by quoting the Bible. God created man with a body, soul and spirit. The spirit is the human entity which communicates with God and enables man to worship God.

The Jews composed the third question when they noticed that the verses from the Quran quoted by Mohammed lacked spirituality, and focused on earthly things. For example, Mohammed claimed an unusual sexual relationship with all women, including the wives of his followers. The Quran claims Mohammed could have married any woman he wished. Each Moslem female was to offer herself to him according to Surah 33: 50, 51, called al-Ahzab. It says:

> Oh prophet, we made it lawful to you to take the wives for which you have paid their dowry. What your hand possesses from the prisoners of war that Allah gave you, and the daughters of your uncles and the daughters of your aunts, and the daughters of your maternal uncles and aunts, those who migrated with you, and any believing woman that gives herself to the prophet, if he wants to wed her, are yours. These privileges are only for you and not for the believers at large, we know what we have appointed for them as to their wives and the females whom they captured in the wars. We established this so no embarrassment would come you. "You turn away any of them that you please, and make any one of them to lodge with you that you please. Of the ones you want to have, whom you previously have sent away, there is no blame on you.

The word used by the Quran is the Arabic word "Al Nikah. "According to ibn Abbass[534] and al Feirusabadi, the word refers to sexual intercourse.[535]

Mohammed claimed his prerogative to take sexual privileges with the wife of anyone he wishes since they were his followers, and with non-Muslims whom he conquered in his military campaigns. He lusted for Zeinab, his daughter-in-law who was Zayd's wife. Zayd was a son whom Mohammed adopted. Then he quoted a verse from the Quran which said that Allah ordered him to marry her.

On another occasion, Mohammed approached Abu Baker, requesting that his daughter Aisha, who was six years old at the time, be given to him as a wife. Mohammed married her when she was nine years old and he was 54 years old.

Mohammed's prerogative was to have any woman he wanted, even if she was already married to a Muslim. During his campaign against the tribe of Mustalaq, Mohammed killed both the husband and father of Jurieh who was the husband of Burrah, who is also called also Jurieh. She then became a wife to one of his followers, Thabet bin Quyes. When Jurieh consulted Mohammed to ask him some questions, Mohammed was fond of her beauty, so Mohammed annulled her marriage with Quyes and married her too.[536]

A considerable part of the Quran revolves around Mohammed's campaigns and those of his followers who must respond to Mohammed's call for Jihad. The distribution of the spoils allowed for him to have a fifth of everything. The Jews, seeing the lack of spirituality in Mohammed's sayings, wanted to reveal his inability to answer when asked the simple question, "What is the spirit?" Mohammed did not answer questions about the spirit immediately, but he promised to answer them the following day. Mohammed did not show up for two weeks. Evidently, he went to look for help. He returned, claiming Allah inspired him. Surah 17, called Isra', verse 85 says, "When they ask you about the spirit, tell them, 'the spirit is the affair of Allah.'" Mohammed did not enter into discussion. He was completely ignorant about the argument, showing that he lacked a spiritual education and was unable to express an opinion.

Concerning the question of Alexander the Great, Mohammed returned with mythological ideas expressing thoughts that were embraced by some superstitious Arabians of his time, derived from the myths found in Pseudo-Callisthenes, and the Syriac writings which depended upon this book, as well.

Mohammed's misinformed understanding of the Legend of the Seven Sleepers of Ephesus.

When questioned concerning the seven young people who slept for centuries, Mohammed naturally turned to his Christian-Byzantine friends, among whom was Jaber. I remind the reader of a saying which we already saw in Ibn Hisham, the book that contains the most significant narration on the life of Mohammed, about one of Mohammed's Christian sources, that is Jaber, a slave to the al Khadrami family.[537] I mentioned that Mohammed used to sit with him and learn from him.

The Meccans noticed that what Mohammed taught others was taught to him by Jaber, a Christian slave. This indicates that the Meccans were acquainted with the teaching of Jaber, and he was active in spreading some of the Byzantine myths.

This accusation by the Meccans to Mohammed was not without foundation. Why would Mohammed sit with a poor slave almost every day? Another thing to consider is that Mohammed despised slaves. He said that a slave cannot testify in a court unless he is beaten.[538] If one of his followers wanted to free a slave, Mohammed objected, insisting that his follower sell the slave instead of freeing him.[539] For example, Mohammed blamed Maimuna bint al Hareth because she freed a female slave. Mohammed said to her:

> If you would have given her to your uncles, it would have been more beneficial for you.[540]

But here is a Christian slave, yet Mohammed took the time to go to him every day. Mohammed came to Jaber. It was not Jaber who came to Mohammed. This reveals Jaber's importance as a source of information (for Mohammed) on the Bible, Christian doctrine, and the Christianized myths of the Byzantine period. Arabic sources speak of Jaber as a "Roman." The term was used in Arabia for the citizen of the Byzantine Empire. I already mentioned that the Islamic narrators stated the family of al-Khathrami had two slaves, Jaber and Yasar. They also recorded that Jaber gathered books. He would read the Old and New Testaments while Mohammed listened to their readings and their teaching.[541]

Al Allusi adds that there were other Christians whom the Meccans say that Mohammed depended upon as sources. He found great benefit from their teachings. He said:

Among them were Addas, Aish عائش , the slave of Huiteb bin Abed alal-
'Uzza حويطب بن عبد العزي , Yasar, a slave of al Ala', who was son of al-
Khathrami العلاء بن الحضرمي , and Jebril جبريل who was a slave of Amer
عامر.[542]

Another contact for Mohammed was "Balaam," also called "Yaish." Balaam was a Byzantine Christian who was a slave to Huitab Bin Abed al-Uzei. The people of Mecca often saw Mohammed when he met with Balaam, and they said Balaam used to teach Mohammed.[543] But it seems Jaber and Balaam were superstitious men, not like the Christian-educated people in their time who distinguished between legends and historical facts, and described the stories of Mohammed as "myths of the ancients." (see the Quran 6:25; 8:31; 16:24)

When we study the Islamic books, we find that Mohammed kept the Syriac books, but he did not want anyone else to know that he had read them. He did this so that his companions would not come to know his Syriac sources. It is known that the Syriacs propagated some myths of their books, such as the one which speaks of Dhu al Qarnayn; his travel to the fetid sea where the sun sets, or his travel to the extremity of the east, where the sun rises from a spot on the earth, and the rocks melt because of the sun's heat, thus no building could be built there. Or Dhu al Qarnayn's imprisoning Gog and Magog behind a dam until the last days of history (myth borrowed from the Syriac letter attributed to Jacob Sarugh). Or the myth of the 7 young men who slept for centuries. This is also found in a letter of Jacob Sarugh.

We read in the Tabaqat al Kubra by ibn Saad:

Zayd bin Thabet said: 'It reach to me books from people, but I do not want anyone to read them. Can you learn the Hebrew or the Syriac?' I said : 'yes.' Then I learned it in 17 nights.[544]

The same saying is confirmed by al Hindi.[545]

Why did Mohammed trust Zayd bin Thabet, and not Omar or any of the companions who were close to him? The answer is because Zayd was a youth, and Mohammed did not want any of his inner circle to discover that some of his stories were found in these Syriac books.

The Quran's version of the Legend of the Seven Sleepers shows that Mohammed failed to understand the legend and its purpose.

In the Quran, Surah 18, al-Kahf, or the Cave, we find Mohammed's answer about the sleepers. He presented the legend as historical fact, yet his variations reflected his lack of understanding and the unreliability of his legendry sources. In verse 17, Mohammed said:

> You would have seen the sun when it rose to the right from the cave, but when it set, it turned away from them toward the left while they were in the open space of the cave.

This verse says the sun entered the cave, but avoided them. This˙ may be a variation of the legend that Christians at Mecca held. Persons, like Balaam and Jaber may have taught that no one could have seen the sleepers during the centuries they slept because the sun had avoided them. This contradicts the original legend which said that the cave was sealed with stones, in a way that neither the sun could penetrate the cave nor could anyone see the sleepers.

In verse 18, we read another development in the legend which only a primitive environment like Arabia at the time of Mohammed could support:

> Their dog stretched his two forelegs on the threshold of the cave. If you had visited them (the Sleepers) and looked, you would have fled from them, filled with terror.

The Quran, through the dog, protected the sleepers during those hundreds of years. According to Mohammed's account, anyone who came toward the cave was filled with terror and fled, because a fierce dog guarded the entrance.

Mohammed picked up on the original legend, which said that after these young people arose from their sleep, they sent one of them with money to buy food for them, thinking that they had slept only one day. The Quran tells us that the people knew about the case of the seven sleepers, but they prevailed against them, and decided to construct a mosque over them to prevent them from coming out from the cave. According to the legend, Mohammed thought that the sleepers arose when the inhabitants of the city and the authorities were angry at the sleepers, to the point they prevailed over them and constructed the place of worship over them to assure that they would be imprisoned in the cave. This shows us that

Mohammed failed to understand the Christian purpose of the legend, which was to show how these seven sleepers were protected when the Roman Empire was persecuting Christians, and arose during a time when the empire espoused Christianity. According to the original legend, the seven were considered saints.

When the Byzantine Church found tombs in the city of Ephesus, they wanted to use the legend to convince atheists of the resurrection, and to profit by making it a popular sacred place. So, they built a church over the tombs. But Mohammed thought the church was built by people who wanted to prevent the legendary sleepers from coming out from the cave.

Mohammed knew his sources about the legend were inferior to the knowledge of those who presented the test to him, so he advanced the argument that Allah prohibited him from discussing the legend.

Mohammed could not come up with a definite number of sleepers in the Ephesian legend. There are two versions of the original legend. One presents seven sleepers and the other, eight. But, among Mohammed's various friends, it seems there were many thoughts about the number of sleepers, which discouraged Mohammed from presenting a specific number for the fear he would be ridiculed by those who tested him. In this case, Mohammed withdrew his claim to present information as coming from Allah, as he always did in the past. Instead, he said Allah ordered him not to discuss the number. In verse 22, he says:

They will say there were three sleepers, the dog being the fourth. They say there were five, the dog being the sixth. Guessing at the unknown, they say there were seven, and their dog is eight. You should say, "My lord knows best their number." Those who know their number are few. Therefore, do not enter into controversies concerning them, except on a matter that is clear, nor consult any one regarding the sleepers.

We ask ourselves: if only a few people, according to the verse, knew the exact number, why was not Mohammed one of them? If he is in contact with God who knows everything, why was not Mohammed among those few who knew the number? We can only conclude that Mohammed was afraid to come with a definite number because he knew the ones who presented the test were more knowledgeable than he was about the legend, and he discovered his sources could not provide a definite number. Thus, he claimed Allah prohibited him from discussing the case.

Mohammed made the sleepers wake up more than 300 years after the authors who Christianized the myth and spread it had died.

Also, in verse 25 of the same Surah (18), we read:

They stayed in their cave 300 years. These years increased by nine.

There is a discussion regarding this verse: some Muslims say that the Christians maintain that the sleepers stayed there for 309 years, but in reality, none of the Christians ever said the sleepers stayed 300 or 309 years, but rather 150 years, up to a maximum of 200 years. If this is the meaning of the verse, Mohammed would have greatly misunderstood the myth.

The majority of the Islamic narrators, however, said that Allah intended that they would sleep for 309 years. Taberi mentioned some of those narrators:

Reported by Mujahed, who said, 'They stayed in their cave 300 years plus nine.' Reported by ibn Hamid, who quoted Salmeh, saying, 'That ibn Ishak said they stayed about the same number of years.' Reported by al Dhahhak bin Musahim, who said, 'the Quranic verse stated that they stayed in their cave 300.' Then they inquired: 'Were they days or months or years?' Thus, Allah inspired, 'They were years.' And Allah added 9 years more.[546]

By this reasoning, the sleepers awoke around the year 559 A.D., when the earlier Syriac translators of the legend from the Greek language were all dead. Even Jacob of Sarugh, who included this legend in his writings, was dead. He died in the year 521 A.D.

Mohammed felt free to establish dates, thinking that no one had the right to refute him. He included myths and legends in the Quran which were spread in his generation, without considering the dates when they were actually spread. Then, he defended the years of sleep he established for them by saying in verse 26, "Say, 'Allah knows best how long they stayed. Allah has the secrets of heavens and earth.'" By this he claimed 309 years as the period they slept as indisputable, because Allah had inspired it. But how did Mohammed's claim fit into the historical framework created by the Syriacs? The Syriacs claimed the sleepers slept during the reign of Emperor Decius, around the year 250 A.D., and the sleep lasted for 150 to 200 years. Then they awoke, either during the reign of Emperor Theodosius, the Great, who reigned between 379 and 395 A.D., or the reign of Theodosius the Younger, who reigned between 408 and 450 A.D. However, Mohammed who claimed the sleepers slept for 309 years, created an impossible scenario. When we add 309 years to 250 A.D., which was the date of the Great Persecution of the church and the date the Syriacs claimed was the beginning of the sleep, we find that Mohammed claimed the sleepers awoke in the year 559 A.D. Nevertheless, the myth as contained in the Syriac writings was one century before that date. In reality however, Mohammed imitated a legend, which was translated by Syriacs. The Syriacs were knowledgeable of the history of the Roman Empire, and they knew the dates of the emperors who persecuted the Christians. This was not an easy task for somebody like Mohammed to complete. Since he lived in Jahiliyyah without accurate knowledge about the Roman Empire and the dates when the legends appeared. Knowledge of these dates were indispensable to any successful imitation of the legend.

The Five Idols
Mohammed's claim about five Arabian idols

In the Quran, Mohammed claimed that five Arabian idols existed during the time of Noah. Mohammed's claim about five Arabian idols is one example that reveals Mohammed's habit of using local elements in Arabia and attributing them to antiquity. In fact, he was known to adopt Arabian names and connect them with Biblical names, or with other famous names in history. Mohammed in Nuh, Surah 71, verse 23, said that Arabian gods were present during the time of Noah. According to these verses, the gods were Wadd, Suwa', Yaghuth, Yauq and Nasr. The verses 21-23 say:

> Noah said: "O my lord. They have disobeyed me. But they follow men whose wealth and children give them no increase, but only lost. and they have devised a tremendous Plot. 'And they said, Forsake not your gods; forsake not Wudd and Suwā' and Yaghuth and Ya'uq and Nasr.'

An Islamic myth was created to connect the five Arabian idols to the time of Noah.

Although these Arabian idols appeared thousands of years after Noah, Islamic tradition created myths in which they connected them with the time of Noah. Hisham Ibn Kalbi and his father, Mohammed ibn al Kalbi, were the first to narrate the myth. They depended partially on Ibn Abbass, Mohammed's cousin. Here is a summary of the myth as told by Hisham Ibn al Kalbi, who reconstructed the story relying on sayings of his father and Ibn Abbass said, "The way the idols were first worshiped, happened as follow: When Adam died, the children of Seth, the son of Adam, buried Adam in a cave in the same mountain where Adam descended from heaven. The mountain, located in India, was named Nawdh[547] نوذ "

Hisham ibn al Kalbi continues narrating about those idols, reporting the words of his father:

Wadd, Suwa', Yaghuth, Ya'uq, and Nasr were righteous people who died within a month of each other, and their relatives were grief-stricken over them. Then one of the children of Cain addressed the relatives saying, 'O people! I shall make unto you five statues after the image of your departed relatives, however, I cannot impart life to them.'

Where upon he carved five statues for them, each one in the image of a departed relative. He then erected the idols over the graves of the relatives. The man often came to honor the statues of his relatives for the next century. The statues were made during the time of Jared (Yarid), the son of Malialcel (Malila'il), the son of Cainan (Qinan), the son of Enos (Anush), the son of Seth, the son of Adam."

Hisham ibn al Kalbi continues narrating about those idols, reporting the words of ibn Abbass:

> The statues soon became idols, and they were worshiped by the people until the time of Noah ...when the flood covered, the whole earth. The flood washed the idols down from the top of Mount Nawdh to the land below. As the waters raged and the billows أمواج عظيمة / او متدحرج مثل الامواج swelled زادت او انتفخت, the idols were tossed here and there, until at last they were cast on the land of Jeddah by the waves. When finally the waters receded, the idols were left on the coast of the city. In time, they were covered by sand which the winds blew from the shore.

Hisham Ibn al Kalbi writes about:

> Amru Ibn-Luhayy (also called Rabi'ah son of Harithah son of 'Amr son of 'Amir son of Harithah son of Tha'labah son of Imru' son of al-Qays son of Mazin son of al-Azd. 'Amru was the father of the Khuza'ah. His mother was Fuhayrah, the daughter of al-Harith son of Mudad al-Jurhumi. He was a kahin or(priest of Jinn). 'Amru had conquered Mecca, drove the Jurhumites out of the city, and took over the custody of the House. He had a Jinn who appeared to him and gave him oracles. One day the oracle addressed 'Amru saying, "To the shores of Jeddah make thy way. There you shall find idols in fine array. Carry them to Tihamah... then bid the Arabs to worship them, one and all., They will hear your voice.[548]

When 'Amru proceeded to the shores of Jeddah, he dug the idols out of the sand and carried them to Tihamah. When the time for the pilgrimage arrived, 'Amru summoned all the Arabs to worship."[549]

How the false Muslim history began

Hisham Ibn Al Kalbi as well his father, Mohammed Ibn al Kalbi, were known to create myths, such as the one I've mentioned. They connect these myths with the Bible and with Biblical names. They wanted to support the words of the Quran by creating a new history for it, built on Biblical names and backgrounds. This falsification was first adopted by Ibn Abbass and Ubeid bin Sharayyahعبيد بن شرية. Ibn Abbass died A.H. 69 which is A.D. 689. Ubeid bin Sharih died in 70 A.H. which is 690 A.D. The same myths of Ubeid bin Sharayyah were embraced by Wahab bin Munabeh who died in 114 A.H. which is A.D. 734. Wahab bin Munabeh added to them. Ibn Ishak who died 153 A.H. which is 773 A.D. and Mohammed Ibn al Kalbi, who died in A.H. 146 which is A.D. 766, developed this false history by adding more genealogies and myths. Hisham, the son of Mohammed Ibn al Kalbi, who died in 206 A.H. which is 826 A.D, created more stories which he recorded in his books.

Their myths began about the end of the 7th century, and they continued through the 8th and 9th centuries. They never appeared before that time, neither were they found in any document or even in Arabian poetry. Yet this false history, written by counterfeiters and fakes, became indisputable facts for Muslims, upon which they document the myths of the Quran.

Analyzing The myth created by the Islamic authors regarding the idols and how they were made reached into Arabia

In analyzing the account which Ibn Abbass, Mohammed Ibn Al Kalbi and Hisham Ibn Al Kalbi concocted about Adam, we can easily see how absurd it is to believe that these men could have information about Adam and his descendants, which never was told before. These men, although they did not claim to be prophets, presented information which only a prophet like Moses could have known. What authority gave them this information?

Their narrations were outrageous. They began by stating that Adam descended from heaven and he placed his feet on a mountain in India. The Quran claims that after Adam and Eve sinned, they were expelled from heaven and sent to earth. (See Surah Tah, that is number 20 and verses 120-123) Why did Ibn Abbass select India as the place where Adam came to earth? It has to do with the Quran's myth about a furnace which caused the earth to flood during the time of Noah. Mohammed claims in the Quran that Noah's flood occurred because "the furnace boiled and fermented."(Surah Hud, that is 11and verse 40) Ibn Abbas placed the furnace in India.[550] Therefore, he claimed all the descendants of Adam until the time of Noah lived in India, around the mountain to which Adam descended. Therefore, he concludes that Noah's family lived there as well.

a furnace in Mesopotamian mythology became the cause of the Noah Flood. Ibn Abbass localized the place of that furnace

As I mentioned above, Mohammed claimed that the Flood of Noah came because the "furnace boiled." This belief finds its origin in Sumerian mythology, which teaches that there are unclean waters which are boiling in the underworld, overflowing from time to time and flooding the Euphrates and Tigris Rivers, making the rest of the Sumerian lands unproductive for agriculture. There are Sumerian Inscriptions which say that the waters of the underground world came from a place called "Kur," replacing the waters in the rivers and killing the crops.[551] (The Sumerians have seen the muddy waters which flood their land from time to time, thinking they were from the hostile underworld. In reality, the muddy waters happened when the Euphrates and the Tigris Rivers flooded, bringing the muddy soil from the mountains of Northern Mesopotamia and Turkey. Thus, this muddy water became the enemy of the Mesopotamians, a hostile enemy which they thought existed under the earth.)

The Sumerian mythology claims that Ninurta, the god of the stormy south wind and the son of Enlil, the famous Sumerian god of the atmosphere, blocked the unclean waters by piling up stones in a certain place in Mesopotamia.[552] The piles of stones became like a hot furnace, underneath which the boiling waters tried to overflow and flood the land. This myth became the base from which the Quran explained where the flood of Noah came from, as we see in Surah 11, verse 40, called Hud:

> The command came, and the Tannur effervesced or bubbled.

The Tannur in Arabic means "furnace of stones." The myth of the Tannur was spread among Arabians. Most of the Arabic narrators, such as al-Shaabi, located the Tannur in Kufa,[553] as well as Mujahed.[554] Kufa is a place a place in the old Sumerians' land, confirming the origin of the Quranic myth. Ibn Abbas says that the Tannur, which flooded the whole earth at the time of Noah, is found in India.[555] Ibn Abbas expressed what Mohammed intended in the Quran by the word "Tannur." We understand from his words that the flood came from a furnace located east of Babel, but he placed it more distant than that. Though the narration of Ibn Abbas is less accurate than that of Shaabi, it reveals the same Mesopotamic myth as the origin of the Quranic verse.

Mohammed spoke about a special mythological furnace during the time of Noah, which effervesced or bubbled until it flooded the earth. This furnace was made from stones,[556] demonstrating that the idea was derived from the Sumerian myth about impeding hostile waters through a pile of stones.

Even ancient Islamic linguists, such as al Zubeidi, ibn Manthur, and al Aini confirmed the word "Tannur" is a foreign word,[557] indicating the myth was originally not Arabic. It probably, spread later in Arabia. Without doubt, it has to do with the Sumerian myth.

The Sumerians have seen the muddy waters which flood their land from time to time, thinking they were from the hostile underworld.

The Sumerians have seen the muddy waters which flood their land from time to time, thinking they were from the hostile underworld. In reality, the muddy waters happened when the Euphrates and the Tigris Rivers flooded, bringing the muddy soil from the mountains of Northern Mesopotamia and Turkey. Thus, this muddy water became the enemy of the Mesopotamians, a hostile enemy which they thought existed under the earth.

The mythological concepts developed by the Sumerians thrived in subsequent generations and were adopted by many religions and sects who lived in Mesopotamia. Among such sects were the Mandaeans, who were also called Sabians. In their sacred books, we find "personalities of light" descending to the underworld, which is formed of the seven earths. They brought the commands of the "King of Light" to people living there. In the Ginza Rba, the main sacred book of the Mandaeans, we read about Mandadahi, one of their "personalities of light." He testified that, after returning from the underworld, he saw the "black waters boiling and trying to effervesce."[558]

The dilemma of bringing the idols through the waters of the Flood from India to Jeddah

Ibn al Kalbi had to find some way to bring the Arabian idols from India to Jeddah near Mecca. Why did the flood waters bring the five idols to Jeddah and place them in one spot along the shore rather than distributing them to many parts of the world? These authors underestimated the intelligence of their followers. The fact is that, the myths created by Mohammed when he claimed the Arabian idols existed at the time of Noah, forced his followers to compose imaginary and childish stories to legitimize Mohammed's historically inaccurate claims.

Early Islamic authors fictionalize history regarding Jurhum

According to these same Islamic authors, Ishmael came with his mother Hager to Mecca, and his mother found a wife for him who was the daughter of Mudad al-Jurhumi.[559] Ibn Ishak said the wife's name was Raalah[560]رعلة. But we know from the Bible that Ishmael's mother found him a wife from Egypt, her country of origin.

The name Mudad al Jurhumi cannot be just pasted into the 20 century B.C. It is an Arabic name bearing the style of Arabic names which existed at the time of these Islamic writers. The Arabic language itself did not exist until the 10 century B. C. It was quite different from the Arabic which spread after the rise of Islam, and became the language of the Quran, and was spoken by the tribe of Quraysh, the tribe of Mohammed.

In addition to Ibn Abbass, Ubeid bin Sharayyah and Ibn Ishak contributed to the creation of stories about the tribe of Jurhum which they said had been living in Mecca since the 20th century B.C., the time of Abraham. However, we know that Mecca did not exist before the 4th century A.D. The tribe of Khuzaah came from Yemen two centuries earlier to build Mecca. If Jurhum dominated Mecca since the time of Abraham, as the Islamic authors of the 8th and 9th centuries A.D. declare, we would have found records about them more, perhaps more material than any tribe who lived in Arabia. Tribes in Yemen and north Arabia which shared a limited span of history centuries before Christ had complete archeological records, yet, neither Mecca or Jurhum turn up in the records.

Furthermore, classical writers and geographers who visited western Arabia, including the area where Mecca was eventually built, mentioned the tiny villages and tribes in Western Arabia, yet, none of them mentioned Mecca or the tribe of Jurhum.

But Hisham bin Mohammed ibn al Kalbi went further than this. He claimed that Jurhum was Hadoram mentioned in Genesis chapter 10 as the son of Joktan, son of Eber, son of Arphaxad, son of Shem.[561]

If the tribe of Jurhum had descended from Hadoram, who was only four generations after Noah, and if they dominated Mecca, and if they existed in Yemen and other parts of Arabia until the time, they were expelled from Mecca by the tribe of Khuzaah, then Jurhum would have been a significantly important tribe in Arabia. Why is there no record in history or archeology about Jurhum? Since there is no similarity of name between the names Hadoram and Jurhum, how could Ibn al Kalbi and Ubeid bin Sharayyah, connect the stories they created with genealogies mentioned in the Bible? It looks simple at first, but it is easy to see their falsity and forgery.

These early Islamic authors were ignorant of historical chronology when they connected Ishmael with the events of the fourth century A.D.

As we saw, Hisham Ibn al Kalbi claimed that 'Amru Ibn-Luhayy was the father of the Khuza'ah. His mother was Fuhayrah, the daughter of Al-Harith Ibn-Mudad al-Jurhumi. Hisham Ibn Al Kalbi also claimed that 'Amru conquered Mecca and drove the Jurhumites out of the city, and took over the custody of the House(means the temple of Mecca). By this, Ibn al Kalbi said 'Amru ibn-Luhayy was grandson of Mudad, the father of the wife of Ishmael. If 'Amru ibn-Luhayy was the chief of Khuza'ah, the tribe that inhabited Mecca in the 4th century A.D. How could he be the grandson of a man who was the father-in-law of Ishmael in the 20 century B.C.? We know that the tribe of Khuza'ah left Yemen after the dam of Maarib was damaged around the year 150 A.D. Islamic historians admit that Khuza'ah came from Yemen after the torrent of "al Irm, سيل العرم" had damaged the dam.[562]

Mecca was built in the beginning of the 4th century A.D., on the caravan route from Yemen northward to Syria and Palestine. For Islamic writers to suggest that Ishmael lived during the time Mecca was built preposterous. I will later discuss this subject with more detail.

Islamic writers claimed the chief of Khuza'ah introduced pagan worship to Arabia, to support another claim that Arabia confessed a monotheistic faith established by the Ishmaelites

Islamic writers said 'Amru ibn-Luhayy, who was the king of Khuza'ah at Mecca, and he was the one who introduced idols worship to Arabia. They claim that before 'Amru ibn-Luhayy, all Arabia followed a monotheistic worship which was established by Ishmael and his descendants. They say 'Amru ibn-Luhayy brought idols from Syria and erected them in the temple of Mecca. We know that Khuza'ah never lived in Mecca until the 4th century A.D., so they intimated that polytheism and paganism began in the 4th century A.D.

We know from archeology that Eastern Arabians were polytheistic long before the 4th century. Their idolatry was well-known three thousand years before Christ; perhaps earlier. The Southern Arabians, especially the Sabeans of Yemen, had many idols and deities since their first kingdom, in the eleventh century B.C. Archeology confirms that the Maini kingdom, other kingdoms in Yemen, and other southern Arabian kingdoms were polytheistic. We have records of the pagan deities and idols of the Kingdoms of the North Arabia dating back to the 8th century B.C. to confirm this.

To claim that the chief of Khuza'ah brought the pagan worship to Arabia is a futile claim: that Ishmael and his descendants controlled Arabia spreading monotheistic worship to all Arabia. Ibn Ishak claims that the Ishmaelites went from Mecca to different parts of Arabia where Allah caused them to conquer everyone who confronted them.[563]

We know from the Bible that Ishmael lived in the wilderness of Paran in northeastern Sinai. We see from Genesis 25:12-18, that Moses in the 15 century B.C. showed the Ishmaelites still living in Sinai. Many of these tribes emigrated to the deserts of the Fertile Crescent such as Syria, Iraq, Jordan, and Palestine, a fact also seen in various Assyrian and Chaldean inscriptions (See the history of Mecca in Dr. Amari's book, Islam: In Light of History.) However, no Ishmaelite tribe had ever lived at Mecca, which we know was not built until the 4th century A.D.

Can the devils wait until the 4th Century A.D., to reveal the idols of Noah's time?

Another major concern is the way Ibn al Kalbi uncovered the five idols. He claimed the water from the flood brought the idols to the shore of Jeddah and the sand covered them. Ibn al Kalbi claimed that a Jinn devil revealed this to 'Amru ibn-Luhayy. Since Islam teaches the Jinn devils have been on earth since the fall of Adam, how could they have kept this secret all those years? Why did they wait until Khuza'ah inhabited Mecca in the 4th century A.D. to uncover these idols and promote their worship among men?

The five idols were considered purely Arabian, and appeared at different times.

There is another important argument against the claims of al Kalbi. Some of these idols are known to have been worshiped by some Arabians before Khuza'ah came to Mecca. Wadd, deity of the moon for the Minaean kingdom in Yemen, was worshiped by the Minaeans centuries before Christ. Nasr was one of the idols of Himyar in Yemen. The Himyarites appeared as a kingdom in 115 B.C. So, in their attempt to create a history for the Quran, ibn al Kalbi and his companions ignored the basic history of Arabia including various deities and kingdoms.

The fact of the matter is, these five idols were known to be Arabian deities which appeared in definite locations and in definite times. They did not all live at the same time. As purely Arabian idols and deities, they belonged to different times and nations or tribes in the history of Arabia. This means their worship began, not in one epoch, but in different ones. If they were idols belonged to the time of Noah, they would have been known in other parts of the ancient world as well, and not just in some isolated areas of Arabia. All of them would have been well-known in Arabia since their beginnings. Yet, apart of Wadd, the other four idols appeared sometime around the Christian era, or even centuries later.

Analyzing those idols will show they were purely Arabian and did not exist at the time of Noah.

Mohammed committed an error when he chose to record these idols as existing in the time of Noah. These idols were of a later period, and each one belonged to an Arabian tribe. They were known to be Arabian idols that appeared in specific places and times. As Arabian idols and gods, they belong in the history of Arabia to different ages and tribes. If they existed at the time of Noah, they would have been known in many regions of the world in ancient times, rather than a limited area of Arabia. At the very least, they would have been known in Arabia since its early history. With the exception of Wadd, the other four idols appeared either around the Christian era or in later centuries. I will analyze the information about these idols to prove that they were Arabian idols, and cannot be attributed to the time of Noah.

Wadd, a Minaean deity of the Moon

Wadd originally was a Minaean deity. Main was a Yemeni kingdom which appeared in the 11 or12 century B.C. Wadd was among the deities they worshiped. They called him the god of the moon.[564]

The Minaeans also had a commercial colony in the city of Dedan among the Lahyanites north of Arabia. The Minaeans of Dedan had a temple just for the worship of Wadd.[565] The spread of the Minaeans' colonies in the north of Arabia among the Lihyanites and Thamud tribes gave Wadd a presence among the deities which the Thamuds honored. The Thamud tribe appeared only after the 8th century B.C.[566]

It is clear that Wadd is originally a Minaean deity. Wadd could not have been worshiped the time of Noah, because this Wadd's worship was born with the Minaeans, and it spread through their colonies in limited areas of the north after the 4th century B.C. The oldest civilization of eastern Arabia never knew this worship.

Yaqut al Hamawi, an Arabic historian, says that Al lat, an Arabian deity which represented the sun, was older than Wadd.[567] This statement confirms the fact that Wadd was unknown in the north before the 4th century B.C. Al lat was also mentioned by Herodotus, the Greek historian who visited Arabia in the 5th century B.C.

This being the case, how did Mohammed hear about Wadd? The answer is simple. Kalb, a northern Arabian tribe, worshiped Wadd. Arabic writers mention that the Yemeni tribe of Khuthaa, who were cousins of Quraysh, the tribe to which Mohammed belonged had carried a statue of Wadd to Duma al Jindel in the northern part of Arabia. Kalb was a branch of Khuthaa, and they worshiped Wadd. According to Yaqut al Hamawi and

Al Bakri al Andalusi, Quraysh had an idol by the name of Wadd.[568] Quraysh was careful to present most of the idols known by Arabians at the temple, so that they could draw as many Arabians as possible to Mecca. This is where Mohammed became aware of these idols.

Kalb in Duma al Jindel worshiped Wadd because Duma was in contact with the Thamud who learned the worship of Wadd from the Minaean colonies.

A study of these arguments shows us that Wadd is a Minaean deity specific to one Arabian tribe which spread after the 4th century to Dedan and then among the Thamud. This could not be attributed to the time of Noah which was five or six thousand years before Christ.

Mohammed's acquaintance with Suwa'

Suwa was an idol known to be worshiped by the tribe of Hudhail[569] هذيل which was descended from Hudhailm, the Son of Mudrakeh مدركة, the 15th ancestor of Mohammed.[570] The idol Suwa, was erected and worshiped by Hudhail in a location called Ruhat رُهَاط in the Yanbu ينبوع area,[571] near al Medina. This is why Mohammed included this idol with the idols he attributed to the time of Noah. Certainly Mohammed was acquainted with this idol.

Arguments support that Suwa' was not an ancient deity.

Suwa' was actually a stone[572] in the form of a woman.[573] However, the meaning of the word in Arabic relates to time, part of the day or night,[574] suggesting they were worshipping time. The Arabian were known to worship night and day. Arabians considered night to be a strong male deity and day to be a female deity. We see this reflected in the Quran, Surah 39:5. The idea of the night tracing the day is expressed in Surah 36: 40, where the sun, moon, night and day all swim in a celestial sea. The night fails to reach the day. I can only conclude Suwa' was a female idol, part of the day, perhaps daybreak or dawn.

Yaqut al Hamawi says about Suwa':

However, I have not heard any mention of it in the poems of Hudhail except in a poem of a man from Yemen.[575]

The Hadhail tribe not mentioning their main deity in their poetry, is something to consider because the deity of a tribe in Arabia is mentioned many times in the poetry of that tribe. Not mentioning Suwa' in the poems of Hadhail is an indication that the idol was not an ancient one. It is worship may have been close to the Islamic period, so that it appeared only once in the poetry. Surely it cannot be an idol from the time of Noah as the author of the Quran claimed. The fact that only one tribe of Arabia revered the idol, confirm that it was a recent local tribe.

Yaghuth and Ya'uq

Yaghuth and Ya'uq are two idols which have opposite meanings and functions for Arabians. Yaghuth was worshiped by Murad, a Yemeni tribe. This idol was placed on a hill called Madhej مَذْحِج . Murad and al Harith حارث began fighting over Yaghuth. Al Harith won the war with the help of Hamdan, another Yemeni tribe. The battle was known as Rismالرزم , and it took place the same year Mohammed defeated the Meccans in the battle of Bader.[576] Mohammed was acquainted with the battle of Rism. He asked Farwah, a Muslim from the tribe of Murad:

> Were you angry or did it please you to see your people fight the battle of Rism? [577]

His question demonstrates Mohammed's knowledge of the idol Yaghuth.

Yaghuth and Ya'uq were Arabian deities under the influence of Zoroastrian dualism.

Ya'uq was worshiped by the Yemeni tribe of Hamadanهمدان , the same tribe that fought over the idol Yaghuth. Ya'uq and Yaghuth had much in common. Their worship was limited to two tribes that were in Yemen. The tribe of Hamadan a one time had both idols. We will see that the worship of these two idols was under Persian Zoroastrian influence.

Yaghuth was shaped like a Lion, Ya'uq like a horse.[578] The word Yaghuth in Arabic means "the one who brings rain." This meaning is confirmed by Arabic writers such as Yaqut al Hamawi and al 'Aini.[579] Worshippers of Yaghuth considered this deity brings them rain contrasted to the word for Ya'uq which means "an obstacle." Yaqut al Hamawi speaks about Ya'uq saying he stops the rain.[580] This suggests to us that the worshipers of Ya'uq revered him, so he would not hinder the coming of the rain. Ibn Hayyan and Al-Allusi confirm that Yaghuth and Ya'uq are two deities which had opposing roles of bringing the rain and opposing it.[581]

This dualism is derived from Zoroastrianism. They believe life is a battle between good forces and wicked ones. There dualism is expressed on each level of animal and natural elements in the universe. For example, for Zoroastrians there are good animals in the kingdom of Ahura Mazda, their main deity, and there are bad animals that follow Ahriman, the god of darkness. There are good stars working with angels and bad stars working with devils.

Zoroastrian dualism has also found a level of the natural phenomena in rain. There is Tistrya, the chief of the stars, who is responsible of bringing the rain from the "celestial sea." But there is also Daeva Apaosha, a devil who opposes the coming of the rain, standing against Tistrya. This devil is usually a wicked planet. Tistrya comes down to battle Daeva Apaosha. The later, according to Tir Yast, a part of the Zend Avesta, "rushes down to Tistrya in the shape of a dark horse with a black coat and black ears and a black tail, stamped with bands of terror."[582] No wonder Ya'uq, the Arabian god who opposes the rain, is the form of horse. When Tistrya overcomes Daeva Apaosha, Tistrya brings the rain down to earth.[583]

But there is more data that confirms the Zoroastrian worship was imposed on Arabian worship. Ibn Manthur and Zubeidi reveal that "Ya'uq was a red planet near the Pleiades constellation, and it got this name because it interfered with the movement of a star called al Dabran."[584] This was certainly derived from the Zoroastrian mythology when the planet devil becomes an obstacle to the star Tistrya, which brings rain down to earth from heaven and from the celestial sea."

It is evident that the Arabian worship of Ya'uq and Yaghuth was under influence of Persian Zoroastrianism. Arabians worshiped the Jinn devils, because they feared their punishment, and the wickedness they could cause to them. So we can understand why Arabian tribes worshiped Ya'uq, though it was seen as a negative deity.

Ya'uq and Yaghuth can be dated to the late Persian Sassanid period, but not to the time of Noah.

The Arabian tribes that worshiped Ya'uq and Yaghuth were both Yemeni tribes. I believe this worship began during the Sassanid Persian Kingdom between the 3rd and the 6th centuries A.D. The influence of the Persians on Yemen during this period was great. We know that the Persians occupied Yemen in the 6th century A.D. They were present in southern and eastern Arabia centuries before this date.

I assume the worship of these two idols was in the last portion of the Sassanid Persian Kingdom, which ended with the rise of Islam. We can date this to the fifth or the sixth century A.D. based on the fact there was only one copy of Yaghuth made of lead,[585]and two or three tribes of Yemen fought one another to have it.[586] This means a short period of time elapsed since the worship of this idol was born in Arabia, so that no other copy of the idol was made.

Yaqut al Hamawi, says he never heard an Arabian naming his son Abed Ya'uq, or the servant of Ya'uq, contrary to the Arabian habit to call their sons after the deities they worshiped. Yaqut goes on to say that he never heard a poem mentioning Ya'uq either.[587]I believe these things indicate that Ya'uq was not an ancient Arabian deity. Certainly we cannot believe Ya'uq and Yaghuth lived during the time of Noah as Mohammed claims in the Quran.

Nasr, an Arabian deity

Nasr is an idol whose name in Arabic means "eagle."

Nasr was found within the idols of the Lahyanites in North Arabia. It must have been an idol of the northern Arabians; In fact, it was mentioned in the Syriac writings as an Arabian idol, especially in the Doctrine of Addai, which dates back to the 4th century A.D., where it was mentioned as Nashra. This was the Aramaic form of Nasr.[588] It was also mentioned in the Hebrew records as being an Arabian deity. The Talmud mentioned "Nashra," a Hebrew word which means Nasr, as being an Arabian idol.[589]

From this, we can conclude that Nasr, as a Lahynite deity, cannot be dated prior to the 4th century B.C., the date the Lihyanites appeared in North Arabia. Later, Nasr worship spread into Yemen, and it was revered by the Himyarite tribe of Yemen. Ibn Manthur and al Asfahani say that Nasr is a symbol of a planet.[590]

The Himyarite Kingdom appeared in 115 B.C.[591]The idol Nasr was in a place called Balkha 'بلخع in the land of Saba.[592] Since Himyar conquered Saba in the year 275 A.D., we can reasonably deduce that the worship of Nasr by the Himyarites began after this date.

Arabic writers agree that Dhi al Kalaa ذي الكلاع, a Himyarite tribe, were the only worshippers of Nasr.[593]

Yaqut al Hamawi says that, like Ya'uq, he never heard anyone from Himyar naming his son after Nasr, nor had he heard anyone mention this idol in the poetry of the Himyarites or other Arabians.[594] I believe this is an obvious indication that the worship of this idol came later from North Arabia to Dhi al Kalaa', a Himyarite tribe. It transferred to this tribe from a definite location in North Arabia — that is, the area the Lihyanites inhabited, knowing that the Lihyanites were the first Arabians to worship Nasr. If Nasr was worshipped by other Arabians prior to the appearance of the Lihyanites in the 4th century B.C., it would have existed and spread throughout many parts of Arabia, and would have been among the deities worshiped by important kingdoms which appeared in Arabia before the Lihyanites, such as the Sabaeans and Minaeans, who appeared in Yemen around the 11th-13th centuries B.C. He would have also existed among the deities of eastern Arabia, such as the kingdoms of Dalmun in Bahrain and Magan in Oman, both dated prior to the 4th millennium B.C. These kingdoms are closer to the time of Noah than the Lihyanites and the Himyarites. If Nasr was an idol at the time of Noah, it would have been logical to find Nasr in the earlier kingdoms that are closer to the time of Noah.

Why these Arabian idols cannot be placed in the time of Noah and still remain historical

The five idols mentioned in the Quran and attributed to the time of Noah, cannot be people, as Islamic writers claim. Only Wadd was in the form of a man, and he was originally the Minaean god of the moon. Suwa' was a stone in the form of a woman, seen as a female idol and part of the daybreak or the dawn. Yaghuth was in the form of a Lion representing a star which an Arabian tribe worshiped and considered as the deity that brings rain. Ya'uq was in the form of horse, and as we saw it was a planet that opposes the movement of the star which brings to them rain. Nasr was in the form of an Eagle, and most probably it was symbolically a planet.

Those idols have Arabic names. We know the Arabic language appeared only after the 10th century B.C. How could those idols be attributed to the time of Noah? Al Khurtubi admits that these five idols were Arabian and no nation had worshiped them other than the Arabians.[595]

The Islamic writers admit that Arabia for a long time did not have these idols.[596] However, they did create the myth that a flood brought the idols from India to the shores of Jeddah. and they were covered by sand until the Jinn ordered Amru bin Lohayy to retrieve them and subsequently the Arabians worshiped them.[597] I have already refuted this myth.

We saw that Ya'uq, Nasr were not mentioned in poetry, and no one named his son after any of them. Hadhail, the tribe that purportedly worshiped Suwa', did not mention Suwa' except in one poem written by a man from Yemen, nor did they name any of their children after the idol. These are important indications that these idols appeared within limited Arabian tribes near the rise of Islam.

Yaqut al Hamawi, the Arabian historian, admits that the Arabians did not revere these five idols like they revered their main idols such as Uzi, al llat (the sun) and Manat.[598] I believe this happened because these five idols were only idols for limited numbers of tribes, and each idol was revered by only one tribe. Another reason for this concerns their origins. They were not ancient Arabian deities like Uzi, al llat (the sun) and Manat. While Yaqut as a Muslim, believe the five idols came from the time of Noah, yet he admits that Al llat is older than the idol Wadd.[599]

Mohammed's lack of a historical base made him unqualified to create reasonable historical frame for the claims he wrote in the Quran.

Mohammed could have chosen other Arabian deities which were much older than those he attributed to the time of Noah. There are ancient Semitic deities which date back to 4500 B.C., such as 'Am and Eil.[600] Mohammed did not have enough knowledge to choose those, but he chose very recent Arabian idols instead.

Mohammed lacked the knowledge of the history of Arabian and Semitic worship. He could not find nor invent a reasonable history for his claims. He addressed listeners who were simple and lived at a time when history did not seem to be important to people. This atmosphere made it easy for people not to question Mohammed's claims.

Mohammed's lack of any historical education made him unqualified to create a structural historicity for his claims in the Quran

Mohammed could have chosen other Arabian gods that were more ancient than the five idols, which he attributes to Noah's time. There are ancient Semitic gods, such as 'Am and El, that go back to 4500 years B.C. It would have been more appropriate to claim them as being idols from Noah's time rather than the late Arabian gods, which the Quran claimed appertained to Noah's era. Mohammed did not possess enough historical education to choose such gods. Instead, he selected more recent gods.

My friend, Professor R. Averbeck, an expert in ancient languages — in particular, the Semitic and Sumerian languages — conducted research about the ancient gods and idols that go back thousands of years prior to Christ. Among those gods, Professor Averbeck did not find any name close to these five Arabian idols.

Mohammed did not possess either knowledge of the history of the Semitic religions, nor the history of the religions inside Arabia. Thus, he was not able to create a logical historical framework within which to base his claims. He addressed simple and naïve listeners who lived in an era and region where history was of no importance. This allowed him to be surrounded by groups who never doubted his claims, with the exception of the educated people of Mecca.

Tubb'a

The destruction of the people of Tubb'a, the Himyarite

The Quran describes the extermination of an ancient people-the Himyarites. This claim is made, in spite of the fact that the Himyarites continued to exist as people until Mohammed's time and beyond.

According to Surah al Dukhan (44:37), the people of Tubb'a were exterminated by Allah, as were other people before them:

What! Are they better than the people of Tubb'a and those who were before them? We destroyed them because they were guilty of sin.

The Himyarites, however, did not perish at the time of Tubb'a. This is one of many serious historical mistakes we find in the Quran.

In Surah Qaf, verses 12-14, the Quran mentions some people along with their prophets, classifying each group according to the prophet sent to that people. The Quran claims that "everyone of them denied (their) Messengers," including the people of Tubb'a. This indicates that the Quran considered Tubb'a to be a prophet to his people, the Himyarites of Yemen.

We want to compare the claims of the Quran alongside of the historical record:

Was this Tubb'a considered by the Himyarites to be a prophet? Were his people destroyed because of their disobedience to his message?

The identity of Tubb'a mentioned in the Quran.

Islamic scholars agree that Tubb'a was intended by the Quran to be Abu Karib As'ad. Al Razi, a famous Quranic expositor, wrote:

Al Kalbi said, 'Tubb'a was Abu Karib As'ad.' The prophet of Allah said: 'Do not curse Tubb'a, because he became Muslim. I do not know if Tubb'a was a prophet or not.'[601]

Ibn Manthur wrote:

A king named As'ad Abu Karib had reigned in the first epochs. It was said that to be named with the title of 'Tubb'a,' a Yemeni king must reign over Hadhramoun, Saba and Himyar.[602]

It is clear from ibn Manthur's words that the Tubb'a of the Quran was the title of As'ad Abu Karib. This is although other Himyarite kings who reigned over Hadhramaut, Saba and Himyar also had the title of Tubb'a. When there is no specification to other Tubb'as, the title is referred to as As'ad abu Karib. He gained this title because he was the first to expand his domain outside Yemen.

Al Zubeidi wrote:

His name is As'ad Abu Karib. Al Leith said, 'The Tubb'as in Himyar were as the Kesras in Persia, and Caesars for the Romans. No king of Himyars called by the title of Tubb'a, unless Himyar and Hadhramaut were submitted to him.' Others add Suba to these two regions.[603]

Islamic writers, such as al Bakri al Andulisi and al Allusi, called the Tubb'a of the Quran Tubb'a al Akbar.[604] (the great) Al Allusi wrote:

The people of Tubb'a,' as it was mentioned in the Quran, refers to Tubb'a al Akbar the Himyarite; his name is As'ad, his nickname is abu Karib. He was a righteous man.[605]

The identification of Tubb'a with As'ad abu Karib, as mentioned by Mohammed, is also clear from Mohammed's Hadith. Al Khurtubi wrote:

Al Waqidi said, '...Abu Hurrerah said, 'the prophet of Allah prohibited cursing As'ad the Himyarite, who was Tubb'a; he was first to clothe al Kaabah.'[606]

Mohammed said about Tubb'a, who clothed the Kaabah, that he was As'ad the Himyarite. Here is Mohammed's Hadith:

Reported by abu Hurrereh, the apostle of Allah said, 'do not curse As'ad the Himyarite, he was first to clothe the Kaabah.'[607]

Ibn Kathir speaks about the Tubb'a mentioned in the Quran:

This Tubb'a is As'ad abu Karib, son of Melkikarib the Yemenite. They said he reigned on his people for 326 years. No one had reigned in Yemen more years than his reign. He died 700 years before the apostle of Allah was called to the role of prophecy.[608]

We see, then, that the Islamic scholars were all united regarding the Tubb'a of the Quran being As'ad abu Karib. This is in spite of their ignoring when, and for how many years he reigned. Historically, it is known that he reigned from 410-435 A.D.

Islamic narrators' confusion in regard to the genealogy of Tubb'a

The confusion of ibn al Kalbi

Hisham ibn al Kalbi claimed that after Balqis (the name of the queen of Saba that visited Solomon according to Arabic tradition), a man reigned by the name of Yasser Amru bin Yaa'fur. We notice that ibn al Kalbi derived the name of Yaa'fur from the name of a son of As'ad abu Karib, that is Sharahbil Yaa'fur. Ibn al Kalbi derived the name Yasser from the name of another Himyarite king, that is Yasser Yahna'm II ياســـر يهنعم الثاني, who reigned between 300-310 A.D. From these two names, ibn al Kalbi formed the name of a king, who he claimed reached North Africa. He claimed this king wrote his name there as "al Himyari." This reveals the ignorance of ibn al Kalbi regarding the history of the Himyarites, who appeared for the first time in 115 B.C. Ibn al Kalbi placed As'ad abu Karib as reigning after this king,[609] hus placing him during the 10th century B.C. This is although As'ad abu Karib appeared in the 5th century A.D.

Thus, the first Islamic narrators attempted to create a history for Tubb'a of the Quran, by making use of some famous kings' names, creating new kings' names and a new history. Their history, however, is contrary to the Himyarite official history, as we know from Yemeni inscriptions written in the Musnad script, and from the rest of the Yemeni archeological findings. The reason they could not discover Mohammed's enormous mistake is because of their ignorance of the Himyarite history, which was very close to their times. As'ad abu Karib was removed from them by less than 200 years (he reigned from 410-435 A.D.). Instead, they thought he lived in a very ancient epoch.

The claim that Tubb'a occupied Asia, including India and China

Some Islamic narrators, such as Ibn Kathir, claimed that Abu Karib reached China and India during his campaigns.[610] Islamic writers, such as Taberi, claimed that As'ad abu Karib led his army to Hira (in Iraq), then proceeded to Samarqand (a city of Uzbekistan in central Asia) and destroyed it.[611]

In order for abu Karib As'ad to reach Samarqand, India and China, he would have had to defeat the Persian Empire which dominated Iraq, Persia, and regions of Asia through parts of India. We do not see, however, that the Himyarites ever defeated the Persian Empire, nor do we see any of the kings of Himyar reigning outside of Arabia.

Did As'ad abu Karib embrace Judaism with his people?

Taberi said that As'ad abu Karib occupied Yathrib-Medina and took two rabbis from the Jews of the Beni Qaritha tribe of Medina. The rabbis influenced him, so he brought them to Yemen and followed their religion.[612] Ibn Kathir repeated the same story.[613] Taberi mentioned that Tubb'a and his people had submitted to the ruling of a fire that devoured the oppressor and did not harm the innocent or the oppressed. The fire ruled in favor of Tubb'a and his two Jewish friends. The fire also devoured the idols of Yemen, causing the people to clap and to embrace Judaism.[614] Without a doubt, at the time of Mohammed this story originated among the Jews who embraced Islam, such as Abdellah bin Salam.[615] We know that this story is an imitation of what is written in the book of Daniel regarding his three companions who refused to bow and worship the statue Nebuchadnezzar had erected. As a result of their disobedience, Nebuchadnezzar ordered them to be thrown into a fiery furnace. The fire, however, did not harm them. When Nebuchadnezzar saw this miracle, he ordered them to be brought out from the fire, and that those who accused them should be thrown into the fire instead. The fire then devoured the accusers. It is clear that Abdellah bin Salam, and the other Jews of Medina who embraced Islam, derived the myth of the fire that ruled in favor of Tubb'a from this story in the book of Daniel.

The myth about Tubb'a helps us to see why the Quran considered him to be a prophet: this is built on unhistorical myths, such as the one we examined. Those myths spread among the Jews of Medina, and had nothing to do with history. Thus, the sayings of Tubb'a regarding the sunset in a muddy fetid spring, which is based on the myths of Pseudo-Callisthenes, became canonical inspiration which was incorporated into the sayings and poems of those who claimed to be prophets in Arabia, such as Umayyah bin Abi al Salt; this was also incorporated into Mohammed's Quran.

Other Islamic narrators, such as ibn Ishak, embraced the same myth regarding Tubb'a and the fire.[616] How can ibn Ishak and Abdullah bin Salam be references to historical facts, without them returning to prior historical documentation?

Assad abu Karib had occupied Medina-Yathrib, because it was a known city built centuries before Mecca. Then he came to Mecca.[617]

The place given to Tubb'a by Mohammed's generation and the generations that followed

Some Yemeni created stories about Tubb'a. As an example, Zayd bin Rabi'a bin Mafragh, a Yemeni poet who died 69 years after Mohammed emigrated to Medina, recited stories about Tubb'a.[618] Ibn Manthur reported some poems that praised David and Tubb'a in accomplishing great works.[619] For the pre-Islamic Jahiliyyah people, attributing the role of prophecy to a person meant that capabilities were given to him to accomplish artistic things. Or, that he was given inventive abilities, such as making iron melt, as the Quran claims that the ability to melt iron was given to David. Those pre-Islamic mythological ideas about Tubb'a as a prophet left its influence on Mohammed and his Quran.

Was Tubb'a a prophet in Mohammed's sight?

In some of his Hadiths, Mohammed was reluctant to consider Tubb'a as a prophet. One of these Hadith says:

> Do not curse Tubb'a, because he became Muslim; I do not know if Tubb'a was a prophet or not.[620]

Another Hadith says:

> Reported by abi Hurrireh, the apostle of Allah said, 'I do not know if Tubb'a was a prophet or not. I do not know if Dhu al Qarnayn was a prophet or not.'[621]

For Mohammed, Tubb'a was a Muslim leader, as Dhu al Qarnayn was, making wars in the name of Allah. But Mohammed did not know if Tubb'a was a prophet or not. Without a doubt, Mohammed was under the influence of the pre-Islamic myths about Tubb'a — that he was a devout leader, and occupied regions of Asia and North Africa, fighting in the name of "Allah" — the same wrong idea that was attributed by Pseudo-Callisthenes to Alexander.

Mohammed's saying that he did not know whether Tubb'a was a prophet or not made Muslims very puzzled regarding Tubb'a; some considered him as a prophet, while others viewed him as a devout Muslim leader. Eventually, however, Mohammed made Tubb'a a prophet in the Quran, as we will see later.

In reality, we do not find the term "Islam" in the Yemeni inscriptions. This term was used by the Sabian Mandaeans, as well as by persons who claimed to be prophets prior to Mohammed. The poems that portray Tubb'a as Muslim were created in the Islamic era.

Tubb'a as a prophet in the Quran

We read in Surah 50, called Qaf, verses 12-15:

Before them was denied (the Hereafter) by the People of Noah, the Companions of the Rass, the Thamud, The 'Ad, Pharaoh, the brethren of Lut, The Companions of the Wood, and the People of Tubb'a'; each one (of them) rejected the apostles, and My warning was duly fulfilled (in them).

We see in the above verse that Tubb'a's people were placed among ancient peoples. According to the Quran, those peoples were: Thumad and Ad, which were, according to the Quran, the second and third generations after Noah. Then came the people of Pharaoh at the time of Moses, then the people of Lot, and "the companions of the wood," — which, according to the Quran, were the Midianites. Then the people of Tubb'a immediately followed. This shows that Mohammed realized that Tubb'a was a prophet who lived in ancient times, to the extent that some expositors of the Quran placed him at least 1,000 years before Mohammed. Here, we see the mistake of the Quran placing Tubb'a in an ancient epoch, even though he reigned from 410-435 A.D. The other mistake is that the Quran said that the people of Tubb'a were exterminated, when we know historically that this never happened to them.

We notice that the Quran names each people by the name of its prophet for example: "the people of Noah," or "the brethren of Lut." He calls the Himyarite people "the people of Tubb'a," indicating he considered Tubb'a to be a prophet. Then the Quran says, "...each one of them rejected the apostles." This means that the people of Noah rejected Noah, Thamud rejected their prophet, and Ad the same etc. The people of Tubb'a rejected Tubb'a. It is clear that the Quran intended to say that Tubb'a was a prophet sent to his people, at the same level as the prophets Mohammed claimed were sent to the Arabian peoples, such as Saleh to Thamud, Hud to Ad, Shuayb to Median, etc., in addition to prophets sent to non-Arabian peoples, such as Lot to Sodom and Gomorrah. This is despite Mohammed's Hadiths regarding Tubb'a as a prophet being written with less assertiveness than his words here in the Quran.

Ibn Kathir explains how the people of Tubb'a became Muslims, and then withdrew from Islam to worship idols. Allah then condemned them, according to the Quranic verse. This shows that Tubb'a was considered a prophet by the Quran expositors. Ibn Kathir wrote:

> About this Tubb'a mentioned in the Quran, his people embraced Islam through him. After he died they returned to worship fire and idols. Allah punished them as he mentioned in Sura Saba.[622]

Al Allusi wrote in his expository book, Ruh al Maani:

> Regarding the people of Tubb'a the Himyarites. He was a believer, whereas, his people were infidels. Therefore, he was not dispraised, but his people were...the meaning of 'rejecting the peoples their apostles' is rejecting what they all were united on monotheism and the belief of life after death. To this end Tubb'a used to call them.[623]

This expresses the Quran and its expositors' idea that Tubb'a was a prophet who called his people to monotheism.

The Yemenites' claim that they were descendants of Yaktan, and that their history had Yemeni prophets, like Tubb'a

As we have seen, at the time of Mohammed, Tubb'a was considered a prophet by some groups. This idea was embraced after the rise of Islam.

There were reasons for the Yemeni to make Tubb'a a prophet, especially after the rise of Islam. The most important was to compete with the people of Hejaz, who after the rise of Islam claimed to be descendants from a figure called Adnan, created by the Islamic genealogists as the 22nd ancestor of Mohammed, and descendent of Ishmael.

Adnan as a descendent of Ishmael is a myth: by studying the Assyrian inscriptions and the Bible, we deduce that the Ishmaelites never reached Mecca.

The Islamic Yemeni claimed to be descendants of Qahtan, whom they identified with Yaktan, mentioned in the book of Genesis, the first book of the Bible. This claim is made despite the descendants of Yaktan never reaching Yemen, but rather East Arabia. The Islamic narrators claimed that Yaktan, mentioned in the book of Genesis as the son of Eber, son of Salah, son of Arphaxad, son of Sam, is Qahtan. There is a difference in Arabic, however, between Yaktan and Qahtan.

From whence did the Islamic narrators come up with the name Qahtan?

When we study the archeological findings, we find a small tribe by the name of Qahten that was subjected to the tribe of Kinda in central Arabia. The first mention of Kinda and Qahten came from the third century A.D., and it was found in an inscription, number 635, deciphered by Jamme, an expert in the southern Arabian inscriptions. The text was inscribed in stone, and listed by Jamme under this term: 635-Brownish sandstone-MaMB 270.

The text speaks about a war erupting between the king of Saba and Raydan against many tribes, whom he subdued. Among these was King Rabiat ربيعت, the king of Kinda and Qahten.[624] According to Kitchen, a famous archeologist and expert in Middle Eastern archeology, including southern Arabia, this Rabiat was the first king of Kinda; his name is Rabi'a Dhu-Al-Thawr. He reigned from 210-230 A.D.[625] We understand from Kitchen that Kinda and Qahten appeared around the year 210 A.D.

Without a doubt, the tribe of Qahten was not the tribe's descendants of Yaktan that spread into eastern Arabia and some regions of eastern south Arabia. Qahten differs in pronunciation from Yaktan. Qahten was a small tribe subdued to Kinda; it could never represent the Yaktan's tribes, who were several nations. Furthermore, the appearance of Qahten was only after the third century A.D. This is contrary to the spread of Yaktan's descendants many thousands of years before Christ.

In their willingness to make Yaktan to have lived in Yemen, the Islamic narrators looked for a name close to Yaktan. The tribe of Kinda lasted until the beginning of the 6th century A.D. The Kinda reign was terminated by Saba in the year 290 A.D. Kinda returned to appear again after the fall of the kingdom of Saba. The last king reigning in Kinda and Qahten was Al-Harith bin' Amr, الحارث بن عمر who ruled from 500-528 A. D.)[626] The Islamic narrators thought that the tribe of Qahten, which was close to their time, was the tribe of Yaktan. They thought its place was Saba. This is although Kinda was located outside the regions of Himyar and Saba. In their first attempt to identify Qahten with Yaktan, the Islamic narrators began calling Yaktan as Qahten[627] (according to the name of the tribe Qahten). Later, they replaced Qahten with Qahtan.

Biblical scholars maintain that the idea of identifying Qahtan with Yaktan is without foundation, but it was adopted by Muslims because of little similarity in pronunciation.

Jawad Ali wrote regarding the Yemeni who created from Tubb'a as prophet:

> Tubb'a Asa'd, is one of the Tubb'a s who had a lot of fortune with the narrators: for them he was a prophet; they claimed he was Dhu al Qarnayn, and the greatest of al Tubb'as, and the most eloquent of all Arabian poets. They bestowed on him great attributions. They went further than this claiming that he was a prophet. Therefore, the prophet Mohammed prohibited cursing him. According to them, he was one of the righteous believers and the men of paradise. These were stories promoted and spread by the Himyarite Muslims, who were zealous to their tribe, and wanted to silence their political foes, the Adnanits, whom the prophecy (the prophetical role of Mohammed) honored them, and elevated their position in Islam. They boasted over the Yemenites. The Yemeni were no less capable of boasting than their foes the Adnanites (the people of Hejaz). They created for their Tubb'as stories, making them to have had great military conquests. They were not satisfied by this. But they said: the prophecy was in the Adnanites, it was also in them. The prophecy was in them before it was in the Adnanites. They claimed (the people of Yemen) to have had many prophets. By this they close the gab from which the Adnanites attacked them.[628]

The words of Jawad Ali reveal that the myth of Tubb'a as prophet took on a new dimension after the rise of Islam. In reality, because Asa'd abu Karib brought two rabbis from Yathrib-Median to Yemen, it was believed by some groups at the time of Mohammed that he became a Jew. This is in spite of the Himyarite inscriptions of Yemen not mentioning this. Some thought that Tubb'a claimed to be a prophet. This idea was embraced by few groups of Yemeni origin during Mohammed's time. To the extent that Mohammed in his Hadiths was reluctant to considering him a prophet. But when he wanted to threaten with judgments, as the ones he claimed happened throughout history, he came up with a series of judgments against nations including the people of Tubb'a. Thus, making him among those through whom Allah warned their peoples, making him an apostle sent by Allah, consequently a prophet.

Tubb'a's trend to support the religions of North Arabia for his political purposes, yet his historical records lack monotheistic interest or faith

When Asa'd abu Karib occupied regions of North Arabia, where some cities existed with a good percentage of Jewish population, such as Yathrib-Medina and Khaiber, he assumed to build a relationship with the Jews. At the same time he showed an interest in being accepted by the pagan tribes of Yemeni origin, which were many, especially in Hejaz. Thus, his purpose in building the Kaabah of Mecca, which was one of the Kaabas built for the worship of the Star Arabian Family. The Star Family had Allah as its head, who in the past was the moon and later became the planet Venus, which was worshiped in Yemen as Athter, and as Radu in northern Arabia. Tubb'a saw that the inhabitants of Mecca, who were of Yemeni origin, worshiped their gods in a tent, so he built the Kaabah for them and clothed it. His behavior of becoming close to the worshipers of the religiosities in the north of Arabia, whether it was Jews, the worshipers of the Arabian Star Family or the rest of pagans there was a political move. He wanted to tighten his control over Northern Arabia as he strengthened his control over Saba, Hadramawt and Yamnat, as well as Kinda in central Arabia. But the historical facts, however, as we deduce from the inscription of Yemen, proved that he did not display any kind of monotheistic religiosity. In reality, he dressed himself with a political manner so as to attract the Jews in North Arabia, who had a strong influence on some northern Arabian cities.

Asa'd abu Karib did not claim to be a prophet. Had he claimed such a role, the Yemeni inscriptions that spoke about him would have showed such a claim. But the inscriptions of Yemen do not have any clue of this regard. Attributing the role of prophecy to Asa'd bin Karib, was an idea born in Mohammed's time, and promoted by few groups. Therefore, the Quranic claim that Tubb'a was an apostle sent to his Himyarite people is an allegation or assertion that contradicts the historical facts about him.

Did an extermination occur to the Himyarites, the people of Tubb'a?

There is something else contradictory to history in the Quranic narration about Tubb'a, that is his people's supposed extermination during his time. We see this in Surah 44, called Al Dukhan, and verse 37:

Are they better, or the folk of Tubb'a and those before them? We destroyed them, for surely they were criminals.

Also in Surah 50 called Qaf, and verses 12-15:

Before them was denied (the Hereafter) by the People of Noah, the Companions of the Rass, the Thamud, The 'Ad, Pharaoh, the brethren of Lut, The Companions of the Wood, and the People of Tubb'a '; each one (of them) rejected the apostles, and our warning was duly fulfilled (in them).

Saying that "our warning was duly fulfilled," means that as Allah warned those peoples mentioned in the verse that if they did not obey the apostles, he would exterminate them. Thus, this warning was fulfilled in exterminating them. In his interpretation to this verse, Taberi wrote:

Allah said that: were the pagans of Quraysh better than the people of Tubb'a and the pagan nations who came before? These (of Quraysh) were not better so we can forgive them and not exterminate them; they are infidel, thus, we exterminated them as we exterminated the infidel's nations before. When Allah said 'they were criminals,' he intended that Tubb'a's people and those who came before them we exterminated because of their criminality and infidelity to their lord.[629]

Thus, the Quran placed the people of Tubb'a alongside of the list of nations, such as Ad, Thamud, Median, and others, whom Mohammed, in the Quran, claimed Allah had exterminated through a cry.

In reality, the idea that the Himyarites were exterminated during As'ad abu Karib's time, as the Quran claims, is contradicted by history. The Quran speaks about an epoch that we know is not ancient; it did not precede the Christian era by thousands of years. It is not actually very distant from the time of Mohammed, since As'ad reigned from 410-435 A.D.

The Himyarite era in Yemen is attested to historically through the Musand inscriptions (Musand was the type of handwriting, used by the southern Arabians.) K.A. kitchen said:

For the later Old-South Arabian historical and epigraphic chronology, the most solid tool we possess is the series of era dates currently attested from 2nd to 6th centuries AD.[630]

The Himyarite era began in the year 115 B.C. There is continuity in the reign of their king without interruption until the reign of Dhu al Nuwas, and the Ethiopian campaign against the Himyarites, around the years 525-526. The campaign was after Dhu al Nuwas burnt the Christians, which occurred around 518-523 A.D. in the city of Nejran.

Discussing the Himyarite period during which As'ad abu Karib and his sons live:

Through an inscription attested by G. Rychman, numbered 509, we know that As'ad's father was Malki-Karib Yuha'min II; he reigned from 375-410 A.D. Then came his son As'ad abu Karib, who reigned from 410-435 (Text 534 numbered by G. Rychmans). As'ad performed military campaigns in central Arabia (Text 509 numbered by G. Rychmans,) and expanded the Himyarite empire; His title was "King of Saba' and Du-Raidan, Hadramawt, Yamanat and the Arabs in the Highlands and on the Coast." As'ad was the one who occupied Yathrib-Medina, and took two rabbis and then occupied Mecca.

We do not see that Judgments and extermination having occurred to the people of As'ad abu Karib as the Quran claims. On the contrary, it was the golden period in the Himyarite history, where they flourished and were empowered over the other peoples around them. The Quran claimed the people of As'ad abu Karib were exterminated. Neither do we see such a claim in any inscriptions from the time of As'ad or in any inscriptions of the periods that came after. Nor do we see this recorded in the writings of the historians who came after that period and wrote about Yemen, such as Procopius, the Byzantine historian. The claim about the genocide of As'ad abu Karib's people is related to Mohammed's trend to exterminate the peoples, whom he heard existed in history, such as his extermination of the people of Ad through a cry, after he replaced them in the second century after Noah., although Ad, according to Ptolemy, the Greek historian of the second century A.D., appeared during his time. Or Mohammed's claim that the Thamud were exterminated in the third century after Noah, when history tells us the tribe of Thamud appeared for the first time in the 8th century B.C. and continued to exist as an organized tribe until close to Mohammed's time. Mohammed claimed that the Midianites were exterminated at a time close to the time of Lot, whereas, they continued to exist after the rise of Islam.

Saying that the Himyarite people of As'ad abu Karib were exterminated by Allah is similar to the Quranic claim that the Midianites were exterminated in an epoch close to the time of Lot. When we examine the history of the Himyarite people we find that they continued to enjoy power over Yemen until a time close to Mohammed's time:

In fact, after As'ad abu Karib, reigned Hassan his son. It seems his son reigned with him for a certain period. Then he reigned alone for five years: from 435-440. His real name as attested to in archeology was Abahsen Yahaaman ابهحسـن يهأمن. Then reigned Sharahbil Ya'afur شـرحبيل اليعفر, the other son of As'ad. He reigned from 440-460 A.D. The reference is a long inscription, inscribed on the dam of Maarib on occasion of Sharahbil Ya'afur's repairing of the dam in the Himyarite year of 564-565, which corresponds to 449-450 A.D. (the difference is of 115 years, because the Himyarites began their kingdom from year 115 B.C.)[3]

The series of Himyarite kings continued until Yusef Athar, called Dh al Nawas, who reigned from 518-525 A.D. He was killed after the Ethiopians occupied Yemen. Then السميفع اشوع Ashwa 'Sumuyafa' reigned after being appointed by the Ethiopians from 525-536. Ashwa' was a chief of Himyarite Christians who were supported by Ethiopia. Then Abraha, the Ethiopian, captured power over Yemen and reigned from 542-553. Then reigned Abraha's sons called Yaksum and Masruq, who reigned consequently until the Persians helped the Himyarites return to reign in Yemen. (The year is not certain; some claim was in the year 570 A.D.) [631] The Himyarites reigned under King Maad Karib III, known as Saif bin Dhi Yazan سيف بن ذي يزن.

Later, another Persian army was sent to Yemen, terminating the Himyarites reign in 597/8. Yemen became a province of the Sassanid Empire under a Persian satrap.

We see that the Himyarites reign continued until 17 -18 years after Mohammed was born (Mohammed was born in 570 A.D.)

---

[3] Corpus Inscriptionum Semiticarum, Pars Quarta, Inscriptiones Himyariticars et Sabaeas continens, I-III,(Paris, 1889-1931) texts number 540:52-54; 98-100

Other references about Sharahbil Ya'afur : Dostal 1 (Neue Ephemeris fur Semitische Epigraphik 2(1974), 139; Garbini 1,2, Proceedings of the Seminar for Arabian Studies, 18('88), 95; cited by K.A. Kitchen, Documentation for Ancient Arabia, page 10

There is also an inscription under the name of (ZM 1) mentions how Sharahbil Ya'afur built a great palace in his capital in the year 457 A.D.

The Himyarites were not exterminated. Their tribes continued to boast of their Himyarites origin even after they entered into Islam. There were many poems of Himyarite poets coming from the Islamic era. Saying that the Himyarites were exterminated during As'ad bin Karib's time, that is in the beginning of the 5th century, reveals the grave ignorance in history of Mohammed's companions. They thought that the As'ad abu Karib's people appertained to very ancient times, and that they had no relation with the Himyarites, who were contemporaries to them. They thought that As'ad abu Karib's people were of the so called the Arab Baedah (A term used by narrators to designate Arabian tribes who, according to them, perished in ancient time, such as close to Noah's time or some centuries after).

How we classify this historical mistake of Mohammed?

This mistake of Mohammed is equivalent to someone in our generation arguing that Giuseppe Garibaldi was a prophet and that his people, the Italians, were totally exterminated. Garibaldi, the well-known Italian leader, was born in 1807 A.D. He helped unify Italy, and raised the Italian identity and national identity after centuries of submission to the various Italian regions to divisions and foreign domains. The distance between Garibaldi's birth and us is around 201 years. The distance between the beginning of As'ad abu Karib's reign, which started in the year 410 A.D., and Mohammed was 200 years. Saying that Garibaldi had admonished his Italian people and declared to them monotheism, and that the Italians rejected his message and were exterminated in Garibaldi's time would be a claim no one would take seriously.

The Splitting of the Moon
The claim that the moon splitting is support that Mohammed was a prophet

Muslims claim that the Quran mentions the moon splitting as support for Mohammed being a prophet. We read in Surah al- Qamar:

The Hour has drawn near, and the moon has been cleft asunder (Surah 54, al-Qamar, verses 1, 2).

The Mandaean myth of the splitting of the earth, and the sign on the moon

The destruction of celestial bodies (the stars, moon etc.) and the earth through the intervention of gods to confirm the claims of a religion is a common theme in mythology. As an example, we find in the Mandaean book, the Canonical Prayer book of the Mandaeans, a poetic saying that talks about the last days of history:

A cleft was cloven in the earth

The being who breached the breach

Was unable with all his might to stop it up[632]

The Mandaean text did not clarify who it is that will split the earth in the last day; whether he is an angel or a prophet. If he was the king of Lights, the main deity of the Mandaeans, the text would not have said "The being who breached the breach was unable with all his might to stop it up." Most probably the text referred to an angel or one of the prophets of the Mandaeans. I can see that the saying of the Quran "The Hour has drawn near, and the moon has been cleft asunder" is an imitation of the Mandaean myth. However, the Quran claimed the splitting happened to the moon rather than the earth.

What the Quran intended by the verse, whether the moon was split in the past or if it is intended to be a phenomenon which will occur during the day of Judgment is unclear. Nevertheless, Mohammed's dependence on Sabian Mandaean mythology and many of its elements regarding the moon, sun and the earth, is encountered in some of Mohammed's Hadiths and the Quran. As an example, we see in Mandaean literature, such as Ginza Rba, that there is a sign placed on the moon that can be viewed when it shines:

> The moon should not know how a sign was placed on his shining.[633]

This claims there is a sign on the moon, which limits its shining. This is close to the idea expressed to Mohammed in his Hadith which says:

> The moon is three times the size of the sun. Gabriel placed his wings on the moon and limited its shining[634]

Al Muqanna' and the wondrous event he claimed about the moon

Mohammed was not alone in his beliefs; other followers also attributed to him a transformation of the moon. These types of events were attributed to individuals who claimed to be prophets with a divine nature. Al Halabieh's book speaks about al Muqanna' Atta al Kharasani:

> He claimed that God was incarnated in the image of Adam, then Noah. Then he was incarnated into his own image. By the magic things he showed, he drew to himself many. He showed a moon, that people can see of two months walk distance from where they stood, then the moon disappeared. When he became famous, the people rebelled against him intending to kill him.[635]

The writer of Taj al Aruss mentions the moon of al Muqanna', saying:

> He was Thawr bin Umeireh, from the sons of al Shaitan bin al Hareth al Waladeh bin Amru bin al Harith the great bin Muayah bin Kinda. He was one of the fakers who claimed to be a deity through reincarnation. Among the things he showed was a shape of a moon, which appeared in the sky through a trick. This moon appeared and was seen by the people from a distance of a two months walk from where they stood, then the moon disappeared. The poet al Maari mentioned this tricky moon of al Muqanna'. Ibn Sana' al Malek speaks about this tricky moon as well[636]

Thus, al Muqanna' was Thaur bin Umeireh al Kindi from the people of Marwa Kharasan (a region of Iran). He lived at the time of the Abbasside Caliph, al Mahdi.

The Islamic records do not deny the moon of al Muqanna', but instead they attributed it to magic. I personally believe that al Muqanna' did not show a moon in front of his contemporaries, but the story demonstrates a phenomenon where if a person who claimed to be a prophet asserted such a thing, he would be immediately believed by his followers. This claim then spreads as reality to many in his generation, as we saw that al Muqanna's moon was viewed by his contemporaries as fact: Many important Arabic writers, like al Zubeidi, and an important poet like al Maari, testified that it occurred, although they attributed it to magic. Therefore, the spread of the claim regarding the splitting of the moon by Mohammed, and the belief of his supporters of the supposed miracle falls under this phenomenon. The thing that proves Mohammed's claim also pertains to the same phenomenon of al Muqanna', who lived 163 years after Mohammed immigrated to Medina. Also, Mohammed lived in a region and epoch where it was not easy to trace the source of news and verify its reliability and trustworthiness. Furthermore, the claim of the moon splitting had no collaborating documentation by historians.

We see then, that claims of these exaggerated and unrealistic phenomena, such as transformational events happening to the moon are attributed to pagan persons in history. We find no prophet of the Bible attributing such things to himself.

The myth of splitting the moon reflects a primitive understanding regarding the moon's size

Islamic claims regarding the moon splitting reflects to the idea among Muslims in Mohammed's generation that the moon was a small lamp that could easily be split, making half to rest on one mountain of Mecca, with the other half on another mountain in Mecca. Ibn Abbass narrated the following:

> The infidels came to the apostle of Allah… they said to the prophet, 'if you are trustful, make the moon to split into two parts, one half to be on Mount abi Qubeis أبي قبيس , the other on Mount Qaiqaan قعيقعان'. The prophet said to them: 'If I do it would you believe?' they said: 'yes.' It was the full moon. Mohammed asked Allah that he would grant him what they asked. The moon became two parts: one on mount abi Qubeis, the other on mount Qaiqaan[637]

The myth of Mohammed splitting the moon is contrary to logic and the true size of the moon, as we know it to be in our day and age. How could half of the moon be sitting on a mountain in Mecca with the other half on another mountain? If the moon had actually split and descended to the earth, its size would have caused the destruction of the earth, and wiped out the region of Hijaz. The reason Muslims, at the time of Mohammed and in subsequent epochs, accepted the claim that the moon split and stayed on two mountains of Mecca was because of their ignorance of the size of the moon as we know it today. This claim is fit for a primitive people and groups lacking total knowledge. Such were Mohammed's followers in his generation.

A claim that lacks historical documentation

Furthermore, this myth lacks historical documentation. If this prodigious event had actually occurred, it would had been recorded by individuals all over the world, as well as all historians who lived on earth during that period. We find, however, that the information about the moon splitting is only mentioned within the Islamic claim, and it has no similar record on earth.

Muslims claim that an Indian king saw the splitting of the moon, and then visited Mecca and embraced Islam. This claim appeared very late in Islamic literature. If a king from India had visited Mohammed, we would have seen this as being the main news in the first pages of the books that narrated Mohammed's life, such as the book of ibn Hisham, or the books of Hadith, such as Sahih al Bukhari and Sahih Muslim. But instead we find the first mention of a Indian king was made by Hakem al Nisaburi. In his work "al Mustadrik," Hakem claimed that an Indian king gave a gift of a jar of ginger to Mohammed. Here is what Hakem wrote:

> Reported by Abi Said al Khuthari, who said: it was given a gift to the apostle of Allah by the king of India a jar that contains ginger. He gave each of his companies a piece including myself. Al Hakem said: I did not record that the apostle of Allah had eaten the ginger except in this case.[638]

Even so, we do not see Hakem al Nisaburi speaking about the coming of this king because he viewed the moon splitting. If the reason for his visit was the moon being split, it would have been the most important thing to mention. Furthermore, Hakim did not allude to this king coming to Mecca and visiting Mohammed, nor did he mention the name of this king. It seems Nisaburi wanted to make Mohammed seem to be an important personality in the world by portraying his prophetic claim as having reached the uttermost parts of the earth, thus inventing the notion that the king of India gave him a jar of ginger. Though the term "king of India" is not historical for that period of time where India was not united under one king, but was formed from many regions, each being ruled by a different king.

Al Hakim is Mohammed bin Abdullah al Hakem al Nisaburi, he died in the year 405 H (H is the Islamic calendar which is reckoned from the year Mohammed emigrated to Medina). This shows that the claim of an Indian king giving a gift to Mohammed was an invention created by either al Hakem himself in his generation, or by someone who lived in his time. This claim did not find acceptance in the subsequent Islamic literature. This is because the books that narrated the life of Mohammed did not mention it. Later, this story was developed to include the claim that this king observed the moon splitting, and came to visit Mohammed. This was only at the time of ibn Hajar al Asqalani. This we find in two books of ibn Hajar: al Isabah, and Lisan al Mizan. Ibn Hajar claimed the name of the Indian king was Sarbanak سَرْبَانَك. When we know that ibn Hajar was born 909 H. that is 909 years after Mohammed emigrated to Medina, we see that for five centuries Islamic scholars disregarded the claim of al Hakem regarding an Indian king giving a gift to Mohammed, even though they mentioned gifts given to Mohammed by less important figures. Furthermore, they never mentioned that an Indian king saw the split of the moon.

The reason Muslims today hold fast to this claim is because Mohammed's claim lacks any historical documentation. They began searching for myths and false stories, which were disregarded by Muslims for many centuries. In the past, Muslims ignored these stories because they were false and had no credibility.

This claim has no documentation outside of Islamic circles. Muslims rely on a book appearing in the 17th century called Kerala Ulppathy; which is the oldest book that displays this claim. The book narrates a story about a king called Cheraman peruma, who saw the splitting of the moon and came to meet Mohammed at Mecca. Later, the account was added to this same story that the king who saw the splitting of the moon was Chakarawati Farmas. Since it is the same story, we can conclude that the later story depended on the book of Kerala Ulppathy.

According to the book of Kerala Ulppathy, Cheraman Perumal entrusted the kingdom to his son and travelled to Mecca. While there he met Mohammed and embraced Islam. When returning to his home country in the company of some Muslims led by Malek bin Dinar, he fell ill. He wrote letters to his son who reigned in Kera, recommending him to take care of the Islamic delegation, but he died and was buried in Yemen. Malek was received by Cheraman's son in the city of Muziris (today known as Kodungallur), which was the capital of Kerala. The king promoted the spread of Islam. This story, however, was not previously mentioned by any Indian historian.

Malek bin Dinar is al Aref billah abu Yahia Malek bin Dinar al Basri. He died in the year 130 H. (that is after Mohammed emigrated to Medina) How then he could have existed during Mohammed's time and accompanied the king who saw the splitting of the moon and came to meet Mohammed and embraced Islam?!

Shungunny Menon, an Indian historian born in the state of Travancore (in the region of Kerala), attributes the book of Kerala Ulppathy to Thunchathu Ramanujen, known also by the name of Ramen Eluthashan, who was born in the 17 century A.D. in the region of Kerala, which was part of Malabar in southern India.[639]

According to the book of Kerala Ulppathy, king Cheraman Perumal from Kerala went to Mecca to meet Mohammed. In reality, Cheraman Perumal was a title of a series of kings which terminated in King Bhaskara Revi Vurmah. [640] This king, however, according to Indian historian Shungunny Menon, died before Mohammed was born.[641]

The book contains Holland, Portuguese and British elements. This indicates the book was written during the 17th century A.D. Indian historians, such as Sreedhara Menon considers the book to be a collection of myths, without any documented value.[642] (Professor Sreedhara Menon is considered the most important historian for the region of Kerala)

Among the historical mistakes by the author of Kerala Ulppathy are his claims that King Krishnadevaraya from the Vijayanagara Empire (a southern Indian empire founded by King Harihara I in the year 1336 A.D.) had appointed a vicar over Kerala in the year 428 A.D. This is in spite of this king reigning from 1509-1529 A.D.[643]

William Logan, author of the <u>Malabar</u> Manual, also refutes the validity of the Kerala Ulppathy and describes it as:

A farrago of legendary nonsense having for its definite aim the securing of the Bramin caste of unbounded power and influence in the country.[644]

K.P. Padmanabha Menon, another native historian, calls the Keralolpathi:

An ill digested and uncollated collection of different versions huddled together in inextricable confusion[645]

Furthermore, there were important Islamic figures who visited Kerala in the middle ages, such as ibn Batuta who was born in 1304 A.D. in Tanja, and Abu al Rihan al Beiruni al Khawarsmi, who was born in 973 in one of the surrounding villages of Khawarism in Peria. Al Kazwini, who was born in 1225 A.D. also visited Kerala. None of these scholars mentioned such a story.

There are other important travelers who visited the region, such as Marco Polo, the important Italian traveler from Venice who was born in 1254 A.D., Friar Odoric, another Italian traveler who was born in 1286. I can name a number of Islamic and European travelers and scholars who visited the same city where it is claimed that Cheraman Perumal reigned. They wrote tens of volumes, but none of them mentioned that story. If this story had happened, it would have been the most important information those scholars would have written regarding that region.

The subject of the moon splitting that would have occurred during the time of Mohammed, that is in the 7th century A.D., would not have been hidden information, so an author of a mythological book written in the 17th century, claimed that a king had seen it in an Indian region. Instead, it would have been a newsworthy event that would have been recorded by multiple historians in various countries of the earth. Since no historian mentioned it during the 7th century A.D., or in subsequent centuries, this makes it a claim that does not deserve attention.

Some Muslims attempt to prove the claim of the splitting of the moon through the existence of fissures on the moon, pretending that the moon was really split. The longest of those fissures, however, is no longer than 300 kilometers. They are superficial fissures, whose depth is no more than 700-800 meters. The natural phenomena that caused these fissures are well-known. These types of fissures exist in greater numbers on other planets such as Mars. Does this mean that one day Mars was divided in two parts?!

An analysis of the Quran indicates that it is not possible for Mohammed to have claimed that the moon was split

Finally, we will demonstrate that the Quran excludes the possibility that Mohammed could have split the moon. Quraysh went after Mohammed, asking that he perform a miracle or phenomenon in order to believe in him. Mohammed, however, used Quranic verses to justify the absence of miracles in his life. According to the chronology of the Quranic inspiration, these verses came after Surah al Qamar (the moon) which was number 37 in the Quran record. The verse upon which Muslims claim Mohammed split the moon is found in Surah al Qamar (see the table below of the Surahs of the Quran and their place according to the time Mohammed brought them). If the moon had split before their eyes, as Muslims claim, Mohammed would had reminded them of the splitting of the moon. Mohammed, however, did not perform any miracle or wonders before their eyes. This is the reason why he repeatedly justified the absence of miracles through various excuses.

Among the excuses Mohammed used to justify the absence of miracles, is the following:

> And when you bring them not a prodigy they say: Why do you not forge it? Say: I only follow what is revealed to me from my Lord; these are clear proofs from your Lord and a guidance and a mercy for a people who believe. (Al-Araf, that is 7:203)

Thus, in Surah Al-Araf, we see that members of the Quraysh tribe demand a miracle from him. But he confessed that he did not bring to them a miracle of a prodigy. He resorts to saying that he only follows what is revealed to him and cannot make a miracle or prodigy. Understand that Surah Al-Araf, came as number 39 chronologically, whereas, Surah al Qamar appeared as number 37, revealing that it is certain Mohammed did not have the miracle of splitting the moon to boast with.

The tribe of Quraysh returned and challenged him to produce a wonder, as told in Surah Taha. Again, Mohammed did not draw their attention to a performance of splitting the moon. Rather, he referred them to the inspiration given to the prophets in the Bible, using the term "al suhuf al Aula," which means ancient sacred scriptures. Mohammed said although there are miracles in these ancient sacred books, he is not compelled to perform a miracle. Here is the Quranic verse:

And they say: If only he would bring us a miracle from his Lord! Hath there not come unto them the proof of what is in the former scriptures? (Surah Taha 20:133)

Taha was number 45 chronologically.

The challenges of Quraysh continued. In Surah al- Ankaboot, another challenge is presented:

And they say: Why are not signs sent down upon him from his Lord? Say: The signs are only with Allah, and I am only a plain Warner. (29:50)

In other words, they said: if his lord would send down a sign or prodigy from heaven, we would believe. He answered that he is only a Warner, and not able to bring signs or prodigies. Chronologically, surah al- Ankaboot is number 85.

The series of Quraysh challenges continued until the last surah he recited, and Mohammed persisted to offer excuses to justify the absence of miracles. Had he split the moon, they would not have asked him for a sign or wonder. He would have changed his speech, boasting of this great miracle.

The Quranic form of the moon-splitting verse is a poetical reproduction from Emriu al Qais. Mohammed did not intend to convey that he split the moon

In reality, the verse in surah al Qamar is a poetical borrowing by Mohammed from the poet Emriu al Qais, and not Mohammed's claim of a miracle. The impact of the Arabic poetry on Mohammed is well-known, particularly the poetry of Emriu al Qais.

Al Manawi said: "Emriu al Qais, spoke the Quran before it was inspired." Al Manawi quoted some verses of the Quran derived from the poems of Emriu al Qais. One of these verses is derived from the following verse of Emriu al Qais:

Man during summer hopes the coming of winter

Until the winter comes, man denies winter

Man is not pleased with any condition

Cursed be man! How ungrateful is he (Qutila al Insan Ma Akfarahu)

يتمنى المرء في الصيف الشتاء حتى إذا جاء الشتاء أنكره

فهو لا يرضى بحال واحد "قتل الإنسان ما أكفره"

Mohammed borrowed the last sentence of this poem which is found exactly the same in surah Abasa 80:17

Here is another case where Mohammed borrows a beautiful stanza of Emriu al Qais. Qais recited:

إذا زلزلت الأرض زلزالها... وأخرجت الأرض أثقالها

تقوم الأنام على رسلها... ليوم الحساب ترى حالها

(transliterated: Etha Zalzalat al Arthu zilzalaha wa Akhrajat al arthu Athqalaha)

When the earth is shaken with her shaking,

And the earth brings forth her burdens.[646]

We read the first two verses of Surah Al-Zalzala, that is number 99, verses 1and 2:

إذا زلزلت الأرض زلزالها... وأخرجت الأرض أثقالها

(transliterated: Etha Zalzalat al Arthu zilzalaha wa Akhrajat al arthu Athqalaha)

The same words exactly.

When the earth is shaken with her shaking,

And the earth brings forth her burdens

The verse in surha al Qamar is derived from the following stanza of an Emriu al Qais' poem:

"اقتربت الساعة وانشق القمر"... من غزال صاد قلبي ونفر

Iqtarabat al Saah wa inshaqqa al qamar

Men gazalen sada qalbi wa nafar,

Which means the following:

The Hour has drawn near, and the moon has been cleft asunder

From a deer who hunted my heart then estranged

Al-Qamar, Chapter ,54# Verse(1# says exactly the same):

Iqtarabat al Saah wa inshaqqa al qamar

The Hour has drawn near, and the moon has been cleft asunder.

If Mohammed would have intended that the moon really split, we would have the surah al qamar (of the moon) focusing on this theme, making it the main theme of the text. The Surah, however, is not explaining this claim to be a miracle, neither is it focusing on it but on various separated themes. It seems that Mohammed's aim was to threaten of the coming hour (the Day of Judgment) which was to be accompanied by great phenomena in the moon and stars. Somewhat later, Muslims added the second verse in order to attribute the miracles to Mohammed; it says:

And if they see a miracle they turn aside and say: Transient magic.

Mohammed's style in using the past tense for what will happen in the future is not exclusive here in surah al qamar. We see it in other verses of the Quran, such as in Surah Al-Haaqqa:

And the heaven was rent asunder, so that on that day it is frail (69: 16)

The scope of the first verse of surah qamar was not originally different from verse 16 of surah 69

Even though the historical contradictions and objective analysis of the Quranic verse reveals otherwise, Muslims nevertheless insist and maintain the claim of the moon splitting, probably due to their awareness of the absence of miracles in Mohammed's life. However, logic follows that if God wanted to confirm his prophecy through a prophet, God's work with him would not be limited to one miracle or wonder. True prophets faced opposition and special challenges that made the presence of miracles essential to confirm their message and silence the enemies who challenged their prophecy. Among examples of these prophets is Moses, who faced great opposition in bringing the Israelites out of Egypt, or Elijah who was confronted by the prophets of Baal, the religion that caused Israel to go astray from God's worship. Or Elisha who faced wicked rulers that led Israel toward paganism. Most important of all was Jesus who declared His divine identity and confirmed it through daily acts of miracles. The miracles Jesus achieved included raising people from the dead, in the case of Lazarus, after four days of death when the body began the process of decay. Jesus raised him with one word, proving His ability to create the cells which had entered into putrefaction. In another incident, he created two eyes for a man who was born blind. Jesus performed this creative miracle through kneading of the dust of the ground, thereby implying that He was the One who created man by kneading the dust of the ground in the first days of creation. He also silenced the wind and sea with one word, demonstrating that He is the creator of nature and able to control it.

In contrast, how could Mohammed's claim be considered credible? Mohammed asserted himself to be a prophet that returned the people to monotheism, yet opposed the worship of the true God of the Bible. The Biblical God was confirmed by God's revelations through all epochs of history; whereas Mohammed's life lacked any miraculous element that would prove he was endorsed by heaven?! The story of the splitting of the moon was not a historical event, nor logical. It contradicted the rest of the Quranic text and was not sufficient to give Mohammed a pretext to challenge the inspiration of the Biblical prophets through whom God worked great wonders which were verifiable by both sympathizers and adversaries. The miracle attributed to the Quran concerning the linguistic claim is not sufficient to defend the Quran and Islamic arguments, otherwise, the merit goes to Emru al Qais from whom Mohammed borrowed the most beautiful of his verses.

Striking Abraha's Army

The myth of striking Abraha's army with stones carried by birds

Muslims boast of the Quranic narration that tells the story of Abraha, an Ethiopian king of Yemen during the 6th century, who marched against Mecca in an attempt to destroy its Kaabah with the use of an elephant. Allah then sent birds to strike Abraha's army with stones, and so defeated the army. The Quran in surah al al-Feel (translates as the elephant) claims that Allah fought against "the people of al-Feel," referring to the Ethiopians led by Abraha.

If the story of Abraha's march against Mecca were true it would have coincided with the date of Mohammed's birth. For the Quran to have mentioned such an event would cause it to become historically unreliable. The story would have spanned the time of Mohammed. It is not like the passage in the book of Genesis where it mentions Abraham's war against the four armies led by Elam, where historians acknowledge the titles of the four kings as corresponding to titles recorded in archaeological findings from that era during the beginning of the second millennia B.C. The same story mentioned in the Quran is not akin to the Bible's mention of hundreds of historical facts referencing events occurring thousands of years prior to its being recorded and which has been confirmed by archeology. Thus, boasting of a story in the Quran which would have occurred a few decades before the date of its narration is something that points to the lack of documented historical facts from events that occurred thousands or hundreds of years ago. We have seen how the Quranic narration about events that it claimed to have happened in ancient times are actually non-historic. Thus, showing the Quran is not a valid source for ancient historical events.

Although the story of striking the army of Abraha, if it really happened, did not bestow upon the Quran reliability and a miraculous narration as

Muslims tend to teach, I will nevertheless discuss this story and show that it has no historical foundation. We read in surah 105 called al-Feel:

> Have you not considered how your Lord dealt with the possessors of the elephant? Did He not cause their war to end in confusion, and send down (to prey) upon them birds in flocks, Striking them with stones of Sijjil (baked clay). And He made them like (an empty field of) stalks (of which the corn has been eaten up by cattle).

We will interpret these verses in the light of the main expositions of the Quran. We read in the book al Baher wal al Muhit, written by ibn Hayan:

> Regarding the elephant of Abraha the Ethiopian and the compliment of soldiers that accompanied him: it seems it was one elephant, this is the saying of many, while the soldiers were 60,000, of whom none returned back except their leader with a small group. When they knew that the rest of the army had been destroyed, they also perished.

> When they went to direct the elephant toward Mecca: as it approached the city it sat. When directing it toward Damascus it walked quickly... every bird carried a stone in its beak, and two stones in their legs: every stone was bigger than the shape of a lentil and less than a pea. On each stone was written the name of the one that it strikes: the stone came down on his head and came out of his anus. Abraha became sick and his body was divided in small pieces, he did not die until his heart came out of his chest. His Wazir, called Abu Maksum, escaped, but his bird followed him until he reached al Najashi (the Arabian name for the king of Ethiopia) and told him what had happened to the army. Then the bird struck him with his stone so he died before the king.[647]

In the expository of Taberi we read:

> Regarding the birds that were sent against them, Ibn Abbass said, 'they were birds that had snouts, and had palms like the dogs palms.' Ekrema said. 'They were green birds that came out from the sea, they had heads like savage beast's heads.'[648]

In the book of Fatah al Qadir we read:

> Bin Jaber said: 'they were birds which came from heaven, no bird alike was seen before and after.' Qutadeh said: 'they were black birds came from the sea; each one carried two stones in his legs and a stone in his beak, anyone reached with this kind of stone was destroyed.' al Zujaj said: 'Sagill (the Quranic word that described these birds) means that the torment was written over the stones ... those were stones baked by the fire of hell, on them were written the names of the people to be destroyed by them.'[649]

The story as was narrated by ibn Ishak:

We were told by ibn Ishak that Abraha built a church in the city of Sanaa. He was a Christian. He named the church Quleis, and it was unique, nothing was seen in earth like it. Abraha wrote to al Najashi, the king of Ethiopia: 'I built for you O king a church, nothing was built like it before. I want to draw to it the Arabians as Hajj.' When the Arabians spoke among themselves regarding the letter Abraha has sent to al Najashi, a man from the tribe of Nassaa, was one of the sons of Fuqim and one of the sons of a king, became angry. He came to the church of Quleis, and stooled (put his feces) in it, then returned to his country. Abraha was told about this and asked: 'who did so' they said to him a man from the worshipers of the house, where the Arabs do Hajj, that is in Mecca, because when he heard your saying that you would draw the Arabians to do Hajj to the church, he was angry and came and stooled in the church. Abraha then was angry and swore to go to Kaabah and destroy it. When he passed by Taif, Masud bin Mu'attab came out to meet him with men of the tribe of Thaqif, and said: 'O king, we are your servants, we listen to your words and to you we are obedient. There is no controversy with you. Our temple (dedicated to Ellat) is not the temple you intend. You want the temple at Mecca, we send with you a guide to that place. They sent with him Abu Righal. Abraha continued, accompanied by Abu Righal until they reached al Maghmas. There died Abu Righal, and the Arabs stoned his tomb… Abraha sent an Ethiopian man called al Assuad bin Maqsud with horsemen until they reached Mecca. He took the money of the people of Quraysh and others of Mecca. He also took 200 camels which belonged to Abdel Mutaleb bin Hashem (the grandfather of Mohammed), who that time was chief of Quraysh…when Hinateh entered Mecca he asked who is the chief of Quraysh and the noble man in the city. He was told that Abdel Mutaleb bin Hashem is the one… then Hinateh said to Abdel Mutaleb: come to the king, he ordered me to bring you to him.

Annis spoke to Abraha: O king, the chief of Quraysh at your door wants to ask permission to enter. He is the owner of the camels of Mecca, he feeds the people in the plains, and the beasts on the tops of the mountains… he was permitted to come before Abraha. Abdel Mutaleb was a great man, handsome and a full sized man. When Abraha saw him he honored him, he got up from his seat and sat with him on his mat. Then he said to his interpreter: 'ask him, what do you have as need from the king?' Abdel Muttaleb answered: 'my need is that the king give me back my 200 camels.' Abraha said to his interpreter: 'tell him when I saw you I was pleased with your look. But when you have talked to me I became surprised: you ask of 200 camels you have lost, and disregarded the issue of your temple, which is your religion and the religion of your father I came to destroy, but you do not speak to me about?' Abed Muttaleb answered: 'I am the lord of the camels, but the temple has a lord who will protect it.' Abraha said: 'this temple will not be protected from my action.' Abdel Muttaleb answered: 'this is an issue between you and him. But give me back my camels'… then Abdel Mutaleb returned and took hold of the door of Kaabah, along with other men of Quraysh, and called for Allah to give them victory over Abraha and his soldiers…at the morning Abraha prepared himself, his elephant and his army to enter Mecca. The elephant's name was Mahmud. Abraha was ready to destroy the Kaabah and then to return to Yemen. When they directed the elephant, Nufayl bin Habib came near him and took the elephant by its ear and said to him: 'set down Mahmud, and return from where you came, because you are in the sacred village of Allah,' then he released his ear. The elephant sat. Nufayl went to the mountain. They hit the body of the elephant so as to stand, but it refused. They hit him on his head to stand, but it refused. They pierced him to stand, but he did not. When they directed it to return to Yemen, it stood walking quickly. When they directed it toward Damascus it did the same; when to the east it did the same. But when they directed it toward Mecca, it sat down. Allah sent against them birds from the sea. With each bird three stones: one carried by his beak, and two stones by his legs. The shape of the stone was like a lentil and a pea. Whoever is hit by the stone was killed. Not all of them were hit. They escaped in the way they came, asking for Nufayl bin Habib to guide them to the way to Yemen. When Nufayl saw what Allah brought upon them he said: 'where is the escape when Allah wants to take revenge against the defeated Abraha.[650]

My comment is that the event is inspired by another story which claims that when Tubb'a passed by the city of Taif in order to destroy its Kaaba, the tribe of Thaqif (who were the inhabitants of Taif) begged him not to destroy their Kaaba but to instead go to Mecca.

The story is placed within a frame that stands in contradiction with Christianity as well as Abraha's purposes

The story portrays Abraha as having built a church to draw the Arabian Hajj to it. This idea could not come from a Christian leader like Abraha or any other Christian leader. Christians do not have the custom or ritual of Hajj, which is exclusively an Arabian pagan custom. Through their Hajj the Arabians visited their Kaabas during specific seasons; circling around the black stones of the Kaabas and presenting their animal sacrifices to the idols worshiped in the Kaabas. It is true that many Christians go on visitations to places such as the tomb of Christ in Jerusalem or the Church of the Nativity in Bethlehem, but it is not a Hajj. Furthermore, Christians of all over the world do not expect pagans to visit their churches. How then could Abraha expect all Arabians to worship in his church that he built in Sanaa? If Abraha had any concerns about spreading Christianity in Arabia, he would have sent missionaries to various cities but he did not do so, proving that he did not intend to spread Christianity but instead desired to confirm his reign in Yemen. His purpose in building a church in Sanaa was to attract the Christians in Sanaa, whether they were Ethiopians or Christian Himyarites. Christianity spread among the Himyarites, for we know that after defeating Dhu Nawas, the last Himyarite king, the king of Ethiopia appointed a Christian Himyarite governor (by the name of Esimiphaeus, as I previously mentioned). It is clear that the story was invented by a person who celebrated the pagan Arabian concept of Hajj, which is contrary to Christian customs.

The story is contrary to the true conditions of Abdel Mutaleb, Mohammed's grandfather

Another concern is that ibn Ishak made Abdel Mutaleb, Mohammed's grandfather, the most prominent member of the tribe, as chief of Quraysh. This statement however, is contradicted by reality: preeminence in Quraysh was given to Beni Umayyah (sons or progeny of Umayyah); their great grandfather was Umayyah bin Abed Shams bin Abdel Manaf. Leadership was then transferred to Abu Sufian bin Hareb bin Umayyah. All the wars of Quraysh were led by this branch called Umayyah. They were the rich people of Mecca, having huge trade caravans that traveled to Syria, Yemen and Hira (in Iraq). The transfer of leadership and preeminence from Beni Umayyah to Beni Hashem (the branch from which Mohammed descended), then to Abdel Muttaleb is an idea originating from Muslims after Islam dominated the Arabs.

Ibn Ishak also claimed that Abdel Muttaleb was rich and owned the camels of Mecca, "and that he fed people in the plains and the beasts on the top of the mountains." It is strange that the Islamic narrators underestimated the minds of their readers. How could Abdel Muttaleb have been the owner of the camels of Mecca and feed people in the plains and the beasts on the top of the mountains when we know that his firstborn son, Abu Taleb, was very poor and unable to feed his son Ali. He sent Ali to live with his nephew Mohammed, after Mohammed married Khadijah, who was a rich widow so that Ali would not die of hunger?!

Ibn Ishak described Abdel Mutaleb as being a man who had monotheistic principles, believing in God and having great faith that God would protect the Kaabah and expressed monotheistic poems. It is known, however, that Abed Mutaleb was born a pagan and died as a pagan. He was a worshiper of Elat, Manat, al Uzza and Hubul- the main idols of Kaabah. He was also a worshiper of Isaf and Naelah to the extent that he wanted to sacrifice his son, Abdullah, who was the father of Mohammed at the feet of a statue of Isaf and Naelah.

The story of ibn Ishak was formulated in a way to portray the family of Mohammed and his ancestors as being protectors of faith in God and as God's co-workers, even though they were pagans. The story was also crafted to occur in the year of Mohammed's birth in an attempt to portray the idea of Mohammed being pre-ordained by God and protected by Him.

The falsity of the story is evident in all its elements. Moreover, there is a strong probability that the myth was created in favor of the Kaabah at the time of Mohammed. For each temple had myths promoted by their worshipers, especially old women. In fact, for a myth to spread throughout a society during pre-Islamic days did not require more than a few years.

Refuting Muslims' claims in their attempt to document the myth

In their attempt to defend the Quranic myth, Muslims say that none of the Meccans objected Mohammed when he recited the Surah al Feel. We submit this is contradictory to the verses of the Quran where we read that the Meccans considered the stories of the Quran to be myths; understood in surahs 25:6 ; 31:8 ; 24:16 ; 83:28 ; 5:25 ; 68:27 ; 15 : 68 "when our verses are recited unto him, he saith: Mere fables of the men of old." Here we see the objection of the Meccans against all the verses of the Quran, saying that they were myths. Why should this story of striking the Ethiopian army, with its clear mythological distinguished character, not be among those which the Meccans considered to be myths? Suppose it was spread during Mohammed's time and accepted by some who tended to believe in superstitions and myths. But because it had no foundation that made it acceptable to the Meccans, the story was not supported by the majority who were intelligent. The objection against all the stories in the Quran is rather obvious in the Quran itself.

Furthermore, Islam was imposed over people in all groups throughout the region of Mecca to the extent that persons who protested Mohammed were killed. No voices remained to oppose the Quran. How then can a religion that imposes its doctrines and kills those who opposed it then claim that its doctrines and stories were documented based on their lack of rejection by the people?

Reasons why the surah of feel is not Meccan

Another important argument against the truthfulness of the story is that it is doubtful the story came during Mohammed's stay in Mecca before he emigrated to Medina. The story reflects an animosity toward Christians during a time when we know that Mohammed at Mecca was always trying to connect to Christians and show friendship with them; especially towards the Ethiopians who received the persecuted Muslims of Mecca that were sent to stay there by Mohammed. However, the Quranic story presents Allah as being antagonistic to the Christians, to the extent that he stood with the pagans of Mecca to fight against the Christian Ethiopians. This spirit resonates with the period when Muslims began invading the Christian Middle East. Thus, we appoint Surah al Feel to a period post-Medina, after Mohammed's death. In fact, there are other surahs and verses which are post-Medina, such as 17:1 which says:

> Glory be to Him Who made His servant to go on a night from the Sacred Mosque to the Aqsa mosque of which we have blessed the precincts, so that we may show to him some of our signs.

We know that the Aqsa mosque was built many years after Mohammed died. I will talk about this subject later.

We conclude, as evidenced in the story Ibn Ishak had narrated, that the purpose of surah al Feel was to demonstrate animosity toward Christians and the Cross, making them infidels and in so doing, justify the occupation and plundering of their lands. This animosity toward Christians is also apparent from a poem by ibn Ishak claiming that Abdel Mutalib had recited:

> Abdel Mutalib holding the door of Kaabah recited: 'let not their Cross to win.'

The notion that the army was hit by smallpox

Some embrace the idea that perhaps a smallpox plague spread among Abraha's army during his military campaigns in Arabia. Especially, when after being instigated by the Byzantines he tried to march against the Persians. However, Procopius, the Byzantine historian, wrote about the appearance of smallpox in the year 554 A.D. In the city of Beilus- an Egyptian city located in the current city of Borsaid, Procopius mentioned smallpox which burst (appeared) upon Constantinople in the year 541-542 A.D. Yet, while Procopius followed the news of Abraha, he neither mentioned his army being affected by smallpox nor his march against Mecca and attempt to destroy its Kaabah.

Would Abraha have chosen to march with elephants instead of camels against a city across the desert?

There is another important aspect to consider. An elephant spends 16 hours eating daily, and another 3-5 hours drinking, wallowing, playing and resting. It also sleeps between 2-4 hours a day. Since the elephant digests only 40% of what he eats, it needs to eat a large quantity of food daily, equal to nearly 5% of its size. According to the African Wildlife Foundation, an elephant requires 30-50 gallons of water daily. The Ethiopian elephant, especially the one known as Loxodonta Africana, is very delicate and spoiled. In order to live, it needs a huge quantity of different kinds of plants.[651]

On the other hand, the Arabian camel possesses one hump where he is able to deposit about 36kg of fat. In the absence of food and water, the camel breaks down the fat in his hump into liquid and energy. Thus, the camel can walk in the desert for a distance of 100 miles without water and rarely sweat even in high temperatures that reach 120°F (49°C).

Marching with elephants toward Mecca in deserted areas for the distance of about 800 kilometers is an improbable plan for a leader like Abraha. When we consider that camels were at his disposal in great number, appertaining to the regions under his domain that were inhabited by Arabian tribes, the thought of such an undertaking by elephants is ridiculous.

When marching against desert regions such as Sinai, the Cushites (which were ancient Ethiopians) never used elephants, but horses. As an example, when Razeh the Cushite marched against Judah he used horses instead of elephants (See II Chronicles 16:8).

The story has no historical foundation

The claim of striking an army with stones carried by strange birds was attributed to an epoch when historians existed; and referred to the destruction of an army that belonged to a nation like Ethiopia, whose history is well known. It was claimed that the story occurred to a king reigning in Yemen, whose enemies the Himyarites recorded important events about in their history through inscriptions. The Himyarites had reigned after Abraha and his two sons. Thus, we cannot ignore important historical facts and instead embrace a tale created in order to promote animosity against Christians and Christianity. It was a myth without historical foundation that was adopted by superstitious groups known for creating mythological stories, such as the she-camel of Thamud that came out of the rock.

The story is contradictory to historical facts

Furthermore, the elements of the story contradict history. This will be examined in the following paragraphs.

The idea of a single elephant being dragged by the army of Abraha is not historical. When Abraha occupied Yemen, he led an army of 100,000 soldiers along with hundreds of elephants.

Another element to discuss is whether Abraha lived until the year of Mohammed's birth in 570 A.D.

Here is an overview of how Abraha came to power in Yemen. Dhu al Nawas, the Himyarite king who embraced Judaism and persecuted and killed the Christians of Nejran and the Ethiopian Christians of Zafar, reigned from 523-525 or from 518-520 A.D. The Byzantines were angered by this and encouraged the Ethiopians to fight Dhu al Nawas, aiding them with their marine fleet. In chapter 20 of his book, Procopius, the famous Byzantine historian, discussed the Ethiopian campaign in Yemen and how Abraha became king of Yemen.[652]

In the year 525, Hellestheaeus, the king of Ethiopia (the Ethiopians called him Caleb or Amda) came and defeated and killed Dhu al Nawas. He then appointed Esimiphaeus as king over Yemen; Esimiphaeus was a Himyarite Christian leader whom the Arabians called Sumoyapha' Ashwa' سوموبافع أشواع. Procopius mentioned that there were among the Ethiopian army a great number of condemned slaves who did not want to return to their homeland. They rebelled against Esimiphaeus and imprisoned him inside of a fortress there, then appointed Abraha as king. The king of Ethiopia was infuriated, and in response sent an army of 3,000 soldiers to take revenge against them and Abraha. The soldiers, however, did not want to leave Yemen because it was a rich land, and secretly contacted Abraha. When war broke out they killed their leader and joined Abraha. The king of Ethiopia again sent another force to engage Abraha in war, but after many losses they returned home. This was king Hellestheaeus' last campaign against Abraha. After Hellestheaeus died, Abraha pledged to send a tribute to the king of Ethiopia who reigned after Hellestheaeus. Thus, Abraha's reign in Yemen was consolidated.

Procopius mentioned how Justinian of the Byzantine Empire sought the Ethiopians and Himyarites to help him in fighting the Persians while he was under Esimiphaeus. The Himyarites were compelled to help the Saracens (who resided in northernmost Arabia) attack the Persians. Although Hellestheaeus of Ethiopia and Esimiphaeus (who during that time reigned over the Himyarites), promised Justinian's ambassador he would send help, neither of the two moved in that direction. When Abraha's reign was consolidated, he promised the Byzantine emperor many times he would rage a war against the Persians. Once he prepared for a campaign against the Persians he quickly withdrew. This campaign was not against Mecca, but against Persia.

These historical facts reveal that Abraha's affairs were of importance to Procopius, who is considered the most important historian of the 6th century. He did not mention anything about birds attacking the army of Abraha. If this event had taken place, it would have been important news for a Byzantine historian like Procopius, who sought to chronicle the events of the region.

Abraha died before what was called "the year of elephant"

Another element worthy of consideration from Procopius is that he spoke of Abraha in the past tense, as if the events happened in the past. There is no hint in his writings that Abraha was alive when Procopius wrote about the region (Procopius died in the year 565 A.D.), this being one of the indications that Abraha died before that date. The claim that Abraha died in the year of Mohammed's birth, in 570 A.D., which was later called "the year of the elephant," was ibn Ishak's allegation, who himself died in 150 H. (after Mohammed emigrated to Medina). That year (I am referring to 570 A.D) was called "the year of the al Feel, or elephant" based on the claim that Abraha marched against Mecca in that year. It was a claim generated by ibn Ishak and has no documentation from any historical sources. On the contrary, all the facts point to Abraha's death before that date.

Historians and archeologists tend to establish an earlier date for the death of Abraha. As an example, the German archeologist Alexander Sima, an archeology specialist of Arabia, gives the date for Abraha's death to be around the year 553 A.D. [653] Prof. Stuart Munro-Hay of Cambridge University in African studies, an expert in the archeology of Ethiopia and south Arabia, appointed a year sometime around 553 A.D. based on an inscription. [654] Abraha's death might have been two or three years after the year 553, but not the year 570 as Islam would like to establish based on the narration of ibn Ishak. Thus, consigning a campaign of Abraha against Mecca to the year 570 A.D. is contradicted by historical facts.

The supposition that Abraha died in the year 570 led to other suppositions: that his sons Yaksum and Masruq who reigned consequently after him, ruled until the year 575 when the Persians occupied Yemen. At this time, the reign of the Himyarites was under Maad Karib III, also called Saif bin Dhi Yazan. However, establishing the year 575 as the date the Persians occupied Yemen with the Himyarites is now doubted. Some scholars date the occupation of the Persians with the Himyarites in the year 570 A.D. [655] They maintain that the sons of Abraha reigned prior to 570. If the year 570 is the year when the Ethiopian domain of Yemen terminated, this would make it after the sons of Abraha reigned and after the death of their father. Thus, the death of Abraha must have been prior to this date by several years. The same idea is supported by Nöldeke, a well-known scholar. He said that 570 was the last year of the reign of Abraha's second son, and that Abraha did not live until the year when Islam claimed and called as the year of the elephant. [656]

Wellhausen said that what Tubb'a (As'ad abu Karib) did in his campaign against Medina and then Mecca, was now attributed by Islam to Abraha. [657]

The lack of Yemeni inscriptions claiming that Abraha campaigned against Mecca

The inscriptions coming from that epoch and subsequent ones as well, contain no mention of Abraha moving his army against Mecca. For example, we have inscriptions of the dam of Maarib, mentioning that in the year 657 according to the Saba calendar, which corresponds to around 540-545 A.D., that Abraha had quieted a rebellion backed by the son of Esimiphaeus, the leader appointed by the Ethiopians in the past over

Yemen. There is another inscription that speaks about the victory of Abraha against the tribe of Maad, in the year 662 (Saba calendar corresponds to 545-550A.D.)[658]

We know that the Himyarites returned to reign with the help of the Persians. Had the story of striking the army of Abraha with stones carried by birds actually occurred it would have been the most important information to record in their inscriptions. Yet, there is no evidence for this claim. There is also lack of mention about such a claim in the Ethiopian writings. Had this happened, the Ethiopians would have recorded it, even in a way which would have justified the failure of the campaign.

The Islamic story portrayed all Arabians performing a pilgrimage to the Kaabah of Mecca, however, at the time the temple of Mecca was just one of many Kaabas where Arabians went for Hajj

Our conclusions thus far show that ibn Ishak is not a dependable and trustworthy historian. He claimed to write about history from the time of Adam, but invented stories without documentation. Ibn Ishak created a story about a church Abraha built in Sanaa, calling it al Quleis, with the purpose of transferring the Arabians' Hajj from Mecca to this church as if all Arabians went to Mecca for Hajj. This was, however, contrary to historical facts because there were several Kaabas in Arabia and many were more prominent than the Kaabah of Mecca. There were more than 23 principal kaabas in addition to many other kaabas that were branches of the Kaaba of the city of Taif. Among the principal kaabas was the Kaabah of Nijran. Another one is Kaabah Dhi al Shara, a temple in northern Arabia near the city of Petra. People used to go on pilgrimages to it like they did for Mecca and even observed a month of fasting similar to what occurs during the month of Ramadan.[659] It was also called "the lord of the house of Dhi Shara" and was probably located at Tabuk. This Kaaba was close to the Nabataeans, and according to classical writers it was a place for Hajj for all Arabian tribes.

There was also the Kaabah Yamanieh for a deity called Dhi al Khelseh, who was, according to many scholars, Athtar-Venus. It also had a system of Hajj.[660] Then there was the Kaabah of Taif for the worship of Allat- the sun. Other kaabas were Kaabah of Yamameh and Kaabah of Ghatfan. Yaqut al Hamawi wrote about this Kaabah, explaining that it bore similarities with the Kaabah of Mecca, such as the service of Sidneh.[661] There was the Kaabah of Sindad in Hirah and al Ableh, where they used to make Hajj.[662] There was a temple or Kaabah for the tribes of Iyad to where they performed Hajj, and called Tha al Kaabat.[663] There was also a temple of al Uzza (a rock that had a Sidneh service and a temple like the Kaabah of Mecca.[664] The circling and Hajj around al Uzza was part of the rituals of the Kaabah of Mecca. Al Azruqi wrote:

> When they finished making Hajj and circling the Kaabah of Mecca, they did not return to their homes till they came to al Uzza Kaabah, they circled it and stayed there for one day. The tribes of Quraysh, and Banu Kinaneh, were with the tribes of Khuzaa and Mather, who revered al Uzza Kaabah. The ones responsible for its service were banu (sons) of Shiban from the tribe of Bani Salim, and were allied with beni Hashem (the branch of Mohammed's ancestors) [665]

We see that the Hajj to the Kaabah of Mecca was part of the Hajj of the Arabian Star Family. The Hajj to Mecca's Kaabah was not considered as being legal without completing the Hajj to other Kaabas that belonged to the Star family.

There was also a temple for Manat (one of Allah's daughters) in the Mashlal- a place about 7 miles distance from Medina. It had a Sidneh service with a rock and pit, like the one at the Kaabah of Mecca where they threw their gifts.[666]

Other famous kaabas were Kaabah of Rida, and Kaaba Siqam (a temple for the worship of al Uzza- Allah's other daughter), it was in a valley called Hirad or Siqam. This Kaabah competed with the Kaabah of Mecca. There was also Kaabah Riam in Sanaa-Yemen. Al Shahrastani said that there was in Yemen a Kaabah similar to the Kaabah of Mecca and it was for the worship of Venus.[667]

There were Kaabas that each had a black stone, where they performed hajj and circled; one of them was the Kaabah of Taif.

Refuting the poems about the campaign that Ibn Ishak put in the mouth of poets

In order for ibn Ishak to back the Quran, he invented the previously mentioned story. Such an encounter would not have been missed by the Byzantine historians and Ethiopians. However, we do not find in their writings anything related to this story.

There are also the poems which ibn Ishak attributed to the Himyarites. Those poems, however, were in the language of ibn Ishak's time; the language of Quraysh. Yet, scholars of the time of ibn Ishak have confirmed that the language of Himyar is different from the Arabic language of their times. Al Jamhi criticized the poems reported by ibn Ishak and others, which they attributed to previous epochs. Al Jamhi wrote:

> Above 'Adnan (Adnan was a name created by the Islamic narrators as a 21st ancestor of Mohammed) there were added names which were not taken from books. These names, no one knew about them and were not mentioned by any Arab." Al Jamhi continued to criticize the poesy which was attributed to ancient times with these words: "We do not consider any lineage or genealogy which they claim to return to a time before 'Adnan. We do not find poesy for the known Arabs of the past, how much more illogical to attribute poesy to Ad and Thamud?! This is a cheap and malicious poesy invented and attributed to older times. No Arab has ever narrated of it even one stanza, and there is no narration for such poesy. Abu 'Amru bin al 'Ala' أبو عمرو بن العلاء said in regard: 'the language of Himyar and Yemen today is not our tongue, neither is their Arabic our Arabic, how much more distant have been the languages of Ad and Thamud. The poesy which was narrated by Ibn Ishak and other narrators is useless and has no evidence of true originality.[668]

Ibn Salam al Jamhi died in the year 232 H. (after Mohammed emigrated to Medina). He quoted Abu Amer bin al Ala' al Basri, who lived between 68-154 H., he was contemporaneous with ibn Ishak who died in the year 150 H. ibn Khalkan says about Abu Amer bin al Ala':

> He was the most knowledgeable in Arabic and poetry. Abu Ubeideh said: Abu Amer bin al Ala' was the most knowledgeable of Arabic literature, language, Quran and poetry.[669]

Yet, Abu Amer bin al Ala' admitted that the language of Himyar in his days was different from the Arabic. How then can ibn Ishak attribute to the Himyarites, poems written during the occupation of the Ethiopians of Himyar, that is in the year 525 A.D., making the language of the poems identical to the Arabic of Quraysh, the language of Ibn Ishak in his era of 760 A.D.?!

The evaluation of Abu Amer bin al Ala' in criticizing ibn Ishak and others who attributed poems to the epochs of Thamud, Himyar and Ad is of significant importance: this is because the languages of these tribes are totally different from the Quraysh language in which the poems were written and attributed to those tribes' epochs.

ibn Ishak recited poems that he claimed were composed about the birds Ababeel (the name of the birds according to the Quran) that hit the Ethiopians with stones. In reality, this was ibn Ishak's custom of creating poems in his own Arabic language, and adding them to every story he attributed to ancient nations.

Ibn Ishak was considered by the educated people of his time to be a liar and deceiver (See my book Islam in Light of History where I discussed the unreliability of the Islamic writers). Besides him, the pre-Islamic poetry suffered forgeries and fraud. Those who reported the poesy were unreliable, how much more worthless is the poetry which ibn Ishak invented in the Arabic language of Quraysh and attributed to Himyar.

Refutation of the poem of ibn Ishak which he attributed to Umayyah bin abi al Salt

Had the story happened, there would have been a great echo present in the poems of the poets of Mecca as the most important event in their history. Yet, there is no such evidence. All we find is that ibn Ishak attributed a poem to Umayyah bin al Salt. I would like to examine these stanzas of this poem:

> He imprisoned the elephant in al Maghmas, until it crawled as if it was wounded...in the day of judgment each religion is perdition except the Hanafieh.[670]

This poesy attributed by Ibn Ishak to Umayyah, contained elements that were originally ideas of ibn Ishak, such as the idea of one elephant being the instrument of destruction. This contradicts the customs of Ethiopian armies which had military legions helped by a large number of elephants. Furthermore, the idea that "the elephant crawled as if it was wounded," is also ibn Ishak's idea. These elements confirm that ibn Ishak created poesy to support his own narration; that this was his custom is based on the testimony of scholars from his time.

There is a Quranic verse expressed in the poem which ibn Ishak attributed to Umayyah: "in the day of judgment each religion is perdition except the Hanafieh." It is actually derived from the Quranic verse:

> The Religion before Allah is Islam. 3:19

The Quran, according to ibn Masud, reads this verse as "The Religion before Allah is Hanifieh." Ibn Masud was one of four individuals Mohammed had chosen to memorize the Quran and recite its verses to Muslims. Ibn Masud had his own version of the Quran which spread in Iraq after Mohammed died. It is clear that ibn Ishak was still under the influence of ibn Masud's version of the Quran.

There is also a Hadith of Mohammed that says:

The most beloved religion to Allah is the flexible Hanifieh.[671]

It is evident that ibn Ishak was influenced by this Hadith of Mohammed when he wrote his poem attributed to Umayyah, who was not a Muslim and thus able to repeat Mohammed's thoughts.

There is something else worthy of consideration: Ibn Ishak, who died in the year 151 H., was the first to recite these stanzas which he attributed to Umayyah bin abi al Salt. Had this important poem with an important subject like this existed prior to ibn Ishak, there would have been evidence of many Muslims quoting it in support of the Quran. This is an obvious indicator as the true composer of the poem being ibn Ishak himself.

Refutation of the poem ibn Ishak attributed to Ruabah bin al-Ajaj

Ibn Ishak mentioned another poem, attributing it to Ruabah bin al Ajaj, al Tamimi, al Rajez, from the Arabs of al Basra. Ruabah was a Muslim who died in the year 145 H. He was born in Islam, and thus cannot be considered a pre-Islamic poet. Though these facts are clear, some Muslims claims that the poem was composed before the Quran was written. A position that proves the lack of the Quranic myth in surah al Feel of any testimony of the pre-Islamic Jahiliyyah period. For them, it is so fundamental to their faith to the extent that Muslims cling to a poem of a poet who died 145 years after Mohammed emigrated to Medina.

Furthermore, Ruabah lived in Basra- Iraq far from the area of Mecca to where the story was attributed. Besides, admitting that the composer was Ruabah carries a lot of doubt because most probably the poem was created by ibn Ishak. Let us discuss these stanzas attributed to Ruabah, as we find them in ibn Hisham and al Qurtubi:

And they were affected by the same which affected the owners of the elephant. Striking them with stones of sajjil"[672] **"and they were affected**

by the same which affected the owners of the elephant. Striking them with stones of sajjil, the birds Ababeel played on them, they became like an empty field of stalks and straw, (of which the corn) has been eaten up.[673]

My comment: in order to consider the probability that such poems are genuine and not composed by ibn Ishak, we would like to see expressions or terms in these poems that are different from what we read in the Quran. Notice for example the term "owners of the elephant." The poet should have said "companions of Abraha," or just "the Ethiopians." But he used the same Quranic words as written in verse one of the Surah al Feel:

Have you not seen how your lord dealt with the owners of the elephant?

The sentence "Striking them with stones of sajjil" is an exact repetition of the wording of verse 4: "Striking them with stones of Sijjil (baked clay). "The birds Ababeel played on them," is taken from verse 3.

The term "they became like an empty field of stalks and straw, (of which the corn) has been eaten up" is repeating exactly what is written in verse 5.

Any comparison between the poem and Surah al Feel suggests that no further proof is needed to acknowledge that the author of the poem had composed it under the influence of the Quran.

A story like this one, had it happened, would have been recorded by many pre-Islamic poets because of its being attributed to a time close to the rise of Islam. It would have been the most dramatic event in Arabia. The attempts of Islam, however, to document this story through a poem of a Muslim poet who died the year 145 H., and through stanzas that ibn Ishak put in the month of Umayyah bin abi al Salt, indicate the inability of Muslims to find documentation to such myths in the Arabian poetry before Islam.

Would God back the pagans against a Christian army? Why God did not intervene when the Qaramitah defiled Kaabah and took the black stone

There is another element to ponder. Why would God back the pagans of Quraysh who had 360 idols in the Kaabah of Mecca in addition to Hubul? They also worshiped Allat, the wife of Allah, and Manat and Al Uzza, the two daughters of Allah. Why would he back them against the

Christians of Ethiopia led by a Christian leader?! We know that when Muslims were persecuted at Mecca during the time of Mohammed, he sent them to take refuge in Ethiopia, where they were received and protected.

Had Abraha intended to destroy al Kaabah, he would have done less than what al Qaramitah did for the Kaabah and Hajj. Destroying the Kaabah would not have been an irreversible critical event. The Meccans could have rebuilt it better than before whenever they desired. Abraha would not have been interested in the black stone because he knew there were many kaabas in Arabia, each with a black stone. But what al Qaramitah accomplished in taking the black stone and killing the pilgrims was something more dangerous for the worship at Mecca. It seems that God forgot to send those birds against them.

Regarding al Qaramitah, in the year 317 H. (corresponds to 929 A.D.) the leader of the Qaramiteh, abu al Taher, marched against Mecca. He killed the pilgrims in the mosque and removed the door of the Kaabah. When the prince of Mecca accompanied by his group of nobles came to implore him, abu al Taher killed them and threw their cadavers in the well of Zamzem and buried many of them in the mosque.

Ibn Taghri Bardi wrote about abu al Taher's exploits to Kaabah and Mecca:

> Abu al Taher, the enemy of Allah, came to Mecca. He killed the pilgrims in great numbers in the center of Mecca and the Kaabah, Allah curses him. He killed ibn Muhareb, the prince of Mecca. He removed the clothing and door of the Kaabah. He removed the black stone and took it with him. He threw the cadavers that he killed in the well of Zamzam. He also performed atrocities in the city, things that neither the Jews nor Christians would have done. He returned to Hajr (his city) with the black stone. The black stone remained with them until it was returned back to its place during the time of Caliph al Muti'. Abu al Taher sat on the door of al Kaabah, while the men were killed around him in the Kaabah. This was in the day of al Tarwiye, which was the most sacred day. Abu al Taher said:
>
> "I am for Allah, and I am in Allah. He creates the creatures, and I destroy them. "
>
> A man of the Qaramteh entered where people used to circle the black stone, while he was drunk and mounting a horse. His horse urinated in the Kaaba. Then the man hit the black stone with his instrument breaking it before removing it. The Qaramitah stayed at Mecca for 11 days.[674]

After 20 years, the Fatimid Caliph, who was governor of Egypt, offered a large quantity of money to the Qaramiteh if they returned the black stone. The Qaramiteh returned 15 small stones claiming that they were the remnants of the black stone. In reality, those small stones had nothing to do with the original black stone. Had they returned another stone the Muslims would have recognized that it was not their black stone that was at Mecca. Thus, they sent small stones, claiming they were the remnant of the black stone they destroyed.

The purpose of al Qaramiteh was to destroy Islam. They fought Islamic rituals such as Hajj, fasting and prayers, and prohibited the performance of these rituals in the regions under their control. They burnt the mosques. Their doctrines were contrary to Islamic teaching. One of those doctrines was that God has hidden himself in a human form. When they took the black stone, how could God remain silent and not send the birds against them to strike them with stones?!

God did not fight the Ommiads when they hit the Kaabah with Mangonel

The Qaramiteh were not the only group that ruined the Kaabah. The Umayyad hit the Kaabah twice with the Mangonel, burning it. The first time was under al Haseen bin al Numeir at the time of their Caliph, Yazid bin Muawiya. The second time was at the time of Caliph Abdel Malek bin Marwan, who sent al Hajaj bin Yusef al Thaqafi to fight Abdullah bin al Zubeir (Mohammed's descendent and a rebel against the Umayyad.)

In the year 64 H. Yazid bin Muawiya sent an army led by al Haseen bin al Numeir to fight Abdullah bin al Zubeir, who fortified himself in the Kaabah. The army besieged the Kaabah striking it until it was burned.

In the year 73 H. Abdel Malek bin Marwan sent al Hajaj to Hejaz and defeated the army of Abdullah bin al Zubeir, besieging Mecca. The city was affected with famine due to this siege. Al Hajaj erected the mangonel on the mount of abu Qubeis and hit the Kaabah until it was burned. Without a doubt, Muslims consider Abdullah bin al Zubeir as the legal Caliph because of his loyalty to the principles which the first Caliphs of Mohammed adopted. But Allah did not stand with him, nor with the Kaabah which was burned twice. How then could God stand with the pagans against Abraha, who was a believer in God and send the birds to strike his army, whereas God remained silent when the enemies of Islam, such as the Qaramiteh, ruined the Kaabah and destroyed the black stones? Or when the Umayyad, who opposed the true Caliphate according to Islam, burned the Kaabah?!

The story that Abraha was hit with stones carried by birds lacks historical documentation, although it was placed in an era where the principal events are attested to by inscriptions and historians. But its substance indicates that the story was weaved in a period subsequent to the death of Mohammed. The reason for this was to justify the wars against the Christians of the Middle East.

Al-Isra'

The trip of Mohammed to the Temple of Jerusalem

Additions to the text of the Quran is a historical fact

After the Muslims occupied regions of the Middle East, especially during the Umayyad period, the Quran of Hafsah became a target for the Umayyad caliphs to destroy. Hafsah was one of Mohammed's wives and a daughter of Caliph Omar, the second Caliph after Mohammed died. Othman, the third Caliph depended on Hafsah's Quran, edited by Zayd bin Thabit with others, to issue one version of the Quran, destroying the other versions which contradicted each other. Othman neglected the other Quran versions, which were more popular than Hafsah's Quran that time, and burnt them.

However, the Quran became under scrutiny and criticism by Christians. This induced the Umayyad Caliph to edit the Quran and omit the things which were mostly criticized. They added some verses that alleviated from the gravity of other verses that had mythological character or illogical meanings. Such as the fifth verse of surah 32 called As-Sajda, which made the distance between earth and heaven as one thousand years walk. The Umayyad added other verse: that is the fourth verse of Sarah Al-Maarij (number 70), which made the distance to be 50 thousand years of walk.

There were other motives for adding new verses: one was that Muslims in those times did not accept to apply any law or legislation that was not derived from the Quran or attributed to the Hadith of Mohammed. This made the caliphs to add verses to the Quran and the Hadith, so that to create new laws that fulfill the needs of the nation.

Though the Umayyad's policy was to gather the copies of Quran under the excuse of editing them, then came up with new copies of Quran, the

Quran of Hafseh, however, which was returned to her after it was edited, was a hindrance before the Umayyads in their plan of developing the Quran. Many Muslims returned to the copy of Hafseh in order to judge in the differences of the verses. Thus, the Umayyads had to destroy the Quran of Hefseh, if they wanted that their Quran would not be judged by a copy of Quran, which was considered by many as a standard copy. Because the process of editing, developing and omitting verses of the Quran, and adding new verses was going on. One of these verses that they added was the first verse of number 17 called al Isra':

> Glory to the one who did take his servant for a Journey by night from the Sacred Mosque to the al Aqsa Mosque, whose precincts we did bless,- in order that we might show him some of our signs: for he is the one who heareth and seeth (all things).

We know that the Aqsa mosque was built during their times. The versions of the Quran became during the first Caliphs numerous, and they were different contradicting each other, especially during Othman's caliphate: one of these Qurans was adopted by ibn Masud in Kofah-Iraq. Other Quran was adopted by Musa al Ashari in Basrah. And other famous version was adopted by Ubei bin Kaab in Syria. There were many versions in Hejaz, such as Ali's Quran and Aisha's Quran. Knowing the tendency of changing the Quran and editing it at the time of Caliphs Abu Baker, Omar bin al Khattab, and Othman, how much more at the time of the Umayyads. The Umayyads felt competition by the Hashimites, Mohammed's branch, regarding the religious and political authority. Abdullah bin al Zubeir, as we have previously seen, rebelled against the Umayyads at Mecca. There was the danger of Hajj which made the Hashemites living at Mecca of great prominence. The Hajj was seen as a danger ritual that attracted Muslims to the cause and ambitions of the Hashemites to dominate Islam. Thus, the need for the Umayyads to create other attractive place of Islamic Hajj; that was toward the Aqsa Mosque which they had built in Jerusalem. There were also some verses of the Quran in favor of "Ahl al Beit," (the family of the house) who were the family descendants from Mohammed through his daughter Fatimah and her husband Ali bin abi Taleb. Thus, the need of omitting those verses, this is though they remained in the Quran that the Shiites still possess today.

When Marwan bin al Hakam was the Umayyad governor of Medina, he asked Abdullah bin Omar, to give him the Quran of his sister Hafseh. She refused strongly to give away her copy of Quran.[675] After she died,

Marwan renewed his request to Abdullah, so he gave him the Quran. Marwan then destroyed this copy of the Quran.

The fact that the Umayyads edited and developed the Quran is something admitted. Among the persons who changed the verses of the Quran was al Hajaj bin Yousef al Thaqafi. He was born in the city of Taif and lived between 660-714 A.D. and was a strong military personality. He then became a governor of Iraq for the Umayyads. Under the excuse of editing the Arabic of the Quran, and by the order of the Abdel Malek bin Marwan then his son al Walid, the Umayyad Caliph, al Hajaj changed at least 11 Quranic verses. The Islamic sources admit that al Hajaj gathered all the Quranic copies existing in his time, and performed amendments to the Quran. The book of al Masahef for al Sajistani mentioned these facts.[676] Also the Quranic encyclopedia of Ibraham at Baiari confirms the fact that al Hajaj gathered the copies of the Quran and dropped many things from the text of the Quran.[677] Al Sajistani said that Ubeidallah bin Ziad added to the Quran 2000 letters.[678]

The claim of the Quran is that Mohammed travelled at night on a winged animal to the Aqsa mosque, yet the Aqsa Mosque was built after Mohammed died, and there was no temple in Jerusalem

We quote again the first verse of Surah al Isra':

Praise to the one who took his servant in a night journey from the mosque of Haram to the Masjid Al aqsa which we blessed around it.

The mosque of Haram was a title for the temple of Mecca. Masjid Al Aqsa means the "the furthest mosque." It was the furthest mosque from Mecca, at the time when it was built by the Umayyads Caliphs. In fact, Masjid Al Aqsa was built by Umayyads Caliph Abdel Malik in the year 687 A.D., the building was completed by Caliph al Walid ben Abdel Malik between 709-714 A.D. more than 80 years after Mohammed died.

The mosque was built on the old site of the Temple of Solomon which was rebuilt by the exiles in the 6th century B.C. then was rebuilt again by King Herod I around the year 18 B.C. It was completely leveled by Titus, the Roman, in the year 70 A.D. The temple never had been rebuilt since that time, and did not exist at the time of Mohammed. We can only conclude that surah 17:1 was added later than 691 A.D., long after the construction of the mosque called Masjed Al Aqsa.

The temple of Jerusalem not being rebuilt is a well-known historical fact; after it was destroyed by Titus in the year 70 A.D., it was never rebuilt to this day. In the year 363 A.D. the emperor Julian II attempted to build the temple, aiming to encourage non-Christian faiths. He failed, however, to rebuild it. In his book Historia Ecclesiastica, the historian Sozomen (400-450), wrote about the failure of Julian II in rebuilding the Temple. Also the Historian Ammianus Marcellinus wrote about the failure of Julian in rebuilding it. The failure was due to fire broke near the foundations, the workers could not continue and many of them suffered scorching. So the people responsible for the project gave up their attempt.

Others attributed the failure to an earthquake, and to the Jews hesitation toward the project. The Christian historians, however, attributed this failure to Divine intervention.[679]

The historical sources inform us that when Muslims occupied Jerusalem, they found the place where the temple was built before, abandoned and full of refuse or garbage... then the Caliph Omar ordered to clean the place where he prayed.[680] It is clear that when Muslims occupied the city of Jerusalem, there was no temple there. Its site was full of refuse.

Other verses were added to the Quran for various scope

Additions to the Quran's text go unquestioned by many scholars. Not only this verse, but other verses, such as surah 98: 6, where the people of the book– Jews and Christians–are said to be "the worst creatures."

> Those who are infidels of the people of the book(Christians and Jews) and the Mushrikin (the pagans)are in hell for eternity, they are the most wicked of all creation.

This verse was probably added after Muslims started the Middle Eastern wars to conquer the Christians. The verse could have been added in order to justify the war against the Christians.

Surah 17:1 shows us the Quran was not compiled exclusively by Mohammed, but by others who had their own agendas and later added verses which reflected this.

The one editing the Quran fell in inattention and distraction. Muslims' attempt to get rid of the dilemma

We see the one who corrected the Quran in the Umayyad period falling in a substantial mistake. In his attempt to present a proof about the Isra of Mohammed on the Buraq (a winged camel), he missed to mention "Beit al Maqdis," (the name of the temple of Solomon as appeared in the Quran). The place after the mosque was built became Masjed al Aqsa. So the one edited the Quran instead of Beit al Maqdis, he mentioned "the Aqsa mosque." This verse is one of many proofs of the development of the Quran by the Umayyads.

To correct the problem and make the Quran sound more authentic, some Muslims claim that the Quran in surah 17:1 was not referring to the building itself but to the site of the Temple of Solomon.

But it is clear this verse is speaking about a specific mosque called "Masjid Al Aqsha", which we saw was an Islamic mosque built in the year 691 A.D. Not only did the verse name a specific mosque, but it mentioned that Mohammed journeyed from the mosque at Mecca to a second mosque – the mosque of Aqsa. Then, the verse adds that Allah blessed around the mosque, distinguishing between the mosque where Mohammed was allegedly transported and the city where the mosque was built. This also we understand from the details of the story of Isra which later I will mention, where is said that Mohammed tied the Buraq by the door of the temple. Later, Gabriel portrait the structure of the building of the temple on his wings so that Mohammed could describe the building to the doubting Quraysh

The people of Jahiliyyah believed the temple of Solomon existed in their time, and Mohammed was influenced by their thinking.

Many of the superstitious people of Jahiliyyah who lived in Arabia at the time of Mohammed believed the Temple of Solomon existed in Jerusalem. They called it "Bayt Al Maqdis," which means "the house of holy." The Arabic name for Solomon's Temple derived its name from the Hebrew, "Bet ha Miqdash." Superstitious Arabians believed that a real house of worship existed at Jerusalem in their generation. It was built by Solomon, that is why they called it "Bayt" which means "house". The pre Islamic poet Emu al qais recited a poem in which he made hint or alluded to the temple in Jerusalem.

فادركته يأخذن بالساق والنسا

كما شبرق الولدان ثوب المقدس

Speaking about the robe which the priest dressed himself in "beit al Maqdes."

Never, however, the Jahiliyyah people called the Temple of Solomon with the term of Aqsa Mosque, but beit al Maqdes. This is an answer to the attempts of Muslims to find a way out of the mistake of the Quran, in mentioning "Aqsa mosque," when it did not exist at the time of Mohammed. Muslims say it was the most distant place of worship from Mecca. We do not find, however, that the term of Aqsa mosque is mentioned in the Arabian pre Islamic poesy or in any other sources, except in the Hadiths of Mohammed which were written after the Aqsa Mosque was built by the Umayyads. Also there was not a building of a temple in Jerusalem under the name of Aqsa mosque or Beit al Maqdes.

Pre Islamic Jahiliyyah Myths regarding "Beit al Maqdes"

The people of Jahiliyyah built myths around the temple of Solomon, which they believed existed at their times. One of the myths they created concerned a rock around which the Islamic mosque was later built. We suppose the Islamic myths around the temple and the rock were derived from previous pre Islamic myths. They believe the rock was suspended between heaven and earth, and no part of the rock touched the earth.

I believe ibn al Arabi was under these myths when he described the rock of Beit al Maqdes:

> The rock of Beit al Maqdes is of the marvels of Allah. It stands independent in the midlist of the Aqsa Mosque. Not connected from any of its edges with anything. Nothing holding it that it will not fall in the ground except the one who holds in his hands heaven... under the rock is the cave which is separated from each side and suspends between heaven and earth. I was afraid because of its prestige and greatness to enter under it, because I was afraid that it would fall on me because of my sins.[681]

Mohammed claimed when he sat on the rock at the temple in Jerusalem the rock tipped because it was suspended between heaven and earth and not anchored.[682]

Many of the people of Jahiliyyah believed in many myths about the Temple of Solomon. One example is found in the book of Halabieh. It is a paragraph attributed to Abia Bin Abi Ka'ab which says, "All the springs which water the earth come out from under the rock which is in the house of holy, Bayt Al Maqdis, the temple of Solomon, then the waters divide and flow into all the parts of the earth."[683]

At the time of Mohammed, many groups believed the Temple of Solomon existed as an indisputable fact. But, in reality, the temple, which you may remember, was rebuilt by the exiles in the 6th century B.C. and was destroyed by Titus in the year 70 A.D. and ceased to exist. The people of Jahiliyyah continued to hold their superstitions and historically false convictions and imaginations. Unfortunately, Mohammed was influenced by them.

Mohammed claimed he visited the Temple of Solomon as a building and not as a site.

When we follow Mohammed's description about the night he claims to have made the trip to the temple of Jerusalem, it is clear he was thinking of a building and not just the site which later became a building. Mohammed claimed while he was sleeping that Gabriel came to him and shook Mohammed with his foot. Then he took him to the door of the temple of Mecca where there was a winged animal called a Buraq. Mohammed mounted the Buraq with Gabriel, and they flew to the temple called Bayt Al Maqdis in Jerusalem.[684]

Mohammed claimed when he arrived at the door of the Bayt Al Maqdis, he tethered the winged camel to the door. Here are the exact words of Mohammed:

> I reached Beit al Maqdes. Then I tied "the Buraq" to the ring of the door.[685]

He clearly claimed the winged camel traveled from the door of the temple at Mecca to the door of the temple at Jerusalem. Once inside the temple of Jerusalem, Mohammed claimed to have discovered Abraham, Moses, Jesus and a multitude of prophets there. He preached to them and led them in prayer.[686]

There is clear imitation of Mohammed to Mani, the founder of Manichaean religion in the third century A.D. Mani claimed to have ascended to heaven. In a Manichaean psalm we read how all the prophets came to welcome Mani and he saluted them.[687]

Mohammed claimed he had the same encounter with the prophets as did Mani, but in his arrogant loftiness Mohammed claimed superiority over them. All this occurred inside the temple of Jerusalem, as we saw in the biography of Mohammed edited by Ibn Hisham.[688] In the book of Halabieh the same idea is repeated concerning Mohammed's alleged encounter with the prophets. Mohammed claimed, "When we entered inside the mosque, a Muezzin called them to prayer."[689]

When he talked about the mosque, he was specifically speaking about the Temple of Solomon, and the Muezzin is the one who calls for prayer in loud voice according to Islamic custom. The Muezzin's custom was exclusive to Arabia at the time of Mohammed, and was adopted by some Kuhhan in the Jinn/devil religion in Arabia. Musielameh Bin Habib who was known for his affiliation with occult worship in Arabia at the time of Mohammed had a Muezzin make the call to prayer in loud voice before him. Musielameh's Muezzin name was Abdullah bin al Nawwaheh[690] عبد الله بن النّوّاحة he used to cry "I testify that there is no god except Allah and that Musielameh is his apostle." Mohammed imitated the Muezzin's custom, adopting the same slogan and wording. Musielameh was known to precede Mohammed in claiming to be prophet. Taberi recorded the reaction of the tribe of Quraysh to Mohammed's announcing about al Rahman:

> When Mohammed said to them: 'bow down to al Rahaman!' they answered : 'shall we worship to what Rahman of Yamama order us to do?!' they meant Musielameh.[691]

Al Suhaili wrote about the time Musielameh claimed to be a prophet :

> As al Zuhri informed, Musielameh was called al Rahman (in relation to his claim about Rahman deity) before the birth of Abdullah, Mohammed's father.[692]

Thus, Musielameh' declaration about al Rahman, and his claim of prophecy goes back to the middle of the sixth century A.D.

But I find it interesting that Mohammed claimed to have the Arabian occult ritual performed inside the Temple of Solomon at Jerusalem during his alleged night trip.

There were people close to Mohammed, including his relatives, who believed that the temple of Solomon was in existence in their time

Mohammed slept in the house of his cousin, Um Hani when he claimed to have made the night trip to the Temple of Jerusalem. She reported that Mohammed said he journeyed in the night to the Bayt Al Makdis and prayed inside it.[693] We see then that all of Mohammed's claims focused on his entering the Temple of Jerusalem called Bayt Al Makdis. We also see his colleagues, such as Abu Baker, and the members of his family including his cousin, Um Hani, all believed the Temple of Jerusalem was in existence during their lifetime.

Ibn Abbass, Mohammed's cousin and authoritative reporter of his Hadith, also spoke about Mohammed's night journey to Bayt Al Makdis.[694]

Therefore, there was among the friends and relatives of Mohammed a mythological notion and ignorance regarding Beit al Maqdes. Mohammed was raised in an ignorant culture and environment who believed in the existence of the Temple of Solomon in the city of Jerusalem in their time.

Abu Baker, the person who became Caliph after Mohammed, asked Mohammed if he visited the Bayt Al Makdis during his trip and Mohammed answered that he did. By this statement, we can see that Abu Baker believed there was a house of worship in his time, called Bayt Al Makdis, that was built by Solomon. When Abu Baker asked Mohammed to describe the building of the house Mohammed complied. Later we will see that Abu Baker claimed to have visited the temple of Jerusalem.

Mohammed claimed that Gabriel showed him the temple building illustrated on Gabriel's wings.

Although Mohammed could deceive his companions when he described the building of the temple at Jerusalem, because he felt at ease with his disciples, when members of Quraysh tribe to which he belonged asked him to describe the building called Bayt Al Makdis he panicked and could not answer

> When Quraysh disbelieved me and asked me things concerning Beit al Maqdes, I could not proved it; they asked me for example: 'how many doors the mosque had' I panicked severely in a way I never ever did[695]

Falsity which was known to appertain to the priests of the Jinn devils, is seen in Abu Baker: when Mohammed claimed he mounted with the company of Gabriel the Buraq and visited Jerusalem. At a time when there was no Beit al Maqdes at Jerusalem, since it was destroyed in the year 70 A.D. by Titus, the Roman leader, and it was not rebuilt until now. After Mohammed claimed of this visit, many Muslims began withdrawing from Islam. Abu Baker wanted to confirm Mohammed's claim through lies. Thus, he claimed of visiting Beit al Maqdes. So he came and asked Mohammed as we see in ibn Hisham:

> 'O prophet of Allah. Did you narrate to this people that you came to Beit al Maqdes this night ?' Mohammed answered : 'yes.' Abu Baker said: 'o prophet of Allah describe it to me because I visited it.' The apostle of Allah said that the temple was portrayed before my eyes. So he began describing him to Abu Baker, whereas, Abu Baker said: 'you said the truth, I testify that you are the apostle of Allah.' Every time Mohammed described some detail of it, Abu Baker said 'you said the truth, I testify that you are the apostle of Allah.' Until Mohammed finished describing it. Then the apostle of Allah said to Abu Baker 'and you Abu Baker you are al Seddiq (the righteous). From that time Mohammed called him al Seddiq.[696]

Abu Baker confirmed Mohammed' claim through lies. In contradiction to history, he claimed that he visited it and that Mohammed had described it as he (Abu Baker) had seen it. By this lie Abu Baker became al Seddiq, and later became the Caliph of Mohamed after the later died. actually, this what Abu Baker looking for in following Mohammed and working to make his religiosity to succeed.

All this demonstrates that the people who were close to Mohammed were not sincere, using lies to save the face of Mohammed. and that Mohammed viewed the Temple of Jerusalem as a building existing in his time, and not a geographical site. Muslims who want to resolve the historical inaccuracy found in the Quran, and the unreliability the claims of Mohammed have a weak excuse.

The flying of the soul through a diabolic spirit is well known phenomenon in the world of magic and sorcery

In reality, the soul flying going to other places is a well-known phenomenon in the lives of many who worship the spirits in our days. The examples are many. I will, however, limit myself in mentioning some:

Corinne Calvet was an actress in Hollywood. She claimed that she no more exists and that she was born again under the name of Corona. She began practicing Yoga, and claimed that she had outside her body a visit to the stars. She always had visions and revelations.[697]

Al G. Manning (Los Angeles – California) he experienced in 1950 his soul coming out of his body and travelling. Later he gained the ability of levitation. This is one of his claims

> One night I had what I would have to term an out-of-body experience. It was as if a searchlight were turned on directly above my head and shining down upon me. I was in the middle of this shaft light... a voice spoke from within the stream of light... after the illumination, I had the power of levitation.[698]

So he was immersed in the light as Mohammed was when he claimed to ascend over the seven layers of heaven. Manning was known to be a professional magician, and wrote books about Clairvoyance, that is the ability to know the secrets of others.

Alister Hardy (died the year 1985) was a professor of Marine biology of Oxford university. After he got retired, he established in the year 1969 Religious Experience Research Center. His purpose was to gather religious experiences of any kind, then classify them. He said:

> In our classification I had thought we should first distinguish these two main categories, the more general kind to be classed as 'A' and the more mystical as B' experiences. We soon realized that the latter could be separated into a dozen or more subdivisions, such as those concerned with seeing visions, hearing voices, ecstatic transfiguration experiences, rapturous Wordsworthian feeling in relation to nature and so no, merging through out-of-the body and lucid dream experiences to "those of a more psychic nature(he meant through contacts with the spirits they gain psychic abilities related to the Mediums of the spirits)[699]

Alister Hardy himself went through dangerous occulted experience, in which he thought he was united with the universe and that God was a mere power. [700] this experience is known to appertain to the wicked spirits mediums, and to some eastern religions. we see that the research and experiences of Alister Hardy expose him to be part of the groups that believe and experience occultism.

My comment is that the experiences of hearing voices, traveling outside the body, and ecstatic experiences are frequent experiences that fall under the psychic occult ones which we find in the life of Mohammed.

Dr. Kurt Koch, a psychiatric and demonologist specialist, speaks about Harry Edwards. Through séances with the spirits, they promised to use him. He went through the demon possessed experiences. He began practicing healing through falling in ecstasy. His practices were accompanied by magical things, such as objects to be transferred from a place to another without any one touching them. Also:

> He has developed the ability to travel out of his physical body to the place where his patient is, the so-called art of spirit travelling or excursion of the soul. [701]

The Shamans, (mediators of the spirits) in north Asia, north Russia and the European Russia, received their inspiration through falling in ecstasy or comas, the spirits appear to them and communicate to them oracles. We can see this by the description of W. Radloff (of the end of the 19 century):

> The ceremony begins with an appeal and invocation to the spirits. Then the shaman appears to set off on a journey through the various regions of the heavens- according to the belief of these peoples the heaven is composed of various regions(or layers). (This reminds us of the alleged ascension of Mohammed so that he brings a message from Allah.). The shaman seeks as best he may to give a vivid picture of this journey, and also makes the spirits talk. [702]

The shamans then go to a superior god, so that to learn about the animal sacrifice if it was accepted or not. Also about the crops. and whether the god Uelguen expects sacrifices, and what kind of sacrifices he expected. it is identical to the ascension of Mohammed through which he obtained instruction from Allah.

The scholar Montegue Summers wrote about the boast of the magicians in claiming to fly upon the back of the animals; their purpose he wrote is to influence their listeners. [703] This applies to Mohammed who boasted to fly over Buraq to influence his followers.

Cirvelo Pedro Sanchez was a judge in the trials, he wrote between the years 1475-1560 a book, which became an important reference in Spain. He mentioned about the magicians claiming that they were carried on the animals to fly. Sanchez said those magicians imagined such flight through the devil effect on them. He attributed such phenomenon to the ecstasy which caused such hallucinations.[704]

Magicians' claims to mount animals and fly to distant places are something old in history. An example, the magicians claimed to fly to distant places in company of goddess Diana, in order to worship her.[705] Ulrich Molitor (year 1489) professor of law at the university of Constance-Germany, said the following paragraph about the issue of transporting the spirits of the magicians to other places:

During sleep as well as during a waking state, devils can produce impressions so vivid that men believe they see or act in actuality.[706]

This reveals the knowledge of the scholars even during those centuries, about the power of the devil in hallucinating the mind of the human, making him to believe that he is flying to distant places.

Jeff Harshbarger says that the trance state enables the person to abandon his body in order to be in communion with the spirits and obtain information. Many of the shamans claim to obtain prophecies through those occult journeys.[707]

Giambattista Porta, known under the name of Giovanni Battista Della Porta (year 1560 A.D.), an Italian scholar from the city of Napoli, mentioned about a sorceress who promised him to come up with information. She fell in trance state. He entered the room and tried to awaken her through hitting her, but she did not wake up. Finally she woke up and said that she travelled during this trance state to mountains, seas and distant places.[708]

Jeffrey Russell and Brooks Alexander spoke about the striking similarities between the African and European magicians. Among these similarities: their souls fly in order to attend meetings in places. They use ointments or cosmetics in order to change how they look. They are in communion with Jin, and practice collective or mass immoral intercourses. There are fifty characters of the European magicians which are found in magicians of other societies.[709]

Mohammed was subjected to such Isra's before his claim to be a prophet

The books of Sirah (that narrated the life of Mohammed), mentioned that Mohammed used to go through these Isra's (his soul flying to distant places) before he claimed of prophecy role.[710] The books of his Sirah reveal that the nature of these Isra were that "while he slept in his spirit."[711] This is actually identical to what the diviners and wizards mention how during their sleep their spirits are transported by a spirit devil in order to have "a journey to the world of spirits."

When Mohammed claimed the Isra occurred, and what are the Isra real purposes?

This was after few days of being rejected by the tribe of Thaqif, the main tribe of the city of Taif. Mohammed was in great state of disappointment and failure. The spirit that plagiarized the identity of the angel Gabriel wanted to console him. So he created two things: first, that the Jinn devils came to Mohammed after they were hit by the stars, while spied on the "ceiling of heaven". They claimed they came to him in order to hear the Quran and embraced Islam. After this, the delegation of devils, came to him to hear the Quran, proposing to him to meet him at al Hujune - a cemetery where Mohammed used to practice his séances with Jinn, proving that those devils were nothing else but the Jinn devils whom he used to meet at Hujune.

Second: then came the Isra'. Without doubt, it was fabricated by the same spirit who plagiarized the identity of Gabriel. The trick was to assume that Mohammed did not need support from the inhabitants of Mecca or from the surrounding villages, because his position is superior to all prophets, as the Isra claimed that all the prophets came to meet him in the temple of Jerusalem and he preached to them. Thus, this phenomenon of Isra of Mohammed is created by the same devils who claimed to embrace Islam.

What occurs to the mediators of the devil during these occult experiences? their bodies remain in their beds, while their souls are captured by the devil in a journey outside the body. The something occurred to Mohammed. Aisha the youngest among the wives of Mohammed said:

> The body of the apostle of Allah remained in its place while Allah made Isra to his spirit[712]

Thus, the experience of Mohammed is equal to the diviners' experiences, who under the hallucinate influence of the devil, their souls are carried to places, where are created in them false convictions about their greatness, so that they can leave impressions on their followers.

These soul journeys are distinguished in that they occur many times to the diviner. This is also recorded in Mohammed's life. We read in the Al Halabieh- that narrates the life of Mohammed:

The Isra occurred to Mohammed 30 times.[713]

Sheik abdel Wahab al Shaarawi said that the Isra of Mohammed were 34 times.[714] What was called Isra was part of the old experiences of Mohammed; his spirit was captured while sleeping to be subjected to hallucinate journeys similar to what the magicians and the religions founders who worship the spirits went through. We already saw some examples in this regard.

Therefore, the case which the Islamic Sheiks wanted to convey to it other meaning: as if he flew in his body, was actually of the nature of his old occult soul journeys. There is the testimony of his cousin, Um Hani, that, the same night he claimed of Isra, he remained sleeping in her house. That is his body did not disappear from the sight of his cousin; he remained sleeping in her house. Her real name is Fakhita.[715] She mentioned the sleeping of Mohammed at her house. When she waked up she saw Mohammed claiming that during the night he flew to Jerusalem. Here her words:

Um Hani said: 'Mohammed was at my house when he had this experience of Isra: he slept at my house that night. He prayed the prayer of dinner, then he slept, and we slept too. When it was before dawn, the apostle of Allah awaked us from our sleep.' in other narration 'he awaked us'. After he prayed the prayer of morning and we prayed with him, he said: 'O Um Hanni. I prayed with you the dinner prayer, as you have seen in this valley. Then I came to Bet al Maqdes, where I prayed inside. Then this morning I prayed with you as you have seen.'[716]

We see that Mohammed prayed the dinner prayer, and slept before his cousin. Then he waked up early mooring to say that he flew to Jerusalem.

Later, Muslims added the story of the ascension of Mohammed to heaven with the Isra. The story became that after Mohammed preached to the prophets in the temple of Jerusalem, he was presented with a cup of milk and another cup of wine, and was told to choose. He chose the cup of milk; he was told that his nation was saved from astray, and that he has chosen wisdom. This story was under the influence of the Zoroastrians, as I will discuss in the following paragraphs.

We notice that when Quraysh objected and criticized the story of Isra' of Mohammed, there was no mention of ascension to heaven. Might be later Mohammed claimed to have ascension to heaven, but the wording and the framing of the story did not belong to him; the story was arranged in way that accords with the Persian, Mandaean, and heretical Christians ascensions to heaven. Thus, this framing of the alleged ascension of Mohammed occurred after Mohammed died.

The alleged ascension of Mohammed is inspired by previous ascensions, especially the Zoroastrians

There are many elements of the alleged ascension of Mohammed in commune with the Middle Eastern religions' ascensions: such as the visiting of the one ascending to seven layers of heaven, where a kind of believers reside according to their works and ritual performances while they lived on earth. In some of the Gnostic sects and heretical Christianity, there is a Biblical figure or name who preside each layer, welcoming the one ascending and opening to him the door of the layer. An angel accompanies the one ascending, until he reaches a point in heaven where he is no more allowed to go further. The one ascending alone proceeds until he reaches a place where the deity resides in an isolated place. The deity then gives the one ascending religious instructions so that he comes down to impose on his followers. There are other particularities of these ascensions, which Mohammed had all adopted.

I do not want to go with more details on the subject of ascension, which requires chapters to cover. I want, however, to present a summary about what was said it occurred to Mohammed before his alleged ascension: he was presented with two cups; one contains milk, the other wine. His choice would have affected the destiny of his Islamic nation. We read in Sahih al Burchari:

> Reported by abi Hurreirah that the apostle of Allah said that the same night that he flew to Jerusalem, he was presented with two cups of wine and milk. He looked to them and took the cup of milk. Gabriel said to him: 'we praise Allah who guided you to act by nature. Had you took the wine, your nation would had went astray.[717]

Actually, these are part of the Zoroastrian mythology. King Vistasp who baked Zoroastrians raging wars to impose Zoroastrianism on the Iranic nations, was presented with a cup to drink. as the king accepts the cup from the hand of the angel, meant the accepting of the religion by all the nation.[718]

The angel gives Vistasp to drink from a cup in order to see the spiritual world.[719] Here we see that the idea that a leader drinks from a cup presented to him by an angel, is essential for the one who is prepared to go to heaven to see the unseen spiritual world, exactly as happened to Mohammed. Zoroaster also is given a honey cup, then he could see heaven and Hell.[720] The idea of presenting a cup to everyone ascending to heaven in Zoroastrianism we see it in the ascension of Firaz, he was presented with a cup to drink before he was enabled to ascend to heaven.[721]

Thus, presenting to Mohammed two cups one of milk and the other of wine was part of protocol, which the ascending man in Zoroastrianism had to go through; it reflects their mythological view of the milk. In book of Sad Dar, we see the relation of discernment of insight with the drinking of Milk.[722] According to the nine books of Dinkard, those who will prepare to the renovation of the cosmos, are giving milk.[723] thus, the Zoroastrians had faith in the magical value of the milk in giving imaginary magic wisdom. Those who will resist the renovation of the cosmos in that period are considered in the Dinkard not wise because they will fail to choose milk. Thus, choosing milk is seen as sign of discernment and wisdom.[724] We see the claim that Mohammed was presented with two cups, one was a cup of milk, and he chose milk, and that all the nation of Islam was saved from going astray, is actually a repetition of a mythological Zoroastrian principle.

Facts that refute Mohammed's claim

First, all these causes us to conclude that his body remained in the house of Um Hani, the thing that was confirmed by Aisha. Thus, his experience was an occult journey which mediums and those connected with negative spirits experience. As we have seen, this was not the first time he had occult experiences.

Second, the experience of Mohammed in mounting the winged Buraq, is derived from the Zoroastrian mythology: We read in Dinkard, book nine, a part of the Pahlavi text, that Kai-Khusroi, a mythological prophet of

Zoroastrianism, transformed Vae, the god of the air, into a winged camel, which Kai-Khusroi mounted to visit the immortals in distant and heavenly places.[725]

The Persians reckoned heaven as a place not far from earth connected to earth through a celestial sea. They thought there was a ceiling that separates the heaven above from the sea underneath. They drew a map of heaven and earth claiming to know all the details about the route to heaven. They claimed to know how to get to each of the different layers of heaven. They considered heaven to be equal in size to the earth. Therefore, they imagined that heaven could be reached when one was transported by things like winged camels. Mohammed borrowed the Zoroastrian concept. Mohammed claimed that the prophets used the winged animal, or Buraq, to go to heaven. He said, "the prophets used to mount the Buraq before my time." He said also, "this Buraq was subjected to the prophets before my time."[726] Mohammed relied on the ignorance of his listeners when he made outlandish statements like these, which he derived from Zoroastrian mythology.

Third, among the incoherent and inconsistent elements of the Isra' is that Mohammed presented two contradictory narrations to this flight over the Buraq: first he made it to be by air then transformed it to be ground:

He first claimed the Buraq flew carrying him in an instant from Mecca to the temple of Jerusalem which was not in existence. Then he returned to give a ground description of his journey, that reflects the journey of the caravans, which required more than month to reach Jerusalem. He made the Buraq to repeat one of his journeys that he used to do when he led the caravans of Khadija, before he married her. He was not attentive that he first presented a fast air journey on the back of the mythological Buraq. But, in his attempt to defend his claim in front of Quraysh who disbelieved him, he stepped down to a very long ground journey, passing through the valleys he used to stop and descend from his camel, when he was a servant leading the commercial caravan of Khadija.

Thus, he stood in his narration on all the stations of the caravans that he knew in his past. He used to pass by families he knew they lived on the caravans' route. As if he now passed by them tired and thirsty because of the length of the journey; to the extent he drunk their water, that was covered, whereas, they were sleeping and were not aware of him ; without knowing that their old friend who used to pass by them in the caravan of

Khadija, now passed by them while they were sleeping mounting a Buraq. In all the stations of caravans where he claimed to pass by them in his Isra', he made the people sleeping:

> I passed by the camels of the sons of so and so, and I found the people sleeping. They had a vessel of water they covered it. I remove the cover, and I drank what was inside. Then I covered it as before.[727]

Then he claimed of passing by a caravan. The Buraq overturned the cover from the water, whose owner had prepared for his ablution. Mohammed drank from the water.[728] Altogether Mohammed presented a description of ground journey in which he passed by caravan stations he knew in his past. He did not, however, present signs or proofs to this journey. Furthermore, this ground journey is contradictory with his previous narration of an air Isra'. In reality, in panicking in front of the Quraysh members who examined him, and in his desire to present proofs to a group who confronted him, he changed the journey. From an instant journey, that is a quick through a flight over a mythological animal, to a ground trip in which he attempted to use his previous knowledge of valleys and caravan stations, so as to support his narration. So he stepped down toward a journey in the desert characterized by tiresome and thirst across his old caravan stations trips. He did not, however, mention any witness of these stations in favor of his journey. He made them all sleeping, not being awake to the voice of the big mythological animal who carried an angel called Gabriel, and Mohammed mounting behind.

Mohammed made a camel to set on the ground, as a sign for his journey

Mohammed mentioned the names of some caravans, which went from Mecca toward Damascus. Those caravans were known to travel during that time. Without doubt, Mohammed knew about the time these caravans left Mecca. He mentioned that when a camel saw the Buraq, it sat on the ground, making it as sign or proof for his journey.[729] We know that camels every day sat for a while during their walk in the desert. He did not, however, mention anyone of members of the caravan, seeing the Buraq, which became walking on the ground instead of flying by the air.

Fourth, the embarrassing element on this alleged Isra' is the personality of Gabriel, who portrayed on his wings to Mohamed the structure of the temple which was not in existence that time, since it was destroyed by the

Roman Titus in the year 70 A.D. but Gabriel wanted to save Mohammed from a very embarrassing position: that is his failure to describe to Quraysh the temple that he claimed to have visited at night on the Buraq. Thus, Gabriel got his way through telling lies and falsification, presenting a portray or picture of a non-existing temple. Thus, Gabriel is not a spirit of truth as the angels are. But a spirit of un-truthiness, falsity and lie. If Mohammed had been a true prophet, why he did not distinguish that this spirit who appeared to him was a spirit of lies? How Muslims trust a prophet led by a spirit of deceit as this one who plagiarized the identity of Gabriel?

Fifth, the Aqsa Mosque being built in the year 691 A.D., and the temple in Jerusalem was not in existence that time; this historical fact, unveiled not only the identity of "Gabriel," who supported the claim of non-existing temple. But it exposed the Quran of this Gabriel and Mohammed himself. But it shed lights on the followers of Mohammed who were close to him, such as Abu Baker whose target is not the truth. But he is ready to embrace lie and falsity by claiming that he visited the temple of Jerusalem and that the description of Mohammed, which depended on the false portray on the wings of Gabriel, was accurate and true. Also it shed light on the rest of the followers of Mohammed who were ignorant in the historical facts of their time, to the extent that they were deceived from "Gabriel," Mohammed and Abu Baker. They thought that Beit al Maqdes as building was in existence in their times. And that Mohammed visited the temple and that Gabriel had described it very well; Abu Baker had visited it praising the description of Mohamed which depended on the portray of it on the wings of Gabriel.

Al Khader

The myth of Al Khader in the Quran, an eternal character that lives on out planet.

Mohammed incorporated the Al Khader story in Surah 18, al Kahf. In addition to Dhu al Qarnayn's journey to the extremities of the earth, and his construction of the dam in which he imprisoned Gog and Magog until the last day of history, we find in Surah 18, other elements taken from Pseudo-Callisthenes. The story of Al Kathir is a main myth Mohammed copied from the myths of Pseudo-Callisthenes.

According to Surah 18, Allah ordered Moses to meet an important wise servant. Moses was ordered to carry a salted fish and travel in search of this "Servant of Allah" who was wiser than Moses. Moses travelled with his servant Joshua, who carried this fish in a pot. Allah gave Moses a sign, "When this fish has been lost- it means it was revived and escaped into the waters, then Moses will find this man, whom Mohammed described in his Hadith as immortal. Moses traveled far to a place where the dead salt fish was revived. Joshua was worried because he lost the fish. But Moses upon hearing this, told Joshua that this is what they were looking for. They had found the immortal wise man in the same location where the fish was revived. Mohammed called the man al Khader.

Moses then asked al Khader to accompany him because he wanted to learn from him because great wisdom had been given to him by Allah. Al Khader objected that Moses would not have patience with him. In the words of the Quran, Surah 18 called al Kahf, verses 60-82, al Khader, said, "Behold, Moses said, 'I will not give up until I reach Majma' al Bahrain, (the junction where two seas meet,) even though I spend years travelling.' But when they reached the junction, they forgot about the fish, swimming through the sea as if it were in a tunnel. When they had progressed some distance, Moses said to his servant, 'Bring us our lunch. Truly we have suffered much fatigue at this stage of our journey.' His servant replied, "You

---

saw what happened when we took ourselves to the rock. I forgot about the fish. Satan caused me to forget to mention it even though it took its course through the sea in a marvelous way.'"

Moses said : 'that was what we were seeking after' So they went back to their footsteps, following the path they had come. So they found one of our servants on whom we bestowed mercy from us, and to whom we taught knowledge from our own.

Moses said to him, "May I follow you so that you can teach me some truth which you have been taught?" Al Khader replied, "You will not have patience with me because your understanding is not complete."

Moses said, "You will find me very patient, if Allah wills. I will not disobey you in anything." Al Khader replied, "Then if you would follow me, ask no more questions about anything until I speak to you concerning it." So they both proceeded until they were in the boat, then he scuttled it. Then said Moses, " You have scuttled it in order to drown those in it? You have done a strange thing." He answered, "Did I not tell you that you cannot have patience with me?" Then Moses said, do not rebuke me for forgetting, nor grieve me by raising difficulties in my case."

Then they proceeded until they met a boy, but Al Khader killed him.

Moses said, "You have slain an innocent lad who never killed anyone. What a foul thing you have done!." Al Khader answered, "Did I not tell you that you would not have patience with me?" Moses said, "If ever I ask you about anything after this, keep me not in your company. Then you will have an excuse to leave me."

Then they proceeded until they came upon the inhabitants of a village whom they asked for food. But the villagers refused to give any hospitality. When they came across a wall that was falling down, al Khader rebuilt the wall so it became straight and true. Moses said, "If you had wished, you could have exacted some recompense for this."

Al Khader answered, "This is the parting between me and you. now I will tell you the interpretation of the things which caused you to lose your patience. As for the boat, it belonged to certain poor men who worked on the water. I desired to render the boat unavailable because a king seized every boat by force. As for the boy, his parents were people of faith. We feared that the boy would grieve his parents by his obstinate rebellion and infidelity to Allah, so we desired that their lord would give them a son who displayed more purity and showed more affection. As for the wall, it belonged to two orphan boys in town. A treasure belonging to them lay beneath the wall. Their father was a righteous man, so your lord desired they should attain to a good age with enough strength to dig up the treasure. A mercy from your lord."

The journey Moses took with his servant carrying a salted fish which had been revived, was taken from the book of Pseudo Callisthenes. When Mohammed in his Hadith explained the story, its original source, the Pseudo Callisthenes book, was obvious. According to Mohammed's Hadith as we see it in the Taberi, " Ibn Abbass said, 'Abi bin Kaab told me that the apostle of Allah said, "Moses the prophet of Israel asked his Lord, 'Is there one of your servants more knowledgeable than myself?

If so, lead me to him.' He answered him, 'Yes, among my servants there is one who is more knowledgeable than you.' Then Allah gave Moses instructions to find his servant, and allowed Moses to find him. So Moses proceeded with his servant, carrying the salted fish. Moses was told when and where the fish would be revived. "Then your friend will be found in that place." Then Moses went out with his servant, carrying the fish. They walked until Moses and his servant were fatigued from the journey. They reached a rock near the water of life. Anyone who drinks from it, becomes immortal. Every dead body which touches the water will be revived. When the fish touched the water it was revived."[730]

The roots of the story of al Khader and the fish in the Pseudo Callisthenes book

This story was told by Pseudo Callisthenes and Syriac writings were based on the book. According to Pseudo Callisthenes, Alexander was looking for the spring of life which promised immortality. He was told that the spring of life exists in the land of darkness where there are several springs. An old man advised Alexander that his cook should carry a salted fish and wash it in every spring of water he passed.

When the fish returns to life by the water of a spring, then that spring is the spring of life.[731] The cook washed the fish in the spring of life and the fish returned to life and dived into the spring.[732]

Alexander returned to wash himself in the spring of life, but he could not find it. God did not allow him to be washed in the spring because He did not want him to have immortality on earth.[733]

I previously mentioned that this myth was originally found in a Greek copy of Pseudo Callisthenes,[734] known as β, that goes back to the third century A.D. - before the year 550 A.D.[735] Among the writings that mention this myth was the Syriac, which is attributed to Jacob Sarugh, and goes back to the sixth century A.D.

In other versions of Pseudo Callisthenes' book, the one who was ordered to carry the salted fish was a leader in Alexander's army.

After he washed the fish in a spring it was revived and went in the water, the leader also immersed himself in the water to search for the fish. However he was changed. His face became green, and he had no desire to drink or eat. He knew that now he was immortal and very wise.[736]

Pseudo Callisthenes and the Epic of Gilgamesh

In this account, the author of the book of Pseudo Callisthenes followed the myths of the Epic of Gilgamesh. As the story unfolds, Gilgamesh looks for immortality too. He went to consult Utnapishtim, called Uta-Napishti, a figure whom Mesopotamian mythology describes as immortal and the wisest man on earth. He is the survivor of the Sumerian flood. The gods bestowed upon immortality for saving the human race. He is called Ziusura in the account of the Sumerian flood. After the flood he went to live in Dilmun, which is Bahrain today. In the Acadian story of the flood his name was Atra-hasis, which means, the very wise one.[737]

Stephanie Dalley, the famous archeologist, says there are many famous names for Atrahasis which are found in Middle Eastern ancient civilizations. In the list of the Sumerian kings Atrahasis is called by his Sumerian name, Ziusudra, which means extra-wise. In the Epic of Gilgamesh he is called Utapishtim or Uta-na'ishtim, which means "He found life." The name Atrahasis appears in Ugaritic mythology as Khothar-wa-hasis, the skilful god of craftsmanship. This is the root of the name al Khader, The Green One,[738] which spread throughout the Middle East.

The survivor of the flood in the Arabic writings

Al Khader survived the Mesopotamian flood and became immortal in writings found throughout many parts of the Middle East. We can trace him in Arabic literature. Ibn Kathir says, Al Khader lived in the time of the Flood and took responsibility of burying Adam.[739]

Al Aini claimed that when the flood was over, and al Khader came out of the ship, became immortal and buried Adam.[740] Arabic writers also emphasized that al Khader became immortal. Ibn Manthur said, " Al Khader is a prophet who is immortal and unseen."[741] He appears to people and knows their names. Al Khader visits the people and greets them, he knows their names and where they live and work. Arabic writers claim that al Khader is immortal no matter when he lived. He was with Dhu al Qarnayn. Many Arabic writers, such as al Halabi and ibn Kathir, wrote that he was the main commander of the army of Dhu al Qarnayn.[742] He obtained immortality through drinking from the spring of life.[743] Ibn Hajar wrote, "It was said that al Khader was in command of the army of Dhu al Qarnayn reached before Dhu al Qarnayn to the "river of life," meaning, "the spring of life" and drank from it without knowing that he became immortal. He is still immortal there."[744]

We can learn a lot from the inconsistencies between various texts. Al Khader drank from the spring of life and became immortal and remained near the spring of life. This is the source behind the claim in the Quran that the fish carried by Moses and his servant was revived in the location where al Khader resided.

The idea that al Khader was commander of Alexander's army is derived from a different version of the book of Pseudo Callisthenes, which claims the one who carried the salted fish was the commander of Alexander's army of instead of the cook. He obtained immortality after he immersed himself in the spring of life, searching for the fish which was revived.

In the Hadiths of Mohammed we find that al Khader was immortal and lived in the time that Mohammed lived. Mohammed claimed al Khader made a Hajj every year.[745]

Al Zubeidi said that al Khader is immortal because he drank from the water of life and his color and face became similar to the color of plants.[746] This reminds us of the Ethiopian version of Pseudo Callisthenes, which was based on the Arabic and Pahlavi versions.

Al Khader in the Arabian mythology

More interesting stories about Al Khader are found in Arabian mythology where he guarded the fountain of life and gave its water to King Sakhr, who's name mean "the rock," and who became immortal. This story is related to one of the Arabian Nights, and is considered a form of Arabian narrative about Gilgamesh. Buluqiya travelled through many lands before he lost his faithful adviser, Affan, in a fruitless attempt to obtain the ring of Suleiman, through which He wanted to travel to the fountain of life and drink the water of immortality.[747]

Mythological aspects about the Mesopotamian immortal figure, which Pseudo Callisthenes had imitated and became incorporated into the Quran

We can conclude there is, according to Middle Eastern mythology, an immortal man who is very wise. He lives near the spring of life. Some men attempted to contact him to benefit from his wisdom and drink from this spring of life as they consult him about his immortality. This thought first appeared in the Epic of Gilgamesh. Gilgamesh travelled to meet with Utapishtim to consult him about immortality. Utapishtim directed him to the plant of life, which gives immortality.

Instead of Gilgamesh, the author of Pseudo Callisthenes had Alexander travel, in search of immortality. Instead of the immortal Utapishtim whom Gilgamesh went to consult, Pseudo Callisthenes created the immortal man from the servant of Alexander. Pseudo Callisthenes had Alexander find the spring of life instead of the plant of life.

Gilgamesh failed to eat the plant of life, because the serpent had stolen it, and ate it and became immortal. Pseudo Callisthenes had Alexander fail to drink from the spring of life.

But the way Pseudo Callisthenes had Alexander's cook discover the spring of life by washing the salt fish in the spring and return it to life. Mohammed copied Pseudo Callisthenes into the Quran perfectly.

There are some other elements from the Epic of Gilgamesh that were copied into the Quran as this epic developed in the Middle East. The archeologist Stephanie Dalley clarified that the immortal Sumerian Acadian man lived under different names at different times. We saw in Ugaritic mythology, he was called Khothar-wa-hasis. From there the immortal man became al Khader who's name spread across the Middle East prior to the time of Mohammed, even among Christians. The name of al Khader was given to Elijah who was called Ilias which is the Greek name for Elijah.

There is another important element in the Gilgamesh myth which was imitated both in Pseudo Callisthenes book and in the Quran. The immortal man, who was originally the survivor of the Mesopotamian flood, went to live in Dilmun, today's Bahrain. Dilmun was viewed by the Sumerians as their paradise. The influence of the idea of Dilmun-Bahrain is seen clearly in Pseudo Callisthenes, "The angel said to Alexander, 'God placed a land of darkness in Arabia, where there is also a treasure in addition to the spring of life. Whoever drinks even one drop from the spring will avoid death. By drinking the water, man gets wisdom and knowledge which no one has ever obtained before. He also gets power to fly through the heavens as the angels fly. He will become immortal forever or until he asks God for death.[748]

It is clear that when Pseudo Callisthenes imitated the Epic of Gilgamesh, he discovered the location where the plant of life existed, according to the epic of Gilgamesh, that is in Arabia. Dilmun was part of Arabia. The Quran is more specific in verifying that the immortal Khader lived in the place where the spring of life (which revived the fish) is. According to the Quran, Moses travelled to the Majmaa' al Bahrain in order to meet al Khader, the one who lives near where the fish was revived. Mohammed explained this place was also the location of the spring of life.

The place where Moses found al Khader is the same place where the immortal personality lived according to the Epic of Gilgamesh, that is Dilmon-al Bahrin, the paradise of the Sumerians

Where is Majmaa' al Bahrain, the place where, according to the Quran, Moses found al Khader?

Its easily seen that it is al Bahrain, the same place where the immortal personality went to live. According to the Epic of Gilgamesh it is called Dilmun, "the paradise of the Sumerians."

Khutadeh said that Majmaa' al Bahrain is where the Persian Sea converges into the Rum Sea, (the Mediterranean Sea.)[749]

It is impossible that the Quran intended this to be the location because the Persian sea, which is part of the Indian Ocean and adjacent to Iran, does not meet with the Mediterranean Sea.

Moses according to the Quran was ready to travel for a period called Huqub حقب », in order to reach Majmaa' al Bahrain. Huqub according to ibn Abbass means "a generation."[750] Others say Huqub would take about 70 or 80 years to reach the destination.[751]

This great distance does not match any location close to Palestine, such as the Mediterranean Sea.

Furthermore, the Sea of Persia does not join the Mediterranean Sea. The two bodies of water which do meet are the Persian Sea and the Persian Gulf. the gulf was considered by the Arabians to be a sea. In fact, they called it " Baher al Qateef," which means " the sea of Qateef."

When the Quran uses the term "Majmaa' al Bahrain," it is also seen by the expositors of the Quran who said it was the island where Moses met with al Khader. Al Taberi also speaks about the fish after it was revived. He said, "Whenever the fish touched the waters, they stiffened and became like rock. Moses followed until the fish brought him to an island in the islands of the sea. There he found al Khader and greeted him."[752] The same idea is expressed by ibn Abbass, the cousin of Mohammed.[753]

It is clear that Moses reached the junction of the Persian Sea with the Sea of the Persian Gulf. Then the fish opened a way in the sea for Moses to follow until he reached the main island in the chain of islands called al Bahrain. There he met al Khader. This also points us to the fact the Quran intended al Bahrain to be the place where Moses encountered al Khader. Al Allusi said "Al Bahra, in intended in the Quranic verse, is where the sweet water unites with the salt water. Without the specifications of two seas."[754] This definition given by al Allusi of Majmaa' al Bahrain or al Bahrain goes well with the country of Bahrain. Bahrain is a country which took its name from the presence of sweet springs of water, called Kawakeb كواكب, inside the salted water of the sea.[755]

The Quran gathered the various insights about the immortal man who lived in Bahrain. According to Mesopotamian mythology, plant life came first. Later, as we saw in Pseudo Callisthenes, spring life came next. Since the fish carried by Moses and his servant was revived in that area, the Quran implicitly expresses the idea that where this man lives the spring of life. lives also. This also agrees with Mesopotamian mythology.

Moses traveled many miles to encounter this man and learn from his wisdom. But Moses eventually became exhausted from fatigue. We also see these ideas as part of the Epic of Gilgamesh. As you remember the story, Gilgamesh travelled many miles risking his life in order to consult the immortal man who is very wise. Gilgamesh found him in the land of Dilmun, or al Bahrain. Finally, the idea of the fish, which was revived is identical to the way Alexander discovered the spring of life according to Pseudo Callisthenes. All this suggests that the Epic of Gilgamesh was a part of the oral tradition in Arabia at the time of Mohammed in a form used by Pseudo Callisthenes. These stories were combined with the myths of the Epic of Gilgamesh. The immortal sage lived in Bahrain, where the spring of life that revived whatever it came in touch with existed.

Different forms of the Epic of Gilgamesh had developed in the area of the Middle East

How could this accumulation of Gilgamesh's epic myths reach Arabia at the time of Mohammed?

Scholars confirm that the myths of Gilgamesh spread in various forms and developed in many parts of the Middle East over a number of years. Some copies of the Epic of Gilgamesh were found in the Arsacid period. The Arsacid dynasty reunited Iran and ruled over it, forming the Parthian empire in the late third century BC. intermittently controlled Mesopotamia between 150 BC and 224 AD. Copies of Epic of Gilgamesh go back to the first or second century B.C. These copies were found in two cuneiform fragments, BM 35174 and 35628.[756] Since we know that the Parthians dominated many parts of Arabia, we can imagine how the Epic of Gilgamesh spread into Arabia.

There is also the appearance of Gilgamesh, Humbaba and the immortal man, Utnapishtim, in the book of Giants. You may remember that Humbaba was a monstrous giant, who appeared in the Epic of Gilgamesh, and was killed by Gilgamesh and his friend Enkidu. This proves that Aramaic versions of the Epic of Gilgamesh circulated among literate circles in the Middle East.[757] The book of Giants was found in a Qumran cave.

Scholars admit that Mani depended on the book Giants when he wrote his book, also called the Giants. It was considered a Manichaean form of the same book. We know the myths in the Epic of Gilgamesh were known and embraced by the Manichaeans. Without doubt, the visit of Gilgamesh to Utnapishtim to ask for wisdom about immortality was well-known to the Manichaeans.

As I previously mentioned, we know that Manichaeism reached the Arabians,

The name of Gilgamesh continued to be popular among the Christian Nestorians, who sent missionaries to Arabia. The ninth century Nestorian bishop Theodore bar Konai includes a list of postdiluvian monarchs synchronized with the generations from Peleg to Abraham among his scholia to the book of Genesis. The tenth name on this roster is Gilgamesh.[758] All these facts, show that the myths of Gilgamesh were known to Arabians, and spread centuries before and after Mohammed. The book of Pseudo Callisthenes was also spread before Islam. When we see how various religious groups borrowed from one another and edited text and ideas, it is little wonder they adopted all kinds of myths. Sharing Biblical names such as Moses at the time of Mohammed is nothing strange.

Elijah – Elias as al Khader

The Immortal Man, who was the survivor of the Mesopotamian Flood lived in many Middle Eastern stories as Atrahasis. In the Ugaritic inscriptions, he was known as Khothar-wa-hasis. He was the skilful God of Craftsmanship. Scholars such as Sephanie Daley, considered his name, as the root of al Khader, which means "the green one."[759] The city of Ugarit was an ancient city located near the Syrian city of al Lathiqia.

However, the name Khader was originally connected with the Immortal Man of Mesopotamia, more specifically with the land of Dilmun-Bahrin. Later, under the influence of the Judaic mythology, he became Elijah.

Because Elijah was taken to heaven and did not die, some Jews at that time considered Elijah to be immortal, and he still lived on earth and appeared from time to time to resolve problems. This belief was reinforced by a verse in I Kings 18:12, where Elijah declared it would not be rain until he gave permission. When Elijah came out from where he had been hiding, he met Obadiah who served Ahab, King of Israel, and told him that he was going to meet with the king. Obadiah answered, "I do not know where the Spirit of the Lord may carry you when I leave you. If I go and tell Ahab and he doesn't find you, he will kill me. Yet I, your servant, have worshiped the Lord since my youth." (I Kings 18:12.) This created the myth that Elijah was led by God in every generation. He appeared and traveled from place to place, carried by the Spirit of God.

Elijah was well known in the book of I Kings. He announced the Word of the Lord which said that it would not rain for three years. When Elijah prayed for the return of rain to the land, God granted him this prayer. Elijah's name became synonymous the one who brings the rain.

He was called upon many times in the Middle East to bring the rain.

Elijah was also called al Khader, which means "green," because he brings green into the desolate and deserted places when he calls for rain. For the Orthodox Christian of the Middle East, the name Khader became Elias[760] which, in turn, became the Greek name for Elijah. M. Hamilton says that this Immortal Man of Mesopotamia who lived in Bahrain, discovered the spring of life and he moved near that spring. However, because he offered help in resolving their problems, he created ambiguity concerning his personality. Therefore, he became identified with Elijah-Elias, who is known by many oriental Christians as the one who brings rain.[761]

I believe these are the roots of al Khader which grew into the Quran. Khader lived near the fountain of life in Dilmun, Bahrain, as the Immortal Man. However, what he said as he traveled with Moses reflected the Judaic/Christian/Oriental myth about Elijah-Elias, who travels from place to place resolving problems.

Elijah, Elias, and al Khader influenced Mohammed as we see by the Hadiths Mohammed wrote. In one Hadith, ibn Abbass reports that Al Khader was Elias. He said that he Apostle of Allah said, "Al Khader is Elias."[762] Also ibn Abbass confirmed that al Khader is Elias, that is Elijah.[763]

Mohammed ignored that Elijah began to prophesy around the year 858 B.C., whereas, Moses lived in the 15th century B.C. How, then could Al Khader- Elijah be contemporaries of Moses and how could Moses visit him in Bahrain?

Elias al Khader was honored in the high places and green hills.[764] This mythology has its resonance on Mohammed. We read in one of his Hadiths which was reported by Abi Hurrerah, "The apostle of Allah said, 'al Khader was named "green," because he sat on white object and it became green under him.' Mujahid said, 'he was called al Khader, because when he prays everything around him becomes green.'"[765]

Mar Jurjes, Serjus and al Khader

Later in the Middle East, two other saints shared the title of al Khader. St. George, a soldier in the Roman army who stood with the persecuted Christians in Palestine. He himself suffered because of his faith and was given the title al Khader. Next was Serjus. Respected by the Armenians and other inhabitants in Asia Minor, he was also given the title al Khader.[766]

Garth Hewitt, an honorary canon of St. George's Anglican Cathedral in Jerusalem, says that St. George also inherited the attributes of Elias. He became protector of the trees and other green environments.

The churches which were built for al Khader also confirm the change from Elias to St. George, who was also called Jerjes. The village of al Teibeh in the West bank is mentioned in the Bible as Ophrah. There is the ruin of a church from the Byzantine period. The church was built for al Khader Elias, but later St. George became al Khader, the saint honored in the church.

All this demonstrates that al Khader was a person who appeared to resolve problems and bring rain and green vegetation. He was the subject of a very famous myth at the time of Mohammed. In some places the name al Khader was given to Elijah, Elias and then St. George. In other places the name of al Khader was derived from the myths of Pseudo Callisthenes, or the immortal wise man in the Epic of Gilgamesh. The form which we encounter in the Quran combines two forms.

The roots of the dialog between Moses and al Khader in the Quran.

Some Jews also described Elijah as the immortal man who appeared on earth to resolve problems. He became very wise, and his wisdom was incomprehensive, even for the rabbis. The Talmud often mentions that Elijah appeared to people including the rabbis, providing them with his solutions derived from his wisdom. One of these encounters was between Rabbi Jochanan and Elijah, which is without doubt the root of the Quran's narration on the dialog between Moses and al Khader in the Quran. A portion of the encounter between Rabbi Jochanan and Elijah, says:

> Rabbi Jochanan, the son of Levi, fasted and prayed to the Lord that he might be permitted to gaze on the angel Elijah who had ascended alive to heaven. God granted his prayer and the semblance of Elijah appeared before him. 'Let me journey with thee in thy travels through the world,' the rabbi said to Elijah. Let me observe thy doings, and gain thy wisdom and understanding.'

> "Nay," answered Elijah. "My actions thou couldst not understand. My doings would trouble thee, being beyond thy comprehension."

> But still the rabbi entreated: "I will neither trouble nor question thee," he said, "Only let me accompany thee on thy way."

> "Come, then," said Elijah, "but let thy tongue be mute. At thy first question or the first expression of astonishment, we must part company." So the two journeyed through the world together. They approached the house of a poor man, whose only treasure and means of support was a cow. As they came near, the man and his wife hastened to meet them, begged them to enter their cottage, and eat and drink the best they could afford. The two men were invited to pass the night under the poor couple's roof. This they did, receiving every attention from their poor but hospitable host and hostess. In the morning Elijah rose up early and prayed to God, and when he had finished his prayer, behold the cow belonging to the poor people suddenly died. Then the travelers continued on their journey.

> Rabbi Jochanan was very perplexed. "Not only did we neglect to pay them for their hospitality and generous services, but we have killed his cow," he said to Elijah. "Why didst thou kill the cow of this good man?" His voice began to trail off.

"Peace," interrupted Elijah. "Hear, see, and be silent! If I answer thy questions we must part." And they continued on their way together.

Toward evening they arrived at a large and imposing mansion, the residence of a haughty and wealthy man. They were coldly received; a piece of bread and a glass of water were placed before them, but the master of the house did not welcome or speak to them. They remained there during the night unnoticed. In the morning Elijah remarked that a wall of the house required repairing, and needed a carpenter. Elijah himself paid the money for the repair. He said that it was for the hospitality they received.

Again Rabbi Jochanan was filled with wonder, but he said naught, and they proceeded on their journey.

As the shades of night were falling they entered a city which contained a large and imposing synagogue. As it was the time of the evening service, they entered and were much pleased with the rich adornments, the velvet cushions, and gilded carvings of the room. After the completion of the service, Elijah arose and called aloud, "Who here is willing to feed and lodge two poor men this night?" No one answered, and no respect was shown to the travelling strangers. In the morning, however, Elijah re-entered the synagogue, and began shaking the hands of its members. "He said, "I hope that you may all become presidents."

Next evening the two entered another city, when the Shamas, who is the sexton of the synagogue, came to meet them and tell the members of his congregation that two strangers had come, the best hotel in town was opened to them and the people all vied to show attention and honor to them.

In the morning when they were to part, Elijah said, "May the Lord appoint over you but one president..."

Jochanan could restrain his curiosity no longer. "Tell me," said he to Elijah, "Tell me the meaning of everything we have witnessed. To those who have treated us badly thou uttered good wishes. But to those who have been gracious to us, thou hast made no suitable return. Even though we must part, I pray thee, explain to me the meaning of thy acts."

"Listen," said Elijah, "and learn to trust in God, even though thou canst not understand His ways. We first entered the house of the poor man, who treated us so kindly. Know that it had been decreed that on that very day his wife should die. I prayed unto the Lord that the cow might prove a redemption for her. God granted my prayers, and the woman was preserved unto her husband.

The rich man, whom we visited next, treated us coldly, and I repaired his wall. I repaired it without a new foundation, without digging to the old one. Had he repaired it himself he would have dug, and thus discovered a treasure which lies there buried, but which is now for ever lost to him.

To the members of the synagogue who were inhospitable I said, 'May you all be presidents,' but with many rulers there can be no peace. I said to the others, 'May you have but one president.' With one leader no misunderstanding can arise. If thou seest the wicked prospering, be not envious. If thou seest the righteous in poverty and trouble, be not provoked or doubtful of God's justice. The Lord is righteous. His judgments all are true. His eyes note all mankind, and none can say, 'What dost thou?' With these words Elijah disappeared and Jochanan was left alone.[767]

The Jewish narration of the encounter between Rabbi Jochanan, son of Levi, and Elijah closely mirrors the Quran's narration to the encounter between Moses and Al Khader which becomes the root of Mohammed's tale. However, when the Quran's myth reached Mecca it was so corrupted that it became illogical. Probably Mohammed heard the story but could not remember the details. However, we see that both stories are built on an encounter with a wise man who does things in an unexpected way without explaining his actions. The only way the wise man will explain his actions is if the person seeking the explanation is prepared to sacrifice the company of the wise man. In the end, in order to learn from the wisdom of the wise man, the person who asked for the company of the immortal wise man loses his patience and prefers to have the explanation at the expense of losing the company of his valuable companion.

The weakness of the Quranic myth compared to the original Jewish myth

The idea in the Jewish story about the prayer of Elijah which included the death of the poor family's cow and Elijah's explanation of his act is more acceptable than the story that appeared in the Quran. You may remember that the Quran says al Khader killed a boy, only because he would become an infidel. This shows that Mohammed lacked an understanding of the grace of God. The Bible never ordered a prophet to kill a boy without reason, under the weak excuse that he might become a wicked person in the future. God does not convey to creatures, whether they were prophets or angels, to act instantly in His wisdom. If they were to have this capability they would become gods, who always have the mind of God and act with His infinite knowledge and wisdom. As we pounder on how God has dealt with people throughout all of history, and as we see it recorded through His dealing in the epochs of hundreds of prophets, whether in the Old or the New Testament), we see that God has never acted this way.

Mohammed's custom was to bring changes to the myths he heard from others, in order to use the myths to justify his own actions, and his directives were sometimes brutal. For example, when he conquered a tribe, he would kill all the males over the age of ten because Mohammed considered them to be infidels. When he conquered the Jewish tribe of Beni Qaritha, he decapitated all the boys age ten and above. He buried them in trenches which he dug for this mass burial. He distributed the younger children to his followers as slaves and the women and girls became concubines.

Not only did he order these despicable acts, but by changing the Jewish account of the myth he made his criminal behavior appear as wisdom, superior to the Law of Moses, which prohibited killing any person unless they committed crime. So Mohammed changed the story to suggest there is a wisdom superior to the law of God spelled out in the Bible and given to Moses. This wisdom is the wisdom of the immortal man of Allah, who is far superior to Moses. So when Mohammed killed children because they were infidels, he saw it as an act requiring special wisdom. But the rest of the world saw it as dangerous satanic deception.

Part of the Jewish myth relates to the setting up of a straight wall, showing clearly that Mohammed failed to understand or even remember the original Jewish account. Either that, or he wanted to modify it to appear that it was a special account that came from Allah. But due to Mohammed's changes, the story became illogical and contradictory.

To reveal the story's true wisdom we need to return to the Jewish account. Let us examine both the Jewish account and the account in the Quran.

The Jewish account:

And they continued on their way together. Toward evening they arrived at a large and imposing mansion, the residence of a haughty but wealthy man. Their reception was cold indeed. The wealthy man placed before them a piece of bread and a glass of water, but the master of the house failed to welcome or even speak to them. During the night they went unnoticed. In the morning Elijah remarked that one wall of the house required repair. So Elijah sent for a carpenter and paid the repair bill. Elijah said it was payment for the hospitality they received."

Now Elijah explained his actions by saying, "The rich man treated us coldly, even though I repaired his wall without digging a new foundation. Had he repaired the wall himself, he would have discovered a buried treasure which now remains forever lost to him.

The rich man was being punished because he failed to decently receive Elijah and the rabbi. If he had prepared the wall himself by digging a foundation for a new wall, he would have discovered a treasure under the old wall. Treasures are not just found under walls. They are placed deep in the ground, hidden from the eyes of everyone except the one who dug so deep to hide them. Without digging deep it was impossible to find the treasure. Did you notice how the Jewish account was logical, and consistent with the customs of the ancient Middle East when they hid their treasures by hiding them deep in the ground.

The Jewish Talmud account reflects the Jewish idea of retaliating against the one who acts improperly, but this is opposed to the spirit of the New Testament which says we should love those who persecute us and do harm against us.

But once we come to the Quranic account, we find it meaningless and not worthy to be considered. The Quran expresses a confused story of a person who did not understand the original Jewish meaning of the myth. Notice the Quran's account. "Then al Khader and his companion, Moses, proceeded on their journey until they came to a small village. Al Khader asked them for food, but they refused to give any hospitality. They found a wall there on the point of collapse. Al Khader set about to straighten the wall. Moses said, "If you desired so, you could have exacted some recompense for it." Al Khader answered, "This is the parting between you and me."

Notice that the Quran replaced the rich man, who did not receive Elijah and the rabbi in a decent manner, with the inhabitants of a village. The members of the village never hide a treasure together. Usually one person or family will hide the treasures for themselves. Furthermore, Elijah or al Khader (in the Quranic narration) should have punished the inhabitants of the village by erecting the wall without digging into the foundation, so as to prevent them finding the treasure. Mohammed, however, did not understand this portion of the Jewish myth. He left the inhabitants of the village, who did not give importance to the two guests, without punishment. This actually contradicts the original myth. The Quran, however, ended up presenting two different contradictory narrations when it made the wall to belong to two orphans. Thus, the Quranic narration became contradictory: first it said the wall was erected by al Khader as a punishment to the village's inhabitants, in order to prevent them from finding the treasure. Then, it went on to say that the wall was erected by al Khader to favor two orphans, so that they would be able to find the treasure when they became mature. This contradiction reflects the confusion of Mohammed regarding the Jewish myth, and not understanding its true meaning. Here are the verses from the Quran:

> As for the wall, it belonged to two orphan boys in the town. There was beneath it a treasure for them. Their father was a righteous man. So your lord desired they should attain their age and strength and get out their treasure, a mercy from your lord.

When Al Khader straitened the orphan's wall, it did not benefit the two boys. They will eventually attain the age, but they will never discover the treasure. They will find the wall erected, but they will never find the hidden treasure in the ground under a wall. You need to dig deeper for that. Repairing an old wall only hides the treasure from the eyes of the people who own the wall. Walls usually stand for hundreds of years, If it happened one day that the wall was destroyed, who would guarantee that the man in charge of erecting it would dig deeply on the ground until he reached the treasure? If he finds it, would he give it to the men who were once two orphans?

So we see once again that Mohammed's knowledge of this famous Jewish myth is weak and illogical. Changing a famous myth which was supposed to convey a specific meaning, was not an easy task for a person like Mohammed. That doesn't mean he lacked experience. He often reconstructed myths without respecting their own original forms. Occasionally he changed the myth because he ignored the details of the original, while at other times he did it to appear as if he received inspiration from Allah through the angel Gabriel.

The antiquity of the Jewish myth is confirmed to have been the origin of the Quranic myth

There is another similar Jewish story. It referred to an encounter between Joshua, the son of Levi, and Elijah. Joshua lived in the first half of the third century. He was the head of the school of Lydda in southern Palestine. And the Midrash tradition made him often to accompany Elijah in his wandering on earth[768] and interlocutor to Elijah.[769]

In the Babylonian Talmud, we find Joshua ben Levi dealing with the angel of death.[770] Many of the myths concerning him were preserved in small books of the Midrash. One book is "Ma'aseh de-Rabbi Yehoshua' ben Levi," which means "The History of R. Joshua bin Levi." Another book is called "Masseket Gan 'Eden we-Gehinnom," means "Paradise and Hell."

Something that explains other myths which were attributed to him, including his dialog with the prophet Elijah, which is similar to the book about the encounter between Rabbi Jochanan, son of Levi, and Elijah.

Nassim ben Shahin, was a well-known Jewish scholar of the 11th century, who lived in the city of Qirawan, an ancient city in Tunisia, North Africa. He is known as important scholar in interpreting the Talmud and the books of Midrash. In his book, "Hibbur Yafe me-ha-Yesua," he mentions an encounter between Joshua ben Levi and Elijah, similar to the conflict between Jochanan and Elijah. This was eventually incorporated into the Quran. An Arabic version of the book called "Comfort" was written by Nassim ben Shahin.

Julian Obermann, another important scholar, attested that many of the myths of the Talmud reached us through the Jews of North Africa. Obermann maintains that the stories narrated by Nassim bin Shahin are authentic and Nassim bin Shahin attests to this fact. Ben Shahin says that most of what he wrote in his book, Comfort, including the stories and proverbs, can be verified in the Talmud and the books of Midrash.[771]

Stories about the encounter between Joshua ben Levi and Elijah were found in a Jewish book from the 11th century. It did not question their authenticity or their presence in the Talmudic and Midrash books which date back to previous centuries. Gaster found material dating from the fourth century AD, which was written outside the Talmud. He published material like this depending on a manuscript written about the 12th or 13th century A.D.[772]

The story of Joshua ben Levi and Elijah are similar to the Quran.

Obermann defended its Jewish origin. He advanced evidence to show that the stories cannot be of Arabic origin. They must be Jewish. For example, one proof is the style he uses to address Elijah. It is identical to the style used by the Jewish Rabbis.

Also Nassim ben Shahin has written that these stories were transmitted by "the masters and the most excellent authorities from among our Sages."[773] This indicates that the stories date back to the Jewish authorities who wrote the Talmud and Midrash.

Obermann wrote, "the two versions of the story, that of the Quran and that of the book of Comfort, are so similar in essence that their genetic identity must be seen to be beyond dispute ; at the same time they appear sufficiently dissimilar in detail to reveal complete independence of one another. This would be only natural if we here have to do with the case of an agadic narrative, which as such had of course first been told in Hebrew or Aramaic, and which was subsequently adapted twice in different ages and environments, for different purposes, and under totally different conditions."[774]

In reality, the original is always more beautiful and more accurate in meaning. But the forms that are illogical, enigmatic and incomprehensible, like the Quran, usually are deviations from the original, whose alteration occurred in a primitive environment like Mecca or Medina.

Obermann continues to defend the authenticity of story written by Nassim bin Shahin. "It is virtually out of question that he (Nassim) one of the foremost expositors of rabbinic literature in his age, the author of a commentary on the Talmud held in high esteem to this day, would have incorporated an apocryphal, oral tale in a work of religious ethical edification for which he pledged to use only such materials as had been handed down by "the masters and the most excellent authorities from among our Sages."[775]

In other words, Obermann says that the story incorporated in the book by Nassim was not an apocryphal story which was transmitted orally, but existed in the books of the Talmud and Midrash during this time.

These facts show that the words which were written in the Quran as occurring between Moses and al Khader, were from a popular Jewish story. Some people claim the conversation occurred between Rabbi Jochanan son of Levi and Elijah sometime between Joshua ben Levi and Elijah. It is of the style used by many dialogs reported in the Talmud, which occurred between Rabbi Joshua ben Levi and Elijah. The fact that we find the story in Jewish communities as far away as the city of Qirawan in North Africa and that a Jewish scholar such as Nassim bin Shahin considered it to be an important piece handed down by excellent authorities, by which he means the writers of the Talmud and Midrash, reflects the spread of the story in other Jewish communities at the time of Mohammed; such as north Arabia, which is nearer to Palestine than the city of Qirawan.

Refuting the Quran's story

We have seen that the story of al Khader in the Quran was developed from the following three sources. First, the immortal wise man, who was supposedly the survivor of the Mesopotamian Flood and lived in Dilmun-Bahrin.

Second, we have the writings of Pseudo Callisthenes which tells us about Alexander's travels searching for the spring of life and find immortality. We have seen that Alexander's cook carried a salty fish, which was revived by the water of the spring of life in the land of darkness, which was some place in Arabia according to Pseudo Callisthenes. Then the cook himself became immortal after bathing in the spring of life.

Third, we have the rabbi who accompanied Elijah and listened to him. The story is the same as when Moses spoke with al Khader. These three roots easily reveal to us that the Quran may tell us about al Khader, but its words do not come from Allah.

Furthermore, if al Khader was a living personality whom Moses encountered and learned from, why did not Moses, who wrote five books of the Old Testament, ever mention his encounter with al Khader? Since Allah, according to the Quran, order Moses to travel and meet with al Khader to learn from his wisdom, this story would surely occupy a central theme in the books which were inspired to Moses. Yet, we do not find in the books written by Moses anything about this immortal and extra wise personality.

Why did this immortal personality appear only to Moses and not to any other Biblical personality in the Old and New Testament? His wisdom and intervention would have been very important for future generations. Why did none of the writers of the Old and New Testament ever mentioned the name of this immortal man? They mentioned the names of others who were not Hebrews yet who were praised by God. It tells the stories of people like Job, of whom God said, "Have you considered my servant Job? There is no one on earth like him; he is blameless and upright, a man who fears God and shuns evil."(Job 1:8) Although he was not an Israelite, Job was praised over the prophets of Israel who lived during his time. In the book of Ezekiel, the Lord emphases the righteousness of three men, two of which were not Israelites. Noah and Job were known by their superior conduct above the rest of the inhabitants of the earth. "As surely as I live, declares the Sovereign Lord, even if Noah, Daniel and Job were in it, they could save neither son nor daughter. They would save only themselves by their righteousness." Ezekiel 14: 19-21.

This shows that the writers of the Bible elevated men and women of other nationalities over their own Hebrew prophets. So why they should ignore al Khader, if he really existed in history?

Finally, we can see that the personality of al Khader contradicts the Biblical account regarding the prophet Elijah. It is against the view of the Bible regarding the real persons that God called for the role of prophecy, wisdom and performing miracles. These prophets were known to their generations and the people among whom they served. People knew where the prophets lived and were in open contact with them. Bible prophets exercised their duties and displayed their gifts openly in front of the eyes of their people, declaring the truth of God. They were not hidden personalities like the ambiguous unseen spirits, whose apparitions are connected with an enigmatic magical or mysterious mythological thing. This is the image of al Khader in the Quran that is contrary to the true prophet of God.

Korah
Korah who became Qaroon in the Quran

One of the characteristics of primitive oriental myths, such as those of Persia and Arabia, is their ability to describe people and things in exaggerated terms. These myths usually flourish among people with primitive knowledge and superstitious traditions. These myths were designed only to entertain small children, yet in these societies with primitive superstitious traditions, the myths easily became reality and consequently became part of the religious system of those societies.

For example, one myth tells of golden flying carpets carrying people. Another myth tells about a wind that carried an army and its king to distant places. The Quran, for example, claims a wind transported Solomon and his entire army to distant locations.

Another primitive myth tells of a distant golden palace, unreachable by anyone except a magician, mythological king or some other special personality. In the Quran we encountered this type of myth in the dam of iron and brass built by Alexander the Great to imprison Gog and Magog.

Other kinds of myths attribute irrational power or riches to people. Although history cannot support these myths, the Quran includes primitive Arabian, Persian and Mandaean myths. One of these myths, found in the Quran, tells of an Israelite, who complained against Moses and was condemned by the Lord in the wilderness; yet, according to the Quran, he became the richest man in Egypt and a leading figure at the time of Pharaoh. We know this man was Korah, but the Quran calls him Karoon.

Why Karoon is actually Korah.

Identifying Karoon with Korah is clear from several aspects.

First, the Quran often changes names. For example, Aaron is called Haroon, so it would not be unusual for Karoon to be derived from Korah.

Second, in Surah, al Qasas 28:76, the Quran states that Karoon was from the clan of Moses. Islamic authors such as Taberi, confirm that Karoon was a cousin of Moses. Moreover, Islamic historians like Ibn Ishak tried unsuccessfully to copy the genealogy of Moses and his uncles as reported in the 6th chapter of Exodus.[776] This clearly shows that the Quran intended Korah, who is mentioned in the books of Exodus and Numbers, when it used the name Karoon. We read about the grandfather of Moses in Exodus 6 :18-22:

> The sons of Kohath – the grandfather of Moses -were Amram, Izhar, Hebron and Uzziel. Kohath lived 133 years. The sons of Merari were Mahli and Mushi. These were the clans of Levi according to their records. Amram married his father's sister Jochebed, who bore him Aaron and Moses. Amram lived 137 years.The sons of Izhar were Korah, Nepheg and Zicri." Korah was the son of Izhar, who as we saw was an uncle of Moses.

Third, concerning Karoon, the Quran in Surah Al Qasas 28:81 states, "then we caused the earth to swallow him up and his house." This statement is copied from the Bible in Numbers 16:28-34, "Then Moses said, 'This is how you will know that the Lord has sent me to do all these things and that it was not my idea. If these men die a natural death and experience only what usually happens to men, then the Lord has not sent me. But if the Lord brings about something totally new, and the earth opens its mouth and swallows them, with everything that belongs to them, and they go down alive into the grave, then you will know that these men have treated the Lord with contempt.' As soon as he finished saying all this, the ground under them split apart and the earth opened its mouth and swallowed them, with their households and all Korah's men and all their possessions. They went down alive into the grave, with everything they owned; the earth closed over them, and they perished and were gone from the community. At their cries, all the Israelites around them fled, shouting, 'The earth is going to swallow us too!'"

This passage removes all doubt that the Quran intended Karoon to be the same person as Korah who rebelled against Moses in the wilderness.

Where the contention between Korah and Moses happen?

The book of Numbers narrates Korah's rebellion and his punishment immediately after Moses sent the 12 spies from the wilderness of Paran to search the land of Canaan. Paran was located in the eastern part of Sinai on the border with south Palestine. While living in the wilderness of Paran, Korah began to complain against Moses.

This is contrary to the claim in the Quran that Korah, or Karoon, challenged Moses in Egypt while Moses was before Pharaoh. Korah was not a unique person as the Quran portrays him. He was a normal Hebrew like all the other Hebrews who came out of Egypt under the leadership of Moses. As slaves in Egypt, none of the Hebrews was free to have his own business and accumulate wealth.

In the Quran, Korah is more pre-eminent and richer than Pharaoh himself.

Contrary to these historical facts, the Quran claims Korah was the richest man in Egypt. Korah's treasure was described as so legendary that even the fictional accounts abstained from repeating them. In Surah 28:76 we read about the riches of Korah:

> Karoon was of the clan of Moses, but Karoon acted insolently. We bestowed so much treasure on him that even a strong man could not carry the keys that protected it.

Al Sabuni, a famous contemporary expositor of the Quran, interprets this verse for us,

> Karoon was given great quantities of treasures so that it was not possible even for a big company of strong men to carry the keys to the places where he stored his treasures.[777]

Evidently, with all we have discovered about the treasures which belonged to the Pharaohs of Egypt, what belonged to Korah, according to the Quran, must have filled hundreds, or perhaps, thousands of storehouses. If they were just few hundred, it would have been possible for a great company of strong men to carry the keys to the storehouses. All the riches and treasures of Egypt and its Pharaohs throughout their history would be trivial compared to the riches which the Quran attributed to Korah.

This legendary narration in the Quran forced the ancient writers of Islamic tradition to explain how Korah carried the keys to the treasure stores. Some of their words are recorded by Taberi,

> Karoon's keys of were made from leather carried by sixty strong mules.[778]

The Islamic tradition says Karoon built his house of gold,[779] yet, with all their imagination, they were unable to express the vast amount of the legendary riches and treasures which the Quran bestowed to Korah, We do not find a similar description in all the ancient fiction of the Orient that attributes such wealth to their mythological kings.

In reality the Pharaohs did not allow anyone, other than themselves, to claim they had great riches in Egypt. How, then, would they have allowed one Hebrew to be far richer than themselves? Rather, they humiliated the Hebrews and enslaved them assigning them the most difficult tasks like building their cities, temples and tombs. As slaves, they were not paid wages. They ate poor man's meals like other worthless and despised slaves.

The Jewish legends as source for the imaginary richness of Karoon in the Quran

The myths of the Talmud speak about Korah, saying that he found one of the great buildings which Joseph built in Egypt and filled with treasures. The keys to these treasure stores of Korah were carried on 300 mules.[780] These keys were made of leather.[781] We find stated in the Midrash and Talmud that Korah and Haman were examples of richness, just as Juliet the Giant is the example of power.[782]

According to Jewish myths:

> when Joseph, during the years of fertile and good harvest, stored crops he sold them and stored great treasures. He built three great buildings, each was 100 yards wide, 100 yards long and 100 yards high. He filled these building with money and delivered them to Pharaoh, being too honest to leave even five silver shekels of this money to his children. Korah discovered one of these three treasuries.[783]

There is another Judaic myth which said that Joseph built four palaces, which he filled with treasures:

> Joseph buried in four different places, in the desert near the Red Sea, on the banks of the Euphrates, and in two spots in the desert in the

vicinity of Persia and Media. Korah discovered one of the hiding- places, and the Roman emperor Antoninus, the son of Severus, another.[784]

This myth is originally taken from the Babylonian Talmud where we read:

> R. Hama son of R. Hanina said: Three treasures did Joseph hide in Egypt: one was revealed to Korah; one to Antoninus the son of Severus; and the third is stored up for the righteous for the future time.[785]

Although the Jewish myth is in accordance with the Quranic narration, it is far removed from the historical facts. Why would Pharaoh allow a Hebrew slave to possess an ancient building full of those treasures, even if this slave had found them? Furthermore, the Pharaohs' treasures are attested to by archaeology and historical research, yet there is no record of even a small part of what this superstitious Jewish narration claimed, and upon which the Quranic narration depended.

Another thing to take into consideration is that the Jewish myths are not in accord with the state in which Korah came out from Egypt, as a slave among slaves in company of Moses. Were he truly the richest man in all the earth as the Jewish myths portrayed, he would have remained in Egypt. How could he have carried all these treasures into the desert and live a life of poverty? Who would protect his treasures in an arid desert, surrounded by hundreds of thousands of Israelites who certainly would have stolen them.

Qaroon as the preeminent political man in Egypt

Not only did the Quran make Pharaoh poor in comparison to the fabulous riches of Korah. But the Quran gave Korah a unique pre-eminency in Egypt, to the extent that he was listed in Surah 29 as the most important personality in Egypt at the time of Moses, even greater than Pharaoh. We read in Surah 29:39:

> Moses came to Karoon, Pharaoh and Haman with clear signs, but they behaved with insolence.
>
> [RA: is "insolence" the right word here? Would the Quran use this word in this context? WK]

We see in this verse that the Quran listed Karoon before Pharaoh, as if Korah was the most important personality in Egypt and held the main political authority. This is contrary to the history of the Pharaohs, who considered themselves as gods and required people to worship them. How, then, could they have allowed one of their despised slaves to hold a position over themselves? Yet, the Quran makes Moses' accountability to Korah, Pharaoh and Haman in Egypt because Korah is the primary person in Egypt.

We notice this verse also places Haman as an important person in Egypt, second only to the Pharaoh. The Bible says in Esther 1:1 that Haman was the prime minister to the Persian King Ahasuerus who lived and reigned during the 5th century B.C. Mohammed committed another historical mistake when he made Haman prime minister to Pharaoh during the time of Moses in the 15th century B.C.

Karoon in the Quran as the man of authority in Egypt has its roots in Mandaean mythology.

The way the Quran portrays Karoon in Egypt suggests that Mohammed was influenced by Mandaean legends. The Mandaeans often tried to imitate the Israelites by taking what happened to the Israelites and saying it actually happened to the Mandaeans. In their ancient legends we find the claim that they were the true religious people in Egypt, and that a Mandaean king named Ardban Melka was given a vision to lead the Mandaeans out of Egypt, rather than Moses leading the Israelites out of Egypt.

History tells us the Mandaeans had never been in Egypt, but they appeared for the first time in the second century in Trans Jordan.

The Mandaeans claimed that king Ardban brought them to the Red Sea, which divided before them leaving a dry road surrounded by mountains of water. It is easy to see that they imitated the miracle which happened to Moses and the Israelites.

The Mandaeans' legend goes on to claim Firukh Melka, the brother of Ardvan Melka, remained in Egypt. Melka is a royal name in Mandaean literature. It reveals the role this mythological king played in their legends. According to their claim, Firukh fought against Moses, but he was defeated and escaped to the Red Sea only to find that the sea was still divided. When he attempted to walk through the sea, the mountains of water collapsed on him and on those who were with him and they drowned.[786]

In this legend, the Mandaeans simply replaced Moses with the mythological king, Ardban Melka. Then they gave the royal Ardban a brother, Firukh Melka. When Mohammed wrote the Quran, he knew that the one who led the Israelites from Egypt was Moses, so Firukh became a brother or relative of Moses.

This royal figure, Firukh Melka, replaced Pharaoh in the Mandaean legend. He remained in Egypt as the man of authority who fought Moses. Firukh, defeated by Moses, had the same fate which the book of Exodus described had happened to Pharaoh's army when they tried to follow the Israelites by walking through the Red Sea and were drowned.

Thus, Firukh was the authority in Egypt rather than Pharaoh, who never appears in the Mandaean legend. In another form, as we see in Ginza Rba, we read that Pharaoh with his army pursued the Jews into the sea where his army was drawn in and drowned. Only Pharaoh and his servants survived. Thus, we see that the Mandaeans claimed that there was a Mandaean king in Egypt while at the same time in another text they admitted the presence of Pharaoh. This made the Mandaean accounts to be contradictory regarding the authority in Egypt. This influenced the Quran narration and made another Israeli man in authority besides Pharaoh.

This explains why Mohammed made Karoon the richest man in Egypt, and placed him above Pharaoh, making him the one who confronted Moses in Egypt. Then it was easy for Mohammed to identify the Mandaean mythological royal figure Firukh with the Biblical figure Korah, since Firukh was described by the Mandaeans as a brother of their leader who led them out of Egypt.

The word "brother" to Semitic people means a relative or kin. Evidently Mohammed was told by Jewish individuals that Korah was the cousin of Moses. All these facts induced Mohammed to replace the Biblical narration about Korah with the Mandaean legend about Firukh, who, according other legend, opposed and fought Moses in Egypt.

There is another thing to ponder: in the beginning the Quran was written in Arabic without punctuation. Firukh in Arabic is written فيروخ which is similar to Qurah, قورح. The letter F was written like the Letter Qaf, before adding punctuation to Arabic. It easy to suppose that the Mandaeans read it in a mistaken way, or that Mohammed thought that the Mandaeans spoke about Korah as being the one he heard the Jews speaking of as a person mentioned in the Old Testament. Therefore, the dependence by Mohammed on the Mandaean myth, which is probably a deviation from the Biblical narration, is a confirmed fact.

The legendary riches of Karoon are easily explained when we understand that the Mandaeans often attributed legendary riches to Biblical people as well as to their own mythological figures.

The riches attributed to Karoon in Egypt can be explained by other Mandaean myths which attribute legendary riches to their mythological figures. As an example, the Mandaean book, Diwan Malkuta Laita, claims one of their mythological figures was surrounded by nine walls of pure diamond.[787] Mandaean literature also claims their mythological figures built legendary palaces and sanctuaries formed by precious stones and crystal. We have, for example, a sanctuary mentioned in "The Great First World or Alma Risaia RBA." It was built entirely of crystal.[788]

Not only did the Mandaeans attribute these events to their own people, but they gave great wealth to Biblical figures such as Adam whom they claimed built houses of Crystal.[789]

These legendary riches attributed by the Mandaeans to their mythological figures and to Biblical figures match the legendry riches attributed by the Quran to Karoon, so it is not unusual that the Mandaeans at the time of Mohammed attributed legendary riches to Firukh Melka in Egypt as described in the verses of the Quran which says that the stores of Karoon's treasures could not be carried by a company of strong men. Also the companions of Mohammed said Karoon, or Korah, had houses made of gold. The Mandaean descriptions concerning Firukh perfectly match the Quran's description of Karoon.

It is most probable that Mohammed had heard, through Mandaean and Sabian sources that Firukh Melka was not only more important than Pharaoh, but he had legendary riches. When such legends were told and retold to naive groups of Jahiliyyah at the time of Mohammed, the people had no problem accepting them as reality, since they were superstitious groups with a tendency to welcome stories like this. They never questioned the irrational elements of the myths and legends.

Luqman
Luqman in the Quran and mythology

I will discuss the subject of Luqman in detail in this book. I do this in order to prove that Mohammed used mythological superstitious sources without distinguishing their origin. But instead made their heroes, such as Luqman, to be prophets and wise men sent by Allah. He did not know, for example, that Luqman was an imaginary figure, who never existed in history.

There is a Quranic surah, number 31, known as Surah Luqman, which cites some instructions of "Luqman," as a wise man. The first verse of the surah introduces Luqman as a man to whom Allah bestowed wisdom. Who was this Luqman? Do we possess the knowledge and sources to help us identify his identity?

Luqman in pre-Islamic Jahiliyyah poetry

Luqman was known outside of the Quran by the pre-Islamic Jahiliyyah people. In their poetry he was known to be a wise man. Some poems made him to be from the tribe of Ad. This we see in a poem attributed to Al Sarim bin Musher bin Thuhil, known with the title "Afnun al Taghlabi."[790] This reflects another Jahiliyyah myth that Ad was an ancient nation.

Al Jaheth quotes a stanza of the poet Lubeid bin Rabia' al Jaafari in which he describes Luqman as having good discernment as a result of providence:[791]

وأُخْلِفَ قُسّاً ليتَني ولو أنَّنِي وأغيَا على لُقمانَ حُكْمِ التدبُّرِ

This is actually a reflection of the Ahikar myth, where Ahikar is said to have the ability of providence in solving the problems and dilemmas in favor of the kingdom and king of Assyria. (Ahikar is a mythological figure that did not exist in history, which I will discuss in detail in this chapter.)

The Arabian myths narrated that Luqman sought immortality. He then was given the choice of having his life being connected with the life of ten cows or ten eagles. He chose for his life to be connected with seven eagles, for as long as they remained alive. The last eagle, called Labed, meaning aeon, died, thus, the life of Luqman terminated with the death of the eagle.[792] This myth is mentioned in a poem of the Arabian poet called Aasha bin Qais bin Thaalabah:[793]

"يقول الشاعر وهو أعشى بن قيس بن ثعلبة: وأنت الذي ألهيت قيلا بكأســـــــه ولقمان إذ خيرت لقمان في العمر

Islamic confusion in determining the identity of Luqman

In the sayings of the Muslim writers there are contradictory ideas regarding Luqman. Some said that he was a nephew of Job, while others said he was from Nuba or Sudan. Here is a Hadith attributed to Mohammed:

> Reported by ibn Abbass. The apostle of Allah said: 'embrace Sudan. Three of them are in Paradise: Luqman the wise, al Najashi and Bilal the Muzzen.'[794]

Others said that he was a contemporary with David, and his tomb is in Palestine. Still others said that he was a judge for the Israelites.

If Luqman was a nephew or cousin of Job, how could be from Nuba? If he were contemporaneous with David and his tomb was in Israel, why did the Bible neglect to mention him when it mentioned all the other prophets at the time of David, such as Jad, Nathan and others.

The Bible never mentions a message from a prophet without mentioning his identity and where he lived. Even in the case of Job, who was not an Israelite, the Bible still specifies that he was from the land of Uz. The book of Job even specifies the tribes of Job's friends, but here the Quran presents a surah after the name of "a wise man or a prophet" without specifying his identity. This shows that Mohammed used the names spread during his time, without being able to determine their identities in the Quran. If Luqman was a prophet or a wise man who received inspired messages from God, how was he inserted in the Quran without specifying his residency, identity, and tribe or family?!

Hadiths attributed to Mohammed about Luqman

Since the Quran does not provide us with information about Luqman, the issue of determining his identity is left to sources that are less important, such as the Hadiths, that we know contradict each other. Some of them appeared many centuries after Mohammed died. There are no Hadiths about Luqman in the books that contain the confirmed Hadiths of Mohammed. That is Sahih al Bukhari and Sahih Muslim. We do find, however, a Hadith attributed to Mohammed by ibn Manthur, who was born 630 years after the emigration of Mohammed to Medina. There are other Hadiths after the time of ibn Manthur. These Hadiths were added by Muslims in later times as part of their attempt to fill in the gap which Mohammed and the Quran left regarding the identity of Luqman.

The Hadith recorded by ibn Manthur says that while Luqman was sleeping he heard a voice, "O Luqman, do you accept that Allah makes you a caliph (a ruler) who rules people with justice?" Luqman hesitated to accept this position, fearing that the love of the world might seduce him. He slept and then woke up finding himself filled with wisdom. The same thing was offered to David. He accepted it, but fell into sin more than one time. David said to Luqman, "bless you O Luqman. You have been given the wisdom, and dismissed the trial." David was given the crown and the sorrow and seduction came upon him.[795]

We do not find at the time of David, however, the existence of a wise man by the name of Luqman. The story reported by ibn Manthur was influenced by a story reported in Second Chronicles about Solomon. The Lord appeared to him at night and said to him "Ask what I will give you?" Solomon asked for wisdom. (II chronicles 1:7-12).

Hadiths attributed to Mohammed and his companions about the identity of Luqman are close to Aesop.

Luqman, as we will later see, is the same mythological Ahikar who appeared for the first time in a Jewish writing dating back to the fifth century B.C., that was written in Aramaic. The proverbs of Ahikar were spread in Arabia under the name of Sahifet Luqman. The figure of Ahikar left its impact on the Greeks, who attributed information about Ahikar to Aesop, who it is also doubtful was a real personality.

There are Hadiths attributed to Mohammed about Luqman as a slave either from Nuba or Ethiopia, these Hadiths were influenced by the Aesop figure.

Aesop was known through the fables that have meanings, which were attributed to him. These fables were characterized by having the animals speak them. They were contrary to the Ahikar proverbs, which were also attributed to Luqman. These proverbs, as we will later see, are identical to Luqman's proverbs, and to the proverbs found in Sahifet Luqman. Some of these proverbs are cited by Mohammed and some by his close relatives. We will see that some of the Quranic verses are derived from the proverbs of Ahikar. All this demonstrates that Luqman is the Arabian name of Ahikar.

If there is a small amount of similarity between what the Greeks attributed to Aesop and what some Hadiths attributed to Mohammed had recorded regarding Luqman, this is because the Greeks attributed the story of Ahikar to Aesop. Thus, the two mythological figures became synonymous with each other.

The Greek tradition describes Aesop as being an emancipated slave that was killed by the people of Delphi. Some see Aesop's name as the Greek name close to Ethiopia. According to some Greek stories, Aesop was the slave of a Greek man called Iadmon, who lived on the island of Samon. He was freed because he defended a man named Samian Demagogue.[796]

There is a similarity between the idea attributed to Mohammed and his companions regarding Luqman with the Greek tradition about Aesop:

> It is reported by ibn Abbass, 'the apostle of Allah said: from Sudan (which was part of Ethiopia) there are from the people of paradise: Luqman, al Najashi and Bilal al Muzzen'.[797]

Ibn abbass says that Luqman was an Ethiopian slave.[798] ibn Qutaibeh said:

> Luqman was an Ethiopian slave to a man from the people of Israel. His lord freed him and gave him money. He was at the time of David the prophet. His son was Tharan.[799]

There are some points in common between the description of Aesop and Luqman: both were wise men. Both were slaves who had been freed because of their wisdom, and both were Ethiopians. Ibn qutaibeh mentioned, however, that the son of Luqman was Tharan, which is derived from Ahikar's adopted son Naran, something that confirms that Luqman was Ahikar, and there was added to him some of the characteristics given by the Greeks to Aesop.

Ahiqar

Ahikar (or Ahiqar) is a mythological name found in Jewish legends about an imaginary person. The legend made him to be an Assyrian personality. He is Aikar in the Talmud; Ahiqar in Arabic; Ahi-Yakar in Assyrian and Akikarus or Achiacharos in Greek. The name is composed of two words: Ah or Ahi, meaning brother and Kar or wakar, which means dignity. Thus, his name means the brother of dignity.[800]

The oldest text that mentions the Ahikar myth is the Aramaic, which was found in the island of al Filah near Aswan in southern Egypt. The tablets were discovered by the Germans under the direction of Dr. Rubensohn during excavations between the years 1906-1908 and published by Sachau E. in the year 1911. The tablets are currently in Berlin.

The tablets belonged to a Jewish colony which lived there. The story of Ahikar is found between tablets number 40-50. The writing dates back to the reign of Darius and Ahasuerus (during the fifth century B.C.)

In each epoch there was added to the story some proverbs and details that agree with the doctrines of the persons to whom the story had reached. It seems the story was a Jewish myth to which the Jewish author added some of his knowledge in the Hebrew literature. After the Christian era some Christian knowledge was added to it.

Conybeare maintain that this Jewish myth was transferred by Greek writers to the myth of Aesop.[801]

The transfer of the myth to Arabia is prior to the time of Mohammed. This is because the Syriac version, as we will see later, dates back to the second century A.D. We know that when the Syriacs sent missionaries into some cities of Arabia they carried many mythological books with them. Furthermore, there are many proverbs of Ahikar which we find in the Aramaic version of the fifth century B.C., that we also find in the sayings of Luqman and the sayings of some close members of Mohammed, as well as in Wahb bin Munabbeh's sayings. Wahb was born in the year 34 H. and he read Sahifet Luqman.

Ahikar in Greek

Clement, the theologian from Alexandria, who lived from 150-215, wrote in his book Stromata," that Democritus, the Greek (died in the year 370 B.C):

> Democritus appropriated the Babylonian ethic discourses, for he is said to have combined with his own compositions a translation of the column of Acicarus.[802]

Clement said that Democritus was distinguished by his journeys, claiming to have visited Babel, Persia and Egypt, and sitting with the Magi and priests in order to borrow from the Persian texts. Without a doubt, he borrowed from these Aramaic tables of Ahikar.[803]

Theophrastus, a Greek philosopher who lived between 370-285 B.C. mentioned the name of Akicharus. We find this in the writings of Diogenes Laertius, who wrote about the Greek philosophers during the third century A.D.[804] Strabo, the Greek historian who lived around the Christian era, mentioned the name of a wise man from the east under the name of Achaicarus.[805] The transfer of the Ahikar myth to the Greeks was because of the spread of this myth in Egypt.

We find part of the story of Ahikar in the life of Aesop: that is the journey of Ahikar to Egypt. This part is recorded for the first time in the life of Aesop.[806] We do not find this part in the Aramaic text that dates back to the fifth century B.C., but we do find it in the Syriac text and others that appeared after the Christian era. It seems that a development of the Ahikar myth occurred after the Christian era, and that the narration in Aramaic by the Jewish sect was incomplete, while the Greek editor of the story of Aesop had a more complete version of Ahikar.[4]

The idea of Aesop as an Ethiopian is derived from the Aesop Romance. The author of this Romance portrayed Aesop's going to Babel and Egypt: resolving problems for the King of Babylon and taking tribute from the king of Egypt in favor of the Babylonian king, which were derived

---

[4] The part regarding Aesop going to Egypt is found in The Aesop Romance, which is also known under the name of Vita or The Life of Aesop or The Book of Xanthus the Philosopher and Aesop His Slave, and dates back to the first or second century A.D.

---

from the Ahikar story. It seems that the author of the Aesop Romance in the first century benefited from a previous Greek translation of the story of Ahikar.[807]

As I previously mentioned, Conybeare maintains that the Jewish myth of Ahikar was transferred through Greek writers to the Aesop myth.

Versions of the story of Ahikar

There are versions of the Ahikar story that we find in different Middle Eastern and European languages. The following are the most important of these versions.

The Arabic version

Many scholars believe that the Arabic version was translated directly from the Syriac. The Catholic encyclopedia gives some proofs for this, such as some Syriac terms that are still extant in the Arabic version. The Armenian version also came from the Syriac.

The Arabic version is seen in manuscripts which now exist in Berlin, Copenhagen, Paris, London, Rome, and Gotha.[808] The Arabian One Thousand Nights also contains a version of the story of Ahikar. The Arabic manuscripts which were written in Arabic letters are few. Most of them were written in the Syriac letters known by the name of al Karshuni (Arabic writings in Syriac letters). This kind of writing was mainly adopted by the Maronites and Syriacs. Without a doubt, these writings were translated from the Syriac. The translators, who had especial knowledge of the Old and New Testament, left many Syriac terms in the translated material.[809]

The Syriac version

The Syriac version is very old and dates back to the first centuries after Christ. Today we possess a Syriac version that came from manuscripts or parts of manuscripts which are kept in Berlin, Cambridge, London, Urmia and in a monastery near Mosul (Iraq).[810] Leonhard Rost wrote:

> The Christian features that appear in the proverbial material at the end of the Syriac recension probably represent the final stage of development; thus the Syriac recension must be dated in the Christian Era, possibly in the second century.[811]

We find many of the Syriac proverbs of Ahikar appearing in the Arabic proverbs, and in proverbs attributed to Luqman. This proves that the Syriac version dates prior to Islam, and that the today's Syriac versions depended on the old Syriac versions dating back prior to Islam. There are other proofs that confirm the antiquity of the Syriac version. Here I present an example: after Ahikar had fettered his nephew, he said to him the following proverb:

> A snare or trap was erected in a muck-heap. Then came a bird, which after seeing the trap said to it: 'what are you doing here?' the trap answered: 'I am praying.' The bird asked 'What is this that is in your mouth?' the trap answered: 'It is bread for the guests.' The bird came closer to it and flipped from the bread. The trap entrapped on him and caught hold of him. The bird said to the trap while jerking: 'If this was your bread for the guest, I do supplication to God to whom you pray that he will not answer to your prayers.'[812]

The same proverb was repeated by Wahab bin Munabbeh, as we see it in the book of al Aqd al Farid:

> One man of the people of Israel erected a trap. A bird came closer and said to the trap: why do I see you bent? The trap answered: 'Because of my fasting, my bones appeared.' The bird asked 'what is this grain in your hand?' the trap answered: 'This is an offering I would give to a poor that would pass.' The bird said: 'I am poor.' The trap answered: 'Then take it.' The bird took hold of the grain, thus, the trap caught hold of its neck. And the bird said: 'From now on I will not be deceived by a hypocrite monk.'[813]

Without a doubt, the form of the proverb as reported by Wahab bin Munabbeh was put in Wahab's language and based on what he could remember of the original proverb. The essence of the proverb, however, is the same as we see in the Ahikar proverb in the Syriac version. Since, as we will later see, Wahab said that he had read in Sahefet Luqman ten thousand paragraphs, this is a proof that he read from Sahefet Ahikar, which we read in the Syriac version. This demonstrates that there existed an Arabic version of Ahikar, and that Sahifet Luqman expressed it or contained it. Today's Syriac version of Ahikar is based on an old Syriac one.

The Syriac versions are old and prior to the 6th century A.D. This is because Sahifet Luqman, which contained the proverbs of Ahikar, as we will later prove, was spread abroad during Mohammed's time. It must have been translated from the Syriac.

Attention should be given to the fact that many of Ahikar's proverbs were added during the Christian era. We see some proverbs containing words such as the deadly sin, eternal happiness, and the kingdom of heaven etc. We understand that those proverbs spread before Mohammed.

We can also see that many of the proverbs in the Syriac version are identical to the Aramaic proverbs that date back to the fifth century B.C. Some proverbs, however, present differences with the Aramaic version due to translation and additions made by the Syriacs. There are proverbs in the Syriac version which are virtually identical to the Aramaic of Ahikar that dates back to the fifth century B.C. This proves the antiquity of the Syriac proverbs of Ahikar and that they have a date from the second century A.D, as I previously mentioned.

The Armenian version

Scholars such as Leonhard Rost believe the Armenian version dates back to 450 A.D. It is extant in many manuscripts that are in Edshmiatsin, Oxford, Paris and Venice.[814] As for the proverbs, they are similar to most of the other versions, but they are abbreviated in the Armenian version.[815]

Before the discovery of the Aramaic version, the story of Ahikar was known in the One Thousand Arabian nights and in India as well.[816]

The Aramaic version of Ahikar in the fifth century B.C.

The oldest version of Ahikar and his proverbs dates back to the fifth century B.C. and was found by a German archeological expedition between 1906-1908 during the excavation on al Filah island near Aswan in southern Egypt. It was written on eleven papyrus tablets that belonged to a Jewish colony. The story of Ahikar is contained between the 40th and 50th tablets.

These Aramaic manuscripts belong to the period when the Persians dominated Egypt. Some of them date back to a period later than 300 B.C.[817] The Jewish sect did not use the Hebrew language during that period, choosing instead to use Aramaic as the language of communication, courts and commerce[818] until the Ptolemaic times, when it was replaced by the Greek language. The Jews in the colony called themselves the "Jewish brigade." when the Persians took over in Egypt, these mercenaries worked for the Persian king.[819]

The author of the Letter of Aristeas, which dates back to the second century B.C., mentions Psammetichus, a title given to three pharaohs from the 26th dynasty, using Jewish mercenaries against Ethiopia. If this is the same Psammetichus of whom Herodotus wrote then the employment of the Jews would be dated to between 595-590 B.C. Later, the Jews were placed in al Fialeh and Syene to defend the Egyptian border with Ethiopia. When. Cambyses came to Egypt in 525 B.C., these Jews were already in al Fialeh.[820] They had developed into a society that had rights such as buying land.[821]

Regarding their worship, they worshiped the God Yahweh but had other gods as well. Cowley said that the description of the prophet Jeremiah regarding the foreign worship which the Jews adopted in his time, continued to exist among the Jews in Egypt for a lengthy period of time. We find the same tendency among the Jews of this colony after one century.[822] This confirms the veracity of the word of God historically; in fact, God had condemned the Jews in Jeremiah's time because of the paganism that had spread among them, even though they continued to claim to venerate Yahweh, God's name in the Old Testament.

The factors in favor of the Jewish origin of myth, and the Persian influence

The name Ahikar is found in the Babylonian Talmud. The name Achish, of which Ahikar -according to the myth- called himself when he went to Egypt, is a Hebrew name. Achish is recorded in the Old Testament as being the king of Gath, where David fled from King Saul (I Sam 21:10).

There are Persian influences on the story, which we would expect since the Jewish author wrote in the 5th century B.C., when the Persians reigned in Egypt. This excludes the possibility that it was originally an Assyrian or Babylonian myth, which preceded the Persian era, that began when Cyrus occupied Babylon in the year 539 B.C. The name of Ahikar's wife is Ishfaghni, which is a Persian name.[823] Nadan, in the original Aramaic is Nadin, the nephew of Ahikar and his adopted son, seems to be a Persian name which means "ignorant or stupid." Anis Frahat says it is a Semitic name, as in Aramaic it means "bestowal or giver"[824] the Persian name, however, seems more probable because it is in accord with the meaning of the story: which is that Nadan, the nephew of Ahikar was ignorant and stupid.

Since the Arabic words used to be written without punctuation, Nadan in pre Islamic myths as the son of Luqman was Taran or Tharan or Naran.[825] This certainly reveals that the Luqman myth was that of Ahikar.

The exact date of the Aramaic papyrus, and the antiquity of the Aramaic writings of the Bible and the book of Proverbs predating it

Cowley says that the Aramaic papyrus was written before 400 B.C. and possibly around 430 B.C. Based on its dialect, the original Aramaic could not have been written prior to the year 668 B.C.[826]

Regarding the antiquity of the Old Testament books, especially the book of Proverbs, over the papyrus tablets of al Fialeh: the papyrus (i) dates back to the year 495 B.C. It must have been written during the reign of Darius I, and is the oldest papyrus of the group. The same is said for papyrus (3). According to Sachau, it contains words similar in spelling to the Old Testament (referring to the few chapters in the Old Testament which were written in Aramaic in the book of Daniel). This papyrus is the oldest among the other papyri of the group. It records an agreement due to a court ruling between two women. The ruling is interesting in that it shows the women both possessed proprieties in their names and went to court.[827]

Since the above papyrus, which has nothing to do with the story of Ahikar, was the oldest, and was closer in its spelling of certain words to the Old Testament book of Daniel, this means that the book of Daniel is much older than the oldest of those manuscripts in this group. Since they verified that this papyrus (that does not contain the story of Ahikar) dates back to 495 B.C., this means that the books of the Old Testament that contain chapters in Aramaic that use a similar dialect are older than this date. Thus, we can date back these Biblical chapters to the time in which the authors, such as Daniel, lived.

There are ten tables of the papyrus that contain the story of Ahikar that are similar to the last papyri in the group. The story is not complete in these papyri. Cowley says that these papyri which contain the story of Ahikar date back to the last part of the fifth century. This is the oldest writing about wisdom outside of the Old Testament.[828] It is clear that the books of the Old Testament that contain wisdom, such as the book of Proverbs and Ecclesiastes, are older than these tablets.

The scholar, Cowley, admits that the name of Assyria is written in these papyri as found in the various Targums, which are of a late date in comparison to the canonical books of the Old Testament. The word is written as we find it in the ancient Assyrian writings such as Sinjirli inscriptions that date back to 850 B.C.[829]

Regarding the book of Proverbs, many of them were authored by Solomon himself in the 10th century B.C. Solomon was known for his wisdom to such an extent that kings of the earth came from near and far to hear his wisdom. We read in I Kings:

> And men of all nations, from all the kings of the earth who had heard of his wisdom, came to hear the wisdom of Solomon. (I Kings 4:34)

The queen of Saba came from Yemen to Jerusalem in order to listen to Solomon's wisdom. With so many heads of state coming to learn from him, it is logical that Solomon would have recorded some of his proverbs during his lifetime.

Cowley states that there are Babylonian proverbs which are similar to Ahikar's proverbs, and that some of the Ahikar proverbs are of Babylonian origin rather than Persian.[830] Having been deported to Babylon, some of the Jews would have had knowledge of the Babylonian education and proverbs.

The Assyrian epoch for the story is excluded

The book of Ahikar mentions King Sennacherib and his son Esarhaddon. We know that Sennacherib succeeded his father Sargon in 705 B.C. and his son Esarhaddon reigned after him. Esarhaddon defeated the Egyptian army in 670 B.C.

There are some Assyrian names in the story, such as the names of the two boys who were made to mount the eagle. Also, Nabu Zaradan, the brother of Nadan, as an Assyrian name means the god Nabu gave progeny. Yet, the mere mention of these names does not by themselves prove that the story was Assyrian. The Jewish author must have been acquainted with the Assyrian names of his time, since they were a known people in the area of the Middle East. Wanting the story to be Assyrian, the author intentionally inserted some Assyrian names into the account. The greatest evidence against the myth being of Assyrian origin is that there is no mention or hint about it in Assyrian or Babylonian writings. If the story were of Assyrian origin, it should have been known to the Assyrians and Babylonians instead of only existing in a text prior to the Christian era that came from the Jews of a distant place near Aswan in southern Egypt. We see this name Ahikar in the Talmud and some Greek writings, but not in Assyrian and Babylonian writings.

Cowley said that we do not need to put the story in the Assyrian epoch because it was born in the Persian epoch. We also do not see the name of Nineveh or Babel in the writing. Cowley added that the language of the Aramaic papyrus is influenced by the Persian.[831]

The story is not real or historical

The Aramaic papyrus makes Ahikar to be a very famous personality, to the extent that Esarhaddon says "let Ahikar live long, he is the wise scribe, councilor of all Assyrian kingdom," as if he were a famous personality during the reigns of Sennacherib and Esarhaddon. The kings of the earth took consideration of Ahikar and feared his wisdom to such an extent that when Pharaoh heard of the death of Ahikar, he reportedly challenged the king of Assyria. We do not see, however, any trace of this throughout history.

The text in the Aramaic papyrus

The Aramaic narration is incomplete and does not contain the journey of Ahikar to Egypt. Here we see a summary of the Aramaic text:

Ahikar had become great and had been the counsellor of all Assyria and bearer of the seal of Sennacherib, king of Assyria. When Ahikar became old he asked Esarhaddon, who succeeded his father Senacherib, to place his adopted nephew Nadin in his place as counselor to the king. Ahikar had taught Nadin in wisdom and Esarhaddon praised Ahikar for this decision and appointed Nadin to be his counselor. Ahikar then returned to his house. Nadin, however, plotted against Ahikar, saying to Esarhaddon that Ahikar corrupted Assyria making the land against the king. The king became infuriated and called for Nabusumiskun, ordering him to go with men and kill Ahikar. But Ahikar said to him:

> I am that Ahikar who formerly saved you from an undeserved death, when Sennacherib the father of this Esarhaddon, the king, was angry with you to kill you. Then I took you to my house... and I hid you from him. I said, 'I have killed him,' until when after time and many days after, I brought you before King Sennacherib and took away your offences before him, and he did you no evil. Moreover King Sennacherib was well pleased with me that I had kept you alive and had not killed you. Now according as I did to you, so do also to me. Do not kill me. Take

me to your house until other days. King Esarhaddon is as kind as any man. Hereafter he will remember me and desire my counsel. Then you shall bring me to him and he shall let me live.' Then answered Nabusumiskun the officer and said to me, 'Fear not. Surely you shall live.'

Nabusumiskun heard Ahikar's supplication. He ordered two of his assistants to kill a slave, a eunuch of his, instead of Ahikar so that when the king would send to see the body of Ahikar they would show him the slave's cadaver, making the king to believe that the sentence of death was executed on Ahikar.

Nabusumiskun hid Ahikar at his house, giving him food daily. He went and told the king that he had executed the sentence of death on Ahikar. The king inquired of the two men who were with Nabusumiskun about what happened. They said that the thing was as Nabusumiskun had reported.

The story ends here in the Aramaic text. After this follows the proverbs of Ahikar. We find the story completed in other versions where we read that the king of Egypt came to know that Ahikar, who used to give Assyria wisdom, was dead. Thus, he precipitated to present a challenge to the Assyrian king, asking him to send an engineer to build a castle suspended in the air between the sky and earth. If the king of Assyria succeeded in sending a man who would build that castle, the king of Egypt promised to give the king of Assyria a large amount of money every year. In the event the Assyrian king failed, he would present to the Egyptian king a tribute. Hearing this, King Esarhaddon regretted killing Ahikar. At this point, Nabusumiskun revealed the secret that Ahikar is alive. Upon hearing this news, the king rejoiced and ordered them to bring Ahikar, and appointed him again to his position.

Ahikar trained two boys to mount an eagle that carried them in flight. He brought them to Egypt and said to the king of Egypt that he was ready to build a castle in the air. He made the eagle to fly carrying the two boys. As instructed previously by Ahikar, the two boys cried with a loud voice: give us stones and brick, because we are ready to begin building. The king of Egypt knew that he lost the round. He knew that this man who prevailed in the challenge was none else but Ahikar. He made him to carry tribute to the king of Assyria. Ahikar asked the king to take Nadin and fetter him. The proverbs were told from Ahikar to Nadin as rebuke and judgment. This is before Nadin died.

Similarities between the characteristics of Ahikar and the description of Luqman by the pre-Islamic Jahiliyyah people

We know that Luqman was Ahikar. The Arabians called him Luqman, after the main characteristic of Ahikar: that is through his wisdom to talk down and debunk the adversary. The word Luqman in ancient Arabic means to prevail against the adversary and silence him. This we see through Lisan al Arab, an ancient dictionary authored by ibn Manthur:

> Reported by abu Turab: 'I heard Arram saying a man who is Laqim is the man who prevailed over the adversary.[832]

Luqman is derived from the root word "laqim," meaning a man who prevails against a challenger. This is also a characteristic of Ahikar, who always prevailed through his wisdom against his challengers. How was the word developed from laqim to Luqman? Ibn Manthur shows how some roots developed as names or adjectives. He gave as an example how the word قمد qamad, which means lion in ancient Arabic, became Qumdan, meaning a strong man like the lion. Thus, we can understand that as Qumdan is derived from qamad, so Luqman is derived from laqim.[833] Ibn Manthur also wrote: laqam means to shut the other mouth.[834] It is an expression in Arabic that means to prevail against him in wisdom silencing him. This ability to silence the foes through his wisdom is actually a characteristic of Ahikar. Since the Arabians assigned foreign names according to their characteristic, they referred to Ahikar as Luqman, because he prevailed in his wisdom against his foes.

Jawad Ali, the renowned Iraqi scholar, admitted that the wisdom of Luqman is derived from Ahikar, and that the pre-Islamic Jahiliyyah people had put Ahikar into their own language as Luqman. In fact, we find in the wisdom or proverbs of Ahikar similarities with ancient Arabian wisdom and proverbs, sometimes a genuine translation of Ahikar's proverbs. Jawad Ali gives an example of a famous Arabic proverb, which is taken from the following Ahikar proverb:

> O my son, if you send a wise man to do a task, do not recommend too much, since he fulfill your need as you desire. Do not send a stupid one, but go yourself and perform your need.[835]

If you study the rest of his wisdom and proverbs, and what was attributed to the pre-Islamic people, we find great similarity in meaning most of the time in the structure of the sentences. This demonstrates that it was taken from the Syriac version of Ahikar and it was Arabized who attributed it to the Jahiliyyah people. Or that the Jahiliyyah people put the proverbs of Ahikar into their own language. Most of his proverbs are directed to his nephew Nadan, as he warns him saying: O my son.[836]

Among the similarities between Ahikar and Luqman are that both were refused a request they made to the gods, and were directed to an alternative. Ahikar besought the gods for a son, but his request was denied, and he was advised to adopt his nephew and teach him wisdom. Luqman requested immortality from the gods. He was denied this request, but was allowed to choose between living as seven cows or eagles.[837] The Arabians recited proverbs about Luqman. One was by Al 'Aasha, the pre-Islamic poet, who spoke about the eagles and that when the seventh eagle died, Luqman died also.[838]

The name of Ahikar was known to the pre-Islamic Jahiliyyah people as Hikar or al-Hikar. The Arabian poet, Adi bin Zayd, mentions in one of his poems that a plot was schemed against Ahikar. This is actually in accord with the original myth about Ahikar. Luis Shikhu quoted a book of Al Buhturi, the Arabic poet, titled al Hamaseh, known also as Hamaset al Buhturi. In page 86, al Buhturi includes a poem of Adi bin Zayd, in which he speaks about the plot against "Al-Hikar".[839] The Arabic writers were confused about Ahikar's name, claiming he was a king of al Jazirah (a region of northeast of Syria) and sometime as a king of Ethiopia. This is seen in the writings of al feirusabadi, who said:

> He is king of al-Jazirah or king of Ethiopia. His name is al Hikar or al Jifar.[840]

We see then the idea by the Arabians of Ahikar being an Ethiopian, the same nationality was given to Luqman and Aesup. Al Zebeidi verified Al Hikar, whom Adi bin Zayd mentioned, as being the king of Al Jazirah or Ethiopia.[841] Ibn Manthur claimed that Al Hikar was the king of Ethiopia.[842]

Luqman for the Arabians is a resolver of great dilemmas in favor of his master, exactly as Ahikar was, according to the myth, a resolver of the dilemmas of Assyria and its king. It was narrated by Luqman that one day his master was drunk and gambled with some people that he could drink all the water in a lake. When he woke up from his drunken state, he perceived the gravity into which he fell. He called for Luqman and said to him: "it is for such a time that I have kept you." Luqman then told his master: "call those people with whom you had this challenge." When they were all gathered together, Luqman asked them, "on what have you wagered with him?" They said: "That he drinks the waters of this lake." Luqman said, "This lake has other material than the water. First separate all these materials." They asked, "how can we could do this?" Luqman answered them, "how could he drink it when it has other material?!'[843]

We notice the statement by Luqman's master "for such moments I have kept you" actually expresses the dilemma of the Assyrian king when Pharaoh had challenged him. The king said, "it was Ahikar for such moments as savior." These words encouraged the man who kept Ahikar hidden in his house to reveal that Ahikar was still alive and was being kept in his house.

Luqman commends his son or tells proverbs to exhort his son, exactly as Ahikar teaches his nephew whom he adopted. This we find, for example, in a poet of the al Saltan al Saadi.[844]

Similarities between Nadan, Ahikar's nephew whom he adopted, and Luqman's son

There are other important facts that proves that Luqman in Arabia was no else but Ahikar, the mythological figure as we have seen. Luqman's son was the same rhyme of Nadan, Ahikar's son, and very close to it. We read about Luqman' son name:

His son name paran and it said was Daran."[845] There are others who say Tharan or Mathan.[846]

The closest name of Luqman's son to Ahikar's son we find in al Ruth and Unf, authored by al Suhaili, and Hayat al Haiwan authored by al Dumeiri, where the name is Tharan or Naran.[847] The old Arabic writing was without punctuation, the letter "Ra" that is "r" was very similar to the letter "dal" that is "d." that is why the Arabians read Nadan as Naran.

Wahab bin Munabbeh mentioned that he read ten thousand words (in another source he said paragraphs) in the wisdom of Luqman, and that Luqman commended his son. We notice that Wahab, who studied Sahifet Luqman, said that Luqman's son was Mathan. This is without a doubt, due to a mistranslation or mistake in copying, or that Wahab could not remember the exact name. This suggests, however, that Sahifet Luqman was the wisdom of Ahikar translated into Arabic, and that Ahikar was given another name, that is Luqman. Al Maqdisi wrote:

Wahab had mentioned that he studied ten thousand words from the
wisdom (of Luqman) and that these proverbs were used in their
sermons and instructions. Luqman continued to preach to his son
Mathan until his son's heart failed and died.[848]

Luqman was like Ahikar without children. Ibn Kathir wrote:

Luqman got married and were born to him children but they all died.[849]

The name of Luqman's son in the pre-Islamic poetry is Luqim.[850] The
pre-Islamic poetry mentions that Luqman's son is also his nephew (son of
his sister) by this repetition of the myth of Ahikar where Ahikar adopted his
nephew. But the Arabians, instead of adoption they presented another
form: al Midani quotes the poet al Nimer bin Taulib, and narrates the story
that Luqman's sister slept with him by a trick:

His sister loved a weak man. She wanted to have a son like her brother
Luqman in intelligence and sagacity. She said to Luqman's wife, 'my
husband is weak, and I am afraid that my progeny come weak because
of him. Please borrow me to sleep in my brother's bed for this night.'
She did … this story was mentioned in a poem of Nimer bin Taulib. He
said: Luqim son of Luqman from his sister. He was his nephew and his
son. It was a stupid night that he was not aware of. He made her
pregnant. And she gave birth to a wise man. [851]

Ibn Manthur also wrote about Luqim that he was Luqman's nephew
and at the same time his son. He quotes the poem of Nimer bin Taulib
explaining how it occurred. [852] We see in the writings of al Baghdadi,
quoting al Aini, about the birth of Luqman's son, which is closer to the
myth of Ahikar. It says that Luqman did not have a son. He was a great,
powerful and wise man. His wife proposed to his sister to dress herself with
her clothes so that he may sleep with her in darkness.[853] This version is
closer to the Ahikar story, which indicates that the Arabian had taken from
the Ahikar myth: that Ahikar was without a son and was a great man who
adopted his sister's son. The pre-Islamic Arabian poets were not familiar
with the idea of adoption. Therefore, they could not reconcile between how
Ahikar's son is his son and at the same time be his nephew. Thus, they
created the story of Ahikar's sister sleeping with her brother and giving birth
to a son.

The envy of Ahikar's son of Ahikar and his tentative desire to get rid of him is inverted in the Arabian culture, where we see Luqman tried to kill his son

The pre-Islamic Arabian mythology borrowed from the story of Ahikar, but inverted it in the other direction. Instead of the nephew of Ahikar resisting Ahikar, as we see in the story of Ahikar, and that Ahikar adopted his nephew and taught him wisdom; the Arabian mythology made Luqman's sister to sleep with him in order for her to give birth to a wise son called Luqim. He became Luqman's son and travelled in his company. Instead of Ahikar's son to envying his father, the pre-Islamic mythology says that Luqman envied Luqim and tried to kill him. We can see, however, that the story is the original one, and that the pre-Islamic Luqman is Ahikar. Al Midani narrates about Luqman persecuting Luqim, and quotes the poet Khufaf bin Nudbeh:

> Luqman's daughter name was Sakhr. Her father Luqman and her brother Luqim went to plunder. They captured many camels. Sakhr killed of the camels that Luqim captured and prepared a meal for her father. Luqman came, and he was jealous of Luqim, when he knew that the meal was Luqim's camel, he gave her a strike that killed her. It became an example for the one who is punished without fault. Khufaf bin Nudbeh recited in his poem about Sakhr who was punished without fault.[854]

Contrary to the myth of Ahikar, we see Luqman persecuting, beating and behaving in stupidly in his house. In the Ahikar myth we find Nadan beating Ahikar's wife and the servants and behaving in stupidity. Ibn Manthur narrated that Luqman schemed to kill Luqim.[855]

There are other Arabian writings, however, that state Luqim schemed plots against Luqman, something that agrees with the Ahikar myth. Al Jaheth wrote: "Luqim schemed against Luqman son of Ad."[856] Al Bagdadi wrote:

> Luqim, the son of Luqman from his sister, left the right path and behaved contrary to the right one without opportunity (he meant with no reason to justify his behavior).[857]

In the proverbs of Luqman to his son we read:

> Luqman the wise said to his son rebuking him: 'when his arm was strengthened he threw me.' It is said for the one who hurts you, whereas, you did good to him.[858]

The above proverb reflects the proverbs of Ahikar to his son who when he was strengthened overthrew Ahikar, and schemed a plot against him to get rid of him. We find this proverb in the Aramaic proverbs of Ahikar that date back to the fifth century B.C.

Sahifeh or Majallah of Luqman

The meaning of Sahifeh or Majallah

Sahifeh is Majallah, or a book that contains wisdom. This we see in the famous Arabic dictionary called Taj al Arus:

> Al Majallah is the sahifeh that contains wisdom. Every book for the Arabian is majallah.[859]

Al Zamkhari mentioned the encounter of Mohammed with Suwaid bin al Samet, when Suyed showed Majallah of Luqmqn to Mohammed:

> Suwaid bin al Samet came to Mecca. The apostle of Allah called him to Islam. Suwaid answered: 'is the source that you have as mine?' the apostle of Allah answered 'what do you have." Suwaid said: 'Majallah of Luqman.' Every book of wisdom for the Arabians is Majallah. The poet al Nabigha said: "their Majallah is their religion.[860]

Thus, the Majallah of Luqman that was displayed to Mohammed was a book of wisdom that contains proverbs of wisdom. Al Zubeidi wrote:

> Majallah is sahifeh that contains wisdom.[861]

Majallah is a well-known word referring to pre-Islamic people. In addition to being connected with Majallah of Luqman, it was used in expressing the books of the Bible. It came in a poem of al Nabigheh, which we have seen was a sacred religious book. Thus, when using it for sahifeh of Luqman, the term Majallah is intended to show that it was a sacred book for the pre-Islamic Arabians, on a par with the books of the Bible.

Khashu wrote on the meaning of Sahifeh or Majallah and its Syriac origin. And that the books inspired by God were called Majallah or sahifeh. He quotes the poet Emriul Qeis: "as the writings of psalms in the Masahif (plural of sahifeh) of monks." Khashu said that the Arabians called the sacred books Majallah. He quoted the poem of al Nabigheh, which I already mentioned. Khashu maintains that the word Mushaf is derived from Suhuf (plural of Mushaf) which means "book" is an Ethiopian word and its root is Syriac.[862]

Thus, Sahifah of Luqman was viewed by many groups as a book inspired by God. That is why Mohammed adopted some of its proverbs into the Quran. Ibn Manthur and ibn Athir said that Majallah of Luqman was translated from Hebrew into Arabic.[863]

Sahifah of Luqman as the book of wisdom spread at the time of Mohammed

Ibn Kathir wrote that there was a book called the wisdom of Luqman. Here are the words of ibn Kathir:

> Many of Luqman's news and preaching were spread. He had a book that was a source, the book is called wisdom of Luqman.[864]

Ibn Kathir had included in his writings many proverbs that existed in the book of Luqman wisdom. We see then that Majallah of Luqman or the book or sahifeh of Luqman was known to the Arabians. It was also called "wisdom of Luqman." This was without a doubt, the wisdom of Ahikar, which was known to many in Mohammed's time. In an occasion reported in the book of al Bukhari, a companion of Mohammed mentioned a Hadith of Mohammed about bashfulness. Then Bashir bin Kaab, mentioned that there was in Sahifah of wisdom about bashfulness:

> Umran bin Husein حُصَـيْن said: the prophet said: 'bashfulness brings goodness.' Bashir bin Kaab said 'it is written in the Wisdom that bashfulness is dignity and peacefulness.' Omar said: I speak to you about the apostle of Allah, and you talk to me about your Sahifeh?!'[865]

Omar was angry because Bashir bin Kaab revealed that the source of that Hadith was from Sahifeh of wisdom, which was in his time. The important thing is that what Bashir quoted was known as Luqman's proverbs. We read in the Tabaqat al Kubri of ibn Saad:

> It is written in the stories of Luqman that some of the bashfulness is weakness and some is a dignity of Allah.[866]

This is an indication that Sahifeh of wisdom which was known to some of Mohammed's companions was none else but Sahifeh of Luqman, from which Mohammed drew many of his Hadiths, and adopted some into Surah Luqman. It is known that bashfulness is one of the subjects which the wisdom of Ahikar dealt with, as we see in the 14th proverb of the Ahikar Syriac version, Ahikar commending his son:

> My son, do not even eat the bread with the one who lacks bashfulness.

Regarding the existence of a book in pre-Islamic Arabia called al-Hikmah (wisdom) that contains proverbs of Luqman, we find that ibn Kathir speaks of a book called al-Hikmah (wisdom), from which he quotes many proverbs of Luqman.[867]

Wahab bin Munabbeh and Sahifeh of Luqman

Mohammed was not the only person who used Majallah or Sahifeh Luqman. Wahab bin Munabbeh said that he read ten thousand paragraphs from the book of the wisdom of Luqman. And that Luqman's words became part of the saying of others:

> I read from the wisdom of Luqman about ten thousand paragraphs. People never heard better sayings. I saw that people adopted these sayings in their. They used them in their preaching and messages. They became part of their eloquence and rhetoric.[868]

Wahab bin Munabbeh was born in the year 34 H. close to the time of Mohammed. He used to read the sahifeh of Luqman, which was spread in Mohammed's time. This tells us how widespread it was among the Arabians. Since Wahab bin Munabbeh had read thousands of proverbs of Sahifeh of Luqman, we see him quoting several proverbs of Luqman, as recorded by the Arabic narrators.

Sahifeh of Luqman was known to others, including Ahnaf group and Umayyah bin Abi al Salat

Jawad Ali writes that the Ahnaf group used to consult the books, the psalms, suhuf (religions sacred books) and Majallah of Luqman.[869] In fact, the Ahnaf group used to read religious books, and religion's sacred books which were available in their times; mostly Gnostic, Manichaean, Sabian and non-canonical Jewish books such as the Apocrypha, and the proverbs of Ahikar. Sahifeh of Luqman contained many myths, as we know from a Hadith of Mohammed reported in the book of Taberi (which I am going to discuss later). It was an important reference for Ahnaf, as if it was inspired by Allah. This is the secret behind Mohammed's attachment to it and his quoting of Luqman, because its teaching and myths were spread in his time and very much esteemed.

It was confirmed by many scholars that Umayyah bin Abi al Salt consulted this Sahifeh or Majallah of Luqman, which contained proverbs and ancient stories. Mohammed consulted the same source. Of these scholars I mention Friedrich Schulthetz, the publisher of the poetry of Umayyah bin Abi al Salt,[870] that showed Mohammed drawing from this source from which Umayyah took many of his doctrines that existed prior to Mohammed. Without a doubt, it is the same Majallah of Luqman.

There were books that Mohammed's companions possessed that instructed people how to treat disease through al Kai. Al kai was an ancient way of treating patients by causing a mild burning on the pain spot. Sahih al Bukhari mentioned about a book written about the use of al Kai as medical treatment. Luqman too had instruction on the importance of al Kai in treating patients. Al Zamkhari reported a saying of Luqman that says:

If the disease is resistant to every medicine then, it must be settled with al Kai. This is what Luqman son of Ad said.[871]

Al Zamkhashri said:

Luqman said: the last resort of treatment is al Kai.[872]

Al Maidani mentioned that Luqman said that the last resort in treatment is Kai. He made it as proverb.[873] There were healthy advices from Luqman to his son, mentioned by al Dainuri.[874] These things make us to suppose that Sahifeh of Luqman also contained instructions on treatments, and that the book mentioned by Sahih al Bukhari was Sahifeh of Luqman.

Sahifeh of Luqman remained as a source which the Arabians returned to consult for many consequent generations. There were proverbs and wisdom of Luqman existing in a sahifeh or book in which ibn Qutaibeh read. Ibn Qutaibeh was born 213 H., equal to 828 A.D. This explains how Ibn Qutaibeh's book is full of Luqman's proverbs.

Verification of Majallah(or Sahifeh) of Luqman as being based on the book or wisdom of Ahikar

This is what demonstrates that Majallah(or Sahifeh) of Luqman was nothing else but the book of Ahikar. Al Maqdisi speaks about Wahab bin Munabbeh saying that he read 10,000 words from the wisdom of Luqman, in which Luqman exhorted his son Mathan. Mathan is a name close to Nadan, the nephew of Ahikar whom he adopted. This indicates that Sahifeh of Luqman was a version of the book of Ahikar. Again, al Maqdisi said:

Wahab had mentioned that he studied ten thousand words from the wisdom (of Luqman) and that these proverbs were used in their sermons and instructions. Luqman continued to preach to his son Mathan until his son's heart failed and died.[875]

It is the same idea we encounter in the Ahikar book that Ahikar continued to preach to his son until his son's heart failed and he died. When we compare the Wahab sayings which he derived from Majallah regarding Luqman with the sayings of Ahikar, we confirm that Luqman's majaleh was the book or wisdom of Ahikar. I previously mentioned in the Syriac version of Ahikar the story of the trap or snare and the bird,[876] something Wahab bin Munabbeh had also mentioned.[877] Since Wahab said that he read in the Sahifeh of Luqman thousands of proverbs, this is a confirmation that he read from the same book that we read today in the Syriac version of Ahikar; proving that there was an Arabic version of Ahikar, which sahifeh of Luqman represented or contained.

In comparison between Luqman's proverbs with Ahikar's proverbs, I found a great similarity. The differences are mild, and were due to translation. As an example, both ibn Kathir and al Thaalabi mentioned a Luqman proverb against lying:

My son, be aware of lie. It is delicious like the meat of bird, but the liar quickly eats?[878]

This is derived from number 23 Syriac proverb of Ahikar:

My son, the words of liar like the fat birds, they are eaten by the one without wisdom.

There is a Luqman proverb identical to an Ahikar proverb with little difference caused by translation:

The father beating his son is like rain to the sowing. His son's name is Tharan.[879]

We notice that Luqman's son here is Tharan. Since there was no punctuation in Arabic, and the letter (tha) was written as letter (Nun) that is (N), thus, Naran was read as Tharan. The letter (d) in Arabic is written close to (r), we can understand how the Arabians wrote Nadan as Tharan.

The previous Luqman proverb is quoted by al Dainuri as follows:

From the wisdom of Luqman. Luqman said: beating the father his son is like compost to the sowing.[880]

We see the same proverb in the Syriac version of Ahikar, proverb number 20:

My son, do not refuse to give correction to your son, because beating a child is like the compost to the garden.

We notice that the Luqman proverbs reads "beating the child is like compost to the sowing," whereas, the Ahikar proverb reads "like the compost to the garden." It is the same proverb. Moreover, the use of the compost to the sowing is more familiar to the Arabians than the compost of a garden, since there were few gardens in Arabia.

Among the principles in common between the proverbs of Luqman and Ahikar is advice in Luqman's sayings to not oppose the man in authority, and not to come close to him when he is angry:

My son, do not come close to the sovereign or man in authority when he is angry. And to the river when it outspreads."[881] Also "my son, do not come close to the sovereign when he is angry and to the sea when it outspreads.[882]

We see the same proverb in the Syriac, Ahikar proverbs number 63. The difference is small and was due to translation:

My son do not contend with a man in time of his glory and authority, and do not stand against the river when it spreads out.

We see in the words of Ahikar from the Aramaic version a similar principle:

Also the word of a king is with wrath of heart. Why should wood strive with fire, flesh with a knife, a man with a king?

Al Thaalabi mentioned Luqman's proverb:[883]

Do not entrust a man on a secret.[884]

Al Dumairi reported a Luqman proverb that explains the importance of hiding the secret:

Concealing secret is keeping reputation or fame.[885]

The same proverb, we find in the Aramaic Ahikar, which dates back to the fifth century B.C.:

Thy secrets reveal not before thy friends, that thy name be not lightly esteemed before them.[886]

This means do not reveal your secrets in order to not lose your reputation with your friends. Thus, it is the same proverb, with a little change occurring because of the translation from Aramaic to Syrian, then perhaps to Hebrew then to Arabic.

The Syriac proverb number 50 of Ahikar is quite similar:

My son, it is better for you to conceal the secret in your heart. Because when you disclose it you lose your friend.

Al Dumari mentioned a Luqman proverb in which Luqman commended his son to not send an ignorant messenger in the event there is no wise messenger to go himself:

My son, do not dispatch an ignorant messenger. If you do not find a wise one, be your own messenger.[887]

This is identical to proverb 39 of the Ahikar Syriac version:

My son, dispatch a wise messenger and do not commend him. Instead of sending an ignorant messenger, go yourself.

We find another proverb with the same meaning in the Syriac version of Ahikar:

My son, if you send the wise in doing a task do not commend him too much, because he will do the job as you require. Do not send the stupid, but go yourself and fulfill your need.[888]

Mohammed's uncle, al Zubeir bin Abdel Mutaleb, was acquainted with this Ahikar proverb that was attributed to Luqman. Al Zubeir recited: "Send a wise messenger and do not commend him." This we read in the book Jamhart al Amthal:

The following proverb is for al Zubeir bin Abdel Mutaleb, in his known stanza:

If you need to send a messenger, send a wise messenger and do not commend him.[889]

There are many proverbs of Luqman that are similar to Ahikar's proverbs. I will limit myself, however, to mention some proverbs that are identical in both. One proverb of Luqman reads:

My son, do not be sweet, lest you are swallowed up. Nor bitter lest you are spit out.[890]

The same proverb we find in Aramaic Ahikar proverbs dating back to the fifth century B.C.:

Be not sweet lest they swallow thee up. Be not bitter, lest they spit thee out.[891]

There is a proverb against debt that we find in Luqman, Syriac of Ahikar, and Aramaic of Ahikar from the fifth century B.C. Al Thaalabi reports the following proverb of Luqman:

It was narrated that Luqman said to his son: my son I have lifted rocks and carried iron, and there is nothing which is heavier than debt.[892]

The same proverb is number 43 in the Syriac Ahikar version:

My son I have lifted salt and carried lead, and there is nothing which is heavier for a man than paying debt that he did not borrow.

The following Aramaic proverb of Ahikar is closer to the Luqman proverb:

I have lifted sand and carried salt, and there is nothing which is heavier than debt.[893]

The above is a further proof that the text of Luqman was translated from Aramaic, perhaps through the Hebrew or sometime from Syriac. And the Syriac was translated from the Aramaic. It is easy to notice the similarity, in spite of mild differences because of translations.

There is a commonality in both Luqman and Ahikar's proverbs regarding poverty:

Luqman said to his son: "I have tasted even the bitter fruit or plant, but there is nothing which is more bitter than poverty.[894]

We read also in the book of Dumeiri, called Hayat al Haiwan al Kubra, the following proverb:

Luqman said to his son: "I have tasted all kinds of bitter, but there is nothing which is more bitter than poverty.[895]

Al Abshihi reported a similar proverb of Luqman:

Luqman said to his son: "I have tasted bitter al Hanthel (a bitter plant), but there is nothing which is more bitter than poverty.[896]

The same proverb of Luqman is identical to the Aramaic, which dates back to the fifth century B.C.:

I have tasted even the bitter sloe, and the taste was strong, but there is nothing which is more bitter than poverty.[897]

The proverbs that made the animals to talk are similar in both the Luqman and Ahikar proverbs

The differences are due to changing the type of animal speaking according to the environment of Arabia. For example, there is a proverb in the Syriac version of Ahikar:

> My son, you were for me as the serpent which mounted a bramble and were thrown in the river. A wolf saw them and said to them: 'a wickedness had mounted a wickedness.' More wicked than they is the wickedness (the river) that leads them.[898]

Luqman spoke about two serpents that were fighting each other. A third serpent came and was reconciling them. A man who saw this incident said to the third serpent: "unless you had been more wicked than they, you should not have succeeded in reconciling them."[899]

The usual correspondence between the Luqman and Ahikar proverbs (whether in the Syriac or Aramaic versions) is a proof that Sahifet Luqman was nothing else but a book of the wisdom of Ahikar; and that Luqman was Ahikar, whom the Arabians gave the name of Luqman.

Mohammed and Sahifat Luqman

Analyzing the encounter between Mohammed and Suwaid bin Samet regarding Sahifat Luqman

There was an occasion where a copy of Sahifat Luqman was presented to Mohammed during his encounter with Suwaid bin Samet, as recorded in the books that narrated the life of Mohammed, such as ibn Hisham and al Halabieh. Among the persons Mohammed showed special concern for was Suwaid bin Samet. Suwaid was from the tribe of Aws, and a cousin of Abdel Muttalib, Mohammed's grandfather from his mother's side. "Suwaid's mother was the sister of Salma, Abdel Muttalib's mother"[900] and he was known for his poetry and patience.[901] We read about this encounter:

> When the apostle of Allah heard about him, he called him to embrace Islam. Suwaid answered, 'is the source that you have as mine?' the apostle of Allah answered 'what source do you have.' Suwaid said, 'Majallah of Luqman.' He meant the wisdom of Luqman. The apostle of Allah said: 'show it to me.' Suwaid then presented it to him. Mohammed sadi responded, 'this is good. But what I have is better than this: it is a Quran which Allah inspired to me.'[902]

The question that may come to the mind of the analyzer is why would Suwaid think that Mohammed may had the same book that he had, that is Sahifat of Luqman? Without a doubt, Sahifat of Luqman was spread in Arabia and known to many who claimed to be prophets, who viewed it as material that elevated them over the average people. They incorporated its proverbs into their poetry and rhymed oracles. Suwaid expected Mohammed to partially base his Quran upon this Sahifat. Sahifat of Luqman was consulted by Umayyah bin Abi al Salt who preceded Mohammed in claiming that he was a prophet.

Here are the differences between Suwaid and Mohammed; Suwaid admitted that he relied on this Sahifat in authoring his poems and became a wise poet because of his reading and continually consulting Sahifat of Luqman. We read about him in the writings of Arabic historians, such as ibn Athir:

> He was a benevolent poet, abundant in wise proverbs in his poetry. Because of his poetry wisdom and honor, his people called him 'the perfect.'[903]

Though he received fame because of his wisdom he never hid its source, which was from Sahifat Luqman. But Mohammed claimed to possess something superior to Sahifat Luqman, which contained the wisdom of Luqman. He made this claim despite using some of the same proverbs as the Sahifat in his Quran. According to Muslim Sheiks, his verses that were taken from Sahifat Luqman were the best verses in the Quran. Because of this, how could Mohammed claim that he had something superior to Luqman's wisdom?!

We see Mohammd as a good reader, who is quick to consult some of the proverbs in Luqman's Sahifat, saying "that is good." There are two possibilities for this statement; the first is that when Mohammed came to know this Sahifat for the first time he quickly became aware of its importance as a source to use in his Quran. The second possibility is that he realized the Sahifat was the same one the Ahnaf group used to read, and thus was known to him and became one of his sources. In my earnest opinion the second possibility is probably the correct one. Regardless of which possibility is correct, he did not want to admit to Suwaid that the proverbs of Luqman were one of his sources, so as not to appear as one who was claiming to be prophet in Arabia while, like Umayyah bin Abi al Salt and others, depending on Luqman's sahifeh.

Thus, we see Mohammed in front of a man who knew an important portion of his commodity and sources, and was unable to contradict the importance of this Sahifat; since it was known to the learned people during his time that many of his verses were coming from sources like Sahifat Luqman, which were already widespread among the learned people. That is why he said regarding Luqman Sahifat that it was good. If he had fought it, he would have also had to fight his verses in the Quran that came from the same Sahifat. Instead, he wanted to convince Suwaid that he possessed something superior, meaning above the good which Luqman had, that consisted of "very good" words from other sources. He, in fact, relied on verses he adopted from the Bible, but in a corrupted form in addition to Zoroastrian and Sabian myths, etc. In reality, if a Sabian would have confronted Mohammed over his verses being similar to the Sabian sayings, we would have seen Mohammed praising the Sabian sayings as good. He would not able to alleviate from their importance, since they were incorporated into his Quran. He would have claimed, however, that he possessed something better to present to the Sabian debater, sayings he took from Luqman and others.

Thus, we see Mohammed counterbalancing himself in regard to the people he encountered, and he was forced to admit how much they knew about the source of his myths. He admitted it to the extent he was obliged to admit it in front of persons who knew the sources of his sayings; but he bargained and hid the truth when others ignored or were unaware of the rest of his sources.

Mohammed left for Ali two Sahifats; Luqman Sahifat was most likely one of them

Mohammed had the ability to quote and build Hadiths based on Luqman's sayings, as I will discuss later in this chapter. This ability was due to his possession of a copy of Luqman Sahifat. Ali bin Abi Taleb, Mohammed's son in-law, admitted that Mohammed had left two Sahifats. We read in Sahih Muslim that it is reported by Ibrahim al Taimi that his father said,

> Ali bin Abi Taleb preached to us saying: 'who claimed that we have other books to read except the book of Allah (the Quran) and this Sahifat.' He said, in addition to other Sahifat hanging (suspended) near his sword.[904]

The saying of Ali reveals that the cotemporaries of Mohammed knew that he was a good reader and possessed books, or Suhuf. To the extent that Ali attempted to get rid of the fact that many close to Mohammed were acquainted with Mohammed's dedication in reading, and reliance on forming the Quran from many other books. Thus, Ali admitted to the use of only two other books. Without a doubt, Luqman's Sahifat was one of these two. This is because of Mohammed's relying heavily on Luqman's sayings in forming many of his Hadiths. Furthermore, we find among the saying of Ali some sayings that were attributed to Ahikar, who was Luqman for the Arabians.

Mohammed quoting Luqman's proverbs

Among the things that confirm Mohammed's reading of Luqman Sahifat and his acquaintance with its content is his quoting from Luqman's proverbs. In addition, many of Mohammed's Hadiths are built on Luqman's sayings. For example, in one of his Hadiths, Mohammed quoted this Luqman proverb:

Luqman the wise said: 'if Allah entrusted something, he would keep it.[905]

Other examples include ibn Omar, who said the apostle of Allah told us that Luqman said,

"if Allah entrusted something, he would keep it."[906]

Ibn Kathir mentioned that al Qasem bin Mukhaimarat claimed that the apostle of Allah said, "Luqman said while preaching to his son, O my son, using the mask is a problematic at night, and dispraise during the day."[907]

We see similar phrasing in Luqman's proverbs:

My son, the mask is bad reputation during the day and problematic at night.[908]

Many of Mohammed's Hadiths are dependent on Sahifat Luqman

That Mohammed was a studier of Luqman's sayings which were included in Luqman's Sahitet, is something that becomes evident when reviewing Mohammed's Hadiths. As an example:

> The good Islam of a person is when he leaves the things that do not concern him." This proverb was narrated by the prophet of Allah, who said that Luqman the wise was asked "what is your most secure work?" He replied, "When I leave the things that do not concern me.[909]

A similar proverb is attributed to Luqman, where he says "my son, do not laugh without amazement or ask about things that do not concern you."[910] The thought conveyed in this proverb attributed to Luqman is similar to the third proverb of the Syriac version of Ahikar. Luqman advised that in some cases a person should walk quickly rather than slowly.[911] Mohammed gave the same advice to his followers.[912]

The idea of whipping a slave is found in Ahikar's proverbs. The Aramaic proverbs of Ahikar records that "A blow for a slave, rebuke for a maid, and for all thy servants discipline. A man who buys a licentious slave (or) a thievish maid brings anxiety into his house, and disgraces the name of his father and his offspring with the reputation of his wantonness."[913]

This proverb of Ahikar undoubtedly influenced Mohammed who, as we see from Sahih al Bukhari, prohibited a slave from testifying unless he was first whipped.[914]

There is a proverb of Luqman and Mohammed about the heart and tongue, which they say are the sweetest organs of the body, while at the same time being the most malicious or malignant. (If they are good the body is good, and if they are corrupted the body becomes corrupted.) Al Dumairy wrote:

> Of the wisdom of Luqman that spread: his master gave him a goat to kill and bring the sweetest organs from it. Luqman killed the goat and brought its heart and tongue. The second day he gave him another goat and asked him to bring the most malignant parts. Luqman brought him the heart and tongue. His master asked him about this. 'Luqman answered: these two organs are the sweetest in the goat if they are good. And they are the most malignant if they became bad.' These are the words of the apostle of Allah, 'there is in the body a part. If it became

good all the body becomes good. If it is corrupted, the whole body becomes malignant, that is the heart.[915]

Among the proverbs of Luqman Sahifat quoted by Wahab bin Munabbeh it says "Luqman said to his son: the beneficial richness is that of the soul."[916]

Mohammed in his Hadith repeated the same idea:

The richness is the richness of soul.[917]

There are proverbs about controlling the tongue found in Ahikar, Luqman and Mohammed's sayings. As an example, the proverb 52 of the Syriac version of Ahikar speaks about burying or storing the word:

My son, if you hear a word of malice, bury it into the earth at seven yards depth.

In the Aramaic version of Ahikar we find storing the word or imprisoning it being likened to imprisoning a bird:

My son, do not chatter overmuch till thou reveal every word which comes into thy mind, for in every place are their eyes and their ears; but keep watch over thy mouth, let it not be thy destruction. More than all watchfulness watch thy mouth, and over what thou hearest harden thy heart, for a word is (like) a bird, and when he has sent it forth. A man does not recapture it." Count the secrets of thy mouth, afterwards bring forth (advice) to thy brother for his help, for stronger is the ambush of the mouth than the ambush of fighting.[918]

The idea of either storing the tongue or imprisoning it is also recorded in the saying of Luqman to his son, where he said, "If you keep your secrets well, and where you store your things is secure, then you have succeeded in your life and eternity. He meant the tongue and heart."[919]

This idea, which we see in the sayings of Ahikar and Luqman, we also observe in the Hadith of Mohammed. Consider the following that is "reported by Anas bin Malek, the apostle of Allah who said, "none of you will complete his faith unless he stores his tongue."[920]

Notice that whenever Mohammed's Hadith takes from the Luqman-Ahikar proverbs they are sometimes taken literally, while at other times the idea of Luqman- Ahikar is placed in another form, but still conserves some of its characteristics, such as this saying of "storing the tongue."

The verses of Surah Luqman and their sources

Verse 12: We gave Luqman wisdom, saying: Give thanks unto Allah; and whosoever giveth thanks, he giveth thanks for (the good of) his soul. And whosoever refuseth, Allah is rich and praised.

Verse 13: Luqman said to his son when he was advising him: "O my son! Join not in worship others with Allah. Joining others in worship with Allah is a great wrong.

In the above verses which are attributed to Luqman, he is addressing them to his son. They each repeated the same form of the wisdom of Ahikar, within all the proverbs where Ahikar likewise addressed his son. This demonstrates that Mohammed drew from Luqman Sahifat, which we have already seen was the wisdom of Ahikar:

14- And we have enjoined man in respect of his parents-- his mother bears him with fainting upon fainting and his weaning takes two years-- saying: Be grateful to me and to both your parents; to me is the eventual coming.

The idea of weaning for two or three years is derived from old Jewish customs:

15- And if they contend with you that you should associate with me what you have no knowledge of, do not obey them, and keep company with them in this world kindly, and follow the way of him who turns to me, then to me is your return, then will I inform you of what you did.

The first part of this verse is taken from Deuteronomy chapter 13:

If thy brother, the son of thy mother, or thy son, or thy daughter, or the wife of thy bosom, or thy friend, which is as thine own soul, entice thee secretly, saying, Let us go and serve other gods, which thou hast not known, thou, nor thy fathers; Namely, of the gods of the people which are round about you, nigh unto thee, or far off from thee, from the one end of the earth even unto the other end of the earth; Thou shalt not consent unto him, nor hearken unto him.

These verses must have been added to the Luqman Sahifat, which is Ahikar's wisdom after the Christian era. Mohammed's attributing them to Luqman, whom we saw was Ahikar shows that he did not receive these verses from Allah, but instead adopted what was available in Sahifat of Luqman and spread during his time in Arabia.

But this Quranic verse stands in contradiction with what Muslims did at the battle of Bader, where some Muslims killed their fathers and uncles after being instigated by other verses of the Quran.

After Mohammed emigrated to Medina he used his followers to ambush the caravans of Quraysh that were going or retuning from Syria to Mecca as well as the caravans going or returning from Yemen. In one of these raids he came out with his followers to plunder a caravan of Mecca, which was returning from Syria carrying the money from the trade. Quraysh knew that Mohammed would be coming out to plunder the caravan and had it take a way near the shore in order to escape. Yet, Mohammed wanted to fight the people of Quraysh who came to protect their caravan.

Mohammed knew that among the people of Mecca who came out to defend the caravan were fathers, brothers and close relatives of the young Muslims who followed him. In order to convince his followers to kill their fathers and brothers, he came up with the following verse:

> You will not find any people who believe in Allah and the Last Day, making friendship or being kind with those who oppose Allah and His Messenger, even though they were their fathers or their sons or their brothers or their kindred (people).(58:22)

Many expositors of the Quran state that the above verse was inspired by Bader, the battle in which Ubeidah killed his father. One of these expositors was al Hafeth bin Kathir. Mohammed came up with this verse to motivate Muslims to have a spirit of hatred toward their relatives and not hesitate to kill them. Mohammed knew that because the Quraysh were known for their forbearance, they would not be hardened to the point where the fathers would kill their sons. However, after being stimulated by this verse, and believing it came from the true God, the Muslims were able to justify killing members of their family. As a result Aba 'Ubeideh bin al Jarrah was able to kill his father in the battle.[921]

We can see that Mohammed approved of Muslims killing members of their family, as we read in this incident by Malik bin Ameer. "A man came to the prophet and said: I faced the enemy and found my father with them. I heard from him a bad saying, so I could not be patient till I pierced him with the spear until I killed him. The prophet was silent."[922]

It is noteworthy that Mohammed did not oppose what this man did, nor did he object, thus showing that he was pleased with his actions. In reality, killing the fathers was something in the heart of Mohammed, as he considered being willing to do so a test regarding a person's willingness to follow him; as we see from the following incident:

> When Talheh bin al Bara' met the prophet, he said, 'O prophet of Allah, order me of what you like and I will not disobey your command.' The prophet was wondered to hear this, especially since Talheh was young. He said to him 'then kill your father.' So Talha left with the intention of killing his father. But the prophet called him and said 'I am not called to destroy the relatives.'[923]

He pretended that he was not called to kill the fathers, but his actions revealed the opposite, showing that following him relied on being willing to fight the fathers and kill them.

At the same battle, Omar bin al Khattab, who became the second Caliph, killed his uncle on his mother's side, as he himself testified, boasting, "I killed my uncle, al 'As bin Hisham bin al Maghira."[924] Omar became a subject of admiration for Muslims. He is titled "al Faruq," which means, the one of discernment. At Muslim schools, students are taught about the "the geniality of Omar, making him out to be one of their most important personalities throughout history. But I do not see what is attributed to Omar as being based on truth. The one who kills his uncle, for the mere reason that he came out to defend his caravan is less wise and has less virtue than the rest of the humans.

At the same battle of Abu Hutheifah, another Muslim contributed to killing his father. He helped the ones who stood to engage in swordplay against his father by striking him. Here are the words of Wakidi when "Utbah bin Rabiah called for swordplay, his son Abu Hutheifah stood to fight against him, but others stood to fight his father. However, Abu Hutheifah helped the ones who fought his father by striking his father."[925] In other words, Abu Hutheifah wanted to engage his father in a sword fight but was preceded by others. Nevertheless, Abu Hutheifah helped kill his father by striking him, which helped the Muslims who fought against his father to be able to kill him. Obviously, the Quranic verse which Mohammed recited regarding the day of the battle of Bader motivated the Muslim sons to hurry in killing their fathers, brothers and uncles as a demonstration of obedience to Allah and his apostle.

Utbah bin Rabiah was an important leader of Quraysh and known for his virtues. Mohammed began throwing the dead bodies of the men of Quraysh into a well. We read in ibn Hisham, that when the body of "Utbah bin Rabiah was taken to be thrown into the well. Mohammed saw that the face of Abu Hutheifah became sad and his visage changed. Mohammed said to him 'O Abu Hutheifah, may there be entered in you something about your father?' he answered: 'No O apostle of Allah. I never doubted in the killing of my father. But I know that my father had good opinions, forbearance, clemency and favor. I hoped these virtues would lead him to Islam.'"[926]

Mohammed would not allow Abu Hutheifah to grieve for the death of his father. Wanting to avoid the wrath of Mohammed, Abu Hutheifah found an excuse to justify the little remorse that existed in his heart. He knew his father was possessed of good virtues, so was it right to kill such a father? Was his father not much better than the Saalik who followed Mohammed in order to plunder the caravans? Without a doubt, he was better than the criminal followers of Mohammed, and certainly better than the one who motivated them with the spirit of hatred and planned to kill their fathers.

Musaab bin 'Amir killed his brother Ubeid in the same battle.[927] It is interesting to note that Musaab was the one whom Mohammed sent to Medina to impose Islam on the city. This occurred after the agreement between Mohammed and the representatives of Aws and Khazraj in the suburbs of Mecca. They agreed to impose Islam on the members of the two tribes as a condition of the agreement, so Mohammed sent Musaab to accomplish this task. But now in the battle of Bader, Mussab manifested the true nature of Islam. What Musaab called others to embrace, that is the Islam of Mohammed, he now displayed in a practical way before all. What Musaab and others called others to embrace of the slogan "there is no god except Allah and Mohammed his messenger," is in reality an introduction to the practice of violence and killing people which aims to get rid of family members who do not embrace this faith. This is actually what we see even in the West. Among the ones who embraced Islam are those who joined al Qaida and enrolled in terrorist organizations to kill their people and fight against their own countries. They are being separated from their own families, and filled with a spirit of enmity against them:

16- O my son! Surely if it is the very weight of the grain of a mustard-seed, even though it is in (the heart of) rock or (high above) in the heaven or (deep down) in the earth, Allah will bring it (to light); surely Allah is Knower of subtleties, Aware.

We see the concept of this verse is similar to a saying attributed to Luqman where we read that Allah sees the trace of an ant in a solid rock.

We read in both Taj al Arus and Lisan al Arab that "it is written in a Hadith of Luqman, 'he sees the trace of an ant in a stone Ayar.' Abu Amru said Ayar is the rock which is very solid."[928]

There is another Luqman Hadith that is very similar to the Quranic verse. Luqman says:

> It was narrated that the son of Luqman the wise asked him. Luqman answered, 'did you see the grain that is in the depth of the sea.' Allah told him that he knows the grain where it is. He knows according to his knowledge and brings to light according to his kindness.[929]

These thoughts attributed to Luqman, without a doubt were added later by the Syriacs to Sahifat Luqman- Ahikar. They agree with ideas we find in the Old Testament, such as the following:

> It is hidden from the eyes of every living thing, concealed even from the birds in the sky. Destruction[a] and Death say, "Only a rumor of it has reached our ears." God understands the way to it and he alone knows where it dwells, for he views the ends of the earth and sees everything under the heavens (Job 28:21-24).

> He reveals the deep things of darkness and brings utter darkness into the light (Job 12:22).

> He reveals deep and hidden things; he knows what lies in darkness, and light dwells with him (Daniel 2:22).

It is obvious there is a similarity between the above Biblical verses and the ideas attributed to Luqman, and the correspondence between Luqman's saying and the Quranic verse. The bridge between Luqman- Ahikar in the Syriac version is the Syriacs themselves, who took some of their thoughts from the Bible and added them to the Aramaic version of Ahikar:

> 17- O my son! Keep up prayer and enjoin the good and forbid the evil, and bear patiently that which befalls you; for this is firmness - the steadfast heart of things)

Notice that the verse is in the same format as Ahikar's address to his son in Ahikar's wisdom. The Quranic verse is an accumulation of more than verses from the Bible, such as:

> Pray continually. (1 Thessalonians 5:17).

> "Turn from evil and do good; seek peace and pursue it" (Psalm 34:14).

> We can rejoice, too, when we run into problems and trials, for we know that they help us develop patience. And patience develops strength of character. (Romans 5:3-4).

Here we see the Quranic verse gathered its words from different verses of the Bible. Since the Quran attributes the verse to Luqman, we see that it is a Syriac addition to the wisdom of Ahikar, which in Arabia was called Sahifat of Luqman:

18- And do not turn your face away from people in contempt, nor go about in the land exulting overmuch; surely Allah does not love any self-conceited boaster.

The idea that God hates pride is found in many verses of the Bible:

Though the Lord is great, he cares for the humble, but he keeps his distance from the proud. (Psalm 138:6).

To fear the LORD is to hate evil; I hate pride and arrogance, evil behavior and perverse speech. (Proverbs 8:13).

From the Aramaic version of Ahikar we see similar declarations:

If thou, my son, wouldst be exalted, humble thyself before God who humbles the lofty man and exalts the humble man.[930]

19- And pursue the right course in your going about and lower your voice; surely the most hateful of voices is braying of the asses.

This Quranic verse is taken from the sixth proverb of Ahikar, according to the Syriac version, which reads, "my son, look down in your eyes, and lower your voice. If man would have been able to build a house through the loud voice, the donkey would have built two houses in just one day. If strength alone was the force to drag the plow, the yoke of the plow would be always on the camel."

We note that Ahikar's proverb is more complete than the Quranic verse, which is an inaccurate translation and abbreviation of Ahikar's proverb:

33- O people! Fear your Lord, and fear (the coming of) a day when no father can avail يفيد aught شــيئاً for his son, nor a son avail aught for his father. The promise of Allah is true: let not then this present life deceive you, nor let the conceit deceive you about Allah.

The first part of the verse is derived from Ezekiel:

The one who sins is the one who will die. The child will not share the guilt of the parent, nor will the parent share the guilt of the child. The righteousness of the righteous will be credited to them, and the wickedness of the wicked will be charged against them. (Ezekiel 18:20).

The second part of the Quranic verse was inspired from other verses in the New Testament, such as:

Beware lest anyone deceive you through philosophy and empty deceit, according to the tradition of men, according to the basic principles of the world, and not according to Christ. (Colossians 2:8)

And the cares of this world, the deceitfulness of riches, and the desires for other things entering in choke the word, and it becomes unfruitful. (Mark 4:19).

34- With Allah is the knowledge of the Hour, he sends down the rain, and knows that which is in the wombs. No person knows what he will earn tomorrow, and no person knows in what land he will die. Allah is Knower, Aware.

The above verse was derived from verses in Ecclesiastes and James which state:

As you do not know what is the way of the wind,[a] Or how the bones grow in the womb of her who is with child, So you do not know the works of God who makes everything. (Ecclesiastes 11:5).

Come now, you who say, "Today or tomorrow we will[a] go to such and such a city, spend a year there, buy and sell, and make a profit"; whereas you do not know what will happen tomorrow. For what is your life? It is even a vapor that appears for a little time and then vanishes away. (James 4:13-14).

As we can see the thoughts are the same. The Syriacs who added Biblical thoughts to the wisdom of Ahikar, which in Arabia became Sahifat of Luqman, while either abbreviating the Biblical verses or just replacing the idea. The Arabic translator wrote them in his way, thus resulting in these proverbs which Mohammed adopted, and he completed additional abbreviations, as he was known to do in the Quran.

It is clear that Mohammed used to read Sahifat Luqman, which was the Wisdom of Ahikar. Since in the Surah he had admitted that the proverbs came from Luqman, thus, he pointed out the source of the Surah of Luqman. We have seen that verse 19 of the Surah Luqman is identical to the 6th proverb of Ahikar.

The family of Mohammed and the proverbs of Ahikar-Luqman

There are enough proofs that the sayings of Luqman, which were copied from the sayings of Ahikar were known to the family of Mohammed, indicating that they were familiar with Sahifat Luqman. Previously I mentioned the poem of al-Zubeir bin Abdel Muttaleb, the uncle of Mohammed, who included a proverb of Ahikar. Al-Zubeir was known to recite poetry and lodge with the Saalik groups, including their leaders and poets such as Abu al Tamhan,[931] The Saaliks were criminals who were disowned by their own tribes. They were later incorporated into Islam by Mohammed, who used them to wage wars against the Arabian tribes and cities. (See the second part of Dr. Amari's book, Star Akbar). Al Zubeir, as the rest of the Saalik leaders, loved and recited poetry. Al Zubeir recited a poem of which the first stanza was taken from a proverb attributed to Luqman and equal to an Ahikar proverb:

> If you need something send a wise man and do not commend him. And if something was difficult to you, consult a rational man and do not disobey him.[932]

As I have previously mentioned, the first stanza of Al Zubeir's poem is a well-known proverb of Luqman and Ahikar. Luqman exhorted his son saying, "My son, do not dispatch an ignorant messenger. If you do not find a wise one be your own messenger."[933]

This is identical to proverb 39 of the Ahikar Syriac version.

> My son, dispatch a wise messenger and do not commend him. Instead of sending an ignorant messenger, go yourself.

It is also similar to another proverb from the Syriac version of Ahikar.

> My son, if you send the wise in doing a task do not commend him too much, because he will do the job as you require. Do not send the stupid, but go yourself and fulfil your need.[934]

This demonstrates that Mohammed lived in a family environment that was acquainted with the Ahikar proverbs, which were known in Mecca as Luqman's Sahifat. Since of Mohammed's uncle recited these proverbs, which were not originally written in Arabic, we should not marvel that the habit of gathering the proverbs was part of the Meccan's circle, including Mohammed's family. At the very least, the proverb's existence in the Syriac version of Ahikar is an indication that the Syriac version preceded the Islamic era. I previously showed that the Syriac version goes back to the second century A.D.

There is an Aramaic Ahikar proverb, which I previously quoted that goes back even further to the fifth century B.C.

> My son, do not chatter overmuch till thou reveal every word which comes into thy mind, for in every place are their eyes and their ears; but keep watch over thy mouth, let it not be thy destruction. More than all watchfulness watch thy mouth, and over what thou hearest harden thy heart, for a word is (like) a bird, and when he has sent it forth. A man

does not recapture it. Count the secrets of thy mouth, afterwards bring
forth (advice) to thy brother for his help, for stronger is the ambush of
the mouth than the ambush of fighting.[935]

Ali bin Abi Taleb, the son in law of Mohammed, repeated the same
idea found in an Ahikar proverb.

Luqman said to his son: 'The words are more severe or harmful than
the stone and more painful than needles...' Ali said: 'Allah never
imprisoned a bird in a fortress as the need of imprisoning the tongue.
Watch the teeth and the lips that imprison the tongue, and then the heart
that imprison (the word) from behind. Fear Allah and do not free or send
forth what is imprisoned except you are sure that its wickedness will not
hurt.'[936]

We observe that both proverbs portray the tongue or the word as
something needing to be imprisoned like the bird. Without a doubt, the
Ahikar proverb of the Aramaic version went through changes when it was
translated into Syriac, then into Arabic to be part of Sahifat Luqman.
Eventually, Ali presented the idea in his own style and words, according to
what he could remember of the proverb. Yet, the main idea of the original
proverb is recognizable.

We can see that Ali bin Abi Taleb adopted specific terms from Sahifat
of Luqman. As an example, there is a saying of Luqman which says, "there
is a Hadith of Luqman: ' I eta al maqir and al sabir.' Ibn Manthur said: 'al
maqir is al sabir. (it is a kind of a bitter medicine. The word sabir means
also to endure or be patient) and that he was patient in taking al sabir. Ali
also said, 'it is more bitter than al sabir and al maqir.'"[937]

Ibn Athir quotes the same proverb of Luqman:

In a Hadith of Luqman: I eta al maqir and have lot of patience. Al maqir
al sabir is the bitter medicine... from here derives Ali's Hadithi which
says: it is more bitter than al sabir al maker.'[938]

The myths of Sahifat Luqman regarding creation

The tenth verse of Surah Luqman features a myth about creation.
Since all the verses of the Surah are connected to Luqman's thoughts, the
tenth verse is also derived from Sahifat of Luqman. For example, the 4th
verse praises those who perform prayer while Luqman advices his son to
perform prayer the 17th verse. In the 10th verse we see the subject of

creation. In the verse that follows, that is the 11th, it says "we bestowed wisdom on Luqman." Thus, we see all the Surahs consist of connecting with Luqman thoughts and containing ideas on how Allah created the earth and sky, followed by the wisdom which was taught by Luqman to his son. Without a doubt, it is based on the Syriac, Manichaean and Arabian myths, which were later added to the Aramaic text of Ahikar, forming Sahifat of Luqman, which we have seen how the family of Mohammed consulted and quoted from its wisdom.

The tenth verse of Surah Luqman says:

He created the heavens without any pillars that ye can see; he set on the earth mountains standing firm, lest it should shake with you; and He scattered through it beasts of all kinds. We send down rain from the sky, and produce on the earth every kind of noble creature, in pairs.

Note that it claims Allah created mountains and placed them on earth, lest the earth shake with its inhabitants. This idea is of a Zoroastrian origin. The Persians reasoned that there happened at the beginning of creation a crisis or dilemma. According to the Zoroastrians, Ahriman, the god of wickedness, lives beneath the earth and shakes it.[939] Ahura Mazda, the main Zoroastrian deity, responded to this earth shaking by creating the mountains. After he set the mountains in place, they grew down into the earth as stakes or anchors, and stabilized it.[940]

The mountains in Indian mythology exist to stabilize the earth from shaking. The Mahabharata presents a myth that one of the gods struck the mountains with their arrows, making them to flee. As a result, the earth shook in all its regions. This led the gods to make peace with the mountains. The earth did not return to its original stability until the mountains returned to their positions as stakes or anchors.[941]

The Arabian mythology shared the view of the mountains as stakes designed to stabilize the earth from shaking. Among the persons who influenced Mohammed was Qis bin Saideh. Mohammed expressed his admiration of Qis and admitted listening to his sayings. Before claiming to be a prophet, Mohammed continuously quoted Qis' sayings. Qis also said that the mountains were anchors to stabilize the earth.[942]

The Sahifat Luqman repeated the same oriental myth that the mountains were anchors to stabilize the earth from shaking, an idea that Mohammed adopted in the Quran. All those who adopted the idea of stabilizing the earth through the mountains did so because of their belief that there existed a being under the earth, which carried it and shook it. In the Quran there is a whale by which Allah swore, according to Mohammed and his companions, was the whale upon which Allah placed the earth.

Mohammed in Surah 68 called Al Qalam, which means "the pen," makes Allah to swear in the Nun and Al Qalam, that is the pen. The Arabic letter "nun," is equivalent to nun, which also means Hut, that is whale. the Quran used the term "nun" for whale more than one time; such as in Surah Al Anbiya' that is 21, and verse 87. In reality, the renaming of this Surah as Al Qalam came later, and in contrast with what Mohammed had named as "Nun and Al Qalam."[943]

The swear of Allah by a letter N has no meaning. Why would Allah swear with the letter Nun and a pen?! Mohammed interpreted the foundation of such swear, as we see from one of his Hadiths, reported by his close companions. Mohammed said, "Allah created the earth on the whale. The whale is the nun whom Allah, be blessed and glorified, mentioned in the Quran in Surah Nun and al Qalam...the whale moved and agitated, therefore, the earth shacked. then Allah placed the mountains on the earth as anchors, so the earth was fixed. The mountains boast over the earth. thus, the words of Allah 'He threw on the earth anchors (the mountains) lest it shakes with you.'"[944] The last sentence of Mohammed, he quoted Surah 16, called Al Nahl, and verse 15.

Thus, the swear of Allah is not in a letter, neither in a normal whale. but in a great whale where the earth was placed. When the whale agitated, the earth quaked, then Allah fixed the earth through the mountains. We saw that Mohammed quoted a Quranic verse that is 16: 15 to support his Hadith. Given the Quranic verses which claim that Allah placed the mountains on the earth lest it should shake with the inhabitants of the earth, we ascertain the belief of Mohammed of the whale. In fact, without the belief of Mohammed of a whale upon which the earth was placed, which threaten to quake the earth, there is no meaning in Quranic phrase of fixing the earth with the mountains, lest it should shake with the inhabitants of the earth.

Al Allusi الالوسي mentioned a Hadith of Mohammed reported by al Dhiya' الضياء and al Hakem الحاكم, in which Mohammed revealed the name of the whale carrying the earth as al Yahmut[945] اليهموت.

The name of the whale, as mentioned by Mohammed and his close companions is derived from the Middle Eastern mythology in his time. in fact, the queen of darkness in Mandaeanism is al Rawha الروهـة. She is called also Hyuwath هيواث . Kurt Rudolph, the expert in Mandaeanism, said that the female of Hyuwath means Haywan (meaning animal), in Aramaic is Haywa حـيـوا or Hayuta [946] حـيـوتـا. He said also that the underground kingdom of darkness according to the Phoenicians called Hut حوت .[947] Which is the same Arabic word for whale. It is interesting to note that the son of al Rawha, the queen of darkness in Mandaeanism, is called Ur اور . He is also called Hyuwath Nimrus.[948] Since Hyuwath or Hywan (animal) in Aramaic is Hyutaحيوتا . Thus, his name in Aramaic is Hyuta Nimrusحيوتا نمروس . The Mandaean manuscripts such as Diwan Abatur, described him as the one carrying the world on his back.[949] From this we see this Haywan (animal) Hyuta, carrying the earth.

The dragon, Hiwath Nimrus or Hyuta Nimrus حيوتا نمروس , as we see from the Ginza Rba, the main scriptures of the Mandaeans, is able to quake the axis of the earth.[950]

The passage in the Quran mentioning Luqman's saying regarding stabilizing the earth through the use of mountains reveals that the Sahifet of Luqman contains various oriental myths which were added to the Ahikar Wisdom. This enabled, Sahifet Luqman to become rich in myths that eventually found acceptance by the pre-Islamic people of Jahiliyyah.

The rock of Luqman, the Manichaean sources and Sahifet Luqman

Mohammed's companions quoted a Hadith, which was most probably his about how the earth was carried by a whale, which in turn was carried by elements such as water which was considered by ancient middle eastern people to be gods, which the Mesopotamians believed was the primordial water goddess. Other elements included a rock and an angel who acted as a porter. We know that Mani, the founder of the Manichaean religion, was believed to have made the earth and universe to be carried by the angel. In this Hadith, the angel stands on a rock. "The angel on a rock, and the rock carried by the wind. The rock is the one mentioned by Luqman. It is neither in heaven nor in earth." This leads us to believe that Sahifet of Luqman was the true source of this mythological tale.

Here the Hadith claims it is reported by the companions of Mohammed:

> Allah's throne was on the waters. He did not create anything before the waters. When he wanted to create his creation, he made the vapor to come out of the waters. The vapor was elevated and became heaven. Then he dried the water beneath making it one earth. He divided the earth into seven earths. He created the earth on a whale. The whale is the Nun which Allah mentioned in the Quran, 'Nun and the pen.' The whale was in the water. The water was on a Safat (a kind of rock). The Safat was on an angel's back. The angel stood on a rock. The rock was on the wind. The rock is the one mentioned by Luqman. It is not in heaven or in the earth. The whale moved, and as a result the earth was shaken. Allah set the mountains on the earth, and then the earth was stabilized. The mountains boasted on the earth. 'This is the meaning of word of Allah: "we set anchors on earth lest it shake with you.'"[951]

The first part of the Hadith was influenced by Sabian Mandaean thoughts as to how the heavens were created by the condensation of the primordial vapor coming out of the waters. The earth was then created by condensing the waters below. In their beliefs there are seven earths, of which ours is the superior. The last thought is expressed in Surah al Talaq in the Quran, which reads:

> Allah is He Who created seven heavens and of the earth a similar number. Through the midst of them (all) descends his command that ye may know that Allah has power over all things, and that Allah comprehends all things in (his) Knowledge. (Surah 65:12 called al Talaq)

Al Sayyuti wrote about the rock which carries the angel porter who carries everything:

> Allah created a rock, which is as thick as the thickness of both heaven and earth. This is the rock of which Luqman spoke to his son: 'If there be (but) the weight of a mustard-seed and it were (hidden) in a rock.' The name of the rock is Saikhur صيخور.[952]

Al Masudi said this rock is the one the Quran mentions in the sayings of Luqman.[953] Al Sayyuti also wrote it was "reported by al Suddi in explaining the words of Allah in Surah Luqman verse 16. He said: 'this rock is neither in heavens nor on earth. It is under the seven earths, on which stands an angel.'"[954]

These mythological ideas describing how the universe and earth were carried are similar to Manichaean ideas. The Manichaeans were Persian

Gnostics founded by the prophet Maniin the third century. The Manichaeans considered both the Jewish mythological books and the Apocrypha books to be canonical. They subsequently went on to add to their canon many other myths of creation. It is highly likely that among their additions they adopted was the book of Ahikar wisdom which they spread throughout Arabia. In fact, the Ahikar story influenced the Manichaean writings. In his book, Jewish Lore in Manichaean Cosmogony, John Reeves discusses the imprint of these Jewish writings on their principles regarding the cosmogonies. He also drew attention to the similarity between the characteristics of Gilgamesh (mentioned in the book of Giant which Mani wrote) and the personality of Ahikar as described in the Aramaic version.[955] Thus, the Manichaeans quoted these types of books which they carried with them as they spread the idea of them being sacred and inspired books from their gods.

When we examine Manichaean ideas about how the universe was transported we can ascertain that the Hadith reported by the companions of Mohammed, such as ibn Abbass and ibn Masud, was derived from the Manichaean editing of Ahiqar, which was their version of Ahikar that believe became known in Arabia as Sahifet Luqman.

Mani claimed there were three huge rocks placed outside the world[956] and there were three earths beneath our earth, which were all carried by the angel porter. The porter then places his feet on another earth.[957] This teaching corresponds to the idea of the rock in the Hadith where an angel carrying everything is standing. According to their Hadith, this is the rock which Luqman spoke of that exists beneath the seventh layer. From this we understand the Quranic statement in surah Luqman verse 16 that Allah is able to bring forth a grain of mustard whether it was on a rock, in the heavens or in the earth. According to mythology this represents three cosmic dimensions. First, the Rock which is far from the earth because according to Manichaeism it exists outside the cosmos. According to the Hadith the rock existed under the 7th earth. After this distant rock, the Quran lists the heavens and then the earth. This shows that the rock was not part of the heavens or earth.

The Manichaean book called "The Kephalaia of the Teacher" speaks of trenches of water that reached the feet of the angel porter who carries the earths.[958] Perhaps the idea of Mohammed's companions that water is among the elements that carries the earth was derived from this Manichaean mythology. All of this leads one to conclude that the Sahifet Luqman went through Manichaean editing in North Arabia.

Conclusion

Mohammed did not realize that Luqman was Ahikar or that Luqman Sahifet was taken from Ahikar Wisdom, which was known for centuries prior to Mohammed's birth. In Mohammed's time people looked on Ahikar as being a historical and wise man who was given wisdom from God. Syriac, Jewish and Manichaean groups all viewed the Majallah of Luqman- Ahikar as containing divine wisdom. Mohammed was concerned about including in his Quran all the important material that was considered in Arabia to have been inspired by God or the gods. He wanted to be sure his Quran was not viewed as being incomplete by any party, whether it be Jewish, Syriac, Manichaean or Sabian.

We can ascertain this trend of Mohammed when we examine his willingness to borrow from other sources and myths commonly known in his time. As an example, there were myths we know that have the book of Pseudo Callisthenes as their source. Later, these myths were adopted and developed by the Syriacs and detail the journeys of Alexander the Great to the extremities of the earth, and how he built a dam to imprison Gog and Magog until the last days of history. To do this, they made Alexander out to be a believer, conducting wars to spread the word of God throughout the earth. Mohammed believed Alexander to be a prophet and subsequently made his name a part of his Quran. This is despite Alexander being known to venerate idols and encourage nations he conquered to honor their own gods.

In the Quran there is an accumulation of material consisting of what naïve groups during Mohammed's time considered to be the words of prophets and wise men sent by God. Luqman- Ahikar is a clear example of this type of compilation.

Ahikar's proverbs are mostly secular and consist of proverbs compiled from pagan populations that were being taught and spread during the time of the Jewish author during the fifth century B.C. The Syriac added some Biblical proverbs around the beginning of the second century A.D. The Quran subsequently adopted some of these proverbs as they were incorporated in Surah Luqman.

There are 31 chapters in the book of Proverbs, most of which were written by Solomon under the inspiration of God. They contained great prophecies about Christ being the everlasting wisdom of God in multiple verses such as Proverbs 8:23 where it says, "I was appointed from everlasting." His role in the Trinity as part of the preparation prior to creating the universe where he says in participation in the cosmos planning before creation that:

> When he prepared the heavens, I was there: when he set a compass upon the face of the depth: when he established the clouds above: when he strengthened the fountains of the deep. (Proverbs 8:27, 28).

This reveals that God Father planned the universe through the use of circles, which we now know are the orbits of galaxies and stars. This idea is actually a key scientific discovery about the nature of the universe that was discovered by a Christian, Johannes Kepler, who discovered that planets have elliptical orbits. This belief is contrary to the Quran's idea about the universe consisting of seven heavens like a building as we see in Surah al Mulk:

> Who has created the seven equal heavens one above another; you can see no fault in the creation of al Rahman. Then look again: Can you see any rifts? (67:3)

This verse claims that the universe consists of seven equal layers that are without rifts, just like a good building. Mohammed describes these layers of heaven in his alleged ascension as being places where believers lived according to their merit. This idea is of Gnostic origin. We have seen in Surah al Talaq how the Quran talks about seven layers of heaven and seven earths, of which ours is the superior. This idea was taken from the Mandaeans. [5]

---

[5] The sacred Mandaean books are attributed to Hibil Ziwa, who they later called Gabriel, of having created seven earths, and our earth is superior. (In some books there are 8 earths). Hibil Ziwa said he appointed over these worlds or earths seven perfect angels (see Rt. Ginza Rba, part 15, page 303). This account bears a remarkable similarity to the Sumerian gods that govern the underworld. The underworld has a current of water called Burdni. Mandadahi, one of the most important light personalities, travelled to these earths where there are rivers. The Mandaean texts claim that these worlds are well-organized. Some trees in these earths are myrrh, such as the Zaqum

In Proverbs 8:30 there is another statement about the role of Christ in creating the cosmos:

> Then I was beside Him as a master craftsman; And I was daily His delight, Rejoicing always before Him.

This means whatever the Triune God plans to do, Christ the Son of God is able to bring into existence. Also He is the subject of divine delight.

In the 30th chapter of Proverbs, there is a declaration about the monotheistic personality of God that contains his eternal persons:

> The words of Agur the son of Jakeh, his utterance. This man declared to Ithiel—to Ithiel and Ucal: Surely I am more stupid than any man, And do not have the understanding of a man. I neither learned wisdom. Nor have knowledge of the Holy One. Who has ascended into heaven, or descended? Who has gathered the wind in His fists? Who has bound the waters in a garment? Who has established all the ends of the earth? What is His name, and what is His Son's name, If you know? Every word of God is pure; He is a shield to those who put their trust in Him. (Proverbs 30:1-5).

After Agur presented the personality of God as monotheistic saying, "knowledge of the Holy One," he declared that before he received a revelation about the divine persons in One God, he was ignorant. Then he spoke about the eternal person in the Godhead, who is responsible for

---

tree which the Quran claims exists in Hell. Rt. Ginza Rba part 3 page 70 speaks of rivers that flow in these earths beneath our earth and describe their inhabitants as being wicked. Mandadhi, the missionary of life for the Sabian Mandaeans, speaks about them during his trip to the lower earths, saying:

"I saw the wicked rebellious, how they put on the weapons of wickedness.

They dress themselves with the weapons of wickedness and plot with maliciousness against the kingdom of light."

According of Rodulph, the water that flow in the underworlds and the description of life there is taken from old Sumerian Semitic imaginations (see al Nusha wa al Khalq Fi al nusus al Mandaeyeh, page 69). The world of darkness was placed as one of the seven earths below according to their imagination. Some texts speak about the kinds of creatures and humans who live in these underworlds (see Rt. Ginza Rba, part 12, page 277, and part 1, 2). In some of these worlds where the wicked live it is said that "their trees taste like poison and myrh, their juice is similar to the oil tanker and asphalt." This like the tree of Zaqum as it is described in the Surah al Saffat 63.

planning, that is the Father and about the everlasting person who is the subject of divine love, that is the Son. We can perceive the idea of a monotheistic God from philosophy and pondering on the greatness of creation. This revelation does not, however, provide a complete knowledge of the true personality of God. Although monotheism is one characteristic of God, it does not reveal his true identity to the soul, nor does it allow for spiritual fellowship with Him

The 31 chapters of Proverbs contain a vast treasure trove from God on how we should live and deal with the various circumstances of life. It is a lamp for our feet as the psalmist wrote:

Your word is a lamp to my feet, And a light to my path. Psalm 119:105.

There are 150 psalms, many of which were inspired to David, that contain scores of prophecies. For example, Psalm 22 describes the agony endured by Christ while on the Cross. Among the prophecies of this psalm we read:

Dogs surround me, a pack of villains encircles me; they pierce my hands and my feet. All my bones are on display; people stare and gloat over me. They divide my clothes among them, and cast lots for my garment. (Psalm 22:16-18).

This prophecy was fulfilled literally when after piercing Christ's hands and feet when placing him on the cross, the Roman soldiers then divided his clothes among themselves by casting lots.

Then the soldiers, when they had crucified Jesus, took his garments, and made four parts, to every soldier a part; and also his coat: now the coat was without seam, woven from the top throughout. They said therefore among themselves, Let us not rend it, but cast lots for it, whose it shall be: that the scripture might be fulfilled, which saith, They parted my raiment among them, and for my vesture they did cast lots. These things therefore the soldiers did. (John 19:23,24)

The Psalms talk about the greatness of God and the importance of enjoying and delighting in Him.

The book of Ecclesiastes, which was written by King Solomon, is another book of wisdom in the Bible and is considered an important guide in understanding the philosophy, meaning and purpose of life and how to avoid its deceitfulness. The book of Job, which is considered to be the oldest book in human history, is similarly unique in dealing with the subject of pain and the reason for human suffering.

The few sentences of Ahikar which we find in the Quran cannot begin to replace this great heritage of wisdom and guidance which God gave through the books of wisdom in the Old Testament. Moreover, Ahikar's proverbs are connected with a mythological figure, Ahikar, who did not exist in history. They are the fruit of the imagination and accumulation of the Jewish author who lived during the fifth century B.C., who incorporated them into an imaginary tale. Mohammed's use of Ahikar's proverbs, which were known during his time as Luqman, is a confirmation that he was a virtual prisoner to the education spread during his generation, and was unable to distinguish the true books inspired by God from the myths. Every book in Arabia and every myth considered by the Arabians to be a fact, Mohammed viewed as a proper source for the Quran. Mohammed intention was to establish a religion founded on many ideas that were adopted by various groups. Sahifet Luqman was only one among many of the other books in Arabia, however it was one of the most well-known. It is for this reason that he adopted some of its sayings and made Luqman to be a wise man coming from Allah.

Monkeys and Pigs

Disfiguring or deforming the Jews and some of Christ's followers into monkeys and pigs.

In Surahs al-Baqarah and al-Aaraf, the Quran claims that Allah disfigured some groups of Jews into monkeys:

> And indeed you knew those amongst you who transgressed in the matter of the Sabbath (i.e., Saturday). We said to them: 'Be you monkeys, despised and rejected.'

Surah al-Aaraf (7:163-166) gives more details about this claim:

> Ask them concerning the town standing close by the sea. Behold! They transgressed in the matter of the Sabbath. For on the day of their Sabbath their fish did come to them, openly holding up their heads, but on the day they had no Sabbath, they came not: thus did we make a trial of them, for they were given to transgression. When some of them said, 'Why do ye preach to a people whom Allah will destroy or visit with a terrible punishment?' the preachers replied: 'To discharge our duty to your Lord, and perchance they may fear Him.' When they disregarded the warnings that had been given them, we rescued those who forbade Evil; but we visited the wrongdoers with a grievous punishment because they were given to transgression. When in their insolence they transgressed (all) prohibitions, we said to them: 'Be ye apes, despised and rejected.'

According to Quranic expositors, a group of Jews in the city of Ilah on the Red Sea began fishing for whales on Saturdays, which was the Sabbath. Allah became angry and transfigured them into monkeys to punish them for their disobedience.

When Mohammed said in Surah al Araf, "Ask them concerning the town standing close by the sea," he purported that the myth of metamorphosis or transfiguring the Jews into monkeys was a famous fact well-known to the Jews. There is no mention about this myth in the Bible, however, or in any other Hebrew book. It is in fact a Mohammedan myth.

According to the Quranic expositors when Surah Al-Maedah speaks about transfiguring the Jews into monkeys and pigs, it is referring to another incident:

> Shall I point out to you something much worse than this, (as judged) by the treatment it received from Allah? It is those who incurred the curse of Allah and His wrath, some of whom He transformed into apes and swine, those who worshipped evil; these are (many times) worse in rank and far more astray from the right path!

When Mohammed issued this verse, Muslims began calling the Jews "O brothers of monkeys and pigs."[959] Mujahed explained the verse, saying:

> Allah had cursed by the tongue of David and Issa, son of Mary, those who disbelieved from the Israelites. They were cursed by David's tongue and became monkeys. They were also cursed by Issa's (Jesus') tongue and became pigs.[960]

There is another interpretation:

> Ibn Jarih and others said, 'The ones of Israel who disbelieved were cursed by David's tongue. David passed by some of them sitting in a house. He asked, "Who is in the house?" They answered, "Pigs." David prayed, "Lord transform them into pigs." They became pigs. Jesus prayed against them saying, "God curse those who spoke evil against me and against my mother and transform them into despised pigs.'[961]

Still others interpret the teaching to mean that God ordered a table full of food to come down from heaven to Jesus. Although God ordered that the table be used exclusively for the poor, many were displeased and complained. The table was then lifted up to heaven and God transformed those who complained into pigs.

Mohammed threatened the Jews and Christians, claiming that if they did not believe in him they would be transformed into monkeys as it happened to those one Saturday:

> O you who have been given the Book! Believe that which We have revealed, verifying what you have, before We alter faces then turn them on their backs, or curse them as We cursed the violators of the Sabbath, and the command of Allah shall be executed. (Surah al-Nisa 4:47).

Without a doubt Muslims claim that Surah al Araf was Meccan (meaning Mohammed recited it while he was still at Mecca), describing the Jews as monkeys and creating hatred in Muslims' hearts against the Jews. This begs the question, why did Mohammed not reveal the subject of the Jews' and Christians' disfiguration into monkeys and pigs until he emigrated to Medina, for we know that the Surahs of al Medina came from Medina and not from Mecca? Why did he transform the followers of Jesus into pigs? The answer reveals Mohammed's willingness to fight the Jews from Medina who were of the tribes of Quraythah, al Nether, and Qainiqa'. Mohammed was hatching a plan to expel and kill them while defiling their women and plundering their possessions. Thus, he sought to reduce them to the level of monkeys and pigs to justify killing them in the same manner as unclean animals. If Allah disfigured the Jews of Ilat into monkeys just because they violated the Sabbath, then the Jews of Medina who opposed Allah and his "prophet" must likewise be transformed into monkeys and pigs and then, as impure beings, be killed.

In addition, at that time Mohammed was preparing for a military campaign against Tabuk (a north Arabian city at the border between Trans-Jordan and Arabia that was annexed to the Byzantine Empire). He also wanted to attack Trans-Jordan, which was then under Christian control. Thus, it was necessary for him to curse the Christians prior to attacking them and reducing them to impure beings in order to justify killing them. Therefore, he came up with the Surah al Maeda, which claims that Allah transformed Christ's followers into pigs.

But, the question as to why Mohammed waited so long before cursing the Christians in this harsh way still needs to be answered. The reality is that he did not dare talk about the Christians using this language while in Mecca because he wanted to get along with the Ethiopians, who hosted his followers when the Meccans were persecuting them. But now Mohammed needed to create a spirit of great animosity against Christians by making them less than human so that it would be easy for his followers to hate them and then fight and kill them.

We must also ask why, if God was furious because the Jews were not observing a particular day, would He not be angry and show His fury and condemnation against the Jews today who fish on Saturdays and the Christians who fish or engage in other activities on Sundays or, for that matter, on Muslims who fish on Fridays?!

The pre-Islamic Jahiliyyah roots of the Quranic myth

The myth of metamorphosis found acceptance and was spread only in pre-Islamic Arabian society. The idea of humans or jinn metamorphosing into another kind of creature was a distinguished feature of Arabian mythology that separated it from all other religions of the world. This was different from the belief in reincarnation prevalent in India and other Asiatic regions in that reincarnation is believed to happen after death, whereas Arabian metamorphosis was believed to happen instantly while a person was still alive. When the gods became angry with a human, they transformed him into another form of being or inanimate object, such as the transformation of the priest and priestess Isaf and Naelah into two stones after they committed fornication inside the Kaabah of Mecca.

Al Japheth, in writing about the Arabian metamorphosis mythology, said that al Theb (a reptilian creature called Uromastyx, which lives in the desert) and the catfish were originally two human nations that were subjected to the metamorphosis process. The shrimp had been a tailor who used her skills to steal while making dresses and for her transgression was transformed into a shrimp. There are some threads or cords left on her body so as to point to the kind of theft she committed. The rat had been a miller, while the serpent was in the form of a camel that God punished by making it creep along the earth. The Arabians claimed that camels were created from the extremities (hands and legs) of devils. The dogs had been a nation of Jinn that were transformed into the animal.[962] Mohammed in one of his Hadiths said that the camels were the extremities of the devils,[963] something that reflects the influence of Arabian metamorphosis mythology on his thinking.

Al Ragheb al Asfahani wrote:

> Some said that the one that endured metamorphosis did not procreate and remains only for a while as a lesson or moral warning. Others, however, believed it procreates, to the extent they made the Theb and dogs were sons of these nations. The serpent was in a form of a camel until it helped the devil at which time it was transformed into a serpent. The Arabs said that God transformed two angels: one into a hyena and the other into a wolf. They also said the star Canopus was a publican, and Venus was a woman called Abaheed.[964]

They claimed that "what underwent metamorphosis had offspring."[965]

In other words, today's rats are the offspring of the woman who was transformed into a rat. Mohammed built on these Arabian myths and used them to fight the Jews by claiming the rats were originally an Israelite tribe or nation that was disfigured:

> Reported by Hirrerah: The apostle of Allah said, 'A tribe of Israelites were lost. I do not know what sin they committed. I see that they are the

rats. Do you not see that when the milk of camels is placed before them, they do not eat? But if the milk of sheep is place before them, they drink it.'[966]

The Arabians believed the serpents were originally Jinn. Ibn Manthur wrote:

The Arabians believed that the serpents are products of Jinn transfiguration. This is why they called the serpent as devil and Jinn.[967]

Mohammed echoed the same belief, saying:

The serpents are metamorphosis of the Jinn, exactly as the monkeys and pigs were metamorphosis from the Israelites.[968]

The Arabians considered black dogs to be dangerous Jinn or devils. Mohammed embraced this teaching from pre-Islamic Jahiliyyah mythology when he said:

'The black dog is a devil. If the dogs were not a nation from the other nations, I would have ordered all of them to be killed. Kill, however, the black dogs.' Abdellah bin al Mughafel reported the words of Mohammed: 'Were the dogs a nation from the other nations, I would order a complete extermination of all. But kill every black one of them. Every household who keeps a dog, their work will fail or decrease every day. Except the dog of hunting, ploughing, and the dog of sheep.'[969]

We have seen that the al Theb (Uromastyx) was a human. Al Ragheb al Asfahani mentioned an incident in which al Theb spoke to the one who was eating it:

Al Theb said to a man who was eating it, 'Know you that you have eaten an elder from the sons of Israel.' It means he was a metamorphosis.[970]

We see Mohammed sharing the belief of the pre-Islamic Jahiliyyah people in this myth that al Qurtubi wrote reporting from Muslims that "about the Hadith of Theb, reported by Muslims reporting by Said and Jaber. Jaber said, 'It was brought to the prophet al Theb, but he refused to comment on it, saying: I do not know, it might be from the old ages which was transfigured from humans.'"[971]

The pre-Islamic Jahiliyyah people viewed metamorphosis as a fact. They viewed the animals as nations that had languages and were capable of speaking. These were nations that would be brought before the Seat of Judgment to be judged according to their works alongside of humans. This belief induced the Jahiliyyah people to bind a camel to their fathers' tombs, so their fathers could mount them on the day of judgment.

This can be seen in the poems of Jaribah bin Ashim, in which he encouraged his son to choose a righteous camel to mount on the day of Judgment:

> O Saud, I recommend you, because you are the closest relative. You know your father will be standing before the Seat of Judgment, which is something terrible. That is why you need to make sure that your father is able to be carried by a righteous camel in the Day of Judgment when they are called to be standing before the Seat of Judgment.[972]

This Arabian mythology regarding metamorphosis left an indelible imprint on the author of the Quran. For example, the Quran says in Al-Anaam, Surah 6:38:

> There is not an animal in the earth, nor a flying creature flying on two wings, who are not peoples like unto you. We have neglected nothing in the Book (of our decrees). Then unto their Lord they will be gathered for judgment.

Mohammed shared a wide variety of supposed metamorphosis events including the transformation into dogs, rats, al Theb, and serpent. When one considers that a story regarding a metamorphosis into Nisnas (a kind of monkey) was spread in Arabia well before the time of Mohammed, it is easy to see that the Quran's claims of people being transformed into donkeys and pigs were inspired by existing Arabian mythology.

The myths of transforming humans to Nisnas

Nisnas are the monkeys, of which Al Nuweiri wrote:

> In Yemen there are many monkeys spread in several regions: some were in the area of Thamar in the region of Sanaa. They are found in the wilderness and in the mountains. The monkeys are also in the land of Nubah and the upper regions of Ethiopia. This kind of monkey has a good-looking, cheerful, rounded face and oblong tail and is of quick intellect. They call it Nasnas.[973]

According to Arabic dictionaries the Nasnas is the gorilla. Al Masudi wrote that "many people claim that the speaking animals are three species: Nas (humans), Nanas, and Nasanis."[974] This same claim is found in the writings of al Jaheth.[975]

Ibn Manthur maintains that there were Arabians who believed the Nasnas were Adam's offspring:

It was said that the Nasnas are of Adam's offspring. It came in the Hadith that the inhabitant of a region of the people of Ad disobeyed their apostle. Allah then transformed them into Nasnas.[976]

The Arabians believed that the Nasnas were originally humans and thus they speak. Al Abshehi and al Qazwini narrated stories about Arabians who hunted Nasnas, which attempted to escape through speaking and asking for mercy.[977]

Because of the similarities between monkeys and humans, the Arabians believed that Nasnas originally inhabited a region of the Ad tribe until their prophet was infuriated with them and transformed them into Nasnas. [978] The Arabians also believed that certain nations were transformed into monkeys. They discussed the possibility that a man who was transfigured into a monkey would keep his height and width.[979]

Clearly, Mohammed built on the Arabian Jahiliyyah mythology that was accepted by many in his generation. This Arabian belief made it easy for him to claim that Allah transformed the Jews into monkeys and pigs. If someone had made a similar claim in any other region of the world, he would have been considered an irrational babbler.

The metamorphosis from humans into monkeys, or nanas, was supposedly wrought by Gods' anger. The Arabians viewed the disfiguration into a Nasnas as being the result of the God's indignation against a man or group of men. Ibn Athir wrote:

> Among the inhabitants of Bahrain and Oman, there were the Banu Umaim bin Lawith. They were the inhabitants of Wabar in the land of Ramel, located between Yamameh and al Shaher. They multiplied and increased in number. This aroused God's indignation because they committed sin. They all perished, except a remnant, which are called Nasnas.[980]

Yaqut al Hamawi also wrote about this mythical land of Wabar:

> The land of Wabar was among the most fertile of the regions and the most watered, abundant in trees and fruits. The tribes there increased, and as their land flourished and their money increased, they became corrupted and oppressors. They were giants in their bodies. They did not know God's righteousness and did not appreciate His grace. Thus, God transformed them into Nasnas: half head for man and woman, half a face, one eye, one hand, and one leg. They came out to the coast pasturing like the animals.[981]

Yaqut al Hamawi traces the genealogy of these monkey-Nasnas back several generations to Noah's son Shem:

> They said they are offspring of Nasnas, son of Umaim, son of Umaim, son of Yalma', son of Lawith, son of Shem. They live between the land of Wabar and Shaher on the outskirts of Yemen. Because they corrupt the crops, the inhabitants there hunt them with dogs and drive them away from their cultivations and gardens.[982]

According to the beliefs of the pre-Islamic Jahiliyyah people, these monkeys were humans who were subjected to this metamorphosis. Stories about their exploits spread among the Arabians, such as the monkeys' stoning an adulterous she-monkey, as narrated by Bukhari and Qurtubi:

> Naim bin Hammad said: Hashim told us reporting from Abi Balj and Haseen, who reported the words of Amru bin Maimun: 'I saw in pre-Islamic times a she-monkey surrounded by monkeys. They stoned her and I stoned her with them.[983]

Since according to the Jahiliyyah people, Allah had disfigured entire nations into monkeys, it was easy for Mohammed's followers to believe his claim that Allah transformed the Jews into monkeys, in spite of the rank stupidity of such an idea. This demonstrates clearly that Mohammed's claims were a product of the Arabian mythology of his time.

The metamorphosis into pigs

We find in Greek mythology the mention of metamorphosis into pigs in the account of the goddess sorceress Circe. Homer, the writer of The Odyssey and The Iliad, described her as living on the mythical island of Aiaia (some Greek authors located this island on the western coast of Italy). Circe lived in a palace situated in a forest surrounded by animals such as lions and tigers, which she transformed into domesticated animals. Circe transformed the crew of King Odysseus-King of Ithaca (a mythological figure) into pigs. This transformation occurred after she invited them to her table and they ate her food, which was mixed with a magical fluid.

But metamorphosis for the Arabians was held to be a fact and not a magical trick performed by mystical beings; it was a divine imposition of punishment on beings.

Al Jaheth wrote why a man is transformed into a pig:

> Some of the reasons why a man is subjected to metamorphosis is the ugliness of his face. If ugliness, treachery, and lies were incorporated

they would not increase over the ugliness of the pig. These are some
of the reasons why man is transformed into a pig.[984]

He believed that the punishment of metamorphosis into a pig brought a man morally to the place where it was impossible for humanity to reach him, implying that God wanted to punish the worst, most depraved man from his human attributions and prevent him from having opportunities for improving his condition and liberation from sin. Metamorphosis requires a type of god who would give man an insensitive and inert status and form, both morally and psychologically, in which, during his life on earth, he loses his humanity forever and belongs to the non-speaking animal world.

This, however, is against the redemptive and graceful character of the true God, who seeks to bring man through repentance and grace to a higher morality and enhanced spiritual state. Those who adopt and embrace the myths of metamorphosis, as did the Jahiliyyah people of Arabia, have absolutely no understanding of the wonderful plan of God, whereby the ugliest, most vile criminal has the potential to be transformed through Christ's redemption into saints and become the best inhabitants on earth.

Al Jaheth presented research on metamorphosis in which he quoted sayings claiming that the Nabataeans had tails:

We were told by enumerable people that they saw Nabataen men from Beisan who had tails like the tails of the alligators, lions, cows, and horses, or like the tails of reptiles and rats. They had long 'Ajub-like tails.[985]

'Ajub, according to the old Arabic dictionary, is a bone in the lower back from which Arabians believed the tail sprang.[986]

Arabian society was full of stories of metamorphosis and testimonies, as if it were a fact. This is why Mohammed's followers readily accepted his statements when he spoke about the metamorphosis of Jews and Christians into pigs and monkeys. Mohammed was not satisfied with transforming Jews into monkeys and pigs, and some followers of Christ into pigs, he also prophesied that in the future even some Muslims would be transfigured into pigs:

In the Mustadrak reported by Abi Imameh, the prophet of Allah said, 'A people of this nation will sleep eating, drinking, making festivity and fun, only to wake up transformed into pigs.'[987]

We see no evidence that Mohammed's prophecy was ever fulfilled, even though Muslims throughout history have experienced periods of fun and exuberance, such as during the Abbasside period. There is a great deal of pleasure in enjoying a Harem and getting drunk in oil-rich Arabic countries today. Cases of drunkenness and frivolity are found in the Islamic world in every time and place, yet we do not see a single case of Muslims' being transformed into pigs.

Despite these facts, however, we see that the myth of metamorphosis is still present in Muslim mind and employed by the Sheiks to terrorize the Muslims under their dominion. From time to time we hear false news reports about a young man who was transformed into a monkey because he committed a transgression, or of a girl who was transformed into a she-monkey because she listened to songs instead of reading or listening to the Quran. Thus, metamorphosis became a weapon in the hands of the Sheiks to terrorize Muslims in order to subdue them. Of course, all these claims are made without a shred of proof. Transforming a girl into a donkey or a young man into a pig is something that would shake the whole world, especially in these days of the 24-hour news cycle. Those who boast these claims should bring the relatives of the young girl or the young man into a TV station and present them along with supporting testimony from the parents, so that it would be part of the public record. But of course, nothing like this has ever happened.

Why is it that we only hear news about these metamorphoses from the Sheiks' tongues, and do not find it occurring in any non-Islamic countries— not even a single case? Would it not be more logical to assume that God would transform humans in non-Islamic countries since they are considered infidels.

Answering the arguments Muslims use to support the metamorphosis

Those who embrace the idea of metamorphosis of the Jews in the Quran use two supposed proofs to support this myth. First, they claim that the ten tribes of Israel disappeared, leaving only the tribes of Judah and Benjamin. They say the probable explanation for this mass disappearance was that the ten lost tribes were transformed into pigs and monkeys.

Those who embrace this argument are either ignorant of historical events or, worse, know the historical facts yet insist on using the argument of the ten tribes to support the Quran to sway the minds of the simple and ignorant.

In the year 930 B.C. ten tribes of Israel rejected the reign of Rehoboam and made Jeroboam their king. Judah and Benjamin continued to serve Rehoboam in the southern kingdom of Judah with Jerusalem as its capital. The ten northern tribes formed the kingdom of Israel with Samaria as its capital.

Due to the Samarian kings' involvement in idol worship, many members of the ten tribes joined the kingdom of Judah, especially when Judah was ruled by a godly king such as King Asa, as recorded in 2 Chronicles 15:9:

> And he (king Asa) gathered all Judah and Benjamin, and the strangers with them out of Ephraim and Manasseh, and out of Simeon: for they fell to him out of Israel in abundance, when they saw that the LORD his God was with him.

This strengthened the kingdom of Judah while weakening the northern kingdom of Israel.

In the year 720 B.C., Sargon II, king of Assyria, occupied the city of Samaria. He removed the inhabitants to the cities of the Medes, north of Mesopotamia. The inscriptions of Sargon II indicate that he deported only those Israelites who were in the city of Samaria. Undoubtedly, those deported were members of the wealthy class and those with close ties to the king and other political leaders. Many of the remaining inhabitants of the northern kingdom fled for refuge in the kingdom of Judah.

Before this incident, in the year 732 B.C., Tiglath-Pileser III, king of Assyria, besieged Damascus and Israel. He deported many inhabitants of the cities of Israel to Assyrian as recorded in 2 Kings 15:29:

> In the days of Pekah king of Israel came Tiglath Pileser, king of Assyria, and took Ijon, and Abelbethmaachah, and Janoah, and Kedesh, and Hazor, and Gilead, and Galilee, all the land of Naphtali, and carried them captive to Assyria.

The northern kingdom of Israel was in a greatly diminished state until it was finally terminated by Sargon II.

Later, the title "Jews" was expanded to refer to all Israelites. Today, we find them spread throughout all regions of the earth. For example, in Egypt under the Persians they formed a military force, which was stationed in the south to protect the border. The greatest migration of the Jews was in the regions that later became known as the Soviet Union. There were Jewish cities in Armenia. The presence of the Jews in those regions dates to before the Babylonian exile. We cannot exclude the possibility that many whom the Assyrians deported from Israel to Assyria and Medes may have emigrated north to the regions that were later under Soviet control.

It is clear that after the fall of the northern kingdom of Israel, the Hebrews saw their national identity in the kingdom of Judah, which remained a kind of Jewish authority until the year 70 A.D. when Titus led the Romans in destroying the city of Jerusalem.

Many nations of the world have disappeared from history and left no trace of their descendants. For example, where are the Ammonites whose capital was in Rabba Ammon (located in modern Amman-Jordan)? This site was uninhabited until the 18th century. Where are the Hittites who were a great empire that dominated Asia Minor and in certain periods extended their domain over north Syria?! By contrast, how can we conclude that the ten tribes of Israel became monkeys and pigs when we can easily trace many aspects or elements of their history even in our generation?

The other argument some Muslims use is that the Bible records the metamorphosis of Lot's wife into a pillar of salt. If he were able to do this, they reason, it would be no small matter for God to transform the Jews into monkeys and pigs.

The response to this claim is that God did not transform Lot's wife into a pillar of salt. Genesis 19:26 says: "But his wife looked back from behind him, and she became a pillar of salt."

The question is: How did Lot's wife become a pillar of salt?

We have to analyze the story in its entirety, including the events that led up to the incident. A reading of Genesis 19 reveals that a pair of angels ordered Lot to flee to the mountain because the time of judgment had come for Sodom and the other cities in the Jordan Valley. They said to him, "Escape for thy life; look not behind thee, neither stay thou in all the plain; escape to the mountain, lest thou be consumed."

The reason for the warning was that looking back would slow down their running towards the mountain since the fires o judgment fell quickly on all the regions of the valley.

The angel's command was for Lot and his family not to look back on the lost elements of Sodom, whether it was their possessions or relatives or friends, because doing so would delay their escape from the unsafe areas. The angel added, "escape to the mountain, lest thou be consumed." The translation is rendered, "nor stay in all the plain; do not stop in the valley."

The idea was that there was no safety anywhere in the valley of Sodom and the surrounding cities. Lot had to continue running toward the mountain and not stop in the valley. Those who remained in the valley were consumed and died. Judgment reached all those who worked or slept in the valley.

We read in Genesis: 18-19:

> And Lot said unto them, Oh, not so, my LORD: Behold now, thy servant hath found grace in thy sight, and thou hast magnified thy mercy, which thou hast showed unto me in saving my life; and I cannot escape to the mountain, lest some evil take me, and I die.

Lot realized that his escape to the mountain would take time. He was scared and in a state of confusion and thus unable to quickly ascend the mountain to avoid the fires of Sodom. He added in verse 20, "Behold now, this city is near to flee unto, and it is a little one: Oh, let me escape thither, (is it not a little one?) and my soul shall live."

The angel agreed and told Lot he could flee to the city of Zoar, saying, "Escape there quickly." Then we read in Genesis 19:24 that "then the LORD rained on Sodom and Gomorrah sulfur and fire from the LORD out of heaven."

Adam Clarke in his commentary on the passage explains the various elements that contributed to the fires coming upon the cities of the valley:

> We may safely suppose that it was quite possible that a shower of nitrous particles might have been precipitated from the atmosphere, here, as in many other places, called heaven, which, by the action of fire or the electric fluid, would be immediately ignited, and so consume the cities; and, as we have already seen that the plains about Sodom and Gomorrah abounded with asphaltus or bitumen pits, (see Gen14:10), that what is particularly meant here in reference to the plain is the setting fire to this vast store of inflammable matter by the agency of lightning or the electric fluid; and this, in the most natural and literal manner, accounts for the whole plain being burnt up, as that plain abounded with this bituminous substance; and thus we find three agents employed in the total ruin of these cities, and all the circumjacent plain:

1.Innumerable nitrous particles precipitated from the atmosphere.

2.The vast quantity of asphaltus or bitumen which abounded in that country: and,

3.Lightning or the electric spark, which ignited the nitre and bitumen, and thus consumed both the cities and the plain or surrounding country in which they were situated."

Scholars maintain that sulfur is available in great quantities on the shores of the Dead Sea. Sulfur is also available in large quantities near volcanos. It has a lemon-yellow color and is odorless unless it is heated, at which time the fumes become asphyxiating. At high temperatures it becomes electrically negative:

> And he overthrew those cities, and all the valley, and all the inhabitants of the cities, and what grew on the ground. (Genesis 19:25)

Some scholars think that a great earthquake occurred, because earthquakes are relatively common in that part of the world. This was accompanied by the phenomenon of chemical materials raining down.

We notice that the whole area and all of its inhabitants were overthrown. Even today aridity continues to exist around the Dead Sea. In the past, however, it was the most fertile of all the regions of Canaan. It is clear that the raining down of burning chemicals was one of the causes of its destruction and continuing aridity.

Genesis 19:26 then states:

> And his wife looked back from behind him, and she became a pillar of salt.

She was walking behind Lot, who did not see her look back. If he had seen her gazing behind them, he would have prevented her from doing so. It seems likely that she was watching to see if her married daughters had fled Sodom or witnessing the destruction of the city with her house. Looking back caused her to delay her escape. This enabled the chemical substances to reach her and fall on her body.

Grill wrote that "Aventinus reports that in Bavaria, in 1348, more than fifty peasants, with the cows they had milked, at the time of an earthquake were struck with a pestilential air, and stiffened into statues of salt, and which he himself saw."[988]

Some believe that Lot's wife was struck by lightning and then covered by sulfur and other chemicals that came down from heaven or were prevalent in the area. Because she was not exposed to fire, the chemicals coated her dead body. The body of Lot's wife, like the bodies of the other inhabitants of Sodom, was covered with sulfur and other chemical agents.

Robert T. Boyed compares the fate of Lot's wife to what happened to the citizens of Pompeii in A.D. 79:

> Some time ago an excavation was conducted at Pompeii, Italy, which may shed some very interesting light on the subject of Lot's wife. Pompeii, much like Sodom and Gomorrah, shows mute evidence of vast volcanic deposits. When Pompeii was destroyed in A.D. 79, it did not suffer destruction by hot molten lava, but first, a volcanic gas settled over the city, asphyxiating many of the citizens in their sleep. The city was then covered with heavy deposits of volcanic ash to a depth of about twenty feet, and forgotten – until the archaeologist went to work...was struck, numerous human and animals forms were found.

What happened to enable humans and animals to retain their physical form? The late Harry Rimmer had this to say:

> Volcanic ash is heavily impregnated with chemicals, which are water soluble. As time went on, the ash later metamorphosed into a soft stone, somewhat similar to pumice stone. Being porous, water penetrated it freely. The chemical content of the ash worked quickly on the forms of the deceased, and wrought a chemical change which turned their bodies into some chemical, crystalline substance of sufficient hardness to permit the surrounding ash to retain a perfect cast of the buried bodies as it slowly formed into a soft stone. Under the action of the water, leaking through the porous rock, the concentration of chemicals which had been a physical form melted, and then disappeared. But the ash-stone matrix retained the shape and features – even the expressions of those dead. After a score of centuries, we are able to look upon the countenances of Pompeii's citizens once again. In plain and simple language, the recovered bodies of Pompeii must have been changed into a pillar of salt of some variety... the term 'pillar of salt' cannot be restricted in its meaning to sodium chloride, but must be understood in its broader meaning and fuller sense as a chemical substance.[989]

All signs suggest that a chemical gas cloud covered the body of Lot's wife while she stood watching the city. Thus, this incident does not support the idea of metamorphosis, which has no attestation in either history or the Bible. On the contrary, it is against divine principles. God will not annul man's opportunity to repent as long as He decides to give him life on earth. God is not a confused being who plays with the standards and principles that He designated for each species He created. He is not an indignant being who suddenly despises and looks down on the value of man and his position as the crown of His creation and then in a moment equates him with the animals, which are without soul and spirit. Instead, God remains waiting until the last moment of man's life in the hope that he may return to Him in repentance.

We ask the question: Has no one repented among all those who, according to Mohammed's claim, were disfigured as monkeys and pigs? Just one, throughout all the years and after all the hardships and misery?! I am sure that if this claim were true, they would have all repented when they found themselves turned into donkeys and pigs. Why do we not see anyone returning to his human form in accordance with God's mercy, which brings the repentant back to his blessings? Why we do not find just one returning and sharing the experience of how he was transformed into a monkey or pig and how God brought him back to his human form after he had repented?

Mohammed's stories of metamorphosis are built on Arabian Jahiliyyah mythology and cannot stand up either to historical scrutiny or to the theology related to the true God and His characteristics. These stories should have been buried in Mohammed's generation along with his society and its myths of metamorphosis, which is extremely primitive and prehistoric in comparison of the rest of the world's mythologies. The other populations of the world buried the myths of their ancestors thousands of years ago. How much more then should these primitive and inhumane myths have been buried so that no one should speak positively of them today?

Abraham

Abraham in Archaeology, the Bible, and the Quran

Can we determine the historical period in which Abraham lived?

In the first part of his life, Abraham lived at Ur, an ancient Sumerian city that dates back to the 4th millennium B.C. Its Sumerian and Akkadic name was Uru and it was situated at Tell el-Muqayyar المقير تل, southwest of the city of Nasirieh in Iraq. The city was on the Euphrates River, but because of the deviation of the river's course it is now distant from it.

Abraham most likely lived the first part of his life during the third dynasty, which began around 2212 B.C. and terminated with the fall of Ur in the year 2004 B.C. This dynasty had united the Sumerian cities and extended the kingdom of Ur by annexing all Mesopotamia and north of Syria. Some historians believe it reached the Mediterranean.

The main deity of Ur was Nana, the moon god, which later was given the title of Sin. The Ziggurat of Ur was built to honor Nana.

It is difficult to determine precisely when Abraham was born. He might have been born during the reign of Shulgi (2095-2047 B.C.), the second king of the third dynasty. King Shulgi was known for accomplishing several building projects in the cities of Sumer and Accad. He built many ziggurats, including the famous Ziggurat of Ur. He extended his domain by annexing Elam, of which Susa was capital at that time, and annexing part of the Persian Gulf. After Shulgi died, his brother Shusin reigned (2036-2028 B.C.). Then reigned Ebiseen (Shusin's son), who was the fifth and last king of the third dynasty. The city of Ur subsequently fell in the year 2004 B.C. under an attack of the Elamites, ending the third dynasty.

Determining the period in which Abraham, Isaac, and Jacob lived in Canaan

Abraham came out of Ur traveling to Haran, accompanied by his wife, his nephew Lot, and his father, Terah. After his father died, he went with his wife and Lot to the land of Canaan.

We can estimate the period during which Abraham, Isaac, and Jacob lived in Canaan. Several historical elements help us in this estimation. The first is the battle of Siddim, mentioned in Genesis 14. The context of the Biblical reference was the campaign of Chedorlaomer, the king of Elam, who led an alliance of three kings against the cities in the valley of Jordan. We know that Elam was liberated from the rule of Ur in 2004 B.C. and thereafter became a power that led alliances in the region of the Fertile Crescent. Thus, we conclude that Abraham lived in the land of Canaan after the year 2004 B.C.

The second element that helps us determine the period in which Jacob, Abraham's grandson, lived is the history of Haran, the city in which Abraham lived for a determined period. Jacob also returned to live in Haran, after he fled from his brother Esau and sojourned with his uncle, Laban, who lived there. Haran was an important commercial center at the time of Abraham and his sons. Since the city was abandoned sometime between 1800-800 B.C.,[990] we can therefore establish that the period in which Abraham and Isaac lived in Canaan was between 2004-1800 B.C. As for Jacob, it is more difficult to determine when he left Canaan with his children and went to live in Egypt because after leaving his uncle Laban in Haran Jacob lived for a period of time in Canaan.

Thus, the Biblical account in book of Genesis about the period in which Abraham lived agrees with the historical facts. (I will discuss this later in greater detail.) This is contrary to the Quran's claims that Abraham had contentions with King Nimrod, who actually lived thousands of years before Abraham and the Quran's erroneous claims about Abraham and Nimrod were adopted from a Jewish book called Midrash Rabbah, which I will discuss later.

Mohammed and the Old Testament

Mohammad's information about the Old Testament relied on weak sources, some of whom were Jews who embraced Islam whose only knowledge of the Bible were various stories they had heard. They had no true knowledge or understanding of the Old Testament on which to draw. Another of Mohammed's sources on the Old Testament was is Zayd bin Thabet:

> Reported by Zayd bin Thabet who said: 'when the prophet came to Medina, he told me: learn the book of the Jews, they did not believe in my book. Zayd bin Thabet said that he learned it in less than one month.'[991]

Zayd bin Thabet was a very weak source of Old Testament knowledge and history. By his own admission, bin Thabet claimed that that he learned the Old Testament in less than one month. Biblical scholars devote decades of their lives to study of the Old Testament and many acknowledge the limits of their understanding of it. One month of study explains the weakness of Mohammed's information about the Old Testament and how he presented the stories of the Old Testament in a distorted way, not understanding the purpose of the Old Testament texts he tried to explain.

The Quran presents errors regarding the relationship of Abraham with his father

The Bible records no contention or strife between Abraham and members of his family, but rather harmony. We see Terah, Abraham's father, going with Abraham to live in Haran (Genesis 11:31-32) after Abraham received a divine call to leave Ur (Genesis 11:31). So Terah accompanied him, which indicates that he supported Abraham's call and decided to help him answer it. This contradicts the Quranic claim that Abraham's father was a worshiper of idols and that there was a conflict or controversy between Abraham and his father. The Quran says:

> Lo! Abraham said to his father Azar: 'Takest thou idols for gods? For I see thee and thy people in manifest error.' (Al-Anaam, Surah 6: 74)

It further claims that his father decided to stone him:

> (The father) replied: 'Dost thou hate my gods, O Abraham? If thou forbear not, I will indeed stone thee: Now get away from me for a good long while!' (Surah Mariam 19:46)

The Quran claims also that Abraham disowned his father:

> But when it had become clear unto him that he (his father) was an enemy to Allah, he (Abraham) disowned him. (Surah al Taubeh 9:114)

The Quranic story in the light of the expositors of the Quran

The story is narrated with details in Surah Al-Anbiya:

> We bestowed aforetime on Abraham his rectitude of conduct, and we
> were well-acquainted with him. Behold! he said to his father and his
> people, 'What are these images, to which ye are (so assiduously)
> devoted?' They said, 'We found our fathers worshipping them.' He said,
> 'Indeed ye have been in manifest error – ye and your fathers.' They
> said, 'Have you brought us the Truth, or are you one of those who jest?'
> He said, 'Nay, your Lord is the Lord of the heavens and the earth, He
> Who created them (from nothing): and I am a witness to this (Truth).
> And by Allah, I have a plan for your idols – after ye go away and turn
> your backs.' So he broke them to pieces, (all) but the biggest of them,
> that they might turn (and address themselves) to it. They said, 'Who has
> done this to our gods? He must indeed be some man of impiety! We
> heard a youth talk of them: He is called Abraham." They said, 'We heard
> a youth talk of them: He is called Abraham.' They said, 'Then bring him
> before the eyes of the people, that they may bear witness.' They said,
> 'Art thou the one that did this with our gods, O Abraham?' He said: 'Nay,
> this was done by – this is their biggest one! Ask them, if they can speak
> intelligently!' So they turned to themselves and said, 'Surely ye are the
> ones in the wrong!' Then were they confounded with shame: (they said),
> 'Thou knowest full well that these (idols) do not speak!' (Abraham) said,
> 'Do ye then worship, besides Allah, things that can neither be of any
> good to you nor do you harm? Fire upon you, and upon the things that
> ye worship besides Allah! Have ye no sense?' They said, 'Burn him and
> protect your gods, if ye do (anything at all)!' We said, 'O Fire! be thou
> cool, and (a means of) safety for Abraham!' Then they sought a
> stratagem against him: but We made them the ones that lost most!'
> (Surah Al-Anbiya: 21: 51-70)

All the expositors of the Quran agree that the king who debated
Abraham and threw him into fire was Nimrod. We read in al Taberi's
exposition on the Quran:

> They made food and placed in the hands of the idols – gods. They said,
> 'When we come back, and the gods bless our food, then we will eat.'
> But when Abraham looked to them and saw the food in their hands, he
> said, 'Do not you eat?' When they did not answer, he said, 'Why you do
> not speak?' and he began striking them with his right hand. Then he
> took an axe of iron and struck each idol. Then he hung the axe in the
> neck of the bigger idol and got out. This was reported by ibn Ishak who
> said: 'The thing that Abraham did in the gods of his people became
> known to Nimrod and the leaders of his people. When he was brought
> in front of Nimrod and the people asked him, 'O Abraham, are you the
> one who did these things to our gods?' he answered 'Their elder did it;
> ask them if they speak. He was angry that the small gods were
> worshiped with him, being the eldest. Thus, he has broken them.' Then
> Nimrod and his people agreed regarding Abraham, saying, 'Burn him

and vindicate your gods. If you want to vindicate your gods, the only way is to burn him' ... they built a fire and threw him into it. We said to the fire, 'O Fire! be thou cool, and (a means of) safety for Abraham.' (Quoting a Quranic verse) ... ibn Abbas said: 'When the fire was put off, they looked to Abraham, and they saw another man with him, wiping the sweat from his face. That man was the angel of shadow. They brought out Abraham.... Qitadah said: 'Every living animal or creature came to extinguish the fire on Abraham except the toad.' Al Zahri said: 'The prophet of Allah ordered to kill the toad and he named it "a small dissolute."'[992]

Al Qurtubi repeated this saying. He added that while Abraham was in the fire, Nimrod saw him while sitting on a bed in his palace, as Abraham was treated by the angel of shadow. Nimrod said, 'Indeed, the Lord is your lord. I will sacrifice to him four thousand cows.' Then he stopped persecuting him." (The exposition of Al Qurtubi.)

The Quranic story is taken from the Midrash Rabbah

This Quranic story is taken from Midrash Rabbah, also called Bereshit Rabbah. The Midrash Rabbah refers its writing to Hoshaiah or Osha'yah (died in 350 A.D.). The Jewish Encyclopedia maintains that the book was not edited after the Jerusalem Talmud, which is in the 4th or 5th century A.D.

Here is the account of this story in the Midrash Rabbah:

Terah, the father of Abraham and Haran, was a dealer in images as well as a worshiper of them. Once when he was away, he gave Abraham his stock of graven images to sell in his absence. In the course of the day an elderly man came to make a purchase. Abraham asked him his age, and the man gave it as between fifty and sixty years. Abraham taunted him with want of sound sense in calling the work of another man's hand, produced perhaps in a few hours, his god; the man laid the words of Abraham to heart and gave up idol-worship. Again, a woman came with a handful of fine flour to offer to Terah's idols, which were now in charge of Abraham. He took a stick and broke all the images except the largest one, in the hand of which he placed the stick which had worked this wholesale destruction.

When his father returned and saw the havoc committed on his 'gods' and property he demanded an explanation from his son whom he had left in charge. Abraham mockingly explained that when an offering of fine flour was brought to these divinities, they quarreled with one another as to who should be the recipient, when at last the biggest of them, being angry at the altercation, took up a stick to chastise the offenders, and in so doing broke them all up. Terah, so far from being satisfied with this explanation, understood it as a piece of mockery, and when he learned also of the customers whom Abraham had lost him during his management, he became very incensed and drove Abraham out of his house and handed him over to Nimrod. Nimrod suggested to Abraham that, since he had refused to worship his father's idols because of their want of power, he should worship fire, which is very powerful. Abraham pointed out that water has power over fire. 'Well,' said Nimrod, 'let us declare water god.' 'But,' replied Abraham, 'the clouds absorb the water; and even they are dispersed by the wind.' 'Then let us declare the wind our god.' 'Bear in mind,' continued Abraham, 'that man is stronger than wind, and can resist it and stand against it.'

Nimrod, becoming weary of arguing with Abraham, decided to cast him before his god--fire--and challenged Abraham's deliverance by the God of Abraham, but God saved him out of the fiery furnace. Haran, too, was challenged to declare his god, but halted between two opinions, and delayed his answer until he saw the result of Abraham's fate. When he saw the latter saved he declared himself on the side of Abraham's God, thinking that he too, having now become an adherent of that God, would be saved by the same miracle. But since his faith was not real, but dependendant on a miracle, he perished in the fire, into which, like Abraham, he was cast by Nimrod. This is hinted in the words (Gen. xi. 28): 'And Haran died before his father Terah in the land of his nativity, in Ur of the Chaldees.'

The author of Midrash Rabbah copied from Daniel chapter 3 the story of Shadrach, Meshach, and Abednego, who refused to worship the statue of King Nebuchadnezzar. He then threw them fettered into fire. The Lord, however, rescued them. Nebuchadnezzar saw them unfettered and saw the Son of God was with them and that the fire did not harm them. Thus, he ordered them to come out and he honored them.

The debate between Nimrod and Abraham as presented in the Midrash Rabbah was put into the Quran in a different form. As we read in Surah al Baqara 2:58:

Have you not considered him (Namrud) who disputed with Ibrahim about his Lord, because Allah had given him the kingdom? When Ibrahim said: 'My Lord is He who gives life and causes to die,' he said: 'I give life and cause death.' Ibrahim said: 'So surely Allah causes the sun to rise from the east, then make it rise from the west'; thus, he who disbelieved was confounded; and Allah does not guide aright the unjust people.

The period in which Nimrod lived

The writer of the Midrash Rabbah committed an egregious historical error when he made Nimrod to reign at Abraham's time. According to

Genesis 8:10, Nimrod was a grandchild of Ham, the son of Noah. Nimrod preceded Abraham by thousands of years. Genesis 10:10 mentioned the city of Erech among the cities that Nimrod built and reigned over. Erech is identified with the Sumerian city of Uruk (its Accadic name), known in Aramaic as Erech. Moses used the Aramaic name. The ancient period of the city is called Uruk XVIII Eridu period, what dates back to 5000 years B.C. Nimrod evidently lived and reigned prior to that period, perhaps as early as 5500 B.C. Thus, between Nimrod and Abraham, who lived in the 20th century B.C., there must have been around 3500 years. How, then, could Nimrod have been a contemporary of Abraham?!

Mohammed fell in this mistake because he depended on the myths of the Midrash Rabbah, a book that was widespread among the Arabians who embraced Judaism in Mohammed's time. Mohammed adopted this myth because he was ignorant of Biblical chronology.

We see that the Bible presents Ur as the city in which Abraham was born and lived during the first part of his life. Ur was a great city, this we know from the archaeological discoveries made by J.E. Taylor in the year 1854 and the discoveries that followed. The city occupied an important role in the history of Mesopotamia; it reigned over all Mesopotamia, north of Syria, and part of the Persian Gulf. The Quran does not mention the name of a city where Abraham lived or was born but, instead, under the influence of the Midrash Rabbah, perpetuates a historical mistake by claiming that Abraham lived during the reign of Nimrod – a historical gaffe because Nimrod lived no less than 3500 years before Abraham.

Abraham's family knew God and Abraham's faith did not come through Abraham's meditation on the stars, moon, and sun as the Quran claims

The Bible clarifies that the God of Abraham was known by members of Abraham's family. The word "the Lord" was on the tongues of members of Abraham's family, such as Laban and his father Bethuel (son of Nahur, Abraham's brother). See for example what they said to Abraham's servant who asked that Rebekah be a bride to Isaac, "Then Laban and Bethuel answered and said: The thing proceedeth from the LORD. we cannot speak unto thee bad or good" (Genesis 24:50). Furthermore, Rebekah, Bethuel's daughter, who became Isaac's wife, was a true worshiper of the Lord who never showed any pagan influence.

Actually, this confirms what the Bible declares –that there was always a monotheistic line of faith throughout ancient history that extended back to Noah. And through the progeny of Shem, Noah's son, and through many centuries, this belief in the one true God continued to exist among groups faithful to God, such as the one to which Abraham's father belonged. Thus, Abraham was born in a family that worshiped God. This proves that Abraham's faith was not a unique phenomenon that reached Abraham through some extraordinary means, as the Quran claims (i.e., that he believed through contemplating the stars, the moon, and the sun). Here is the Quranic explanation of how Abraham became a believer in the one God:

> So when the night over-shadowed him, he saw a star; said he: 'Is this my Lord?' So when it set, he said: 'I do not love the setting ones.' Then when he saw the moon rising, he said: 'Is this my Lord?' So when it set, he said: 'If my Lord had not guided me I should certainly be of the erring people.' Then when he saw the sun rising, he said: 'Is this my Lord? Is this the greatest?' So when it set, he said: 'O my people! Surely I am clear of what you set up (with Allah). Surely I have turned myself, being upright, wholly to Him Who originated the heavens and the earth, and I am not of the polytheists.' (6:76-79)

The Book of Genesis is in accordance with the historical facts of the period of which it speaks

The War of Seddim

The Lord's call to Abraham came for the second time while he was in Haran. The Lord said to Abraham:

> Now the LORD had said unto Abram, Get thee out of thy country, and from thy kindred, and from thy father's house, unto a land that I will shew thee: And I will make of thee a great nation, and I will bless thee, and make thy name great; and thou shalt be a blessing: And I will bless them that bless thee, and curse him that curseth thee: and in thee shall all families of the earth be blessed. (Genesis 12:1-3)

Abraham departed to the land of Canaan accompanied by Sarah, his wife, and Lot, his nephew. The twelve chapter of Genesis narrate how a famine occurred in the land of Canaan. Abraham went to Egypt and then returned to Canaan. In Chapter 13, Abraham and Lot were separated, and Lot went to live in Sodom in the Valley of Jordan.

The book of Genesis shows that at Abraham's time Elam was a leader of alliances in the region. This is actually in agreement with the official history of Abraham's time that is the beginning of the second millennium B.C. Genesis 14 tells about a war between four kings against five kings of the cities of the Valley of Jordan:

> And it came to pass in the days of Amraphel, king of Shinar, Arioch, king of Ellasar, Chedorlaomer, king of Elam, and Tidal, king of nations; That these made war with Bera, king of Sodom, and with Birsha, king of Gomorrah, Shinab, king of Admah, and Shemeber, king of Zeboiim, and the king of Bela, which is Zoar. All these were joined together in the vale of Siddim, which is the salt sea. Twelve years they served Chedorlaomer, and in the thirteenth year they rebelled. And in the fourteenth year came Chedorlaomer, and the kings that were with him, and smote. (Genesis 14:16)

Does the political picture of that period agree with the narrative presented in Genesis chapter 14?

After the kingdom of Ur fell in the 2004 B.C., a great political vacuum existed in the area of the Fertile Crescent. Before that date, Ur was the empire that dominated many regions of the Fertile Crescent, especially Mesopotamia and northern Syria. After 2004 B.C., city-states emerged, each one governed by a king, in addition to small districts surrounding the cities. The fall of Ur was brought about by the attacks of the Amorites on the northern cities and the Elamites in the south. Elam was the only organized power in the region in the midst of these city-states and small districts, who from time to time banded together to form alliances. Thus, the emergence of Elam as a power presiding over alliances in that period is the picture that perfectly matches what the book of Genesis recorded about this alliance led by the Elamites. The account of Elam as the power that defeated Ur, which was the great power in the Fertile Crescent, to flex its muscles and to plunder in that region, is in perfect accordance with the account of Genesis chapter 14 about the attack of this alliance against many regions, including the Jordan Valley.

Most of the cities and places mentioned in Genesis, which this alliance led by Elam attacked, are recorded in the inscriptions of the Middle East. There is no space here to mention them. Instead, I will focus on the titles of the kings who were part of this alliance.

Chedorlaomer, and his title, and the dominance of the Elamites

The first part of the name (Chedor) is identified with Kutir, a title of the kings of Elam as it is attested in long series of kings. (Kenneth Anderson

Kitchen quotes many scholars who attest to this fact.)[993] Some scholars maintain that it is possible that Laomer was Lagamar, known in the inscriptions of Mari.[994] There is another possibility that Chedorlaomer was a second name of one of Elam's kings, who was Kudur Lagamar. Kudur means "servant"; Lagamar is Lagamaru, an Elamite god mentioned by Assurbanipal. This possibility is supported by David Rohl, a famous scholar who is a specialist in the Middle Eastern inscriptions, and also by Sayce.[995]

As I previously mentioned, Elam tried to fill the vacuum created by the fall of Ur. The Elamites were active in that period in contacting the important cities of the region in order to create alliances. The emissaries of Elam reached important cities of that period, such as Qatna.[996] Qatna was in the region known today as al Mashrafeh, which is a site of an ancient Amorite civilization, which is about 18 kilometers from the Syrian city of Humus. Its history dates back to the middle of the third millennium B.C.

The dominance of Elam over regions in Syria and Palestine is clear when we study the history of the region. For example, there was Kudur-Mabug (1770-1754 B.C.), an Elamite king who reigned in the city of Larsa, which was about 25 kilometers southeast of Yuruk City (in the south of Mesopotamia). Albert Tobias Clay, an American archeologist (who died in the 1925) wrote:

> In a number of inscriptions, Kudur-Mabug also calls himself Adda Martu, which means 'prince of the Land of Amurru (Palestine and Syria).' In other words, in inscriptions prior to the over-throw of Elam and Larsa record the supremacy of Elam over this region. This is in strict accordance with Genesis. [997]

Notice that the name of this Elamite king begins with Kudur, as Chedorlaomer or Kodorlaomer. Thus, the book of Genesis calls an Elamite king with the title of Chedor or Kodor, which is an ancient title of the kings of Elam. Genesis also reveals that Elam dominated the region through alliances, which reflects the historical situation at the time of Abraham.

Tidal as a Hittite title

The second king in the alliance was Tidal. Tidal according to the Biblical text here is "Tidal king of Goyim" (i.e., Tidal king of the peoples). He carried a Hittite title. Saying that he was "a king of peoples" indicates that he was not a king in a kingdom but a king of a tribe. The Hittites lived as a people in the Anatolia – Asia Minor, and later occupied Syria, and had some penetration into the land of Canaan. Before they created their kingdom in Anatolia in the 18th century B.C., however, they were known as groups of fighters:

> Tudkala was a title of leaders in Anatolia between the 20th and 19th centuries B.C., leaders of groups of fighters.[998]

Victor P. Hamilton wrote:

> The connection between the Hebrew word tid'al and Hittite Tudhalia is evidenced by the Ugaritic spelling of the Hittite royal name as tdg'l. [999]

Thus, the book of Genesis mentioned Tidal as a title of a Hittite leader who was known by the people at the time of Abraham.

Amraphel as a title of some Amorite kings

Shinar was a kingdom in Babylon (Genesis 10:10). Shinar is also found in the Hittite, Syrian, and Egyptian inscription, which date back to the second part of the second millennium B.C. [1000] It was a name of Mesopotamia especially in the region of Babel.[1001] It seems that the name Shinar is derived from Shene nahar, which means "the two rivers."[1002]

We find in the letters of Amranah as well in other Egyptian writings the word Sanhar or Sangar (Sankhar), which scholars identified with Shinar, which represented a region in Mesopotamia.[1003]

The use of this word cannot be dated to a time after Moses wrote the book of Genesis. In describing the king of a region in Mesopotamia that was part of the alliance led by Elam in attacking the Jordan Valley, Moses used the term Shinar, the name of Mesopotamia known at his time.

Kitchen says that Amraphel might be Amudpiel.[1004] K. Jaritz says that Amudpiel was an Amorite king, whose name means "Enduring the command of El".[1005] It seems that this name was a title of the Amorite kings.

Arioch as a royal title known in that period

Arioch, king of Ellasar, was a known title for a group of kings in Mesopotamia. Some of them are attested in Mari Archive[1006] to have lived at the beginning of the second millennium B.C. We find the name of King Ariukki in Nuzi, [1007] a center near Haran. Arioch must have been a king for the northern region of Mesopotamia. We also find a name similar to that mentioned in the Bible in the Execration texts (Mirgissa F.3).[1008]

Execration texts were magical inscriptions that contained names of leaders or kings whom the Egyptians abhorred. They belonged to nations that disturbed the Egyptians.[1009] Their names were inscribed on statues or vessels and then broken and buried. The Egyptians thought such acts would hurt the named parties represented by the statues through magic. These kinds of inscriptions are of special importance to reveal the names of some leaders or kings in the Middle East in the period between 2000-1800 B.C. This shows that one of the kings who had the title of Arioch was well known to the Egyptians as a worrisome king who competed with them in the regions of Syria and Palestine.

As for the location of Ilasar, some scholars say that it is Larsa, originally a Sumerian city 25 kilometers from Uruk in southern Mesopotamia. Larsa continued to be an important city even after the fall of Ur. Others identify Ilasar with Alsiya in northern Mesopotamia on the Tigris River. There is also Ilansura, which was a kingdom in northern Mesopotamia, between Kerkamish and Haran.[1010] There was also Telassar mentioned in the book of Isaiah 37:12.

The titles of the four kings and their alliances are in agreement with the political circumstances at Abraham's time

We thus see an alliance among four kings: the king of Elam, a king of a Hittite tribe, an Amorite king, and a king of northern Mesopotamia (likely near Haran). The names of the kings of this alliance recorded in the Biblical book Genesis chapter 14 agree with titles of that period. Kitchen says:

> Thus, the personal names fit the regions they ruled and correspond with real names and known name types, even if the individuals are not yet identified in external sources. This is hardly surprising, given the incompleteness of data for most regions in the ancient Near East for the third, and much of the early second, millennia, even the great Mari archive covers only about fifty to seventy years.[1011]

In reality, after the fall of Ur around 2004 B.C., Mesopotamia was divided into a number of small kingdoms, such as Isin, Larsa, Eshnunna, Assyria, in addition to cities-states such as Mari in the northwestern region. This situation persisted until the appearance in the 18th century B.C. of Hammurabi in Babel who dominated the region. Later the Assyrians began dominating around the beginning of 1600 B.C. Thus, alliances such as that mentioned in Genesis emerged between 2000-1700 B.C. Mari's Archive attests to these alliances:

> No single king is strongest by himself; 10 or 15 kings follow Hammurabi of Babylon, and so for Rim-Sin of Larsa, and so for Ibalpiel of Eshnunna, and so for Amutpiel of Qatna. But 20 kings follow Yarim-Lim of Yamhad.[1012]

Therefore, as Kitchen maintains, the period between 2000-1700 B.C. was the only period during which Elam intervened in the politics of Mesopotamia and its armies. Kitchen writes:

> It is only in this particular period (2000-1700) B.C. that the eastern realm of Elam intervened extensively in the politics of Mesopotamia – with its armies – and sent its envoys far west into Syria to Qatna. Never again did Elam follow such wide-reaching policies. So in terms of geopolitics, the eastern alliance in Gen. 14 must be treated seriously as an archaic memory preserved in the existing book of Genesis.[1013]

Were the cities mentioned in the war of Seddim verified?

Ham: Among the cities mentioned in the war of Seddim was Ham. Albright, a famous American archeologist, speaks about Ham as a place that was occupied by Chederlaomer and the kings who were allied with him as described in Genesis 14:5. Albright found the place in eastern Gilead. After studying the site, he verified that it belonged to the Bronze period. The name of the city of Ham is mentioned among the cities that Pharaoh Tuthmosis III had occupied in the year 1480 B.C. Albright cites proofs indicating that the war of Seddim was indeed historical.[1014]

Ashteroth Karnaim: Nelson Glueck has verified Ashteroth Karnaim (two words) mentioned in Genesis 14:6 with two neighboring sites located in southern Syria, known as Tel Ashtarah and Sheikh Sa'ad. Sheikh Sa'ad was known in the Christian era as Carnaim. Albright says that Ashteroth and Karnaim were occupied in the same period as revealed in the excavations.[1015]

Enmishpat, which is Kadesh: This is mentioned in Genesis 14:7:

> And they returned, and came to Enmishpat, which is Kadesh, and smote all the country of the Amalekites, and also the Amorites, that dwelt in Hazezontamar.

This place was verified as the spring known as Ain el-Qudeirat situated in Sinai.[1016]

The city-states and the leaders of tribal folks in the period of Abraham, Isaac, and Jacob

The Egyptian inscriptions known as Execration texts reveal the political circumstances in the first part of the second millennium B.C. The region consisted of cities, each governed by one person. There were also the tribal folks such as the one Abraham hailed from. The same inscriptions mentioned about 30 tribes or chieftains existing in the same regions.[1017]

An Egyptian story, called the story of Sinuhe, referred to the time of the death of Pharaoh Amenemhat I, who was the founder of the 12th dynasty, at the beginning of the second millennium B.C. When the Egyptians began campaigning against Libya, Sinuhe accompanied Senwosret I, the crown prince, in the campaign. Suddenly, Amenemhat I died, perhaps through a conspiracy, and Senwosret returned to Egypt to claim his throne. Sinuhe feared that struggles would ensue, and he fled to the land of Canaan and Syria to begin a new life in those regions. Sinuhe was rescued by Ammunenshi, one of the shepherds' chiefs or leaders there, who was a shepherd leader similar to Abraham and Isaac.

The authority was in the hand of governors or kings or chiefs. Those chiefs we find wandering as nomads carrying their tents from regions of Canaan toward the south and vice versa, exactly as Abraham used to do in his travels.

We find similar political structures of migratory chiefs of shepherds sometimes in alliance with governors or kings of cities in other regions as well. Thus, in the beginning of the 2nd millennium B.C., authority was shared between the local kings of the cities and the chiefs of tribes who lived in tents on the outskirts of the cities. This status is verified in city-kingdoms such as Kish, Babylon, Sippar, Isin, and Kisurra. Those chiefs were called rabianu.[1018]

This type of political structure in Canaan was completely different from that which prevailed during the time the Egyptians dominated Canaan, dating back to 1460-1160 B.C. The existence of these tribal chiefs, or shepherds' chiefs, such as Abraham, led to the creation of treaties or alliances between those chiefs and the leaders or kings of the cities, either in Mesopotamia or in Canaan and Syria. From the tables of the city of Mari, which date back to 1750 B.C., we see the relationships of Mari with various groups of nomadic peoples who lived dwelled in tents and inhabited the surrounding regions. Treaties were issued between these tribes and the city of Mari.[1019] The same treaties or alliances were struck between Abraham and Amorite leaders (Memra and his brothers). Later we see a treaty between Abraham and Abi Malek, the king of Jerar, and between Abi Malek and Isaac.

The wandering of the tribes or shepherds' chiefs

The tribes who lived around the cities were semi-nomadic in that they wandered from time to time in search of grass for grazing their livestock. We know from the tablets of Mari that Mare-Yamina lived around the city of Mari and sometimes wandered east of the Tigris river and to the south toward Uruk, Larsa, and Sippar. There were tribes that surrounded Haran, exactly as did Terah, Abraham's father. There were tribes that wandered in north Syria as far as the range of the Lebanon mountains.[1020] Nomadic or semi-nomadic wandering tribes and shepherds emigrated to the land of Canaan and Trans-Jordan in the period between 2000-1800 B.C.[1021]

The big cities were abandoned in the period in which Abraham lived. The period was characterized by the emigrations of mostly shepherd groups to the land of Palestine from different regions of Mesopotamia. Small cities appeared with chiefs on the level of Abraham, to the point that treaties were established between Abraham and some leaders of these small cities, as previously mentioned. The rarity of archeological discoveries in that period of great buildings, fortifications, and big cities supports the Biblical narrative.[1022] This picture had changed at the time of Isaac and Jacob. When Abraham visited Shakim it was just a place (Genesis 12:6). But, by the time Jacob returned to Shakim, it had developed into a city (Genesis 33:18).

It would be impossible for any author who came later to invent such a narrative, which is in accordance with the historical facts. This is contrary to the Quranic narrative.

Thus, the account of Genesis regarding Abraham agrees with the political circumstances that we encounter in archeology with all its elements. When we come to the story of Abraham in the Quran, however, we find it very simple without any historical reference that would bestow any credibility on it. All that the Quran narrates about Abraham is a myth derived from the Midrash Rabbah, whose author connected Abraham with Nimrod who lived thousands of years before Abraham. It is impossible that such an erroneous narrative could be inspired by the God of history. Instead, it is an account born of mythological thoughts without any historical support that would render it deserving of the searcher's or the thinker's attention. It is easy to narrate or recount a story under mythological influence as we see in the story of Abraham in the Quran. But it is impossible for any writer who lived in a later epoch to create a narrative that expresses accurately the political picture during the 20th and 19th centuries B.C. This shows that Moses, the writer of Genesis, relied on written records that came from Abraham, Isaac, and Jacob's times, transmitted by Joseph and kept by the Israelites in Egypt where Moses acquired them.

The names in the patriarchs' generation and their similarities with the patriarchs' names

Kaiser wrote about the importance of these names:

A parallel line of evidence on the validity of the patriarchal age comes from the form of the names given in this era, for names do tend to reflect a unique cultural setting in time. Just as one can determine the age of a modern photograph by noting the style and shape of an automobile (if one is included), or even by noting the style and length of dresses worn by the women in the picture, so names are usually pretty much of a dead give-away of the era one is in by the particular form of the names.[1023]

We understand from the list of Abraham's ancestors in Genesis 11 that his father, grandfather, and great-grandfather were Terah, Nahur, and Sarug. These names we encounter in the Assyrian and ancient Babylonian writings in the upper Euphrates region around the city of Haran where the family lived. That historical evidence cannot be considered a mere coincidence or chance.[1024] The Abraham family names indicate that the family belonged mainly to the northernmost region of Mesopotamia, which had Haran as its center, and then to Ur. This supports the notion that Haran was the origin of this family, then the family migrated to Ur because of its economy and returned to Harran after Ur fell. Among the proofs of the connection of Abraham's family with Haran is the fact that Abraham's brother was called Haran and his second brother was Nahur, the name of a city mentioned in the tablets of Mari that dates back to the 18th century B.C. Abraham's father, Terah, was the name of a town or village located in the site of Tel-Turakhi. His grandfather, Sarug, is the name of a town named Sarugi. His ancestor Peleg is similar to the name Phaliga.

Names in Genesis such as Isaac, Ishmael, Joseph, and Jacob are found in abundance in the inscriptions that date to the beginning of the second millennium B.C. For example, we find those names in the tablets of Mari, which dates back to the 18th century B.C. The scholar Ignace J. Gelb gathered 6,000 such names dating from that period. Though we encounter these names in each epoch, its great use applies to the period in which the patriarchs lived. These are west Semitic names, such as the Amoritis' names, that begins with the letter I, like Ishmael and Isaac. And names like Joseph and Jacob, which begin in the letter Y. These names were widespread in the first half of the second millennium B.C., which was the time of the patriarchs. But they went down to 55% during the second half of the second millennium B.C. The name Benjamin was found among these names of the same period.[1025]

The trips between Mesopotamia, Syria, and other regions, and vice versa

The archeologists say that not only livestock owners, but also the envoys of the rulers and merchants travelled between southern Mesopotamia, passing through Haran to north Syria and Canaan. They travelled not only to Canaan and Syria but also to Anatolia and other destinations. The historical evidence is in stations of rest and itineraries.[1026] For example, a rental contract for a wagon that dates back to the first part of second Millennium B.C. has been found in the writings of Mesopotamia. Among the articles of the rental there is one that prohibits driving the wagon towards the Mediterranean coasts.

The following is the text of the contract

A wagon

From Mannum-balun-Shamash,

Son of Shelibia,

Khabilkinum,

Son of Appani {bi},

On a lease

For one year

Has hired.

As a yearly rental

2/3 of a shekel of silver

He will pay.

As the first of the rent

1/6 of a shekel of silver

He has received.

Unto the land of Kittim

He shall not drive it.

In the presence of Ibku-Adad,

Son of Abiatum;

In the presence of Ilukasha,

Son of Arad-Ilishu;

In the presence of Ilishu.......

Month Ululu, day 25,

The year the king Erech from the flood

Of the river as a friend protected.[1027]

As we know from many verses of the Old Testament, such as Ezekiel 27:6, Kittim means the Mediterranean Sea. This contract was written in the city of Sippar, which in ancient times was called Agade, located on the Euphrates river north of Babylon.[1028]

It is clear that there were wagon rentals because of the heavy transportation among Mesopotamia, Palestine, and Syria. No doubt the wagon owners prohibited the wagons from reaching the coasts out of fear that the waters of the sea would destroy the wagons.

This explains the ease with which Abraham's family travelled about as narrated in the book of Genesis. Bible scholars believe that Nahur (and the family of Abraham in general) lived first in the area of Haran, then migrated to Ur, and then returned to Haran, the original family home. The migratory phenomenon was known to occur from the Haran region to the south toward Ur and vice versa. This helps explain the return of Terah, Abraham's father, to Haran[1029] and the ease with which Abraham travelled with his wife Sarai and his nephew Lot from Haran to Canaan.

The Quranic claim that Abraham went to Mecca is contrary to history and the principles of geography

We conclude that Abraham's trip from Ur to Haran and then to the land of Canaan was a routine part of life in that period. Such migration was nothing unusual in the historical reality of Abraham's time. This contradicts the Quran's claim that Abraham went to Mecca, as is stated in the following Quranic verses:

> And (remember) when Ibrahim (Abraham) said, 'My Lord, make this city (Makkah) a place of security and provide its people with fruits, such of them as believe in Allah and the Last Day.' He (Allah) answered: 'As for him who disbelieves, I shall leave him in contentment for a while, then I shall compel him to the torment of the Fire, and worse indeed is that destination!' (Al Baqara 2:126)

The Quran also claims that Abraham prayed at Mecca asking that some of his offspring, (the Ishmaelites) dwell there by the Kaabah and that the peoples go there for Hajj. Here is the verse:

> O our Lord! I have made some of my offspring to dwell in a valley without cultivation, by Thy Sacred House; in order, O our Lord, that they may establish regular Prayer: so fill the hearts of some among men with love towards them, and feed them with fruits, so that they may give thanks. (Surah Ibrahim 14:37)

This Quranic claim—that Abraham went to Mecca—conflicts, however, with both history and geography. We know that Mecca did not exist in Abraham's time, as I will discuss later. There was no route whatsoever between Yemen and Palestine to justify the construction of Mecca on the route (as happened only much later when the route appeared). There is no historical evidence that anybody walked this land route until the third century B.C. Western Arabia where Mecca was later built was an unknown place for the inhabitants of Mesopotamia and Canaan. Furthermore, there was no mention of Yemen in any inscription before the 15th century B.C. The first Egyptian writing that speaks about Yemen (or possibly Somalia) was about a chief named Genebtyu who presented a tribute to Pharaoh Thutmose III, who reigned between 1479-1425 B.C.[1030] Today scholars doubt that Genebtyu was a Yemeni leader and tend to identify him as Somali. We do not have any reference about western Arabia and Yemen in any Mesopotamian, Syrian, or Canaan inscriptions. This confirms that western Arabia was completely unknown to the populations of the Fertile Crescent and Egypt. No knowledge was available to the inhabitants of those regions about western Arabia before the Sabaeans and Maini appeared in

Yemen between the 13th and 11th centuries B.C. when a commercial communication began to take place between Yemen and the area of the Fertile Crescent. How then could Abraham have gone to a place where nobody had gone before, where nobody had heard of in his generation?!

Furthermore, the alleged trip Abraham made to Mecca was not mentioned in the book of Genesis, the only book through which the world came to know about Abraham's life. Why would the Hebrews have hidden Abraham's trip to western Arabia if really it happened?! Genesis narrated Abraham's journey to Egypt through the negative events that occurred during the trip; we know he lied in claiming that Sarah was his sister, which resulted in Pharaoh's taking her to his palace as a concubine. She was liberated only when the Lord intervened on her behalf. Abraham went to Egypt even though the Lord had called him to live in the land of Canaan and in no other place; thus, he went to Egypt against God's will. Why then given its unrelenting honesty would the Bible hide the alleged trip of Abraham to western Arabia?! The authors of the books of the Bible were in the habit of not hiding anything about the important figures of the Bible, such as Abraham, Moses, and David, no matter how negative the events of their lives were at times, and despite the fact that the writers were not pleased with it—such as the fall of David in adultery; or Abraham's cowardly denial of his wife Sara twice, claiming she was his sister, out of fear for his own life; or Moses' killing the Egyptian and then fleeing to Sanai. Why, then, would those writers hide Abraham's trip to Mecca if it had really happened?!

The tribes of Canaan at the time of Abraham

The book of Genesis mentions some tribes or groups living in Canaan at the time of Abraham. Do history and archeology agree that these tribes existed in that era or were they rather names created by a later writer? This question is vitally important because the Quran lacks any information regarding tribes or nations who lived in western Arabia (where Mecca was built) in Abraham's time. So the question is whether the historical and archeological evidence confirms the historicity of what the Quran claimed.

Among the tribes and peoples mentioned by Genesis are the Canaanites, Hittites, Horites, Amorites, Jebusites, Girgashites, and Kadmonites (Genesis 14:6;15:19-21).

The Canaanites: They lived in the coastal area, also the lowlands toward the Jordan river. The origin of the tribes that descended from Canaan, son of Ham, was that they first lived in Mesopotamia. They then occupied regions in northern Syria and Palestine. The Canaanite archeological records from Abraham's time are abundant. Their language influenced the Hebrew language to a great degree.

The Hittites: The center of the Hittites was in Anatolia in Asia Minor. From there they extended to north Syria and the land of Canaan. The Hittite Empire reached its golden period during the 14th century B.C. The empire was divided in the 12th century B.C. Scholars debate whether the Hittites of Asia Minor are the same Hittites who lived in Canaan at the time of Abraham.

In 1906 Professor Hugo Winckler of Berlin, discovered 20,000 tablets in Boghaz-keui, the capital of the Hittites.[1031] Kitchen wrote:

> **By circa 1800 B.C. we already have Kukun' son Luqqa (the Lycian) named on a small obelisk at Byblos; these are ancestral to Lycian, i.e., Luvian, a sister dialect of Hittite.[1032]**

He also said that if this was in the city of Byblos in Phoenicia, then it would be easy to find Nesites (the Hittites, inhabitants of Anatolia) 160 miles farther.[1033] (He was referring to the sons of Heth who sold the field and the cave to Abraham, where he buried Sarah.) There are scholars who maintain that the obelisk of Byblos contains the name of Kukun' son Luqqa and was originally an Egyptian obelisk dating to the 21st century B.C.[1034]

About the penetration of the Hittites in the land of Canaan and their antiquity: During the 18th and 17th centuries B.C., the Hittites intervened in Syria[1035] and there has been attested an early penetration of Hittites in Phoenicia and Palestine.[1036]

The Horites: The book of Genesis mentions them in more than place (e.g., 14:6 and 36:20). Historically the Horites were mentioned for the first time in a document that dates back to the Accadic Sargon's period during the 24th century B.C. when they had a kingdom behind the Tigris River. In the 19th century B.C., they extended their domain in Mesopotamia and occupied Assur. Then they went to Syria and penetrated Syria and Palestine.

In the year 1931, during excavations in Yorghan Tepe, the site of the city Nuzi, near Karkuk, archeologists discovered thousands of tablets written in cuneiform that date back to the 14th and 15th centuries B.C. The inhabitants of Nuzi were Hurrians, the Horites of the Old Testament. The name of the city was Gasur, originally an ancient Accadic city. In the middle of the second millennium B.C. the Horites occupied the city and called it Nuzi.

The Amorites: Many scholars maintain that the Amorites were the cause of the Ur kingdom's fall. Around 1900 B.C. the Amorites dominated a large area of Mesopotamia. They dominated Babylon between 1800-1530 B.C., the period known as the ancient Babylonian era. Hammurabi, who reigned during the 18th century B.C., was one of them. They extended their domain to northern Syria and part of Canaan. Mari was an important city of the Amorites.

Mari is located 200 miles southeast of Haran and was a large fluorescent city between 2800-1760 B.C. Found there was a palace that consists of 300 rooms and contains an archive of 15,000 documents: mostly letters, treaties, and religious texts. From these letters we see custom identical to what we find in Genesis, such as killing animals when issuing treaties. We find in the Mari texts names of various gods mentioned in the Old Testament. There are names such as Abram, Noah, Laban, and Jacob. This means that those names we encounter in the book of Genesis were common in that day. We find names of cities such as Haran and Nahur, which might have been named after Abraham' grandfather. Also we find the name of the city of Hasur. The letters of Mari prove the social correspondence of Abraham and the rest of the patriarchs' time with the customs and conventions of that historical time period.

The Kadmonites: The Hebrew tradition tells us that the Kadmonites were "the sons of the east," a people living east of the land of Canaan. There is mention in the Egyptian writings of a political man named Sinuhe, mentioned earlier, who fled from Egypt during the 12th dynasty and found refuge in Canaan in the land of Kedem.[1037] This was most likely a Canaanite tribe that lived east of Canaan.

The Girgashites: They descended from Girgash, the fifth son of Canaan. They lived in Trans-Jordan. They were mentioned in the Hittite inscriptions as Qaraqishaor Qarkisa and in the Egyptian inscriptions as Kirkash.[1038]

The Jebusites: They were a tribe descended from Canaan (see Genesis 10:16). They inhabited the city of Jerusalem. Their king at the time of

Abraham was Melchizedek. When Israel reached the land of Canaan, Adonizedec reigned over Jerusalem (see Joshua 10:1). Though the Jebusites were defeated by Joshua, they remained in their city Jebus (Jerusalem) until it was occupied by David who made it his capital. We know that the inhabitants remained in David's time and that David bought a field from Arnan the Jebusite, in which he built an altar to the Lord.

The Jebusites were identified under the name of Yabusium in a cuneiform letter in the city of Mari.

The lack of any mention in the Quran of any tribe who lived in Abraham's time to give to its narrative any historical credence

We see then that most of the peoples mentioned in Genesis at the time of Abraham are historically attested, establishing through historical and archeological evidence that they lived in his time. This was not a story inserted into history during a later epoch. Rather, the narrative of Genesis is an account of historical facts, events that happened to particular people at a historical time and place. They are not myths invented by later writers. The more we advance in knowledge and archeology, the more we discover information about the population who lived at the time of Abraham mentioned in the book of Genesis. This proves that we can trust the accuracy of the Genesis account about Abraham and the political and social circumstances in Abraham's time and place.

When we examine the claims of the Quran, however, we find no historical reference that indicates the author was led by the Spirit of God who is knowledgeable of the details of history. Mohammed did not mention any tribe existing in western Arabia, which would encourage us to search and verify his claim that he was inspired by the God of history.

Filling the gap through innovations created by later writers

In the early centuries after Islam was born, Muslims became aware of the great historical vacuum in the Quran. They attempted to invent an ancient history for Mecca by claiming that Mecca was inhabited by tribes before the alleged trip of Abraham and Ishmael to Mecca. One of these tribes was Amalek. They also claimed that a tribe called Jurhum had emigrated from Yemen to Mecca and got permission from Hagar to live in Mecca. Thus, they made it out as though Hager was in possession of Mecca and hence dominated Amalek, the tribe the Muslims held to be the main inhabitants of Mecca when Hagar reached Mecca. All this contrived history was invented after Mohammed died; it was not known before that in any book or inscription. Among the named individuals who contributed to such invented claims were ibn Ishak, ibn Abbass, Ubeid bin Sharayyeh, ibn al Kalbi, Wahab bin Munabbeh and Kaab al Ahbar.

Among those who claimed that the Amalek tribe inhabited Mecca was ibn Abbass. Ibn Ishak claimed that some members of Amalek went to live in Damascus and that the pharaohs were descendants of Amalek.[1039] It is known that Amalek (for whom the tribe was named) was son of Aliphaz, son of Esau, son of Isaac, son of Abraham (see Genesis 36:9-13). Thus, Amalek was an Edomite tribe (the tribe descended from Esau). They inhabited the eastern part of Sinai. Ibn Ishak, however, made them the third offspring of Sam. He followed the claim of ibn Abbass that they were the inhabitants of Mecca.[1040] All of these claims were made to create an ancient history for Mecca where there was none, for we know from analyzing the historical facts that Mecca did not appear before the 4th century A.D. (For more on this topic, see Dr. Amari, Islam in Light of History.) Ibn Ishak claimed that Amalek was the origin of the pharaohs. Sadly, these fabrications of ibn Abbass and ibn Ishak remain today still the foundation upon which Muslims build the history of Mecca, on the fictional history that the Amalekites had inhabited Mecca since thousands of years B.C.

Regarding Jurhum: The Islamic narrators claimed that he was a son of Qahtan, whom they identified with Joktan who was mentioned in Genesis 10:25-26. The first to claim this was Ubeid bin Sharayeh. We have seen that Qahtan is derived from the name of the tribe of Qahten, which was dominated by the tribe of Kinda. We see in the Arabian inscriptions that Rabi'at the king of Kinda was given the title of "king of Kinda and Qahten."[1041] In their attempt to make Joktan live in Yemen, they found that the tribe of Qahten is relatively close in spelling to Joktan. They then changed Qahten into Qahtan and claimed that he was Joktan. They claimed Qahtan was the father of all Yemen, despite the fact that the descendants of Joktan in the Bible lived in the area of the Persian Gulf and southeastern part of Arabia. In our discussion of the five idols that Mohammed attributed to the time of Noah, we saw that Ibn al Kalbi claimed that Jurhum was the Hadoram[1042] who was mentioned in Genesis 10:27, as son of Joktan, son of Eber, son of Arphaxad, son of Sam. This is a historical mistake, however, for the two words are quite different.

Muawiya and Ubeid bin Sharayyeh

Mauwiya bin Abi Sufian, founder of the Umayyad dynasty, used to call Ubeid bin Sharayyeh so that Ubeid could narrate to him "the news of the ancients." Thus, every night Ubeid created and narrated stories without any documentation to support them. Muawiya in turn recorded these stories, which became for Muslims the most important reference to the invented history that replaced the true and official history. These undocumented stories became the substance by which they support the Quranic narration. The genealogies Ubeid created became famous and widespread and were believed by the later Islamic writers who wanted to write about the ancient history – even the history never mentioned in the official history. They could not find anything earlier than what Ubeid claimed when he entertained Muawiya. For example, the Masudi holds Ubeid to be more important than the rest of the Islamic writers. Here is his comment:

> Among those narrators who had access to Muawiya who had knowledge of the ancients, whether they were Arabs or non-Arabs, the best was Ubeid bin Sharayyeh. He told him the chronicles of the ancient days, what they contained of incidents and how the genealogies were born. Ubeid bin Sharayyeh's book is widespread and famous.[1043]

Among the ridiculous claims of Ubeid is that he created a genealogy of the kings of Saba that began with "Saba," whom he claimed was son of "Ya'rib, son of Qahtan." His genealogy passes through the Himyarites whom he placed immediately after Rehoboam, son of Solomon (that is, at the end of the 10th century B.C). We know, however, that the Himyarites appeared and reigned in southern Yemen beginning in the year 115 B.C., whereas the Sabaeans continued to reign until the third century A.D. Ubeid invented history without having any knowledge of historical chronology.

The interesting thing is that Ubeid created the list of names of the kings of Saba who reigned during a historical period that no other historian besides him mentioned. We do not find any book or inscription, such as the Musnad inscription of Yemen, that mentions any name for the period Ubeid claimed to know. The historical list of kings assembled from archeological findings begins in the middle of the 8th century B.C. and it is very accurate and complete and has no gaps. Ubeid did not mention a single name that occurs on this attested list of kings. Ubeid had no grounds (and no historical reference) to create a list of all kings of Saba, from the first king till the end, during a time when archeologists maintain that the Sabaeans of Yemen were not using written records. They began using writing only from the 11th century B.C. at the earliest; the oldest Saba inscription dates back to the year 820 B.C.[1044]

Was Muawiya convinced of what Ubeid narrated to him? Why he recorded the buffoonery of Ubeid's stories.

It is obvious that Muawiya was not convinced of the accuracy of the stories of Ubeid. Muawiya was known to be shrewed and cunning and knew that most Muslims looked to him as abductor of the caliphate, especially after defeating Ali ibn Abi Taleb, Mohammed's son-in-law, who became the fourth caliph. Muawiya wanted to distract his contemporary Muslims from politics and get them to focus instead on attractive things as their topics of discussion and study. Thus, he found in the stories of Ubeid bin Sharayah and Kaab al Ahbar a huge amount of mythological material that, if he recorded it, would become in the eyes of Muslims an official history that would draw Muslims to it. By accomplishing this recording, Muslims would consider Muawiya a person who had provided a great benefit to Islam.

The "talkative history"

Dr. Abdellah bin Ibrahim al Askar, Professor of History at King Saud University, wrote an article about the "popular history."[1045]

In this article, al Askar debunks the "talkative history" Ubeid bin Sharayyeh created and discusses how Muslim historians, such as al Taberi and ibn Khaldoon, accepted this "history" despite the fact that they were not convinced by it. The Islamic historians accepted the stories of Ubeid bin Sharayyeh and his colleagues and used them even though they doubted their veracity. The important consideration for them was not historical truth but rather an eagerness to use anything, even the mythological stories created by Ubeid and his colleagues, to validate the Quran.

What is the place of these myths in the Muslim historians' writing? Do the Arabs today still suffer from this forgery?

Dr. Abdellah al Askar wrote:

> As a result of mixing the talkative popular history with the official history, the talkative-poplar history affected the Arabic mentality and still affects it today. Till now this mentality suffers from it... Two narrators who played an important role in transforming the talkative history into a recorded official history were Daghafel bin Hanthalah al Dosi al basri ودغفل بن حنظلة الدوسي البصري, who died in the year 60 H.(60 years after

Mohammed emigrated to Medina), and Ubeid bin Sharayyeh (who died 70 H.). The Umayyad Caliph, Muawiya bin Sifian, prepared the way for them and for others of Syria to take this role... but what they did influenced the Arabic mentality and education and the way the Arabs began to view history.

In other words, the Islamic historians neglected the official history and adopted instead these invented stories and myths. As Dr. Abdellah al Askar admitted, this practice influenced the Arabic mentality and the way Muslims view history. They came to view history from the mythological point of view of Ubeid bin Sharayyeh. As a result, they missed the official history. If they had studied the official history and ignored the fictional "history" Ubeid bin Sharayyeh and his colleagues invented, they would have discovered the mistakes of the Quran and the forgery on which it is built.

Jurhum and Qaturah and Mecca

The Islamic narrators invented a narrative in which Ishmael went to Mecca and married a wife from Jurhum, whom Ibn Abbass called al Saideh bint Mathath bin Amru al Jurhumi.[1046] Ibn Ishak transformed her name into "Raaleh bint Mathath bin Amru al Jurhumi."[1047] Ibn Abbass and Ibn Ishak did not know that the names they chose for Ishmael's wife were of a later Arabic style that belonged to the generation in which ibn Abbass and Ibn Ishak lived. In the 20 century B.C., the time in which Ishmael lived, there was no Arabic language, the language of Hejaz in which the Quran was recited, which, after Muslims spread by occupying the Middle East, became the language of the Arab world.

This fictional account continued to assert that while Jurhum had been defeated by the tribe of Khuzaa (the tribe that built Mecca in the 4th century A.D.) and fled from Mecca, Jurhum hid the black stone with two golden gazelles in the well of Zamzam. They then buried the well, the black stones, and the two gazelles under the dust.[1048] They created this story to justify the absence from Mecca during all ancient eras of the Black Stone and the well of Zamzam, which was later dug by Abdel Muttalab, grandfather of Mohammed. But it would be impossible to bury a well in western Arabia and conceal it from the eyes of the Bedouins who had drunk and watered their camels from it. It would be easier to hide the Red Sea from their eyes than to hide a well. They would return to uncover the well the day after.

According to these stories, Jurhum would have inhabited Mecca from the time of the ruination of the dam of Maareb (in Yemen), which signaled the time the tribe of Khuzaa exited Yemen around 150 A.D., until Khuzaa came to the mountains around Mecca around the 4th century A.D.

Ibn Ishak created cousins of Jurhum, which he named Qatura'.[1049] He claimed that these Qatura' came from Yemen and became the inhabitants of Mecca. They fought against Jurhum, but were defeated and left Mecca. We find the oldest mention of Qatura' and the struggle between them and Jurhum in Ibn Ishak's book the Sirah according to ibn Hisham.[1050] Since there is no mention of Qatura' before Ibn Ishak wrote about them, it is clear that he was the creator of these stories.

Ibn Ishak claimed that Ishmael learned Arabic from Jurhum and lived at Mecca.[1051] We answer this claim by saying that the language of Yemen during the 13th century B.C. was the Sabaean language, which was similar to the Accadic and Amharic languages, and very different from Arabic. How, then, could Jurhum in Yemen have spoken Arabic and taught it to Ishmael?!

To bolster his myth, Ibn Ishak claimed that Qatura' were the first to learn Arabic when the language of the nations were confounded in Babel.[1052] He made this claim despite the fact that the Arabic language is not ancient; the oldest proto-Arabic is the Thamudic, which goes back to the 8th century B.C., and compared to the Arabic of the Quraysh—the language of the Quran—it is not at all similar. Ibn Ishak composed poetry and attributed it to Jurhum; but the poetry was in the style of the Arabic language at the time of Ibn Ishak.[1053]

Contrary to the other tribes in western Arabia, the tribes that Islamic narrators claimed existed at Mecca were not attested throughout history by any source

If Jurhum or the Ishmaelite tribes were the inhabitants of Mecca since the ancient epochs, they would have been noted first by Moses, the one who wrote the book of Genesis, which mentioned the ramifications of the nations from Noah. Genesis mentioned many tribes in Arabia but makes no mention of Jurhum or the existence of Ishmaelite tribes in the mid-western Arabia, where Mecca was eventually built. This absence is all the more striking given that this region was geographically closer to Moses than were the other tribes' he mentioned. Furthermore, we find that the tribes on the land route between Yemen and the Fertile Crescent, such as Saba and the Midianites, are mentioned in the Assyrian inscriptions. Mention is even made of Ephah, the main Midianite tribe. Scholars maintain that the tribe of Hayappa, mentioned in the inscriptions of Tiglath-Pileser III and Sargon II, is Ephah. We do not find, however, any mention of Jurhum. We find mention in the Assyrian writings of many Ishmaelite tribes in many regions, but no mention of any Ishmaelite tribe in mid-western Arabia where Mecca was eventually built.

The classical writers, geographers and historians alike, mentioned the tribes who lived on the land route that connected Yemen to the Fertile Crescent. Many of these geographers walked this route. They mentioned the Nabataeans, the Midianites, the Thamudi, the Lahyanites, and many other tribes. When they reached the region where Mecca was later built, however, they did not mention any tribe. This indicates that the region was uninhabited until a time close to the birth of Christ. For example, Pliny (who lived during the 1st century A.D.) in his survey did not ignore any region in Arabia that was inhabited in his time. He wrote in such detail that he mentioned the tribes who inhabited the Nafud Desert. One of these tribes was Agraei. But he made no mention of Mecca or any tribe inhabiting the area where Mecca was later built.

The absence of tribes from the surveys that preceded Pliny's survey, such as those of Artemidros, Aghtharchides, and Strabo, is proof positive that the Muslim narrators wanted to back the Quran in its false claims regarding Mecca. Muslim narrators invented names of tribes that they claimed inhabited Mecca. They also created a false history for Mecca that did not agree with the official documented history written by the Greek and Roman geographers and historians. If the Islamic claims were true—that Jurhum in fact lived at Mecca since the time of Abraham and that the Ishmaelite tribes dominated Arabia—then Jurhum would have been greater than all the other tribes, such as Saba and Main, that history richly attests to. The presence of the Ishmaelite tribes would have been attested by the facts of history and archeology and the journeys of the geographers and historians. We find, however, no mention by these historians and geographers of Jurhum or that the Ishmaelite tribes had lived in the area where Mecca was later built.

Given these facts, only one rational conclusion can be drawn: The Quran does not present a history for the time of Abraham, especially for the region of Mecca that the Quran claims Abraham visited and where Ishmael lived and built the Kaabah. The Muslims of the 7th and 8th A.D.

centuries who invented a spurious history for Mecca and claimed that various tribes lived there did not rely on any recorded historical documentation and created a history contrary to the official history.

Archaeology documents the cities mentioned in Genesis to exist at the time of Abraham and his children

I already mentioned some cities that Kederloamer and his allied kings attacked. We saw archaeological testimony to those cities. I discussed the city of Ur in southern Mesopotamia that Genesis cites as the city where Abraham was raised. It is a city that is very rich in archaeological records, and its history is well-attested by historians and archaeologists. Abraham then emigrated to Haran.

The book of Genesis mentions names of various cities that existed at Abraham's time, such as Salem (Jerusalem), Dan-Laish, and Jerar. Genesis mentioned Isaac's connection with the city of Beersheba and Jacob's with Bethel, Shechem, and Dothan. These cities are all attested to exist at the time of the patriarchs Abraham, Isaac, and Jacob.

Albright wrote:

Every town mentioned in the narratives of the Patriarchs was in existence in the Middle Bronze Age, examples are Shechem, Bethel, Ai, Jerusalem (Salem), Gerar, Dothan, Beersheba.[1054]

Here is a little information about these cities:

Haran: Haran was an important center of commerce at the time of Abraham and his children. It was abandoned, as I previously mentioned, from 1800-800 B.C. If the author of Genesis had lived, as some claim, in a later period, he would not have chosen Haran as the city where Abraham's family lived.[1055]

Dan or Laish: These are places, known to exist during the Middle Bronze Age, that Abraham and the rest of the patriarchs visited. For example, Laish, which was later called Dan, was a city with walls. It was mentioned as Dan in Genesis 4:14 (because the book was later edited in the 12th century B.C. or later than that date). We read in the Old Testament book of Judges 18:29:

And they called the name of the city Dan, after the name of Dan their father, who was born to Israel. However, the name of the city formerly was Laish.

Laish is mentioned in the Egyptian inscriptions known as Execration texts that date back to the 19th and 18th centuries B.C.[1056]

Dothan: Dothan is mentioned in Genesis 37:17. It was about 10 miles from Samaria and existed in the Middle Bronze Age. Excavations led by Joseph P. Free of Wheaton College beginning in 1953 proved through successive layers the occupations of the cities between 3000- 100 B.C.[1057]

Shechem: Shechem was known in Stela of Khu-Sobec under the name of Sakmum at the time of Pharaoh Sesostris III, the fifth pharaoh of the 12th dynasty, around the year 1860 B.C.[1058]

Bethel: Bethel is called Luz in Genesis 28:19:

> And he called the name of that place Bethel: but the name of that city was called Luz at the first.

Bethel was known in the first and second Middle Bronze Age.[1059] The excavations on its site prove that it was in existence as a Canaanite place at least since 2500 B.C. It was destroyed when the Israelites entered Canaan. Then it was rebuilt. It was occupied many times in the Byzantine period.[1060]

Jerusalem is mentioned in Genesis 18:14 as Salim, and it was an important city at the time of Abraham.[1061] The excavations in the year 1909 under Parker at Jerusalem demonstrated that the city was built many centuries before Abraham.[1062]

Gerar: Scholars and archaeologists believe that Gerar was the site of Tel abu Hureirah (Tel Haror). According to recent excavations, Gerar was a large city in the Middle Bronze Age.[1063]

Hebron: In the Middle Bronze Age Hebron was a place with walls. Hebron was among the important centers in the land of Canaan. A tablet found there contains western Semitic names written in Cuneiform in addition to names that were likely Horites names.[1064]

Thus, we notice that the book of Genesis gave a realistic and historical picture of the names of the cities that existed in Mesopotamia and Canaan, some of which flourished at Abraham's time. Some of these cities, such as Bethel and Haran, later disappeared and then reappeared at a very late date. The life of Abraham could not have reached us through a late writer after Moses' time, for Moses benefitted from Abraham's records that were passed down to him through Joseph son of Jacob. Joseph asked that his bones be kept and buried in the land of Canaan. How then could they not keep his family records, the records of his great grandfather Abraham, his grandfather Isaac, and his father Jacob?!

There is no information supporting Mohammed's claim in the Quran regarding Abraham

When we come to the Quran's narration of Abraham and his times, however, we see a complete lack of mention of the cities of the patriarch's day, except the verses that claim that Abraham placed his offspring in an uncultivable valley:

> Our Lord! Lo! I have settled some of my posterity in an uncultivable valley near unto your holy House, our lord! That they may establish proper worship; so incline some hearts of men that they may yearn toward them and provide them with fruits in order that they may be thankful. (Surah Ibrahim 14:36-37)

All the Quran tells us is that Abraham put his offspring, meaning Ishmael, in an uncultivable valley, unproductive without trees nor crops, near al Beit al Haram (the Kaaba). If Abraham had gone to Mecca, it would have been an important journey. Confirming such an alleged journey would have been a vitally important argument in supporting a religion that claims to be based on Abraham and on his alleged trip to western Arabia where he built a temple for God in order to establish the foundations of a religion on which Islam was built according to the Quran and Mohammed. Did not such a momentous journey merit some historical and geographical clarification in the Quran?

Abraham's life in the Bible is richly attested with historical and theological facts. This is contrary to the absence of information in the Quran about Abraham, though Islam claims to base its claims on Abraham

The Bible devotes 14 chapters (nearly one third) of the book of Genesis to the life of Abraham, detailing his journeys from Ur to Haran and from the Canaanite cities to Egypt, and then his return to Canaan and his residency there. Chapters 12-24 provide a detailed life of Abraham, including myriad incidents, mention of cities, tribes, treaties, wars, alliances, and the Lord's visitations to him in which He gave him the promises. Genesis records various prophecies, such as the one foretelling his descendants' subjection to slavery in a foreign land for four centuries and their subsequent return to possess the land of Canaan and God's judgment of the nation that subjected them to slavery. Other prophecies foretold the coming of the Messiah from his seed so that all the nations would be blessed by Him. Later, that same promise was confirmed to Isaac and Jacob. There was also the unique symbolic prophecy involving Abraham's willingness to sacrifice his son on the mountain of Moriah that foreshadowed the Lord God's order of sacrificing His own son on the mountains of Jerusalem. Then Isaac was redeemed through a ram from heaven, symbolizing Christ who came from heaven and died on the same mountain for the redemption of mankind. How, then, we could make verse 37 of Surah Ibrahim to annul the truth declared in 14 chapters of Genesis with all that these chapters prove in the way of historical, geographical and theological facts, which are a unique foundation of the faith that God established for the human race?!

Mecca is absent before the 4th century A.D.

Mecca is absent in the classical geographers' and historians' surveys before the Christian era

The expeditions commissioned by Alexander the Great were of great importance. He had planned to occupy Arabia, but he died before he accomplished this purpose. We understand from Arrian, the Greek historian, that Alexander sent three naval expeditions from Babylon to Arabia. The most important was the one under Hieron, who sailed "round the greater part of Arabia,"[1065] meaning that he sailed around western Arabia. Another very important expedition was the one Alexander commissioned while he was in Egypt. He sent Anaxicrates from Hierapolis to explore western Arabia. Scholars consider Anaxicrates' survey to be very extensive and successful. In his book The Archaeology of Seafaring in Ancient South Asia, Dr. Himanshu Prabha Ray wrote: "Anaxicrates surveyed the whole of the Western coast of Arabia as far as the Bab-al-Mandeb."[1066] Dr. Stanley Burstein, an expert in the ancient geography of Arabia, stated that Anaxicrates provided an "accurate account of political conditions in Western Arabia."[1067] This means that Anaxicrates rendered an accurate account of the nations, cities, and tribes that dominated the region of western Arabia. Anaxicrates' expedition was an important reference for later Greek geographers, who added the results of their surveys to other surveys that preceded them. Since Mecca is not mentioned in any of their writings, whereas other cities are mentioned, we conclude that

Mecca was not in existence during the 4th century B.C. Nor is there any mention of any tribe in the area where Mecca was later built.

The absence of any mention of Mecca is repeated in the survey of Agatharchides, who wrote between the years 145-132 B.C. Agatharchides studied and analyzed the writings of the geographers who were sent by the Ptolemy's kings.[1068] He also depended on eyewitnesses, among whom were envoys of the kings, in addition to explorers and merchants who visited the regions of the Red Sea and the cities around.[6] We find the most important summary of his book in Photius book Bibliotheca.[7]

The importance of Agatharchides' survey is that that he described the western coast of the Red Sea, including some populations and tribes that were farther inland than Mecca. This coastal region covers the area from the Gulf of Aqaba in the north to Yemen in the south. But when he reached the middle region of western Arabia, the area where Mecca was eventually built, he did not find any city or village. This proves that the area was inhabited. That arid area had no village or temple.

The same fact is seen in Artemidorus' survey. Artemidorus was from the city of Ephesus, in Asia Minor, and lived around 103 B.C. Artemidorus included information gathered during his own travels and additional information gathered by others in his time. [1069] Like Agatharchides, Artemidorus described the nature of each tract along the coast of the Red Sea and the population who lived there. When he came to the very central western Arabian tract where Mecca was later built, he did not mention any people living there. It is clear that this region of western Arabia was not inhabited in his time. He had to walk very much farther south of that region in order to find a small port. To the south of the port was a land inhabited

---

[6] Many passages in On the Erythraean Sea clearly point to the fact that Agatharchides consulted eyewitness merchants and others who visited the region. See especially fragment 41.

[7] Although the book of Agatharchides is no longer in existence, it has been preserved through the synopsis of the classical authors Photius, Diodorus, and Strabo. We find a good summary of the fifth book of Agatharchides in the work of Diodorus, Library of History, chapters 12-48. The summary of Photius in his work Bibliotheca, especially Codex 250, is very important.

by the so-called "Debae" people. He encountered Bedouins traveling in the area and a few farmers but no cities in that area. Artemidorus had to travel much farther south to near the border of Yemen to find, as he said, "more civilized" people.[1070] In other words, the tract of central western Arabia where Mecca was later built was still uninhabited as of 103 B.C. This tract was divided from Yemen by an area that was inhabited only by uncivilized Bedouin tribes.

The Roman campaign to western Arabia confirmed the absence of Mecca during that time

The Roman military expedition around the year 25 B.C. confirmed the fact that Mecca was not in existence at that time. The Romans wanted to occupy western Arabia to fight piracy and to occupy Yemen to control the spice route. Rome appointed Gallus, the governor of Egypt, to lead the military campaign and the famous geographer and historian Strabo accompanied the expedition. He wrote about it in his 16th book of Geography (for details of this expedition, see Geography of Strabo, Book XVI, 4, 24).

Strabo described the army's march to the city of Leuce Come, meaning the "white village," on the Red Sea. This city was located in what is today called the Hora' region in Saudi Arabia, some 280 miles from where Mecca was later built. The army then marched toward the city of al-Hijr, which was under Nabataean control, and from there onto the region of mid-western Arabia where Mecca was later built. Strabo described their arid lands. Strabo wrote:

> The next country Gallus traversed belongs to nomads, and most of it was truly desert. It was called Ararene, and he travelled 50 days before arriving at the city of Negrani.

Negrani is the city of Nejran, situated on the Yemeni border, about 385 miles from Mecca and 125 miles from the coast of the Red Sea.

Another historical fact worth mentioning is that after Gallus failed to occupy Maarb, he dismissed Syllaeus, the Nabataean guide, and depended thereafter on local experts on his return to Nejran and then on to the Nabataean city of Leuce Come. As a result, his return was quicker, and he passed by the villages built on the land route where Mecca was later built. Strabo mentioned these villages by name but did not mention Mecca. For instance, Strabo reports that the expedition came to a village called Hepta

Phreata, and from there moved to another city called Chaalla and then on to a village called Malotha (most probably Malothan), which was situated near the modern Saudi city of Jeddah, about 30 miles from Mecca.

Strabo, the historian and geographer who accompanied the expedition, made no mention of any village between Malotha (or Malothan) and Egra or al Hijr (which was situated north of the site where Mecca was later built). Strabo notes that Gallus' expedition party had an urgent need for water and food supplies, but found in the region where Mecca was later built no villages that could provide him and his soldiers with urgently needed supplies and rest.

The Periplus of the Erythraean Sea confirmed the absence of Mecca during the 1st century A.D.

The fact that Mecca was not in existence (i.e., had not yet been built) in the 1st century A.D. is established by more than source, such as The Periplus of the Erythraean Sea. This book was written between 58-62 A.D.[1071] by an unnamed author who resided in the city of Berenice across from central Arabia located about 200-220 miles from the place where Mecca was later built. The author was an expert on that area. He mentioned various cities and villages of western Arabia within about 100 miles of the shore. He made no mention of Mecca.

Pliny's survey confirms the absence of Mecca during the 1st century A.D.s

There is also the book of Pliny, the renowned Roman historian. He wrote Natural History between 72-76 A.D.[8] His extensive survey covered the entire Arabia peninsula. In his sixth book of Natural History, chapters 32 and 33, Pliny wrote about Arabia in great detail. For instance, he mentioned 92 nations and tribes and various cities and villages that were in Arabia in his time. But, for all his meticulous detail, Pliny mentioned neither Mecca

---

[8] Scholars concur that Pliny wrote his Natural History after the compilation of The Periplus of the Erythraean Sea because Pliny includes many elements and descriptions of Arabia Felix that the author included in The Periplus of the Erythraean Sea. It is known that Pliny wrote his work Natural History between 72-76 A.D.

nor any tribe living in the area where Mecca was later built. He made no mention of the tribes that the Islamic narrators claimed inhabited Mecca, such as the Jurhum.

Ptolemy's survey confirmed the absence of Mecca during the 2nd century

In the 2nd century A.D. Ptolemy, the famous Greek geographer who lived in Alexandria, wrote about the cities and villages of Arabia. But he made no mention of Mecca.

In his work Geography, book six, chapter seven, Ptolemy documented the latitude and longitude coordinates of several landmarks in Arabia.[1072] As we study these locations and coordinates, we notice once again that Ptolemy did not mention Mecca. In fact, Ptolemy does not mention any cities on the strip of land where Mecca was eventually built.

Macoraba was not Mecca

Ptolemy mentioned a city in the Arabian interior called Macoraba. Some Muslims wanted to assume that Macoraba was actually Mecca. This is not the case, however, for Ptolemy located Macoraba near the Omani coast. He placed its longitude east of Lathrippa, which is Yathrib- Medina. Ptolemy placed the city of Macoraba at 73 20 longitude, which means about 3.33 degrees east of Yathrib, while Mecca is west of Yathrib. So Macoraba could not possibly be the city of Mecca nor any city in the direction where Mecca was later built. Regarding the latitude Ptolemy gave for Macoraba, it was not the next city south of Lathrippa, or Yathrib, but the sixth city to the south. That is, the city of Carna is the first city to the south of Lathrippa, whereas Macoraba is the sixth city to the south. Carna was a well-known Yemeni city that belonged to the Minaean kingdom that Strabo mentioned.[1073] In the past Carna was the capital of the Maini nation. According to the latitude Ptolemy identified, we conclude that Macoraba was in southern Arabia, south of the city of Carna. Pliny mentions a city with the name Mochorbeand, he said it was a port of Oman on the Hadramawt shore in South Arabia. It is also possible that Macoraba is derived from Mochorbe.[1074]

Since Macoraba appears in no other literature except Ptolemy's narration, it must have been a small settlement or tiny village that disappeared in Ptolemy's time during the 2nd century A.D.

The absence of Mecca during the 3rd century A.D. is confirmed from analysis of the Ethiopian, Syriac, and Coptic writings, all of which mentioned details of Arabia and its cities. Crone researched the Ethiopian, Syriac, and Coptic writings and found no mention of Mecca in those literatures.[1075]

The northern temple described by Agatharchides in the Aqaba Gulf region

In the face of the absence of Mecca in Greek and Romans geographers' writings, some Muslims try to identify a temple mentioned by Agatharchides in the past as the Kaabah of Mecca. As we understand from Diodorus, Agatharchides mentioned a temple close to Ilat in the region of the Gulf of Aqaba. He described it as existing in a land inhabited by the tribe of Batmizomaneis. He noted that it was "highly revered by all the Arabs."[1076]

To accurately determine the location of this temple, however, it is necessary to follow the narration of Agatharchides himself as quoted by Photius and Diodorus. Agatharchides began by describing the regions north of the temple, including those inhabited by the Nabataeans who were in the area of the Gulf of Aqaba. (The northern part of the Gulf of Aqaba was called Laeanites Gulf in Agatharchides' time.). He then described the regions south of the temple, the Thamud regions, and we know that the Thamudi were in the area of the Gulf of Aqaba, very far from where Mecca was later built.

After mentioning the Thamud region, Photius mentioned the segment directly to the south of Thamud.[1077] Scholars have identified this segment as the portion of the coast between رأس كركمة Ras Karkama (25 54 N, 36 39 E) and راس ابو مد Ras Abu Madd (24 50 N, 37 08 E).[1078] Ras Abu Madd is about 450 kilometers (280 miles) north of Mecca. This accurate study shows clearly that the temple that Diodorus mentioned was in the Aqaba Gulf region, north of the Thamud region, and thus cannot be identified with the Temple of Mecca (see Fig.2).

In the 6th century A.D., Nonnosus mentioned the same temple. He located it in the oasis called Phoinikon, whose inhabitants were Saracens, [1079] who in the 6th century A.D. inhabited the area of Gulf of Aqaba and southern Transjordan. (See the detailed examination of the northern temple in my book "The Star Akbar").

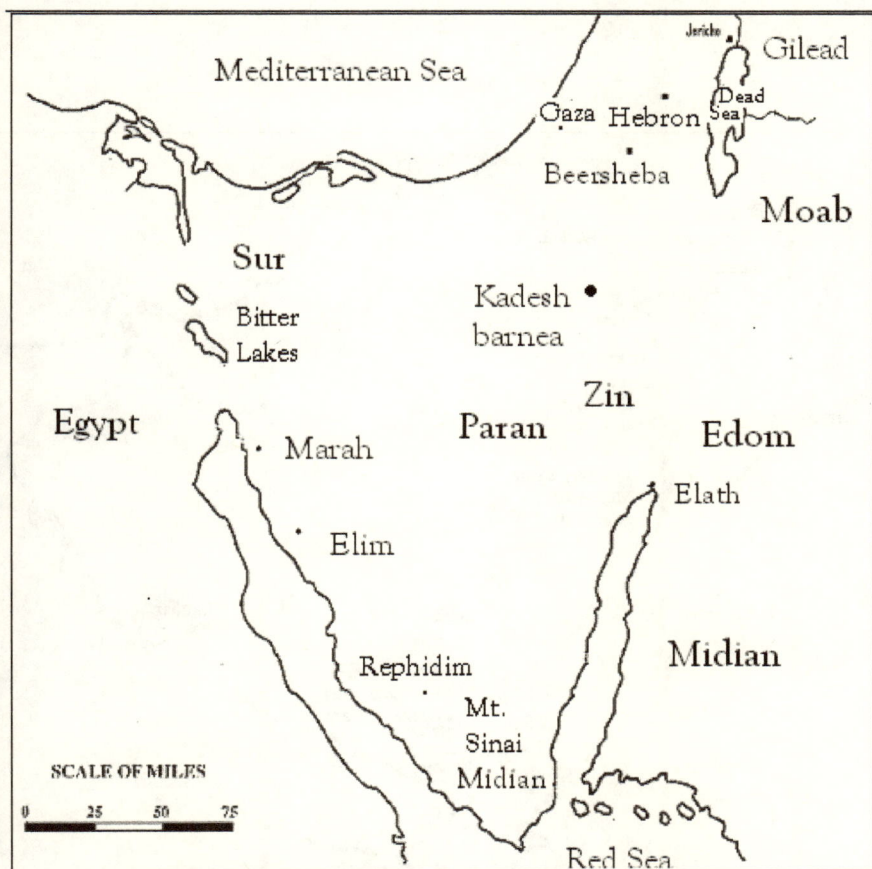

Fig. 1 The Sinai at the time of Moses

Fig. 2 Arabia in ancient times.

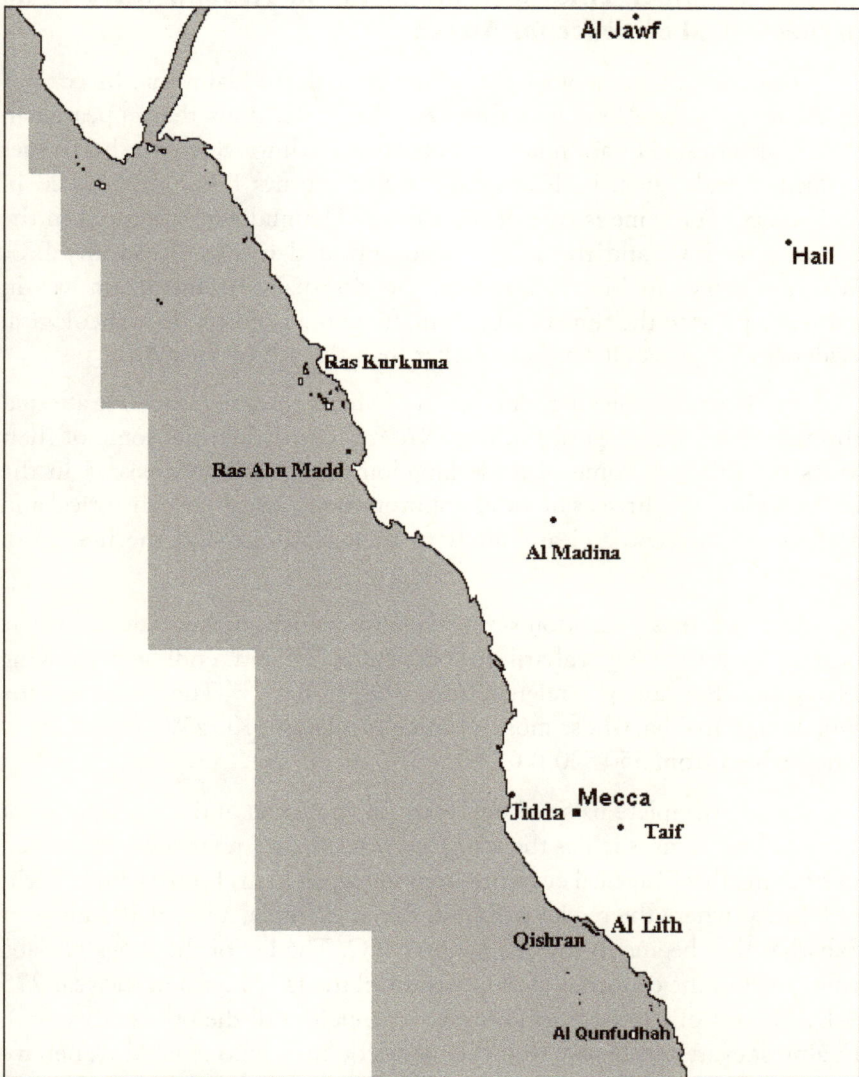

Fig. 3 North-central Western Arabia.

Archeology and the Absence of Mecca

Unlike the other cities and kingdoms in Arabia, there is no archeological evidence for Mecca

There are no archeological findings to back the claim that Mecca was in existence since Abraham's time. All the civilizations that appeared in Arabia are attested by abundant archeological findings. Such northern cities as Dedan and Tema, built around the 9th century B.C., are attested in archeology. The same is true of the tribe of Thamud who appeared in the 8th century B.C. and the Lihyan who appeared in the 4h century B.C. When it comes to Mecca, however, the city that Muslims claim was in existence prior to the time of Abraham, there is absolutely no archeological evidence that proves it was built earlier than the 4th century A.D.

Furthermore, the kingdoms south of Mecca toward Yemen are attested through rich archeological findings. We can clearly identify some of their kings even though some of these kingdoms are small and existed in the centuries before Christ as modest, not prominent, kingdoms. Historical and archaeological records clearly attest to their existence and the lineage of their kings.

One of these kingdoms was Haram, which had a line of rulers beginning with King Yaharil in 600 B.C., [1080] and ending with King Maadikarib Raydan, who reigned from 190-175 B.C.[1081] Then there was the kingdom of Inabba, whose most prominent ruler was King Waqahil Yafush, who reigned from 550-530 B.C.[1082]

Nearly complete lists of kings exist for the larger and more important Yemeni kingdoms, such as the kingdom of Qatban. I refer those interested in studying this historical evidence in more depth to my book Islam in Light of History, where the reader will find, for an example, a list of 102 kings of Sabathat that begins in the 9th century B.C. The list of the kings of Saba continued in the centuries after Christ until the fall of Saba in the year 275 A.D. The list of the kings of Himyar continued until the 6th century A.D. In almost every century we find the names of kings who reigned. When we compare the historical evidence of these other cities and kingdoms with Mecca, however, we come to the conclusion that it is impossible that Mecca existed in ancient times. If it had existed, Mecca would have a record listing names of its kings in each century. The lack of a historical record is even more acute when we consider the fact that Mecca has a much lower annual rainfall average than Yemen, where those well-attested kingdoms were born. The scarcity of rain is an important factor in preserving the archeological findings.

Furthermore, abundant archaeological evidence chronicles the ancient kingdoms in eastern Arabia—such as Dilmon, which was situated in the region called in our day Bahrain and Magan in Oman. The Dilmon kingdom existed for many millennia before Christ dating back to the time of Abraham. This is further evidence that Mecca, which has no such record, could simply not have existed during Abraham's lifetime.

Mecca is not mentioned in the inscriptions of other cities and kingdoms

Another important factor is the absence of any mention of Mecca in the inscriptions of other Arabian regions. Mecca is absent from the Yemeni inscriptions and from the inscriptions of the northern cities of Arabia, despite the fact that these inscriptions mention other Arabian cities.

Furthermore, Mecca was absent from the records of the nations—both Arabian and foreign—that occupied the region. We do not find Mecca mentioned in the records of the Maini, Nabataeans, Lahyanite, or Himyarite writings and inscriptions, despite the fact that these nations colonized the land route, including the desert of central western Arabia, on which Mecca was eventually built. They mentioned names of various cities in northern Arabia but not Mecca.

The Assyrians, Babylonians, Persians, and Romans all had ancient empires that occupied northern and central western Arabia. Yet not a scintilla of evidence from the historical and archaeological records of these empires suggests the existence of Mecca.

The Chaldean records also exclude any record of Mecca during the 7th and 6th centuries B.C. Nabonidus, the king of Babylon who reigned from 556-539 B.C., left many interesting records. Information about this king and his occupation of North Arabia is documented in the Harran Inscriptions of Nabonidus (known as H2), Nabonidus and the Royal Chronicles, and the so-called Verse Account of Nabonidus.

Nabonidus left the empire in the control of his son Belshazzar and traveled to the Arabian city of Teima. He occupied the city of Teima and took up residence there.[1083] The Harran Inscriptions of Nabonidus tell us that during his sojourn in Teima, Nabonidus went farther south to conquer the cities of Dedan, Fadak, Khaybar, Yadi, and Yathrib (which is Medina).[1084] Since Nabonidus controlled the entire region, he was assured of dominating all three land routes from Yathrib. Yet, although he controlled the entire region including Hejaz, not once did he mention Mecca in the inscriptions he left behind. If Mecca had existed in Nabonidus' time, he would certainly have attacked and conquered it, for it would have been the only city in the region south of Yathrib that was not under his control. (See figure 4)

Mecca is not mentioned in any of the military campaign records from the Assyrian and Chaldean period that chronicle how the tribes and cities of North Arabia formed alliances from time to time and attack the borders of the Assyrians and the Chaldeans.

Mecca is absent in records of the trade activity

Mecca is also absent from the records of trading activity. The cities and tribes on the Arabian routes used to pay tribute to the Assyrian and Chaldean kings so as to facilitate their commerce with the nations of the Fertile Crescent. Yet, despite the fact that commerce was its fundamental source of living, we find no mention of Mecca.

Another important point is that although the inscriptions of great nations such as the Assyrians and Egyptians mention the names of the Arabian merchants who traded with them, we find no mention of any merchant of Mecca in any of the inscriptions. (For further details on this topic, see my book, "Islam in Light of History")

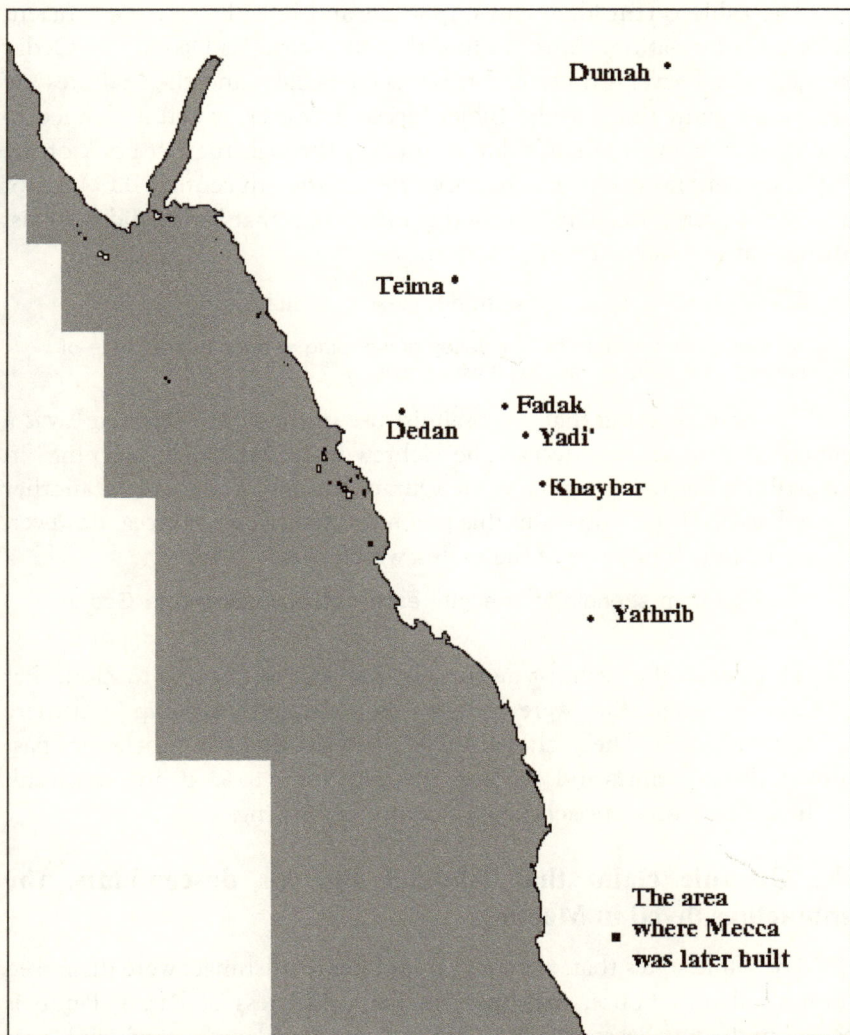

Fig. 4 The cities occupied by Nabonidus, king of Babylonia, during his 10 years' sojourn in north and central western Arabia; Mecca is missing in his records.

The Bible mentions the other cities and tribes in Arabia, Mecca is not mentioned in the Bible

The Bible is considered an important and reliable source of ancient historical information. Thus, we find that such cities as Dedan and Qedar are mentioned several times and tribes such as Saba and the Mainites are mentioned many times in the Bible. Mecca, however, which is claimed to have existed from Abraham's day all the way through the last book of the Old Testament (Malachi, which was written in the 5th century B.C.), is not mentioned even once. This is a solid confirmation that Mecca did not exist during that extensive historical period.

Some Muslims look to Psalm 84, verse 6, which says:

As they pass through the dry valley of weeping, it becomes a place of springs; the autumn rain fills it with pools.

They are claiming that the psalmist use of the word "weeping" was a reference to the city of Mecca. The Hebrew word translated "weeping" in this psalm is baca. According to the Quran, the city of Mecca had another name, Bacca. Those who claim this psalm was referring to Mecca, however, ignore the following verse of the psalm, which says:

They go from strength to strength; each one appears before God in Zion.

Thus, what the psalmist meant was that they were going to Zion, that is Jerusalem, where they were going to the Temple to worship God there and not to Mecca. The psalmist intended to say that when believers pass through difficult times and weeping, they pray more to God, and as a result the difficult circumstances become a source of blessings.

The Quranic claim that Ishmael and his descendants, the Ishmaelites, lived in Mecca

The Bible states that, after Hagar and her son Ishmael were dismissed from Abraham's house, they lived in the wilderness of Paran. Paran is located in the northeastern region of Sinai. It is the place from which Moses sent 12 spies to surveil the land of Canaan. It is not possible that Hager would travel to a land that was unknown in her generation. There was no land route to connect her with western Arabia. The land route appeared only after the 9th century B.C. when the cities of northern Arabia, such as Dedan, Tema and Qedar, were built. These cities began providing the caravans with water and food. Those land routes connected Yemen with the Fertile Crescent. Before the 13th century B.C. when the kingdom of Saba appeared, no connection existed between Yemen and the Fertile Crescent.

How could a maiden bearing her son walk across this vast arid desert spanning thousands of kilometers in an epoch when no one before had crossed this route? The caravans that traveled this land route between Yemen and the Fertile Crescent after the northern cities of Arabia were built in the 9th century B.C. included thousands of camels and men charged with guarding the caravan against the threat of pirates and savage Bedouins. These caravans were also outfitted with sufficient food and water for a months-long journey. Was a single woman and her son, alone with a small skin of water, capable of crossing those vast deserts, walking alone for months to reach a land that was uninhabited in her time?!

Ishmael and the Ishmaelites lived in the wilderness of Sinai

Another important fact that proves that Ishmael did not in fact inhabit Mecca is this: Ishmael lived all his life in the wilderness of Paran. He had a relationship with Esau, Isaac's elder son. Esau married Ishmael's daughter. When Abraham died, Ishmael attended the funeral with Isaac as we read in Genesis 25:9. If he had in fact resided in Mecca, he would have needed months to travel to the site where Abraham lived. This was impossible since in that day a cadaver had to be buried on the day of death because of the hot weather conditions and the absence of refrigeration.

The Ishmaelites were known to live in Sinai throughout their history. Moses mentioned their 12 tribes as residents of Sinai in his day—the 15th century B.C. (see Genesis 25:12-18).When we study the Assyrian inscriptions, we find that the Ishmaelites inhabited Sinai until the 10th century B.C. After the 10th century B.C., many of their tribes emigrated to the deserts of the Fertile Crescent. Only the tribes of Qedar and Tema emigrated inside Arabia and settled on the northern border of the peninsula. There is no record, however, of any tribe emigrating toward the area where Mecca was later built.

The names of Abraham and Ishmael never appeared in Arabia before the introduction of Judaism and Christianity to the Arabian tribes.

But, there is more to consider. The Israelites are the offspring of Abraham, a fact attested to in every Israelite generation. You will find the names of Abraham and his sons expressed clearly in Hebrew literature in each and every era. The fact that Abraham was the father of the Hebrews has influenced the spiritual, cultural and sociological life of the Israelites throughout history, causing them to follow in the faith of Abraham.

Within the Arab history there is no mention of Abraham – even in the Jahiliyyah period, the time period prior to Islam's appearance in Arabia. The use of Biblical names among the Arabs occurred because many Arabic tribes embraced Judaism or Christianity. However, al-Kalbi, an ancient famous historian, mentioned two names, which were derived from the name of Abraham. He wrote:

Ibrahim (that is Abraham), grandfather of Adi, son of Zayd, son of Hamad, son of Zayd, son of Ayuob (that is Job) from the sons of Emrea' al-kais (who is a famous Christian Arabian poet), son of Zayd Manat, son of Tamim. The other was Mukatil, son of Hassan, son of Thaalabeh, son of Aws, son of Ibrahim (that is Abraham), son of Ayuob. Ibn al-Kalbi said, "I do not know in the Jahiliyyah period any other person from the Arabs, other than these two who called themselves with such Biblical names. And these two were called so because they were Christians."[1085]

When we study the period before Judaism and Christianity penetrated Arabia, we do not find any Biblical names, including Abraham and Ishmael, in any Arabian inscriptions. Historically, the ancient names of a nation's founding fathers, and other great national figures, are always recorded and repeatedly mentioned as their stories pass from generation to generation. Thus, it would be most unusual if the Arabs were actually descendants of Abraham through Ishmael, and failed to ever mention them. For example, we see the name, Israel, which God gave to Jacob, the father of the Israelites. We see his name mentioned in Hebrew literature down through the generations. The Israelites also mention Ishmael, who is not the father of the Israelites, many places in their history. The names of Abraham, Isaac and Jacob are common names attesting to the lineage of the Israelites.

When we consider other people, such as those in Mesopotamia, we find the important figures in their history are listed by each succeeding generation. For example, in Genesis 10:8-11, we learn that Nimrod is the father of the Babylonians and the Assyrians. Nimrod is common to both Assyrian and Babylonian literature. Many people, and even locations, were named after Nimrod. The ancient capital of the Assyrians was called Nimrod. This attests to the fact that the important figures, such as the father of a nation, cannot be forgotten by the following generations in those nations.

In contrast to this, we find that Arabian inscriptions never mention Abraham or Ishmael. Instead, they record the names of men and deities of a separate and distinct Arabian culture. How could Ishmael be the father of the Arabs when we do not find his name mentioned in any of the old Arabian inscriptions? The answer is simple: Ishmael could not be the father of the Arabs.

The claim that the Arabians had a prophetic role is without foundation and had no preparation for this alleged divine call

How could there have been a prophetic calling to Arabs, when we consider God never planted the seeds for an Arab calling anywhere in history. God never planted promises, empowered Arab prophets, or inspired Arabian sacred books. Would God choose a prophet from China to be the head of a religion that would be God's final revelation to the world? I think not. God chose all the prophets from Israel, and He directed them to prepare the way for the coming of the Savior. God promised that the Messiah would be a descendent of Abraham, Isaac and David, not Abraham and Ishmeal. Competing with the plan of God, creating another way where God has never worked before is a malicious and baleful imitation of the Truth.

A historical testimony about the name of Abraham outside the Bible

We find Abraham's name in the Egyptian list of King Shoshenq I (Shishak) (dating to 925 B.C.) Kitchen says: "The only suggested extra Biblical mention of Abraham is in the topographical list (nos. 71-72) of Shoshenq I (Shishak) of Egypt in 925 B.C., giving what may be read as 'Enclosure of Abram,' which is fairly widely accepted." Kitchen also says that the place is Negev, which agrees with place where Abraham and Isaac lived.[1086] In fact, we read in Genesis:

And Abraham journeyed from thence toward the south country, and dwelled between Kadesh and Shur, and sojourned in Gerar"(Genesis 20:1) and also "And Isaac came from the way of the well Lahairoi; for he dwelt in the south country. (Genesis 24:62).

This suggests that the place was named after Abraham. Archeologist Yohanan Aharoni maintains that the Egyptians knew that the city of Beersheba by this old name, which indicates that it was so named because Abraham was the original founder of the city as we see in Genesis 21:31-32.

Roland Hendel states:

Yohanan Aharoni believed that the Egyptians knew the Israelite city of Beersheba by this older name, thereby indicating that it was so named because Abram was the original founder of that city. (Genesis 21:31-32)

Roland Hendel suggests:

When a government builds fortifications, it is natural to name them for illustrious or national heroes. Abram of Biblical fame fit this bill.[1087]

Did Ibraham and Ishmael build the Kaabah?

The Quran claims in Surah 2:127 that Abraham and Ishmael were the builders of the Kaabah:

And when Abraham and Ishmael were raising the foundations of the House, (Abraham prayed): Our lord! Accept from us (this duty). Lo! You are the hearer, the knower.

History, however, does not agree with this claim

From the writings of al Azruqi, who wrote the history of Mecca, we know that in the place of the Kaabah there was a tent.[1088] This was during the 5th century A.D. when As'ad Abu Karib (also called Tubaa, who ruled from 410-435 A.D. as the king of the Himyarites of Yemen) occupied Mecca. The Khuzaa built the city of Mecca in the 4th century A.D. after emigrating from Yemen. There are ample proofs that the tribe of Khuzaa did not build Mecca in the valley of Mecca where the Kaabah was later built. Rather, they inhabited the mountains. This was because a devastating torrent often flowed through the valley of Mecca and swept away everything. Thus, it was not convenient to build a village or a town in the valley of Mecca. Another thing is that the valley required protecting the city through erecting defensive walls and fortresses. Khuzaa was not equipped for the task of building walls and fortresses to protect the city from invasions and thus preferred to inhabit the mountains around the valley of Mecca. We understand that before Qusei bin Kilab, the fifth ancestor of Mohammed, occupied the mountains of Mecca and expelled Khuzaa from them, Mecca did not exist in the valley where the Kaabah was later built. Jawad Ali, the famous Iraqi scholar, wrote:

> It seems because the narrators did not mention that any fortress existed at Mecca to defend the city, this city which was safe and had no fortification, stronghold, or towers and a wall to avoid the attack of the Bedouins or any enemy. This suggests that Mecca before the time of Qusei was not in the valley where the Kaabah was built but was rather on the surrounding mountains.[1089]

The Black Stone and the sacredness of Mount Abu Qubais to the pagans

The black stone was an idol that the pagan Khuzaa tribe worshiped on the mount of Abu Qubeis, one of the mountains of Mecca.

The Arabian sources tell us that because the black stone was in the mountain of Abu Qubeis the mountain was called "the faithful."[1090] Al Zubeidi confirms that Abu Qubeis was called the "faithful, and that it is the mountain that overhangs Safa."[1091] Here we see that the sacredness of Safa, which is one of two rocks that the Muslims walk between in the pilgrimage called Umrah, is due to its vicinity to Mount Abu Qubeis, where the black stone was. It seems that the tribe of Khuzaa, which worshiped the black stone, used to walk between Safa and Marwa and then returned to kiss and worship the black stone on Mount Abu Qubeis. But after the Kaabah was built, the ritual of Safa and Marwa became connected with the Kaabah.

It is also clear that the spot where the Kaabah was built was selected because of its vicinity to the mount of Abu Qubeis. Ibn Manthur wrote: "Abu Qubeis is a mountain overhanging the mosque of Mecca."[1092]

Abu Qubeis was one of the sacred places of the pre-Islamic people in the area of Mecca. Thus, we understand why the black stone was there before it was transferred to Kaabah. These facts annul the Islamic claim that Abraham leaned on the black stone while building the Kaabah. Dr. Jawad Ali writes about the sacredness of Abu Qubeis for the pagans:

"Abu Qubeis was one of the sacred places for the Jahileah people (the pre-Islamic Arabians). When performing ascetic practices the people of Mecca or those who wanted to become like monks went to Abu Qubeis and made their retreat there. Abu Qubeis was also a place of residency for the rich people of Mecca; this was before the tribe of Quraysh came down to live in the valley of Mecca."[1093]

Qusei was first to bring down the Black Stone and part of Quraysh to reside in the valley of Mecca

Qusei bin Kilab, the fifth ancestor of Mohammed, was the one who moved the families from the mountains they inhabited to the valley of Mecca. This was after he occupied Mecca and expelled Khuzaa.

It seems they worshiped in a tent, as we know from the writings of Azruqi, who wrote that before the building of Kaabah there was a tent.

When Qusei brought the black stone from Mount Abu Qubeis, there was no Kaabah in which to house the black stone. Qusei did not place the black stone in the Kaabah, which he most certainly would have done if the Kaabah were in existence at his time. Some Islamic authors claimed that the tribe of Iyad buried the black Stone in the mountain until Qusei brought it forth. He brought it down from the mountain and it remained with a group of Quraysh until Quraysh built the Kaabah and placed the stone in the corner of the house.[1094]

It is clear that there was no Kaabah in which Qusei could put the black stone. So the black stone remained with a group of Quraysh whom Qusei brought to the valley from the mountains. Because the families who descended from him and from his close relatives were the ones whom he made to live in the valley, he wanted the idol worshiped on Mount Abu Qubeis to be in control of his close relatives. He did this to ensure the prominence of his tribe because those who had control over the idols and oversaw their rituals were believed to enjoy a favored status. Qusei's act of securing the black stone ensured that after the Kaabah was built such privileges would accrue to the families who descended from him.

In reality, Qusei was not a man of monotheistic belief but rather was attached to idols and saw the black stone as one such idol. In fact, he named his sons after his idols. How, then, can it be said that this man was a worshiper of the God of Abraham?!

Al Taberi wrote:

The narrators mentioned Qusei's sons' were four. They claimed he said: were born to me four sons. Of which I called two of them after my idols.[1095]

The pagan symbols were changed into Abrahamic symbols

Two important elements in the pagan worship of Mecca were the black stone, which the Khuzaa worshiped on mount Abu Qubeis and the Qusei brought down to the valley of Mecca, and the well dug by Abdel Mutaleb. In Islam, however, the black stone was held to be a jewel descended from paradise that Abraham leaned on in building the Kaabah. The Muslims also attributed the well to Abraham's time and claimed that the angel Gabriel dug the well with his foot to provide water for the child Ishmael, who according to the Islamic narrators reached Mecca with his mother Hagar on the brink of death. The Muslims distorted the Biblical account of the event, which states that when Hagar and Ishmael ran out of water while wandering in the wilderness of Beershebaon on their way to the wilderness of Paran (in the northeastern part of Sinai where Ishmael lived all his life with his descendants), God opened the eyes of Hagar to see a well of water.

Estimating the date when the Kaabah was constructed. Tubb'a the Himyarite as the original builder of Kaabah

Al Allusi wrote that Qusei reigned when Munther bin al Numan reigned on al Hira (in Iraq) at the time of King Bahram Jur, which is Bahram V.[1096]

Bahram Jur reigned from 421-439 A.D., that is, during the first part of the 5th century A.D.[1097] Considering that, as some narrators claim, Qusei was contemporary to this Persian king, Qusei would have reigned after the year 420. Since we know that Asaad Abu Karib reigned until the year 435 A.D., it is easy to see that Asaad had occupied Mecca at the time of the Quraysh, which is after Qusei passed away. Asaad built the Kaabah when some of the Quraysh came from the mountains and lived in the valley and worshiped in a tent. Asaad wanted to attract those families of the Quraysh who were, like him, of Himyarite origin. So he built for them a small temple—the Kaabah.

Many Islamic writers confess that Tubb'a built the Kaaba of Mecca. We find in the biography of Mohammed, "Ibn Hisham," that Tubb'a "built the Kaaba and dressed it. His reign was before the reign of Rabieh bin Nasser."[1098]

The Arabic word 'Ammara عَمَّر," is used by Ibn Hisham. It means "built". Tubb'a is said to be the first one to open the door of the Kaaba and to close and lock it.[1099] Other Islamic historians and scholars confirm that he was first to make a key, or series of keys, for the Kaaba.[1100]

The question in this case is logical, who was first to open a door to the building and close and lock it with a key? It has to be the one who built it in the first place. How could the Kaaba, for thousands of years, be without doors, and have its door unprotected without a lock or key, knowing that people had donated gold and other valuable gifts by throwing them into the well which was in the Kaaba? Could a sacred place such as this have been left vulnerable from the time of Abraham as Muslims claim?

Islamic scholars, historians and expositors of the Quran said the same, that Tubb'a was first to cloth the Kaaba.[1101] Islamic writers say that Tubb'a was first to establish "Woolat وُلاة," people responsible for the religious services in the temple[1102] Who can accept the idea that a temple in existence since the time of Abraham had been without people who were responsible for its religious services? It is clear that Tubb'a first appointed the men responsible for temple services. Both the religious services and the construction of the temple were in Tubb'a's hand, and no temple existed before his occupation of Mecca. For example; Worshippers were prohibited from offering dead sacrifices. If a woman was menstruating, she should not enter the Kaaba and present her offering.[1103]

The regulations that Tubb'a instituted show clearly that he was not just the constructor of the Kaaba but the founder of its religious ceremonies. If a temple had been built in the time of Abraham, it surely would have rich rituals well-documented in addition to sacred literature. For example, the rituals and traditions of Judaism are well developed and documented in hundreds of books in addition to the Biblical texts and the writings of several prophets.

Yet, when we come to the Kaabah of Mecca we see that everything started with Tubb'a, the Yemeni monarch, who sought to connect Mecca with Yemen by building a temple there. The temple he built was of the same building style as the Kaabas that were in existence in Yemen and in other northern cities of Arabia. Most of the Kaabas contained a black stone around which they circled. When Tubb'a found that Mecca was the only city without a Kaabah and that the inhabitants worshipped in a tent, he wanted to do the inhabitants a favor and built the Kaabah, something that indicates the city was built recently, close to Tabbaa's time, around the end of the 4th century A.D., which accords well with the true date of the building of the city of Mecca.

Was Abraham a founder of a religion called Hanafieh?

The Quran claims that the religion of Abraham was called al Hanafieh. All the men of the Bible were Muslims Hanif. The Quran further states that Allah called Mohammed to follow Abraham's religion and to be, like him, a Hanif. Here some verses of the Quran:

> And they say: Be Jews or Christians, you will be guided. Say: Nay! (we follow) the religion of Ibrahim, the Hanif, and he was not one of the polytheists. (2:135)

> Say: 'Verily, my Lord hath guided me to a way that is straight, a religion of right, Abraham's religion Hanif. He was not polytheistic.' (6:161)

> We have sent the revelation to you: 'Follow the religion of Ibrahim (Abraham) Hanif).' (16:123)

As for the claim that Abraham and his descendants were Muslims, we find the following verses of Surah al Baqarah:

> When his Lord said to him, 'Be a Muslim,' he said: 'I submit myself to the Lord of the worlds.' When his Lord said to him, 'Be a Muslim,' he said: 'I submit myself to the Lord of the worlds. Or were you witnesses when death approached Ya'qub (Jacob)?' When he said unto his sons, 'What will you worship after me?' They said, 'We shall worship your God, the God of your fathers, Ibrahim (Abraham), Isma'il (Ishmael), Ishaq (Isaac), One God, and to Him we submit in Islam.' (2:131-133)

The Israelites, however, did not know a separated religion of Abraham named Hanafieh. Furthermore, we do not see in any Arabian inscriptions or even in pre-Islamic Jahiliyyah poetry any mention of this alleged religion.

The main founder of the group of Ahnaf

The group of Ahnaf was established by four individuals: Zayd bin Amru bin Nufayl, Waraqa bin Nofel, Ubeid allah bin Jhash, and 'Uthman bin al Huweireth. These four men agreed on their opinions.[1104] All four of these men were relatives of Mohammed, descending from Luai لُؤَيّ , one of

Mohammed's ancestors. Waraqa, the second figure in the group, was a cousin of Khadija, the first wife of Mohammed. Of the four men, Zayd bin Amru was seen as the pioneer in the group. He claimed that while searching for a religion to follow he met a monk in Damascus who pointed him to the "religion of Abraham," telling him:

> You ask for a religion no one today practices, this was Abraham's religion. He was Hanif, neither Jew nor Christian.[1105]

Zayd returned to Mecca spreading the idea of Hanif, claiming for the first time that Abraham built the Kaabah and established Hajj around the hills of Mecca. He made his Qubleh (the direction of prayer) toward Mecca instead of Jerusalem as the Jews prayed.

Additional proofs point that Zayd bin Amru was the founder of Ahnaf group

The Ahnaf claim that Abraham was the founder of their sect originated at the time of Mohammed by Zayd, the founder of Ahnaf. In turn, Mohammed embraced this erroneous claim. Mohammed, in one of his Hadiths, said: "Zayd will be considered as the chief founder of a nation between Jesus and me."[1106] Mohammed also said: "Zayd will be one nation at the day of the resurrection from dead."[1107]

This claim of Mohammed reveals that Mohammed and other members of the group of Ahnaf believed that Zayd was the founder and head of the Ahnaf. Just as Moses was the head of Judaism and Jesus was the head of Christianity, Zayd was the head and initiator of the belief of Ahnaf.

There is additional evidence which reveals that Zayd was the founder of Ahnaf. He declared that he alone followed the religion of Abraham.[1108]

The relationship of Ahnaf with Jinn; Mohammed's relationship with the founder of Ahnaf

There are indications that the Ahnaf group had a relationship with the Jinn. Dr. Jawad Ali notes that "the old narrators mentioned that the sayings of Ahnaf are similar to the words of the Kuhhan (priests) of the Jinn in that they use the same kind of rhyme."[1109]

The Ahnaf was a group that Mohammed joined in his early youth and spent time with them in the caves of Harra'. Zayd bin Harithah, Mohammed's adopted son, described an encounter between Mohammed and Zayd bin Amru as the two walked around two silver idols of Isaf and Naelah:

> We presented to Zayd the food that contained roasted meat. When Zayd said, 'What is it?' we answered, 'It is the goat...,' and he said, 'I do not eat anything slaughtered to anyone except Allah.' There were two copper idols there. They were Esaf and Naelah. The prophet of Allah walked around them, and I walked with him.[1110]

Zayd attributed the pagan Hajj of Mecca to Abraham

Zayd bin Amru attributed certain pagan rituals to Abraham that Mohammed adopted (see the subject of Ahnaf in my book The Star Akbar). For instance, Zayd promoted the practice of Hajj to the hills around Mecca, which he claimed had originated with Abraham and Ishmael, although in fact some of the pagan tribes around Mecca practiced the Hajj for the purpose of pleading for rain.

They used to stop at Mina, which was a place where they worshipped Manat, a daughter of Allah, to plead for rain. Arafa was the place in the pre-Islamic Hajj where they worshipped the sun. Muzdalifeh was the place where they worshipped the moon and the devil Quzah. (For more information, see Dr. Amari's book The History of Mecca and Jerusalem.)

Zayd bin Amru bin Nufayl and the immoral Hallah sect

Zayd also contradicted his own tribe, the Quraysh. The Arabians who used to encompass the Kaaba belonged to one of two parties: the first group was Hallah الحلة , which included women, who encompassed the Kaaba in the nude; the second group, called Hummas الحُمْس , was conservative and more hard-line. They were offended over the nakedness of the al Hallah. Quraysh belonged to the Hummas.[1111]

Al Hallah was a word derived from the Arabic word "Halla حَلَّ." Ibn Manthur said:

> Halla means that the one who is consecrated is freed from his consecration. It means it is permissible for him to leave his consecration. And 'Ahlah' means permissible.[1112] Ibn al Athir said the word grants him permission to him to do what was unlawful and forbidden in the Hajj...and the word 'Halal الخَلال 'means permissible and is opposite of al Haram الحرام – unlawful.'[1113]

Al Hallah made lawful various practices that were originally unlawful and illicit, even some that the religion prohibited, such as having another man's wives. That was why the Hallah walked naked around the Kaaba.

Ibn Hajar said there was a pre-Islamic Jahiliyyah group that claimed, "It is lawful for those who walk around the Kaaba doing that which is unlawful to change and do what they see as sinful. These include both things that are desired and things which are illicit."[1114]This means that the group itself allowed things such as walking around the Kaaba naked.

Something else distinguishes al Hallah from al Hummas. Hallah proselytes treated 'Arafa, also called 'Arafat, as a special religious stop on the Hajj. Hummas proselytes, including the tribe of Quraysh, did not stop at 'Arafa. Instead, they stood in a place called Nimrah, which was near the Kaaba. The Hummas did not consider 'Arafat as a station in the Hajj.

Al Azruqi said, "In the day of Arafa, al Hallah went to 'Arafa, and al Hummas went to Nimrah, near the temple. When the people of al Hallah stop over from 'Arafa, the Hummas stay near the Kaaba. The Hallah walk from 'Arafa until all will meet at Muzdalifah."[1115]

We find Zayd bin Amru bin Nufayl with the Hallah, sharing the ritual of standing on 'Arafa. Al Hafeth ibn Kathir and Sa'ad said, "Zayd stood at 'Arafa and used to say, 'We come to you. You, who have no partner with you, nor an equal to you.' Then he moved from 'Arafa to the next station of Hajj."[1116] This reveals the affiliation of Zayd with al Hallah, which was an immoral group, as evidenced by the fact that they compassed naked around the Kaabah, including the women. Men and women marching naked around the Kaaba is an attribution of occult religious sects.

Mohammed joined Zayd bin Amru and the Hallah sect in the ritual of stopping at Arafa

One proof that Mohammed joined Zayd bin Amru in this practice is the fact that Mohammed contradicted his tribe Quraysh and stood at Arafa:

Jabeer bin, Mut'am bin, 'Adi bin, Nofel bin and Abdel Manaf جبير بن مطعم بن عدى بن نوفل بن عبد مناف, who was a relative of Mohammed, said, 'A camel went astray in the day of 'Arafa (when al Hallah made their religious stop at 'Arafa). So as I came out toward 'Arafa, tracking the camel, I saw Mohammed at 'Arafa. I said to myself, 'He is from Hummas. What made him stand here? I wondered about the matter.'[1117]

Though Mohammed was of Hummas, Jabeer was surprised that he, like al Hallah and Zayd bin Amru, stopped at Arafa.

Zayd married his stepmother

Another action that unveils the immoral life of Zayd came when he married his stepmother,[1118] which was a despised custom in the pre-Islamic Jahiliyyah period. Al Asfahani said, "When a person marries his stepmother, it is called the marriage of Maqetالمقت ." Al Asfahani defined the word Maqet "as the severe hate for the one who practiced something nasty and ugly."[1119] Abi al Fidaابي الفداء says, "The people of pre-Islamic Jahiliyyah placed shame on anyone who married his stepmother. They called him al Thaisenالضيزن which means iniquitous."[1120]

One could only conclude that Zayd bin Amru bin Nufayl was immoral and perverted. His generation and the Jahiliyyah viewed him as a man of low moral standards and one who practiced nasty things. How then can one take seriously his claims as the founder of a religion that was supposed to follow the faith of Abraham?

Mohammed began his activity as leader of Ahnaf and promoter of a religion under the name of "flexible Hanafieh"

Waraqa bin Nofel prepared Mohammed to be the leader of the Ahnaf when Mohammed first claimed to be a prophet. Waraqa grew old and blind. Because of his close ties with his cousin Khadijah, the first wife of Mohammed, he pictured her young husband Mohammed to be his successor as leader of the Ahnaf group.

Mohammed called people to join the religion of Ahnaf, or Hanifieh. It was the basis for his religious claim.[1121] He said that Allah created men as "Muslim Hunaffa'."[1122] The Jinn used to recite poetry in a loud voice, such as during the battle of Bader, in order to encourage Mohammed in his claim, calling the Muslims "Hanifs."[1123] Mohammed used to say, "I was entrusted with the flexible easy Hanifieh."[1124] Flexible means not imposing any moral boundaries on Muslims. Thus, we find in the Quran verses that allow Muslims to keep however many women they gain through wars, as in Surah al Nisa' (4:3):

Inkahu (marry or have sex with) as many women as you desire: two or three or four... or whatever women you capture.

We can say that Mohammed was a reformer of the religion that Zayd bin Amru bin Nufayl established, which was the Hanafieh. Waraqa added Christian heretical doctrines to it. Mohammed built on this religion, adding to it various elements from the religions of his day, such as Zoroastrianism and Sabianism. He called it "flexible easy Hanifieh." He adopted some of Zayd's slogans, such as "Abraham was neither a Christian nor a Jew, but a Hanif." Mohammed repeated this slogan in Surah 3: 67:

> Abraham was neither a Jew nor a Christian, but a Muslim Hanif.

This justification for founding a new religion was founded on Zayd's claim that a monk in Damascus told him that Abraham was neither Christian nor Jew, but a Hanif.

A Quranic myth was based upon the fact that Mohammed did not understand the covenant God established with Abraham

Some of the stories in the Quran were the result of changing a text in the book of Genesis into a myth. As we read in Surah 2:260 called al Baqarah:

> When Abraham said: 'Show me, Lord, how You will raise the dead,' He replied: 'Have you no faith?' He said, 'Yes, but just to reassure my heart.' Allah said, 'Take four birds, draw them to you, and cut their bodies to pieces. Scatter them over the mountaintops, then call them back. They will come swiftly to you. Know that Allah is Mighty, Wise.'

This myth is derived from a story in Genesis 15 in which God appeared to Abraham and gave him a promise:

> 'I am the Lord who brought you out of Ur of the Chaldeans, to give you this land to possess it.' He said, 'O Lord God, how may I know that I will possess it?' So He said to him, 'Bring Me a three year old heifer, and a three year old female goat, and a three year old ram, and a turtledove, and a young pigeon.' Then he brought all these to Him and cut them in two, and laid each half opposite the other; but he did not cut the birds.

We see that the Quranic version changed Abraham's question "O Lord God, how may I know that I will possess it?" into another question: "Show me, Lord, how You will raise the dead."

When making a treaty or covenant, it was customary to kill animals by cutting them in two.[1125] There is a reference in Jeremiah 34 that proves that cutting the calf in two had continued in Israel when making a treaty (Jeremiah 34:18-19):

> And I will give the men that have transgressed my covenant, which have not performed the words of the covenant which they had made before me, when they cut the calf in twain, and passed between the parts thereof, the princes of Judah, and the princes of Jerusalem, the eunuchs, and the priests, and all the people of the land, which passed between the parts of the calf.

Cutting the animals in two represented the two parties in the treaty; one of the two parties walked between the two parts of the animal as a sign of commitment to the articles of the covenant. The animals in the verses represent Abraham's descendants, and what will happen to them in the future.

Placing the two parts of the animals in front each other, in a way that made them appear as one, easy to restore their unity, signified the unity of the two parties in the treaty. The strong party was committed to protect the weak party and ready to be united with it. In Genesis, the custom served as a symbol of the Lord's assurance as the strong who would fulfil the purposes of the covenant: which issued in the birth of a nation from Abraham's progeny and the coming of the Messiah, in the flesh according to Abraham's progeny in order to save the world from sin.

We notice that Abraham "did not cut the birds."

Leviticus 1:17 states that the birds should be offered as a complete sacrifice without being cut. It was a type of the body of Christ; although pierced with the nails and spear, it was not divided on the Cross. Also His body when was buried did not go into decomposition.

The three big animals that were cut in two represented Abraham's descendants, the Israelites, who were going to be divided first into two kingdoms and spread throughout the world. But God would restore them as one nation.

We read in Genesis 15:11:

> And when birds of prey came down on the carcasses, Abram drove them away.

Without a doubt, Abraham expected a sign to come from God who ordered him to present an offering of animals and birds. Abraham obeyed the Lord's instructions. There were, however, opposing forces who wanted to devour the elements of the treaty, which represented Israel. The birds of prey were a falcon and a hawk, which were unclean birds according the Law.

Those symbolized hostile pagan nations that wanted to destroy Israel as happened in Egypt and later by other nations.

Genesis 15:12 continues:

As the sun was going down, a deep sleep fell on Abram. And behold, dreadful and great darkness fell upon him.

Clarke says that the Hebrew word for "deep sleep" is tardemah, the same word used when Adam fell asleep so that Eve could be created from one of his ribs. The verse that follows explains the "dreadful and great darkness" that fell upon him. Abraham wanted to know how to inherit the land. The Lord, however, shows him in a vision what would happen before his descendants inherited the land: They would suffer a dreadful period, which actually occurred in Egypt for four centuries, during which they were enslaved by the Egyptians and endured a dreadful bondage and oppression under the pharaohs.

God's promise to Abraham was not fulfilled to him personally because it was not to be fulfilled in his time. Since he was the one who first received the promise, however, he received a vision showing what would happen to his descendants before they inherited the land. This was to prevent them from being dismayed and in despair over their humiliation during their slavery in Egypt. They would see that there will be an exodus from Egypt into the land of promise as was revealed to their father Abraham in the vision.

Genesis 15:13:

Then the LORD said to Abram, 'Know for certain that your offspring will be sojourners in a land that is not theirs and will be servants there, and they will be afflicted for four hundred years.'

This means that the inheritance would be preceded by a severe slavery. This is to reveal man's condition under the slavery of Satan and sin. He needs liberation through Christ so that he can walk spiritually with God and inherit eternal life.

The promised land was not just a gift to Abraham's descendants. God called the Hebrew people in order to fulfill in them a special pattern through which humanity would learn about man's horrible slavery to sin and the devil and about the liberating divine power and the foundation of human salvation through Christ's redemption. This redemption was symbolized in the protection (salvation or saving) of the Israelites in Egypt from perishing through the sprinkling of the blood of the lamb on the two side posts and on the upper door post of the houses. The believer's walk in new life was symbolized by God's leading of the Israelites in the wilderness of Sinai. The entrance into the land of Canaan through Joshua, a type of Jesus (whose name Joshua is Hebrew for the Greek Jesus and means deliverer), who leads the soul to inherit fellowship with God and then to enter God's heaven in eternity.

When the Lord responded to Abraham's question "How am I to know that I shall possess it?" with the declaration "Know for certain" He was giving him assurance, based on a sign that the Israelites would remain in slavery in a foreign land. Moses must have relied on this sign while a he was a prince who was adopted by the Pharaoh's daughter. He noticed that the 400 years were drawing to a close.

Genesis 15:14 says:

But I will bring judgment on the nation that they serve, and afterward they shall come out with great possessions.

This was given to Abraham so that his descendants would not despair under horrific slavery at the hand of the Egyptians. For although cruelty and slavery by the strong were not deterred and there was no hope of liberation from a strong nation such as Egypt, the Lord left a promise to them that He would break the arms of the nation who enslaved the people whom God Himself had chosen to be a holy nation worshiping the Lord. This promise was given before this progeny came into existence.

The Lord ordered each Israelite family to slay a perfect lamb, which was a symbol of Christ who, as a perfect man was without any blemish, and was sacrificed on the cross for man's redemption. They had to sprinkle the blood on the "the two side posts and on the upper door post of the houses," representing the structure of the cross. The blood was to protect them from being stricken while God judged the Egyptians, killing their firstborn (Exodus 12:13):

And the blood shall be to you for a token upon the houses where ye are: and when I see the blood, I will pass over you, and the plague shall not be upon you to destroy you, when I smite the land of Egypt.

This symbolizes the fact that there will not be any condemnation for anyone who takes Christ's redemption as his refuge.

Genesis 15:16-17 says:

> And they shall come back here in the fourth generation, for the iniquity of the Amorites is not yet complete. When the sun had gone down and it was dark, behold, a smoking fire pot and a flaming torch passed between these pieces.

"The smoking fire" symbolized the entrance of the Israelites into the fire of distress in Egypt, as Daniel's friends were thrown into the fiery furnace in Babylon. Though it was burning them with pain and agony, God's presence as a flaming torch would enlighten the way for them. But He would devour their opponents as happened when the ten plagues came down on Egypt. The Lord led them through a pillar of cloud by day and a pillar of fire by night (Exodus 13:21).

The flaming torch passed between the two pieces of the animal symbolized God's presence in the covenant promising that Abraham's progeny would inherit the land and that He would be with them during times of tribulation. This Biblical narrative describes the practice of issuing covenant as it was done in Abraham's time in which both parties to the covenant would pass between the pieces of the animal. But here we see only the presence of God passed between the pieces of the animal, which indicates that the Lord—not Abraham—is the guarantee of the fulfillment of the covenant. Our salvation is assured through God's commitment to His covenant; our salvation is based on Christ's redemption, what He did for us, and not on our ability to save ourselves.

Genesis 15:19 says:

> In the same day the LORD made a covenant with Abram.

In establishing this covenant with Abraham, we see that God passed in His presence between the pieces as sign of His intention to come down Himself in a human form in order to be the sacrifice of the Covenant and its great lamb on the Cross. Christ had to be cut off, as Daniel prophesied in the 6th century B.C.:

> Shall Messiah be cut off, but not for himself. (Daniel 9:26)

In Daniel chapter 9, Daniel prophesied as to the exact time Christ was to come and die. Daniel's prophecy "not for himself" means that Christ's death was for us, for our benefit rather than His own.

This was a reference to what was to occur to Him when He became the lamb of the Covenant between God and man. In reality the covenant with Abraham, and then with Moses and David, was established according to animal sacrifices, which pointed to Christ's death, the sacrifice God prepared for the redemption of humanity. Here we see the animal sacrifices were cut, but when the covenant was made with Moses, blood was shed. Though this covenant with Abraham was to guarantee the bestowal of the land to Abraham's descendants, it was also a phase in preparing the way for the coming of Christ, who made the New Covenant through His blood for the salvation of humanity.

What a striking contrast between the spiritual meaning of the Bible and the Quran's notions as adopted from groups who did not understand the meaning of the Biblical text.

The account of the covenant between God and Abraham was widespread among groups who were ignorant of the Old Testament, such as those Arabians who embraced Judaism in the form of a myth. The recounting of this myth is found in Surah 2 called Baqarah and verse 260. It is the Quranic mythological version of the Biblical account we have just examined that Mohammed adopted from stories he heard narrated by individuals who neither knew the Old Testament nor studied it. But they learned stories that were widespread among a people who studied the apocryphal books (Hebrew books that were not included in the Bible) or heard the stories of the Old Testament and changed them into mythological stories that fit the tastes of the pre-Islamic Jahiliyyah people.

There are, however, a few sentences in the Quran that contained a summary in Arabic of some stories of the Old Testament. This was due to Mohammed's relationship with certain groups that had the Old Testament. Among these paragraphs are the story of Joseph, the story of Abraham's celestial guests, and the story of God's testing Abraham's willingness to present his son as a burnt offering. The latter was merely a summary that made no mention of the place where God ordered Abraham to offer his son. We examine the celestial guest's visit to Abraham first.

Mohammed did not understand the identity of the guest who visited Abraham and promised him a son (the birth of Isaac)

Surah al-Hijr 15:60 states:

And inform them of the guests of Ibrahim:

When they entered upon him, they said, Peace. He said: Surely we are afraid of you. They said: Be not afraid, surely we give you the good news of a boy, possessing knowledge. He said: Do you give me good news (of a son) when old age has come upon me? Of what then do you give me good news! They said: We give you good news with truth, therefore be not among those who despair. He said: And who despairs of the mercy of his Lord but the erring ones? He said: What is your business then, O apostles? They said: Surely we are sent towards a guilty people, except Lot's followers: We will most surely deliver them all, except his wife; We ordained that she shall surely be of those who remain behind.

The story is repeated in Surah Adh-Dhariyat, Chapter 51:24-34:

Has there come to you information about the honored guests of Ibrahim? When they entered upon him, they said: 'Peace. Peace,' said he, a strange people. Then he turned aside to his family secretly and brought a fat (roasted) calf near them. He said: 'What! Will you not eat?' So he conceived in his mind a fear on account of them. They said: 'Fear not.' And they gave him the good news of a boy possessing knowledge. Then his wife came up in great grief, and she struck her face and said: An old barren woman! Thus says your Lord: Surely He is the Wise, the Knowing. He said: 'What is your affair then, O apostles!' They said: 'Surely we are sent to a guilty people.'

Without a doubt, Mohammed heard this story told or read by a Jew. He then summarized it according to his understanding and his known Quranic rhyme. He mentioned how the guests came to Abraham and Abraham went to his wife and brought a fat calf to feed them. They gave Abraham good tidings of the birth of Isaac. He noted that Abraham's wife doubted the promise saying that she was an old barren woman. Then Abraham asked them about their mission, which was the destruction of the city or the people where Lot resided. Lot and his family escaped destruction, all except his wife.

The Quranic story is a summary of the visit of three celestial beings mentioned in Genesis chapter 18 and two additional sentences about the destruction of Sodom, the rescue of Lot and his two daughters, and the perishing of his wife mentioned in chapter 19.

Mohammed did not specify the number of these guests, which was three. Furthermore, the one who narrated the story or read it to Mohammed was not aware of the identity of the Person who was in the middle of the two angels—who was the Lord Yahweh before the incarnation, that is Christ. This visit was described in the book of Genesis as follows:

The LORD appeared to Abraham at the sacred trees of Mamre. As Abraham was sitting at the entrance of his tent during the hottest part of the day... he looked up and saw three men standing there.

He must have felt the sacredness of the place so that he suddenly looked up to see what accounted for the feeling of solemnity because he was in the presence of a glory such as he had never experienced in his life. The fact that the Lord appeared in human form between two angels was not to hide His divine presence. The viewer could not fail to recognize His divine identity. Abraham distinguished Him as the One who called him and used to speak to him in the same manner in which Peter the disciple distinguished Him when He sat in his boat and performed the miracle of filling the net with fish. We read in the Gospel of Luke:

> When Simon Peter saw this, he fell at Jesus' knees and said, 'Go away from me, Lord; I am a sinful man!' (Luke 5:8)

> Thus "when Abraham saw them, he hurried from the entrance of his tent to meet them and bowed low to the ground to worship the one in the middle."

It was a unique opportunity to have direct fellowship with the One who had called him, to strengthen his fellowship with Him, and to honor Him in his tent. Thus, he went toward them and worshiped the One in the midst of the two angels. Verse three says:

> And said, 'O Lord, if I have found favor in your sight, do not pass by your servant.'

The word "Lord" in Hebrew here is Adonai. Abraham distinguished Him as the Lord because he had seen Him in the past; He had appeared to him more than once. Abraham had experiences with God: he saw Him and talked to Him. Though we do not know how the Lord used to appear to Abraham, in this case, the divine personality and its sublimity or highness is so evident even though He was appearing in human form between two angels. Abraham felt the same awe and holiness when seeing God in human form. This was actually a prophetical sign of God's intention to be incarnated. This was the same feeling that many experienced when encountering Christ during His life on earth, to the extent that Jairus, a ruler of the synagogue who had never bowed in front a man in his life, since worship was reserved for God alone, yet bowed down and worshipped Christ because he saw in Christ the highness that belongs only to God.

A celestial visit in which the Lord of heaven was seen standing near his tent was a unique opportunity that Abraham had not experienced at that level in the past, when God had appeared to him for a brief moment. But, here the God of revelations treaded on the earth in a form that suggested

He wanted to be closer to Abraham. He was nearby Abraham's tent walking in human form. Do we not recognize here that the Son of God's determination to exist in our world as man was an ancient desire of His.

When Abraham saw the Creator close to him in a human form, he did not want to miss this opportunity for intimacy, to sit with him for the first time and contemplate His glory, to take advantage of a rare opportunity when the Lord entered his tent and blessed his family. He was determined not to miss this opportunity because if he had not urged Him, He would have passed him by.

Abraham extended the following offer in verses 4 and 5:

> Let a little water be brought, and wash your feet, and rest yourselves under the tree, while I bring a morsel of bread, that you may refresh yourselves, and after that you may pass on—since you have come to your servant.

Abraham had seen a picture of the incarnation 2,000 years before it took place

Abraham spoke in a humble language and in human terms "a morsel of bread, that you may refresh yourselves." The appearance of the Lord and the two angels was in a perfect human appearance such that Abraham thought they had bodies that needed to eat, or that these bodies that appeared as men were able to eat as they walked on the earth.

Abraham who pre-saw the redemption on Mount Moriah 2,000 years before it occurred (in his willingness to sacrifice his only son), now saw how the incarnation would take place 2,000 years before it happened. The Lord who appeared to him in human form, walking on the earth and ready to eat with the one whom He loves and who serves Him, came literally in the flesh 2,000 years later. He came walking on our earth, eating with the disciples, sitting with the sinners in order to bring them out of sin and attract them to His blessed person.

We see in the Lord's acceptance of Abraham's offer as a pre-sign of His incarnation. The house of Abraham is where the Lord wanted to sit, eat, and give a prophetical indication of His determination to come incarnate (in human flesh) and enjoy full intimacy with the human race.

When Abraham heard of the Lord's acceptance to be honored in this way, we see Abraham hurry. How great was this opportunity for the Lord to sit with His two angels under his tree and in front of his tent. It was an opportunity that no one in his generation had been given before. We see that the Lord ate from what Abraham prepared. The sitting of the Lord to eat under Abraham's tree was something rare in history before the incarnation; it was a prophetic example of the truthfulness of His incarnation.

Mohammed neither understood the Divine identity of the Person who visited Abraham nor the purpose of this revelation

Then the Lord presented a promise one year after His visit that Sarah will bear a child. Sarah, however, laughed, excluding the fulfillment of the promise because of her barrenness and old age. Verses 13 and 14 say:

> The LORD said to Abraham, 'Why did Sarah laugh and say, "Shall I indeed bear a child, now that I am old?" Is anything too hard for the LORD? At the appointed time I will return to you, about this time next year, and Sarah shall have a son.'

The Hebrew word "Lord" in this text is Yahweh. This confirms that the identity of the One who was between the two angels was indeed Yahweh God Himself. He is Christ before the incarnation. The Lord revealed to Sarah that her idea about God and His power was limited and not correct. When the Lord told her, "Is anything too hard for the LORD?" He wanted to elevate her eyes that He was the omnipotent, that nothing was impossible for Him to do in this life and in the universe. Her barrenness was something trivial in regard to His unlimited great potency. We see Jesus in the book of Revelation confirming that He is omnipotent.

> 'I am the Alpha and the Omega,' says the Lord God, 'who is and who was and who is to come, the Almighty.' (Revelation 1:8)

We say in concluding our discussion of this divine visit to Abraham in human form, that Mohammed did not recognize the identity of the divine personality who walked between the two angels. He did not understand why He appeared in human form, which is as we have seen was a prophetic sign of the incarnation.

The great prophecy of Moriah, which Mohammed did not understand

Furthermore, Mohammed in the Quran summarized in a few sentences the great prophetic experience recorded in Genesis 22, without understanding its meaning or mentioning what Genesis specified as the place where Abraham was ordered to offer his son—Mount Moriah. That is a mountain range outside Jerusalem where Christ was crucified as redemption for the human race. We read in Surah as-Saaffat (37:102-107):

> And when he attained to working with him, he said: O my son! Surely I have seen in a dream that I should sacrifice you; consider then what you see. He said: O my father! Do what you are commanded; if Allah please, you will find me of the patient ones. So when they both submitted and he threw him down upon his forehead, and We called out to him saying: O Ibrahim! You have indeed shown the truth of the vision; surely thus do We reward the doers of good: Most surely this is a manifest trial. And We ransomed him with a great sacrifice.

Mohammed mentioned, in verse 107, "We ransomed him with a great sacrifice." He must have heard this sentence from the Christians in the area of Mecca. The ram that God brought from heaven when He stopped Abraham's knife to fall down on Isaac's neck cannot be described as "great sacrifice." But the sentence points to the fact that the Redeemer is a great personality, which is a clear reference to Christ. Thus, Mohammed was either not aware or simply ignored this sentence that pointed to Christ. He heard the sentence without being able to understand its obvious prophetic significance.

Abraham's great test is recorded in Genesis chapter 22:

> And it came to pass after these things, that God tried Abraham, and said to him, Abraham! and he said, Here am I. And he said, Take now thy son, thine only son, whom thou lovest, Isaac, and get thee into the land of Moriah, and there offer him up for a burnt-offering on one of the mountains which I will tell thee of.

> And Abraham rose early in the morning, and saddled his ass, and took two of his young men with him, and Isaac his son; and he clave the wood for the burnt-offering, and rose up and went to the place that God had told him of. On the third day Abraham lifted up his eyes and saw the place from afar. And Abraham said to his young men, Abide ye here with the ass; and I and the lad will go yonder and worship, and come again to you.

> And Abraham took the wood of the burnt-offering, and laid it on Isaac his son; and he took the fire in his hand, and the knife, and they went both of them together. And Isaac spoke to Abraham his father, and said, My father! And he said, Here am I, my son. And he said, Behold the fire and the wood; but where is the sheep for a burnt-offering? And Abraham said, My son, God will provide himself with the sheep for a burnt-offering. And they went both of them together.

And they came to the place of which God had told him. And Abraham built the altar there, and piled the wood; and he bound Isaac his son, and laid him on the altar upon the wood. And Abraham stretched out his hand, and took the knife to slaughter his son.

And the Angel of Yahweh called to him from the heavens, and said, Abraham, Abraham! And he said, Here am I. And he said, Stretch not out thy hand against the lad, neither do anything to him; for now I know that thou fearest God, and hast not withheld thy son, thine only son, from me.

And Abraham lifted up his eyes, and looked, and behold, behind was a ram caught in the thicket by its horns; and Abraham went and took the ram, and offered it up for a burnt-offering instead of his son. And Abraham called the name of that place Yahweh-jireh; as it is said at the present day, On the mount of Yahweh will be provided. And the Angel of Yahweh called to Abraham from the heavens a second time, and said, By myself I swear, saith Yahweh, that, because thou hast done this, and hast not withheld thy son, thine only son, I will richly bless thee, and greatly multiply thy seed, as the stars of heaven, and as the sand that is on the sea-shore; and thy seed shall possess the gate of his enemies; and in thy seed shall all the nations of the earth bless themselves, because thou hast hearkened to my voice.

An essential aspect of Abraham's call was that through Abraham's obedience God revealed important aspects of the redemption as well about God as giver and about the personality of the Redeemer

The significance of Abraham's call was not simply that he sired a beloved son, nor even that great nations would arise through his progeny. There was something even more important than that—the fact that God revealed through Abraham's obedience—his faith—important aspects about the great and blessed promise of the Redeemer of mankind who was to be born from his progeny: Christ the Lord. Abraham's relationship with his promised son Isaac expressed the nature of the relationship between the Heavenly Father and His Son Christ and the Father's willingness to offer Him as a sacrifice on Mount Moriah, the very mount on which Abraham was ordered to offer his son Isaac, whom he loved, as a burnt offering. It reveals and foreshadows also the Son's obedience to the Father in His willingness to be the Lamb of the burnt offering.

Though in old age Abraham through a miracle begat Isaac, from whom the nation of Israel would come and give rise to all the prophets throughout history before Christ, Abraham's long walk with God had not yet reached the mount of Moriah. For it was there on Mount Moriah that occurred the most important prophetic message in history regarding redemption. It perfectly foreshadowed God's love in sacrificing His only Son on the same mountain where Abraham was asked, but not required, to sacrifice his only beloved son Isaac. This illustration was made possible by the characteristic obedience to which God had called Abraham and trained and prepared him for.

Abraham's experience unveils the Father's giving heart, the One who sacrificed to bring redemption

In Genesis 22:2 the Lord said to him:

And he said, Take now thy son, thine only son, whom thou lovest, Isaac, and get thee into the land of Moriah, and there offer him up for a burnt-offering on one of the mountains which I will tell thee of.

Why did God use the term "Your only Son" and "whom You love"? This command caused Abraham great emotional anguish, for after he sent away Ishmael, he was left with only one son—a son who was the great subject of his love, on whom rested the hope of the promise of inheriting the land, for the blessings were expected to come through Isaac. God's command caused a great crisis in an old man's heart. Abraham saw that Isaac was the subject of his call, his life, and the continuation of the great promise of blessing. It was a crisis too great for a man to bear. It was, however, a picture of what a great divine personality was going through at and prior to Abraham's time: the beloved Son in the Godhead was dedicated to be offered as a burnt offering on the same mountain. Those were sentiments or emotions Abraham had endured for three days. For God, however, the path leading to such an offering of the beloved Everlasting Son on the same mountain was everlasting.

This was not a literal prophecy typical of many prophecies of the Old Testament, but the prophet in this case, Abraham, was required to pass through a difficult decision, to make an offering that weighed on his heart, his most precious and beloved treasure. This was so that the world might see through Abraham's three days of anguish the great heart of the true Giver, the Heavenly Father, who was willing to sacrifice His only beloved Son on that very mountain to the disgrace, shame, humiliation, and death in the flesh.

The Bible proclaims Mount Moriah as the place God appointed for redemption

Why was Abraham ordered to travel for three days from the place where he lived in Beersheba in the south to the land of Moriah?

2 Chronicles 3:1 says:

> Then Solomon began to build the house of the LORD in Jerusalem on Mount Moriah, where the LORD had appeared to David his father, at the place that David had appointed, on the threshing floor of Ornan the Jebusite.

Thus, the Lord revealed to David 1,000 years later that Mount Moriah was the place He had appointed for redeeming His people. It happened after David fell into depending on himself instead of attributing his success to the Lord. As a punishment, the plague struck Israel. God commanded David to build an altar on Araunah, the Jebusite field, which was on Mount Moriah in Jerusalem. When David made sacrificial offerings, the plague was lifted from Israel. David knew then that this mountain was appointed by God for the people to be redeemed. God used this Old Testament event to reveal the place where He was to offer His Son as a ransom for the human race and the importance of that place in removing the wicked epidemic of sin from man.

This was so that Abraham and the world would know about the place where the greatest offering and sacrifice throughout history would occur; it was a definite place. Abraham was directed to go to no other place in order to offer Isaac, but to the mountain of Moriah.

Here we see that the Old Testament has an obvious purpose, which is to present a prophetic image of Christ as a person walking on earth and to make known His identity, His redemptive work, details about His relationship with the Father, as a beloved everlasting Son, and even the very place where He had to be offered as an atoning sacrifice for the human race. The word "Moriah" means "seen of Yahweh" or "vision of Yahweh" (see Hamilton, page 103).

We find another reference to the place of the divine sacrifice for all the nations of the earth in Isaiah 25:6-9, that is Mount Zion in Jerusalem, which is part of the range of the mountains of Moriah:

> On this mountain the LORD Almighty will prepare
>
> a feast of rich food for all peoples,
>
> a banquet of aged wine—
>
> the best of meats and the finest of wines.

On this mountain he will destroy

the shroud that enfolds all peoples,

the sheet that covers all nations;

he will swallow up death forever.

The Sovereign LORD will wipe away the tears

from all faces;

he will remove his people's disgrace

from all the earth.

The LORD has spoken.

In that day they will say,

Surely this is our God;

we trusted in him, and he saved us.

This is the LORD, we trusted in him;

let us rejoice and be glad in his salvation.

From the above verses, we see that the shame of sin as well as the spiritual death from which man suffers is removed on this mountain. The veil on the eyes of the nations will be taken off (removed) there. Because of Christ's death and redemption, man will discover his true God who redeemed him.

Without the light shed by the New Testament, Abraham's experience cannot be understood in its true meaning and purpose

That Abraham would place the knife to his son's throat and then kill him and burn him over the wood as a burnt offering is an outrageous and atrocious thing for a father to do to his son. How a man could be called to do such an unexpected thing—to slay his son and offer him as burnt offering—in the most important calling in ancient history is impossible to comprehend without the revelation of the New Testament. It was interpreted as only a test throughout the 2,000 years before Christ. Before Abraham heard the Lord's voice commanding him not to kill his son and saw that God presented him with an expiatory ram, most likely Abraham saw no benefit in it and feared only losing the most important treasure in his life, his only son whom he loved. Before God intervened, he saw himself behaving against his love and passion as a father and in cruelty as if his son were a real lamb. Only obedience enabled Abraham to be part of a prophetic picture in which he was cast in the role of the Father and stood in the place the Father would stand 2,000 years later.

It was a specific mountain, not just any mountain, which is something the Muslims did not comprehend

There were many mountains in the land of Moriah, the region of Jerusalem. Abraham, however, was not left to choose the mount because it was not a normal offering that would be accepted on any mountain. The matter instead was to trace a prophetic map that depicted a future walk: The Son of God was carried by the Father; and the Son carrying a Cross scaled that same mount on which He was offered as ransom for the human race. Abraham voluntarily went with his son to that mountain, which pointed to the fact that the Father by His own will arranged that His Son be dragged to that mountain so that He could offer Him up. The sacrifice is of God the Father, as it is written:

> For God so loved the world, that he gave his only Son, that whosoever believes on him may not perish, but have life eternal. (John 3:16)

Unfortunately, Islam did not understand God's command to Abraham in offering his son on the mount of Moriah at Jerusalem. Muslims followed Zayd bin Amru bin Nufayl, the founder of the Ahnaf group, who claimed that Abraham went to Mecca and tried to offer Ishmael there. They did not know that God, who opposed human sacrifice and the offering of the children as burnt offerings, intended to present a prophecy about the place where He had to present His son as atonement for the human race.

God's determination did not fade (weaken) throughout eternity and history

Genesis 22 says that Abraham rose early in the morning, saddled his ass, took two of his young men and Isaac his son, and clave the wood for the burnt offering. He then rose up, and went unto the place of which God had told him. Verse 22 says:

> Then on the third day Abraham lifted his eyes and saw the place afar off.

It was three days' journey. If it was a precipitance or rush by him not comprehending God's will, the journey was enough to dissipate from Abraham extreme positions of obedience. The distance toward Jerusalem, could have exposed his decision to fade, making him to turn back. Thus, the consistency of his decision was tested through his steadiness for enough time, three days.

The Father's determination in offering His Son was not weakened through Everlasting and history. He revealed it to the prophets in various epochs. Christ determination to offer Himself as a burnt offering never was weakened during His life on earth. He rebuked Peter who said to him "God be favorable to thee, Lord; this shall in no wise be unto thee." But turning round, he said to Peter, "Get away behind me, Satan; thou art an offence to me, for thy mind is not on the things that are of God, but on the things that are of men." (Matthew 16:22-23)

The prophetical dimension of the Biblical term "the third day"

When the Bible states "the third day," it expresses the length of time man or the people of the Old Testament must endure a period of testing or wait after a severe judgment for the solution to come on the third day. It is a prophetical sign of the resurrection after the Cross. Several scripture passages point to this fact. In Exodus 5:3 they journeyed three days before they found water. In the book of Joshua (1:11), God said, "In three days you will cross the Jordan River and take possession of the land the LORD your God is giving you."

This means they needed three days in order to possess the land. This was a symbol of our spiritual possession through the death of Christ, which was represented by the River Jordan.

Here Isaac was considered dead from the time Abraham accepted God's instruction to sacrifice him as a burnt offering. But on the third day on the mountain, Abraham restored him as symbol of Christ's resurrection, as we read in the letter to the Hebrews 11:17-19:

> By faith Abraham, when he was tested, offered up Isaac, and he who had received the promises offered up his only begotten son, of whom it was said, 'In Isaac your seed shall be called,' concluding that God was able to raise him up, even from the dead, from which he also received him in a figurative sense.

Isaac, who carried the wood on his shoulder, is a prototype of Jesus, who carried the Cross while going up into the mountain of redemption

In Genesis 22:5, Abraham commanded the two young men to stay with the ass while he placed the wood on Isaac's shoulders as he climbed the mountain. Was not the ass necessary to carry the wood onto the mountain? Why was the wood left for Isaac, who was tired and exhausted from walking on his feet during the long journey, to carry? Abraham was led on a prophetic journey all the way to the point at which the suffering and sacrifice of Isaac was to begin, so as to point to the suffering and sacrifice of Jesus who carried the Cross toward Golgotha. Isaac's carrying the wood on his shoulders toward the top of the mountain so as to be offered as a sacrifice by his father was a prototype of what had to happen to Jesus 2,000 years later.

Abraham's faith in the resurrection of Isaac pointed prophetically to Christ's resurrection

In spite of Abraham's distress and his submission to the severest test of obedience in his life, he had faith that he was not ordered to lose the promise that he obtained in his old age regarding Isaac. We see God raise up faith in Abraham's heart in a resurrection of Isaac, even though Abraham did not know that it was part of the prophetic scene he was called to draw in his life that foreshadowed the Father's own walk in offering His Son. He had faith in a resurrection without knowing the Person to whom the prophecy pointed. The writer of the letter to the Hebrews, as we saw previously, revealed Abraham's faith, through which he pointed to the resurrection of Christ (Hebrews 11:17-19).

The responsibility for redemption was laid on Jesus because He is the only One able to redeem all humanity

Genesis 22:6 says:

So Abraham took the wood of the burnt offering and laid it on Isaac his son.

He laid the wood on his back. He took the responsibility, the burden, hat should have been borne by the ass and the two slaves and laid it on Isaac's shoulders. Abraham was led by the Spirit of prophecy so that

Isaac's walk was a figure of Christ who carried the wood of the Cross. He also carried our sins as we read in 1 Peter 2: 24:

> Who Himself bore our sins in His own body on the tree, that we, having died to sins, might live for righteousness—by whose stripes you were healed.

Why was the wood laid on Isaac and not on his two slaves? Because if the slave had carried the wood, that would have pointed to an angel—for angels are servants of God. An angel cannot carry the sins of humanity because an angel is a limited being. The need was for a divine Personality, the Creator Himself, that is Christ, who is unlimited, to bear the burden of redemption. Why was the wood not laid on the ass? Because animals and animal sacrifices cannot server as substitutes for man nor remove his sins.

Isaac is the only one who possessed characteristics that are in accord with those of Christ. He was the only son, beloved and innocent, carrying the wood. Christ alone is able to carry the sins of humanity; He alone is perfect, unlimited in value, and beloved and accepted by the Father as atonement for all. Christ accepted the responsibility of carrying the wood of the Cross.

God's justice came down against the substitute of humanity

The second part of Genesis 22:6 says: "and he took the fire in his hand, and a knife."

The fire and knife that slew the sacrifice were in the hand of Abraham the father. This indicates that the fire of the divine justice and its sword was in the hand of God the Father. When Christ accepted His assignment as a substitute for the human race in paying the price of all human transgression, God the Father did not throw away or set aside His justice, holiness, and truth in punishing the substitute laid upon the altar of redemption. The prophet Zachariah prophesied about the determination of God the Father to make the sword of divine justice come down upon Christ, the shepherd of His creatures, and the Person of everlasting fellowship with the Father in the Trinity. Here is Zachariah's prophecy (Zachariah 13:7):

> 'Awake, O sword, against My Shepherd, Against the Man who is My Companion,'
>
> says the Lord of hosts. 'Strike the Shepherd, And the sheep will be scattered';
>
> Then I will turn My hand against the little ones.

The journey throughout the Old Testament was headed toward a definitive purpose—the redemption of mankind on the same mountain

Isaac did not know that the fire and knife were to slay him as a burnt offering. He walked in ignorance of the purpose of the trip. The everlasting Son, however, knew of the divine justice and its fire He was to face because He accepted His role since the world's creation to redeem sinners. Perhaps if Isaac had known the purpose of the journey, his journey would have become painful from the beginning. But Abraham hid this information from him so as to spare Isaac suffering from the moment he left Beersheba. The everlasting Son, however, always knew that one day His body would be offered up by the very creatures He created, and that they would spit on Him and humiliate and revile Him. He did not flee from this because He looked to remove judgment from man as something important and essential.

In Genesis 22:7 Isaac asked his father:

Then he said, 'Look, the fire and the wood, but where is the lamb for a burnt offering?'

The preparation for burnt offering, such as wood and fire, were ready from the beginning of the journey, but without the animal, which was essential for sacrifice. The sacrifice of Christ was not generally known to the people before Christ in their journey with God (as recorded in the Old Testament). It was revealed only to a number of prophets, such as Isaiah, David, Zachariah, and Daniel, who prophesied of the coming of the Messiah as a lamb to be slaughtered for the people. Just as Isaac did not realize that he was to be sacrificed during his journey with his father, much preparation without a sacrifice is a journey without purpose. The sacrifice existed and was prepared by Abraham, and it was to be an offering most precious, his beloved son. Yes, the journey of the Hebrew people was not without a purpose. It was headed toward an essential offering, which was the redemption of humanity from sin. Though man ignored the proper sacrifice that removed his sins, the prospect of the sacrifice accompanied the people, pastoring, leading, and providing Christ the Son of God and the Creator, the redeemer who had to be placed on the burning altar. Abraham answered his son:

And Abraham said, 'My son, God will provide for Himself the lamb for a burnt offering.'

It is the burnt offering of God. God provides the lamb, not Abraham. Abraham's words were of great prophetic value, indicating that he had a spiritual conviction that he was going to a place where in the future God Himself would provide the lamb for the burnt offering, a ransom greater than Abraham's son. Thus, the Lord said in Jonah 8:56:

> Your father Abraham rejoiced that he would see my day. He saw it and was glad.

Isaac's was an embarrassing one for Abraham who was to present his son as a burnt offering. But since God had ordered it at the time He promised Abraham that he would have descendants from Isaac, Abraham thus believed in Isaac's resurrection from the dead, knowing that there must exist a true permanent ransom that God saw instead of Isaac.

Isaac's acceptance to be the lamb of the burnt offering was a symbol of Christ's acceptance of the plan of our redemption

Isaac did not resist his father when he wanted to bind him because he trusted that his father was fulfilling a divine command in offering him as a burnt offering to God. It was as if he accepted of his own accord offering himself to God. Here he was a prototype of Christ who offered Himself by His own accord, as we read in John 10:18:

> No one takes it from me, but I lay it down of my own accord. I have authority to lay it down, and I have authority to take it up again. This charge I have received from my Father.

Many Bible expositors agree that Isaac had a prior agreement to be the lamb on the altar on Mount Moriah. Perhaps this agreement came when they reached the mountain. There is no sign of resistance or discussion or dialogue with his father about binding him and laying him on the wood. He continued to sit on the wood quietly, waiting for the knife to come down on his neck. This is a symbol of Jesus' hanging on the Cross, not coming down when he was challenged by religious men, as we see in Matthew 27:42:

> 'He saved others,' they said, 'but he cannot save himself! He is the king of Israel! Let him come down now from the cross, and we will believe in him.'

Abraham who stretched out his knife toward his son's throat pointed to a real scene on the very same Mount

Genesis 22:10 says:

And Abraham stretched out his hand and took the knife to slay his son.

Slaughtering Isaac would be to no avail, for there is no redemptive benefit in a sinner's death. Like the rest of humans, Isaac was born in sin and thus could not redeem others. But the knife's coming down toward him was a scene that pointed to another real scene in which the sword of divine justice came down on the substitute who sat voluntarily by His own accord in the place of sinner in front of the justice of God. Therefore, the Lord said in book of the prophet Zachariah, which we previously quoted (Zachariah 13:7):

'Awake, O sword, against My Shepherd, Against the Man who is My Companion,'

says the Lord of hosts. 'Strike the Shepherd, And the sheep will be scattered;

Then I will turn My hand against the little ones.'

Then God called out to Abraham and told him: "Lay not thine hand upon the lad, neither do thou anything unto him."

The Lord knew of Abraham's obedience, otherwise he would not have chosen him for this prophetic and critical call. But he left him to walk all the way to Mount Moriah, lay his son on the wood, and hold the knife in his hand over his son's throat to draw an accurate prophetic picture of the real scene, which is the Father's offering His Son as ransom on the same mountain.

He said to him in Genesis 22:12:

For now I know that thou fearest God, seeing thou hast not withheld thy son, thine only son from me.

God acknowledged that Abraham did not withhold the most beloved one in his life, the son of his love, when the order was to offer him to God. God was saying, in effect, "You did not choose the fatherhood of an only son over my will of offering him to Me on the altar. You did not choose your emotions as father over pleasing Me. You did not attempt to spare and feel pity for your son and put his safety before My command to offer him up to pain and death."

Abraham was found in a scene that pointed to a true scene in which the Father did not spare His Son but delivered him up for us all, as we read in Romans 8:32:

> He that spared not his own Son, but delivered him up for us all, how shall he not with him also freely give us all things?

The ram God provided for Abraham to offer on the mountain was a symbol (or prototype) of the Great Lamb of redemption

We read in Genesis 22:13:

> Then Abraham lifted his eyes and looked, and there behind him was a ram caught in a thicket by its horns.

Abraham lifted his eyes toward the voice that talked to him and saw a ram, which was a provision of God. Isaac did not fulfil all the requirements of the prophetic scene to symbolize the redeemer fully. The scene must be completed through slaughtering a ram provided by heaven. The sacrificial ram is mentioned in Leviticus 9:2-4. It was to be killed in the day of expiation or atonement (Leviticus 16:1, 3). Atonement is a divine heavenly provision and not a human initiative through human or animal offerings and sacrifices. The ram that was bound on Mount Moriah was a symbol of the celestial redeemer identity of Jesus Christ, to which the scene pointed. Though the journey of Abraham to Mount Moriah was prophetically accurate because it drew the outlines of an important prophecy, it did not carry the essence of the true ransom of Mount Moriah. It finished without the offering of Isaac, his son, whom Abraham had carried on his journey. Whatever sacrifices we carry are unable to fulfil the requirements of redemption and atonement. The Redeemer has the characteristics of a meek lamb, who descends from heaven, without sin, and who is able, because of the greatness of His deity, to expiate the sins of humanity. Abraham knew that his journey was to draw the outlines of a prophetic scene in which God would offer the Lamb of Redemption on the same mount. Thus, Abraham saw, through the spirit of prophecy, the Redeemer of Mount Moriah 2,000 years before His incarnation.

Christ has voluntary caught Himself in the bonds of redemption

The second part of Genesis 22:13 says that the ram was "caught in a thicket by its horns." What kind of bounds had caught the ram by its horns? The verse does not clarify this. There was no man to subject or subdue the ram and bind it so that Abraham could slaughter it. It is a symbol of Jesus who accepted being caught in the human nature as a lamb to be offered on the altar of redemption on Mount Moriah. There was no power that could overcome Jesus and compel Him to the death of the Cross. He proved His ability to avoid the Jews when they wanted to throw him from the top of a mountain near Nazareth. He passed through the midst of them and went His way. The soldiers who came to Gethsemane to arrest Him fell on the ground when He said to them, "I am He." He could easily have left them and withdrawn from the painful scene. Instead, He yielded Himself to them, expecting them to lay hands on Him. Thus, He caught Himself as the ram of Moriah.

A complete prophetic journey in pointing to the Christ's redemption on the Moriah mountain

Genesis 22:13 continues:

So Abraham went and took the ram, and offered it up for a burnt offering instead of his son.

Abraham's preparations for a burnt offering was not without fulfilment. He was led to offer a burnt offering that pointed to Christ the Redeemer, the Lamb of God. He obeyed and followed a path that had special prophetic significance in offering his only son whom he loved reflecting the Father's determination to offer His beloved Son on the same mountain. He obeyed perfectly in his role. He carried, however, a prototype that did not have all the meanings of a full prototype of Jesus. Isaac was not without defect or blemish, as Jesus the Redeemer was. Isaac also needed redemption, which was a symbol that pointed to the Redeemer. Thus, it would be reckoned to him according to the acceptance of the One to whom the symbols pointed, to descend from heaven at the same place and die for the sins of the world.

Thus, Abraham was given to offer the proper sacrifice, a ram caught by its two horns, which was a symbol of the incarnate Christ in human nature, prepared and available to be slaughtered, in the same place where Christ the Redeemer had to be slaughtered. Abraham was given the ram to complete the symbol of the journey to which he was called to take so that the characteristics of the redeemer were manifested through his obedience and through God's intervention in completing the symbol on Mount Moriah through the ram caught by his two horns.

God is seen by the soul through the Cross of redemption

Genesis 22:14 says:

And Abraham called the name of the place, The-Lord-Will-Provide; Yahweh-jireh.

The translation is "Yahweh will see or Yahweh will provide." The meaning is that God will see and provide whatever is required. God foresaw humanity's need for redemption throughout history. The Father's providence came in the fullness of times at the same place where Abraham was ordered to offer his beloved son, at the same place where God provided a ram for the burnt offering, at the same place God offered His Son for the atonement for the sins of humanity. The Septuagint renders: "in the mountain the Lord is seen," which means that in offering a ram instead of Isaac, Abraham had discovered God's providence for a substitute for Isaac and for every other sinner. God is seen on the mount of Golgotha, at the same place, as substitute and reconciler between man and Himself. God is known by the soul when man comes spiritually to the Redeemer who was Crucified on Golgotha.

A man's going to the Cross of Jesus in order to obtain salvation is a submission to the Lord's command. However, Christ's reveals Himself to the one who comes to the Cross to obtain salvation, and he finds salvation. In addition to salvation, he experiences a great and marvelous encounter with the Lord. It is a beautiful thing when we present ourselves on the altar of dedication in submission to the Lord. But Christ's coming into our life, a life dedicated to Him, and making use of our lives is the amazing thing that we testify to and that is seen by others.

Mohammed did not understand the purpose of Abraham's call

A few sentences of Surah as-Saffat 37:101-107 indicate clearly that Mohammed did not understand God's purpose in testing Abraham. It was not just a test, but to draw an important prophecy about the place of redemption, that is Mount Moriah at Jerusalem, where Jesus was crucified. Mohammed did not understand the Redeemer's identity, Christ the everlasting subject of God's love, and the subject of love in the Trinity.

There is something else that Mohammed did not understand, and as result, Islam has not understood throughout its history: that there is no blessing in Abraham's life for the nations of the earth. A religion could not be built on Abraham, a religion separated from God's providence and His purpose in History and His inspiration to all prophets. God's purpose in history was to prepare for His coming through incarnation, to be the victorious man over the devil for our sake.

Jesus' virgin birth fulfilled one of the first Biblical prophecies about the Cross.

This divine plan was revealed from the moment man fell into sin in the paradise (the Garden of Eden) recorded in Genesis 3:15:

> I will put enmity between you and the woman, and between your offspring and her offspring; he shall bruise your head, and you shall bruise his heel.

After Adam fell and was defeated, God declared the principles of victory. This victory is in the coming of One Person from the woman's offspring (which means without intercourse with a man) in order to crush the devil's claims in reigning over man. This prophecy is fulfilled only in Jesus, who is the only Person in history who was born from woman without the intervention of a man. He lived a perfect, sinless life and accepted the death of the Cross as redeemer, paying for the sins and transgression of man. Thus, he crushed the claims of the devil who enslaved humanity through man's fall in sin. Jesus disarmed the devil's claims of having authority over a fallen, weak, and rebellious man unworthy of fellowship with God. Through His perfect, sinless life and substitutionary death for man's sins, Jesus crushed the devils claims and ensured the right of each man who believes in His redemptive work to regain God's fellowship.

The devil, however, bruised Jesus' heel on the Cross according to the prophecy "and you shall bruise his heel." This prophecy was one of the first prophecies in the Bible about the Cross.

Our transgression against the Law of God was subject to the devil's protest and his arguments that the Holy God cannot accept us. On the Cross, Christ disarmed the devil's power and his complaint. By the Cross He canceled the unfavorable record of our debts and sins against God's Law. He crushed the enemy's power and liberated man from the yoke of his slavery because through His death Christ Jesus liberated man from the bondage of the devil.

We find reference to this prophecy in the New Testament (Galatians 4:4-5):

But when the fullness of time had come, God sent forth his Son, born of woman, born under the law, to redeem those who were under the law, so that we might receive adoption as sons.

And also in Colossians 2:14-15:

By canceling the record of debt that stood against us with its legal demands. This he set aside, nailing it to the cross. He disarmed the rulers and authorities and put them to open shame, by triumphing over them in him.

Through the Spirit of prophecy Abraham foresaw the seed through whom all the nations of the earth would be blessed, who was originally a divine Personality

God's plan preceded Abraham's call. That plan was for the coming of the Person through whom all nations of the earth would be blessed. Before Abraham, God accepted fellowship with man only through the animal sacrifices that symbolized the redemptive death of Christ. One example of this fact is seen in God's refusing the offerings of Cain, which were the product of his field, symbolizing his attempt to have communion with God through works. But God accepted Abel's offering of firstlings of his flock, confirming that God's plan of human redemption existed before creation and man's fall. The birth of a Person in which all nations of the earth would be blessed clearly revealed to Abraham. As we see from God's word to him in Genesis 22:18, the same chapter in which God commanded him to offer his son on mount Moriah. Abraham foresaw the Redeemer whom both Isaac and the ram symbolized. He knew from God's word on that occasion that this redeemer was to offer Himself as ransom for humanity on the same mountain and would be, according to the flesh, from his offspring:

In your seed all the nations of the earth shall be blessed.

In the New Testament, Galatians 3:16 provides a clarification of the prophecy given to Abraham:

Now the promises were spoken to Abraham and to his seed. He does not say, 'And to seeds,' as referring to many, but rather to one, 'And to your seed,' that is, Christ.

It is impossible for all humans to have a blessing through one man, even if he was a prophet or king. The blessing, however, is expected to come from the Creator. Thus, the promise mentioned above indicates that the Promised One who was to come is a divine personality, the Creator Himself, who came from the offspring of Abraham according to the flesh.

The promise of the coming of the divine Person was repeated and confirmed to other members of the Messianic genealogy

This promise was repeated to Isaac, as we see in Genesis 26:4:

I will multiply your offspring as the stars of heaven … And in your offspring all the nations of the earth shall be blessed.

The promised was renewed to Jacob, in Genesis 28:14:

Your offspring shall be like the dust of the earth, and you shall spread abroad to the west and to the east and to the north and to the south, and in you and your offspring shall all the families of the earth be blessed. (This offspring is Christ.)

This promise was renewed to Judah, the fourth son of Jacob. The prophecy Judah's father gave him was (Genesis 49:10):

The scepter will not depart from Judah, Nor the lawgiver from between his feet, Until Shiloh come, And to him will be the obedience of peoples.

Genesis was inspired by God and given to Moses fifteen centuries before Christ.

The great promise given to David around 1,000 B.C. was that the Messiah would come from his seed. Then the promise was renewed to other members of the Messianic genealogy until Jesus was born.

The importance of Jacob's prophecy to Judah about Christ in showing that the God of the Bible is the true God of History

Without doubt, this prophecy demonstrates that the One who inspired the books of the Bible is the God of history, who supervises each detail, and who holds everything in His will.

Here we see that Jacob, the son of Isaac, the son of Abraham called his 12 sons together in order to bless them before he died. To each of his children he gave a description of normal blessings. Jacob described the kind of circumstances which the tribes and those who came from them, should encounter. Jacob prophesied about the nature of each tribe and where some of the tribes would live. However, when Jacob, led by the Spirit of the prophecy, reached Judah, his fifth son, he exclusively prophesied that special blessings would come to the tribe which was descended from him. He said to Judah:

Judah, thou art he whom thy brethren shall praise: thy hand shall be in the neck of thine enemies; thy father's children shall bow down before thee. Judah is a lion's whelp: from the prey, my son, thou art gone up: he stooped down, he couched as a lion, and as an old lion; who shall rouse him up? (Gen 49:8-9)

No one has ever bowed down to worship Judah, the son of Jacob. He was a normal brother among normal brothers. We know that Judah's brother Joseph obtained honor when he became the second person in importance in Egypt under Pharaoh. Thus, the prophecy given to Judah was not fulfilled in his time.

But what about a prophecy concerning another person descended from Judah who was to be born according to the flesh? Jesus Christ will return to earth and all the tribes of Israel are going to bow and worship Him.

The Bible says when Jacob addressed Judah he said, "Judah is a lion's whelp. From the prey, my son, you have gone up. He couches. He lies down as a lion, and as a lion, who dares rouse him?"

The Lion of the tribe of Judah

Judah was not a lion's whelp. This was a prophecy about a Person who was to be born from his lineage—Christ, who was described in the book of Revelation with the words, "The Lion that is from the tribe of Judah, the root of David."

When the apostle John was taken to heaven to obtain a revelation from God, he was shown a book, "a book written inside and on the back, sealed up with seven seals. He saw a strong angel proclaiming with a loud voice, 'Who is worthy to open the book and to break its seals?' And no one in heaven or on the earth or under the earth was able to open the book or to look into it. Then John began to weep greatly because no one was found worthy to open the book or to look into it.

And one of the elders said to him, "Stop weeping; behold, the Lion that is from the tribe of Judah, the root of David, has overcome, so he can open the book and its seven seals." (Revelation 5:1-5)

In the book of the Revelation John reports that there "stood a Lamb as it had been slain," indicating that the traces of the Cross wounds still existed on the glorified body of Christ in heaven. This was to remind those going to heaven of the cause of their residency there was because of Christ's redemption. John saw Jesus coming and opened the book and began to open its seals.

This book and its seals symbolize creatures who are unable and unworthy to deal with the dimensions of judgment over sin and sinners. The seals of judgment can only be executed by someone who lived on earth without being involved in any of this world's sin. He was the Lion about whom Jacob prophesied when he said that He would come from the tribe of Judah. That is no one except Christ. He lived on earth in obedience to the commandments of His Father. As a man, he lived a sinless life. He announced His righteousness and worthiness to judge wickedness, and execute judgment over the wicked.

Furthermore, He has the right to remove judgment from His people who believed in His redemptive work on the cross. He paid the price of our transgressions through His blood, providing for our justification when we stand before the righteous angels of heaven, who will be watching the final judgment executed by Christ on the inhabitants of the earth.

Jacob prophesied about the tribe of Judah remaining in legislative authority until Christ's coming

Returning to the prophecy of Jacob, we see him continuing to prophesy about the blessing which the tribe of Judah will enjoy in leadership and authority. Jacob prophesied that the tribe will continue to keep its legislative authority. He said:

> The scepter shall not depart from Judah, Nor a lawgiver from between His feet, until Shiloh comes; And to Him shall be the obedience of the people. (Genesis 49:10)

It means Judah would keep this special authority until the coming of Christ, whom the words of this prophecy described with the word Shiloh: "He whose it is," or "the One to whom it belongs." He has been the Person in authority since everlasting.

The authority is also His as a perfect man without sin who overcame sin and the devil. He also returned the lost inheritance of spiritual fellowship with God which had been lost by our father Adam and mother Eve.

Jacob prophesied, describing that the tribe of Judah would keep its legislative authority until the coming of the Messiah in these words, "The scepter shall not depart from Judah, nor a lawgiver from between his feet." The last part of this sentence means holding the authority to legislate and to issue laws.

As the history of Israel and Judah unfolds, we verify the accuracy of his prophecy. The kingdom, though divided into 12 tribes, was always united under one king. No one thought of the possibility that Judah would become separated from the other tribes, and have a special separated authority, which will continue throughout history even after Israel will cease to be in power.

However, God who promises and controls the present and future, intervened during the reign of Rehoboam, Solomon's son. God tore the kingdom out of the hands of David's descendants and gave 10 tribes to Jeroboam, Solomon's servant. They became known as the kingdom of Israel. Some kings did come from the descendants of David. They became known as the tribe of Judah which became the kingdom of Judah, and they annexed the small tribe of Benjamin. This was to fulfill the prophecy of Jacob regarding Judah.

In 722 B.C. Sargon II, the Assyrian king, besieged and captured Samaria. He carried Israel away into exile to Assyria, and settled them in the cities of the Medes, hundreds of miles north of Mesopotamia. Judah alone remained in power under the reign of the kings who were descendants of David. This occurred because God wanted the tribe of Judah to keep alive the genealogy which was to include Christ.

The people of Judah were disobedient to the Lord, and in 586 B.C., He gave Judah and its capital, Jerusalem, into the hands of the Chaldeans. Although the inhabitants of Judah were deported to Babylon, there still remained a remnant in the country. Eventually, the Jews returned to Jerusalem after 70 years of captivity and a Jewish governor from the lineage of David was appointed to govern the country.

The legislative independence of the tribe of Judah remained even when it was dominated by the Chaldean kingdom, and by other empires that followed. During the occupation enforced by the Persian empire, Zerubbabel, a descendant of David, became the governor of Judah and exercised the full legislative authority. Zerubbabel, was an important ancestor in the Messianic line.

The legislative power continued for the tribe of Judah during the reign of the great empires that dominated the region. During Greek control in the Middle East, the Jewish Maccabees came to power in the land of Judah and remained in power from 142 B.C. to 63 B.C.

Even when the Roman commander Pompey defeated the Maccabees and occupied Jerusalem, Judah continued enjoying special authority till the year 6 B.C. when the Romans added Judah to the Roman Empire as province. This date corresponds with the date of Jesus' birth. In fact, the Gospel of Matthew and Luke reveal that the birth of Jesus was during the reign of Herod the Great, who is believed to have died around 4 B.C. Thus, 6 B.C. can be easily identified as the true year of Jesus' birth.

We know then that we are witnessing the fulfillment of the prophecy of Jacob recorded in Genesis. During the year Jesus was born, a Roman governor, rather than a Jewish one, ruled over Judah for the first time. Judah ceased to exist completely in the year 70 A.D. when the Jews rebelled and the Romans destroyed Jerusalem and exiled the Jews from their land.

It is not possible to take Abraham out of God's plan and use him in the claims of Zayd, the founder of Ahnaf

It is impossible to cut Abraham out of God's plan. God has called Abraham to point to the redemptive work of Christ through his obedience in offering his only son Isaac on the Mount of Moriah where Jesus later died. Then God has chosen him so that Christ the Redeemer comes from his seed. This was confirmed to other members of his descendants and was proved historically in the fact that the tribe of Judah remained in authority until the birth of Christ. Thus, it is impossible to remove Abraham from God's plan and place him instead in Zayd bin Amru bin Nufayl's plan, that immoral man who belonged to the immoral group of Hallah, and established the Ahnaf group, in order to compete with Jews in their affiliation with Abraham. Zayd also wanted to compete with the Christians, who declared Jesus as the fulfillment of all prophecies. The truth is that Christ was promised before Abraham was born.

Zayd wanted to create an Arabian religion. He took Abraham out of the Bible and claimed he was the founder of this new religion. Zayd claimed that Abraham came to Mecca and connected Abraham's name with the pagan religiosity of the Kaabah, and the Hajj on the hills around Mecca. Zayd disregarded all the prophets of the Old Testament who prophesied in various epochs. The Bible prophesied about the Son of God who was to come in the flesh and to die in His human nature on the mount of Moriah at Jerusalem and then rise again (the resurrection). This prophetic heritage does not come through one prophet's claim, but by a rich revelation of God that came through many epochs of history. When Christ was incarnate, He was attested historically for His power in raising the dead and for His holiness, which was unique in history, and of His moral perfection over all humans. He is the same One who was promised to Abraham and his descendants as well was the fulfillment of the promise established before Abraham came to existence.

It is impossible to disregard this great heritage and to place it in another land. Zayd bin Amru bin Nufayl and Mohammed his disciple stole the true heritage of Abraham in what amounts to an act such as stripping the skin of a lion and placing it on the body of a cat and then claiming the cat is a lion. This kind of forgery will be taken by a person who has never seen a lion in his life or studied the description of one. Such a forgery as the one created by Zayd, and spread by Mohammed, would be accepted by those who never studied the characteristics of the divine plan and the historical chronology in which God revealed it.

It is not possible that a historical credibility that confirms the revelation of God stands on the claim of one person

An individual who created a religion at the time of Mohammed—in the 7th century—would not be able to imitate the historical credibility the Bible enjoys. He would be just one person, separated from the prophets of the Bible. How then could he offer a historical credibility throughout all ancient historical epochs? It would be like an individual in our day claiming to be an heir to the throne of Rome. He would be believed only by those who either were ignorant of or chose to ignore Roman history.

Furthermore, we have seen that the Quran reflects the mistakes of the pre-Islamic Jahiliyyah people, some Arabians Jews who ignored the Biblical facts, and the views of some Persian and Mandaean groups who were ignorant regarding historical facts. Thus, the chronology of the Quran of Mohammed is not accurate whereas the Biblical narrative is directly parallel to official historical chronology.

Given his enormous historical mistakes, Mohammed cannot be considered a reliable source for ancient history. Nor can we trust the Islamic writers who came after Mohammed and invented stories with no support of written documentation.

The summary I have presented concerning the historical mistakes of the Quran confirms Mohammed's lack of education regarding official history. What Mohammed said about historical figures and nations is incorrect and is not supported by the official historical record.

We know that no source in history confirms what Mohammed claimed about Mecca, Abraham, and Ishmael. On the contrary, we also know that official documented history contradicts Mohammed's claims. If we cannot trust Mohammed to tell us the truth about the issues we have been discussing, how can we trust him to tell us the truth about anything?

Finally, certainty regarding God's plan through history, as He declared it through His prophets through all ages and which was fulfilled in Christ, is available to everyone who studies the Bible with honesty and a sincere desire to know the Truth. This truth is far from Zayd bin Amru bin Nufayl's influences that misguided and misled Mohammed and with him the Arabs and other peoples of the world.

Word Index

References' Abbreviations

AAB: Robert G. Hoyland, *Arabia and the Arabs: from the Bronze Age to the coming of Islam*, (Routledge. Taylor & Francis Group: London and New York), 2002

ABB: George Barton, *Archaeology and the Bible*, seventh edition, (American Suday-School Union: Philadelphia, 1937)

ABE : *The Alexander book in Etheopia, the Etheopian book of Pseudo Callisthenes*, translated by Ernest A. Wallis Budge, (Oxford University Press: London, 1933)

ABF: Joseph Free, *Archaeology and Bible History*, (Zondervan: Grand Rapids-Michigan, 1969)

ABH : James K. Hoffmeier, *The Archaeology of the Bible*, (Lion Hudson plc: Oxford, England, 2008)

AFI: Niklas Holzberg, *The ancient fable: an introduction*, (Indiana University: Bloomington & Indianapolis, 2002)

AFR: ibn Rabbuh al Andalusi, *al Ekd al Farid*, (Dar al kutub al Ilmiyah: Beirut-Lebanon, 1983

العقد الفريد لابن عبد ربه الاندلسي، دار الكتب العلمية، بيروت-لبنان، 1983

AGH : Abi Faraj al-Asfahani, *Al Aghani*, in 25 volumes, (Dar Sader: Beirut, 2008)

الاغاني لأبي فرج الا صفهاني، في 25 جزء ، دار صادر بيروت، طبعة 2008

AGHS: ibn al Atheer, *Asad al ghabah fi maarifat al sahabah*, (Dar al Kutub al Ilmiyah: Beirut-Lebanon, first edition 1996)

أسد الغابة في معرفة الصحابة، ابن الاثير، دار الكتب العلمية، بيروت، الطبعة الاولى 1996

AHJ: Bader al Deen al Shabli, *Ahkam al-Jin*, (Dar ibn Zeidun, Beirut, 1985)

احكام الجن ، بدر الدين الشبلي، دار ابن زيدون، بيروت، 1985

AHK: Anis Freheh, *Ahikar Hakim men al Sharq al Qadim*, (American University: Beirut, 1962)

أحيقار حكيم من الشرق الأدنى القديم، أنيس فريحة ، الجامعة الاميركية بيروت 1962م

AHM : Kuhrt and Heleen Sancisi-Weerdenburg, *Achaemenid History* III. *Method and Theory*, (Netherland Instituut nVoor Het Nabue Oosten: Leiden, 1988)

AJ : *The Apocryphon of John; Synopsis of Nag Hammadi Codices II,1;III,1 And IV,1* with BG 8502,2, Edited by Waldstein and Wisse, (E.J.Brill: Leiden, 1995)

AJF: *Antiquities of the Jews*, Flavius Josephus, Translated by William Whiston

AKHZ : Al-Masudi, *Akhbar al Zaman*, (Abdel Hamid Ahmad Hanafi press: Cairo, 1938

اخبار الزمان، للمسعودي، مطبعة عبد الحميد احمد حنفي، القاهرة، 1938 ،

AKM: Al Imam Abi al Walid Mohammad bin Abdellah Al Azruqi, *Akhbar Meccah wa ma jaa fiha men Athar*, published by Abdel Malek bin Abdellah bin Daheesh, 2003

ALF: Ibn Nadim, *Alfahrest*, Maktabet Khayyat, Beirut- Lebanon

---

583

AM: De Lacy O'Leary, *Arabia before Muhammed*, (AMS Press: New York), 1973

AN: Bert Hölldobler and Edward O. Wilson, *The Ants*, (The Belknap Press of Harvard University Press: Cambridge, Massachusetts, 1990)

ANET : James Bennett Pritchard: *Ancient Near Eastern Texts Relating to the Old Testament*, second ed., (Princeton University Press: Princeton, New Jersey, 1955)

AOO: K. A. Kitchen, Ancient Orient and Old Testament, (InterVarsity Press: Downers Grove, Illinois, 1975)

AP: *Aramaic Papyri of the fifth century B.C.*, edited with translation and notes by A. Cowley, (Oxford University Press: Oxford, 1923)

APB: W. F. Albright, *The Archaeology of Palestine and the Bible*, (The American Schools of Oriental Research, Cambridge, Massachusetts, 1974)

APC : *The Romance of Alexander the Great by Pseudo-Callisthenes*, Translated from the Armenian Version with introduction by Albert M. Wolohojian, (Columbia University Press: New York and London 1969)

AR : F.V.Winnett and W.L.Reed, *Ancient Records from North Arabia*, (University of Toronto Press: Toronto and Bufalo, 1970)

ARN: Arrian, *Anabasis of Alexander*, translated by P.A. Brunt, Harvard University Press, 1983

ASSA: Himanshu Prabha Ray, *The archaeology of seafaring in ancient South Asia*, Press of the University of Cambridge, 2003

BA: Irfan Shahîd, *Byzantium and the Arabs in the fourth century*, (Dumbartun Oaks: Wathington), 2006

BAS : John H. Sailhamer, *Biblical Archaeology*, (Zondervan: Grand Rapids, Michigan, 1998)

BE: The Book of Enoch, From-The Apocrypha and Pseudepigrapha of the Old Testament, R.H. Charles Oxford: The Clarendon Press

BEA: Mahmud Shukri Al Ayyusi, *Bulug al Erab fi Maarifat Ansab al Arab*, Dar al Kutub al Ilmiyah, Beirut

محمود شكري الألوسي، بلوغ الأرب في معرفة أحوال العرب، دار الكتب العلمية، بيروت ـ لبنان

BG: Victor Hamilton, *The Book of Genesis, two vol.*,(Grand Rapids: Eerdmans, 1995)

BNH : Ibn Katheer, *al Bidayah wa al Nihayah*, first ed., (Dar al Hadith: Cairo, Egypt, 1992)

ابن كثير، البداية والنهاية، دار الحديث ـ القاهرة، الطبعة الاولى، 1992

BNK: ibn Katheer, *al Bidayah wa al Nihayah*, second ed., Dar ibn Katheer, Damascus, 2010

ابن كثير، البداية والنهاية، دار ابن كثير، دمشق، 2010، طبعة ثانية

BT :Al-Jaheth, *al Bayan wa al tabiyeen*, (Maktabat al Khanji, seventh edit., Cairo, 1998)

الجاحظ، البيان والتبيين، مكتبة الخانجي، القاهرة، طبعة سابعة عام 1998

CEI: Cyril Glassé, *The Concise Encyclopedia of Islam*, Harper & Row, 1989

CIS: F.W. Hasluck, *Christianity and Islam under the Sultans,* 2 vols. (Oxford University Press: Oxford, 1929)

CP: *The Canonical Prayerbook of The Mandaeans*, translated with notes by E.S. Drower, (E. J. Brill: Leiden 1959)

DA : Maria Vittoria Cerutti, *Dualismo e Ambiguita', Creatori a creazione nell dottrina mandea sul cosmo*, (Edizioni dell'ateneo s.p.a.: Roma, 1981)

DAA : K.A. Kitchen, *Documentation For Ancient Arabia*, Part I, (Liverpool University Press: Liverpool, 1994)

DAB : *Diwan Abatur*, or Progress Through The Purgatories, Text with translation notes and appendices by E.S. Drower, (Biblioteca Apostolica Vaticana: Citta' Del Vaticano, 1950)

DL: Jeff Harshbarger, *From Darkness to Light*, (Bridge-Logos : Gainesville, Florida, 2004)

DTZ: R.C. Zaehner, *The Dawn and Twilight of Zoroastrianism*, (Weidenfeld And Nicolson: London), 1975

DUBS: *Diwan Umiayah bin Abi Al –Salt*, edited by Dr. Saje' Jamil al Jubeili, first edition,(Dar Sader: Beirut- Lebanon, 1998)

ديوان امية بن ابي الصلت، جمعه الدكتور سجيع جميل الجبيلي، دار صادر بيروت، الطبعة الاولى 1998

EFTS: Ahmad bin Ali bin Hajar, *al Esabah fi Tamyeez al Sahabah*, in 8 volumes, (Dar al Jeel: Beirut-Lebanon, 1992)

احمد بن علي بن حجر، الاصابة في تمييز الصحابة، في ثمانية اجزاء، دير الجيل ، بيروت- لبنان، 1992

EI: *Encyclopedia of Islam*, in 12 volumes, Leyden, Brill, Lond. Luzae, 1911-14

EIM: *Encyclopedia of Islam and the Muslim world*, edited by Richard C. Martin, Gale Group.

ERE : James Hastings, *Encyclopedia of Religion and Ethics*, edited by James Hastings with the assistance of John A. Seible, in 13 volumes,(Charles Soribner's Sons, New York)

ES : *Agatharchides of Cnidus, on the Erythraean Sea*, translated and edited by Stanley Burstein, (The Hakluyt Society: London, 1989)

ETQ : Al-Sayuti, *al Etqan fi Ulum al Quran*, (Majma' al Malek Fahed litibaat al mashaf : Saudi Arabia, 2005)

السيوطي، الاتقان في علوم القرآن، مجمع الملك فهد لطباعة المصحف الشريف، السعودية، 2005

EW: Rossell Hope Robbins, *The Encyclopedia of Witchcraft and demonology*, (Crown Publishers: New York, 1959)

FAH: Bin Hajar al Askalani, *Fateh al Bari bisharh al Bukhari*, (Dar al Maarifah: Beirut-Lebanon)

فتح الباري بشرح صحيح البخاري، بن حجر العسقلاني، دار المعرفة، بيروت

FB: Al Balathri, *Futuh al Buldan*, (al Maaref: Beirut- Lebanon, 1987)

البلاذري، فتوح البلدان، مؤسسة المعارف، بيروت، 1987

FBAS :Ibn Taimiyah, *al-Furqan bein auliya allah wa auliya al sheitan*, (Dar al Fathila: Riyad, Saudi Arabia)

ابن تيمية، الفُرْقَان بين أولياء الله وأولياء الشيطان، دار الفضيلة، الرياض- المملكة العربية السعودية

FBH:Al Hanbali, *Fateh al Bari sharh Sahih al Bukhari*, in ten volumes, (Maktabat al Ghuraba' al Athariyah: Medina- Saudi Arabia, 1996)

فتح الباري شرح صحيح البخاري، للحنبلي، في عشرة اجزاء، مكتبة الغرباء الاثرية، المدينة – السعودية، 1996

FQJ : Mohammed al Shokani, *Fateh al qadeer bein fini al riwayah wa al dirayah men Ilem al tafseer*, in five volumes, (Dar al Wafa', Egypt)

فتح القدير الجامع بين فني الرواية والدراية من علم التفسير ، محمد بن علي بن محمد الشوكاني، في خمسة مجلدات، دار الوفاء، مصر

FQS : Al-Manawi, *Feith al qadeer shareh al-jame' al saghir*, (Dar al Maarifah: Beirut-Lebanon, second edit., 2012

المناوي، فيض القدير شرح الجامع الصغير، دار المعرفة ببيروت، الطبعة الثانية، 2012

FVQ: Jeffery, Arthur, *The Foreign Vocabulary Of The Qur'an*,(Oriental Institute, Baroda: 1938)

GA: Stoneman, Richard, *The Greek Alexander Romance*, (Penguin Books, UK., 1991),

GAS: Howard F. Vos, *Genesis and Archaeology,* (Moody Press: Chicago, 1963)

GD: Gods‹ Demons and Symbols of Ancient Mesopotamia Jeremy black and Anthony green, (University of Texas Press: Austin, 1995), p.162

GMM: Richard F. Burton, *The Gold Mines of Midian*, (Dover Publications, INC., New York, 1995)

GP: Claudius Ptolemy, The *Geography*, Translated by Edward Luther Stevenson, (Dover Publications, INC.:New York), 1991

GR: *Ginza Rba*, translated by Yousef Matta Khuzi and Sabih Madlul al-Suheiri, Bagdad, 2001

GS: *The Geography of Strabo*, with an English translation by Horace L. Jones, in eight volumes, (Harvard University Press: Cambridge, Massachusetts;William Heinemann LTD: London),1966

HCV : By A. H. Sayce, *The Higher Criticism and the Verdict of the Monuments*, (Society for promoting Christian Knowledge: London 1894)

HE : *A history of Ethiopia*, by Harold G. Marcus, (University of California Press: Berkeley, Los Angeles, 2002)

HFAM: Al-Sayuti, al Habaek fi akhbar al malaek, (Dar al Kutub al Ilmiyah: Beirut-Lebanon, second edition 1988)

الحبائك في أخبار الملائك، للسيوطي، دار الكتب العلمية، بيروت- لبنان، الطبعة الثانية 1988

HG ; *Haran Gawaita*, (Citta del Vaticano, Biblioteca Apostolica, 1953,)

HGA: Charles Forster, *The Geography of Arabia*, THE PATRIARCHAL EVIDENCES OF REVEALED RELIGION, in two volumes

HGR: John C.Reeves, *Heralds of that good realm*, (E.J. Brill: Leiden-New York-Koln, 1996)

HJ : *Kitab al Haywan*, al Jaheth, in 8 volumes, second edition, published by Mustafa al Halabi, second edition, 1965 كتاب

الحيوان، تأليف ابي عثمان عمرو بن بحر الجاحظ، بثمانية اجزاء، تحقيق وشرح عبد السلام محمد هارون، الناشر: مصطفى البابي الحلبي، الطبعة الثانية ، 1965

HJA: *Tarikh al Yahud fi bilad al Arab, (The History of Jews in Arabia Pre-Islamic and Early Islam*, Dr. Ben Zeev

اسرائيل ولفنسون : تأريخ اليهود في بلاد العرب في الجاهلية وصدر الاسلام، مطبعة الاعتماد، القاهرة 1927

HM: *Hindu Myths*، a sourse book translated from Sanskrit، with an introduction by Wendy Doniger O'Flaherty, Penguin books, 1975

HTT: Shungunny Menon, *History of Travancore From the Earliest Times*, (Forgotten Books: Madras- India, 2012)

HW: Jeffrey Russell & Brooks Alexander, *A New History of Witchcraft*, (Thomas & Hudson: London, 2007)

HWS: Montague Summers, *The History of Witchcraft and Demonology*, Citadel Press, Carol Publishing Group 1993

IAA; Israel Eph'al, *The Ancient Arabs*, (E.J.Brill: Leiden), 1982

IAI : S.M. Zwemer, *The Influence of Animism in Islam*, Macmillan Company, New York, 1920

ION : C. M. White, *IN SEARCH OF ... THE ORIGIN OF NATIONS*, (1stBooks: 2003)

ISBE : *The International Standard Bible Encyclopedia.*, The Howard-Severance company: Chicago, 1915)

JAD : Ibn Duraid, *Jamharet al-lugha*, (Daerat al Maaref: Hyder Abad, India, 1924)

جمهرة اللغة، ابن دريد، دائرة المعارف، حيدر آباد، الهند، 1924 ،

JAM: Abu Hilal al Askari, *Jamharat al amthal*, (Dar al Kutub al Ilmiyah: Beirut-Lebanon, first edit, 1988)

جمهرة الأمثال، أبو هلال العسكري، دار الكتب العلمية، بيروت، لبنان، طبعة اولى 1988

JCF: Hans-Joachim Schoeps, Jewish Christianity: Factional Disputes in the Early Church, pages 136-140, (Fortress Press: Philadelphia, 1969)

JMC: John Reeves, *Jewish Lore in Manichaean Cosmogony*, (Hebrew Union College Press: Cincinnati), 1992,

JOC: Leonhard Rost, *Judaism Outside the Hebrew Canon*, An Introduction to the Documents, (Abingdon: Nashville 1976)

KA : Alaa al Deen al Mutaqi al Hindi, *Kinz al Ummal fi Sunan al Aqwal wa al Afaal*, (Muassasat al Risalah: Beirut- Lebanon, 1989)

علاء الدين المتقي الهندي، كنز العمال في سنن الاقوال والافعال، مؤسسة الرسالة، بيروت- لبنان، 1989

KFT : Ibn al Atheer, *al Kamil fi al Tarikh*, in 10 volumes, (Dar al Kotob al-ilmiyah, Beirut Lebanon)

ابن الاثير ، الكامل في التاريخ، في عشرة مجلدات، دار الكتب العلمية، بيروت- لبنان،

KL : Sinasi Gunduz, *The Knowledge of Life*, (Oxford University Press: Oxford, 1994)

KMS : al Sajestani, *Kitab al Masahef*, (Muassat Qurtubah, Cairo)

كتاب المصاحف للساجستاني، مؤسسة قرطبة، القاهرة

KMW: al-Waqidi, Kitab al maghazi, (Oxford University Press: London, 1966)

كتاب المغازي للواقدي، جامعة اكسفورد للنشر، لندن عام 1966

KT: *The Kephalaia Of The Teacher*, the edited Coptic Manichaean Texts, translated by Lain Gardner, (E.J.Brill, Leiden, New York, Koin, 1995)

LA: ibn Manthur, *Lisan al Arab*, (Dar Ehyaa al Turath al Arabi: Beirut- Lebanon, 1999)

ابن منظور، لسان العرب، الطبعة الثالثة، دار إحياء التراث العربي، بيروت- لبنان، 1999

LOT: Albert T. Clay, *Light on the Old Testament from Babel,* (The Sunday School Times Company: Philadelphia, 1907)

MA: Andrew Welburn, *Mani, the Angel and the Column of Glory*, An Anthology of Manichaean Texts, (Floris Books: Edinburgh, 1998)

MAE : Geraldine Pinch, *Magic in Ancient Egypt*, (British Museum Press: London, 2006)

MAHA: Louis Cheikho, *Majani al- adab fi Hadaiq al- Arab*, (the Jesuite fathers Press: Beirut-Lebanon 1912)

لويس شيخو، مجاني الأدب في حدائق العرب، مطبعة الاباء اليسوعيين، بيروت، 1912

MAQ : Mohammed bin Habib al Baghdadi, *almonammaq fi akhbar Quraysh*, (Dar al Maaref al Uthmaniah, Haidar abad-India, 1964

محمد بن حبيب البغدادي، المنمق في أخبار قريش، مطبوعات دائرة المعارف العثمانية بحيدر آباد-الهند، 1964

MAR : Ibn Qutaibah al-Deinuri, *Al Maaref*, (Dar al Maaref: Cairo-Egypt, fourth edit.)

المعارف، ابن قتيبة الدينوري، دار المعارف، القاهرة ، الطبعة الرابعة

MAS:Al Hafeth Abi Abdellah al Hakem al Nisabori, *Al-Mustadrak 'ala al-Sahîhayn* (Dar al Haramyen, Cairo-Egypt, 1997)

المستدرك على الصحيحين، الحافظ ابي عبدالله الحاكم النيسابوري، دار الحرمين للطباعة والنشر، القاهرة، 1997

MAY: Yaqut al Hamawi, *Maajam al Buldan*, (Dar Sader: Beirut, 1977)

ياقوت الحموي، معجم البلدان، في خمسة مجلدات، دار صادر -بيروت- 1977

MBH: *Musnad al Imam bin Hambel*, (Muassat Qurtuba, Cairo) in six volumes

مسند الإمام أحمد بن حنبل، في ستة اجزاء، مؤسسة قرطبة ـ القاهرة

MF: Jawad Ali, *al Mufassal Fi Tarikh al Arab Qabl Al-Islam*, in nine volumes, (Dar al Elm: Beirut), 1968,

الدكتور جواد علي، المفصل في تاريخ العرب قبل الاسلام، في تسعة مجلدات، دار العلم للملايين، بيروت، 1968

MFAA: al Zamekhshari, *al mustaqsa fi amthal al arab*, (Daerat al Maaref al Uthmaniyah: Heidarabad- India, 1962)

المستقصى في أمثال العرب، الزمخشري، دائرة المعارف العثمانية، حيدر اباد- الهند، 1962

MFM: Shihab al Deen al Abshihi, *al Mustatref fi killi fannen Mustathref*, (Dar Maktabat al Hayat: Beirut- Lebanon, 1992)

شهاب الدين أحمد الأبشيهي، المستطرف في كل فن مستظرف، في مجلدين، دار مكتبة الحياة، بيروت، لبنان، 1992

MFTB : Abi al Fida', *al Mukhtasar fi tarikh al basher*, four volumes, (al Matbaah al Huseiniya al Misriya: Cairo, 1909)

ابي الفداء، المختصر في تاريخ البشر، في اربعة اجزاء، المطبعة الحسينية المصرية، القاهرة، 1909

MH: Bin Habib al Bagdadi, *Al Mahber*, (Dar al Afaq al Jadideh, Beirut-Lebanon)

المحبر، لابي جعفر بن حبيب البغدادي، دار الافاق الجديدة- بيروت

MIS: Ibn Sedu, *al Mukhassas*, in 18 volumes (Dar al Kutub al Ilmiyah: Beirut-Lebanon)

المخصص، ابن سيده، في 18 مجلد، دار الكتب العلمية، بيروت- لبنان،

ML : *Manichaean Literature*, translated by Jes P. Asmussen, (Scholars' Facsimiles & Reprints: Delmar,New York, 1975)

MM: Geo Widengren, *Mani and Manichaeism*, by Geo Widengren, translation into Arabic by Dr. Suhail Zakkar, (Dar Hassan: Damascus, 1985,

ماني والمانوية ، جيو وايدنغرين ، ترجمة الدكتور زكار ، دمشق ، دار حسان للطباعة ، 1985

MMC: Stephanie Dalley, *Myths from Mesopotamia: creation, the flood, Gilgamesh and others*, Revised edition, (Oxford University Press, Oxford, New York, 2000),

MME : Al-Bakri al-Andalusi, *Maajam ma Istaajam*, (Alam al Kutub: Beirut, third edit., 1983)

البكري الاندلسي ، معجم ما استعجم، عالم الكتب بيروت، الطبعة الثالثة، 1983

MNS: Al Shahrastani, *al Milal wa al Nahil*, Maktabat al Anglo al Masriyah, first ed., Cairo-Egypt, 1977

الشهرستاني، الملل والنحل، مكتبة الانجلو المصرية، القاهرة، طبعة اولى ، 1977

MP: *A Manichaean Psalm-Book*, Part II, edited by C. R. C. Allberry, Manichaean Manuscripts in the Chester Beatty Collection, Volume II, (W. Kohlhammer: Stuttgart, 1938)

MSM: Najia Murani, *Mafahim Sabieh Mandaeh*, (Sharikat al-Times: Bagdad, second edition1981)

ناجية مراني، مفاهيم صابئية مندائية، شركة التايمس للطبع والنشر، بغداد- 1981 ، طبعة ثانية

MT: Patricia Crone, *Meccan Trade*, (Princeton University Press: Princeton, New Jersey, 1987)

MTD : Ibn Manthur, *Mukhtasar tarikh Dimashq*, in 29 volumes, (Dar al Fiker: Damascus- Syria, 1996)

مختصر تاريخ دمشق، ابن منظور، في 29 مجلد، دار الفكر، دمشق- سوريا، 1996

MTM: al Masudi, *Muruj al thahab*, first edit., (al Aalami: Beirut-lebanon, 1991)

المسعودي، مروج الذهب، مؤسسة الاعلمي للمطبوعات، بيروت، طبعة اولى 1991

NA: Abi Al Abbass Ahmad al Qalqashindi, *Nihayat al Arab fi Maarifat Ansab al Arab*, (Dar al Kitab al Lubnani, Beirut-Lebanon, 2ⁿᵈ edit., 1980)

نهاية الارب في معرفة أنساب العرب ، ابي العباس احمد القلقشندي، دار الكتاب اللبناني، بيروت، الطبعة الثانية، 1980

NAFA : Shihab al Deen al Nuwairi, *Nihayat al Arab fi funoon al Adab*, (Dar al Kutub al Elmeyyeh: Beirut- Lebanon, 2004)

شهاب الدين النويري، نهاية الأرب في فنون الأدب، دار الكتب العلمية، بيروت لبنان، 2004

NH: Alois Musil, *The Northern Hejaz,* A Topographical Itinerary, (Published under the Patronage of the Czech Academy of Science and arts and of Charles Crane: New York), 1926

NHCVII: *Nag Hammadi Codex VII*, Volume editor: Birger A. Pearson, (E.J. Brill: Leiden, New York, Koln, 1996)

NM : Sabaih al Suhairi, *al Nushu wal Khalq Fi al Nusus al Mandaeah*, Mudamedan ala Kurt Rudolph, al Lahut wa Khalq al Kawain wa al Insan Fi al Kitabat al Mandaeah, (University of Bagdad, Bagdad, 1994)

صبيح السهيري، النشؤ والخلق في النصوص المندائية، جامعة بغداد، بغداد 1994 ، معتمدا على كتاب كورت رودولف " اللاهوت وخلق الكون والانسان في الكتابات المندائية "

NZM: ben Taghri Bardi al Atabaki, *al-Nujum al zahirah fi muluk messer wa al qahirah*, (Dar al Kutub al Ilmiyah: Beirut-Lebanon, first edit., 1992

النجوم الزاهرة في ملوك مصر والقاهرة، بن تَغْري بَرْدي الاتابكي، دار الكتب العلمية، بيروت- لبنان، طبعة اولى 1992

OB: Dr. Kurt Koch, *Occult Bondage and Deliverance*, (Kregel Publications: Grand Rapids, Michigan, 1972)

OC: Origen, *Contra Celsum*, early Christian, writings

OTD: Walter C. Kaiser Jr., *The Old Testament Documents*, (InterVarsity Press, Downers Grove, Illinois, 2001)

PC: *A pair of Nasoraean Commentaries*, Two Priestly Documents, The Great "First World" And The Lesser "First World", translated by Drower, (E. J. Brill: Leiden, 1963)

PD: T. K. Oesterreich, *Possession Demoniacal And Other*, London, Kegan Paul, Trench, Trubner & CO., LTD. : (London, Great Britain, 1930)

PEC: *The Periplus of the Erythraean Sea*, translated by Wilfred H. Schoff, (Munshiram Manoharial Publishers Pvt Ltd.:New Delhi, 1995)

PM: Vesta Sarkhosh Curtis, *Persian Myths*, (University of Texas Press: Austin, 1993)

PNH : *The Natural History* of Pliny, Tr. With copious notes and Illustrations, by the late John Bostock and H. T. Riley, (Published London: H.G. Bohn, 1855-57)

PPS: A. H. Sayce, *Patriarchal Palestine*, (The Echo Library: Teddington, 2006)

PPW: Procopius, *History of the Wars, The Persian War, Books I & II*, H..B. Dewing, Translator, Cosimoclassics: New York), 2007

RA: Al-Suhaili, *al Rauth al Anuf*, in seven volumes, (Maktabet ibn Taimiyah: Cairo-Egypt, 1990)

الروض الانف في شرح السيرة النبوية لابن هشام، لامام عبد الرحمن السهيلي، في سبعة اجزاء، مكتبة ابن تيمية، القاهرة 1990

RC: *The Recognitions of Clement*, Edited & Revised by Douglas F Hatten, (Lulu.com: 2007)

RD: Brad Steiger, *Revelation The Divine Fire*,(Foresthill, CA: Reality Press, 2006)

RDS: Nelson Glueck, *Rivers in the Desert*,(Farrar Strauas and Cudahy: New York, 1959)

ROTK : K. A. Kitchen, *On the Reliability of the Old Testament*, (William B. Eerdmans Publishing Company: Grand Rapids, Michigan/ Cambridge, U.K., 2006)

SA : E.S. Drower, *The Secret Adam, A Study of Nasoraean Gnosis*, (the Clarendon Press: Oxford, 1960)

SAH: *The Story of Ahikar, from the Aramaic, Syriac, Arabic, Armenian, Ethiopic, Old Turkish, Greek and Slavonic Versions*, by F. C.Conybeare, J. Rendel Harris, and Agnes Smith Lewis (Glasgow, 1898).

SAN: Sheldon Oberman, *Solomon and the Ant*, (Boyds Mills Press: Honesdale, Pennsylvania, 2006)

SBE *Sacred Books of the East Series*, Motilal Banarsidass:Delhi, 1969-1970

SC: *The Stromata, or Miscellanies*- Clement of Alexandria, Early Christian Fathers

SE : *The Scroll of Exalted Kingship*, Diwan Malkuta Laita, translated by J. J. Buckley, (American Oriental Society: New Haven, Connecticut, 1993)

SHB: al Sira al Halabiya, Ali bin Burhan al Deen al Halabi, in three volumes, Dar al Maarifa: Beirut- Lebanon

السيرة الحلبية ، علي بن برهان الدين الحلبي، في ثلاث مجلدات، دار المعرفة، بيروت- لبنان

SHC: Samuel Noah Kramer, *The Sumerians Their History, Culture, And Character*, The University of Chicago Press:London, Chicago, 1971

SHM: Rushdi Iliayyan, *al-Sabiun Harraniyyen wa Mandiyen*, (Matabaa Dar al Salam: Bagdad, 1976)

رشدي عليان، الصابئون حرانيين ومندائيين ، مطبعة دار السلام-بغداد 1976

SHSL : Wright, *A Short History of Syriac Literature* (Adam and Charles Black: London, 1894),

SIH: *al Sirah al Nabawiya ibn Hisham*, Dar al Khair, Beirut, 1992 :

السيرة النبوية لابن هشام، دار الخير، بيروت، 1992

SIHT: Leon James Wood, *Survey of Israel's History*, (Zondervan: Grand Rapids, Michigan, 1986)

SIM: A. Jamme, W.F., *Inscriptions from Mahram Bilqis (Marib)*,(The Johns Hopkins Press: Baltimore, 1962)

SJA : al-Hamadani, *sifat jazirat al arab*, (Maktabat al irshad: Sanaa, Yemen, 1990

الهمداني، صفة جزيرة العرب، مكتبة الارشاد، صنعاء، اليمن، 1990

SKB:Al-Bahiqi, *al Sunan als Kubra*, in 11 volumes, (Dar al Kutub al Elmiyah: Beirut-Lebanon, third edit., 2003)

السنن الكبرى للبيهقي، دار الكتب العلمية، بيروت، طبعة ثالثة، 2003

SKH : A. Sreedhara Menon, *A survey of Kerala history,* (DC books: Kottayam, Kerala State, India, 2012)

SKN: Ahmad bin Shuaib al Nisai, *al Sunan al Kubra*, in six volumes, (Dar al Kutub al Elmiyah: Beirut- Lebanon, 1991)

أحمد بن شعيب النسائي، السنن الكبرى، في ستة اجزاء، دار الكتب العلمية، بيروت- لبنان، 1991

SKS: Muhammed Abedel Hamid al Hamad, *Sabiat Harran wa Khwan al Safa*, (al Ahali: Damascus-Syria, 1998)

محمد عبد الحميد الحمد ، *صابئة حران واخوان الصفا* ، (الاهالي ، دمشق سوريا 1998)

SNK: ibn Katheer, *al Sirah al Nabawyah*, the electronic version by Shabaket Mishkat al Islamiyah, 1976

السيرة النبوية لابن كثير، النسخة الالكترونية شبكة مشكاة الإسلامية، 1976

SPC: Ernest A. Wallis Budge, *The history of Alexander the Great, being the Syriac version of the Pseudo Callisthenes*, (Gorgias Press: New Jersey, 2003)

STE: *Second Targum of Esther*, an Explanatory Commentary on Esther, with four Appendices, consisting of The second Targum translated from the Aramaic, Paulus Cassel, (Edinburgh, T. & T. Clark, 1888)

STS : Mohammed Ali al Sabuni, *Safwat al Tafaseer*, in three volumes, (Dar al Quran al Kareem: Beirut, 1981)

محمد علي الصابوني ، صفوة التفاسير ، في ثلاثة مجلدات، دار القرآن الكريم، بيروت 1981

SUT: Mohammed bin Isa al Tarmathi, *Sunan al Tarmathi*, (Dar Ihya' al Turath al Arabi, Beirut- Lebanon

محمد بن عيسى الترمذي، سنن الترمذي، دار إحياء التراث العربي، بيروت

TA: Mohammed Murtatha al Huseini al Zubeidi, *Taj al Aruss*, in 40 volumes, (al Majles al watani lelthaqafa wa al funun wa Adab, Kuwait, 2004)

محمد مرتضى الحسيني الزبيدي، تاج العروس، في اربعين جزءا، المجلس الوطني للثقافة والفنون والاداب، الكويت، 2004

TAT : Jaafar Mohammed bin Jarir al Tabari, *Jamea al Bian an Taweel al Quran, known as Tafseer al Tabari*, (Dar al Feker, 1995)

جعفر محمد بن جرير الطبري، جامع البيان عن تأويل آي القرآن المعروف بتفسير الطبري، دار الفكر للطباعة والنشر والتوزيع، 1995

TES : Julian Obermann, " Two Elijah Stories In Judeo-Arabic Transmission", *Hebrew Union College Annual*, 1950-1951, Volume XXIII (Part I),

TFMH : Wahab bin Munabbeh, *Kitab al Tijan fi Muluk Himyar*, (Daerat al Maaref al Uthmaniyah: Heidar Abad, India, first edit., 1928)

كتاب التيجان في ملوك حمير، وهب بن منبه، دائرة المعارف العثمانية، حيدر آباد، الهند، طبعة اولى سنة 1928 ،

TFR: Al Razi, *Tafseer al fakher al razi*, in 32 volumes (Dar al Feker : Beirut-Lebanon, 1981)

الرازي، تفسير الفخر الرازي، في 32 جزء، دار الفكر، بيروت، 1981

TFS : Ibn Salam al Jamhi, *Tabaqat Fuhool al Shuara'*, Dar Almaaref, Second Edition, prepared by Abu Faher Mahmood Mohammed Shaker, (Dar al Maaref-Cairo-Egypt, 1974)

طبقات فحول الشعراء لمحمد بن سلام الجمحي، تحقيق ابو فهر محمود محمد شاكر، طبعة ثانية (دار المعارف - القاهرة- مصر، 1974م)

TFT: Ibn Jezy al Kalbi, *al tasheel fi Ulum al tanzeel*, (Matbaat Mustafa Mohammed: cairo- Egypt, first edit., 1936

التسهيل في علوم التنزيل لابن جزيّ الكلبي، مطبعة مصطفي محمد، طبعة اولى، القاهرة، 1936

TIK : Ibn Khaldun, *Tarikh ibn Khaldun*, in 8 volumes, (Dar al Fiker: Beirut-Lebanon, 2001)

ابن خلدون، تاريخ ابن خلدون، في ثمانية مجلدات، دار الفكر، بيروت- لبنان، 2001

TKB : al Bukhari, *al Tarikh al Kabeer*, (Dar al Kutub al Elelmiyah: Beirut-Lebanon)

البخاري، التاريخ الكبير، في ثمانية مجلدات، دار الكتب العلمية، بيروت- لبنان

TKIS: ibn Saad, *al Tabaqat al kubra*, (Maktabat al Khanji: Cairo, 2001

كتاب الطبقات الكبرى لابن سعد، مكتبة الخانجي- القاهرة، الطبعة الاولى 2001

TMD: Ibn Asaker, *Tarikh Madinat Dimashq*, (Dar Al-Fiker: Beirut-Lebanon, first edit., 1997

ابن عساكر، تاريخ مدينة دمشق، دار الفكر، بيروت-لبنان، الطبعة الاولى 1997

TMTH: al Thaalibi, *al Tamtheel wa al muhathara*, (al dar al arabiya lelkitab: cairo, Egypt, 1983)

التمثيل والمحاضرة ، الثعالبي، الدار العربية للكتاب، القاهرة، مصر، 1983

TQTH: al Thaalibi, *Thimar al Qulub fi al muthaf wa al mansub*, (Dar al Maaref: Cairo-Egypt, 1965

ثمار القلوب في المضاف والمنسوب، الثعالبي، دار المعارف، القاهرة، 1965

TS: H. Polano, *The Talmud Selections*, (Frederick Warne& CO., LTD: London and New York, 1978)

TSE: Bernard Grossfeld, *Targum of Sheni to the Book of Esther*, (Sepher-Hermon Press: New York, 1993)

TSK: *Testament of Solomon*, translated by F. C. Conybeare, Originally Published as The Testament of Solomon The Jewish Quarterly Review, Vol II, No 1. (October, 1898)

TTA : *Tarikh al Tabari*, Tarikh al Rusul wa al Muluk, Abi Jaafer bin Jarir al Tabari, in 10 volumes, second edition, Dar al Maarif, Egypt.

تاريخ الطبري، تاريخ الرسل والملوك، لابي جعفر محمد بن جرير الطبري، في عشرة اجزاء ، الطبعة الثانية ، دار المعارف بمصر،

TTB : *Tarikh al Tabari*, Tarikh al Rusul wa al Muluk, Abi Jaafer bin Jarir al Tabari, in 5 volumes, (Dar al Kutub al Elmeyiah: Beirut-Lebanon, 1991)

تاريخ الطبري ، تاريخ الامم والملوك، لابي جعفر بن جرير الطبري ، في خمسة مجلدات ، دار الكتب العلمية ، بيروت- لبنان ، الطبعة الثالثة 1991 ،

TTH: Abed al Rahman Al Thaalibi, *Tafsir al Thaalibi al musamma bil-jawaher al hisan fi tafseer al quran*, (Dar Ehya' al Turath al-arabi: Beirut-Lebanon, first edition, 1997)

عبد الرحمن الثعالبي، تفسير الثعالبي المسمى بالجواهر الحسان في تفسير القرآن، دار احياء التراث العربي بيروت - لبنان الطبعة الاولد - 1997

TTL : Mohsin Ashraf, *Top Ten- Lives of the Greatest Monarchs of History*,(Lulu Publications: London, 2007)

TTQ: *The Thousand and Twelve Questions, Alf Trisar Suialia*,Translation by E.S. Drower, (Akademie-Verlag: Berlin, 1960)

TTT : Robert T. Boyd, *Tells, Tombs and Treasure,*(published by Bonanza Books by arrangement with Baker Book House, New York)

UQ : Bader al Deen al Aini, Umdet al Qari Shareh Sahih al Bukhari, in 25 volumes, (Dar al Kutub al Ilmiyah: Beirut-Lebanon, 2001)

بدر الدين العيني، عمدة القارئ شرح صحيح البخاري، في 25 مجلد، دار الكتب العلمية، بيروت لبنان، طبعة اولى، سنة 2001

WQ : Al-warraq, electronic version

النسخة الالكترونية لموقع الوراق

ZMT:ibn al Jozi, *zad elmaseer fi elm al tafseer*, (al Maktab al Islami: Beirut-Lebanon, 1984)

زاد المسير في علم التفسير، ابن الجوزي، طبعة الثالثة، (المكتب الاسلامي، بيروت، 1984)

ZS : A.V. Williams Jackson, Zoroastrian Studies, The Iranian Religion And Various Monographs, AMS Press, New York, 1965

ZT : *Textual sources for the study of Zoroastrianism*, edited and translated by Mary Boyce, (The University of Chicago Press: Chicago, 1990)

References

Chapter 1

[1] Charles Forster, *The Geography of Arabia*, Vol. 2, HGA, page 32.

[2] Wellhausen: cited by encyclopaedia of Islam, EI, volume 1, page 169

[3] Quoted by Jawad Ali, in al Mufassal fi Tarikh Al Arab Qabel Al Islam, MF, part I, page 308

[4] Ibin Hisham, SIH8 : 1

[5] Introductio to Ibin Hisham SIH‹ pages L and M

[6] Tarikh ibn Khaldoon, TIK, part II, pp. 21-22

[7] Diwan Ummiah Bin Abi Alsalt, version Bashir Yamut, p. 58, Beirut 1938

[8] Quoted by Jawad Ali, in al Mufassal fi Tarikh Al Arab Qabel Al Islam, MF, part I page75

[9] Tafseer aj Taberi, TAT, 1, 217

[10] I Enoch :73, (BE)

[11] Haran Gawaita, (HG), page 13

[12] E.S.Drower, A Mandaean Book of Black Magic, Journal of the Royal Asiatic Society. 1943, page 169 ; cited by Maria Vittoria Cerutti, Dualismo e Ambiguita',(DA), page 96

[13] John Reeves, Jewish Lore in Manichaean Cosmogony, (JMC), page 88

[14] Al Masudi, Muruj al Dahab. MTM, part 1, pp.258 and 259; ;Al Firozabadi, al Qamus al Muhit, part 3, chapter Zein
‹ Ibn Hajer, Fiteh al Bari, FAH, part 12, pp.270-271
;Al Zubeidi, Taj al Alarus, part 6, under "Nshj", and part 7, under "zind", and part 22, under "zendiq" ; Ibn Manthur, Lisan al Arab, LA, part 6, under "zendiq"

[15] Yaqut al Hamawi, Maajm al Buldan, MAY, part 2, p.24

[16] Al Abshihi, al Mustatref fi kuli fin Mustethref, MFM, volume 2, p.83

[17] Al Hakem al Neisaburi, al Mustadrak ala al Sahihein, MAS, part 2, p. 643, no 4068

[18] Al Yakubi, WQ, p.101

[19] Geo Widngrain, Mani and Manichism, MM, pp. 162-163

[20] Geo Widngrain, Mani and Manichism, MM, p. 163

[21] Manichaean Literature, (ML), translated by Jes P. Asmussen, page 2

[22] Manichaean Literature, (ML), translated by Jes P. Asmussen, page17

[23] Al 'Ani, Umdet al Qari, UQ, part 15, p.311.

[24] Al Bakri al Andalusi, Maajam Ma istujem, MME, part 1, p.119.

[25] "Hud and other Pre-Islamic prophets of Hadramaut" (Muséon, 67{1954}, pages 121-179; see especially pages 166-171;F.V.Winnett and W.L.Reed, Ancient Records from North Arabia, (AR), page 45

[26] F.V.Winnett and W.L.Reed, Ancient Records from North Arabia, (AR), page 45

[27] Von Kremer, Uber die Suedarabishe Sage, S., 21; Cited by Jawad Ali, al Mufassal fi Tarikh al Arab Qab al Islam, MF, part 1, page 312

[28] Al Sabuni, Sauft al Tafaseer, STS, 2, 309

[29] Al Abshihi, al Mustatref fi kuli fin Mustethref, MFM, volume 2, p.83

[30] Al Yakubi, WQ, p. 101

[31] Ram Yast I, 2 and 3, SBE, Volume 23, Zenda Avesta Part II, page 250

[32] Ram Yast V, 20, SBE, Volume 23, Zenda Avesta Part II, page 254

[33] Dinkard,VII, chapter II, 44-46, SBE, Volume 47, Pahlavi Texts part V, page 28

[34] Al Shahrastani, al Milal wa al Nahl, MNS, p.259

[35] Cited by Al Sabuni, Sauft al Tafaseer, STS, 3, p.199

[36] Al 'Ani, Umdet al Qari, UQ, part 15, p.311

[37] Al Bakri al Andalusi, Maajam Ma istujem, MME, part 1, p.119

Chapter 2

[38] Inscriptions of Sargon, (Ta-mu-di, Lie, The Inscriptions of Sargon II, King of Assyria, 20:120; quoted by I. Eph'al, The Ancient Arabs, IAA, page 230

[39] De Lacy O'Leary, Arabia before Muhammed, AM, page 51

[40] Sahih al Bukhari, Kitab al Al Anbiya, chapter about the words of Allah: Saleh telling Thamud his brethern;Sahih Muslim, kitab al Zuhd wa al Raqaeq

[41] Al Qalqashandi, Nihayet al arab fi Marifat Ansab Al Arab, NA, p.198

[42] F.V.Winnett and W.L.Reed, Ancient Records from North Arabia, AR, page 130

[43] The Geography of Strabo, Book XVI. 4. 24 (GS volume vii, page 359)

[44] F.V.Winnett and W.L.Reed, Ancient Records from North Arabia, AR, page 130

[45] F.V.Winnett and W.L.Reed, Ancient Records from North Arabia, AR, page 117

[46] K.A. Kitchen, Documentation For Ancient Arabia, Part I, DAA, page 237

[47] A. Jaussen and R. Savignac, Mission archéologique en Arabie, II, (Paris 1914), page 56 and 57 cited by F.V.Winnett and W.L.Reed, Ancient Records from North Arabia, AR, page 42

[48] Tafseer aj Taberi, TAT, 12, surat Hud, verses 67-8 Hadith 14187

[49] Van den Branden, in Le Museon, LXIII, (1950) 1-2, pages 47-51; Cited by Jawad Ali, al Mufassal Fi Tarikh al Arab Qabl Al-Islam, vol. I, MF, page 328

[50] Preislamiques p. 23; Cited by Jawad Ali, al Mufassal Fi Tarikh al Arab Qabl Al-Islam, MF, vol. vi, p. 324

[51] F.V.Winnett and W.L.Reed, Ancient Records from North Arabia, AR, page 44

[52] Enno Littmann, JESUS IN A PRE-ISLAMIC ARABIC INSCRIPTION, The Muslim World, Volume 40, Issue 1, January 1950, Pages: 16–18, Article first published online : 3 APR 2007

[53] Tafseer al Qurtubi fi Surat al Araf, Tafseer aj Taberi, TAT, 19, surat al shura', Hadith 20322

[54] Al Thaalibi, Tafseer Al Thaalibi, TTH, 3, page 49; Al Masudi, Muruj al Dahab. MTM, part 2, pp.45-46

[55] Tafseer Ibn Kathir In his comment on Surah al Araf

[56] Tarikh al Tabari, TTB, volume 1, p.140

[57] Diwan Umiah ben abi al Salt, DUBS, p.76

[58] Diwan Umiah ben abi al Salt, DUBS, p.76

[59] See: R.C. Zaehner, The Dawn and Twilight of Zoroastrianism, DTZ, page 142

[60] Azruqi, akhbar Mecca, AKM, p.198

[61] Al Aghani, al Asfahani, AGH, part16 , p. 260

[62] Al Allusi, Bulugh al arab fi Marefat Ahwal al Arab, BEA, 2, pp.307-308

[63] Selection of Zad-Sparam, Chapter XII:7-19, SBE, V.47, Pahlavi Texts, Part V, pages 135- 137

[64] Selections of Zad-Sparam, Chapter XII, 7-9, SBE, V.47, Pahlavi Texts, Part V, page 135

[65] Dinkard, book VII, Chapter II: 63-66, SBE, V.47, Pahlavi Texts, Part V, page 32

[66] Selections of Zad-Sparam, Chapter XII, 19, SBE, V.47, Pahlavi Texts, Part V, page 137

[67] F.V.Winnett and W.L.Reed, *Ancient Records from North Arabia*, AR, pages130-131.

[68] Irfan Shahîd, Byzantium and the Arabs in the fourth century, BAFO, pages 393- 394

[69] Notitia Dignitatum, OR. 28.17, 34.22; cited by Robert G. Hoyland, Arabia and the Arabs: from the Bronze Age to the coming of Islam, Routledge. AAB, p. 69

[70] Notitia Dignitatum, 52.5

[71] F.V.Winnett and W.L.Reed, Ancient Records from North Arabia, AR, page 70

[72] F.V.Winnett and W.L.Reed, Ancient Records fom North Arabia, AR, page 138

Chapter 3

[73] Ptolemy, Geography, book VI, chapter 7, GP, page 137

[74] Alois Musil, The Northern Hejaz, NH, page 279

[75] Eusebius, Onomasticon, section M, Genesis, Madiam

[76] Procopius,Persian War, I, xix, PPW, p. 181

[77] Richard F. Burton, The Gold Mines of Midian, GMM, pages 317-369

[78] Ibn Hisham, SIH, 4, p.196

[79] Yaqut al Hamawi, Maajm al Buldan, MAY, 5, p.78

[80] Ibn Manthur, Lisan al Arab, LA, part 3, under "jahl"

[81] Tafseer al Qurtubi fi Surat Hud

[82] Al Allusi, Ruh al Maani, in his expository on Surah Al Aaraf ;Tafseer Ibn Kathir ln his comment on Surah al Araf ؛ Tarikh al Tabari, TTB, volume 1, p. 198

[83] Al Masudi, Muruj al Dahab. MTM, part 1, p.66

Chapter 4

[84] Tafseer ibn Kathir in his expository on Surah Yaseen

[85] Al Allusi, Ruh al Maani, in his expository on Surah Yaseen

[86] Tafseer al Qurtubi fi Surat Yaseen

[87] Tafseer al Qurtubi fi Surat Yaseen

[88] Abu Hayyan, Tafseer al Bahr al Muhit in his expository of Surah yaseen

[89]Tafseer Ibn Kathir ln his comment on Surah Yaseen

[90] Al Masudi, Muruj al Dahab. MTM, part 1, pp.73-74

[91] Ibn Juzei al Kalbi, al tasheel fi Ulum al tansil, TFT, part 3,p.161

[92] Tafseer Ibn Kathir ln his comment on SurahYaseen

[93] Al Masudi, Muruj al Dahab. MTM, part 1, page 73

[94] Al Maqdisi, al Bada' w ail Tarikh, WQ, p. 164 ؛ Tarikh al Tabari, TTB, volume 1, pp.79&380; Ibn Kathir, Al Bidayah wa Al Nihaya, BNH, 1page 235

[95] Tafseer al Qurtubi fi Surat Yaseen

[96] Tarikh al Tabari, TTB, volume 1, pp.379-380

[97] Tarikh al Tabari, TTB, volume 1, pp.379-380

[98] Sahih al Bukhari, chapter Surah read in the name of your lord who created. Hadith No 3043

[99] Al 'Ani, Umdet al Qari, part 1, p.53

[100] Ibn Manthur, Lisan al Arab, under "saab"

[101] Ibn al Athir, al Nihayat fi Ghareeb Al Hadith wa ather, p.392

[102]Al Suheili, Al Ruth al Anuf, RA, part 2, page 399

[103] Ibn Hisham, Part 1, 190

[104] Al Munjed, a famous Arabic dictionary, p.544

[105] Halabieh, SHB, 1, 385

[106] Tarikh al Tabari, TTB, volume, 1, p.531

[107] Halabieh, SHB, 1, pp. 38&384; Ibn Hisham, Part 1, p. 190; 5

[108] Hyppolytus, The Refutation of All Heresies, book VI, Chapter xiv

[109] Irenaeus, Against Heresies, Chapter XXIV: 4, Ante-Nicene Fathers, Volume I, Hendrickson, Peabody, Massachusetts, 1995, page 349; Sahih al Bukhari, kitab the begging of inspiration, chapter I

[110] Sahil al Bukhari, kitab badi al wahi, chapter 1

[111] Ibn Hisham, SIH, 2, 26

[112] Tafseer aj Taberi, TAT, Hadiths 16554-6; Al Allusi, Ruh al Maani, in his expository on Surah al Nahl

[113] Ibn Hisham, SIH, 1, pp.147-148

[114] Ibn Hisham, SIH, 1, p.147, fotenote 6

[115] Ibn Hisham, SIH, 1, p.148

[116] Tranquillus, Gaius Suetonius (2011-03-24). The Lives of the Twelve Caesars, Volume 06: Nero. Kindle Edition

[117] Tacitus, The Annals, book 15.22

Chapter 5

[118] Bundahis XIX :1,2, SBE, Volume V, Pahlavi Texts part I, pages 67-8

[119] Darmesteter, (Ormazd et Ahriman), page 148-151 quoted by West in his comment on Palavi Texrs part I page 67

[120] *Bubdahis* XIX: 3, SBE, Volume V, Pahlavi Texts part I, page 68

[121] *Bundahis* XIX,7, SBE, Volume V, Pahlavi Texts part I, page 68

[122] *Bundahis* XIX,8,9, SBE, Volume V, Pahlavi Texts part I, page 69

[123] Introduction to Vendidad, SBE, Volume 4, Zenda Avesta Part I, pages lxxv- lxxvi

[124] Bahman yast III: 59,60, SBE, Volume V, Pahlavi Texts part I, page 235

[125] *Bundahis* VII : 12, SBE, Volume V, Pahlavi Texts part I, page 28

[126] *A Manichaean Psalm-Book*, MP, page 138

[127] *Paraphrased of Shem,* chapter 6: 2-6, *Nag Hammadi Codex VII*, NHCVII, page 39

[128] John C.Reeves, *Heralds of that good realm*, HGR, page 179

[129] *The Thousand and Twelve Questions*, 231, TTQ, P.168

[130] Ginza Rabba, GR, book 5, p.109

[131] *The Thousand and Twelve Questions*, 256, TTQ, P. 179

[132] *The Thousand and Twelve Questions*, 256, TTQ, Pages. 179-180

[133] The Great First World (Alma Risaia RBA), VII, 435, *A pair if Nasoraean Commentaries*, PC, page 32

[134] *The Thousand and Twelve Questions*, 83, TTQ, P.133

[135] *The Scroll of Exalted Kingship*, Diwan Malkuta Laita, SE, page 66

[136] Ginza Rabba the Right, G, Book 17, praise 7, p.293;
(Ginza Rabba 15, page 351, cited by Kurt Adulf, reported by Sabih al Suheiri in his book: al Nushu wa Khalq in Mandaean Texts, MN, pages 68&107 where he translates Cry instead of called

[137] Ibn Hisham, SIH, 1, p.186

[138] The prophet biography according to Ibn Kathir, SNK, part I, page 157

[139] The prophet biography according to Ibn Kathir, SNK, part I, page 156

[140] Al Nisae, al Sunan al Kubra, SKN, no 8188

[141] Al 'Ani, Umdet al Qari, UQ, part 4, p.49

[142] giving a passage from Thabit b. Kurra, quoted by Barhebraeus, Chronicum Syriacum,Paris 1890,168); cited by Encyclopaedia of Islam, EI, volume III, page 166

[143] (cf. N. A. Faris and H. W.Glidden,The development of the meaning of the Koranic Hanif, in Journal of the Palestine Oriental Society, xix (1939), 1-13, esp. 6-9; cited by Encyclopaedia of Islam, EI, volume III, page 166
[144] Noldeke, Zeitschrift der deutschen Morgenländischen Gesellschaft, xli, 721; de Goeje, Bibl. Geogr. Arab, viii, Glossary, p. xviii.;cited by Jeffery, Arthur, *The Foreign Vocabulary Of The Qur'an*, FVQ, page 114

Chapter 6

[145] Ibn Hisham, SIH, 1, p.173 ᵻ Halabieh, SHB, 1, 303
[146] Halabieh, SHB, 1, 310
[147] Dinkard-Book IX, Chapter XXXIII, 5, SBE, Volume 37, Pahlavi Texts part IV, page 262-see note 2
[148] *Sad Dar*, Chapter XCVIII, 2-3, SBE, Volume 24, Pahlavi Texts part III, page 360
[149] Dinkard-Book VIII, Chapter XXXVIII, 49-51
[150] Introduction to Vendidad, SBE, Volume 4, Zenda Avesta Part I, pages lxxv- lxxv .
[151] Bahman Yast (part of Pahlavi Texts) Chapter III: 47, 48, SBE, Volume V, Pahlavi Texts part I, pages 231-2
[152] Sahih al Bukhari, kitab al Riqaq, chapter 40: the sunrise from the West; Sahih al Bukhari, Kitab al iten, chapter 26
[153] Comment on Mihir Yast, XXIV: 95, SBE, Volume 23, Zenda Avesta Part II, page 143-fotenote 5
[154] Mihir Yast, XXIV: 95, SBE, Volume 23, Zenda Avesta Part II, page 143, see also fotenote 5
[155] Sahih al Bukhari, kitab the beginning of creation, chapter 4
[156] Sahih al Bukhari, kitab monotheism, chapter 22
[157] Dinkard book VII, chapter X, 2, SBE, Volume 47, Pahlavi Texts part V, page 112
[158] Introduction to Pahlavi Texts, 12-13, SBE, Volume 47, Pahlavi Texts part V, page XIII
[159] R.C. Zaehner, *The Dawn and Twilight of Zoroastrianism*, DTZ, Weidenfeld And Nicolson, London 1975, page 318
[160] Sahih al Bukhari, kitab al Anbya, chapter 5
[161] Farvardin Yast, XVI: 57
[162] *Introduction to Pahlavi Texts*, SBE, Volume 47, Pahlavi Texts part V, page XIII, 12.
[163] Sikand-Gumanik Vigar, Chapter XIV, 39, SBE, Volume 24, Pahlavi Texts part III, page 225
[164] Jawad Ali, al Mufassal fi Tarikh al Arab Qab al Islam, MF, part 2, p.384
[165] Halabieh, SHB, 2, p.6 ᵻ Ibn Hisham, SIH, 2, p.5, fotenote 1
[166] Halabieh, SHB, 2, p.6
[167] Sahih al Bukhari, kitab the Quran worship, chapter 4 ;Halabieh, SHB, 2, 6
[168] *Bundahis*,Chapter XXX : 6, SBE, Volume V, Pahlavi Texts part I, page 123

[169] Dinkard, book VII, Chapter I:9; SBE, Volume 47, Pahlavi Texts part V, page 6, see also fotenote number 2

[170] Dinkard, book VII, chapter II: 36, SBE, Volume 47, Pahlavi Texts part V, page 26

[171] Farvardin Yast I :11, SBE, Volume 23, Zenda Avesta Part II, pages 182-3

[172] Sahih al Bukhari, kitab al Tafseer, chapter 415

[173] Yasna LXV(LXIV): SBE, Volume 31, *Zenda Avesta Part III*, pages 317-320

[174] The Gathas, Yasna LI.,9, SBE, Volume 31, *Zenda Avesta Part III*, page 182,see also fotenote 1; Dinkard-Book IX, Chapter XXXII, 25, SBE, Volume 37, Pahlavi Texts part IV, page 259-260

[175] Dinkard-Book IX, Chapter XLIV,11, SBE, Volume 37, Pahlavi Texts part IV, page 296

[176] *Bundahis*,Chapter XXX : 19-21, SBE, Volume V, Pahlavi Texts part I, pages 125-6 ; *Dadistan-I Dinik*, Chapter XXXII, 12-13, SBE, Volume 18, Pahlavi Texts part II, page 73; Dadistan-I Dinik, Chapter XXXVII, 110, SBE, Volume 18, Pahlavi Texts part II, page 115

[177] Sahih al Bukhari, kitab al Anbya, chapter 2

[178] Sahih al Bukhari, kitab al Taabir, chapter 45.

[179] Sahih al Bukhari, kitab al Tauheed, chapter 24.

[180] Sahih al Bukhari, chapter about the prestige of worship.

Chapter 7

[181] Oriental Institute of the University of Chicago, Revised: February 7, 2007; under : "Mud brick stamped with the cartouche of Rameses II"can be accessed at http://oi.uchicago.edu/museum/highlights/tools.html

Chapter 8

[182] Can be accessed at : http://www.israelofgod.org/esther.htm

[183] *The International Standard Bible Encyclopaedia.,* ISBE, I, p. 80-81

[184] *The International Standard Bible Encyclopaedia.,* ISBE, I, p. 80

[185] Babylonian Talmud - Mas. Megilah 16b

[186] Babylonian Talmud, Mas. Megilah 15b, footnote 1 a

[187] A.L. MCMAHON For Esther Woodall From the Catholic Encyclopedia

[188] Babylonian Talmud, Mas. Megilah 10b, Footnote 42

[189] Babylonian Talmud - Mas. Megilah 16b

[190] Encyclopedia Judaica CD-ROM Edition 1.0 1997, under *Haman*

Chapter 9

[191] Hyppolytus, The Refutation of all heresies, Book X, Chapter VIII.—Simon Magus.

[192] Hyppolytus, The Refutation of all heresies, Book X, Chapter VIII.—Simon Magus.

[193] Hyppolytus, The Refutation of all heresies, book X, Chapter VIII

[194] The Recognitions of Clement, book 2.1, RC, page 59

[195] Clementine Homilies, book 2. 22

[196] The Recognitions of Clement, book 2. Chapter 9, RC, pages 64-5

[197] Pseudo-Clementine Homilies, book 2, chapter 32,

[198] Pseudo-Clementine Homilies, book 4, chapter 4

[199] Pseudo-Clementine Homilies, book 2, chapter 26

[200] The Recognitions of Clement, book 2. Chapter 15, RC, page 69

[201] Epiphanius, Against Heresies (Panarion), xxx, 15

[202] Irenaeus, Against Heresies, book I, chapter.26.2,

[203] Epiphanius, Panarion 30:18,1

[204] Epiphanius, Panarion 30: 2,7-9

[205] Al Aghani, al Asfahani, AGH, part 3, p.82 ; al Ishtiqaq p. 164

[206] Epiphanius, Panarion XXX

[207] Irenaeus, Against Heresies, book I, chapter.26.2

[208] Epiphanius, Panarion 30: 2,4-5

[209] Epiphanius, Panarion 30: 3,7

[210] Epiphanius, Panarion 30: 13, 2

[211] Epiphanius, Panarion 30: 15, 3

[212] Epiphanius, Panarion 30: 21,2

[213] Epiphanius, Panarion 30: 26,1

[214] Epiphanius, Panarion 30:18,4

[215] Epiphanius, Panarion 30:18, 2

[216] Epiphanius, Panarion 30:18, 3

[217] Hans-Joachim Schoeps, Jewish Christianity: Factional Disputes in the Early Church, JCF, pages 136-140

[218] Tafseer aj Taberi, TAT, Hadith 18338

[219] The Epistula Apostolorum, chapter 1, section 9

[220] Sahih al Bukhari, kitab the tricks, chapter 14

[221] Tarikh al Tabari, TTB, volume 1, p.251

[222] Tafseer al Razi, TFR, part 22, p. 103

[223] Tafseer al Qurtubi fi Surat Al Araf, verse 148

[224] Tafseer aj Taberi, TAT, 16, on verse 148 of Surah al Araf, Hadith 18313

[225] Bundahis,Chapter XXXI : 32, SBE, Volume V, Pahlavi Texts part I, page 138

[226] Pseudo-Clementine Homilies, book 18, chapter 12

[227] Al Sabuni, Sauft al Tafaseer, STS, 2, p.245

[228] Ginza Rabba, GR, book 1, praise 2, page 8

[229] The Canonical Prayerbook of the Mandeans, CP, chapter 379, pages 294-5

[230] Ginza Rabba, GR, book 5, pp. 94 and 95-100

[231] Ibn Kathir, Al Bidayah wa Al Nihaya, BNH, 1:19;

232 Ginza Rabba, GR, book 15, p. 250

[233] Ginza Rabba, GR, book 12, page 198

[234] The Apocryphon of John, AJ, page 59

[235] The Kephalaia Of The Teacher, KT, Introduction page xxviii

[236] Ginza Rabba, GR, book 17, praise 7, p.292

[237] A.G. Lie, The Inscriptions of Sargon II, King of Assyria, I: The Annals, Paris, 1929, 22: 120; The Ancient Arabs, I. Eph'al, IAA, page 230

[238] Antiquities of the Jews, Flavius Josephus, Book xi,chapter 8. (AJF)

[239] Antiquities of the Jews, Flavius Josephus, xi, chapter viii (AJF)

[240] Bible dictionary, daert al Maerf, a Christian Biblical publisher, chapter Mim p.196 about Land of Moriah

[241] www.jewishvirtuallibrary.org/mount-moriah

[242] Tarikh al Tabari, TTB, volume 1, p.251

[243] Al Munjed, famous Arabic dictionary, page 107

[244] Al Allusi, Ruh al Maani, in his expository on Surah Tah

[245] Tafseer al Razi, TFR, part 22, p.48

[246] Tafseer aj Taberi, TAT, 16, Hadith 18339

[247] Ibn al Jozi, zad al maser fi Elm al Tafseer, on his expository of Surah Tah

Chapter 10

[248] Halabieh, SHB, 2, p.109

[249] Haran Gawaita, (HG), page 3

[250] Haran Gawaita, (HG), page 8

[251] Tarikh al Tabari, TTB, volume 1, p.345

[252] Sahih al Bukhari, kitab ablutions in dust, chapter 5 ؛ Al 'Ani, Umdet al Qari, UQ, part 4, p. 38؛ Al Hambali, Fath al Bari, FBH, part 2, p.270, Hadith 344

[253] Al Aghani, al Asfahani, AGH, part 17, p.46

[254] Cited by Kurt Adolf, reported by Sabih al Suheiri in his book *al Nushu wa Khalq in Mandaean Texts*, MN, page 127.

[255] Cited by Mohammed Abdel Hamid al Hamed, Saebat Harran wa Ikhwan al safa, SKS, p.30.

[256] al Saebah al Mandayeen by E.S. Drower cited by Dr. Rushdi Elian, al sabyun Harraniyeen wa Mandaeyen, SHM, p. 27.

[257] Najia Murani, Mafahim Sabieyeh Mandaeyeh, MSM, p. 180

[258] Cited by Mohammed Abdel Hamid al Hamed, Saebat Harran wa Ikhwan al safa, SKS, p.37

[259] Tarikh al Tabari, TTB, volume 1, pp.346-7

[260] Tarikh al Tabari, TTB, volume 1, p.347

[261] Tarikh al Tabari, TTB, volume 1, p.347

[262] Tarikh al Tabari, TTB, volume 1, p.495

Chapter 11

[263] Al Sabuni, Sauft al Tafaseer, STS, 2, p. 270

[264] Al Jaheth, Al Hiwan, HJ, 6, pp.225-272

[265] Gods‹ Demons and Symbols of Ancient Mesopotamia, Jeremy black and Anthony green, GD, p.162

[266] A.V. Williams Jackson, Zoroastrian Studies, ZS, page 83

[267] A.V. Williams Jackson, Zoroastrian Studies, ZS, page 83 ‹ Persian Myths‹ Vesta Sarkhosh Curtis, PM, page 32

[268] Tarikh al Tabari, TTB, volume 1, p.298

[269] Targum to Ecclesiastes. i. 13;Babylonian Talmud Pesachim 110a

[270] Testament of Solomon, translated by Conybeare, TSK, verses 2-11, pages 15-17

[271] Testament of Solomon, translated by Conybeare, TSK, verses 13-15, page 18

[272] Testament of Solomon, translated by Conybeare, TSK, verses 124-125, pages 43-4

[273] Ginza Rabba, GR, book 2, praise 1, p.28

[274] Tafseer al Qurtubi fi Surat WQ, page 2261;Diwan al Asha p.243

[275] Al Zubeidi, Taj al Alarus, under "jin" cited by Jawad Ali, MF, 6, pp. 722-723

[276] Al Jaheth, Al Hiwan, HJ,6, p.223

[277] Al Masudi, Muruj al Dahab. MTM, part 1, p.283

[278] Al Nuwairi, Nihayat al arab fi funoon al adab, NAFA, part 14, p. 110

[279] Tafseer al Taberi, TAT, 22, 21967

[280] Al Nuwairi, Nihayat al arab fi funoon al adab, NAFA, part 14, pp. 108-109

[281] Midrash Tehillim (in Yalk., I Kings, 182); cited by Jewish Encyclopedia

[282] Tafseer aj Taberi, TAT, 23, on Surah Sad, verses 30-33, Hadith 22949-22951

[283] Tafseer al Qurtubi fi Surat sad, verses 30-33

[284] Pliny the Elder, Natural History 8. XXX;
Tafseer aj Taberi, TAT

[285] Al Tabrizi, Mishkat al Masabih, chapter ishrat al nisa'

[286] Taberi, TAT, 23, verse 34 of surah Sad, Hadith 22967

[287] Tafseer al Taberi, TAT, 23, on Surat Sad verse 34 Hadith 22971

[288] Sanh. l.c.; Git. 68b; Ecclesiastes Rabbah, i. 12; Cited by Jewish Encyclopedia on Solomon

[289] Midrash (Ruth Rabbah 5:6)

[290] (Git. 68; parallel passages, Midrash Tehillim on Ps. lxxviii. 45; Yalk. ii. 182; compare Num. R. xi. 3; Targum Ecclesiastes, i. 12, and the extract from a manuscript Midrash in "Z. D. M. G." xxi. 220, 221); cited by Jewish encyclopedia

[291] Yer. Sanh. ii. 6; Pesik., ed. Buber, 169a; Tan., ed. Buber, iii. 55; Eccl. R. ii. 2; Simon b. YoHai of the middle of the second century is quoted as the authority ;cited by Jewish Encylopedia

[292] Tobit iii. 8; vi. 13 and14

[293] Emek ha-Melek, 14a-15a

[294] Emek ha-Melek, 14a-15a

[295] Origen, Contra Celsum, (OC) sixth book, chapters 28-30

[296] Ibn Hisham, SIH, 1, p. 128

[297] Sahih Muslim, chapter 16

[298] Al Tabrizi, Mishkat al Masabih, chapter al waswaseh; Ibn Kathir, Al Bidayah wa Al Nihaya, BNH, 1:84-85.

[299] Halabieh, SHB, 2, 65

[300] Halabieh, SHB, 2, 66

[301] Tarikh al Tabari, TTB, volume 1, pp.573-4

[302] Creation of the Physical Earth, Turfan Fragments M 98 and 99, cited by Andrew Welburn, Mani, the Angel and the Column of Glory, MA page185

[303] Testament of Solomon, translated by Conybeare, TSK, verses 122, page 43

[304] Al Jaheth, Al Hiwan, HJ, 6 p.190

[305] Sheldon Oberman, Solomon and the Ant, SAN, page 18

[306] The Ants, by Bert Hölldobler and Edward O. Wilson, AN, page 259

[307] The Ants by Bert Hölldobler and Edward O. Wilson, AN, page 257

[308] The Ants by Bert Hölldobler and Edward O. Wilson, AN, page 258

[309] The Ants by Bert Hölldobler and Edward O. Wilson, AN, page 254- 255

[310] Deuteronomy/Devarim Rabbah 5.2

[311] The Ants by Bert Hölldobler and Edward O. Wilson, AN, page 256

[312] The Ants by Bert Hölldobler and Edward O. Wilson, AN, page 256

[313] Vendidad,Fargard X :14 , SBE, Volume 4, Zenda Avesta Part I, page136 ; Look also to fotenote 7

[314] Appendix to Pahlavi Texts, Part II, SBE, The Sacred books of the East, Volume 18, page 372, footnote 2

[315] Bundahis,Chapter XXVIII : 24, SBE, Volume V, Pahlavi Texts part I, page 110

[316] Appendix to Pahlavi Texts, Part II, SBE, The Sacred books of the East, Volume 18, p. 377

[317] Aban Yast XXVIII, 120, SBE, Volume 23, Zenda Avesta Part II, page 81

[318] Tarikh al Tabari, TTB, volume 1, p.109

[319] Dinkard-Book IX, Chapter XXIII, 2-7, SBE, Volume 37, Pahlavi Texts part IV, pages 224-225

[320] Testament of Solomon, translated by Conybeare, TSK, verses 117-123, pages 41-43

[321] Al Masudi, Muruj al Dahab. MTM, part 2, page 263

[322] John C.Reeves, Heralds of that good realm, HGR, page 184

[323] The paraphrase of Shem, chapter 34:6-12, Nag Hammadi Codex VII, NHCVII, page 97

[324] The Thousand and Twelve Questions, 243, TTQ, P.173

[325] The Scroll of Exalted Kingship, Diwan Malkuta Laita, SE, page 41

[326] Ginza Rabba, GR-Left, book1, praise 1, page 7

[327] The Kephalaia Of The Teacher, chapter 8, KT, page 41

[328] R.H. Charles and M. Whittaker, "the Life of Adam and Eve," 153, cited by John C.Reeves, Heralds of that good realm, HGR, page 193. See also note 56, page 203

[329] Quoted by Jewish Encyclopedia

[330] Ecclesiastes Rabbah. ii. 25; cited by by Jewish Encyclopedia

[331] Al Jaheth, Al Hiwan, HJ, 6 p.223

[332] Bet Hamidrash, ed. Jellenek - collection of smaller midrashim] V, 22–26 ; Louis Ginzberg, The Legends of the Jews, volume iv, chapter 5, Solomon

[333] Tafseer Ibn Kathir In his comment on Surah saba Al Buhturi, Kitab al Hamaseh p. 90 [334]

[335] Al Masudi, Muruj al Dahab. MTM, part, 1, p.283

[336] Ibn khadun, Tarikh ibn khaldun, TIK, volume 2 p.203

[337] Halabieh, SHB, 1, 252

[338] Halabieh, SHB, 2, 252

[339] Al Suheili, Al Ruth al Anuf, Al Waraq electronic version, page 418

[340] Al Masudi, Muruj al Dahab. MTM, part 1, p.79; Ibn Kathir, Al Bidayah wa Al Nihaya, BNH, part II, pp.231-2

[341] Ibn Kathir, Al Bidayah wa Al Nihaya‹ , BNH part II, page 231

[342] Sahih al Bukhari, kitab of dress, chapter 2

[343] Halabieh, SHB, 1, 469

[344] Sahih al Bukhari, kitab al Anbya, chapter about the sleepers in the cave

[345] Halabieh, SHB, 1, 253

[346] Al Zubeidi, Taj al Alarus, under "Humur"

[347] Ibn Saad, Al Tabaqat al Kubra, TKIS, part 10, p.201

[348] Ibn Asaker, Tarikh madinet Dimashq, TMD, volume 4, p.232

[349] Ibn Taimiah, al Furqan bein Auliya Allah wa Auliya al shaitan, FBAS, p.324

[350] Al Masudi, Muruj al Dahab. MTM, part 1, page 80

[351] Bader al deen al shabli, Ahkam al jin, AHJ, p. 66

[352] Al Azruqi, akhbar Mecca, AKM, p. 828

[353] Sahih al Bukhari, Kitab al Hajj, chapter 22

[354] Halabieh, SHB, 2,632 ; Al Bukhari, al Tarikh al Kabeer, TKB, part 2, pp.200-1 Hadith 2191

[355] Halabieh, SHB, 2,63

[356] Sahih al Bukhari, kitab al Hajj, chapter 22

[357] Halabieh, SHB, 2, 63

[358] The prophet biography according to Ibn Kathir, SNK, part I, page 373

Chapter 12

[359] Cf. Das Targum Sheni Scheni zum Buche Esther, Frankfurt a.M., 1893, page 12; cited by Bernard Grossfeld, Targum of Sheni to the Book of Esther, TSE, page x

[360] Targum Ketubim {Hebrew}, New York, 1945, p. 233, cited by Bernard Grossfeld, Targum of Sheni to the Book of Esther, TSE, page xi

[361] Second Targum of Esther, chapter V, Paulus Cassel, STE, page 288

[362] Second Targum of Esther, chapter 1, Paulus Cassel, STE, page 263

[363] Diwan Umiah ben abi al Salt, p.26

[364] Diwan Umiah ben abi al Salt, p. 26

[365] Ibn Hajer, Fiteh al Bari, FAH, part 6, pp.384-385

[366] Tarikh al Tabari, TTB, volume 1, p.426

[367] Yaqut al Hamawi, Maajm al Buldan, MAY, 3, p.110 ;Tarikh al Tabari, TTB, volume, 1, p.426; Al Yakubi, WQ, 1, p. 101

[368] De Lacy O'Leary, D.D., Arabia before Muhammed, London, AM, page 172- 173

[369] Israel welfinson, tarikh il yahud fi bilad al arab, HJA, page 13

[370] Second Targum of Esther, chapter IV, Paulus Cassel, STE, pages 276-278

[371] Second Targum of Esther, chapter IV, Paulus Cassel, STE, page 278

[372] Second Targum of Esther, chapter IV, Paulus Cassel, STE, page 279, 280

[373] Second Targum of Esther, chapter IV, Paulus Cassel, STE, pages 282-3

[374] Tafseer al Qurtubi fi Surat al taubeh;Tarikh al Tabari, TTB, volume, 1, p.128 ;Tafseer Ibn Kathir ln his comment on Surah al Bakarah

[375] Tarikh al Tabari, TTB, volume 1, pp.144-146; Tafseer aj Taberi, TAT, Hadiths 1668 and 16291

[376] Tarikh al Tabari, TTB, volume 1, pp.142-3

[377] Ibn Kathir, Al Bidayah wa Al Nihaya, BNH, part I, p.152 ; Tafseer al Qurtubi fi Surat al kahf ; Abu Hayyan, Tafseer al Bahr al Muhit in his expository of Surah al naml

[378] *Second Targum of Esther*, chapter 1, Paulus Cassel, STE, page 263

[379] *Second Targum of Esther*, chapter 1, Paulus Cassel, STE, page 266

[380] *Second Targum of Esther*, chapter 1, Paulus Cassel, STE, page 267

Chapter 13

[381] Agatharchides of Cnidus, on the Erythraean Sea, book I, 17, ES, page

[382] The Geography of Strabo, Book XVI.I. 11, Volume VII, (GS), page 211

[383] Discourse of Jacob of Serugh, 185-190, SPC, page 174

[384] Pseudo-Callisthenes, II. chaps. xxxix.-xli. (version B)

[385] Stoneman, Richard, The Greek Alexander Romance, GA, page 28

[386] The Alexander book in Ethiopia, the Ethiopian book of Pseudo Callisthenes, EPC, page 156-159

[387] Tafseer aj Taberi, TAT, 16, Hadith 17552

[388] Syriac version of the Pseudo Callisthenes, book III, VII, SPC, page100

[389] Ernest A. Wallis Budge, The history of Alexander the Great, being the Syriac version of the Pseudo Callisthenes, SPC, page civ

[390] A Christian Legend concerning Alexander, SPC, page148

[391] Tafseer al Qurtubi fi Surat al kahf;Al Thaalabi, in his expository of Surah al kahf

[392] A Christian Legend concerning Alexander, SPC, pages 144-145

[393] A Christian Legend concerning Alexander, SPC, page 146

[394] A Christian Legend concerning Alexander, SPC, page 147

[395] A Christian Legend concerning Alexander, SPC, page 148

[396] Discourse of Jacob of Serugh, 80-85, SPC, page 167

[397] The Alexander book in Ethiopia, the Ethiopian book of Pseudo Callisthenes, EPC, page xxviii

[398] Al Masudi, Muruj al Dahab. MTM, part I, page 172

[399] Yaqut al Hamawi, Maajm al Buldan, MAY, 1, p.20

[400] Nishwan al Himyari, khulest al seir al jamiah liajab akhbar, WQ, p.39

[401]The Alexander book in Ethiopia, the Ethiopian book of Pseudo Callisthenes, EPC, page xxviii

[402] A discourse composed by Jacob Sarugh, 130-160, SPC, page170 -172

[403] Dinkard-Book VIII, Chapter XXXI, 30, SBE, Volume 37, Pahlavi Texts part IV, page 103

[404] Dinkard-Book VIII, Chapter XXXI, 30, SBE, Volume 37, Pahlavi Texts part IV, page 103

[405] Syriac version of the Pseudo Callisthenes, book III, IV- V, SPC page 92

[406] A Christian Legend Concerning Alexander, SPC, page 148

[407] Al Allusi, Ruh al Maani, in his expository on Surah al Kahf

[408] Tafseer al Taberi, TAT, 16, Hadiths 17577-17580

[409] Abu Hayyan, Tafseer al Bahr al Muhit in his expository of Surah al kahf;Al Thaalabi, in his expository of Surah al kahf

[410] Tarikh al Tabari, TTB, volume 1, p.49

[411] Ibn al Nadim, al Fahrest, ALF, p. 350

[412] Tafseer aj Taberi, TAT, 16, Hadith 17591

[413] Yaqut al Hamawi, Maajm al Buldan, MAY, 3, p.198.

[414] Al Thaalabi, in his expository of Surah al kahf; Ibn Hisham, SIH, 1, p.244.

[415] Ibn al Jozi, zad al maser fi Elm al Tafseer, ZMT, on his expository of Surah al kahf

[416] Tafseer al Qurtubi fi Surat al kahf

[417] Tafseer Ibn Kathir In his comment on Surah al Kahf ؛ Tafseer al Qurtubi fi Surat al kahf ;Tafseer aj Taberi, TAT, 16, surat al kahf, Hadith 17580

[418] Aban Yast, IX, 34; SBE, Volume 23, Zenda Avesta Part II, page 61; Bahman Yast III, 55-63, SBE, Volume V, Pahlavi Texts part I, pages, 234-5

[419] Dinkard-Book IX, Chapter XXI, 17- 19, SBE, Volume 37, Pahlavi Texts part IV, pages, 216-7

[420] Dinkard-Book IX, Chapter XXI,17- 19

[421] Dinkard-Book IX, Chapter XXI, 22-23, SBE, Volume 37, Pahlavi Texts part IV, page 218

[422] Sahih al Bukhari, kitab the beging of creation, chapter 11

[423] A Christian Legend Concerning Alexander, SPC, page 151

[424] Dinkard-Book IX, Chapter XXII, 4-9, SBE, Volume 37, Pahlavi Texts part IV, pages 220-221

[425] Pseudo-Callisthenes primum edidit Carolus Mullerus, Parisiis, 1877; cited by Ernest A. Wallis Budge, The history of Alexander the Great, being the Syriac version of the Pseudo Callisthenes, SPC, page Lii

[426] C.E. Wilson "The Wall of Alexander against Gog and Magog; and the Expedition Sent out To Find it by the Khaliph Wathiq, in 842 A.D." Hirth Anniversary Volume, Asia Major, London: Probsthain and Co, 1922, pp. 577-579.

[427] C.E. Wilson "The Wall of Alexander against Gog and Magog; and the Expedition Sent out To Find it by the Khaliph Wathiq, in 842 A.D." Hirth Anniversary Volume, Asia Major, London: Probsthain and Co, 1922, pp. 577-579.

[428] Tafseer al Qurtubi fi Surat al kahf

[429] Tafseer al Razi, TFR, part 21, page 81

[430] Tafseer al Qurtubi fi Surat al kahf; Al Thaalabi, in his expository of Surah al kahf

[431] Ibn al Jozi, zad al maser fi Elm al Tafseer, ZMT, on his expository of Surah al Kahf

[432] Sahih al Bukhari, kitab al Tafseer, chapter 234

[433] Abu Hayyan, Tafseer al Bahr al Muhit in his expository of Surah al kahf; Ibn Hajer, Fiteh al Bari, FAH, part 13, p. 107 ;Yaqut al Hamawi, Maajm al Buldan, MAY, 3, p.197

[434] A Christian Legend Concerning Alexander, SPC, page 153

[435] Ernest A. Wallis Budge, The history of Alexander the Great, being the Syriac version of the Pseudo Callisthenes, SPC, page lxxvii

[436] Pseudo-Callisthenes primum edidit Carolus Mullerus, Parisiis, 1877; cited by Ernest A. Wallis Budge, The history of Alexander the Great, being the Syriac version of the Pseudo Callisthenes, SPC, page Lii

[437] C.E. Wilson "The Wall of Alexander Against Gog and Magog; and the Expedition Sent out To Find it by the Khaliph Wathiq, in 842 A.D." Hirth Anniversary Volume, Asia Major, London: Probsthain and Co, 1922, pp. 577-579.

[438] A Christian Legend Concerning Alexander, SPC, pages 154-155

[439] Sahih al Bukhari, kitab al Manaqeb, chapter about the signs of prophecy in Islam; Ibn al Athir, al Nihayat fi Ghareeb Al Hadith wa ather, under "Halaq"

[440] Tafseer Ibn Kathir In his comment on Surah al Kahf

[441] Sahih al Bukhari, kitab al Anbya, chapter about the story of Gog and Magog

[442] Ibn Hajer, Fiteh al Bari, FAH, part 13 pp.107-108

[443] A Christian Legend Concerning Alexander, SPC, page151

[444] Ibn al Jozi, zad al maser fi Elm al Tafseer, ZMT, on his expository of Surah al anbiya

[445] A Christian Legend Concerning Alexander, SPC, page151

[446] Tarikh al Tabari, TTB, volume, 1, 49

[447] A Christian Legend Concerning Alexander, SPC, page 151

[448] Tafseer aj Taberi, TAT, 16, Hadith 17592; Al Termithi, Sunan Al Termithi, SUT, part 5, Hadith 3153; Al Thaalabi, in his expository of Surah al kahf ;Tafseer Ibn Kathir In his comment on Surah al kahf; Tafseer al Qurtubi fi Surat al kahf

[449] Ernest A. Wallis Budge, The history of Alexander the Great, being the Syriac version of the Pseudo Callisthenes, SPC, page152; quoting Knös, Chrestomathia Syr., page 80

[450] Dinkard-Book IX, Chapter XXI, 17-22, SBE, Volume 37, Pahlavi Texts part IV, pages 216-8

[451] Tafseer al Qurtubi fi Surat al kahf; Al Thaalabi, in his expository of Surah al kahf

[452] A Christian Legend Concerning Alexander, SPC, page 151

[453] Tafseer al Qurtubi fi Surat al kahf; Al Thaalabi, in his expository of Surah al kahf

[454] A Christian Legend Concerning Alexander, SPC, page 152

[455] Dinkard-Book IX, Chapter XXII, 4-9, SBE, Volume 37, Pahlavi Texts part IV, pages 220-2

[456] Tafseer Ibn Kathir In his comment on Surah al kahf: Tafseer al Taberi, TAT, 16, Hadith, 17552

[457] Wright, A Short History of Syriac Literature, SHSL, page 68

[458] Ernest A. Wallis Budge, The history of Alexander the Great, being the Syriac version of the Pseudo Callisthenes, SPC, page lxxvii

[459] Discourse of Jacob of Serugh, 520, SPC, page 191

[460] Discourse of Jacob of Serugh, 215- 250, SPC, pages 176-178

[461] Ibn al Jozi, zad al maser fi Elm al Tafseer, on his expository of Surah al kahf

[462] Discourse of Jacob of Serugh, 255-270, SPC, pages 178, 179

[463] Tafseer aj Taberi, TAT, 16, Hadith 17552

[464] Discourse of Jacob of Serugh, 290-335, SPC, pages 180-181

[465] Discourse of Jacob of Serugh, 340-380, SPC, pages 182-184

[466] Discourse of Jacob of Serugh, 375, SPC, page 184

[467] Discourse of Jacob of Serugh, 425-470, SPC, pages 186-188

[468] Discourse of Jacob of Serugh, 475-485, SPC, pages 189

[469] Discourse of Jacob of Serugh, 490-515, SPC, pages 189-191

[470] Tafseer aj Taberi, TAT, 9,Hadith 17617

[471] Al Hakem il Neisaburi, al Mustadrak ala al sahihein, MAS, part 2, p.452, Hadith 3505

[472] Ibn Saad, Al Tabaqat al Kubra, TKIS, part 2, p.309: Al Hindi, Kinz al Ummall fi sunan al Qal wa afal, KA, Hadith 37059

[473] See also Tafseer aj Taberi, TAT, 16, Hadith 17552; Tafseer al Qurtubi fi Surat al kahf : Ibn Hajer, Fiteh al Bari, FAH, part 6, p.382 and the pages that follow;Tafseer ibn Kathir in his expository on Surah al kahf

[474] Abu Hayyan, Tafseer al Bahr al Muhit in his expository of Surah al kahf

[475] Tafseer al Razi, TFR, part 21, p.77

[476] Tafseer al Qurtubi fi Surat al kahf

[477] Al Allusi, Ruh al Maani, in his expository on Surah al kahf

[478] Ibn al Jozi, zad al maser fi Elm al Tafseer, on his expository of Surah al kahf

[479] Al Suheili, Al Ruth al Anuf, RA, part 3, p. 179

[480] Al Zubeidi, Taj al Alarus, under "Saab"

[481] Ibn Hajer, Fiteh al Bari, FAH, part 6, p.384

[482] Al Allusi, Ruh al Maani, in his expository on Surah al kahf

[483] Ibn Hajer, Fiteh al Bari, FAH, part 6, pp. 384-385

[484] K.A. Kitchen, Documentation For Ancient Arabia, Part I, DAA, page 5

[485] K.A. Kitchen, Documentation For Ancient Arabia, Part I, DAA, page14

[486] M. Boyce, "The Religion of Cyrus the Great," in A. Kuhrt and Heleen Sancisi-Weerdenburg, Achaemenid History III. Method and Theory, AHM, pp. 15-31.

[487] James Bennett Pritchard, Ancient Near Eastern Texts Relating to the Old Testament (ANET), pages 315 - 316

[488] Ernest A. Wallis Budge, The history of Alexander the Great, being the Syriac version of the Pseudo Callisthenes, SPC, page 146

[489] Ernest A. Wallis Budge, The history of Alexander the Great, being the Syriac version of the Pseudo Callisthenes, SPC, page 146

[490] Ernest A. Wallis Budge, The history of Alexander the Great, being the Syriac version of the Pseudo Callisthenes, SPC, page xi

[491] The Book of Ser Marco Polo the Venetian, Vol.I, Introduction, page 110; quoted by Ernest A. Wallis Budge, The history of Alexander the Great, being the Syriac version of the Pseudo Callisthenes, SPC, page xxxvi

[492] The Book of Ser Marco Polo the Venetian, Vol.I, Introduction, page 110; quoted by Ernest A. Wallis Budge, The history of Alexander the Great, being the Syriac version of the Pseudo Callisthenes, SPC, page xxxvi

[493] First book of Maccabees, I.1-9

[494] Josephus, Antiquities, book xi, chapter viii, (AJF)

[495] First book of Maccabees, I.1-9

[496] Muller, Pseudo Callisthenes, Introduction, p.vii.col.2, No.13, Paris, 1877; cited by Ernest A. Wallis Budge, The history of Alexander the Great, being the Syriac version of the Pseudo Callisthenes, SPC, page Lii

[497] The Alexander book in Ethiopia, the Ethiopian book of Pseudo Callisthenes, EPC, page xvii

[498] Müller, Pseudo Callisthenes, Paris, 1877; cited by Ernest A. Wallis Budge, The Alexander book in Ethiopia, the Ethiopian book of Pseudo Callisthenes, EPC, 1933, page xvii

[499] Stoneman, Richard, The Greek Alexander Romance, GA, pp. 28-29

[500] Historia Alexandria Magni (Berlin, 1926, repr. 1958); Bucephalus: various versions of Alexander's taming of his horse, AN EXTRACTION FROM: Ancient History Bulletin 9.1a, Volume 9.1 (1995) 1-13;The Alexander Romances within Alexander Historiography, by E. Baynham (University of Newcastle, Australia)

[501] Stoneman, Richard, The Greek Alexander Romance, GA, page 22-23

[502] Ernest A. Wallis Budge, The history of Alexander the Great, being the Syriac version of the Pseudo Callisthenes, SPC., page Liv

[503] Ernest A. Wallis Budge, The history of Alexander the Great, being the Syriac version of the Pseudo Callisthenes, SPC, page Liv

[504] The Romance of Alexander the Great by Pseudo-Callisthenes, APC, page 10 ; quoting S.Malxasian, The Armenian History of Movses Xorenaci, (Erevan, 1961), pp.53-58

[505] Dashian, Studies on Pseudo-Callisthenes' life of Alexander, (Viena, 1892), pp.56-60; 73-74; cited by Albert M. Wolohojian, The Romance of Alexander the Great by Pseudo-Callisthenes, APC, page 11-13

[506] Dashian, Studies on Pseudo-Callisthenes' life of Alexander, (Viena, 1892), pp.56-60; 73-74; cited by Albert M. Wolohojian, The Romance of Alexander the Great by Pseudo-Callisthenes, APC, page 11-13

[507] K'nnaser, II, (1887), 7-28; cited by Albert M. Wolohojian, The Romance of Alexander the Great by Pseudo-Callisthenes, APC, page 13

[508] Pseudo-Callisthenes, p. 192; quoted by Ernest A. Wallis Budge, The history of Alexander the Great, being the Syriac version of the Pseudo Callisthenes, SPC, page lx

[509]Ernest A. Wallis Budge, *The Alexander Book in Ethiopia, the Ethiopian book of Pseudo Callisthenes*, EPC, page xix; quoting 'Beiträge zur Geschichte des Alexanderromans', in the Denkschriften der Kaiserlichen Akademie der Wissenschaften in Wien, Bd. Xxxvii. Wien, 1890.

[510]Dr. Ausfeld, Zur Kritik des griechischen Alexanderromans, Karlsruche, 1894; cited by Ernest A. Wallis Budge, *The Alexander Book in Ethiopia, the Ethiopian book of Pseudo Callisthenes*, EPC, pagexix.

[511] Ernest A. Wallis Budge, *The Alexander Book in Ethiopia, the Ethiopian book of Pseudo Callisthenes*, EPC, page xix.

[512] Tafseer al Qurtubi fi Surat al kahf

[513] Al Allusi, Ruh al Maani, in his expository on Surah al Kahf

[514] Tafseer al Qurtubi fi Surat al kahf

[515] A Christian Legend Concerning Alexander, SPC, page 154

[516] A Christian Legend Concerning Alexander, SPC, page 155

[517] A Christian Legend Concerning Alexander, SPC, page 154

[518] A Christian Legend Concerning Alexander, SPC, page 154

[519] Discourse of Jacob of Serugh, 521, SPC, page 191

[520] Discourse of Jacob of Serugh, 630, SPC, pages 196 and 197

Chapter 15

[521]Aristotle, Physics., IV, xi

[522] Koch, Die Siebenschlafereigende, ihr Ursprung u. ihre Verbreitung (Leipzig, 1883), pp. 24-40; Quoted by the Adrian Fortescue, The Catholic Encyclopedia, Volume V

[523] Wright, A Short History of Syriac Literature, SHSL, page 68

[524]Tacitus, Annals XV, 44

[525] Lucian of Samosata, the Passing of Peregrinus, 11, 13

[526] Julius Africanus, Chronography, 18.1

[527] Babylonian Talmud, Sanhedrin 43a

[528] Ibn Hisham, SIH, 1, p.240 ٤Tafseer al Qurtubi fi Surat al anam٤ Tafseer ibn Kathir in his expository on Surah al Aaraf

[529] Ibn Hisham, SIH, 1, p.239

[530] Ibn Hisham, SIH, 1, p.282 ;Tafseer al Qurtubi fi Surat Luqman

[531] Ibn Hisham, SIH, 1, pp. 239& 282;Tafseer al Qurtubi fi Surat al Anam٤ Tafseer ibn Kathir in his expository on Surah al aaraf

[532] Ibn Hisham, SIH, 1, p.240

[533] Tarikh al Tabari, TTB, volume 1, pp.46-7

[534] Tafseer al Qurtubi fi Surat al Nur

[535] Al Firozabadi, al Qamus al Muhit, 1, chapter noon

[536] Ibn Saad, Al Tabaqat al Kubra, TKIS, part 10, p.113 ٤113 صفحة ; Al 'Ani, Umdet al Qari, UQ, part, 4, p.130٤ Halabieh, SHB,2,587٤ Al Hakem il Neisaburi, al Mustadrak ala al sahihein, MAS, part 4, pp.109-110, Hadiths 6858-6860; Sunan Abi Dawood, Hadith 3931

[537] Ibn Hisham, SIH, 2, p.26

[538] Sahih al Bukhari, kitab al shahadat, chapter 8

[539] Sahih al Bukhari, kitab al Buya', chapter 59

[540] Sahih al Bukhari, kitab the gift and its credit, chapter 14

[541] Al Allusi, Ruh al Maani, in his expository on Surah al Furqan;Tafseer aj Taberi, TAT 14, Hadiths 16558-16559

[542] Al Allusi, Ruh al Maani, in his expository on Surah al furqan, verses 3-5

[543] Al Allusi, Ruh al Maani, in his expository on Surah al Nahl؛ Tafseer aj Taberi, TAT, 14, Hadiths 16553-4

[544] Ibn Saad, Al Tabaqat al Kubra, TKIS, part 2, p.309

[545] Al Hindi, Kinz al Ummall fi sunan al Qal wa afal, KA, Hadith 37059

[546] Tafseer aj Taberi, TAT, 15, comment on verse 25 of Surat al kahf

Chapter 16

[547] Hisham ibn Alkalbi, al Asnam, WQ, page 9

[548] Hisham ibn Alkalbi, al Asnam, WQ, page 9

[549] Hisham ibn Alkalbi, al Asnam, WQ, page 10

[550] Ibn Kathir, Al Bidayah wa Al Nihaya, BNH, I, page 114

[551] The Sumerians Their History, Culture, And Character, Samuel Noah Kramer, SHC, page 151

[552] The Sumerians Their History, Culture, And Character, Samuel Noah Kramer, SHC, page 152

[553] Ibn Kathir, Al Bidayah wa Al Nihaya, BNH, I page 114؛ Ibn Atheer, al Kamel fi al Tarikh, KFT, part 1, p.56

[554] Al 'Ani, Umdet al Qari, UQ, part 15, p. 300

[555] Ibn Kathir, Al Bidayah wa Al Nihaya, BNH, I page 114 ; Al Hakem il Neisaburi, l Mustadrak ala al sahihein, MAS,part 2, p.406, Hadith 3369;Ibn Atheer, al Kamel fi al Tarikh, KFT, part 1, p.56

[556] Ibn Atheer, al Kamel fi al Tarikh, KFT, part 1, p.56؛ Al 'Ani, Umdet al Qari, UQ, part 15, p.300 ؛ Abu Hayyan, Tafseer al Bahr al Muhit in his expository of Surah hud ؛ Tafseer al Qurtubi fi Surat Hud

[557] Al 'Ani, Umdet al Qari, UQ, part 15, page 300 ؛Al Zubeidi, Taj al Alarus, under "tnr" ؛ Ibn Manthur, Lisan al Arab, LA, part 2, under "tnr"

[558] Rt. Ginza Rba, book 3, first Hymn, GR, page 51

[559] Al Azruqi, akhbar Mecca, AKM, pp.140-1

[560] Ibn Hisham, SIH, 1, p.6

[561] Tarikh al Tabari, TTB, volume 1, 127

[562] Al Qalqashandi, Nihayet al arab fi Marifat Ansab Al Arab, NA, p.17

[563] Ibn Hisham, SIH, 1, p.94

[564] Jawad Ali, al Mufassal Fi Tarikh al Arab Qabl Al-Islam, volume 6, MF, page 299

[565] F.V.Winnett and W.L.Reed, Ancient Records from North Arabia, AR, page 118

[566] Wellhausen, Reste, Arabischen Heidentums, Berlin, 1927, S. 14; quoted by Jawad Ali, al Mufassal Fi Tarikh al Arab Qabl Al-Islam, volume I, MF, page 331

[567] Yaqut al Hamawi, Maajm al Buldan, MAY, 5, p.386

[568] Yaqut al Hamawi, Maajm al Buldan, MAY, 5, p.365;Al Bakri al Andalusi, Maajam Ma istujem, MME, part 1, p.51 (see fotenote 2)

[569] Al Zubeidi, Taj al Alarus, under "S-waw-Ain" ; Hisham ibn Alkalbi, al Asnam, WQ, page 1;Al Bakri al Andalusi, Maajam Ma istujem, MME, part 2, p. 679 ؛ Yaqut al Hamawi, Maajm al Buldan, MAY, part 3, p.276

[570] Hisham ibn Alkalbi, al Asnam, WQ, page 10

[571] Hisham ibn Alkalbi, al Asnam, WQ, page 10; Ibn Kathir, Al Bidayah wa Al Nihaya, BNH, part II, page 194; Yaqut al Hamawi, Maajm al Buldan, part 3, p.276

[572] Tarikh al Tabari, TTB, volume 2, page 163

[573] S.M. Zwemer, The Influence of Animism in Islam, IAI, p. 5.

[574] Ibn Manthur, Lisan al Arab, LA, part 6, under "Saua'"

[575] Yaqut al Hamawi, Maajm al Buldan, part 3, p.276

[576] Yaqut al Hamawi, Maajm al Buldan, MAY, part 5, p.439

[577] Tarikh al Tabari, TTB, volume 2, p.297

[578] Tafseer al Qurtubi fi Surat Noah ; Al Thaalabi, in his expository of Surah Nuh ;Abu Hayyan, Tafseer al Bahr al Muhit in his expository of Surah Nuh

[579] Yaqut al Hamawi, Maajm al Buldan, MAY, part 5, p.439 ; Al 'Ani, Umdet al Qari, UQ, 7, p.57

[580] Yaqut al Hamawi, Maajm al Buldan, MAY, 5, p.439

[581] Abu Hayyan, Tafseer al Bahr al Muhit in his expository of Surah Nuh ;Al Allusi, Ruh al Maani, in his expository on Surah Nuh

[582] Tir Yast :VI, 27, SBE, Volume 23, Zenda Avesta Part II, page 100

[583] Tir Yast:VI, 27-34, SBE, Volume 23, Zenda Avesta Part II, page 100

[584] Ibn Manthur, Lisan al Arab, LA, part 9, under "Auq"؛ Al Zubeidi, Taj al Alarus, under "Auq"

[585] Al Allusi, Ruh al Maani, in his expository on Surah Nuh; Ibn Kathir, Al Bidayah wa Al Nihaya, BNH, 9: page 391

[586] Yaqut al Hamawi, Maajm al Buldan, MAY, 5, p.439

[587] Yaqut al Hamawi, Maajm al Buldan, MAY, 5, 438

[588] The Syriac Doctrine of Addai, p.24; Cited by James Hastings, Encyclopedia of Religion and Ethics, ERE volume I,662-663

[589] The Talmud, ('Abodah zara, 116) cited by James Hastings, Encyclopedia of Religion and Ethics, ERE volume I,662-663

[590] Ibn Manthur, Lisan al Arab, LA, part 14, under "nser"; Al Asfahani, Mufradat al Quran, kitab al Noon, under "Niser"

[591] K.A. Kitchen, Documentation For Ancient Arabia, Part I, DAA, page 5

[592] Hisham ibn Alkalbi, WQ, page 2 ; Ibn Habib al Baghdadi, al Munamq men akhbar quraish, MAQ, page 407

[593] Sahih al Bukhari, Yauq ;Al Allusi, Ruh il Maani fi tafsir Surah Nuh; Tafseer ibn Kathir in his expository on Surah Nuh;The prophet biography according to Ibn Kathir, SNK, I, pp.68-69 ; Al Suheili, Al Ruth al Anuf, RA, part I, p.353; Tafseer aj Taberi,

TAT, 29, hadiths 27107-10 ; Al Thaalabi, in his expository of Surah Nuh; Al Zubeidi, Taj al Alarus, under "Nesser"

[594] Tafseer al Qurtubi fi Surat Noah

[595] Tafseer al Qurtubi fi Surat Noah

[596] Ibn Habib al Baghdadi, al Munamq men akhbar quraish, MAQ, pages 405-407

[597] Hisham ibn Alkalbi, al Asnam, WQ, page 10

[598] Yaqut al Hamawi, Maajm al Buldan, MAY, part 4, pp. 117-8

[599] Yaqut al Hamawi, Maajm al Buldan, MAY, part 5, p. 386

[600] Encyclopedia of Religion and Ethics,edited by James Hastings, I, ERE, page 387

Chapter 17

[601] Tafseer al Razi, TFR, part 27, page 55

[602] Ibn Manthur, Lisan al Arab, LA, part 2, under "Tba'"

[603] Al Zubeidi, Taj al Alarus, under "Tabia'"

[604] Al Bakri al Andalusi, Maajam Ma istujem, MME, 2, p.510

[605] Al Allusi, Ruh al Maani, in his expository on Surah al dukhan

[606] Al qurtubi in his expository of Surah al Baqareh

[607] The prophet biography according to Ibn Kathir, SNK, part I, p.23 ; Al Suheili, Al Ruth al Anuf, RA, part I, p.164

[608] Tafseer ibn Kathir in his expository on Surah al-Dukhan

[609] Tarikh al Tabari, TTB, volume 1, p.331

[610] Ibn Atheer, al Kamel fi al Tarikh, KFT, part 1,page 211.

[611]Tafseer aj Taberi, TAT, 25, Hadith 24081

[612] Tarikh al Tabari, TTB, volume 1, p.426

[613] Ibn Kathir, Al Bidayah wa Al Nihaya, BNH, part II, pages 168-167

[614] Tarikh al Tabari, TTB, volume 1, pp.427-8

[615] Tafseer aj Taberi, TAT, part 26, Hadith 24657

[616] Tafseer aj Taberi, TAT, part 26, Hadith 24659 ;Yaqut al Hamawi, Maajm al Buldan, part 3, p.108

[617] Ibn Hisham, SIH, 1, pp. 18-21

[618] Al Aghani, al Asfahani, AGH, part 18, p.187

[619] Ibn Manthur, Lisan al Arab, LA, part 2, under "tba'"

[620] Tafseer al Razi, TFR, part 27, p.55; Ibn al Jozi, zad al maser fi Elm al Tafseer, on his expository of Surah al Dukhan; Ibn Manthur, Lisan al Arab, LA, p. 16, under letter Ta

[621] Al Hakem il Neisaburi, al Mustadrak ala al sahihein, MAS, part 1, No 104

[622] Tafseer ibn Kathir in his expository on Surah al-Dukhan

[623] Al Allusi, Ruh al Maani, in his expository on Surah qaf

[624] A. Jamme, W.F., Inscriptions from Mahram Bilqis (Marib), SIM, pages 136 and 137

[625] K.A. Kitchen, Documentation For Ancient Arabia, Part I, DAA, page 226

[626] K.A. Kitchen, Documentation For Ancient Arabia, Part I, DAA, pages 38,39 and 226

[627] Tarikh al Tabari, TTA, volume 1, p.209

[628] Jawad Ali, al Mufassal fi Tarikh al Arab Qab al Islam, MF, part 2, p.18
[629] Tafseer aj Taberi, TAT, part 25, Hadith 24082
[630] K.A. Kitchen, Documentation For Ancient Arabia, Part I, DAA, page 1
[631] A history of Ethiopia, by Harold G. Marcus, HE, page 10

Chapter 18

[632] The Canonical Prayerbook of the Mandeans, CP, chapter 153, page 132
[633] Ginza Rabba cited by Kurt Adulf, reported by Sabih al Suheiri in his book: al Nushu wa Khalq in Mandaean Texts, MN, page 117
[634] Tarikh al Tabari, TTB, volume 1, p.47
[635] Halabieh, SHB, 1, 410
[636] Al Zubeidi, Taj al Alarus, under "qana'"
[637] Ibn Kathir, Al Bidayah wa Al Nihaya, BNH, part III, page 356
[638] Al Hakem il Neisaburi, al Mustadrak ala al sahihein, MAS, part 4, p.241, Hadith 7270
[639] History of Travancore From the Earliest Times, by Shungunny Menon, HTT, page 38
[640] History of Travancore From the Earliest Times, by Shungunny Menon, HTT, page 85
[641] History of Travancore From the Earliest Times, by Shungunny Menon, HTT, page 86
[642] V.Nagam Aiya, Travancore State Manual, TSM, Volume I, page 223-4
[643] V.Nagam Aiya, Travancore State Manual, TSM, Volume I, page 223-4
[644] A. Sreedhara Menon, A survey of Kerala history, SKH, page 25
[645] A. Sreedhara Menon, A survey of Kerala history, SKH, page 25
[646] Al Manawi, Feith Al Qadir, part 2, FQS, part 2, p.187

Chapter 19

[647] Abu Hayyan, Tafseer al Bahr al Muhit in his expository of Surah al Feel
[648] Tafseer aj Taberi, TAT, 30, hadiths 29314, 29323-4
[649] Mohammed al Shokani, Feth Al Qadir al Jamea bein finei al Riwayah wa al Dirayeh men Elm al Tafseer, FQJ, part 5, p. 667, on his expository on Surah al Feel
[650] Tafseer aj Taberi, TAT, 29344
[651] Food habits of African elephant (Loxodonta africana) in Babile, Elephant Sanctuary, Ethiopia, Tropical Ecology 53(1): 43-52, 2012 ISSN 0564-3295
© International Society for Tropical Ecology, www.tropecol.com
[652] PROCOPIUS OF CAESAREA, HISTORY OF THE WARS: BOOK I THE PERSIAN WAR, chapter xx, PPW, pages 189-195
[653] Alexander Sima, "Abraha" in Siegbert von Uhlig, ed., Encyclopaedia Aethiopica: A-C (Wiesbaden: Harrassowitz Verlag, 2003), p. 42.; Quoted from an article of Andrew Vargo
[654] Stuart Munro-Hay, "Abraha" in Siegbert von Uhlig, ed., Encyclopaedia Aethiopica: A-C (Wiesbaden: Harrassowitz Verlag, 2003); cited by Wikipedia "under Abraha."

[655] A history of Ethiopia, by Harold G. Marcus, HE, page 10

[656] E.J. Brill's first Encyclopaedia of Islam, 1913-1936, Volume 2, by Martijn Theodoor Houtsma, page 72

[657] E.J. Brill's first Encyclopaedia of Islam, 1913-1936, Volume 2, by Martijn Theodoor Houtsma, page 72

[658] Abraha in Dictionary of African Christian Biography. 2007, (DACB is a digital resource hosted by the Center for Global Christianity and Mission at Boston University School of Theology)

[659] Patricia Crone, Meccan Trade, MT, page, 197

[660] Pfannmüller, Handbuch der Islam-Literatur, (Berlin und Leipzig 1923), I, S. 232; Cited by Jawad Ali, MF, VI, page 172

[661] Yaqut al Hamawi, Majmaa al Buldan, MAY, part 4, p. 116 under "al Uzza"

[662] Al Zubeidi, Taj al Alarus, under "snd"

[663] Al Hamadani, Sifat Jaziret al Arab, SJA, p.286

[664] Jawad Ali, al Mufassal fi Tarikh al Arab Qab al Islam, MF, part 6, page 236

[665] Al- Azruqi, akhbar Mecca, AKM, p.199

[666] Yaqut al Hamawi, Majmaa al Buldan, MAY, part 5, p. 203 under "Manat"

[667] Al Shahrastani, al Milal wa al Nahl, MNS, p.575

[668] Ibn Salam Al Jamahi, Tabaqat Fuhul Al Shaara', TFS, page 11

[669] Ibn Khalkan, Wafiat al Ayan, WQ, p.476

[670] Ibn Hisham, SIH, 1, p.51

[671] Ibn Manthur, Lisan al Arab, LA, part 3 under "Hanaf"

[672] Ibn Hisham, SIH, 1, p.46

[673] Al qurtubi in his expository of Surah al Feel

[674] Ben Taghri Bardi al Atabaki, al Nujum al Zahireh fi Muluk Masser wa al Qahireh, NZM, part 3, pp.252-253

Chapter 20

[675] al Sajastani, kitab al Masahef, KMS, p.24

[676] al Sajastani, kitab al Masahef, KMS, p. 49-50;117-118

[677] Al Musuah al Quranieh of Ibrahim al Abiari, part 1, pp. 361-and the pages after

[678] al Sajastani, kitab al Masahef, KMS, p.117

[679] The Emperor Julian and the Jews,Michael Alder, The Jewish Quarterly Review

[680] Cyril Glassé, The Concise Encyclopedia of Islam, CEI, p. 102

[681] Halabieh, SHB, 2, 81

[682] Halabieh, SHB, 2, 81

[683] Halabieh, SHB, 2, 82

[684] Ibn Hisham, SIH, 2, pp.30-31

[685] Halabieh, SHB, 2, 79

[686] Ibn Hisham, SIH, 2, p.30

[687] Manichaean Literature, translated by Jes P. Asmussen, ML, page 66

[688] Ibn Hisham, SIH, 2, p.30

[689] Halabieh, SHB, 2, 82

[690] Tarikh al Tabari, TTB, volume 2, p.276

[691] Tafseer aj Taberi, TAT, 19, Hadith 20070

[692] Al Suheili, Al Ruth al Anuf, RA, part 3, page 195

[693] Ibn Hisham, SIH, 2, p.33

[694] Sahih al Bukhari, Kitab al Tafseer- 207

[695] Halabieh, SHB, 2, p.92

[696] Ibn Hisham, SIH, 2, 31

[697] Brad Steiger, Revelation The Divine Fire, RD, page 45-6

[698] Brad Steiger, Revelation The Divine Fire, RD, page 62-63

[699] Brad Steiger, Revelation The Divine Fire, RD, page 22-24

[700] Brad Steiger, Revelation The Divine Fire, RD, page 22-24

[701] Dr. Kurt Koch, Occult Bondage and Deliverance, OB, page 44-6

[702] W. Radloff, Aus Sibirien, ii, pp. 49 sq. quoted by T. K. Oesterreich, Possession Demoniacal And Other, PD, pages 305- 306

[703] Montague Summers, The History of Witchcraft and Demonology, HWS, page 5

[704] Rossell Hope Robbins, The Encyclopedia of Witchcraft and demonology, EW, page 96 and 98

[705] Montague Summers, The History of Witchcraft and Demonology, HWS, page 121

[706] Rossell Hope Robbins, The Encyclopedia of Witchcraft and demonology, EW, page 511

[707] From Darkness to Light, Jeff Harshbarger, DL, page 105- 106

[708] Rossell Hope Robbins, The Encyclopedia of Witchcraft and demonology, EW, page 514

[709] Jeffrey Russell & Brooks Alexander, A New History of Witchcraft, HW, page 22

[710] Halabieh, SHB, 2, 71

[711] Halabieh, SHB, 2, 71

[712] Ibn Hisham, SIH, 2, p.31

[713] Halabieh, SHB, 2, 71

[714] Halabieh, SHB, 2, 71

[715] Halabieh, SHB, 2, 72

[716] Ibn Hisham, SIH, 2, p.33; Halabieh, SHB, 2, 72

[717] Sahih al Bukhari, kitab al Tafseer, 200

[718] Dinkard, book VII, Chapter IV: 85- 87, SBE, Volume 47, Pahlavi Texts part V, pages 71-2

[719] Dinkard, book VII, Chapter IV: 84, SBE, Volume 47, Pahlavi Texts part V, page 70

[720] Introduction to Pahlavi Texts part V, SBE, Volume 47, page, xxiii

[721] Mary Boyce, Textual sources for the study of Zoroastrianism, ZT, page 84

[722] Sad Dar, Chapter XXIV, 2, SBE, Volume 24, Pahlavi Texts part III, page 287

[723] Dinkard-Book IX, Chapter XLV, 6, SBE, Volume 37, Pahlavi Texts part IV, page 300

[724] Dinkard-Book IX, Chapter XLV, 7, SBE, Volume 37, Pahlavi Texts part IV, pages 300-301

[725] Dinkard-Book IX, Chapter XXIII, 2-7, SBE, Volume 37, Pahlavi Texts part IV, pages 224-225

[726] Halabieh, SHB 2, 77;Ibn Hisham, SIH, 2, p.30

[727] Ibn Hisham, SIH, 2, 34;Halabieh, SHB, 2, 94

[728] Halabieh, SHB, 2, 94

[729] Halabieh, SHB, 2, 96

Chapter 21

[730] Tafseer aj Taberi, TAT, 15,Hadith 17500

[731] Discourse of Jacob of Serugh, 170

[732] Pseudo-Callisthenes, II. chaps. xxxix.-xli. (version B); Discourse of Jacob of Serugh, 185-190

[733] Discourse of Jacob of Serugh, 190-195

[734] Pseudo-Callisthenes, II. chaps. xxxix.-xli. (version B)

[735] Stoneman, Richard, The Greek Alexander Romance, GA, page 28

[736] The Alexander book in Etheopia, the Etheopian book of Pseudo Callisthenes, ABE, page 156-159

[737] Gods، Demons and Symbols of Ancient Mesopotamia, Jeremy black and Anthony green, GD, page 189

[738] Stephanie Dalley, Myths from Mesopotamia, MMC, page 2.

[739] Ibn Kathir, Al Bidayah wa Al Nihaya, BNH, part I, p.336

[740] Al 'Ani, Umdet al Qari, UQ, part 2, p. 91

[741] Ibn Manthur, Lisan al Arab, LA, part 4, under "khuder"

[742] Halabieh, SHB, 1, 500; Ibn Kathir, Al Bidayah wa Al Nihaya، , BNH, part 2, page 108

[743] Ibn Kathir, Al Bidayah wa Al Nihaya, BNH, part I, page 338

[744] Ibn Hajer, al Isabeh fi tamyees al Sahabeh, EFTS, 2272

[745] Ibn Kathir, Al Bidayah wa Al Nihaya, BNH, part I, page 343

[746] Al Zubeidi, Taj al Alarus, under "Khuther"

[747] Stephanie Dalley, Myths from Mesopotamia, MMC, page 2.

[748] The Alexander book in Etheopia, the Etheopian book of Pseudo Callisthenes, ABE, page 156

[749] Tafseer aj Taberi, TAT, 15, fi tafsser surat al kahf, hadith 17467

[750] Tafseer aj Taberi, TAT, 15, Hadith 17473

[751] Tafseer aj Taberi, TAT, 15, Hadiths 17471-2

[752] Tafseer aj Taberi, TAT, 15, Hadith 17502

[753] Tafseer ibn Kathir in his expository on Surah al kahf

[754] Al Allusi, Ruh al Maani, in his expository on Surah al furqan

[755] Wikipedia, under "al Bahrin"

[756] Tigay, Gilgamesh, page 251 cited by John Reeves, Jewish Lore in Manichaean Cosmogony, JMC, page 158

[757] John Reeves, Jewish Lore in Manichaean Cosmogony, JMC, page 120

[758] John Reeves, Jewish Lore in Manichaean Cosmogony, JMC, pages 120 -121

[759] Stephanie Dalley, Myths from Mesopotamia, MMC, page 2.

[760] Palmer, Desert of the Exodus, p. 57

[761] F.W. Hasluck, Christianity and Islam under the Sultans, CIS, volume I, page 324

[762] Ibn Hajer, al Isabeh fi tamyees al Sahabeh, EFTS, no 246

[763] Al Hindi, Kinz al Ummal, KA, Hadith No 34046

[764] F.W. Hasluck, Christianity and Islam under the Sultans, CIS, volume I, page 324-336

[765] Al Thaalabi, in his expository of Surah al kahf

[766] F. W. Hasluck, Ambiguous Sanctuaries and Bektashi Propaganda, (Published by: British School at Athens, 1913/1914), page 102; quoting Molyneux-Seel, in Geog. Journ. xliv (1914), p. 66

[767] H. Polano, The Talmud Selections, TS, pages 325-328

[768] Midrash Pesikta 36a; Babylonian Talmud, Sanhedrin 98a

[769] Babylonian Talmud, Sanhedrin 98a

[770] Babylonian Talmud: Tractate Berakoth- Folio 51a

[771] Julian Obermann, " Two Elijah Stories In Judeo-Arabic Transmission", TES, p. 388

[772] Exempla of the Rabbis(London and Leipzig, 1924) pp.39ff cited by Julian Obermann, "The Two Elijah Stories In Judeo-Arabic Transmission", TES, p. 388

[773] Julian Obermann, "The Two Elijah Stories In Judeo-Arabic Transmission", TES, p. 399

[774] Julian Obermann, "The Two Elijah Stories In Judeo-Arabic Transmission", TES, p. 400

[775] Julian Obermann, "The Two Elijah Stories In Judeo-Arabic Transmission", TES, p. 401

Chapter 22

[776] Tarikh al Tabari, TTB, volume 1, pp.262-3

[777] Al Sabuni, Sauft al Tafaseer, STS, 2, p.445

[778] Tarikh al Tabari, TTB, volume 1, p.263

[779] Tarikh al Tabari, TTB, volume 1, p.265

[780] Pesachim 119a (part of the Babylonian Talmud) ; Babylonian Talmud, Sanhedrin. 110a, 30 and 31

[781] Babylonian Talmud, Pesachim, fol. 119a, 25.

[782] Exodus Rabbah, Sacred Texts Judaism, Midrash, page 83

[783] Louis Ginzberg, The legends of the Jews, volume iii, Chapter V, "The Rebellion of Korah"

[784] Louis Ginzberg, The Legends of the Jews, Volume II, chapter I, Joseph, "Joseph's Kindness and Generosity"

[785] Babylonian Talmud, Pesachim 119a, 21 and 22

[786] The Mandaeans of Iraq and Iran. Their cults, customs, Magic legends and Folklore, Drower,(Oxford 1937) pages 10, 261 (Quoted by Sinasi Gunduz, The Knowledge of Life, KL, page 64

[787] The Scroll of Exalted Kingship, Diwan Malkuta Laita, SE, page 61

[788] The Great First World (Alma Risaia RBA), VI, 164, A pair of Nasoraean Commentaries, PC, page 10

[789] The Secret Adam, E.S. Drower, SA, page 71

Chapter 23

[790] Al Jaheth, al Bayan wa tabyeen,BT, part 1, page 190

[791] Al Jaheth, al Bayan wa tabyeen,BT, part 1, page 189

[792] Al Midani, Majma' al Amthal, chapter 3, proverb No 657

[793] Al Maqdisi, al Bada' w ail Tarikh, WQ, p.134

[794] Ibn Kathir, Al Bidayah wa Al Nihaya, BNH, part II, pp. 128-129

[795] Ibn Manthur, Mukhtasar Tarikh Dmashq, MTD, part 8, pp.107-108

[796] Aristotle, Rhetoric, ii. 20

[797] Ibn Kathir, Al Bidayah wa Al Nihaya, BNH, part II, p.129

[798] Ibn Kathir, Al Bidayah wa Al Nihaya, BNH, part ii, p.125

[799] Ibn Qutaibah al Deinuri, al Maaref, MAR, p.55
55

[800] Anis Frehah, Ahikar hakim men al shareq al adna al qadim, AHK, p. 152

[801] The Story of Ahikar, from the Aramaic, Syriac, Arabic, Armenian, Ethiopic, Old Turkish, Greek and Slavonic Versions, by F. C.Conybeare, J. Rendel Harris, and Agnes Smith Lewis, SA, introduction, Page XVII

[802] Clement of Alexandria, Stromata, book I, chapter 15, (SC)

[803] Clement of Alexandria, Stromata, book I, chapter 15, (SC)

[804] Diogenes Laertius, Lives of Eminent Philosophers, book V, 50

[805] Strabo, Geographica 16.2.39, Volume VII, (GS), page 289

[806] Leonhard Rost, Judaism Outside the Hebrew Canon, JOC, pages 192- 193

[807] The ancient fable: an introduction, by Niklas Holzberg, AFI, page 78

[808] Leonhard Rost, Judaism Outside the Hebrew Canon, JOC, page 191

[809] Anis Frehah, Ahikar hakim men al shareq al adna al qadim, AHK, p.111

[810] Leonhard Rost, Judaism Outside the Hebrew Canon, JOC, page 191

[811] Leonhard Rost, Judaism Outside the Hebrew Canon, JOC, page 194

[812] A proverb from the Syriac version cited by Anis Frehah, Ahikar hakim men al shareq al adna al qadim, AHK, p.103 (it was taken from a Syriac version published by Cambridge university

[813] Ibn Abed Rabbu al Andalusi, al qed Al Farid, AFR, 3, p. 171

[814] Leonhard Rost, Judaism Outside the Hebrew Canon, JOC, page 192

[815] Leonhard Rost, Judaism Outside the Hebrew Canon, JOC, page 193

[816] Aramaic Papyri of the fifth century B.C., AP, page 209

[817] Aramaic Papyri of the fifth century B.C., AP, page xiv

[818] Aramaic Papyri of the fifth century B.C., AP, page xv

[819] Aramaic Papyri of the fifth century B.C., AP, page xv and xvi

[820] Aramaic Papyri of the fifth century B.C., AP, page xvi

[821] Aramaic Papyri of the fifth century B.C., AP, page xvii

[822] Aramaic Papyri of the fifth century B.C., AP, page xix

[823] Anis Frehah, Ahikar hakim men al shareq al adna al qadim, AHK, p.153

[824] Anis Frehah, Ahikar hakim men al shareq al adna al qadim, AHK, p. 155

[825] Al Suheili, Al Ruth al Anuf, RA, part 4, page 67 ;Al Dumairi, Hayat al Hywan al kubra, under "shat"

[826] Aramaic Papyri of the fifth century B.C., AP, page 207

[827] Aramaic Papyri of the fifth century B.C., AP, page 1

[828] Aramaic Papyri of the fifth century B.C., AP, page 204

[829] Aramaic Papyri of the fifth century B.C., AP, page 205

[830] Aramaic Papyri of the fifth century B.C., AP, page 207

[831] Aramaic Papyri of the fifth century B.C., AP, pages 207-8

[832] Ibn Manthur, Lisan al Arab, LA, part 10, under "faqam"

[833] Ibn Manthur, Lisan al Arab, LA, part 11, under "qamed"

[834] Ibn Manthur, Lisan al Arab, LA, part 12, under "luqum"

[835] Aghnatius Efram I Barsum, al Lulu al Manthur fi Tarikh al ulum wa adab al syrianeyah, Humus 1943, p.67 ;Jawad Ali, al Mufassal fi Tarikh al Arab Qab al Islam, MF, part 8, p.341

[836] Jawad Ali, al Mufassal fi Tarikh al Arab Qab al Islam, MF, part 8, p.341

[837] Wahab bin Munabbeh, Kitab al Tijan fi Muluk Himyar, TFMH, p.70

[838] Al Masudi, akhbar al zaman, AKHZ, p.82

[839] Luis Shikhu, al nasranieh wa adabaha bein Arab al Jahilyiah, WQ p.124

[840] Al Firozabadi, al Qamus al Muhit, chapter Kha (an Arabic letter)

[841] Al Zubeidi, Taj al Alarus, under "Khafter"

[842] Ibn Manthur, Lisan al Arab, LA, part4, under "khafter"

[843] Luis Shikhu, Majani al Adb fi Hadaeq al Arab, MAHA, PART 1, P.60

[844] Al Jaheth, Al Hiwan, HJ, 3 p. 478; Ibn Qutaibah al Deinuri, al Shar wa al Shura', WQ, p. 107

[845] Al Sayuti, al itqan fi Ulum al quran, ETQ, part 6, pp.2053-2054

[846] Al Safuri, Nuzhat al Majales wa Muntakhab al Nafaes, WQ, p. 89; Al Suheili, Al Ruth al Anuf, RA, part 4, p. 67

[847] Al Suheili, Al Ruth al Anuf, RA, part 4, p.67;Al Dumairi, Hayat al Hywan al kubra, under "Shat"

[848] Al Maqdisi, al Bada' w ail Tarikh,WQ, p.156

[849] Ibn Kathir, Al Bidayah wa Al Nihaya, BNH, part II, p.126

[850] Ibn Duraid, Jamhart al Lughah, JAD, part 3, p.163

[851] Al Midani, Majma' al Amthal, chapter 27, proverb No 4514

[852] Ibn Manthur, Lisan al Arab, LA, part 3, under "hamaq"

[853] Abd al Qader Baghdadi, Khazant al adb, WQ, p.1626

[854] Al Midani, Majma' al Amthal, chapter 24, proverb No 3760

[855] Ibn Manthur, Lisan al Arab, LA, part 7 under "sharj"

[856] Al Jaheth, al rasael, WQ, p.57

[857] Abd al Qader Baghdadi, Khazant al adb, WQ, p.1626

[858] Al Midani, Majma' al Amthal, chapter 23, proverb No 3410

[859] Al Zubeidi, Taj al Ala'rus, under "Jalal"

[860] Al Zamkhashri, al Faeq fi Ghareeb Al Hadith wa ather, WQ, p.72

[861] Al Zubeidi, Taj al Alarus, under "Jalal"

[862] Luis Shikhu, al nasranieh wa adabaha bein Arab al Jahilyiah, WQ, p. 82

[863] Ibn Manthur, Lisan al Arab, LA, part 2, under "jalal" ;Ibn al Athir, al Nihayat fi Ghareeb Al Hadith wa ather, under "Jalal"

[864] Ibn Kathir, Al Bidayah wa Al Nihaya, BNH, part II, p.128

[865] Sahih al Bukhari, Kitab 77, chapter al Haya'

[866] Ibn Saad, Al Tabaqat al Kubra, TKIS, part 9, p.66

[867] Ibn Kathir, Al Bidayah wa Al Nihaya, BNH, part II, pp. 126-129

[868] Al Thaalibi, Thimar al qulub fi al Muthaf wa lmansub, TQTH, p.125

[869] Jawad Ali, al Mufassal fi Tarikh al Arab Qab al Islam, MF, part 6, p.508

[870] Tar Andrea، Die Entstehung des Islams und das Christentums، Upsale، 1926. S. 48 ; Cited by Jawad Ali, al Mufassal fi Tarikh al Arab Qab al Islam, MF, part 6, pp.494-5

[871] Sahih al Bukhari, kitab al teb, chapter 25

[872] Al Zemkhari, al Mustaqsa fi Amthal al arab, WQ, p.3

[873] Ibn Qutaibah al Deinuri, Uyun al Akhbar, p.369

[874] Ibn Qutaibah al Deinuri, Uyun al Akhbar, WQ, p. 369

[875] Al Maqdisi, al Bada' wa il Tarikh, WQ, p. 156

[876] A proverb from the Syriac version cited bymAnis Frehah, Ahikar hakim men al shareq al adna al qadim, AHK, p.103 (it was taken from a Syriac version published by Cambridge university

[877] Ibn Abed Rabbu al Andalusi, al qed Al Farid, AFR, 3, p.171

[878] Ibn Kathir, Al Bidayah wa Al Nihaya, BNK, part X, p. 112 ; Al Thaalibi, Thimar al qulub fi al Muthaf wa lmansub, TQTH, p.125

[879] Al Safuri, Nuzhat al Majales wa Muntakhab al Nafaes, WQ, p.89

[880] Ibn Qutaibah al Deinuri, Uyun al Akhbar, WQ, p.200

[881] Al Thaalibi, Thimar al qulub fi al Muthaf wa lmansub, TQTH, p.125

[882] Al Thaalibi, al tamthil wa al muhathara, TMTH, p. 35

[883] Aramaic Papyri of the fifth century B.C., the words of Ahikar, plate 45, lines 104, AP, page 223

[884] Al- Thaalibi, al shakwa wa al-itab, WQ, p.5

[885] Al Dumairi, Hayat al Hywan al kubra, under "shat"

[886] Aramaic Papyri of the fifth century B.C., the words of Ahikar, AP, plate 47, lines 141, page 224

[887] Al Dumairi, Hayat al Hywan al kubra, under "bird"

[888] Aghnatius Efram I Barsum, al Lulu al Manthur fi Tarikh al ulum wa adab al syrianeyah, Humus 1943, p.67

[889] Abu Hilal al Askari, Jamhart al Amthal, JAM, chapter 1, p.83

[890] Al Dumairi, Hayat al Hywan al kubra, under "bird"

[891] Aramaic Papyri of the fifth century B.C., the words of Ahikar, AP, plate 47, line 148, page 225

[892] Al Thaalibi,Thimar al qulub fi al Muthaf wa lmansub, TQTH, p.668

[893] Aramaic Papyri of the fifth century B.C., AP, plate 46, lines 111, page 223

[894] Ibn Kathir, Al Bidayah wa Al Nihaya, BNK, X, pp. 81&82

[895] Al Dumairi, Hayat al Hywan al kubra, under "bird"

[896] Al Abshihi, al Mustatref fi kuli fin Mustethref, MFM, part 2, chapter 51, p. 28

[897] Aramaic Papyri of the fifth century B.C., AP, the words of Ahikar, plate 45, lines 105, page 223

[898] The Syriac version of the book "Ahiqar the wise," by bishop Ghrigurius Bulos Bahnam

[899] Anis Frehah, Ahikar hakim men al shareq al adna al qadim, AHK, p.202

[900] Halabieh, SHB, 2, 160

[901] Halabieh, SHB, 2, 160; Ibn Hisham, SIH, 2, pp.51-52

[902] Ibn Hisham, SIH, p. 146

[903] Ibn al Athir, AGHS, part 2, p.595

[904] Sahih Muslim, kitab al Hajj, chapter 85

[905] Al Hindi, Kinz al Ummal, KA, Hadith No 17475

[906] Ibn Kathir, Al Bidayah wa Al Nihaya, BNH, part ii, p.348

[907] Ibn Kathir, Al Bidayah wa Al Nihaya, BNK, part II, page 348

[908] Al Thaalabi, Arayes al Majales fi qisas al anbiya', cited by Anis Freha, Ahiqar, AHK, p.190

[909] Al Midani, Majma' al Amthal, proverb No 4115

[910] Ibn Abed Rabbu al Andalusi, al Eqed Al Farid, AFR, part 3, p.96

[911] Ibn Manthur, Lisan al Arab, LA, part 14, under "Nasl"

[912] Ibn Manthur, Lisan al Arab, LA, part 14, under "Nasl"

[913] Aramaic Papyri of the fifth century B.C., AP, the words of Ahikar, plate 44, lines 83-85, page 222

[914] Sahih al Bukhari, kitab al shahadat, chapter 8

[915] Al Dumairi, Hayat al Hywan al kubra, under "Shat"

[916] Al Marzabani, Nur al qabs, WQ, p.127

[917] Sahih al Bukhari, kitab al riqaq, chapter 15

[918] Aramaic Papyri of the fifth century B.C., AP, the words of Ahikar, plate 45, lines 96-100, page 223

[919] Ibn Manthur, Lisan al Arab, LA, part 4, under "khazen"; Ibn Seedu, al Mukhassas, MIS, part 12, p.273

[920] Usama bin al Munqeth, Lubab al Adab, WQ, page 79

[921] Al Hakem il Neisaburi, al Mustadrak ala al sahihein, MAS, part 3,p.321, Hadith 5218

[922] Abu Dawood al Sajastani, al Maraseel, Hadith 328 ;Al Beihaqi, al Sunan al Kubra, SKB, part 9, pp.46-47, No 17836

[923] Al Beihaqi, al Sunan al Kubra, SKB, part 9, p.46, no 17834

[924] Al Waqidi, al Maghazi, KMW, 1, 92

[925] Al Waqidi, al Maghazi, KMW, 1, p. 70

[926] Ibn Hisham, SIH, 2, p. 213

[927] Tafseer al Qurtubi fi Surat al Mujadalah, verse 58

[928] Al Zubeidi, Taj al Alarus, under "yarr": Ibn Manthur, Lisan al Arab, LA, part 15, under "yarr"

[929] Ibn Manthur, Lisan al Arab, LA, part 13, under "maqal"; Al Zubeidi, Taj al Alarus, under maqal

[930] Aramaic Papyri of the fifth century B.C., AP, the words of Ahikar, plate 47, lines 149, page 225

[931] Al Aghani, al Asfahani, AGH, part 13, p. 5

[932] Abu Hilal al Askari, Jamhart al Amthal JAM, chapter 1, pp. 83-84

[933] Al Dumairi, Hayat al Hywan al kubra, under "bird"

[934] Aghnatius Efram I Barsum, al Lulu al Manthur fi Tarikh al ulum wa adab al syrianeyah, Humus 1943, p.67

[935] Aramaic Papyri of the fifth century B.C., AP, the words of Ahikar, plate 45, lines 96-100, page 223

[936] Luis Shikhu, Majani al Adb fi Hadaeq al Arab, MAHA, 3, P.116

[937] Ibn Manthur, Lisan al Arab, LA, part 13, under "maqar"

[938] Ibn al Athir, al Nihayat fi Ghareeb Al Hadith wa ather, under "Maqr"

[939] Dadistan-I Dinik Chapter xxxvii : 45, SBE, Volume 18, Pahlavi Texts part II, page 94

[940] Dadistan-I Dinik Chapter lxx : 2, SBE, Volume 18, Pahlavi Texts part II, page 213

[941] Hindu Myths‹ with an introduction by Wendy Doniger O'Flaherty, HM, page 112

[942] Al Qalqashandi, Nihayet al arab fi Marifat Ansab Al Arab, NA, pp.95-6; Al Aghani, al Asfahani, AGH, part 15, p.164; Ibn Kathir, Al Bidayah wa Al Nihaya, BNK, 2:538

[943] Al Thaalabi, in his expository of Surah al qalam

[944] Tarikh al Tabari, TTB, volume 1, p.40

[945] Al Allusi, Ruh al Maani, in his expository on Surah al qalm

[946] Cited by Kurt Adulf, reported by Sabih al Suheiri in his book: al Nushu wa Khalq in Mandaean Texts, MN, page 65, see also fotenote 194;cited also by the Mandaean dictionary page 142

[947] Cited by Kurt Adulf, reported by Sabih al Suheiri in his book: al Nushu wa Khalq in Mandaean Texts, MN, page 65, see also fotenote 194

[948] Cited by Kurt Adulf, reported by Sabih al Suheiri in his book: al Nushu wa Khalq in Mandaean Texts, MN, page 65

[949] Diwan Abatur, Appendix I, DAB, page 44

[950] Ginza Rabba Cited by Kurt Adulf, reported by Sabih al Suheiri in his book: al Nushu wa Khalq in Mandaean Texts, MN, page 125

[951] Ibn Atheer, al Kamel fi al Tarikh, KFT, part 1, p. 20; Tarikh al Tabari, TTB, volume 1, p.40;Tafseer al Qurtubi fi Surat al Baqarah;Ibn Kathir, Al Bidayah wa Al Nihaya, BNH ‹part I, page 17

[952] Al Sayuti, Badae' al zuhur fi waqae' al duhur, WQ, p.7

[953] Al Masudi, Muruj al Dahab. MTM, part 1, p.33

[954] Al Sayuti, al Habaek fi Akhbar al Malaek, HFAM, p. 113,No Hadith 417

[955] John Reeves, Jewish Lore in Manichaean Cosmogony, JMC, pages 158 and 159-(in reference to note 366 in page 120)

[956] The Kephalaia Of The Teacher, chapter 62, KT, page 163

[957] The Kephalaia Of The Teacher, chapter 72, KT, page186

[958] The Kephalaia Of The Teacher, chapter 95, KT, page 249

Chapter 24

[959] Tafseer al Qurtubi fi Surat al maedah

[960] Tafseer aj Taberi, TAT, 6, Hadith 9681

[961] Tafseer aj Taberi, TAT, 6, Hadith 9681

[962] Al Jaheth, Al Hiwan, HJ, 1, p.297

[963] Ibn Manthur, Lisan al Arab, LA, part 9, under "anan"

[964] Al Ragheb al Asfahani, Muhatharat al udaba', WQ, p.632

[965] Al Hindi, Kinz al Ummal, KA, Hadith No 40024

[966] Sahih Muslim, kitab al Zuhd wa Al Rqaeq, chapters 11 and 12

[967] Ibn Manthur, Lisan al Arab, LA, part 5, under "rai"

[968] Musned Ahmad, MBH, part 1, p.348, Hadith No 3254 (a correct Hadith according to Bukhari); Ibn Haban, 1080; al Tabarani in Maajem al Kabir, 11946

[969] Al Hindi, Kinz al Ummal, KA, Hadith No 40037 & 40258

[970] Al Ragheb al Asfahani, Muhatharat al udaba', WQ, p.625

[971] Tafseer al Qurtubi fi Surat al Baqareh

[972] Al Allusi, Bulugh al arab fi Marefat Ahwal al Arab, BEA, 2, pp.307-308;Ibn Manthur, Lisan al Arab, LA, part 15,under "Hoom"

[973] Al Nuwairi, Nihayat al arab fi funoon al adab, NAFA, part 9, page 209

[974] Al Masudi, Muruj al Dahab. MTM, part 2, p.230

[975] Al Jaheth, Al Hiwan, HJ, 7, p.178

[976] Ibn Manthur, Lisan al Arab, LA, part 14, under "nasnas"

[977] Al Abshihi, al Mustatref fi kuli fin Mustethref, MFM, part 2, pp.162-163; Al Qazwini, Athar il bilad wa akhbar il Ebad, WQ, p. 17

[978] Al Zubeidi, Taj al Alarus, under "waber"

[979] Al Jaheth, Al Hiwan, HJ, 4, p.73

[980] Ibn Atheer, al Kamel fi al Tarikh, KFT, page 61

[981] Yaqut al Hamawi, Maajm al Buldan, MAY, 5, pp.356-357

[982] Yaqut al Hamawi, Maajm al Buldan, MAY, part 5, p.358

[983] Al Bukhari, al Tarikh al Kabeer, TKB, part 6 page 367 Hadith 2659; Tafseer al Qurtubi fi Surat al baqareh

[984] Al Jaheth, Al Hiwan, HJ, 4, pp. 50-51

[985] Al Jaheth, Al Hiwan, HJ, 4, p.72

[986] Ibn Manthur, Lisan al Arab, LA, part 9, under "Ajb"

[987] Al Dumairi, Hayat al Hywan al kubra, under "the wild peg"

[988] Annal. Bojor. apud Heidegger. Hist. Patriarch. tom. 2. exercitat. 8. p. 270. & Witsii Miscellan. tom. 2. exercitat. 7. p. 201. (i) Argonaut. Americ. l. 14. c. 2. apud Witsium, ib. p. 202.;Quoted by Grill in his exposition on Genesis 19:26

[989] Robert T. Boyd, Tells, Tombs and Treasure, TTT, pp 85, 86

Chapter 25

[990] Walter C. Kaiser Jr., Old Testament Documents, OTD, p.88

[991] Ibn Saad, Al Tabaqat al Kubra, TKIS, part 2, p. 309

[992] Tafseer aj Taberi, TAT, 17, surat al Anbya, verses 51-70, Hadiths 18602, 18611, 18622, 18612, 18624, 18623, 18636

[993] Various editors, The Cambridge Ancient History, third edition, (Cambridge Univercity Press, 1973), II/1, pages 272 and 820-21; Cited by K. A. Kitchen, On the Reliability of the Old Testament, ROTK, page 568

[994] J. M. Sasson, Revue d'assyriologie et d'archeologie Orientale, 92, (1998): 114; after Mari, Annales de Recherches Interdisciplinaires, 7, {1993}: 372, no. 117; Cited by K. A. Kitchen, On the Reliability of the Old Testament, ROTK, page 568

[995] A. H. Sayce, The Higher Criticism and the Verdict of the Monuments, HCV, page 164

[996] W.Hinz, in Various editors, The Cambridge Ancient History, third edition, (Cambridge Univercity Press, 1973), II/1, page 263; Cupper, Archives Royales de Mari, Textes(Tradutions) vi, (Paris: Imprimerie Nationale, I-XXII-XXVIII, 1954, letters 19,22; Cited by K. A. Kitchen, On the Reliability of the Old Testament, ROTK, page 568

[997] Albert T. Clay, Light on the Old Testament from Babel, LOT, page 137

[998] K. A. Kitchen, On the Reliability of the Old Testament, ROTK, page 320

[999] Victor P. Hamilton, The Book of Genesis, 1-17, BG, page 400

[1000] K. A. Kitchen, On the Reliability of the Old Testament, ROTK, page 320

[1001] Sir A.H. Gardiner, Ancient Egyptian Onomastica, I(Oxford: Oxford University Press, 1947, pages 209-212)

[1002] The New York Review, a journal of the ancient faith and modern thought, St Joseph's Seminary, 1907, p. 205.

[1003] A. H. Sayce, Patriarchal Palestine, PPS, page 24

[1004] K. A. Kitchen, On the Reliability of the Old Testament, ROTK, page 568

[1005] K. Jaritz, wer ist the Amraphel in Genesis 14, Zeitschrift fur die alttestament Wissenschaft, 70(1958), pages, 255-56; Cited by Victor P. Hamilton, The Book of Genesis, 1-17, BG, page 400

[1006] Cupper, Archives Royales de Mari, Textes (Tradutions) vi, (Paris: Imprimerie Nationale, XXVIII, (1998), pages, 221-28; Cited by K. A. Kitchen, On the Reliability of the Old Testament, ROTK, page 568

[1007] K. A. Kitchen, On the Reliability of the Old Testament, ROTK, page 320

[1008] Cited by K. A. Kitchen, On the Reliability of the Old Testament, ROTK, page 568

[1009] Geraldine Pinch, Magic in Ancient Egypt, MAE, pp.92-93

[1010] Albright, Journal of the Palestine Oriental Society, 1(1920)74-75

[1011] K. A. Kitchen, On the Reliability of the Old Testament, ROTK, page 320

[1012] K. A. Kitchen, On the Reliability of the Old Testament, ROTK, pages 320 - 21

[1013] K. A. Kitchen, On the Reliability of the Old Testament, ROTK, page 321

[1014] W. F. Albright, The Archaeology of Palestine and the Bible, APB, p. 141-2

[1015] W. F. Albright, The Archaeology of Palestine and the Bible, APB, p.142

[1016] Nelson Glueck, Rivers in the Desert, RDS, page 73

[1017] John H. Sailhamer, Biblical Archaeology, BAS, page 45

[1018] K. A. Kitchen, On the Reliability of the Old Testament, ROTK, page 335

[1019] James K. Hoffmeier, The Archaeology of the Bible, ABH, p. 42

[1020] To see the wanderings of of these tribes, see Kupper, Nomads, 47, 53,49, 179; Quoted by Kitchen, On the Reliability of the Old Testament, ROTK, p. 317

[1021] Albright, Archaeology of Palestine, APB, p. 82

[1022] John H. Sailhamer, Biblical Archaeology, Zondervan, BAS, page 41

[1023] Walter C. Kaiser Jr., Old Testament Documents, OTD, p.88

[1024] Walter C. Kaiser Jr., Old Testament Documents, OTD, p.88

[1025] I. J. Gelb et al, *Computer-Aided Analysis of Amorite* (Chicago: oriental Inst., 1980); quoted by Kitchen, *On the Reliability of the Old Testament* (William B. Eerdman's Publishing Company: Grand Rapids, Michigan/ Cambridge, U.K., 2006), pages 341-342.

[1026] For old Babylonian "itineraries", cf. long ago W.W. Hallo. *Journal of Cuneiform Studies*, 18, (1964): 57-88, with A. Guetze, 112-19, with schematic route maps, pp. 71, 87; see map, M. Roaf, *Cultural Atlas of Mesopotamia and the Ancient Near East* (New York and Oxford: Facts on File, 1990), 113.; Quoted by Kitchen, *On the Reliability of the Old Testament*, page 317.

[1027] George Barton, *Archaeology and the Bible*, ABB, pages 346-7.

[1028] George Barton, Archaeology and the Bible, ABB, page 347

[1029] Kitchen, On the Reliability of the Old Testament, ROTK, p. 317, 318

[1030] Annals of Thutmose III, cited by *Documentation For Ancient Arabia*, Part I, K.A. Kitchen, page 110.

[1031] Howard F. Vos, Genesis and Archaeology, GAS, page 119

[1032] See Albright, Bulletin of the American schools of Oriental Research, 155 (1959), pp. 33-34 along with, Bulletin of the American schools of Oriental Research 176 (1964), p. 42 n. 17 (on order of names); on date of Luqqa's obelisk, cf. Helck, Die Beziehungen Ägyptens zu Vorderasien.... 1962, p. 646 to p. 64; S. H. Horn, Andrews University Seminary Studies,1 (1963), pp. 58-59, and Kitchen, 'Byblos, Egypt and Mari in Early 2nd Millennium BC', Orientalia 36 (1967), in press. Helck's doubts on the Asianic linguistic affiliation of the names are not justified.; Quoted by K. A. Kitchen, Ancient Orient and Old Testament, AOO, p. 52

[1033] K. A. Kitchen, On the Reliability of the Old Testament, ROTK, page 327

[1034] I. E. S. Edwards, N. G. L. Hammond, C. J. Gadd, The Cambridge Ancient History, Cambridge University Press 1975, p, page 836; K. A. Kitchen, Ancient Orient and Old Testament, AOO, p. 52

[1035] 89 Note Albright, Bulletin of the American schools of Oriental Research, 14.6 (1957), PP. 30-31 (Zukrasi, etc.) and H. Otten, Mitteilungen Der Deutschen Orient-Gesellschaft zu Berlin, 86 (1953), pp. 61,63; Wiseman, New Bible Dictionary, (ed. J. D. Douglas, F. F. Bruce, J. I. Packer, R. V. J. Tasker, D. J. Wiseman), 1962, p. 66b. For nondocumentary data, cf. note 91 below.; Quoted by K. A. Kitchen, Ancient Orient and Old Testament, AOO, p. 52

[1036] K. A. Kitchen, Ancient Orient and Old Testament, AOO, p. 52

[1037] James Bennett Pritchard: Ancient Near Eastern Texts Relating to the Old Testament, ANET, 19-21

[1038] C. M. White, IN SEARCH OF THE ORIGIN OF NATIONS, ION, p. 292

[1039] Tarikh al Tabari, TTB, volume 1, pp.126-7

[1040] Al Azruqi, akhbar Mecca, AKM, pp.151-2

[1041] A. Jamme, W.F., Inscriptions from Mahram Bilqis (Marib), SIM, pages 136-7

[1042] Tarikh al Tabari, TTB, volume 1, p.127

[1043] Al Masudi, Muruj al Dahab. MTM, part 2, p.269

[1044] K.A. Kitchen, Documentation For Ancient Arabia, Part I, DAA, page 13

[1045] http://faculty.ksu.edu.sa/834/Pages/topicacd2.aspx#_ftn23

[1046] al Azruqi, akhbar Mecca, AKM, chapter about Ibrahim, p.135

[1047] Ibn Hisham, SIH, 1, page 6

[1048] Tarikh al Tabari, TTB, volume 1, p.524

[1049] Ibn Hisham, SIH, 1, p. 93

[1050] Ibn Hisham, SIH, Part 1, pp.93-94

[1051] Al Qalqashandi, Nihayet al arab fi Marifat Ansab Al Arab, part 1, page 9

[1052] Al Zubeidi, Taj al Alarus, 8, p.227 ; cited by Jawad Ali, al Mufassal fi Tarikh al Arab Qab al Islam, MF, part 1, MF, p.361

[1053] Al Azruqi, akhbar Mecca, AKM, p.144

[1054] W. F. Albright, The Archaeology of Palestine and the Bible, APB, p. 133

[1055] Walter C. Kaiser Jr., Old Testament Documents, OTD, p.88

[1056] Ephraim Stern et al., eds.,The New Encyclopedia of Archaeological Excavations in the Holy Land, 1: 324-26; Quoted by K. A. Kitchen, On the Reliability of the Old Testament, ROTK, pages 335, 572 (note 67)

[1057] Howard F. Vos, Genesis and Archaeology, GAS, page 120

[1058] James B. Pritchard, The Ancient Near Eastern Texts Relating to the Old Testament, ANET, p. 230

[1059] Ephraim Stern et al., eds., The New Encyclopedia of Archaeological Excavations in the Holy Land, 1: 192-94: Quoted by K. A. Kitchen, On the Reliability of the Old Testament, ROTK, pages 336, 573

[1060] Howard F. Vos, Genesis and Archaeology, GAS, page 118-9

[1061] Ephraim Stern et al., eds., The New Encyclopedia of Archaeological Excavations in the Holy Land, 2: 701-2: Quoted by K. A. Kitchen, On the Reliability of the Old Testament, ROTK, page 336

[1062] Jewish Quarterly Review, 1930, p. 165 f.; Quoted by W. F. Albright, The Archaeology of Palestine and the Bible, APB, p. 35

[1063] Ephraim Stern et al., eds., The New Encyclopedia of Archaeological Excavations in the Holy Land, 2: 580-82: Quoted by K. A. Kitchen, On the Reliability of the Old Testament, ROTK, pages 336, 573

[1064] Ephraim Stern et al., eds., The New Encyclopedia of Archaeological Excavations in the Holy Land, 2: 606-9: for the tablet, see M. Anbar and N. Naaman, Tel Aviv, 13/14, (1986/87):3-12, pl.1.; Quoted by K. A. Kitchen, On the Reliability of the Old Testament, ROTK, pages 336, 573

[1065] Arrian, Anabasis, book vii, chapter 20: 7, 8, ARN, page 275

[1066] Himanshu Prabha Ray, The archaeology of seafaring in ancient South Asia, ASSA, pages 169- 170

[1067] Stanley M. Burstein, Agatharchides of Cnidus, On The Erythraean Sea, ES, pages 2-3

[1068] Peremans, W., Diodore de Sicile et Agatharchide de Cnide', pp. 447-55, cited by Burstein, Agatharchides of Cnidus on The Erythraean Sea, ES, page 32

[1069] Leopoldi, Helmuthus, De Agatharchide Cnidio (Diss.Rostow, 1892) pp.13-17 ; Cited by Burstein, Agatharchides of Cnidus on The Erythraean Sea, ES, page 39.
Strabo made abridgement of Agatharchides's book, adding material from the lost book of Artemidorus. The work which Artemidorus developed, especially about Arabia, is contained in Strabo's chapters, especially 16.4.5-20, (GS), pages 315-349. See Bunbury, E.H. A History of Ancient Geography, 2nd ed. (London 1883), pages 61-69; Cited by Burstein, Agatharchides of Cnidus on The Erythraean Sea, ES, page 38

[1070] The Geography of Strabo, Book XVI.4.18, Volume VII, (GS), pages 345

[1071] Wilfred Schoff, introduction to The Periplus of the Erythraean Sea, PEC, pages 14,15

[1072] Claudius Ptolemy, The Geography, GP, book VI chapter VI, page 137-138

[1073] The Geography of Strabo, Book 16, chapter iv, 2, Volume VII, (GS) page 311

[1074] Natural History of Pliny; Book VI, chapter 32, (PNH), page 85

[1075] Patricia Crone, Meccan Trade, MT, pages 134,135

[1076] From book 5 of Agatharchides of Cnidus, on the Erythraean Sea, excerption from Diodorus, Library of History, cited by Burstein, ES, page 153, fragment 92b

[1077] From book 5 of Agatharchides of Cnidus, on the Erythraean Sea,, excerption from Photius, Bibliotheca, cited by Burstein, Agatharchides of Cnidus on the Erythraean Sea, ES, page 155, fragment 95a

[1078] Burstein, Agatharchides of Cnidus, on the Erythraean Sea, ES, page 155, see note 2

[1079] Nonnosus cited by Photius, Bibliotheca, 1,5

[1080] C.Robin, Inventair des Inscriptions Sudarabiques, 1ff. Paris/Rome, 1992 ff.1, 67-68, Haram 3 & 4; Repertoire d'Epigraphie Semitique, esp.V-VIII, Paris, 1929-1968, 2751/M.15; Quoted by K.A. Kitchen, Documentation For Ancient Arabia, Part I, DAA, page 180

[1081] K.A. Kitchen, Documentation For Ancient Arabia, Part I, DAA, pages 181; 239

[1082] C.Robin, Inventair des Inscriptions Sudarabiques, 1ff. Paris/Rome, 1992 ff.,1, 5-6, pls.2b,3a; Inabba; Quoted by K.A. Kitchen, Documentation For Ancient Arabia, Part I, DAA, page 181; See also K.A. Kitchen, DAA, page 239

[1083] For "Verse Account of Nabonidus," see J.B. Pritchard, Ancient Near Eastern Texts Relating to the Old Testament, ANET, page 313; Sidney Smith, Babylonian Historical Texts, London, 1924, Chapter III, pp. 27-97 ;Quoted by F.V. Winnett and W.L. Reed, Ancient Records from North Arabia,AR, page 89

[1084] See C.J. Gadd "The Harran Inscriptions of Nabonidus," Anatolian Studies, 8 (1958) page 59; Cited by F.V. Winnett and W.L. Reed, Ancient Records from North Arabia, AR, page 91; The exact part in the Harran Inscriptions is (Nab. H2 I 26; ii 11) see I. Eph'al, The Ancient Arabs, IAA, page 180

[1085] Al Zubeidi, Taj al Alarus, under "Aub"

[1086] Kitchen, On the Reliability of the Old Testament, ROTK, p.313

[1087] Roland Hendel, "Finding historical memories in the Patriachal narratives," Biblical Archaeology Review 21, no. 4 (July- August 1995): 58; Quoted by Walter C. Kaiser Jr., Old Testament Documents, OTD, p. 89

[1088] al Azruqi, akhbar Mecca, AKM, part 1, pp.80-81

[1089] Jawad Ali, al Mufassal fi Tarikh al Arab Qab al Islam, MF, part 4, page 8

[1090] Al Zubeidi, Taj al Alarus, under "qabas" ;Abbas al Musawi al Mekki, Nuzhat al Jalis wa Muniat al Adib Alnis, 1, p.27; Cited by Jawad Ali, al Mufassal fi Tarikh al Arab Qab al Islam, MF, part 4, page 7

[1091] Al Zubeidi, Taj al Alarus, under "Khashab"

[1092] Ibn Manthur, Lisan al Arab, LA, part 11, under "qabas"

[1093] Jawad Ali, al Mufassal fi Tarikh al Arab Qab al Islam, MF, part 4, p.8

[1094] Al Balathri, Ansab al Ashraf, WQ, p. 22;Abbas al Musawi al Mekki, Nuzhat al Jalis wa Muniat al Adib Alnis,1, p.26 ; Nihayet al arb 16, p.31 ; Cited by Jawad Ali, al Mufassal fi Tarikh al Arab Qab al Islam, MF, part 4, page 54

[1095] Tarikh al Tabari, TTB, volume 1, p.505

[1096] Al Allusi, Bulugh al arab fi Marefat Ahwal al Arab, BEA, 1, 247

[1097] Encyclopedia Of Islam And The Muslim World, EIM, page 526

[1098] Ibn Hisham, SIH, Part 1, p.18 ;Al Suheili, Al Ruth al Anuf, RA, part I, p.159

[1099] Al Allusi, Ruh al Maani, in his expository on Surah al dukhan; The prophet biography according to Ibn Kathir, SNK, part I, p.21; Al Hambali, Fath al Bari, FBH, part 3, p.388

[1100] Al Zubeidi, Taj al Alarus, under "qalad" ;Yaqut al Hamawi, Maajm al Buldan, MAY, 4, p.465

[1101] Yaqut al Hamawi, Maajm al Buldan, MAY, part 4, p.465;Tafseer aj Taberi, TAT, 25, Hadith 24082;Al Zubeidi, Taj al Alarus, under "KhSF" ; Al 'Ani, Umdet al Qari, UQ, part 4, 260;Ibn Kathir, Al Bidayah wa Al Nihaya,BNH, part 2, p.170 ;Ibn Hisham, SIH, 1, pp.18-22 ;The prophet biography according to Ibn Kathir, SNK, part I, page 21;Al Allusi, Ruh al Maani, in his expository on Surah al Dukhan

[1102] Ibn Hisham, SIH, 1, p.22;The prophet biography according to Ibn Kathir, SNK, part 1, p.21 ; Al Allusi, Ruh al Maani, in his expository on Surah al Dukhan

[1103] Ibn Kathir, Al Bidayah wa Al Nihaya, p. 168 ;Ibn Hisham, SIH, 1, p.22 ;Al Allusi, Ruh al Maani, in his expository on Surah al Dukhan

[1104] Ibn Hisham, SIH, 1, pp.179-180 ;Ibn Habib al Baghdadi, al Mahbar, MH, p. 171

[1105] The prophet biography according to Ibn Kathir, SNK, I, p.157 ;Ibn Hajer, al Isabeh fi tamyees al Sahabeh, EFTS, 2, no 2925;Ibn Hisham, SIH, 1, 186; Sahih al Bukhari, chapter 54:Hadith Zayd bin Amru bin Nufeil ;Ibn Saad, Al Tabaqat al Kubra,TKIS, part 3, pp. 352-353

[1106] The prophet biography according to Ibn Kathir, SNK; Al Nisae, al Sunan al Kubra, SKN, no 8187;Al 'Ani, Umdet al Qari, UQ, 16, p.392

c

[1107] Ibn Hisham, SIH, 1, page 181;The prophet biography according to Ibn Kathir, SNK,I, 156 Ibn Kathir, Al Bidayah wa Al Nihaya, BNH, part II, p.24 ; Al Asfahani, Mufradat al Quran, under "Um" ; Ibn Hajer, al Isabeh fi tamyees al Sahabeh ; Ibn Saad, Al Tabaqat al Kubra, EFTS, part 2, Hadith 2925

[1108] Ibn Saad, Al Tabaqat al Kubra, TKIS, part 3, p. 353 ;Sahih al Bukhari, kitab Fathael al Sahabah, chapter 54 about Zeyd bin Amru bin Nufeil ;The prophet biography according to Ibn Kathir, SNK, part 1, p.154; Ibn al Athir, AGHS, part 2, pp. 360 &370;Ibn Hisham, SIH, 1, 181; Al Nisae, al Sunan al Kubra, SKN, no 8187

[1109] Jawad Ali, al Mufassal fi Tarikh al Arab Qab al Islam, MF, part 6, p.461

[1110] Al Nisae, al Sunan al Kubra, SKN, no 8188

[1111] Al Azruqi, akhbar Mecca, AKM, pre-islamic Hajj, pp.272-273

[1112] Ibn Manthur, Lisan al Arab, LA, part 3, under "halal"

[1113] Ibn Manthur, Lisan al Arab, LA, part 3, under "halal"

[1114] Ibn Hajer, Fiteh al Bari, FAH, part 3, pp.482-483

[1115] al Azruqi, akhbar Mecca, AKM, pp.281-2

[1116] The prophet biography according to Ibn Kathir, SNK, part 1, p.159;Ibn Saad, Al Tabaqat al Kubra, TKIS, part 3, p.353

[1117] Al Azruqi, akhbar Mecca, AKM, p. 28 ;Ibn Hajer, Fiteh al Bari, FAH, part 3, p.516

[1118] The prophet biography according to Ibn Kathir, SNK, part I, p.153

[1119] Al Asfahani, Mufradat al Quran, under "maqet"

[1120] Abi al Fida', al Mukhtasar fi Tarikh al Basher, MFTB, part 1, p.99

[1121] Al Hindi, Kinz al Ummall fi sunan al Qal wa afal, KA, part I, Hadith 1063

[1122] Al Hindi, Kinz al Ummall fi sunan al Qal wa afal, KA, part 10, Hadith 32124

[1123] Al Suheili, Al Ruth al Anuf, RA, part 5, p.224;The prophet biography according to Ibn Kathir, SNK, 3, p.478

[1124] Ibn Manthur, Lisan al Arab, LA, part 3,under "hanf"

[1125] E. Lipinski "Notes on the Mesa inscriptions," or 40 (1971) 337 n. 50.; Quoted by Victor P. Hamilton, The book of Genesis chapter 1-17, BG, p. 430

www.ingramcontent.com/pod-product-compliance
Lightning Source LLC
Chambersburg PA
CBHW031934090426
42811CB00002B/176